Visual Test™ 6
Bible

Visual Test™ 6
Bible

Thomas R. Arnold II

IDG Books Worldwide, Inc.
An International Data Group Company

Foster City, CA ✦ Chicago, IL ✦ Indianapolis, IN ✦ New York, NY

Visual Test™ 6 Bible

Published by
IDG Books Worldwide, Inc.
An International Data Group Company
919 E. Hillsdale Blvd., Suite 400
Foster City, CA 94404
www.idgbooks.com (IDG Books Worldwide Web site)

Library of Congress Catalog Card Number: 98-073342

ISBN: 0-7645-3255-3

Printed in the United States of America

10 9 8 7 6 5 4 3 2 1

1B/RZ/RR/ZY/FC

Distributed in the United States by IDG Books Worldwide, Inc.

Distributed by Macmillan Canada for Canada; by Transworld Publishers Limited in the United Kingdom; by IDG Norge Books for Norway; by IDG Sweden Books for Sweden; by Woodslane Pty. Ltd. for Australia; by Woodslane (NZ) Ltd. for New Zealand; by Addison Wesley Longman Singapore Pte Ltd. for Singapore, Malaysia, Thailand, Indonesia, and Korea; by Norma Comunicaciones S.A. for Colombia; by Intersoft for South Africa; by International Thomson Publishing for Germany, Austria, and Switzerland; by Toppan Company Ltd. for Japan; by Distribuidora Cuspide for Argentina; by Livraria Cultura for Brazil; by Ediciencia S.A. for Ecuador; by Ediciones ZETA S.C.R. Ltda. for Peru; by WS Computer Publishing Corporation, Inc., for the Philippines; by Unalis Corporation for Taiwan; by Contemporanea de Ediciones for Venezuela; by Computer Book & Magazine Store for Puerto Rico; by Express Computer Distributors for the Caribbean and West Indies. Authorized Sales Agent: Anthony Rudkin Associates for the Middle East and North Africa.

For general information on IDG Books Worldwide's books in the U.S., please call our Consumer Customer Service department at 800-762-2974. For reseller information, including discounts and premium sales, please call our Reseller Customer Service department at 800-434-3422.

For information on where to purchase IDG Books Worldwide's books outside the U.S., please contact our International Sales department at 650-655-3200 or fax 650-655-3297.

For consumer information on foreign language translations, please contact our Customer Service department at 1-800-434-3422, fax 317-596-5692, or e-mail rights@idgbooks.com.

For information on licensing foreign or domestic rights, please phone +1-650-655-3109.

For sales inquiries and special prices for bulk quantities, please contact our Sales department at 650-655-3200 or write to the address above.

For information on using IDG Books Worldwide's books in the classroom or for ordering examination copies, please contact our Educational Sales department at 800-434-2086 or fax 317-596-5499.

For press review copies, author interviews, or other publicity information, please contact our Public Relations department at 650-655-3000 or fax 650-655-3299.

For authorization to photocopy items for corporate, personal, or educational use, please contact Copyright Clearance Center, 222 Rosewood Drive, Danvers, MA 01923, or fax 978-750-4470.

 is a trademark under exclusive license to IDG Books Worldwide, Inc., from International Data Group, Inc.

ABOUT IDG BOOKS WORLDWIDE

Welcome to the world of IDG Books Worldwide.

IDG Books Worldwide, Inc., is a subsidiary of International Data Group, the world's largest publisher of computer-related information and the leading global provider of information services on information technology. IDG was founded more than 25 years ago and now employs more than 8,500 people worldwide. IDG publishes more than 275 computer publications in over 75 countries (see listing below). More than 90 million people read one or more IDG publications each month.

Launched in 1990, IDG Books Worldwide is today the #1 publisher of best-selling computer books in the United States. We are proud to have received eight awards from the Computer Press Association in recognition of editorial excellence and three from *Computer Currents'* First Annual Readers' Choice Awards. Our best-selling *...For Dummies®* series has more than 50 million copies in print with translations in 38 languages. IDG Books Worldwide, through a joint venture with IDG's Hi-Tech Beijing, became the first U.S. publisher to publish a computer book in the People's Republic of China. In record time, IDG Books Worldwide has become the first choice for millions of readers around the world who want to learn how to better manage their businesses.

Our mission is simple: Every one of our books is designed to bring extra value and skill-building instructions to the reader. Our books are written by experts who understand and care about our readers. The knowledge base of our editorial staff comes from years of experience in publishing, education, and journalism — experience we use to produce books for the '90s. In short, we care about books, so we attract the best people. We devote special attention to details such as audience, interior design, use of icons, and illustrations. And because we use an efficient process of authoring, editing, and desktop publishing our books electronically, we can spend more time ensuring superior content and spend less time on the technicalities of making books.

You can count on our commitment to deliver high-quality books at competitive prices on topics you want to read about. At IDG Books Worldwide, we continue in the IDG tradition of delivering quality for more than 25 years. You'll find no better book on a subject than one from IDG Books Worldwide.

John Kilcullen
CEO
IDG Books Worldwide, Inc.

Steven Berkowitz
President and Publisher
IDG Books Worldwide, Inc.

Eighth Annual
Computer Press
Awards ≥1992

Ninth Annual
Computer Press
Awards ≥1993

Tenth Annual
Computer Press
Awards ≥1994

Eleventh Annual
Computer Press
Awards ≥1995

IDG Books Worldwide, Inc., is a subsidiary of International Data Group, the world's largest publisher of computer-related information and the leading global provider of information services on information technology. International Data Group publishes over 275 computer publications in over 75 countries. More than 90 million people read one or more International Data Group publications each month. International Data Group's publications include: **ARGENTINA:** Buyer's Guide, Computerworld Argentina, PC World Argentina; **AUSTRALIA:** Australian Macworld, Australian PC World, Australian Reseller News, Computerworld, IT Casebook, Network World, Publish, Webmaster; **AUSTRIA:** Computerwelt Österreich, Networks Austria, PC Tip Austria; **BANGLADESH:** PC World Bangladesh; **BELARUS:** PC World Belarus; **BELGIUM:** Data News; **BRAZIL:** Annuário de Informática, Computerworld, Connections, Macworld, PC Player, PC World, Publish, Reseller News, Supergamepower; **BULGARIA:** Computerworld Bulgaria, Network World Bulgaria, PC & MacWorld Bulgaria; **CANADA:** CIO Canada, Client/Server World, ComputerWorld Canada, InfoWorld Canada, NetworkWorld Canada, WebWorld; **CHILE:** Computerworld Chile, PC World Chile; **COLOMBIA:** Computerworld Colombia, PC World Colombia; **COSTA RICA:** PC World Centro America; **THE CZECH AND SLOVAK REPUBLICS:** Computerworld Czechoslovakia, Macworld Czech Republic, PC World Czechoslovakia; **DENMARK:** Communications World Danmark, Computerworld Danmark, Macworld Danmark, PC World Danmark, Techworld Denmark; **DOMINICAN REPUBLIC:** PC World Republica Dominicana; **ECUADOR:** PC World Ecuador; **EGYPT:** Computerworld Middle East, PC World Middle East; **EL SALVADOR:** PC World Centro America; **FINLAND:** MikroPC, Tietoverkko, Tietoviikko; **FRANCE:** Distributique, Hebdo, Info PC, Le Monde Informatique, Macworld, Reseaux & Telecoms, WebMaster France; **GERMANY:** Computer Partner, Computerwoche, Computerwoche Extra, Computerwoche FOCUS, Global Online, Macwelt, PC Welt; **GREECE:** Amiga Computing, GamePro Greece, Multimedia World; **GUATEMALA:** PC World Centro America; **HONDURAS:** PC World Centro America; **HONG KONG:** Computerworld Hong Kong, PC World Hong Kong, Publish in Asia; **HUNGARY:** ABCD CD-ROM, Computerworld Szamitastechnika, Internetto online Magazine, PC World Hungary, PC-X Magazin Hungary; **ICELAND:** Tolvuheimur PC World Island; **INDIA:** Information Communications World, Information Systems Computerworld, PC World India, Publish in Asia; **INDONESIA:** InfoKomputer PC World, Komputek Computerworld, Publish in Asia; **IRELAND:** ComputerScope, PC Live!; **ISRAEL:** Macworld Israel, People & Computers/Computerworld; **ITALY:** Computerworld Italia, Macworld Italia, Networking Italia, PC World Italia; **JAPAN:** DTP World, Macworld Japan, Nikkei Personal Computing, OS/2 World Japan, SunWorld Japan, Windows NT World, Windows World Japan; **KENYA:** PC World East African; **KOREA:** Hi-Tech Information, Macworld Korea, PC World Korea; **MACEDONIA:** PC World Macedonia; **MALAYSIA:** Computerworld Malaysia, PC World Malaysia, Publish in Asia; **MALTA:** PC World Malta; **MEXICO:** Computerworld Mexico, PC World Mexico; **MYANMAR:** PC World Myanmar; **NETHERLANDS:** Computer! Totaal, LAN Internetworking Magazine, LAN World Buyers Guide, Macworld Netherlands, Net, WebWereld; **NEW ZEALAND:** Absolute Beginners Guide and Plain & Simple Series, Computer Buyer, Computer Industry Directory, Computerworld New Zealand, MTB, Network World, PC World New Zealand; **NICARAGUA:** PC World Centro America; **NORWAY:** Computerworld Norge, CW Rapport, Datamagasinet, Financial Rapport, Kursguide Norge, Macworld Norge, Multimediaworld Norge, PC World Ekspress Norge, PC World Nettverk, PC World Norge, PC World ProduktGuide Norge; **PAKISTAN:** Computerworld Pakistan; **PANAMA:** PC World Panama; **PEOPLE'S REPUBLIC OF CHINA:** China Computer Users, China Computerworld, China InfoWorld, China Telecom World Weekly, Computer & Communication, Electronic Design China, Electronics Today, Electronics Weekly, Game Software, PC World China, Popular Computer Week, Software Weekly, Software World, Telecom World; **PERU:** Computerworld Peru, PC World Profesional Peru, PC World SoHo Peru; **PHILIPPINES:** Click!, Computerworld Philippines, PC World Philippines, Publish in Asia; **POLAND:** Computerworld Poland, Computerworld Special Report Poland, Cyber, Macworld Poland, Networld Poland, PC World Komputer; **PORTUGAL:** Cerebro/PC World, Computerworld/Correio Informático, Dealer World Portugal, Mac*In/PC*In Portugal, Multimedia World; **PUERTO RICO:** PC World Puerto Rico; **ROMANIA:** Computerworld Romania, PC World Romania, Telecom Romania; **RUSSIA:** Computerworld Russia, Mir PK, Publish, Seti; **SINGAPORE:** Computerworld Singapore, PC World Singapore, Publish in Asia; **SLOVENIA:** Monitor; **SOUTH AFRICA:** Computing SA, Network World SA, Software World SA; **SPAIN:** Communicaciones World España, Computerworld España, Dealer World España, Macworld España, PC World España; **SRI LANKA:** Infolink PC World; **SWEDEN:** CAP&Design, Computer Sweden, Corporate Computing Sweden, Internetworld Sweden, it branschen, Macworld Sweden, MaxiData Sweden, MikroDatorn, Natverk & Kommunikation, PC World Sweden, PCaktiv, Windows World Sweden; **SWITZERLAND:** Computerworld Schweiz, Macworld Schweiz, PCtip; **TAIWAN:** Computerworld Taiwan, Macworld Taiwan, NEW ViSiON/Publish, PC World Taiwan, Windows World Taiwan; **THAILAND:** Publish in Asia, Thai Computerworld; **TURKEY:** Computerworld Turkiye, Macworld Turkiye, Network World Turkiye, PC World Turkiye; **UKRAINE:** Computerworld Kiev, Multimedia World Ukraine, PC World Ukraine; **UNITED KINGDOM:** Acorn User UK, Amiga Action UK, Amiga Computing UK, Apple Talk UK, Computing, Macworld, Parents and Computers UK, PC Advisor, PC Home, PSX Pro, The WEB; **UNITED STATES:** Cable in the Classroom, CIO Magazine, Computerworld, DOS World, Federal Computer Week, GamePro Magazine, InfoWorld, I-Way, Macworld, Network World, PC Games, PC World, Publish, Video Event, THE WEB Magazine, and WebMaster; online webzines: JavaWorld, NetscapeWorld, and SunWorld Online; **URUGUAY:** InfoWorld Uruguay; **VENEZUELA:** Computerworld Venezuela, PC World Venezuela; and **VIETNAM:** PC World Vietnam.   5/7/98

Credits

Acquisitions Editor
John Osborn

Development Editors
Vivian Perry
Denise Santoro

Technical Editors
Joe Benner
Dan Hodge

Copy Editors
Robert Campbell
Anne Friedman

Project Coordinator
Ritchie Durdin

Cover Coordinator
Constance Petros

Cover Design
Murder By Design

Graphics and Production Specialists
Mario Amador
Linda Marousek
Hector Mendoza
Dina F Quan

Quality Control Specialists
Mick Arellano
Mark Schumann

Proofreader
Christine Sabooni

Indexer
York Production Services

About the Author

Tom Arnold graduated from Purdue University in 1990 with a Bachelor of Science degree in computer science. He began his career in the computer industry at Asymetrix Corporation, where he was the Senior Test Lead and contributing developer for their Multimedia & Tools Group. Tom has dedicated the majority of his career to testing, working at Software Testing Laboratories (ST Labs, Inc.) and Microsoft Corporation. He has also developed and taught testing courses for Microsoft employees and other companies (such as MCI, IBM, Traveling Software, Spry/CompuServe, Attachmate, Hewlett-Packard, Delrina, Asymetrix, Aldus/Adobe, Peachtree, Compaq, Entergy, and Corel). As a Vice President at ST Labs, Inc., he led the development teams for ST Labs' add-on products, Test Now 1.0 and 2.0, and built the training department, which continued to provide training on Visual Test and other quality assurance topics.

In late 1996 Tom consulted on the Visual Test 4.0b update (later renamed to Visual Test 4.0r when it was purchased by Rational Software Corporation). In 1998 he left ST Labs to join a new company focusing on the creation of instructional digital media (DVDs, CD-ROMs, streaming content, and plain old videos) for software products. Tom also moved onto the Rational Software development team as a Development Manager for the release of Rational Visual Test 6.0. He has written *Software Testing with Visual Test 4.0* for IDG Books Worldwide, plays host and instructor in a Visual Test 6.0 video series, and teaches hands-on Visual Test classes. Visit www.vtindepth.com to get updates on all Visual Test–related topics or to contact Tom.

Charlotte, I thought this world held nothing for my spirit until I met you.

Foreword

I was honored when Tom asked me to write the foreword for the update of his book on Visual Test. Not only because Tom is a cofounder of ST Labs and one of my closest friends, but largely because Tom embodies the art and skill of today's best software test automation engineers.

Why do I say art and skill? Some believe that writing good automation is simply a matter of how many tests you can automate, how reusable the automation is, and how it can be optimized for highest performance. All of these are notable and worthy achievements but have little to do with shipping quality software.

The art of the automation has to do with the engineer's understanding of what the overall project objectives are. Even today, I see more test automation scrapped than used. I believe the basic problem stems from whether test engineers understand the business/financial implication of their actions. What business objective will the automation solve (feature coverage, costs control, schedule constraints, quality)? What are you going to automate and why? Have your fellow project team members bought in to the automation effort? Are they aware that automation is *another* software development project in its own right? Have you successfully identified the risks associated with the automation effort and communicated them to the rest of the project team members?

Software quality has become big business. By 1995, only 16.2 percent of application development projects in mission-critical client/server environments succeeded by being delivered on time, within budget, and with all of the functional capabilities intact. It's estimated that, in 1996, 175,000 custom applications were created at a cost of $250 billion. It's further estimated that $140 billion was wasted due to lack of the best practices. (My source for this information is the Standish Group.) How can this be? Aren't the people working on these projects smart? Aren't they experienced? Of course they are. Sadly, it's estimated that 80 percent of project problems are due to poor communication.

These are very startling statistics in light of software becoming ever more complex. With software development moving to "Internet time" and the multiple layering of systems, an infinite number of test scenarios is created. Because of this, I consider myself to be a tremendous advocate for test automation. That is, thoughtful, pragmatic test automation. What I've learned from Tom is that the most successful automation projects are the ones where expectations are set carefully, team dependencies are well understood, project progress is tracked and measured, and the overall business objectives are achievable.

I see a bright future for us to solve both complex and not-so-complex problems. I hope to see more in the way of automated test case generators, cross-platform technology, and better systems for the integration of test results from a variety of tools. In sum, test automation is here to stay. Let's just not forget it's more about the quality of the software we deliver and less about how whizzy the tools we used to create it are.

I wish you happy reading and great success in your pursuit of software quality.

Rob Arnold
Cofounder and Chairman, ST Labs, Inc.
E-mail address: roba@stlabs.com
Web address: www.stlabs.com

Preface

I had a few different goals when writing this book. First, I wanted to show a realistic view of Rational Visual Test 6.0 and explain how to approach an automation project effectively and flexibly. I also wrote the book to help readers already familiar and comfortable with Visual Test move on to advanced topics. In short, this book is meant to stay with you as you grow in your knowledge and abilities as a Visual Test programmer.

What's in This Book

This book has a lot of information and can be used as a reference as you're learning the tool, or can be read straight through if you want to "know it all." I'm the type who likes to have a roadmap so I can jump in and go directly to the parts that interest me. This preface is my attempt to provide you with such a roadmap.

Introduction: Chapters 1 through 3

This part starts with a history of Visual Test. It's interesting reading to find out the who, what, where, and why of this tool, especially as you come to love Visual Test. I then attempt to answer the question, "To automate or not to automate?" That is, without a doubt, the *important* question. When you're on a tight deadline and your manager or manager's manager thinks that test automation is going to be the answer to all your woes, for goodness sake read Chapter 2; it's essential. You'll then find out what's on Rational Visual Test's CD-ROM and what files get installed in which locations on your computer when you install the product.

An Overview of Visual Test: Chapters 4 through 7

It's here that you get more into the touring mode of Visual Test, its language and utilities. This part starts off with an introduction to the Microsoft Developer Studio, which is the integrated development environment (IDE) used by many of Microsoft's programming tools. Because Visual Test came from Microsoft's "Visual" family of tools, it remains integrated into this editing and debugging utility. You'll then get to the Visual Test programming language. (Known as the *Test language* for short, it is also still referred to as *TestBasic* even though Microsoft tried to do away with this term in version 4.0.) This overview doesn't teach you how to program; it only tells you about the Test language and how it compares to other structured programming languages (such as C, Pascal, and Visual Basic). You'll look at the utilities that accompany Visual Test. These include the scenario recorder, the Window Information (Winfo) Utility, the Suite Manager, and the Screen Capture/Comparison utility. Finally, you'll take a look at writing your first script in Visual Test. Having laid the groundwork in the previous chapters, we now jump in and put to use what we have learned. It's only a first script and isn't the prettiest thing you've ever laid your eyes on, but it's a start.

Building a Test Suite: Chapters 8 through 12

Here's where it all starts to come together. I'll begin by giving you some guidelines to follow either by yourself or with your teammates. These are based on what I've learned on automation projects and as a consultant when visiting companies doing automation with Visual Test. Then you'll be introduced to an approach for writing your scripts; Chapter 9 points out a couple of different approaches and describes the pros and cons of each. You will then write a couple of simple test cases, which will evolve as you progress. The goal is to point out how a test script begins and eventually evolves into something useful. You will then learn how to mine your existing scripts to create sharable and reusable utilities. This will save you and your team time when writing your scripts. And if you're working for a large company where there are other testing teams doing automation work, you can share the fruits of your labor to save your company even more time and money. Finally, you will review the whole, final test suite that was created in this part of the book.

Advanced Topics: Chapters 13 through 17

Here's where the fun begins. First, you'll get into advanced Visual Test methods, starting off with some advanced techniques for writing to or reading from different kinds of files. From there this part moves on to benchmark testing and pointers, Windows APIs, and callback functions. You'll also learn how to distribute your tests in a compiled form and learn from those on the front lines. Bill Hodghead, an automation test engineer at Microsoft; Dan Hodge, formerly my student and now a Visual Test instructor and consultant; and Joe Benner, a developer and test engineer on the Visual Test 6.0 project, share helpful information with you about localization issues, testing OLE controls, working with databases via Visual Test, and putting the new Microsoft Active Accessibility features to use.

Noel Nyman, a test engineer at Microsoft, then shows you one of the really cool tools that Microsoft uses in their testing: "Monkey." It takes a predefined set of logic and uses it to guide an automated script to work its way randomly through a product. This chapter is based on an internal Microsoft white paper and is provided in this book by Noel with Microsoft's permission. The source code is included on the CD-ROM. You'll then learn how to add a user interface to your test scripts so that you can communicate with the test engineer running your scripts and get to know the functions and subroutines in the Visual Test language that allow you to run scripts across a network.

The final chapter in this part gets into the new Web functions introduced in Visual Test 6.0. Learn how to write scripts with Visual Test that will test your HTML documents as they are displayed in Microsoft Internet Explorer.

Appendixes

Appendix A is a language reference that allows you to quickly see the syntax of all of the commands available in the Visual Test language.

Appendix B points you to other sources of information about Visual Test, such as hands-on classes and videotape training.

Appendix C is James Bach's "Useful Features of a Test Automation System." This paper is reprinted with permission from ST Labs, Inc., and James Bach, a well-known author and quality assurance consultant, and contains a great list of things to keep in mind when you have decided to embark on the path to automation.

Appendix D points you at other resources for your software quality assurance needs. This includes discussion groups, Web sites, newsgroups, newsletters, and books.

Appendixes E–H are the listings for the final scripts that were built in Chapters 10–12. If you don't have access to a computer but you're itching to see what the final, full test suite looks like, here are the routines in all their glory.

Appendix I is a log file — with "verbose" mode turned off — listing the results of the full run of the final test suite. This will give you an idea of what a simple log file looks like and what kind of information your scripts can provide while running tests.

Appendix J tells you more about what's on this book's CD-ROM. The CD contains all kinds of cool things, including video interviews with Dr. Cem Kaner, author of *Testing Computer Software*, and James Bach; evaluation copies of some tools you might find interesting to fill out your team's requirements (including bug tracking systems); and, of course, every single piece of code you find in this book.

Glossary

The glossary is new in this edition. When you see a word with which you aren't familiar, and it is italicized, it's likely that this word is in the glossary. I tried to include everything I could think of, and hopefully I hit the lion's share of relevant terms.

Conventions Used in This Book

I was given four icons to play with when I wrote this book. Those icons are *Note*, *Tip*, *Caution*, and *On the CD-ROM*, shown here:

 The Note icon is used when I want to draw your attention to something, give you an extra tidbit of information, or just make a side quip or comment. It's my way of saying, "By the way...."

 I use the Tip icon when I want to point out something that might not be obvious to the first-time user or that might be hidden in Visual Test's online documentation.

 When something could cause you to lose work or cost you time down the road, I use the Caution icon to alert you to the situation.

 I've put a lot of time into putting cool stuff on the CD-ROM. This icon focuses on something on the CD that you might want to explore further.

A Note About the Code in This Book

Finally, please note that while the majority of the source code examples in this book were written by myself, others have contributed source code (such as ST Labs, Noel Nyman, Dan Hodge, Bill Hodghead, Joe Benner, Microsoft, and Richard Wartner) that is copyrighted. You are free to use it in your own automations, but you cannot sell it with a retail product without prior written permission from the appropriate folks. Send me e-mail if you need such permissions.

Finding Technical Support

While I cannot provide any technical support help on any of these files or for Visual Test in general, I can direct you to a mailing list I set up that currently has over 800 subscribers. This e-mail list (or listserver) allows you to send a question or comment to the discussion group. That message is then broadcast to the members of the group, allowing others to answer your questions. Or, hopefully, it allows you to help others with their Visual Test problems. Subscribe to this group by sending e-mail to `MT_Info-request@eskimo.com`. In the subject line of your message, type in the word *SUBSCRIBE*. Leave the rest of your message blank (verify that an auto-signature line doesn't add text into the body of your message).

When you subscribe, you will receive a confirmation e-mail message describing how to use this service. I hope you find this to be an ongoing source of help.

Acknowledgments

A few people deserve to be recognized because I consider them key to the creation of this book. First I'd like to thank Shabbir Dahod for twisting my arm so that I learned Microsoft Test. Thank you Rick Fant of Microsoft Consulting Services. Rick gave the testing team the time we needed to develop robust and maintainable scripts for the Boeing 777 project. I'd also like to thank Bill Barry, James Tierney, and Rebecca Reutter of the Microsoft Worldwide Products Group for the opportunity to develop courses on Microsoft Test and Visual Test for Microsoft and its employees.

Thank you to Steve Fuchs (Program Manager, Visual Test 1.0–4.0), Bob Saile (Development Manager, Visual Test 1.0–4.0), Michael Scheele (Product Manager, Visual Test 4.0), and the rest of the Visual Test 4.0 team for their help in answering my questions on how to push the envelope of their great tool. Thank you to Daryl Wray (Program Manager, Visual Test 4.0b/r) for allowing me to be a part of the Microsoft development project. Thank you to Ed Humphrey (Product Manager, Visual Test 6.0) and Ilya Rozenberg (Quality Engineer, Visual Test 6.0) of Rational Software for letting me be a part of the development process. You guys have a killer product with a strong following. Take good care of it.

Brian Malcolm (Lead Developer, Visual Test 6.0), Arlene Kagi (Developer, Visual Test 6.0), and Joe Benner (Developer/Quality Engineer, Visual Test 6.0), thank you for your hard work on Rational Visual Test 6.0. It paid off! It was a great pleasure working with you! Thank you to Cory Low, my ski buddy and author of three successful Internet books. It was Cory's guidance and willingness to act as a sounding board during our skiing and chair-lift rides that helped keep me sane. Michelle Drewien, thank you for your graphics-artist abilities and sparing the readers of this book from my diagrams.

Thank you to everyone at IDG Books who put this book together, especially John Osborn, Jim Sumser (my editor-extraordinaire on the Visual Test 4.0 book), and Tim Lewis, who helped me appear to be a somewhat coherent writer. Denise Santoro, thank you for being such a cool editor on this Visual Test 6.0 update. Vivian Perry, thank you for your great editing and encouragement as we rode the "scheduling roller-coaster" together. Thanks to Dan Hodge for doing the technical edits on the first half of this book and for writing a section that discusses OLE testing with Visual Test. Joe Benner, thank you for your willingness to review the harder, more technical last half of this book and for sharing your knowledge on MSAA. Noel Nyman of Microsoft, thank you very much for sharing your knowledge on automated monkeys by writing an entire chapter on the topic (Chapter 14)!

Mary Sweeney, thank you for the hallway chats and for making me feel good by asking me to speak in your VT classes. Bill Hodghead, thank you for providing great advanced topics material for the book and examples on the CD-ROM about working with databases. Thank you Shannon Cooper and Keith McMahon of ST Labs, Inc., for providing the readers with expert articles on this book's CD-ROM. Thanks to Richard Wartner and his team of contributors for providing a great online book on using Visual Test (found on this book's CD-ROM).

Thank you Charlotte for putting up with my long hours, late nights, and booked (pun intended) weekends in writing this new edition. Special note to DDI: take good care of ST Labs. She's a fine company with great people. And finally, thank you to Rob Arnold (chairman, co-owner, and founder of ST Labs, Inc.), for your kind words and insights in the foreword. Also for your ever-appreciated business advice and the excellent, weekly rounds of golf (I'm going to take the money I no longer spend on beer and use it for golf lessons, so watch yourself, Mr. Trout). Lisa, thank you for putting up with me every time I call and say, "Can Rob come out and play?"

And finally, thank you to the readers of *Software Testing with Visual Test 4.0* who were kind enough to write me to let me know what they found helpful about the book. Thank you to the MT_Info discussion group for e-mailing me suggestions on what to make sure is included in this new edition. And thank you, the reader (wow, did you really read this far?), for buying this book and thereby contributing to my golf lessons so that I can eventually beat my brother Rob at golf.

Contents at a Glance

Appendixes

Contents

Appendixes

Introduction

It was in January 1992 that I was first introduced to what was then called Microsoft Test. It was a beta of the 1.0 version, and because Asymetrix (now Asymetrix Learning Systems) and Microsoft Corporation had strong ties with each other, we were on Microsoft's beta program.

I was the Senior Test Lead on the ToolBook 3.0 project at Asymetrix, responsible for leading the quality assurance effort for that product. The Director of Development had heard of this new tool and how it would automate testing. He asked me if I would be interested in putting together a demonstration for the company's founder, Paul Allen, who cofounded Microsoft with Bill Gates those many years ago. "Er. . . uh. . . No, I think I'll pass on that one," was my first reply, mostly because I didn't want to be put on the spot in front of Paul, but also because I was busy getting our testing effort under way for the latest version of ToolBook.

Then he posed the question to me differently. Actually, the question became more of a command. "Let me put it this way: Learn how to use Microsoft Test and be ready with a demo for Paul on Friday." You can probably guess my second reply: "Uhm, sure! Happy to!" Considering it was Wednesday, there was a bit of pressure to get this done. So I cleared the decks, sat down in front of my computer, installed and ran Microsoft Test, and. . . where to start? I wasn't sure.

It seemed a simple task: Learn what the product is about and what it can do for our development teams. Simple, yet the cursor in the Microsoft Test editor just kept blinking at me, offering neither help nor direction on how to proceed. It just kept flashing, waiting for me to do something, anything!

I fumbled around with different approaches and ideas until I pieced together something for Paul based on the examples that came with the Test 1.0 beta and my background in programming. Fortunately he had to cancel the Friday meeting, so I had the entire weekend to continue to prepare for the demo that had been moved to the following Monday.

As much as I'd like to say my scripting and layout were works of art, they weren't. It was my first attempt at an automated script. I wasn't sure to what degree I should be testing the product using automation, and I didn't have any idea of how much time it would take me to automate an entire product. Even so, the presentation left the executives with high hopes in what automation promised to contribute to delivering a quality product to market.

A successful demonstration, then, right? Well, no. Not really, because they weren't given the entire picture. And I wasn't in the position to give them the entire picture because of my newness to the realm of test automation. What wasn't impressed upon them was the time it took to come up to speed with the tool, the effort required to write automated scripts, and the number of people it would take not only to guarantee that the product received the same level of testing it had before but also to allow for the scripts to be written correctly and maintained over the full product cycle.

After that, using Microsoft Test became a part of Asymetrix's testing efforts. Unfortunately, the number of testers didn't increase. We were to provide the same level of testing that we'd given before this new tool made its debut and begin putting our testing into automated scripts.

We did our best, shared our efforts with other testing teams at the company, and figured out what worked and what didn't. We even started building some common utilities and scripting libraries that we could share throughout the company. And we refined our efforts from there.

We were encouraged to automate the entire product. Because script development is truly a parallel development project, it takes time to develop scripts to automate some or much of the testing on a product. Because the number of testers wasn't allowed to increase, the bug count dropped — we were spending all of our time automating. We were then asked to increase the bug count to help keep up pressure on the developers. Because we were still laying the groundwork for our automated scripts and still understanding the full potential of this automation tool, we weren't at a point where the scripts would help test the product. So we returned to manual testing. The bug count increased; the script development dropped. We were then asked to redouble our scripting efforts; the bug count dropped again — in a vicious and all-too-common cycle for companies new to automation.

Taking my experiences from Asymetrix, I moved on to a project at Microsoft, where I was given the chance to "do it right." After building a solid yet flexible foundation, adding automated tests, and introducing new team members into the mix, I understood how it could all come together when one is given the opportunity to do it right. Having had this experience, I constructed a course on Visual Test for ST Labs, Inc., which I taught at Microsoft, Compaq, IBM, Corel, Hewlett-Packard, and so on. And you know what I learned? The companies that already had solid automation processes in place were taking very similar approaches.

Since the first Visual Test class and the *Software Testing with Visual Test 4.0* book, I've had a chance to become more deeply involved in the enhancement of Visual Test. I was hired by Microsoft to manage the development effort for the Visual Test 4.0b release (which was later released as Rational Visual Test 4.0r). Then I was hired by Rational Software to help manage the development effort for Visual Test 6.0.

The methods, approaches, and tidbits that I've picked up along the way as a Test programmer, instructor, and player in the design of the latest version of Visual Test are what I'm looking forward to sharing with you in this book.

Tom Arnold
E-mail address: `toma@inproduction.com`
Web address: `www.vtindepth.com`
`www.inproduction.com`

Introduction

A History of Visual Test

Back in 1996, when I wrote the first edition of this book, then known as *Software Testing with Visual Test 4.0*, I had the opportunity to talk with Bob Saile, Development and Quality Assurance Manager for the Microsoft Visual Test 4.0 team. Bob had been at Microsoft since the beginning, and he told me something about the history of Visual Test and how it got its start. The reason Microsoft Visual Test — known as Microsoft Test for versions 1.0 through 3.0 — became a product was that enough of Microsoft's customers asked for it to be made available to them, instead of being used exclusively by Microsoft Corporation as an internal testing tool.

At the end of the 1980s, Microsoft was working on ways to automate some of its testing efforts. Specifically, it was interested in capturing mouse movements and keystrokes. Its first efforts involved a hardware device it called the Versatile Computer Recorder (VCR) that was to be used for testing DOS applications and that worked by plugging the mouse and keyboard directly into the VCR hardware. This project was overseen by Byron Bishop, the development lead, and Marv Parsons, the test manager.

Applied to the predecessor to Microsoft Access, the VCR tool was responsible for blazing the trail into the area of test automation and was responsible for bringing the tracking and finding of system problems (*bugs*) to new levels. Its biggest task was ensuring that problems fixed in the software didn't recur as the development cycle came to an end. It broke Microsoft's project bug-count records, so Microsoft and its quality assurance groups realized the value of this kind of automation early on.

After realizing the potential of test automation, Saile approached Mike Maples, then Vice President of Development at Microsoft, to increase the head count in Saile's group, so that he could improve upon the existing automation schema. It wasn't possible because there weren't any projects that could afford to lose developers at that time. Test automation advances were temporarily put on hold.

A few months later, Saile was approached by an internal tools group at Microsoft that wanted him to help develop a software version of the VCR system. After 10 months of development time, and feedback from over 300 testers at Microsoft who had played with the tool, the group developed a new system it referred to as WATT: the Windows Application Testing Tool. The team had taken what it had learned from the VCR hardware used under DOS, avoided the problems the VCR system had faced, and created a new tool that worked in the Windows 3.0 environment.

All of this was going on around spring 1990, the time that Windows 3.0 made its debut. A number of Windows 3.0 developers outside Microsoft were developing new programs that would run under this latest version. One of Microsoft's major clients heard about the tool and decided to use it to help the software development efforts for its new Windows 3.0 product. The client fell in love with the tool and provided feedback to Saile's team to help improve it even further.

Later that same year, Saile presented the tool at a Microsoft Windows developers' conference in Seattle, Washington. Those attending were intrigued by the possibilities and wanted to hear more about it; then they wanted copies of it so that they could use the tool in their development cycles.

Because such a small group of people were interested in the tool, Microsoft wasn't interested in turning it into a product. The company decided to release it to developers as an unsupported tool. Saile's group's only focus was to support the 300 to 400 testers at Microsoft; there wasn't enough time to support those outside the company. Incredibly, the WATT group was made up of only two developers, two testers, one group leader, and a program manager.

Next came a crucial turning point in the decision whether or not the product would remain an internal tool, unsupported for developers outside Microsoft. The outside developers continued to call Saile and Steve Fuchs, the Program Manager of WATT, telling them that they would pay for support on the tool. They were using it, liked it, and wanted to continue to get updates on it. Plus, they wanted some kind of technical support to help them with their questions.

It was then that Maples approached Saile and asked him how much effort was needed to enhance the documentation and add a script recorder to turn the tool into a product that could be shipped to clients. Microsoft Test was born.

Microsoft Test 1.0

Microsoft Test 1.0 showed up in beta form around the end of 1991, and as a fully fledged product in spring 1992. It provided the ability to work with Microsoft Windows controls, capture and compare dialog boxes and screens, and generate *Test Basic* (a language very similar to Microsoft Visual Basic) *scripts* using a *script recorder*. As a result, Test 1.0 was a good first version of an automation tool (see Figures 1-1 and 1-2).

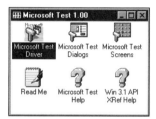

Figure 1-1: Test 1.0 installation

Figure 1-2: The Microsoft Test 1.0 About box

The first version included tools for capturing the contents of the screen and the controls of dialog boxes. It also came with some simple scripts that served as examples of how to use the tools.

Microsoft Test itself was considered a *test driver* (a program that steps through and runs a group of test scripts); it wasn't until version 2.0 that a driver appeared that ran each test script file in turn (later titled the *Suite Manager*). And when it did, the driver itself was considered a sample script. Version 1.0's main window can be seen in Figure 1-3.

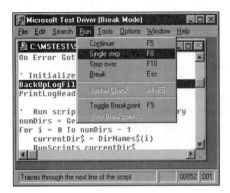

Figure 1-3: The Microsoft Test 1.0 main window

Microsoft Test 1.0 was a pretty good starting point and gave developers and testers an automation tool with which to begin their work. What it lacked as a programming environment (for example, it lacked a way to view the values of local or global variables, and it lacked a way to force a variable to be explicitly declared, a deficit that resulted in mistyped variables being automatically declared as new variables), it made up for in value, with a $99 retail price.

Microsoft Test 2.0

In 1993, version 2.0 hit the market. It was a big leap forward, offering a number of new features for automating Windows 3.1 products (see Figure 1-4).

The new *integrated development environment* (IDE) made its appearance, allowing users to access all the product's different tools from one window. Also included with this version were the latest advances in user interface (UI) design, including a scalable toolbar, a status bar, and child windows for tracking the values of the local and global variables used in a script.

FastTest, a feature of Microsoft Test 1.0 that allowed for the quick development of test suites, went undocumented in the 2.0 version to encourage testers to move over to the normal Test Basic scripting language. In version 3.0, FastTest was removed completely.

One of the biggest features of Microsoft Test 2.0 was the capability to precompile large declaration files into *header files*. With large blocks of declarations and utilities combined into one precompiled file, compilation time decreased dramatically. The theory was, "Why recompile sections of code that aren't changing between executions of the scripts?"

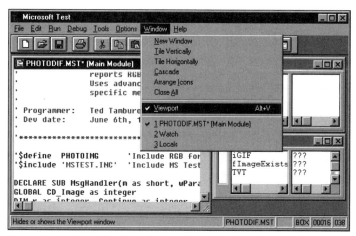

Figure 1-4: Test 2.0 offered a number of welcome new features.

Along these same lines was the ability to compile scripts into a *pseudocode,* or *.PCD,* file. This further decreased the compilation time because the scripts were already in a compiled state. It didn't increase the run-time speed, however, because scripts were interpreted just as they were when a non-PCD file was compiled and run. However, it did allow them to be run without reincluding external files, to check syntax and to perform parse-time checks. It also opened up another possibility. Tests the automation engineer didn't want modified without his or her knowledge could now be distributed in compiled form for other testers to use. Those scripts could also be run on multiple machines without violating any software licensing agreements.

Context-sensitive help was also added, a foreshadowing of what was to come with documentation. Microsoft was slowly moving its documentation online; a controversial move made company-wide that was encouraged by many users but discouraged by others. The printed documentation was slowly shrinking.

Personally, after getting the general idea of how to lay out an automated test suite, I rarely returned to the book. The online help described how each feature worked and offered a number of coding examples to clarify how each Test Basic command was used.

Some new and enhanced *dynamic link libraries* (DLLs) were added to version 2.0. These allowed three specific functions:

✦ Automation of DOS applications with DOS Virtual Machine (VM) routines

✦ Communication between other Microsoft applications using Dynamic Data Exchange (DDE)

✦ Remote distributed testing using the new Test Talk routines, which allowed for running tests on more than one machine across a Network Basic input/output system (NetBIOS)–compatible network

A driver made its first appearance that would allow testers to specify which tests to run. While many thought it hideous because of the colors used in its user interface, it definitely served a positive purpose by providing a way to run multiple scripts, and it served as an example of how to create a test driver. The test case driver is shown in Figure 1-5.

This first implementation of the test driver was written using Microsoft Test's own language: Test Basic. It was a useful tool for batch-running all automated tests, and it provided an excellent example of how to use the latest feature of Microsoft Test: the User Interface Editor. Test 2.0 enabled testers to add dialog boxes and menus to their test scripts. They could now either use the driver that was included with Microsoft Test or design their own. In addition, they could create countless other tools that required a user interface of some kind.

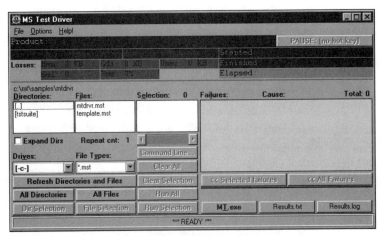

Figure 1-5: The Microsoft Test 2.0 test case driver

Microsoft Test 3.0 and 3.0a

The next version of Microsoft Test, version 3.0, was born in fall 1994. Its installation program can be seen in Figure 1-6.

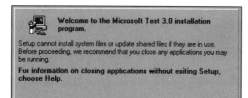

Figure 1-6: The Microsoft Test 3.0 installation program

When it was launched, Microsoft Test 3.0 didn't seem to be much of an upgrade from 2.0. Actually, it looked very similar, at first glance, to the previous version. When people looked a little deeper, however, they found that Microsoft had been busy once again.

All of the DLLs had been rewritten to be compatible with 32-bit versions of Microsoft Windows. As a result, those software companies that were busily upgrading their 16-bit applications to 32-bit found this latest version of Test invaluable. They could now take their existing scripts and run them on a 32-bit platform, with little or no modification.

The error numbers were another big change to the way Microsoft Test worked. Previously, each DLL had returned error numbers specific to itself. In some cases, tracking down an error number was tricky because some DLLs would begin numbering their errors in the same range as another DLL's routines. Some would return negative numbers for their error return values; others would return large positive numbers. And then, the Test Basic language itself would return its own run-time error numbers.

In Test 3.0 this issue was addressed by assigning a base number to each DLL as it was loaded and by having all DLLs start numbering their error return values at zero (0). The return value was then added to the base number assigned to the DLL returning the error, to arrive at a unique error number. This solution was very creative because it provided automation programmers with a unique error numbering system, and it left the error numbering scheme open-ended for future expansion.

While no discernible change was made to the *Test Talk* routines that allowed for distributing tests across a network, the name that collectively referred to those routines was changed to *Network Distribution Libraries*.

Note   Network Distribution Libraries was in turn changed to *Network Distribution Procedures* in Visual Test 4.0.

Last of all, the screen capture and comparison utility was updated. A screen no longer needed to be referred to as an index position in the capture file; each screen capture could now be associated with a string describing the image. A new user interface was given to the capture utility as well. No modifications were made to the dialog capture and comparison utility, however. This was a foreshadowing of what was to happen to the dialog comparison utility in version 4.0; that is, the dialog utility was not included with Visual Test 4.0.

In spring 1995, a 3.0a version of Test was made available, which added support for Windows 95 controls. It was now possible to work with the new desktop layout, tree controls, tabs, sliders, spinners, and so on.

Microsoft Visual Test 4.0

As Microsoft's language group was moving into all-visual tools, it was decided that Microsoft Test 4.0 should go into that same group. The result was to rename the product Microsoft Visual Test and move it to a different development environment. An example of this new, visual approach can be seen in Figure 1-7, with the splash screen.

Figure 1-7: The splash screen displayed when Visual Test 4.0 was started. Depending on what programming tools were installed and how the Developer Studio was set up, different sections of this splash screen were highlighted.

Microsoft Developer Studio

Part of creating the vision of Visual Tools entailed having them share one integrated development environment (IDE). Therefore, they all used the Microsoft Developer Studio, including Microsoft Visual J++. (Back then, Visual Basic remained the rogue development tool that used its own specialized development environment. For the moment, anyway.)

As a result, when working with most of the visual tools, you needed to learn only one programming environment, and you had access to all your tools in one place.

The Move to 32-bit Only

This latest version of Microsoft Test worked only on 32-bit versions of Microsoft Windows: Windows NT and Windows 95. To make sure that 16-bit users weren't forgotten, however, the Microsoft Visual Test team followed the example of the then-current version of Visual C++ by including the previous 16-bit version (Microsoft Test 3.0) on the installation CD-ROM.

Snap-On Parts

This version 4.0 made Visual Test more modular than before. If Visual C++ was installed at a later date, it integrated right into the Developer Studio. If version control was an issue, and Microsoft SourceSafe was installed, it snapped into place in the "studio" as well. NuMega Technologies worked closely with Microsoft, so BoundsChecker 3.0 integrated into the IDE for use by both Visual C++ and Visual Test. Additionally, Software Testing Laboratories (now ST Labs, Inc.) created an add-on tool (Test Now 2.0) for Visual Test that snapped into place on the Tools menu, just like BoundsChecker, so that the goal of having all tools available in one place was realized.

On the CD-ROM

Test Now 2.0, by ST Labs, Inc., has since been discontinued and is no longer supported. Because it is still helpful to many test engineers seeking to dissect code and take sections for use in their own scripts, ST Labs was kind enough to make it available for inclusion on this book's CD-ROM. Keep in mind that it is completely unsupported.

Intrinsic Language

Microsoft Test versions 1.0 through 3.0 all relied on DLLs to provide the special functions for working with Windows controls, network protocols, and basically everything that elevated the tool above and beyond being another BASIC language. All of these DLLs were rolled into the Visual Test language in version 4.0. This format provided better support for working with keywords, and by encapsulating the multiple .DLL files into a single DLL, it cleaned up the product's footprint. The problem was, however, that people who used Visual Test via other languages, such as Visual Basic and C/C++, could no longer do so since these routines were now invisible to them.

Rational Visual Test 4.0r

Around the same time that Microsoft was cutting the deal with Rational Software for the purchase of Microsoft Visual Test (in October 1996), a team of testers and programmers were busily creating a Visual Test 4.0b. This "b" version was developed specifically to fix known bugs in Visual Test. It also reexposed or *exported* the functions that were previously rolled into a single DLL so that Visual Basic and Visual C/C++ programmers could use those Test functions.

The first quarter of 1997 saw a Rational Visual Test 4.0r release of this tool, which was basically the Microsoft Test 4.0b release with one big exception: The product was now relabeled such that all occurrences of "Microsoft" were replaced with "Rational Software."

Rational Visual Test 6.0

What happened to version 5.0? The version number was skipped so that Visual Test had the same version number as the latest version of Microsoft Developer Studio, the editing environment used by Visual Test (version skipping is not an uncommon practice for achieving more synergy between integrated products and the public's understanding of how they integrate). In September 1998, Visual Test 6.0 was announced as an updated and even more powerful version of the product.

Visual Test 6.0 has been upgraded so that it now works with the latest version of Microsoft Developer Studio, which Microsoft recently renamed from Microsoft Developer Studio 97 to *Microsoft Developer Studio 6.0*. Having Rational Visual Test use Microsoft Developer Studio 6.0 (or *Dev Studio* for short) as its editor and debugger keeps Visual Test on the same path it has followed for the last couple of years and spares Rational from having to create their own editor and debugger for Visual Test. But using Microsoft's development environment comes with a price: Rational's schedule could be affected by Microsoft's schedule. If Microsoft Developer Studio 6.0 slipped, so did Rational Visual Test 6.0. Wondering why it took so long for the next version of Visual Test to come out? 'Nuff said.

Web Functions

One of the coolest features added to Visual Test 6.0 is its Web functionality. These functions allow you to test HTML documents by using Microsoft Internet Explorer 4.0 (or newer). Clicking on links, finding pages within frames, and filling in forms are just a few of the things that you can do with these functions. You can also set many of the attributes of a Web page by using the Set* forms of these new functions. This is because the object model that Internet Explorer uses allowed the Visual Test programmers to modify a currently displayed page. That means that through these

Web functions you can modify the attributes of an HTML document being displayed in Microsoft Internet Explorer (not the actual HTML source found on the server). These modifications allow you to put in your own instrumentation so that you can more easily test a page.

MSAA

Microsoft Active Accessibility is a new feature of Visual Test 6.0 that allows you to work with applications that are Active Access–compliant. MSAA applications can receive a request from Visual Test 6.0 and return information about that application. For example, if you're testing a word processor that supports MSAA and allows for the contents of the main window to be returned via an Active Access function call, you will be able to easily grab the contents of a word processor — something that in the past was much more difficult to do.

Registry Functions

New functions for working with the Windows 95 and 98 and Windows NT Registries are now available. These allow for searching through keys, modifying their values, and even deleting them. This is a very helpful feature when you are running tests that rely upon the Registry being in a known state.

New Controls

New controls have been included in Windows 98 and Windows NT 5.0. The same is true in Visual Basic 5.0 and 6.0. These are supported in Visual Test 6.0 to make testing applications that much more easy. Specific controls include the Rebar tool (a dockable menu bar and toolbar) and the datetime picker used by programs requesting date and time information from the user.

The Competition: Merged

In the earlier edition of this book I listed the different competing automation tools on the market. The list wasn't all that extensive, but it gave the reader a clear understanding that other competing companies were in the marketplace offering excellent automation tools. Rational Software not only acquired Visual Test, it has been acquiring other tools companies since 1996. So what does one do with one's competitors? In Rational's case, they simply acquired them.

The Timeline

The software quality assurance community has seen a number of changes in recent years as companies began merging or acquiring tools from other companies. In 1995, two companies — Pure Software and Atria Corp. — merged to create Pure Atria Software. Their tools focused mostly on the UNIX world with an emphasis on supporting Windows NT as well. Their key tools — Purify, Quantify, Coverage, and ClearCase — offered some of the best testing, analysis, and management software products available.

On October 2, 1996, Rational Software announced it had acquired Visual Test from Microsoft for a $23 million cash payment. At the time of the announcement Bob Muglia, Vice President for Developer Tools at Microsoft said, "Microsoft selected Rational because of its excellent record of working with the developer community. We are confident in Rational's ability to continue the development of Visual Test and support the large installed base of Visual Test users, including Microsoft's own development teams. Rational's continued evolution of the product will extend its support for component-based development. The combination of Rational and Microsoft tools provides a scalable end-to-end solution for enterprise and Internet application development."

On November 12, 1996, Rational Software and SQA, Inc. (creators of SQA Robot, SQA Manager, and SQA LoadTest) jointly announced a definitive merger agreement to "create a worldwide company providing a comprehensive solution for component-based software development." The press release also stated that "the companies plan to integrate their respective products, creating a comprehensive suite of tools for modeling, assembling, testing, and managing components. Combining SQA's comprehensive automated software quality (ASQ) product suite with the Visual Test product that Rational recently acquired from Microsoft provides a broader ASQ solution for Rational. The merged solution will be integrated with leading component-construction tools, such as Microsoft Visual Basic, Visual C++, Java, and PowerBuilder."

February 27, 1997, saw the announcement of the completion of the Rational/SQA merger. "This merger with SQA is a key part of our strategy for providing the leading solution for automated development of component-based systems," said Mike Devlin, president of Rational. "By adding SQA's industry-leading line of Windows-based testing tools, we will be able to offer our customers a complete integrated solution."

This merger with SQA brought Visual Test's biggest competitor into the same company. The question became, "What now?" Will they sell SQA Robot as a higher-end automation tool and keep Visual Test as a lower-priced tool? Or will they somehow combine the two technologies to make an end-all, be-all automation tool? Only time will tell. As for now, with the release of Visual Test 6.0, they are following the model of two separate products.

In the first quarter of 1997, Visual Test 4.0r was released by Rational. The product was mostly a maintenance release with many bugs fixed, and it was relabeled to bear the company name "Rational Software" instead of "Microsoft Corporation." It also made visible again the functions that were previously made invisible (to Visual C/C++ and Visual Basic users in the first release of 4.0).

On March 31, 1997, Rational acquired Performance Awareness, their flagship product being an automated performance testing tool called *preVue-C/S*, which according to its marketing materials is "the only client/server testing tool with a virtual user recording technology that is completely independent of the client environment."

One week later, on April 7, 1997, Rational announced its agreement to acquire Pure Atria Software, which added the Purify, Quantify, Coverage, Performix, and ClearCase tools to the Rational family of products. The merger was completed on July 30, 1997.

Fast-forward to March 10, 1998, and Mainsoft Corporation (www.mainsoft.com) releases a ported version of Visual Test 4.0r for Solaris Sparc 2.5.1. Don Gallagher, Vice President of Sales, said, "By utilizing Visual Test 4.0r, MainWin developers can now test applications ported to UNIX efficiently and in a timely manner by taking advantage of Visual Test's ability to rapidly validate Windows applications on UNIX. Also, the scripting language, Test Basic, is easy for programmers to use since it provides them with access to familiar programming features such as Windows API on UNIX platforms, allowing for the writing of powerful and maintainable application test scripts."

In September 1998, after a long wait and with high expectations, Rational Visual Test 6.0 is announced. This version follows the same path as the previous version in that it is integrated with the Microsoft development environment, Microsoft Developer Studio 6.0. It adds support for HTML testing, registry settings, and MSAA-compliant applications, as well as new controls for Windows 98 and Windows NT 5.0.

The Aftermath

Wow! So who are the remaining players in the automation tools market? A few are still around, with three of the key companies being *Segue Software* (www.segue.com), creators of QA Partner, *Mercury Interactive* (www.merc-int.com), makers of WinRunner and LoadRunner, and *AutoTester* (www.autotester.com), creators of the AutoTester tool. The two key things about these Segue Software and Mercury Interactive products is that they support X-Windows on the UNIX operating system. QA Partner by Segue even runs on the Macintosh. But Visual Test isn't out of the running for UNIX, because a company called *Mainsoft Corporation* ("Microsoft Development Technologies on UNIX") ported Microsoft Test 3.0 to run on their MainWin product, which in turn runs with X-Windows. And in March 1998, they released the Visual Test 4.0r port to UNIX.

The big question on everyone's mind is, "What's going to happen to Visual Test?" When concerns were voiced about the product's future, Ed Humphrey, the Product Manager for Visual Test at Rational Software, posted a message to the MT_Info discussion group. In a message to that group on January 22, 1998, Ed's response was, "You, as customers and as representatives of a very significant segment of the QA/QE population, are very important to Rational. VT provides us with insight and access to Microsoft development, making it strategic for us. If you don't believe that, then perhaps the fact that we are contractually obligated to support VT at Microsoft through 2002 will lessen concerns. We know you're concerned about the product's future. Our hope is that [this] release will provide proof that we are investing in this product."

The MT Info group is a listserver discussion group consisting of over 800 people. Refer to the appendix of this book or the CD-ROM for more information on how to join. Rational uses MT Info as one of its venues for releasing information to the Visual Test community.

The Future

And what does the future hold for Visual Test? In his January 22, 1998, message to the MT_Info listserver, Ed Humphrey speculated that in future versions of Visual Test, Rational Software would:

✦ Ensure that test assets developed today can be used with it.

✦ Improve the reusability of test assets and make it easier to build reusable test code.

✦ Maintain and expand upon VT's lead as a test programming tool.

✦ Use common core technologies between VT and SQA Robot wherever possible (as he said, it "makes sense and saves us some money").

Without a doubt, Visual Test has a large following. The MT_Info group that I started years ago currently has over 800 active subscribers who all work together to answer each other's questions. The user base is there, and we all hope that Visual Test continues to be developed well into the Year 2000. It's also doing very well in the Japanese market, for which a localized version of Visual Test 4.0r exists.

The key advantage to Visual Test is that it is used heavily by Microsoft to test its own applications. Because of Rational's strong ties with Microsoft it will hopefully continue to be on the leading edge of support for new controls and features found in future versions of Windows NT and Windows 9x.

Summary

Visual Test was known as Microsoft Test for versions 1.0 to 3.0a. It started as a purely internal development tool, but when external clients became interested in it, it was developed for wider use. It gradually improved its user interface, and Version 2.0 introduced header files, pseudocode (.PCD) files, and context-sensitive help. Version 3.0 rewrote the DLLs and updated the screen capture and comparison utility. In Version 4.0, Visual Test instigated a fully visual set of tools, all available on the same screen, giving full support for Windows 95 and Windows NT.

After it was acquired by Rational Software Corporation in 1996, Microsoft Visual Test became Rational Visual Test. The first Rational release of this product was the rebranded version called Rational Visual Test 4.0r, which had all traces of the word "Microsoft" replaced with "Rational Software." Also, many bug fixes had been made. Finally, the latest version, which is the main focus of this book, is Visual Test 6.0. Dubbed "Version 6.0" (skipping 5.0) to stay in line with the version number of Microsoft Developer Studio — the editor used by Visual Test — this product boasts many new features to make it an even more powerful automation tool.

✦   ✦   ✦

Why Automate Software Testing?

Over the last few years, testing software has become increasingly complex and fraught with danger. Windows NT (4.0 and 5.0) and Windows (95 and 98) both present highly intricate programming needs, and so the opportunity for bugs and poor software performance is very real. Yet the time available to check for all these bugs and performance problems, in the present cutthroat software development market, means that a product's success depends on quickly and efficiently removing them. This, in turn, makes automated testing an essential tool.

Because of this, automated testing is now becoming integrated into the general development cycle. We shall look, first, at the cycle as a whole, then at the role and benefits of automated testing within it. Finally, we shall consider three of the perceived drawbacks of test automation.

I would like to say up front, before we get too far into this book, that no test automation tool is a silver bullet. Automation takes time, effort, and commitment from all involved, including an understanding from management about the realities of what automation can and cannot do. The purpose of this book is to provide you with a *how to* approach to using Rational Visual Test 6.0. These approaches and side comments about the realities of automation are based on my experiences and the experiences of people whom I've spoken with who've participated on test automation teams.

Attitude Is Everything

An important aspect of this book for me is the attitude in which it is written. I am as much a student as you are. I had to pick up how to use Microsoft Test on my own and then had to defend when it did and did not make sense to use it in a particular way. To a certain extent, I was feeling my way along a dark passage without a flashlight.

Fortunately, as it turned out, when I created a class on Visual Test and started teaching that class, the people I spoke to who were getting the most out of their automation happened to be doing it the same way that I was. This reinforcement of my methods helped me realize how best to use this tool and how to share these approaches with others.

Be like them: Be open minded; be willing to try some of these ideas; be willing to fail; be willing to dive in, move forward, make mistakes, and come back later and tweak the work you've already done.

If you aren't willing to do that, then you're making your job harder than it needs to be. Whether you're making mistakes or writing code that Bill Gates would be proud of, the only way you're going to learn is to start putting down some code and tweaking from there.

The first thing I would ask you to do is be willing to try different things and be willing to fail. If you're not making mistakes, you're not learning. Even those of you who think you already know much of this should at least browse the next chapters. Even if you think you know most of it, you might pick something up along the way. Every time I go into a company using an automation tool, I learn a new approach that can be added to my bag of tricks. In turn, they also learn tricks and methods from me to help them improve upon their existing processes. No one knows it all. The more we can share information, the better the results of our automation efforts.

The Development Cycle

Development cycles for computer software vary from company to company and depend on how long a firm has been in the software development business. For the sake of establishing the big picture, in this chapter I will include only a broad overview of the development process. I'm speaking broadly about the development cycle because it varies so greatly between companies. This book is about how to automate portions of testing through Visual Test, so please pardon some of the broad strokes.

To begin with, a group of people get together and decide to build a product. This group is run by a *Program Manager*, who orchestrates the development process by managing the Quality Assurance (QA), Development, and Technical Writing Leads, as shown in Figure 2-1.

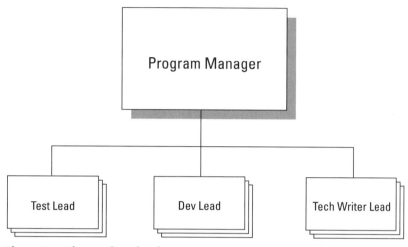

Figure 2-1: The product development group

Usually, the process starts with the engineers telling the marketers, or the *Product Manager*, which features they can get into the product based on the suggested timeline. If the team has been through enough development cycles in the past, and if it has learned from those efforts, it'll then put together a *functional specification* that outlines the features and milestones of the product.

Note The Product Manager, not to be confused with the Program Manager, works on the marketing side, taking care of building the marketing messages, art work, timelines with manufacturers, and advertising. Depending on which company you work for, usually the Product Manager reports to the Director of Marketing, while the Program Manager reports to the Director of Development.

The quality assurance engineers then come on the scene (some argue that they should be involved from the beginning, but that's a matter of program management style and depends on how mature the company is in its experience in developing software) and begin designing their overall *test plan* for the features of the product. The documentation team will also come in around the same time as the quality assurance team and will begin designing its approach to documenting the product.

The goal is to have the test plan and checklists laid out and ready to be manually stepped through by the test engineers when each feature is completed by the programmers. Each item on a test checklist is considered a *scenario,* and related scenarios are grouped into *test cases*. These test cases are organized into *suites* of tests that focus on such testing concerns as benchmarks, stress testing, functionality testing, and so on.

The other part of that goal is to have the documentation reach completion at the same time as the developers and testers are finalizing the development of the product. This is basically the theory of how the development cycle works, not including the marketing side of things.

The Real World

The reality of what tends to happen in the development cycle, especially in a young software company, is that a group of people get together over hamburgers, decide to develop a product, get a lead developer to put the product together, and then decide that it needs to be documented and tested before it is released onto the market. Quality Assurance and Documentation find themselves on the back end of the development cycle, where all the time pressures build up because the schedule has been underestimated.

It can be argued that this is a cynical view, but I guarantee that a high percentage of the people reading this book are nodding their heads and saying, "Yup, that's exactly what happens!"

An experienced Program Manager knows not only to have as accurate a project timeline as possible, but to also add time for "feature creep" caused by overzealous developers, marketing types, and, sometimes, the company's owner. She also keeps in mind the bugs that can be caused by junior developers, incompatibility issues with another company's software or hardware, staff turnover, and other potential complications.

While this padding can help take some of the pressure off those who find themselves on the back end of the schedule, that pressure still exists to some degree. In many cases, though, it is actually positive, since it keeps everyone focused and moving forward toward getting the product finished and out the door on time and with high quality. The trick is finding the fine line between the amount of pressure that is positive, as opposed to negative — where everyone on the team is thrashing around in their efforts to reach their intended goals.

The Role of Test Automation

What is the role of automated testing in this process? What benefits can it produce for those harried test engineers and for the overstretched and understaffed development process as a whole? First, let's take a look at what test automation is, and then we'll consider its benefits.

What Is Test Automation?

A number of people, when first hearing about test automation, assume it's meant to replace the human aspect of testing. As it turns out, just the opposite is true. Automated tests are helpful in performing tests quickly and precisely, but they don't replace the human tester, who has to run the tests, check that all is going satisfactorily, and *think* about what other items need to be checked to ensure quality. Where automation wins is in doing the same steps the same way over and over again. As a way of catching errors early and allowing for the production of much more reliable software, it can cut up to 80 percent from testing time, as Microsoft has boasted of the results its projects have realized.

Simply put, test automation emulates user actions such as clicking on buttons, typing, dragging and dropping, and selecting menus. Above all, it lends speed and reliability to tedious, repetitive tasks. It also ensures that those tasks are repeated in the same order again and again, helping to verify that features are working as documented and that known bugs aren't recurring.

Take, for example, a test to verify the state of an application's menus. Test automation can run through this for you, checking that the accelerator keys haven't changed from the previous build, verifying that menu items haven't been added or removed, and ensuring that the menus still display the dialog boxes that they displayed in the build from the previous week. This alone is a powerful mechanism that provides the tester with a reasonably good idea of what sections of the product may have changes that weren't reported by the development team. It also validates portions of the program, letting the tester know that the features that worked in a previous build appear to still be hooked up.

But pushing a button and clicking on a menu item does not a test make. Tests that verify that menus haven't changed are helpful in identifying changes, but they don't delve deeply into the functionality of a product. A structure must be built by someone using Visual Test (from now on referred to as a *Test programmer*) who will exercise key components of a product. A decision must also be made by the Program Manager and *Test Lead* as to how much of the testing will involve automation. As you continue to read through this book, you will begin to understand the task ahead of you in automating testing. Take care to weigh the advantages and disadvantages of automation, which are both discussed next, beginning with the benefits of automation.

Benefits of automation

Imagine yourself near the end of a project. Management has you in late every evening and on weekends, pounding on the code; your family hasn't seen you for three months; the developers are complaining about the testers and the fact that bugs are being found now that should have been found earlier; new code drops and releases of the code are being thrown over the wall to the testers every hour, on the hour. . . . *Everything's going nuts!*

It is in the final days of a project that test automation can really pay off. Imagine being able to run through the majority of your known list of system problems or bugs every time the programmers provide a new compilation of the product. Imagine not only being able to run through a huge portion of the known and fixed bugs, but being able to verify that those bugs are still closed in a fraction of the time it would take someone to perform such a verification by hand. Further imagine being able to run whatever tests have been created for testing the product on a number of machine configurations, all at the same time, all using the same steps, and all in a fraction of the time it would take to perform those tests manually. The result is being able to quickly determine whether or not a build provided by the development team is stable enough to be accepted by the testing team. If it doesn't pass specific tests deemed important by the QA group, it goes back over the wall to the programmers to fix the major bugs that have broken the build. Not only that, but the scripts can be included to provide a way of reproducing those problems for the developers.

Rational Visual Test

Specifically, Rational Visual Test (or simply "Visual Test" for short) offers considerable benefits over and above those just mentioned. Not only can it provide a means to automate testing, it's a powerful tool that will allow you to build other tools that can help in the testing process.

Visual Test is truly a development tool that has the capabilities for building standalone applications (with help from a run-time engine) that can be used by one's fellow test engineers. An example of these capabilities is ST Labs' Digger utility, which was written completely in Visual Test. This utility, which reads in an executable file and spits out a Visual Test template based on that file's menus and dialog boxes, shows how capable Microsoft's test automation tool really is.

ST Labs, Inc. was kind enough to provide the full version of Test Now 2.0, which includes the Digger utility and its source code. This can be found on the CD-ROM in the \Apps\Test Now 2.0 folder.

Since acquiring Visual Test, Rational Software has taken care to keep close ties with Microsoft so that Visual Test can continue to move up the ladder. This relationship keeps Visual Test current by integrating it with Microsoft Developer Studio, the same integrated development environment (IDE) that Visual C++, Visual J++, and many of the other Microsoft development tools use. Visual Test has been updated so that its network scripts can communicate with and synchronize over a hundred machines to perform the same or different tests at the same time. Its scenario recorder has been updated to have more robust script generation capabilities. And its report generation capabilities allow for writing to everything from a simple text file on up to a database-compatible file. Not only that, but support has been added for working with the Microsoft Internet Explorer browser so that testing of HTML documents is now possible.

Advanced programmers who are already aware of Visual Test's capabilities appreciate how open-ended this tool really is. It supports such advanced features as pointers to functions, pointers to variables, linking to the user's own dynamic libraries, and working with Windows APIs. In other words, it's extensible such that you can write your own utilities in C and use them from Visual Test as if those routines were a part of Visual Test's own language.

So Why Use an Automation Tool?

What's making the idea of automating tests such a big deal? A big part of it is management buying into the marketing hoopla: "You'll get higher-quality products out to the market faster if you automate your testing." And it's true to a certain extent: Once a testing team really gets an automation library built and a process in place, automation can play a big part in getting a quality product to the market. It's just that the initial investment required isn't part of that marketing message.

So your company decides to try it out. Consider this scenario: You are on a testing project and someone comes to you and suggests that you look into automating your testing. Maybe it's the Director of Development of your company, who'd like to standardize the testing efforts on using an automation tool. Or perhaps it's the Program Manager, who thinks she can help you get your testing done more quickly and effectively. Or maybe you're in the lucky minority and your QA Manager, who has a realistic view of automation, has broken the testing team into two groups: those who will automate and those who will perform manual testing.

Whatever's the case, most likely your first response will be the same as mine was, and you'll think that you have enough to do as it is: You've got a product to test and not much time to do it in, and you want to make sure you get the best darned product out to market. Why do you want to spend what little time you have learning how to automate your testing, when you have tight deadlines to meet? That's a fair question.

Let's look at some of the key reasons for using an automation tool like Visual Test:

- ✦ Regression testing
- ✦ Reproducible steps
- ✦ Compatibility testing
- ✦ Accurate benchmarking
- ✦ Reusing scripts
- ✦ Specialized needs

Regression testing

On most development projects, a time is set for when the developers can expect to make a *build* that will be handed off to the testing team. As a result, the development team is pushing to have their bugs fixed and new features checked in, so that testing can continue on the product.

Once the build is finished, it is handed off to the testing team to verify whether it's a good build or not. Typically, this happens once a week. If the build is no good, the testers will stay with the previous version and usually ask the development group to fix the high-priority bugs. Eventually, a build is accepted by the testing team, so that testing can be done for yet another week on the latest and greatest build of the product.

Bugs have a tendency to resurface, or a programmer will fix one problem within the system only to cause a new bug to surface. Fixing that new bug might break the previous fix of a feature someplace else in the system — perhaps in an area that is seemingly unrelated.

If the testing team sets up a process, such that all known and reported bugs in the system are put into an automated test file, those tests can be run with each new release of the product. This process is commonly referred to as *regression testing*: the process of stepping through all known bugs to verify that they have either been fixed or remained fixed from the last time they were regression-tested.

By the end of the project, when thousands of bugs have been filed on the product, running a group of regression tests is a valuable tool to determine the stability of the product.

Reproducible steps

After your department receives a new build from the development team, tests are usually run that exercise the main features of the product. If, after a few minutes of the tests running, an error occurs that causes your application to shut itself down, a critical bug has been found. Because the testers wrote their scripts such that they logged each step taken during the testing, a list of steps now exists that can be used in tracking that bug down.

If you rerun that script and the error occurs again in the same place, count yourself among the fortunate, because you have a reproducible error and a script that can reproduce it. Using the script, the error can be tracked down by working backward from where the error occurred. Was it as simple as displaying the Open dialog box, or was it crucial that the user selected New Document just before doing so? You can track this sequence down by retracing your automated script's steps.

Once these steps are refined to the minimum reproducible case, a problem report (*bug*) can be communicated to the developer who owns the area where the error was found.

Compatibility testing

Imagine yourself on a project where you need to verify that the product you are testing works on a number of different configurations: low memory, low disk space, a specific video board, a particular printer driver, a sound board that has given your company fits in the past, a particular computer brand, and so on. Now imagine taking a number of tests that you and the other test automation engineers have written and running them on each machine configuration. The workload is enormous. But with test automation, in addition to running those key tests, you have the time to test specific areas of concern by hand.

Compatibility testing is a definite area to focus on when automating tests. The intention isn't to automate the entire product; it's to automate some of the key features that can be tested on the different configurations. This gives testers the time they need to use their skills to their fullest. They can pound on the areas of concern they know have caused problems in the past. And they can do this while the automated tests are busily exercising the mundane pieces of the product, verifying that the obvious pieces of the product haven't deteriorated unexpectedly.

Benchmarking

Just like many other testers, I've performed benchmarking by using a hand-held stop watch. This is effective on really slow sections of a program where time can be accurately estimated in fives or tens of seconds.

It's not so effective when dealing with two seconds or less, and it is in this area that Visual Test comes in very handy. Let's take a drawing program as an example. Say a particular picture takes up to five seconds to draw because of the graphical richness involved in it: multiple irregular polygons, ellipses, shading, layers, and so on. Let's also assume that efforts are being made by the developers to optimize their code to speed up that drawing process.

Setting up an automated test to load a complicated picture and cause it to redraw a number of times is a breeze with test automation. Not only that, but it will do it multiple times, performing the exact same steps, so that an average time can be computed, resulting in cutting down on the timing errors relating to benchmarking. These results can be saved and compared with future versions of the product to determine if it is truly being sped up by the efforts of development.

Once that speed is finally realized, the last thing you want to happen is to have it drop back to a slower speed again. If a suite of tests exists that determines the speed of specific risk areas in the product, each build can be tested to verify that something hasn't changed to cause the drawing or imaging to become slow once more.

Bugs can occur in more ways than one. They can be obvious bugs, such as a crash that brings the product down, or bugs in logic that cause the imaging of a program to slow to such a slight degree that a human operator might not notice any change between builds of the product, but which becomes very noticeable with complex drawings. Test automation can spot these changes, in a way that human testers might not be able to.

Re-using scripts

The internationalization teams in software companies typically have the hardest jobs on the shortest time lines. The software has been written; all they have to do is translate it into a foreign language. What's the big deal?

Take someone from your company's international team to lunch some day and ask them about their job. You'll find that they have one of the shortest timelines of any group in the company. You think documentation and quality assurance folks have it tough since they're commonly on the back end of the development cycle? These folks have it tougher because the domestic version of the product is out and the owners of the software company are eager to get localized versions for foreign markets selling as soon as possible.

Let's take just two typical nightmares.

Because a number of resources need to be changed to allow for another language, an executable file needs to be recompiled so that resources can be reattached. If even a small change is made, or if somehow the build that was released to manufacturing is not the same as that given to the international team, you're no longer certain exactly where you stand on the stability of that product.

And what happens if a word that only took eight characters in English takes 12 in another language? Is there anything hard-coded in the code base that relies on the size of that character string? When the developers made the changes for the internationalization group, did they use the same compiler flags that specify code compaction and optimization? You can't be sure.

Now imagine how nice it would be if there were automated scripts available from the original domestic testing teams that the internationalization group could run on the builds of the localized product they're testing. Also, think how handy automated tests could come in for a quick check on the stability of a product. In addition, if the testing team working on the domestic version of the product has programmed with flexibility in mind, the internationalization team can make use of those scripts in helping them bring their localized product to market faster.

These scripts do not replace the need for manual testing, however, they merely act as a virtual tester that painstakingly checks the same sections of a product that were checked in the domestic version of the product. The manual testing must still be done to verify that other problems haven't surfaced.

Specialized needs

Other, more specialized needs can be met by using an automated script. An example is testing the record-locking on a database when there is high network traffic. A good way of testing this is to have a test suite running on multiple machines, hitting the same area of a database, allowing the tester to verify, manually on another machine, that the record-locking is working.

There are countless specialized needs that can be met with an automation tool. One business in New Orleans where I provided training used Visual Test as a way of installing new versions of software across the company network. When a new version of a product came out, it would run this script and distribute the latest version onto everyone's machines. Pretty slick, but not your typical use of a test automation tool.

Note   All of these potential uses for an automation tool can be a reality if the proper amount of effort is placed up front from the beginning of the development cycle and carried throughout to its completion. As you will see when reading through this book, *automation is much like a parallel development cycle* that is carried out at the same time as the development of the product itself. Because of this, it is necessary to have testers who focus on manual testing and those who focus on automation. Focusing solely on automation will lead to a poorly tested product because of the time and effort it takes to write, debug, and maintain automated scripts.

Automation Rears Its Ugly Head

Of course, nothing wonderful in this world is without a few attendant difficulties. Let's look at two of the main concerns encountered with automation:

✦ It's too time-consuming to learn the testing tool, and it will use up valuable extra resources.

✦ If the team is new to automation, no one is sure where to begin.

Each of these worries is valid. Let's look at them individually.

Test Automation Consumes Time and Resources

It's a fact that automating tests does take time; a fact that has to be embraced rather than avoided. First you have to sit down and learn how to use the automation tool, whether it's Visual Test or something else. Next, you need to figure out exactly the approach you want to take. Then you need to assess how dedicated your company is to automating testing on the product. And finally, you need to either hire automation engineers or bring your existing team up to speed on an automation tool.

Furthermore, test automation does not replace testers, although this is a common belief in some companies. What it allows you to do is automate repetitive tasks so that those tests can be run automatically and allow you to *work smarter* as a software testing engineer. Let me restate that: *It doesn't replace testers, it increases testers' effectiveness*. In fact, it is necessary to have automatic testing run in parallel with normal "human" testing.

All this takes time and money. But this unspoken message about needing initial investment isn't necessarily what the management of a software company wants to hear. It just wants to get the product out the door in a reasonable amount of time, so that it can grab more market share than the competition. This is a fair goal for management to have, but it cannot be achieved without adding more resources to a development team to make automation come together and function correctly.

It takes time and it takes commitment to learn a tool and get an automation process in place. Plus, it takes *more* people, not less, if you are on any kind of critical path. This is because you need the regular number of testers to do the manual testing that was already being done, and a separate group of testers to put the automation in place.

The company's production goal can be attained if the time and resources (in other words, people) required to put together a realistic automated testing approach are available. If your Development Managers are thinking they can pick up a test automation package and increase productivity and bug count without adding to the head count of the testing department, they will soon, and painfully, realize their error. If they don't have the resources to spare, they should reassess whether or not they really want to automate all, or even automate just part of the testing of a product.

It is your job as a test engineer to communicate the realities of test automation to the company's management. Automation pays off big at the end of a project and also when a product is internationalized to another market, but as the saying goes, you can't get something for nothing.

Note It is my opinion that very little test automation should be done on a version 1.0 of a product. This is because the testing staff is setting up test plans and checklists as they are working to understand what it is they are helping to create. On a version 2.0 of a product, automation can be started using version 1.0 while the developers are busy pulling the guts out of what will turn into version 2.0. When the version 2.0 begins to settle and come together, many of the scripts that were written using the stable version 1.0 can then be moved over and executed on the more stable builds of the new version.

Where Do We Begin?

This is the question everyone asks themselves when they sit down with an automation tool: "Where do I begin my automation approach?" It doesn't matter which tool you use; it's always a challenge to figure out where to start.

Buying this book was certainly a good move. With it spread out on the desk beside you, you can begin by typing in some code, trying to run it, and tracking down the errors from there. Hopefully, this book will get you past some of the obvious hassles facing you and point you in the right direction. Above all, you need to keep your scripts flexible, both for your own benefit and for the benefit of those who will be charged with maintaining your code in the future.

Your best bet is to work carefully through this book, working with the examples as we go along, and then going back and sorting out glitches as you come to understand them. Chapter 1, "A History of Visual Test," and Chapter 3, "The Lay of the Land," provide you with the background on how this quality tool came about, and what you can look forward to in the next chapters of this book. Chapter 4, "Visual Test User Interface," introduces you to the basic development environment you will be using when building your scripts. Chapter 5, "Visual Test Language," introduces you to what Visual Test offers as a programming language, whereas Chapter 6, "Visual Test Utilities," explains the Scenario Recorder, the Window Information Utility, the Screen Utility, and the Suite Manager.

We will specifically look at a beginning example of a simple script in Chapter 7, which is a very good place to start if you just want to dive in. In Chapters 8 through 12 you'll be taken, step by step, through the creation of automated tests for a common Windows text editor. And finally, the last chapters focus on some of the more advanced areas of this tool.

Ignore the Man Behind the Curtain

Don't be pulled in by all the magic and promises of automated testing. They may not all turn out to be feasible. Test automation is *not* meant to replace existing testing methodologies, only to enhance them. It is a tool to be used in addition to your regular testing. And the level of this enhancement depends strictly on the skills and thoroughness of those who wrote the automated tests.

You're not going to be able to write tests that will find all the bugs in your program. Not all bugs show up by simply clicking on a feature of the product. Sometimes it requires something specific to have occurred just before a particular action is taken. This is a big part of a tester's job, to think about what's going on underneath; to figure out what the developer of the product has missed. To ask himself, "I wonder if she thought to put a check in her code for this situation?" This isn't something an automated test can do; it reinforces the old axiom that computers will never be able to replace humans.

On the other hand, you can certainly achieve a significant number of beneficial returns when using an automated testing tool, as I've explained in this chapter. It takes time and effort, though, to put automation together.

Summary

At present, the reality of the development process is that companies wait to consider testing a product until the last moment, and enough time is never given to it. This is where test automation can help. It can provide significant benefits, in terms of speed, reliability, regression testing, creating reproducible steps, compatibility testing, benchmarking, reusing scripts, and meeting specialized needs. In particular, Visual Test offers specific advantages, such as providing the Test programmer with a common editor used by Microsoft's development tools, the capability to extend the language through the use of dynamic libraries (DLLs), and the same advantages of other programming languages, such as the use of pointers.

Don't buy into the shuck and jive of an automation tool vendor's spiel. Automation is not the magic bullet, and it won't be the answer to all of your testing problems. It is one of the tools found in a test engineer's toolkit to be used in specific situations. You can't tighten a bolt with a screwdriver, so don't even try. Use test automation when and where it makes sense, and use it effectively so that you get the most return on your investment.

✦   ✦   ✦

The Lay of the Land

This chapter is basically your jumping-off point to figure out the lay of the land and where to go to meet your needs. I begin by identifying what is on the Rational Visual Test 6.0 CD-ROM and move on to what the CD-ROM's setup program installs onto your computer. This includes where things get installed and why they're installed. As the CD-ROM and the installed directories are explored, I'll point you to other chapters in the book for finding out more specific information on those components.

Note

Note that this section is based on a prerelease version of Rational Visual Test 6.0 approximately two weeks before the product was released to manufacturing. It is possible that some of the files discussed have shifted to other directories or have been removed altogether. It is also possible other files have been added. Most of this information is current, however.

Exploring Rational Visual Test's CD-ROM

Figure 3-1 shows what your Visual Test 6.0 CD should look like when you right-click your CD-ROM drive and select the Open menu item. Visual Test is installed like most other shrink-wrapped software products today, and that is by double-clicking the SETUP.EXE file. Rational Software is using the industry standard setup program: InstallShield.

Figure 3-1: What's provided on the Visual Test installation CD-ROM

As with most software installation disks, the Visual Test CD-ROM has a Readme file that you need to make sure you read prior to running the installation. Going through this Readme file — provided in both HTML (README.HTM) and rich-text (README.WRI) formats — can save you time and hassles. For example, when the Beta version of Visual Test was released, a warning was included for those MSDN (Microsoft Developers Network) sites using prerelease versions of Microsoft Visual Studio. Installing Visual Test 6.0 over the top of a prerelease version of Microsoft Visual Studio caused the Microsoft Developer Studio (Visual Studio's integrated developer environment, or editor) programs (for example, Visual C++) to stop working as expected. This was because Rational Visual Test was using the final, Gold release of Developer Studio in the Visual Studio suite.

Caution   Last minute bugs and issues that didn't make it into the documentation will also be mentioned in this file. Take the time to read through the Readme file *before* you begin installation — or risk the consequences.

All of Visual Test's main components are compressed into the different .CAB files. The other files are files that are required by the setup program. These aren't the files I want to draw your attention to. The folders are the main topic of this section. We'll discuss Daosetup, IE 4.0, MSAA, MSDN98, and Samples. The reason I bring these folders to your attention is because not all of them may be installed as you run the Visual Test setup program, depending on which Setup type you select when running the installer. Should you want to install these additional utilities later, you can go directly to their folders instead of rerunning the Visual Test installation program.

Daosetup

The Daosetup folder (shown in Figure 3-1) contains the version 3.5 release of Microsoft Data Access Objects (DAO). The feature in Visual Test Suite Manager that allows you to log your test results to a database instead of a simple, flat text file needs to use MS DAO 3.0 or later. If you find that you would like to take advantage of this capability, run the SETUP.EXE program found in the Daosetup folder.

Note   Chapter 6 gives you more information about working with the Suite Manager. Chapter 13 also addresses topics related to working with databases via the Visual Test language.

You only need to install this if you want to use the built-in functionality in Visual Test to log to a database. If logging to a text file will meet your needs, you can save disk space by not installing MS DAO. Also, if you are working with other databases, you do not necessarily need to install MS DAO.

IE 4.0

Microsoft Internet Explorer 4.0 (IE 4.0) is provided on the Visual Test CD-ROM in the Ie4 folder shown in Figure 3-1. This is a full copy of Internet Explorer that can be used with Visual Test's new functionality for testing HTML 4.0–compliant (or earlier) documents. If you don't plan to refer to the online help and you don't plan to use the new Web functions in Visual Test 6.0, then you can skip installing this browser. If you want to do Web page testing, however, you must install — or already have installed — IE 4.0 or newer.

Caution   At the time Visual Test 6.0 was under development, IE 5.0 was just reaching its Beta milestone. Some light testing was done with that beta version of IE 5.0, and no problems were found. It should be noted that no intensive testing could be done at the time Visual Test 6.0 was under development and that future releases of IE 5.0 could potentially be incompatible with the Visual Test 6.0 Web functions. If you encounter such incompatibilities, you will need to use the IE 4.0 version provided on the Rational Visual Test CD-ROM (service pack 1, version 4.72.3110.8).

The new Web functionality in Visual Test depends on Microsoft Internet Explorer. Currently those functions will only support Microsoft's browser and won't work with other browsers, such as Netscape Navigator. The reason for this is that the new Visual Test 6.0 functions rely on the IE 4.0 object model that is maintained behind the scenes. This object model allows Visual Test to be more flexible in how it works with links, tables, forms, and frames that are used by HTML 4.0.

Note These new Web functions are covered in Chapter 17.

MSAA

Microsoft Active Accessibility (MSAA) is an alternate way to gather information about an *application under test* (AUT). It was originally created to make Microsoft Windows more accessible for people with disabilities, particularly those who are blind or have poor vision. An example of an MSAA-compliant application is Microsoft Word. Because of its use of the MSAA tools, Word can be queried by another program, such as a program that will gather the text content from a document and read it back to a visually impaired user. Previously this was a difficult task because the program would need to understand the format of the Word document so that it could open it and interpret the data itself. Now, with MSAA, a helper application that performs such services as reading back content will be able to work with any MSAA-compliant application.

Note For more information on what was added to Visual Test 6.0 for making use of the MSAA interface read Chapter 6 (the section about the Window Information utility) and Chapter 13 (the section about the new MSAA functions).

With these additional hooks added to an application via the MSAA interface, and with the new MSAA functions added to Visual Test 6.0, Test programmers now have yet another way to gather information about an application.

Rational has provided the MSAA Software Development Kit (SDK) on the Visual Test 6.0 CD-ROM (MSAA\MSAASDK.EXE); when installed, this kit will allow the MSAA functions in Visual Test 6.0 to work.

MSDN98 and Samples

The last two folders are part of the installation of Visual Test. They weren't compressed into .CAB files so that the *Compact* setup type can be selected during setup. The result is that the help and sample files are left on the CD-ROM instead of placed on your hard drive.

The MSDN98 folder holds the main Visual Test help files that use the new hypertext file format for help files that Microsoft adapted for their Microsoft Visual Studio product. This allows Visual Test's help to integrate cleanly into the Developer Studio editor.

Figure 3-2 shows what the help directory looks like. The directory structure is such that if Visual Test is installed in addition to another Microsoft Visual Studio installation, the help files will be placed in an organization similar to any other help files that are installed.

Figure 3-2: The help files for Visual Test follow Microsoft's new hypertext standard for help files.

The HHVT6.DAT file is a data file that is used to provide information on all of the help files, including the VT6.COL collection file (described next), and is used by the Developer Studio to determine how to attach help into its list of available online help documents. Basically, it describes each of the help files (.CHM) and assigns an identifier to each of those help files that is then used by the VT6.COL file.

The main collection file is the VT6.COL file. This file is a text document, using HTML-style scripting, that tells the Microsoft HTML Help engine (HH.EXE) how the individual help files should be displayed and in what order (see Figure 3-3). This includes defining what title should be displayed for each help file along with the identifier declared in the HHVT6.DAT file so that the HTML Help engine knows where to find the associated help file. To display the Visual Test help outside of the Microsoft Developer Studio editor, you can run the help engine with the .COL file as an argument on the command line. For example:

```
C:\winnt\system32\hh.exe d:\msvs\msdn98\98vs\1033\vt6.col
```

This has been done for you as a shortcut when Rational Visual Test was installed. If you use the *Compact* setup, the path for VT6.COL should be to your CD-ROM drive.

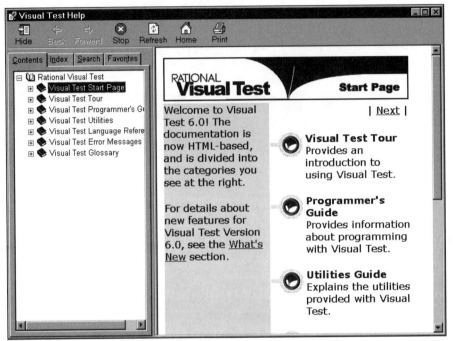

Figure 3-3: When the VT6.COL file is run with Microsoft's HTML Help engine, this window is displayed. A shortcut was created in the Rational Visual Test 6.0 folder during installation.

The .CHM files are the actual help text that is displayed when the F1 key is pressed and the Visual Test help is the active help collection (or the VT6.COL file is run via the shortcut in the Rational Visual Test 6.0 application folder on the Start menu). These are compiled HTML files and have an associated .CHI file that is the index for each of those .CHM files. These files are

✦ VTHOME.CHM: "Visual Test Start Page"—Includes Welcome, What's New, Copyright.

✦ VTTOUR.CHM: "Visual Test Tour"—Constitutes an online book that introduces you to the main features of Visual Test: designing tests, simulating user actions, verifying results, building test projects, running suites, and other places to look for information on VT.

✦ VTPRGMR.CHM: "Visual Test Programmer's Guide"—Gives detailed information about programming with Visual Test: working with projects, using the Test language, simulating and verifying user actions, using screen procedures, logging, using the Test debugger, handling errors and events, advanced programming techniques, using resources, and so on.

Why Are You Telling Me All This?

If you're like me, you're moving stuff around on your machine all the time so that you have room for the application you're testing, or for compatibility testing (and so on). Knowing what files are where and why, and how they affect Visual Test, can help you minimize Visual Test's installation size and hook everything back up when things stop working because of your activities. A lot of this information is also a great catalyst for pointing you in different directions for more information.

In short: We're test engineers. It's our job to rip our software installations apart and put them back together again. Where else are you going to find this kind of information when you're trying to get it back together and running again?

✦ VTUTIL.CHM: "Visual Test Utilities"—Includes help information on Visual Test's set of utilities: Scenario Recorder, Screen capture/comparison, Suite Manager, and Window Information utilities.

✦ VTREF.CHM: "Visual Test Language Reference"—Is an alphabetical list of the commands that make up the Visual Test language.

✦ VTRTE.CHM: "Visual Test Error Messages"—Includes run-time error and compiler error messages defined to help you track down problems in your scripts.

✦ VTGLOSS.CHM: "Visual Test Glossary"—Includes definitions for terms used by Rational Visual Test.

The last folder is the Samples folder and is exactly the same as the version that is installed. And with that, let's look at what gets installed when you run the Visual Test setup program.

Visual Test Installed

When you install Rational Visual Test 6.0, it will prompt you to install into:

```
C:\Program Files\Microsoft Visual Studio
```

This is the standard directory where the full version of Microsoft Visual Studio will be installed for Microsoft Visual C++. Remember, Rational Software has integrated Visual Test into the Developer Studio editor, so they've done their best to integrate cleanly into Microsoft's model.

Note   In my example I'm using D:\MSVS as my installation directory. Keep that in mind when you look at my screen shots and my comments about directories.

Caution   If you already have Visual Test 4.0 installed, do *not* install Visual Test 6.0 over the top of that installation.

Java Virtual Machine

Even if you already have Microsoft Internet Explorer installed, you will most likely see the message box shown in Figure 3-4. When you install Visual Test you shouldn't see this message box if you have the latest Java VM (virtual machine) installed. This file is installed so that you can view the Visual Test online help.

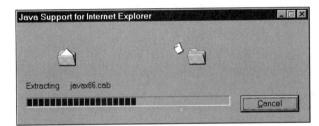

Figure 3-4: The Java Virtual Machine needs to be installed so that Visual Test online help can be viewed.

On the CD-ROM   I used a program called "INCTRL 3 — Installation Control for 32-bit Windows" (available from Ziff-Davis Publishing's Web site) that tracks what exactly gets installed where on your computer. It also tracks Registry changes. At this writing I was using the prerelease of Visual Test so some final changes may have been made, but, for the most part, this information will be the same for Rational Software's final release. This information can be found on this book's CD-ROM in \OTHER\SETUPINFO.TXT.

Environment Variables

There are a couple of environment variables set when Visual Test 6.0 is installed. These are used by Developer Studio when compiling your automated scripts. These variables are

✦ INCLUDE = d:\MSVS\vt6\include

✦ LIB = d:\MSVS\vt6\lib

✦ PATH = d:\MSVS\vt6\bin;d:\MSVS\common\msdev98\bin

The LIB variable is defined in case you have Microsoft Visual C++ installed. It is not used by Visual Test 6.0 nor its scripts. In Visual Test 4.0 the external dynamic-link libraries (DLLs) were put into one large DLL (VTEST60.DLL), which effectively cut off Visual Basic and Visual C++ users from linking into Visual Test's libraries. This was rectified in Visual Test 4.0r (Rational Software's first release of Visual Test). Anyone who wants to access Visual Test's automation routines can do so via C++, but it requires access to a library file called VTEST60.LIB and a header file called VTCTRL.H. The LIB and INCLUDE variables tell the Microsoft Developer Studio where to find those files.

The INCLUDE variable is used by Microsoft Visual Studio when searching for Visual C++ and Visual Test include files.

Tip   VTEST60.LIB and VTCTRL.H are used by Microsoft Visual C++ so that Visual C/C++ users can link into many of Visual Test's capabilities. These files are found in \msvs\vt6\lib and \msvs\vt6\include, respectively. VTCTRL.BAS is included for Microsoft Visual Basic users who want to link into Visual Test's functions. This file is found in \msvs\vt6\include. Visual Basic and Visual C++ users will be able to determine what functions are available to them by viewing these .BAS and .H files in a text editor.

The PATH variable has Visual Test directories prepended to it so that Visual Test and all of its components know where to look when trying to find their own supporting executables and DLLs.

Installed Files

Visual Test doesn't have a lot of its own files to install because it's pretty well encapsulated into just a few files. However, because Visual Test 6.0 (and 4.0, for that matter) relies on Microsoft Visual Studio's editor, called Developer Studio, a number of other files get installed into multiple directories. This is because Developer Studio was designed to work with many of Microsoft's tools so that the user need only learn one set of editing tools for many different programming languages. Visual Test 4.0 was integrated into Developer Studio, and Visual Test 6.0 remains integrated into that editor to this day, even though Visual Test is no longer owned by Microsoft.

These files are arranged so that when the other Microsoft tools are installed — if they get installed — they will fit into the existing directory structure. That way the user will be able to create a Visual Test project or a Visual C++ project, and so on, depending on which tools you purchase from Microsoft and install.

The following sections explain what each directory contains and the roles the files in those directories play in your installation of Rational Visual Test 6.0.

\Common

The Common directory is where files common to Developer Studio can look for and place information. With a fresh installation of Visual Test 6 — and only Visual Test — you will find a lone folder called MSDEV98 in the Common directory. The contents of the \Common\MsDev98 directory are shown in Figure 3-5.

Figure 3-5: The contents of \Common\MsDev98 show the shared files of the Microsoft Developer Studio integrated development environment (IDE). These are used by Rational Visual Test 6.0.

 Note   An interesting side note is that the previous version of Visual Studio was called *Microsoft Visual Studio 97*. Microsoft dispensed with using the release year as part of the name and has returned to release numbers instead. So this version of Visual Studio is called *Microsoft Visual Studio 6.0* (instead of *Microsoft Visual Studio 98*), yet they didn't rename the MsDev98 directory to reflect this name change. It doesn't hurt anything, but I thought I'd point it out just in case you were wondering where that "98" came from. (Most likely what happened was that multiple groups at Microsoft were trying to come together to use this one editor. Some groups probably finished earlier than others, and it would have been too expensive to update their contribution to use 6.0 instead of 98 after the decision was made not to use the release year as part of the naming conventions.)

All but two of the folders shown in Figure 3-5 are empty. The empty folders are places where you can store common add-in tools, macro files, and templates. The two folders that contain anything are the bin and help folders.

\Common\MsDev98\Bin

The Bin directory contains all of the Developer Studio binary files that, together, define and control how that program runs. It's pretty cool the way Microsoft put this together, really. There are a number of package files that control what additional tools appear depending on which language you're working with. The key package files modified for Visual Test are DEVEDIT.PKG, DEVPRJ.PKG, and VTEST6.PKG (found in the Ide folder). These files define how the editor works with Visual Test files (keyword coloring), how a Visual Test project is defined (creating include folders, entry scripts, and exit scripts), and specific information about how Visual Test integrates itself into the IDE. Other common package files are found in the Ide folder and are generic enough to be used by all tools integrated into Developer Studio.

The main file to be aware of in the Bin directory is the VTDEV.EXE file. This is what the shortcut in the Start menu for the Rational Visual Test 6.0 folder links to. If you ever lose those shortcuts, you now know where to look to get Visual Test running.

The Ide subdirectory is where all of the common components for this integrated development environment are stored. These files are used by Visual Test and any other programming language that is integrated into the Developer Studio.

\Common\MsDev98\Help

The Help directory holds the context-sensitive help specific to Microsoft Developer Studio. For example, if you go into a dialog box and press the F1-key, a little pop-up help box will be displayed telling you more about that dialog box and how to use it. This is where that help information is stored. Visual Test–specific help is stored in another directory.

\Msdn98\98vs\1033

Refer back to Figure 3-2 earlier in this chapter to see what this folder looks like. What is installed into the \<root>\msdn98\98vs\1033 folder (where, in my case, <root> is equal to MSVS) is exactly what is on the Rational Visual Test installation CD-ROM. Read that section for more information on the specific help files.

\VT6

The VT6 directory, found in the \<root> directory of your installation of Visual Test 6.0, contains five folders and three files. This folder's contents are shown in Figure 3-6. This directory includes Visual Test binaries, "What's This?" help files, include files, a Visual C library, and samples. Also included are the Readme notes (in rich-text and HTML format) and a list of files that cannot be redistributed.

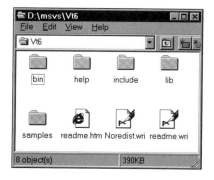

Figure 3-6: The guts of Visual Test 6.0 are installed into the VT6 folder.

✦ The README.WRI and README.HTM documents display the same last-minute information about known issues in Visual Test 6.0. Although they contain the exact same information, these two files are accessed from two different places. The README.WRI document has a shortcut on the Start menu in the Rational Visual Test 6.0 program group. The README.HTM document is accessed via the Help menu using the Visual Test Release Notes menu item.

✦ NOREDIST.WRI contains a list of files that cannot be redistributed without written permission from Rational Software Corporation. These files are mostly the Microsoft binaries that Rational is using along with other Visual Test bits that aren't needed for running your compiled scripts. The major pieces that can be redistributed are VTEST60.DLL (the guts of Visual Test) and MTRUN.EXE, the run-time engine for running your compiled (.PC6) scripts. These files can be redistributed so that you can install your scripts on multiple machines without having to buy multiple licenses of Visual Test.

\VT6\BIN

The Bin folder, shown in Figure 3-7, contains the main compiled files that make up the Visual Test tool. Four of these files are executables, six are DLLs, and two are compiled Visual Test scripts (.PC6), which leaves us with an .OCX (OLE control), a .BAT file, two icon files, and an .INI file.

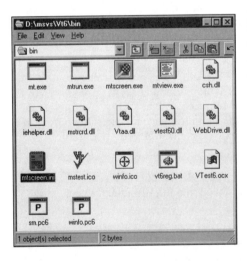

Figure 3-7: The \VT6\BIN folder holds the main, proprietary Rational Visual Test components. Any binaries that are proprietary to Microsoft are in the \Common\MsDev98 folder.

✦ MT.EXE is a program that can run your uncompiled Visual Test scripts (files with an .MST extension). It can also be used to quickly parse and verify that your file is syntactically correct. And it can be used to take your existing, uncompiled scripts and compile them into pseudocode (.PC6) files.

✦ MTRUN.EXE is the run-time engine that runs compiled Visual Test files that have a .PC6 extension. Having compiled scripts allows you to distribute your tests to multiple machines without worrying about licensing problems. It's also a great way to distribute your scripts without having to worry about your source code being modified without your knowledge.

Note

Compiling scripts using MT.EXE and MTRUN.EXE for standalone execution is discussed in more detail in Chapter 13.

✦ MTVIEW.EXE is the standalone viewport that serves as Visual Test's standard output window. Whenever the PRINT statement in the Test language is used, but not as part of a file output operation, the results are written to the Viewport. Microsoft Developer Studio has a viewport integrated into the utility, and that is where output is displayed when a script is run within the IDE. However, standalone scripts that require a way to display information easily use the MTVIEW.EXE version of the Viewport.

Tip

The Window Information utility discussed in Chapter 6 has a toolbar control that allows you to dump information to the system clipboard or to the Viewport. When using the Viewport tool on the Window Information toolbar to send this information to the Viewport, you must run this Viewport program (also available through a shortcut in the Start menu) to see the output.

✦ MTSCREEN.EXE is the Screen Capture and Comparison utility that allows you to view Visual Test screen capture (.SCN) files. While screen captures can be made with this utility, that's not the typical way in which it is used. Normally, people will use MTSCREEN.EXE to verify that a screen was captured as expected.

✦ CSH.DLL provides a hook into the "What's This?" help for Visual Test. Some dialog boxes will respond to the F1 key being pressed or, if available, a Help button or Question mark being clicked. This links into the help files in the \VT6\Help directory.

✦ IEHELPER.DLL is new to Visual Test 6.0. This library acts as intermediary between WEBDRIVE.DLL and Microsoft Internet Explorer. For every instance of Internet Explorer (IE) that is run while Visual Test is running, a copy of IEHELPER.DLL is loaded, providing hooks into that browser's object model. This is the magical DLL that allows Visual Test to get its hooks into IE.

✦ WEBDRIVE.DLL is the heart of the new Web functionality. It contains the meat of the Web functions that allow you to get and set information about a page that is currently displayed in IE.

Note

For information on using the new Web functions turn to Chapter 17.

Caution   The new Web functionality will only work if you have Microsoft Internet Explorer 4.0 (or newer) installed and accessible to Visual Test.

✦ MSTRCRD.DLL is the dynamic-link library that houses the Script Recorder functionality. When you're running the Script Recorder and it is recording your every move, mouse click, and keyboard action, this is the DLL that's doing the work.

✦ VTAA.DLL contains the new support for working with Microsoft Active Accessibility applications. These are the applications that provide extra support for visually challenged users. Applications making use of the MSAA routines provide users of Visual Test with much easier access to testing that application's capabilities.

Note   For more information on MSAA refer to the section in Chapter 6 on the Window Information Utility. Also refer to Chapter 13 for information on the new functions available in Visual Test.

✦ VTEST60.DLL holds the Visual Test language. In versions 1.0–3.0 the language was stored in multiple DLLs, allowing Test programmers to link only to those DLLs that held the functions that they needed. To make it easier, these files were merged into a single DLL, which became VTEST60.DLL.

✦ MSTEST.ICO is just an icon file.

✦ WINFO.ICO is the icon file used for the Winfo program.

✦ VT6REG.BAT was added for Rational technical support's use. Every now and then some of the Visual Test DLLs get unregistered from the system. It's not exactly clear what causes this; in some situations it has been caused by uninstalling seemingly unrelated programs. To help you avoid the process of going through a complete reinstallation of Visual Test, this file was added. If you suddenly find that MSAA or Web functionality stops, you can try running this batch file to see if it helps the situation. It causes the DLLs to register themselves with the system, and running it won't hurt anything.

✦ VTEST6.OCX is an OLE control that is used by those who want extra information about OLE/ActiveX controls used by Visual Basic. Simply include VTEST6.OCX as part of your Visual Basic application, and you've provided Visual Test with a hook into any other control your VB application uses.

Note   For more information on using VTEST6.OCX refer to Chapter 13.

✦ SM.PC6 and WINFO.PC6 are compiled Visual Test scripts that serve as powerful utilities. SM.PC6 is the Suite Manager that allows you to organize your Visual Test scripts so that you can run them in any order, any number of times, against the program being tested. WINFO.PC6 is a utility that allows you to gather more information about the windows or controls in an application. It also allows you to gather information on any MSAA support, ActiveX controls, and even HTML documents displayed in Internet Explorer.

Note For more information on using the Suite Manager and Window Information utilities refer to Chapter 6.

Note Curious about the "MT" prefix on some of these filenames? The product was originally called Microsoft Test. Then it became Microsoft Visual Test. And finally Rational Visual Test. Some filenames were left alone to preserve backward compatibility.

\VT6\Help

The Help directory contains online documentation for the Visual Test utilities, such as the Script Recorder, the Screen Comparison utility, Visual Test Suite Manager, and the Window Information tool. There is also context-sensitive help and "What's This?" help that is stored in the VT6.HLP file.

\VT6\Include

The Include directory, shown in Figure 3-8, holds a number of helpful files. The first are the VTCTRL.BAS and VTCTRL.H files. These are meant to be used by Microsoft Visual Basic and Microsoft Visual C++ users, respectively. These files provide function declarations that link into the VTEST60.DLL so that many of Visual Test's automation functions are available outside of Visual Test. The good news is that you don't have to use Visual Test's language if you don't want to: You can use Visual Basic or Visual C/C++. The bad news is that if you don't use the Test language, you can't as easily redistribute your files. The functions that the Visual Basic and Visual C++ files link into check to see if VTEST60.DLL is running on a machine that has a licensed copy of Visual Test installed. If not, the functions won't work. You can avoid this problem by using the Test language and compiling to a .PC6 file.

Figure 3-8: The Include directory contains prewritten source code that you can use in your scripts.

While you can use Microsoft Visual Basic or Visual C++ to easily link into Visual Test's capabilities, you won't be able to distribute your final files easily because of the licensing checks in the code. Using the Test language avoids this problem.

T4CTRL.BAS and T4CTRL.H are files that contain only comments that tell you to use the new versions of these include files: VTCTRL.BAS and VTCTRL.H.

Microsoft came up with a cool way to avoid backward-compatibility issues as the Visual Test language evolved. Rational Software has continued this tradition.

✦ VTCTRL.BAS and VTCTRL.H are Microsoft Visual Basic and Microsoft Visual C++ declarations that allow you to link into the VTEST60.DLL and make use of Visual Test's features.

Visual Basic and C++ programs that link into VTEST60.DLL will only work on a system that has a registered copy of Rational Visual Test installed. Licensing code has been put in place to help avoid illegal usage of this library. VTEST60.DLL remains a freely distributable file, however, because compiled Visual Test scripts (.PC6 files) can use it whether a licensed copy of Visual Test is installed on the destination computer or not.

✦ DECLARES.INC automatically creates a *precompiled header* file to cut down on your compile times. It includes MSTEST.INC and WINAPI.INC, and if a compiled header doesn't exist or the files have been updated since the last compilation, it creates a compiled version of those two files.

✦ MSTEST.INC contains Test language *wrappers* that, when included by your Test scripts, will take the place of previously available functions in the Visual Test language. Did your old scripts use a function that has since been wiped out in Visual Test 6.0? Not to worry, just include MSTEST.INC with your other .INC files. (Refer to Chapter 8 and Chapters 9–12 for more information on including .INC files.)

✦ RECORDER.INC contains constants, variables, and routines used by the source code generated when the Script Recorder completes its recording task. This file is automatically added to the top of the generated script as an include file.

✦ TOOLS.INC is a simple example of how to link into the Rational Software line of tools when used with Visual Test. It's merely a template to let you see what form the syntax should take.

✦ WINAPI.INC is a file that provides you with predefined constants, structures, and function prototypes that link into the Windows APIs. This file was originally modeled after the WINDOWS.H file that was the main header file used by anyone writing Windows programs.

Note For more information on linking into Windows APIs, refer to Chapter 13.

✦ TEMPLATE.TPL is a template provided to give you a place to start when writing your test scripts. If you don't like the template provided, you can modify this .TPL file; from then on, anytime you create a new script your template file will be used. This is very helpful when you're on a team and trying to get a common look-and-feel to your script files.

Note Refer to Chapter 8 for examples of other styles of templates. Cut and paste from the existing template and the templates in Chapter 8, and add your own company's programming style to create your very own end-all, be-all template.

\VT6\LIB

The Lib directory contains a single file: VTEST60.LIB. This file is required only if you are planning on using Visual C/C++ with Visual Test's VTEST60.DLL. If you are a Visual C++ programmer you already know what to do with this file.

\VT6\SAMPLES

This folder contains Visual Test samples that you'll want to play with to get a feel for what Visual Test can accomplish. Look through these sample projects, get a sense for what it is that you can do, and get a sense for the language. These files illustrate both the testing capabilities of Visual Test and the flexibility of the tool and its language.

Summary

Rational Visual Test is a huge product with a lot of nooks and crannies. I hope I've helped you get a better foothold on the purpose of the files on the CD-ROM. Also, I hope you find it helpful knowing what gets installed where on your computer. This has been a great opportunity, as well, to explain where to find more information on each of the pieces that make up the overall Visual Test tool.

Rational's online documentation gives great details about how to use the tool, and the last thing I'd try to do would be to replace those online documents with this book. Instead I'm trying to give you a good leg up and fill in the gaps.

✦   ✦   ✦

Overview of Visual Test

Visual Test User Interface

Visual Test was given a major facelift between versions
3.0 and 4.0. Where previous versions of Microsoft Test
had their own integrated development environments (IDE),
Microsoft Visual Test was integrated directly into a common
IDE used by Microsoft Visual C/C++, Microsoft Fortran Power
Station, and the Microsoft Development Library. Part of the
deal Rational Software cut with Microsoft when it purchased
Visual Test was to allow Visual Test to continue to make use of
Microsoft's IDE. The Developer Studio (see Figure 4-1) is not
only used by Rational Visual Test but is also the main editor
used by the Microsoft Visual Studio, a suite of development
tools from Microsoft.

If you have already used Visual C++ from version 2.0 and up,
you may be familiar with the features of the IDE and you can
quickly browse this chapter looking for the key components of
Microsoft Visual Test that are different. If you've not done any
development using the Developer Studio IDE, then you'll
probably want to read all the sections in this chapter so that
you have a good overall understanding of what it offers.

Note   In the interest of clearly communicating which features are
available through the Developer Studio IDE when used
with Visual Test, the IDE is looked at and discussed as if
only Visual Test were installed. Microsoft Visual C/C++
users will notice some differences depending on whether
they are working on a C/C++ project or a Test project.

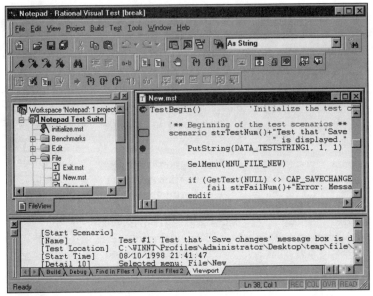

Figure 4-1: The Microsoft Developer Studio is an integrated development environment (IDE) used by many of Microsoft's development tools.

Three Views of the IDE

There are three principal windows that appear in the Developer Studio's main window:

✦ **Workspace:** The Project Workspace shows a graphical representation of the project's file hierarchy, making it easier to organize all related files in the test suite.

✦ **Output:** The Output window provides a container for information on errors encountered while compiling the script, information helpful when you are debugging a script, results of any searches performed on your source code files, and any text written out by a test script.

✦ **Source File:** The Source File window is where the actual programming is done. This window is a text editor allowing you to type in your test script. As keywords are typed into this window, they are highlighted depending on their functionality.

These windows provide easy access to information about the script you're writing and testing. We will now look at each one in more detail.

Workspace

The workspace keeps track of your settings and the projects on which you are currently working. In Developer Studio 6.0 (the version that is used by Visual Test 6.0), you can have multiple projects open in a single workspace. No longer is *workspace* synonymous with *project*.

In addition to tracking a programmer's preferred settings, the workspace also tracks which projects it is viewing and the state of the windows in those projects. That means that if a source code file is open when the workspace is saved and the program exited, the next time the workspace is loaded into Developer Studio it reverts to the way it was originally.

Note The version of Microsoft Developer Studio in Visual Test 4.0 had an InfoView tab at the bottom of the Workspace window. This was to provide access to online documentation. In version 6.0 of Developer Studio that tab is gone and the standalone online help viewer from Microsoft is used when referencing the electronic documentation.

If the programmer is making use of a version control program — such as ClearCase by Rational Software or Visual Source Safe by Microsoft — a project's source code files can be checked in and out of a source code database via the Workspace window.

In some cases, the window won't appear as shown in Figure 4-2. Instead, it will appear *attached* to the IDE's main window. This is known as the *Docking view* and is a difficult view to work in when using the IDE at a low resolution (800 × 600, or less). To get out of this docking mode, right-click anywhere in the project window and select the Docking View menu item, so that it toggles the check mark off. The window becomes a separate MDI (multiple document interface) window, or child window. You can now minimize it when it's in the way: It will appear as an icon at the bottom of the IDE's main window.

Figure 4-2: The Workspace window shows your project(s) in a tree view.

If you are working at a high resolution (1024 × 768 and up), you can tear off the window so that it isn't even a part of the IDE's main window. To do this:

1. Return it to Docking view by right-clicking the contents of the window.

2. Select the Docking View menu item, so that the check mark toggles on.

3. Click the banded portion of the window (where a caption would be on a normal window) and drag the window out of the IDE's main window to make it a separate window.

This is really cool to do when you're taking advantage of Windows 98's or NT 5.0's multimonitor support. You can place these windows and toolbars out of the way on a separate monitor. Optionally, the Project Window can be moved to snap to the other side of the IDE's main window.

Tip   To avoid the now-detached window's attempt to reattach to the IDE main window when moving it across the Developer Studio's window, hold the Ctrl key down while dragging.

Note   The Output, Watch, and Locals windows (discussed shortly) can also be manipulated through the same methods as described for the Workspace window and can be torn off or minimized in the main window. The toolbars can also be manipulated in this way.

Output

The Output window (see Figure 4-3) has five tabs that provide different kinds of information. The first tab, *Build*, provides information about the progress and results of the compilation of the source code. If an error occurred while the script was compiling, double-clicking the line displaying the error information will cause the Source File window to display the line of code causing the error. The *Debug* tab displays information generated by the debugger. The *Find in Files 1* and *Find in Files 2* tabs display the results of the last search for information in a file by using the Find in Files menu item under the Edit menu. The final tab is the *Viewport* tab, which provides a place for common output information and takes the place of the Viewport window — a separate executable file that comes with Visual Test — when running scripts from the Developer Studio.

Tip   If an error occurs during the compilation of your script and your attempts to double-click the error message in the Build section of the Output window don't take you to the line of code causing the problem, save the file so that it isn't considered an untitled file. This should fix the problem.

The MTVIEW.EXE version of the Viewport is used by the Visual Test Suite Manager and by the Window Information utility. Both of these utilities are discussed further in Chapter 6.

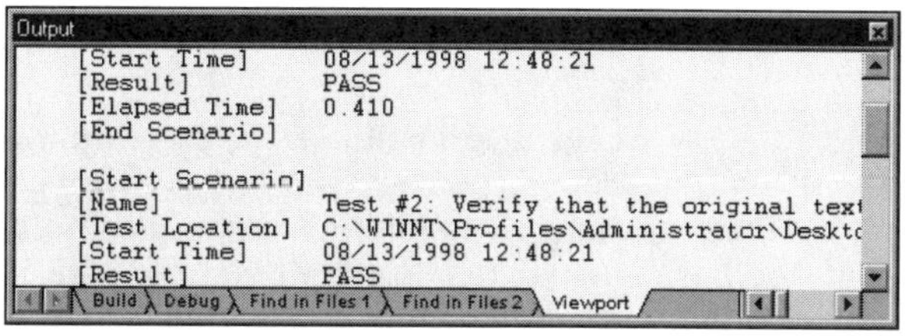

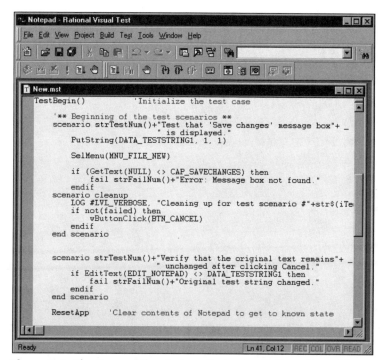

Figure 4-3: The Output window communicates information to the user about compilation errors and run-time test information.

Source File

The Source File window, shown displaying NEW.MST in Figure 4-4, is where the scripts are written using the Test language. As keywords are typed in, they will become highlighted depending on their usage. By default, keywords appear in blue; comments appear as green text; the keywords of the language that existed in separate DLLs in version 1.0 to 3.0 of Microsoft Test appear as red; and so on. This editor is also where you can place breakpoints to cause the script to halt and bookmarks to simplify the process of relocating sections of code, as was previously shown in Figure 4-1.

Figure 4-4: The Source File window displays and allows the editing of source code.

Using Toolbars

Eight toolbars are available with the Visual Test installation in the Developer Studio. More may be added as other development tools are installed. Users can create their own toolbars via the Customize menu item found under the Tools menu. Only three of these eight toolbars are fully functional when used with Visual Test. The others can be used but only in a limited manner, since they were mostly created with Visual C++ in mind. We'll take a look at each of these in turn:

- ✦ Standard
- ✦ Build
- ✦ Build MiniBar
- ✦ Resource
- ✦ Test
- ✦ Edit
- ✦ Debug
- ✦ Browse

Tip   The toolbars and their displayed status can be controlled by right-clicking any visible toolbar or on the menubar.

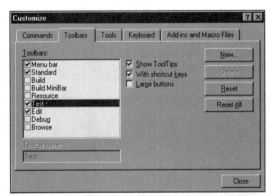

Figure 4-5: The Customize dialog box allows the user to control which dialog boxes are displayed in the environment. New toolbars can be created as well.

Each toolbar is described briefly in this section.

If the toolbars in your installation of Visual Test don't appear the same as the toolbars shown in this book, it could be because either you have other development tools installed that work with the Developer Studio, or you're not working with a fresh installation of Visual Test and the toolbars have been modified.

Standard

The Standard toolbar is basically just that: the standard toolbar you find in almost every application that uses toolbars. This can be seen in Figure 4-6. It provides a shortcut for creating new files, opening files, saving files, and saving all of the opened files in the environment. It also has shortcuts for the Edit menu allowing the user to cut, copy, and paste, as well as offering multiple levels of undo and redo.

The three icons to the right of the *undo* and *redo* icons allow the user to easily display the current open Workspace window and the Output window, and also a dialog box that allows the user to see a list of all windows open in the Developer Studio (allowing you to easily find and display a window).

It also has search capabilities. The first search icon (the binoculars) allows you to perform a search for a keyword across multiple files. The second search icon allows you to search for a keyword in the online documentation.

Tip If you find that the wrong online help files are being displayed, you can select the appropriate help files via the Help System tab in the Options dialog box, which is accessed via the Tools menu.

Figure 4-6: The Standard toolbar

Build and Build MiniBar

The Build toolbar, shown in Figure 4-7, is meant for Visual C++ developers. Aspects of it, however, can be used by Visual Test programmers, but I suggest using the Test toolbar for your Visual Test needs instead.

Figure 4-7: The Build toolbar

The combo box that appears on the left side of this toolbar allows you to select which project is the *active* project. Because Developer Studio allows multiple projects to be open within a workspace, the tools (such as the compiler) must know which project to act upon. This combo box allows the user to easily specify which project is considered the active project.

Other than the last two icons at the far right of this toolbar, the rest of its components aren't useful to Visual Test. These last two icons, from left to right, allow the user to begin the execution of the current source code file and to break or stop the execution of the currently executing file.

The Build MiniBar, shown in Figure 4-8, is a watered-down version of the Build toolbar.

Figure 4-8: The Build MiniBar

While both the Build and Build MiniBar toolbars can be used to a small degree by Visual Test, the Test toolbar should instead be used. It contains these and other options that are specific to using Visual Test.

Resource

The Resource toolbar is put to use in the Advanced Topics section of this book (see Chapter 15 for more detailed information). Its purpose is to provide easy access to the resource editor that comes with the Developer Studio. By using this toolbar and the resource editor, developers can add dialog boxes, menus, and other resources to make test scripts easier to use (see Figure 4-9).

Figure 4-9: The Resource toolbar

Test

The Test toolbar, shown in Figure 4-10, is the main toolbar that you will be using when working with Visual Test. It contains buttons for running a script that is under development.

Figure 4-10: The Test toolbar

Starting, stopping, and breaking

The first button on the Test toolbar is the Go button, which compiles and runs the script (its keyboard equivalent is F5). The second button will break or stop the execution of a script so that debugging and programming can be done.

> **Tip** To bring an executing script to a complete stop, select the Break Execution button, or its Break menu item equivalent, twice. The first time will pause the script so that variables can be examined and the script's execution can continue one line at a time. In this paused state, selecting Break again will bring the script to a complete stop.

The third button (it shows a hand) is used to mark *breakpoints* in the script. Its keyboard equivalent is F9, and it acts as a toggle to turn on/off breakpoints. (For further information on breakpoints, see the note that follows.)

> **Tip** You can determine the state of a script's execution by looking at the Rational Visual Test caption bar. If it says "[run]," then the script is currently executing. If it says "[break]," then it is paused. If neither of these appear in the caption, then the script isn't running.

> **Note** A breakpoint is used to mark a line on which the execution of the script should be temporarily halted. This allows you to examine the values held in the program's variables and to step through the rest of the code, line by line if necessary.

Stepping through code

The next three buttons on the Test toolbar allow you to Step Into, Step Over, or Step Out of a function or subroutine. These options are great when you want to debug a script and watch its execution — and the effects of the execution on variables and other factors — one line at a time.

When you are stepping through a file's source code and you encounter a subroutine or function name, it's sometimes preferable to *step into* the source code for the subroutine so that every single line being executed can be observed. This is where the Step Into button comes in handy. The keyboard equivalent for this command is F11.

At times, however, it isn't necessary to step into a subroutine's or function's section of code. Perhaps you know that the routine isn't the source of the problem, so why look at its code? This is where the Step Over button comes in handy. The keyboard equivalent for this button is the F10 key, as can be seen under the Test menu in the Test Debug submenu.

Finally, for those occasions when it's no longer necessary to step through the code of a subroutine or function, the Step Out button allows the function or subroutine to continue its execution. In this situation, the debugger will stop on the line of source code that immediately follows the function or subroutine call. The keyboard equivalent to the Step Out button is Shift+F11.

Scenario recorder

The next button is for the Scenario Recorder. This button is only active when a script is not running. Clicking it allows you to record your actions and generate test scripts based on those actions. This is a great tool when you are learning the Visual Test language, but don't rely on it too heavily. These generated scripts are simply a sequential list of steps taken while the recorder was on. The script is not making use of common coding guidelines or practices that allow you to create scripts that are usable for years to come. (See Chapter 8 later in this book.)

Visual test utilities

The next three buttons allow you to easily run Visual Test's other utilities. These are the Window Information (Winfo) utility, the Suite Manager, and the Screen utility. These utilities are discussed in Chapter 6 and Chapter 12. You'll also notice that the menu items for accessing these utilities are found under the Test menu.

Watching variables

The last two buttons are only available while a script is running; they allow you to display the Test Watch and Test Locals windows. These two windows allow you to see the values your variables are assigned during the execution of your script, but only when you are stepping through your script. These two windows are discussed later in this chapter.

Edit

The first four icons on the Edit toolbar, shown in Figure 4-11, are ones that I use frequently when editing a test case file in the development environment. These icons, shown as flags, allow the programmer to place bookmarks on individual lines of source code. The reason for doing this is that many times it is necessary to jump from one section of the file to another, but it's a hassle to relocate where you were in the source window. Setting a bookmark lets you mark important locations (such as declaration blocks to determine the type of a variable or the parameters of a function) to jump to them quickly. These four icons allow you to set a bookmark, jump to the next or previous bookmark, and remove all bookmarks. There's also an icon showing a pair of binoculars that allows you to search for specific text and place bookmarks next to the matches it finds.

Figure 4-11: The Edit toolbar

The next group of buttons makes it easier to indent and un-indent text. Highlighting a block of text makes these buttons active. The same thing can be accomplished using the keyboard by pressing Tab to indent and Shift+Tab to un-indent a block of text when it is selected.

The last button on this toolbar is a toggle that causes the Source File window to show periods and chevrons (two greater-than signs) to represent spaces and tab characters in your source code. Clicking it again turns this mode back off.

Debug and Browse Toolbars

The Debug toolbar is the Visual C++ version of the Test toolbar. Not all of its icons are active, and only those buttons described already in this chapter are active. Use the Test toolbar instead of the Debug toolbar shown in Figure 4-12.

Figure 4-12: The Debug toolbar. Use the Test toolbar for Visual Test–specific actions.

The Browse toolbar, shown in Figure 4-13, is also a Visual C++–specific toolbar and isn't used by Visual Test.

Figure 4-13: The Browse toolbar is not used by Visual Test.

Note

So why are toolbars that aren't used by Visual Test available to us when *only* Visual Test is installed? This is because Rational is using Microsoft's Developer Studio editor, and some sections of code in the Developer Studio couldn't be changed without risking problems down the road should someone choose to install Microsoft Visual C++ into Developer Studio.

Finding Help Online

The previous version of Visual Test had an InfoViewer tab on the Workspace window and also an InfoFinder toolbar. These are no longer a part of Microsoft Developer Studio because of Microsoft's move to a more generic help engine. Online Help can be found in a number of ways. The first is to use the Contents, Search, and Index menu items under the Help menu. This will cause a window similar to the one shown in Figure 14-14 to be displayed.

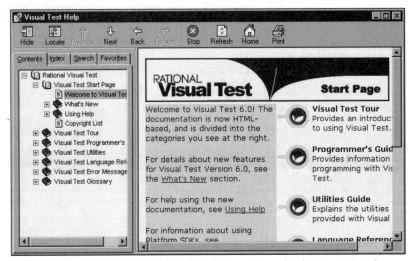

Figure 4-14: The new Microsoft online Help engine displaying Rational Visual Test documentation

When running only Visual Test under Microsoft Developer Studio, you shouldn't see any problems with the online help. However, when you have other products installed that make use of this same help engine, you might find the "preferred" online help setting changing unexpectedly, which will cause other online help contents to be displayed.

To set the preferred online help to Visual Test, you need only go to the Tools menu and select the Options menu item. This will display the Developer Studio options dialog box. You will need to use the right arrow at the top-right corner of that dialog box to scroll to and select the Help System tab that controls which help file gets displayed. Selecting that tab will result in the dialog box looking something like the one shown in Figure 14-15.

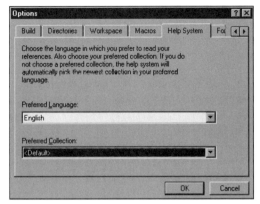

Figure 4-15: The Help System tab in the Options dialog box controls which help collection is displayed.

The Preferred Collection combo box shows which Help Collection is used when the Help menu's items are used. This is also the help file that is polled for information when F1 is pressed while the cursor is in the Source File window. Use this combo box to select Visual Test as your preferred help.

Making a Project

A project in the Developer Studio is a group of files that, together, make up a suite of tests. For a project to exist in Developer Studio, it must be part of a Workspace. When a project is created, a new file with a .DSP extension ("Developer Studio Project") is created. Another file is also created with a .DSW extension (you guessed it: "Developer Studio Workspace"). The .DSP file tracks the specific information for a given project, such as which files are considered part of that project and which subfolders in the tree structure those files are kept in. A workspace can track multiple projects at the same time, so the .DSW file's job is to keep track of which projects need to be displayed when that workspace is opened in the Developer Studio.

The easiest way to create a new project is to go to the File menu and select the New menu item. This causes the dialog box shown in Figure 14-16 to be displayed.

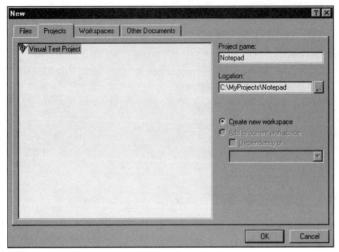

Figure 4-16: Creating a new project isn't as complicated as this dialog box makes it look.

There are four tabs in the New dialog box: Files, Projects, Workspaces, and Other Documents. The Files tab is usually used when you're adding a file to an existing project. The Projects tab is what we'll use to create a new project and workspace. The Workspaces tab can be used to create a blank workspace so that you can add existing projects to a new workspace. And the Other Documents tab allows you to create other kinds of documents in the editor, depending on which of the Microsoft Office tools you have installed.

If you have only Visual Test installed, your dialog box will look similar to the one in Figure 14-16. Otherwise, if you have Visual C++ or other tools installed that use this IDE, you will have other options available to you for creating projects.

In this example we're creating a new project called "Notepad" so that we can create tests for exercising the Microsoft Notepad application. The first thing to do is to type in the name of the directory in which the project should be stored. In this case I've used "MyProjects." The next step is to type in the name of the project to be created. As the name of the project is typed in, a subdirectory with the same name is added to the directory I specified for storing my projects. In this example, the result of typing in "Notepad" as the project name has created a path of C:\MYPROJECTS\NOTEPAD.

Verify that the Create new workspace option button is selected, click the type of project you want to create — in this case Visual Test Project — and click the OK button.

Note   If any other Visual tools are installed, the dialog box shown in Figure 4-16 will offer more options. In this example, only Visual Test is installed to clearly show the Visual Test components.

After you click the OK button, the Workspace window will look similar to the one shown in Figure 4-17. A new directory structure of C:\MyProjects\Notepad will have been created, and four files will exist in the Notepad subdirectory: NOTEPAD.DSP, NOTEPAD.DSW, NOTEPAD.OPT, and TEMPLATE.TPL.

Figure 4-17: A new workspace shows one file — a template (.TPL) that is used when new Visual Test Case files are created.

 Tip   If you find that no Workspace window is shown, then it is currently hidden and can be displayed by selecting the Workspace menu item from the View menu. Alternatively the workspace can be shown or hidden by clicking the Workspace button on the Standard toolbar, which was discussed earlier in this chapter.

 Tip   The .DSP file that is created contains machine-independent information about the project hierarchy and its contents. If you move your files over to another machine, you may need to delete the .DSW and .OPT files. Don't worry, though, because opening a .DSP file automatically generates new .DSW and .OPT files for your project.

The .DSP and .DSW files have already been explained — they're project and workspace files. The .OPT file holds additional configuration information for the Workspace, and the .TPL file is a generic template that will be used every time a new .MST (Visual Test Case file) is created.

 Tip   Edit the .TPL file in your new project directory and all of your new test case files will use that template. Or edit the .TPL file found in the \VT6\Include installation directory; any new Visual Test Project you create will use that .TPL file.

Adding to a Project

Now that the project has been created, it is possible to add test cases to it. This is done by using the New menu item found under the File menu. When the New dialog box is displayed this time, however, the Files tab is automatically selected, as shown in Figure 4-18.

Note   This exact same result can be achieved by selecting the New menu item via the Add to Project submenu found under the Project menu. Dealer's choice.

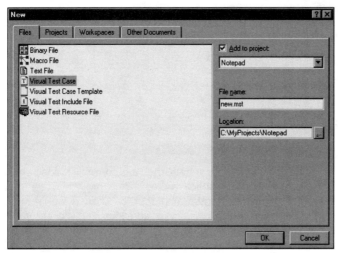

Figure 4-18: Creating a new file in the project is as easy as creating the project itself.

This dialog box will allow you to add a new file to the current project. Selecting Visual Test Case, typing in NEW.MST, and clicking the OK button, for example, will result in NEW.MST being added to your project and the Source File window being opened to display the newly created file, as shown in Figure 4-19. Note that this new file is showing the contents of the template (.TPL) file that was automatically added when the project was first created.

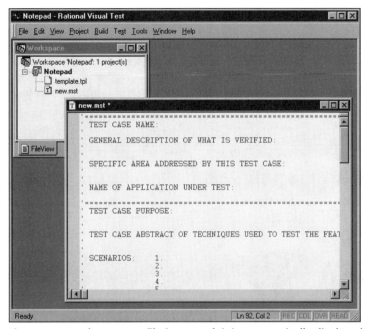

Figure 4-19: When a new file is created, it is automatically displayed in a Source File window and added to the current project.

The easiest way to add files

The previous section showed how to add files to a project. That approach used the standard menus to accomplish that task. Adding a folder and then a file into that folder using those same methods is a hassle. First you need to go to the Project menu, select the Add to Project submenu, and select the New Folder menu item. After that you can select the New menu item from the same menu and submenu to add a new file. In the New dialog box you then need to update the Location setting so that it takes advantage of the newly created folder/subdirectory. What a hassle!

Here's the easy way to do all of this: right-click the project item in the tree view of the Workspace. Or right-click any folders found in that tree; this will allow you to add folders and new files, import files, and so on. In my opinion, right-clicking is the only way to go.

Importing files

First you need to have an active project in your workspace. You can either create one as we've already discussed or open an existing project. Importing files is simple: right-click the project in the workspace's tree view and select the Import menu item from the pop-up menu, as shown in Figure 4-20. The result is a dialog box that allows you to select files or folders that are brought directly into the project.

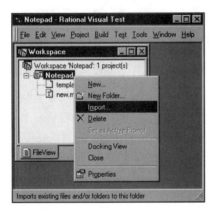

Figure 4-20: Right-clicking a project is the easiest way to add files to your project, whether they're newly created files or files to be imported.

Once the Import menu item is selected, the Import Test Project Items dialog box is displayed. This allows you to import existing files or folders. Figure 4-21 shows six test case files previously created for testing the menu items under Notepad's File menu.

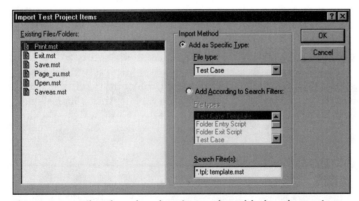

Figure 4-21: Files that already exist can be added to the project by using the Import Test Project Items dialog box.

An alternative method for importing files is to use the Project menu. This supplies you with the same methods as the right-click pop-up menu, plus one more: the Files menu item. The Files menu item is found under the Add to Project submenu in the Project menu. Using this feature allows you to add files that are at the same directory level as the project, or that are at lower levels. That is, if there is a file deep down in a subdirectory under your project's directory, you can navigate down to it and add it to the project. The result is all of the subfolders being created in the project itself. It's pretty slick. Unfortunately it only works for directories within your project's directory. That is, you can't jump to another drive or local area network path to add a file. A pity.

Note Deleting files from a project is as simple as right-clicking a file or folder and selecting the Delete menu item from the pop-up menu. This will remove the file from your project but won't remove it from your disk drive.

The Main Components of a Project

In the first half of this book we'll build a test suite for the Windows Notepad application. This application has been selected because it's available on everyone's system and most people are familiar with it and its functionality. The goal is to have a final project that is similar to the one shown in Figure 4-22.

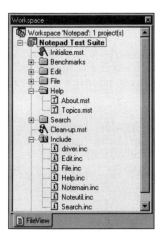

Figure 4-22: This project is similar to the one we build in Part III of this book.

When a new project is created, the name of the project appears at the top of the project tree. As each new item is added, it falls in place underneath.

In Figure 4-22, INITIALIZE.MST is known as a *folder entry script* and appears as a green starting flag in the project window. This script is automatically run every time another script on the same level, or the levels below, is executed. This only happens through the Suite Manager, however, so the entry script won't run when the test case files (.MST files) are executed in isolation, using the Developer Studio.

> **Tip**   Clicking the Suite Manager icon in the Test toolbar will run the Suite Manager utility using the project that is currently active in Developer Studio.

A folder entry script provides a place where initialization routines can be stored for tasks that need to be accomplished before each test case is executed. Entry scripts can also be placed in subfolders. In this case, they will only run when scripts in those subfolders, or in subfolders of those subfolders, are executed.

The folders in the project are known as *test folders* and hold test files related to a given area of the product (such as the File menu in Notepad) or to a particular task that needs to be performed (for example, benchmarking). One test folder can be placed within another, allowing for very structured projects. (In fact, an almost limitless number of folders can be placed inside other folders.)

A special folder appears in Figure 4-22 that isn't a standard folder: It's an *include folder* and is identified by the lowercase *i* on its icon. This folder contains *include files* (.INC files) and is searched by all *test case* files (.MST files) when they reference an include file as part of their requirement to execute correctly. It's searched by all .MST files at the level of the include folder and below.

Subinclude folders can be created at lower points in the project tree. These also contain .INC files, which can only be accessed by files lower in the hierarchy. In the Notepad test suite example, only one include folder is used because of the suite's simple design.

An *include file*, delineated by the .INC extension in the filename, holds all the declarations for constants, user-defined types, global variables, and, sometimes, sharable subroutines and functions. Except for sharable subroutines and functions, an .INC file is comparable to an .H file in C, or an .HPP file in C++. These .INC files will be discussed in more depth in Chapter 8.

Finally, the *test case file* type holds all tests that exercise the functionality of the product being automated. This file has a simple, dog-eared document icon with a letter T on it. An example can be seen in Figure 4-22 in the Help test folder: ABOUT.MST and TOPICS.MST are two test case files holding one or more test scenarios. We create and dissect a simple test case file in Chapter 7. They also are discussed in more depth in Part III, when we build the initial structure for a test suite.

Adjusting Script Execution Order

Creating a folder entry or exit script in Visual Test 6.0 isn't as obvious as it was in version 4.0. This is now accomplished by right-clicking the project or a project folder and selecting the Properties menu item from the pop-up menu. Either the Project Properties dialog box, shown in Figure 4-23, or the Test Folder Properties dialog box is displayed.

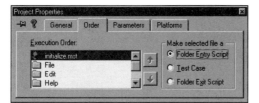

Figure 4-23: The Properties dialog box allows the order of execution to be selected for a test project's files.

Recall, however, that adjusting the order of execution does not affect how the scripts run when executed in the Developer Studio. It only affects how they execute when they are run via the Suite Manager.

Tip
Right-click windows and objects often. You might be surprised at the features you find.

The Test Menu

You will use the Test menu — or a version of it via the toolbars and accelerator keys — when you're writing and debugging test scripts. These scripts can either be part of a project or separate, standalone scripts. The Test menu and its contents are shown in Figure 4-24.

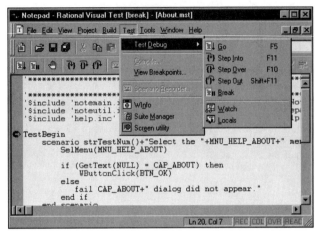

Figure 4-24: The Test menu is specific to Visual Test and contains many of the same operations as the Test toolbar.

Compiling Scripts

Every time a script is executed, it must first be compiled to a form understandable by the Visual Test interpreter. You can save the compiled, interpretable form of a test script in a *p-code* or *pseudo-code* file, with a .PC6 file extension (versions previous to Visual Test 6.0 used a .PCD extension). This feature has been available since the 2.0 version of Microsoft Test.

By saving a compiled script into a p-code file, as shown in Figure 4-25, you can skip the compilation step for future executions of that script. While a p-code file doesn't run any faster than a script that must go through the compilation step, it does allow you to skip the compile time of the script. By doing this, you make the process quicker, even though the actual execution time of the scripts is the same.

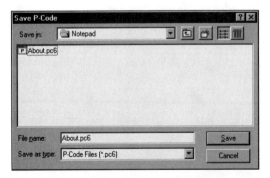

Figure 4-25: Save the compiled form of a test case file with the Compile menu item found under the Test menu.

Another reason for compiling a script to p-code is so that it can be distributed with the MTRUN.EXE run-time engine to other machines. The Visual Test license agreement says that only one copy of Visual Test can be installed on a single machine at any given time, but the MTRUN.EXE engine is freely distributable, as are any p-code files that you generate. Therefore, you could create a shipping product by using Visual Test as the development tool, compiling your product's source code into p-code, and distributing it with the MTRUN.EXE engine. Because p-code is machine independent, the process of distribution is that much easier. (For more information on which files are required to distribute compiled scripts, read Chapter 13.)

Since p-code is a compiled or tokenized version of the source code text, comments and source code recognizable by humans are stripped out. As a result, you can distribute a file throughout your company without losing sleep about people making changes to it. This form of version control means you can ensure that changes are only made with your knowledge.

Running a Test

If you select Go from the Test menu, or press F5, the script in the active Source File window will compile and run. The Output window will become active during the compilation process so that compilation errors can be reported back to the Test programmer (see Figure 4-26).

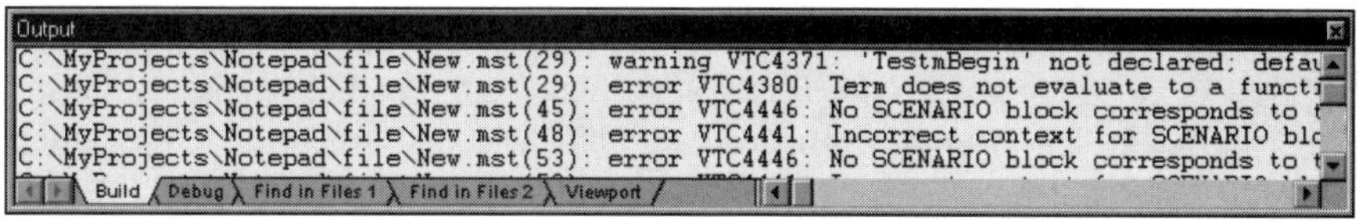

```
Output                                                                          ⨯
C:\MyProjects\Notepad\file\New.mst(29):  warning VTC4371:  'TestmBegin' not declared; defau▲
C:\MyProjects\Notepad\file\New.mst(29):  error VTC4380:  Term does not evaluate to a functi
C:\MyProjects\Notepad\file\New.mst(45):  error VTC4446:  No SCENARIO block corresponds to t
C:\MyProjects\Notepad\file\New.mst(48):  error VTC4441:  Incorrect context for SCENARIO blc
C:\MyProjects\Notepad\file\New.mst(53):  error VTC4446:  No SCENARIO block corresponds to t▼
◄ ► \ Build / Debug \ Find in Files 1 \ Find in Files 2 \ Viewport /     ◄           ►
```

Figure 4-26: Errors and warnings that occur during the compilation of a script are displayed in the Output window.

In the event that errors or warnings occur during compile time, the run of the script is terminated so that you can track down the root of the problem(s). Depending on how Visual Test is configured in its Options dialog box, you can ignore warnings that occur and allow the script to run. However, if an error does occur, it's because a fatal problem exists that will keep the script from running. Therefore, the script won't begin its execution step.

Tracking Down Problems

When errors or warnings occur while a script is being compiled, the Output window reports information about them, as was shown in Figure 4-26.

The compiler does its best to not stop at the first error it encounters, so it can continue and report as many errors as possible in the compilation of the file. This is a great improvement over previous versions of Test, which would stop at the first error encountered.

When an error is encountered, you can jump to the offending line by double-clicking the error message in the Output window (under the Build tab). The line causing the problem is marked with an arrow on the left of the editor, and it's up to the programmer to determine what the compiler is attempting to communicate.

Tip   Frequently, if you have a whole number of errors in a listing, they are based upon the first error. As a result, when you fix one specific problem, it might well result in all the other problems fixing themselves. Therefore, fix a couple of the obvious errors and recompile your script to get a fresh list of errors.

Tracking down compilation errors can be time-consuming and frustrating. There's no way around these errors other than becoming more familiar with Visual Test through using it more and more. Don't get too frustrated when an error is staring you in the face; just keep trying different things to track it down.

Tip   One thing I always do is to create a temporary, untitled text file in the Developer Studio to try out different things, so that I can better understand how a feature works. Once I've got it figured out, I cut and paste the code into the main test case file. To create a temporary file, click the New Text File button on the Standard toolbar, right-click the resulting Source File window, and select Properties. In the Language combo box, select Visual Test to make it act as a Visual Test source file even though it hasn't yet been saved.

Another way to understand what the compiler is trying to tell you is to press F1, so it will bring up more information about the error that has occurred. When an error or warning is reported in the Output window, a number (such as "VTC4371") is given with the message. Click that number to place the insertion cursor in the text of the Output window, then press F1. The context-sensitive help will search for information on it and provide a more thorough description of what's happening, as shown in Figure 4-27.

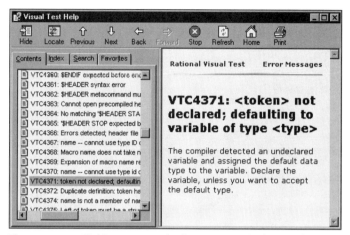

Figure 4-27: Clicking an error in the Output window and pressing F1 provides additional information on an error message.

Stepping through code

Even if a script is able to compile itself fully without errors or warnings, errors may still be encountered during the execution of the script. These types of errors are called *run-time errors*.

A simple example of a run-time error is when a script attempts to act upon a Windows control that doesn't exist. At compile time, the compiler checks to see if you used the function, subroutine, or statement correctly. If so, the script is allowed to run. But if a line of code instructs Visual Test to click a button that doesn't exist, the result is a run-time error.

Here is a script that will compile without any warnings or errors but will generate a run-time error before completing its execution. It will generate the run-time error shown in Figure 4-28.

```
dim i as integer
dim j(5) as integer
    for i = 1 to 7
        j(i) = i
    next i
END
```

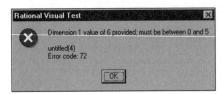

Figure 4-28: A run-time error has occurred. The compiler couldn't catch it because it couldn't determine that it would happen.

Another example of a run-time error is an out-of-bounds error. This type of error occurs when the program attempts to access an element of an array that doesn't exist. The compiler is unable to confirm that this will happen, so the error doesn't occur until the script actually runs.

When these types of errors are encountered, it is sometimes necessary to track down what is going on by stepping through the source code line by line. This can be accomplished by setting a breakpoint on or around the line where the error is occurring. A breakpoint is a marker that tells the interpreter where to stop execution of the current script and turn control back over to you. Figure 4-29 shows a script where a breakpoint has been set and execution has come to a halt.

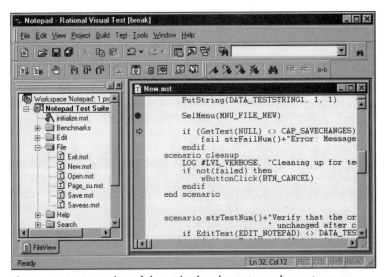

Figure 4-29: Execution of the script has been turned over to your control so that the script can be stepped through one line at a time.

There are two symbols on the left-hand side of Figure 4-29. The first is a large dot. (In earlier versions it looked like a little red stop sign. Now it's just a red dot.) The second item is an arrow that marks the line of code about to be executed. When the breakpoint was encountered, the script stopped before executing that line of code. (I had it execute that line of code so that the arrow and breakpoint symbol weren't overlapping.)

Now that the script is back under the programmer's control, Visual Test is in its debug mode (denoted by the "[break]" text placed in the caption bar) and you can explore exactly what's going on with each variable as you execute the script one line at a time — as slowly or quickly as you want. (Just think how much fun it must have been tracking down problems in the days of punch cards, and you'll appreciate this debugger even more.)

If you want to step through the source code, you can use the Test toolbar or the keyboard equivalent of the menu items found under the Test Debug submenu in the Test menu. This is where the Step Into, Step Over, and Step Out menu items and toolbar buttons come into play.

Step Into (F11) will step into a function or subroutine for which source code is available. Step Over (F10) will allow a subroutine or function to perform its action and then move on to the next line of code. Step Out (Shift+F11) will allow you to get out of a function or subroutine you've stepped into.

Meanwhile, when you step through a script, Visual Test hides itself as each line of code gets executed, so that the application becomes active again (although only as that line of code executes). This allows you to step through a section of code without causing the Visual Test commands to act upon the Developer Studio instead of upon the application.

Note If you find that Visual Test isn't hiding itself automatically, select the Options menu item under the Tools menu, click the Test tab to display the Visual Test settings, and make sure that both the Minimize on Start and Restore on End check boxes are checked.

Caution Although using breakpoints and stepping through code is often absolutely invaluable, sometimes it is impossible and it can be frustrating. For example, if you display a window's context menu (by right-clicking or using Shift+F10) and set a breakpoint in Visual Test after that, the menu will disappear during the switch to Visual Test and will not be restored on continuation.

Watching variables

Although stepping through a program one line at a time is helpful to make sure all the steps are being executed correctly, there's yet another detail that can be invoked to make tracking scripts even easier. These are windows for watching the values of a script's variables.

Visual Test supplies two types of these windows: the Test Watch window and the Test Locals window, both of which are available under the Test Debug submenu in the Test menu. They're also available via the Test toolbar.

Test watch window

The Test Watch window is shown in Figure 4-30. It tracks only those variables it is told to track. In this case I've typed in the global variable named `giTestCount` and am just about to hit Enter after typing in the other global variable named `giFailCount`.

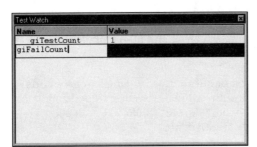

Figure 4-30: The Test Watch window shows the values held by variables it is told to track.

If you want to add a variable to the Test Watch window, click an empty line and type in the name of the variable in your program whose value you'd like to watch. Don't worry about using upper- or lowercase characters, since Visual Test's compiler and interpreter aren't case-sensitive. The minute you hit Enter, the value of that variable, if the variable exists, is displayed in the right-hand column.

Test locals window

When working with variables in a function or subroutine, it isn't necessary to use the Test Watch window to track the values of those variables. This is because another window is provided, called the Test Locals window, which automatically displays the variables currently in *scope* (available for use) with the exception of global variables. (You will find more details on global variables in Chapter 5.) Figure 4-31 shows the Test Locals window.

Test Locals	
Name	**Value**
strOut	Now is the time for all good people...
strDirection	NULL
iLoopLimit	0
iLoop	0
iChar	1
iCurrChar	0
iLine	1
iCurrLine	0

Figure 4-31: The Test Locals window automatically shows variables local to a section of code.

The Test Locals window will update itself automatically when moving in and out of functions and subroutines.

When execution is leaving a routine, the window's variables are no longer used and are considered to be out-of-scope (no longer available). Therefore, the Test Locals window updates itself to show those variables that are still available. In the event that the Test Watch window is set to view the values of a variable that goes out of scope, it will put a message next to the variable that says, "<Error: Variable is not declared or is not in current scope>." Typically, the Test Watch window is used only to track global variables or local variables that can't be seen because the Test Locals window is so full.

Tip One really cool feature of the Test Watch and Test Locals windows is that a variable's value can be changed while you're stepping through the script. By double-clicking the value displayed to the right, you can change that value, as is shown in Figure 4-31.

Bookmarks

Bookmarks were mentioned briefly when the Edit toolbar was discussed earlier in this chapter. However, this feature is helpful enough to be mentioned again.

When working with source code, whether you're stepping through one line at a time or coding it for the first time, you may well want to move around the source code file to recall how something was written, declared, or used. The problem is that, when this happens, you lose your place and waste time trying to find where you were before you went on your search.

A bookmark allows tags to be set at specific lines of code so that you can then search through those tags to return to a marked location (see Figure 4-32). To use a bookmark, do one of these things:

✦ Have the Edit toolbar up and available.

✦ Use Ctrl+F2 to add/remove a bookmark and F2 and Shift+F2 to cycle through them.

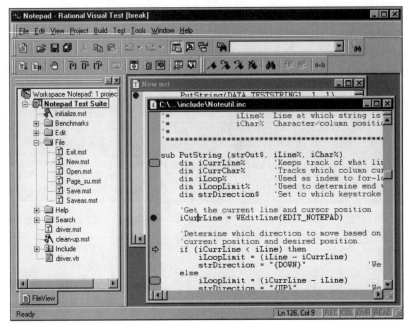

Figure 4-32: Bookmarks make it easy for Test programmers to mark important sections of code so they can be found and referenced more easily.

On a color monitor, a bookmark appears as a blue, rounded rectangle.

Customizing the IDE

The development environment provided by the Developer Studio has gone through usability testing based on programmers' feedback, and a number of new features have been added for each major release. However, you may well have specific requirements that have to be addressed if the tool is to be as helpful as possible. To help you with some of these personalized needs, Microsoft has made many features in the IDE customizable.

The Customize dialog box can be accessed in the Tools menu by selecting the Customize... menu item. This displays the dialog box shown in Figure 4-33 and makes available five customization areas:

✦ Commands

✦ Toolbars

✦ Tools

✦ Keyboard

✦ Add-ins and Macro Files

Figure 4-33: The Customize dialog box makes it possible for you to customize the development environment to your needs.

Commands

The Commands tab of the Customize dialog box allows you to view which shortcuts are available for the different menus and toolbars. These can then be dragged to a menu or a toolbar so that you have easy access to the commands you use most often. As you drag one of these commands over a toolbar or menu, a line will appear to show where the command will be placed.

To remove a menu, menu item, or toolbar button, simply go into this dialog box, click the object you wish to remove, and drag it out of the window until an X appears on the cursor.

Tip If you get yourself into trouble, which isn't hard to do with this feature, simply click the Reset All Menus button to return your menus to normal. Mess up your toolbars? Go to the Toolbar tab and click the Reset All button.

Toolbars

The Toolbars tab on the dialog box makes it easy for you to display the available toolbars or create your own toolbars with the features you need the most. Once you've created your toolbar, you can select it and then return to the Commands tab in this dialog box. When you're back in the Commands tab, you can drag the items you want to your new toolbar. Easy! This new toolbar not only shows up in the list with the standard IDE toolbars, it also shows up when you right-click a toolbar when you're in the main editor, so that you can easily turn it on and off.

Tools

As you can see in Figure 4-34, the Tools tab in the Customize dialog box allows the developer to add her own external tools to the Developer Studio's Tools menu. This way the tools are always within easy reach and are integrated into the development environment. Some third-party, add-on programs have even been known to place themselves into this menu when they're installed. These tools can be removed or modified via this customization dialog box.

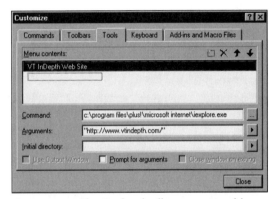

Figure 4-34: The Tools tab allows you to add your own tools to the Developer Studio Tools menu.

Keyboard

The Keyboard tab provides a means of adding accelerator or shortcut keys to commonly used menu items. If, for example, you're an old-timer when it comes to using Visual Test, you'll recall that F8 has always been the key for stepping into a function while debugging a script. This has recently changed to F11. This is a way for you to remap your accelerator keys.

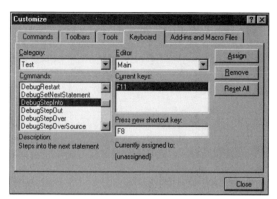

Figure 4-35: The Keyboard tab in the Customize dialog box makes it easy to add, remove, or modify shortcut keys for commonly used menu items.

Add-ins and Macro Files

The final tab on the Customize dialog box allows you to determine which macro files should or should not be active in Developer Studio. The MYMACROS file appears in the dialog box in Figure 4-36 automatically because it was placed into the \common\msdev98\macros folder that is found in the installation directory created when you installed Visual Test. If you create additional macros and want to take advantage of them, place them in this folder and activate them from this dialog box.

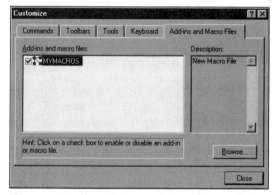

Figure 4-36: The Add-ins and Macro Files tab in the Customize dialog box allows you to turn on/off macro and add-on behavior.

Options Dialog Box

Another form of customization is done through the Options dialog box, which is also accessed via the Tools menu. Selecting the Options... menu item displays the dialog box shown in Figure 4-37. By stepping through the individual tabs in this dialog box, you can tweak features of Visual Test for best performance, depending on your needs.

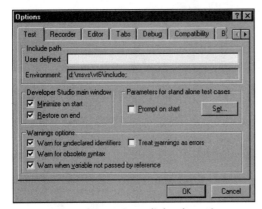

Figure 4-37: The Options dialog box gives you the flexibility to control how Visual Test and Developer Studio features should work.

Many of these tabs are discussed in this book as the relevant topics arise. The Test tab, however, is important enough to mention here even if it gets repeated in other parts of this book.

The Include path section of this dialog box allows you to specify where your include files (.INC files) reside. Any path you type into this section will cause Visual Test's compiler to search that path for files included by your test cases.

The Minimize and Restore check boxes allow you to instruct the Developer Studio to get itself out of the way as your scripts begin to execute. Both boxes are typically checked, as shown in Figure 4-37.

The Parameters section of this dialog box allows you to specify information that may or may not be used by your test scripts, depending on how you wrote them. For example, if you have a script that adjusts which files it includes depending upon which operating system it is running on, it will probably be using the predefined symbols shown in the dialog box in Figure 4-38. You can also add your own symbols to control how your scripts work.

Note Chapter 8 goes into more detail on using symbols, and Chapter 13 has more information about COMMAND$ and TESTMODE$.

Figure 4-38: This dialog box allows you to specify run-time parameters that can be used by your scripts.

Summary

Because the Developer Studio is the main editing tool, those already familiar with the environment can focus on learning the Visual Test language and need to spend less time learning how to use the user interface. While a lot of features make up this integrated development environment, they'll soon become second nature to you as you start using the features and developing scripts. Don't feel too overwhelmed, because you don't need to know all the features at once, and you should pick them up as you need them.

Three principal windows appear in the Developer Studio's main window: WorkSpace; Output; and Source File. These provide easy access to information about the script you're writing and testing. Also, eight main toolbars are available: Standard, Build, Build MiniBar, Resource, Test, Edit, Debug, and Browse.

You can create and work with your own projects. A project is a group of files that, together, make up a suite of tests. It is represented by a tree, or hierarchical view, of subfolders, such as test folders and include folders. You can also create a Project Workspace window, so your files are organized into one area. The Test menu allows you to write and debug scripts. The Test Watch window and Test Locals window allow you to watch variables and keep track of them. You can also use bookmarks when you need to jump around to key sections of your source code quickly.

Finally, it is possible to customize the IDE by adding or selecting the features you want, by changing menus, toolbars, and tools; by modifying the keyboard shortcuts; or by adding macros and add-on tools.

In the next three chapters we look at the Visual Test language and the utilities found under the Test menu. We dive into a simple scripting example designed especially for those new to programming in the Test language. The key is to push forward, not get too frustrated, and look back now and then to realize how much you've learned in such a short period of time.

✦　　✦　　✦

Visual Test Language

Visual Test's language is a robust version of BASIC that gives you enough flexibility to write complex scripts to meet your testing needs. The price to be paid for this flexibility, however, is the steep learning curve to understand all of the functions available. This learning curve is commonplace when learning any language, especially a language that works with a windowing environment. Don't get discouraged or overwhelmed by the amount of information, because you'll pick it up in time.

Fortunately, once you get the overall idea of the functions available to you, you'll know where and what to look for. The purpose of this chapter is not to step you through the Visual Test language piece by piece, but to give you an overview of what's available and tell you how to find more detailed information about those features. It isn't meant to replace the Visual Test online help documentation, but to provide a road map to what's available and where to look for information. As you write your scripts, knowledge of what statements and functions to use and which are available will come to you.

Note Appendix A in this book provides you with a reference to the Visual Test language. It isn't exhaustive like the online help; its purpose is to let you know at a glance what is available to you in the Visual Test language. It also helps you when you're new to the language to determine which part of the language you want to use to achieve your goals. For more detailed information refer to the online help provided with Rational Visual Test 6.0.

This chapter is a jump start on what the Test language has to offer. This way you can focus on what's important now — getting started in using Visual Test. As you get more comfortable with the language, move into the later chapters to discover some of the more advanced features. Some of these advanced features are discussed in Chapter 13. Chapter 7 is also a good place to begin when you're interested in seeing a first attempt at a test script.

Some Programming Experience Required

If you are a programmer from the olden days of Applesoft BASIC, FORTRAN, or COBOL, or if you're new to programming altogether, I strongly recommend that you enroll in a local community college's *Introduction to Programming* class as soon as possible. These classes tend to be taught using the Pascal or C programming languages, structured languages after which the latest versions of BASIC are modeled. You might also consider taking a Microsoft Visual Basic class, since the Test language is very similar to Visual Basic.

Taking a class like this will give you the general introduction you need to pick up the Test language quickly. It's important to understand that Rational Visual Test is a programming language that has testing-centric utilities included to help simulate users' actions. This book does not teach basic programming methodology; it assumes you have some background in programming with a structured, procedural language like Visual Basic, Pascal, or C. It points out how to do comparable tasks using the Test language.

The Basics of the Test Language

In this section, we go through the basic features of the Visual Test language. Some are extremely easy to use; some, more complex. Let's start with a real easy nut to crack that will continue to help us as we learn the language: *context-sensitive help*.

Context-Sensitive Help

I believe context-sensitive help to be one of the most important features of Visual Test. It's also the easiest to use. Therefore it's the first aspect of the language we're going to learn. It's extremely simple: Type in the keyword that you want to look up, making sure the flashing cursor is in or next to the word, and press the F1 key. That's it! The result is the Visual Test Help being displayed in its new HTML format, as shown in Figure 5-1.

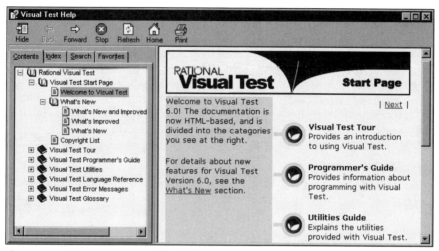

Figure 5-1: Use context-sensitive help extensively whether you are a beginner or an old hand at Visual Test.

Declaring Variables

Unfortunately, it's all uphill from here. But declaring variables is also pretty straightforward.

There are three main ways a variable can be declared in the Visual Test language. The visibility of a variable—or scope—to other sections of the source code you've written is determined by which method you use when declaring each variable:

✦ **Global variable:** The value of a *global variable* declaration (declared using the GLOBAL statement) can be referenced from any place within the source code, including other files (if they are included using the '$INCLUDE metacommand), functions, subroutines, and error handlers. The scope of the variable is *global*, and therefore it is always available.

✦ **Local variable:** A *local variable* (declared using the DIM statement) is accessible only by the function, subroutine, or main block of source code in which it is declared. The scope of a local variable is limited to the block of code in which it has been declared. If, for example, a variable has been declared within a function or subroutine, the main section of code cannot reference the variable within that subroutine or function. In the same way, a function or subroutine cannot access any variables outside itself, unless those variables are globally declared.

  ✦ **Static variable:** A *static variable* (declared using the STATIC statement) is typically used only in functions and subroutines and causes those routines to retain the value of a static variable, so that it is still available the next time the function or subroutine is called. A local variable in a routine is created and set to zero (0) when the routine starts and disposed of when the routine terminates. This is not the case for a static variable, however. It remains unchanged or, well, *static* even between calls to the routine. It is not like a constant, however, since its value can be modified by the routine in which it was declared.

The DIM statement

A variable is declared in the Test language using the DIM statement. In previous versions of BASIC, this statement was used only when working with arrays, but it now applies to variables that hold only a single value as well. The format for declaring a variable is

```
dim variable[(subscripts)][AS type][,variable[(subscripts)][AS
type]]…
```

Items in square brackets are optional as part of the declaration. An example declaration, one that results in three variables of type INTEGER, STRING, and LONG, is

```
dim A as integer, B as string, C as long
```

Variables can be declared anywhere in the test script. A common place to put declarations is at the top of the main script where the variables are being used, instead of interspersed throughout the script. This ensures that variables can be easily found.

An array of a given type can be declared by adding parentheses and the number of subscripts that make up that array. This is peculiar to the Test language — array indices can start and end anywhere (3 to 6). If not explicitly specified, the value of the lowest subscript defaults to 0, but the default can be set to 1 with the OPTION BASE 1 statement. When only one value is specified in the declaration, it represents the upper bound of the array. An array's upper and lower bounds can be determined at run time with Visual Test's ubound and lbound functions:

```
dim D(10) as integer, E(5) as string, F(3 to 6) as long
```

A global variable is declared using the GLOBAL statement and is the same as the local declaration, except that GLOBAL is used in place of DIM. The situation is the same for a static variable; the keyword STATIC is used in place of DIM. For example:

```
global G as integer
static H as string
```

Shorthand declarations

Optionally, variables can be declared using *shorthand notation* instead of writing out the full name of the type. These abbreviated symbols, which represent the different types, are shown in Table 5-1.

Table 5-1
Single-Character Symbols Representing Variables

Data Type	Shorthand
short	%
integer	%
long	&
single	!
double	#
string	$

An example of a variable declared using the shorthand notation is

```
dim MyVariable%, YourVariable$
```

where `MyVariable` is an `INTEGER` type and `YourVariable` is a `STRING`.

Tip

In Microsoft Test 3.0 the `SHORT` data type was introduced to guarantee that a script executing under version 3.0, which used a `SHORT` type, would continue to use a 16-bit form of an `INTEGER`. This was done because an integer's size would fluctuate between 16 bits (2 bytes) and 32 bits (4 bytes) when moving between two environments such as Windows 3.1 (a 16-bit system) and Windows 95 or NT (32-bit systems). In Visual Test 4.0 and 6.0, however, the `INTEGER` and `SHORT` data types are both 16 bits (2 bytes), which is why they now both use the same shorthand notation (%).

Force Explicit Declarations

For better or worse, Test programmers can *implicitly* declare variables simply by using the shortcut character of a variable in the source code (for example, A$ = "Test"). By doing this, it is no longer necessary to use the DIM statement. This is a poor practice to follow because it increases the chances for errors.

If, for example, you use the variable iBook% but later accidentally refer to it as iBooks% (with an *s*), you now have two variables floating around when you think you only have one. Modifying the variable in one place and then referring to it (incorrectly) later will lead you to believe that somehow the variable didn't get set or was inadvertently modified somewhere else in the source code. Tracking down problems like this can be time consuming and frustrating.

To force *explicit declarations* to be used, two check boxes need to be set in the Options dialog box. Those check boxes are Warn for Undeclared Identifiers and Treat Warnings as Errors, both of which are located under the Test tab in the Options dialog box. I suggest you turn these on to help you and your team avoid problems down the road.

The Main Section

When working in languages such as Pascal or C, you always have a main section of code that starts all the execution. The C language has a function named main() that is called by the operating system to get the program running. Pascal uses the program and begin statements, so that it's clear where execution begins.

The fact that Visual Test begins execution on the first line of code without a main() function or begin keyword throws most programmers who are familiar with other programming languages.

In the Test language, the first line is the beginning of the program. Any executable source code from the first line forward will be compiled and executed by Visual Test. Typically, a Visual Test script looks like Listing 5-1. This is an example of a simple Visual Test script that demonstrates commenting, declaring variables, clearing the output viewport, using loops, and printing Hello World! to the viewport.

Listing 5-1: A typical Visual Test script

```
'Just for fun
dim i%, j%, k%
    viewport clear  'Clear the Output window
```

```
    for i = 1 to 5
        for j = 1 to 20 step 5
            for k = 20 to 1 step -4
                print i,j,k
            next k
        next j
    next i
    print "Hello World!"
end
```

If you type the code shown in Listing 5-1 into the Developer Studio's editor for a Visual Test file and then select Go from the Test Debug submenu found under the Test menu, a bunch of numbers will print to the Output window along with a `Hello World!` at the end.

Tip   Comments to yourself or other programmers can be placed into the source code without being misunderstood by the compiler. Use the `REM` statement, or its short-hand notation, which is a single-quote mark ('), as used in Listing 5-1.

Writing Routines

Subroutines and functions provide a means of encapsulating code that is used multiple times so that it doesn't need to be replicated throughout the entire code base. By using a subroutine or function, you will find it easier to change the behavior of the source code from one location. This practice also results in source code that is easier to read and to share with other testing teams.

Typically, subroutines and functions are placed after the `END` statement, outside the main section of source code. This is not a requirement, however, just a style that many programmers follow to make their code resemble C, with its initial `main()` block of code. Separate routines are then referenced from that block of code to get everything running.

Other programmers will place all of the functions and subroutines at the top of the source code file and the main block of code that calls those routines at the bottom, which resembles the way a lot of beginning Pascal programmers were taught.

And others, who want to keep their code clean, sharable, and easy to read, will put their routines in a separate file — an *include file* — that can be programmatically added to their source code file during compilation.

The fact is, it doesn't really matter, just as long as a style is chosen and adhered to. I advocate placing functions and subroutines after the `END` statement or into an include file so that the first thing a programmer sees when opening up a test case file is the main section of code that gets everything started. What it comes down to is that, no matter where a function or subroutine is placed, its section of code isn't executed until it's called — either by the main program or indirectly from the main program by another function or subroutine originally called by the main program.

Subroutines

A subroutine is the same as a function, with one significant difference: It doesn't return a value. C programmers can relate to a subroutine as a function with a `void` return type.

Subroutines and functions no longer need to be declared, as was the case in versions preceding Visual Test 4.0. There's no need for a forward prototype or declaration to be there to tell the compiler that the function or subroutine exists, except in the case of a function or subroutine that's in a dynamic-link library. (DLLs are discussed in Chapter 13.) The only part that needs attention is the actual definition of the function or subroutine. Listing 5-2 shows a typical subroutine definition.

Listing 5-2: **An example of a subroutine definition**

```
'*************************************************************
'* Subroutine:   ResetApp
'* Purpose:      Attempts to reset the application to a known
'*               state. This routine will likely grow in
'*               complexity as strange circumstances are
'*               discovered where it isn't able to reset the
'*               application.
'*
'*************************************************************

sub ResetApp()
    wMenuEnd
    wMenuSelect("FILE\NEW")

    if (GetText(NULL) = "Save changes?") then
        wButtonClick("No")
    endif
end sub 'ResetApp()
```

This subroutine performs a simple yet important task used when testing almost any application: It resets the application to a known state or condition. No local variables are used in this example, but if they were, they would be declared using the DIM statement and be placed directly under the first line of the subroutine in

Listing 5-2. No parameters are required for this subroutine, either, which is why there are no variables listed inside its parentheses.

To activate the source code in the `sub ResetApp()` subroutine, it must be *called*. This can be done by the main script, or by way of another function or subroutine.

Functions

A function is similar to a subroutine, except that it returns a value when it has finished its task. Listing 5-3 shows a typical function (it returns a string with a value representing how many times this function was called). In addition to showing you what a typical function looks like in Visual Test, this listing also demonstrates the `STATIC` variable type and the use of the continuation mark (the underscore character '_') that allows source code to be broken across multiple lines.

Listing 5-3: An example of a function definition in the Test language

```
'*****************************************************************
'* Function:    strFailNum
'* Purpose:     Keeps a counter of the total number of
'*              failures that have occurred using the fail
'*              command for the current test case file. For
'*              this to work, it must be called for each
'*              failure and is therefore designed to work with
'*              the FAIL statement.
'*
'* Parameters:  NONE
'*
'* Returns:     STRING  The string that is returned is
'*                      formatted to fit in front of the text
'*                      being included in the fail statement.
'*
'* Format
'* returned:    "Fail #<num>: "
'*
'* Use:         FAIL strFailNum()+"<descrip-of-failure>"
'*
'*****************************************************************

function strFailNum() as string
    static iCount%

    iCount = iCount + 1
    strFailNum = "Fail #"+trim$(str$(iCount))+ _
                 ": "end function 'strFailNum()
```

Pay less attention to what this function does and more to how it is structured. The front part declares the name of the function to be strFailNum. The function doesn't take a parameter, either, but it does make use of a STATIC variable. Recall that a STATIC variable retains its value even after the function has been exited. Therefore, this function not only returns a nicely formatted string with error information, it also keeps a counter of how many times it was called. This function works by only being called when an error occurs so that the counter is updated only in those situations.

A line of source code can be up to 256 characters long. Because it is difficult to read long lines of source code, especially in an editor at low resolution, it's preferable to break those single lines into multiple lines. This can be done by using the underscore character (_), as seen in Listing 5-3.

As you may recall, a function must return a value when it terminates, and in this case the value must be an INTEGER. A function returns a value by setting the name of the function equal to the value to be returned. This is not the same as the return statement used in the C language, which will immediately exit the function. Instead, the value isn't returned until the end of the function is reached or an EXIT FUNCTION statement is used (use the EXIT statement sparingly, if at all, since common coding practices encourage routines exiting at a single point in the routine. In this case that single point would be at the END FUNCTION statement). Assigning the name of the function to the value to be returned is the same way Pascal's functions return values.

Macros

A macro is similar to a function in the way it operates: It can take parameters and returns a value to the section of code calling the macro. A macro takes a single expression instead of multiple lines of code, unlike functions and subroutines, which can take multiple lines of code:

```
MACRO ConvNum(theNum) = trim$(str$(theNum))
```

Another difference that macros bring to the table is that they don't allocate a chunk of memory to execute a task and then free that memory up, as do subroutines and functions. Instead, the compiler replaces every instance of where the macro is called with the expression that defines that macro. The result is a larger compiled form of the code but faster execution, since the run-time engine doesn't need to take care of allocation and deallocation of memory.

User-Defined Types

The term *type* refers to the kind of value held by a variable in the Test language. The standard types available in Visual Test are shown in Table 5-1. But at times it is helpful to encapsulate a number of variables that are related to each other. The way to do this is for you to create your own type. In Pascal this is known as a record, in C it's known as a structure, and in Visual Test it's known as a *user-defined type*. Here is an example of a user-defined type that might be created to help track information about a test:

```
type TESTINFO
     iTestID          as long
     strDescrip       as string
     strExpResult     as string
     strRecResult     as string
     fPassed          as integer
end type 'TESTINFO
```

Notice that when declaring a field in a user-defined type, the longhand form of declaration is used. That is, a $ isn't used to declare a STRING; it is actually written out as AS STRING. This is a requirement of the compiler, I know not why. Notice too that the declarations inside the user-defined type definition are not accompanied by DIM, GLOBAL, or STATIC.

Once a new type has been declared, it can be used like any other type by declaring a variable with either the DIM, GLOBAL, or STATIC statements. An array of the type can also be created, if desired:

```
type TESTINFO
     iTestID          as long
     strDescrip       as string
     strExpResult     as string
     strRecResult     as string
     fPassed          as integer
end type 'TESTINFO

dim tiTestOne as TESTINFO
dim tiMenuTests(5 to 20) as TESTINFO
global tiAllTests(100) as TESTINFO
```

The first variable declaration creates a local variable called tiTestOne that is a single variable of type TESTINFO. The second declaration creates a local variable that is a 16-element array (indexed from 5 to 20) of type TESTINFO. The third declaration is a global variable that holds 100 array elements of type TESTINFO.

The fields or members of the user-defined type can be accessed by using the variable name along with the dot (.) operator as shown in Listing 5-4. The dot operator, used to access a user-defined type's elements, is similar to how such access to data is accomplished in other languages such as C, Pascal, and Microsoft Visual Basic.

Listing 5-4: **The dot (.) operator must be used to access the elements of a user-defined type.**

```
'User-defined type declaration
type TESTINFO
    iTestID        as long
    strDescrip     as string
    strExpResult   as string
    strRecResult   as string
    fPassed        as integer
end type 'TESTINFO

'Variable declarations
dim tiTestOne as TESTINFO
dim tiMenuTests(20) as TESTINFO
global tiAllTests(100) as TESTINFO

    'Setting values to variables declared using a
    'user-defined type.
    tiTestOne.iTestID = 1
    tiTestOne.strDescrip = "Verify Open menu works"
    tiTestOne.strExpResult = "The Open dialog box"
    tiTestOne.fPassed = TRUE

    tiMenuTests(1).iTestID = 1
    tiMenuTests(1).strDescrip = "Verify Open menu works"
end
```

When a variable is declared in Visual Test, it is automatically initialized to zero (0), or in the case of strings, set to an empty or null string. The VARIANT type, introduced in Visual Test 4.0, is originally declared as *empty*, a value unique to that type. Therefore, it isn't necessary to set unused values to zero or NULL yourself. You need only set those items in the user-defined type you wish to give a particular value to. Programming styles vary on this approach, however; some programmers still prefer to set each value to zero, to ensure it's initialized properly.

Conditional Branching

Two types of statements in the Test language allow for a situation to be assessed and acted upon, based on a true or false situation. They are known as control structures, and they cause conditional branches, allowing you to control how the execution of the source code flows into other sections of your program depending on a given condition. They are:

✦ IF/THEN branching statements

✦ SELECT CASE branching statements

IF/THEN branching

The first type of branch is an IF/THEN branch statement. The form this statement
takes is very similar to C and Pascal programming languages. Listing 5-5 shows a
couple of typical IF/THEN statements. In them, the PutString subroutine takes a
text string, line, and character position and places the provided string at the
specified line and character positions in the active window. (The special w*
functions are discussed later in the *Working with Windows Controls* section of this
chapter).

Listing 5-5: **A couple of typical IF/THEN statements**

```
'*************************************************************
'* Subroutine:   PutString
'* Purpose:      Places a string into the Notepad editor at a
'*               specified line and character position.  If the
'*               line or character doesn't exist, this routine
'*               adds the necessary carriage returns and spaces.
'*
'* Parameters:   strOut$ String to be written to the editor
'*               iLine%  Line at which string is to be written
'*               iChar%  Character/column position to place
'*                       string
'*
'*************************************************************


sub PutString (strOut$, iLine%, iChar%)
    dim iCurrLine%          'Keeps track of what line the cursor
                            'is on
    dim iCurrChar%          'Tracks which column the cursor is in
    dim iLoop%              'Used as an index to for-loop
    dim iLoopLimit%         'Used to determine end value of for-
                            'loop
dim strDirection$    'Set to which keystroke should be used

    'Get the current line and cursor position
    iCurrLine = wEditLine("@1")

    'Determine which direction to move based on
    'current position and desired position.
    if (iCurrLine < iLine) then
        iLoopLimit = (iLine - iCurrLine)
```

continued

Listing 5-5 *(continued)*

```
        strDirection = "{DOWN}"              'We need to move down
    else
        iLoopLimit = (iCurrLine - iLine)
        strDirection = "{UP}"                'We need to move up
    endif

    'Move to the desired position, adding lines
    'if necessary.
    for iLoop = 1 to iLoopLimit
        if (wEditLine("@1") < wEditLines("@1")) then
play strDirection
        elseif (strDirection = "{DOWN}") then
play "{END}"
            play "{ENTER}"
        else
            play strDirection
        endif
    next iLoop

    'Get the current character position
    iCurrChar = wEditPos("@1")

    'Based on the current position, determine which
    'direction to move.
    if (iCurrChar < iChar) then
        iLoopLimit = (iChar - iCurrChar)
        strDirection = "{RIGHT}"
    else
        iLoopLimit = (iCurrChar - iChar)
        strDirection = "{LEFT}"
    endif

    'Move to the desired position added spaces if needed.
    for iLoop = 1 to iLoopLimit
        if (wEditPos("@1") < _
            wEditLineLen("@1",wEditLine("@1"))) then
play strDirection
        elseif (strDirection = "{RIGHT}") then
            play " "
        else
            play strDirection
        endif
    next iLoop

    play strOut    'Type the string at the
                   'current location
end sub 'PutString()
```

This subroutine will place a string at a specific line and character position in a text editor. The text string, line, and character positions are provided by the caller. The subroutine determines where the cursor is in the editor, as well as whether or not spaces and carriage returns need to be added, and then types the string into the editor using the Test language's PLAY statement. A number of conditions need to be checked, which is why the IF/THEN statement is so important.

The key to any conditional branch is that it must somehow evaluate to a TRUE (−1 in Visual Test) or FALSE (0) value (also known as a Boolean value). If it evaluates to TRUE, then the execution steps into the IF statement. If it evaluates to FALSE, then the code in the IF statement isn't executed. In the situation where it evaluates to FALSE and an ELSE branch exists as part of the IF statement, the ELSE branch is executed.

Caution   The fact that TRUE is −1 is a dramatic distinction for C programmers where TRUE is any nonzero value. Although it is correct that any nonzero value will be evaluated as true in the Test language, the trouble arises when you try to use the NOT operator in conjunction with an arbitrary nonzero value. Visual Test doesn't have a Boolean NOT, only a bitwise NOT. The only value that will return FALSE (0) when a bitwise NOT is applied is −1. So it is very important for the Test programmer to get in the habit of using only −1 for TRUE.

Some of the IF/THEN statements can get quite elaborate and hard to read. One way to cut down on this is to assign some of the values to individual variables and then test the conditions of those variables. Listing 5-6 shows both a convoluted IF/THEN statement and two other versions of it that are a little easier to read.

Listing 5-6: **An example of a complex-looking IF/THEN statement broken down into two more readable alternatives**

```
'*** original form of IF/THEN statement taken from Listing 5-5
    if (wEditPos("@1") < _
        wEditLineLen("@1",wEditLine("@1"))) then
        play strDirection
    elseif (strDirection = "{RIGHT}") then
        play " "
    else
        play strDirection
    endif


'*** alternate form of the above IF/THEN statement
```

continued

Listing 5-6 *(continued)*

```
'(Extra declarations that would be placed at the top of
'the subroutine)
dim iCurrPos%        'Current position of the cursor in the text
                     'line
dim iCurrLine%       'Current text line the cursor is in
dim iLineLen%        'Length of a given line of text

'(The modified IF/THEN statement requiring the new variables
'to be initialized first.)

    iCurrPos = wEditPos("@1")
    iCurrLine = wEditLine("@1")
    iLineLen = wEditLineLen("@1", iCurrLine)

    if (iCurrPos < iLineLen) then
        play strDirection
    elseif (strDirection = "{RIGHT}") then
        play " "
    else
        play strDirection
    endif


'*** alternate, alternate.
'(Going to extremes just for the sake of an example, the first
'line of the IF/THEN statement could be modified yet another
'way by adding a fourth variable)

dim fMoveCursor as integer

    fMoveCursor = (iCurrPos < iLineLen)

    if fMoveCursor then 'et cetera...
```

While the second version of the IF/THEN statement in Listing 5-6 is easier to read, it requires three extra variables to be declared. The style to be used must be determined by the automation programming team and weighed against the experience of the users on that team.

In the third version, the first line of the IF/THEN statement uses a fourth variable that is set to a Boolean value (TRUE or FALSE). That variable can then be used as the sole expression. The last example goes to extremes but can be helpful when a TRUE/FALSE value needs to be used multiple times, as it can be evaluated and stored once using a variable.

Select case

The second form of conditional branching is the Test language's SELECT CASE statement. This is very similar to C's switch statement and Pascal's case statement; it takes the form shown in Listing 5-7.

Listing 5-7: **A Select Case statement**

```
'In this example we propose that a variable called
'iTestResult is used in a test script.  There are
'four different values it can be assigned to
'depending on the problem that may have resulted
'during the test execution: The test passed without
'problems; it failed; it was interrupted by the
'tester running the script; or an unknown error
'occurred causing the script to terminate un-
'expectedly. In this proposed example, the case
'statement might look something like this:

'Constants declared at the beginning of the script.
const RESULT_PASSED  = 1
const RESULT_FAILED  = 2
const RESULT_STOPPED = 3
const RESULT_UNKNOWN = 4

dim iTestResult as integer


'Select case statement encountered lower in the
'script and used to write out summary information.
select case iTestResult
    case RESULT_PASSED
        log "The test script passed."
    case RESULT_FAILED
        log "The test script failed."
    case RESULT_STOPPED, RESULT_UNKNOWN
        log "Test script terminated unexpectedly."
    case else
        log "Unknown value set to iTestResult!"
end select
```

The SELECT CASE statement is easier to read in a situation like that shown in Listing 5-7 than is an IF/THEN statement with a number of ELSEIF branches.

Caution

The GOTO statement is known as an *unconditional branch* and should be used sparingly. Heavy use of GOTO, especially when it jumps backward or up in a source code listing, leads to what programmers commonly call *spaghetti code*, since it's difficult to trace the path of the source code's execution. Using GOTO is commonly considered poor programming style. Avoid it or be prepared to face the wrath of fellow programmers. Note also that the uses and abuses of unconditional branching are discussed in Chapter 8.

Loops

There are three different loops for controlling the execution of sections of code multiple times. These are the FOR/NEXT, WHILE/WEND, and DO/WHILE/UNTIL loops. Refer to the documentation for complete details on each of these loops. We focus on brief introductions to each loop in this chapter.

FOR/NEXT loops

The FOR/NEXT loop is the easiest of the three and is the most unlikely to get caught in a never-ending loop. A typical FOR/NEXT loop takes the form shown in Listing 5-8.

Listing 5-8: The FOR/NEXT loop allows you to specify a beginning and end value along with an optional STEP form of this statement.

```
'SYNTAX:
'for <counter> = <start> to <end> [step <increment>]
'      [<tasks to be carried out>]
'      [EXIT FOR]
'next [<counter>]
'
'Example:
dim iLoop%
    for iLoop = 2 to 20 step 2
        print "Counting by 2's: ";iLoop
    next iLoop
end
```

Here, the iLoop variable is initialized to the value 2, the PRINT statement prints out the string and the value set to iLoop, and then the FOR statement increments the iLoop counter by 2. If iLoop is still less than the <end> value, then the loop executes its contents again, using the new value of iLoop.

WHILE/WEND loops

The WHILE statement requires the condition it evaluates to be TRUE before it allows the script it encapsulates to be executed. Listing 5-9 shows a very simple search algorithm using a WHILE/WEND loop.

Listing 5-9: **A simple search algorithm using the WHILE/WEND loop**

```
'SYNTAX:
'while <condition>
'     [<tasks to be carried out>]
'     [EXIT WHILE]
'wend
'
'Example:
OPTION BASE 1 'Causes arrays to be 1-based (index starts at 1)

const MAX_NAMES = 100    'Max. # of names allowed

dim strNames(MAX_NAMES) as string    'Name array
dim iIndex as integer                'Index into array
dim strTheName as string             'Name to search for

    'Assume the array strNames gets filled with up to 100
'random names (index positions 0 to 99) taking the form
    '<FIRSTNAME>,<LASTNAME>, all in capital letters.  Now,
'search for a name in that array and terminate when the
'name is found or when the end of the array is reached.

    strTheName = "JOE,BENNER"
    iIndex = 0

    while (iIndex < MAX_NAMES) _
         AND (strNames(iIndex) <> strTheName)
       iIndex = iIndex + 1
    wend

    if (iIndex < MAX_NAMES) then print "Found!!"
    'example of a single line IF/THEN
    '(has no ENDIF)

    'source code continues ...
end
```

The conditional section of the WHILE/WEND statement does all of the work by determining if the name has been found or if the index has exceeded the total number of names in the list. When this statement is terminated, iIndex will either hold the location of the name in the array (a value between 0 and 99), or it will hold the value 100, signifying that the name wasn't found in the array.

DO/WHILE/UNTIL loops

This form of loop is used when the task needs to be done at least once, and possibly multiple times. If you use the DO/WHILE/UNTIL loop with the syntax shown in the Listing 5-10, the statements will be executed and then it will determine whether or not the process needs to be repeated. What's different about a DO/WHILE/UNTIL loop is that the source code in the loop will always execute at least once. The determination of whether or not to loop is made at the back end of the loop instead of the front.

You can also use the WHILE option. If you do, the execution will be repeated as long as a condition is true. Alternatively, the UNTIL option will keep the execution going until a condition is met.

Listing 5-10: **An example DO/WHILE/UNTIL loop**

```
'Syntax:
'do
'    [<tasks to be carried out>]
'loop [ UNTIL | WHILE ] <condition>
'
'Example:
'Assume a function called RunTest that returns TRUE
'if the test has been executed successfully, and FALSE
'if an error occurred. Assume further that the tester
'wants execution of the tests to stop in the event any
'one of the tests fails. The code might look similar
'to the following:

dim fTestResult%

    do
        fTestResult = RunTest()

        if (fTestResult) then
            print "This test passed."
        else
            print "This test failed."
        endif
    loop while fTestResult
end
```

Working with Windows Controls

Visual Test's language is very similar to the Visual Basic language. Most people assume that they're so similar because when Visual Test was first designed at Microsoft the Visual Test development team worked closely with the Visual Basic team and shared the sections of the two languages that intersected. However, that wasn't the case: They went down two separate paths, with notable divergence in the areas of pointers, Windows controls (that is, Windows 95/98 or Windows NT buttons, check boxes, menus, and so on), and other significant areas.

One of the key areas where Visual Test differs from Visual Basic is in the functions and statements it provides for working with Windows controls. In previous versions of Test, these functions were kept in separate DLLs and linked to Test by the MSTEST.INC include file. But in the 4.0 version of Test this was changed; the functions were brought into the language and made *intrinsic* to it.

We'll start our introduction to working with Windows controls by taking a simple example of clicking a button. This is the easiest statement for working with Windows controls and allows us to both demonstrate the basics and point generally to how all of the routines work with Windows controls.

Then we shall look at another example: working with controls that don't have a caption as part of their configuration.

Control with a Caption

Figure 5-2 shows the Open dialog box used by the Microsoft Notepad editor. It contains a number of Windows control types:

- ✦ Static
- ✦ Combo box
- ✦ Edit
- ✦ Toolbar
- ✦ Listview
- ✦ Button

Figure 5-2: The Open dialog box is a good example of a dialog box that contains a number of Windows controls that can be acted upon using Visual Test.

All these types can be worked with using the functions and statements provided in the Test language.

The easiest control to work with is a control that has a caption, or label, associated with it. A button, for example, has text on it that is considered a caption. To work with a button, the user need only use one of the many wButton* functions or statements. These are shown in Table 5-2.

Table 5-2
Functions and Statements for Working with a Windows Command Button

Keyword	Type	Description
wButtonClassLen[1]	Function	Returns the number of characters in a button's class name.
wButtonClick	Statement	Clicks on a button given a caption.
wButtonDefault	Function	Determines whether a button is a default button or not.
wButtonDefaults	Function	Returns the number of default buttons in the active window.
wButtonEnabled	Function	Determines whether the specified button is enabled or grayed out.
wButtonExists	Function	Determines whether a button with a specific caption exists.
wButtonFind	Function	Returns the handle of a specified button.

Keyword	Type	Description
wButtonFocus	Function	Returns true if the specified button has focus.
wButtonGetClass[1]	Statement	Fills a buffer with the names of classes associated with buttons.
wButtonMoveTo	Statement	Moves the mouse pointer to a specific location in the specified button.
wButtonSetClass	Statement	Informs the Test language what class names are associated with buttons.
wButtonSetFocus	Statement	Sets the input focus to the specified button.
ButtonGetClass[2]	Function	Returns the names of classes associated with buttons.

[1] Remains only for backward compatibility.

[2] Replaces the need for wButtonGetClass and wButtonClassLen.

The functions and statements shown in Table 5-2 are typical of all of Visual Test's routines that work with Windows controls. That is, some routines are found for each control, and some are specific to how each control works. An example of a common routine is the wButtonSetFocus statement. This is available for virtually every control, except that it varies in its name. So for a check box control, instead of using wButtonSetFocus, the Test programmer would use wCheckSetFocus.

When in doubt as to what routines are available for working with a particular Windows control:

1. Go into the Developer Studio and type a W, followed by the class name or type of control.

2. Highlight it.

3. Press the F1 key to get online help.

Windows Controls Have Class

Each control in Windows has a class name associated with it. A command button has the class name BUTTON. An edit control is EDIT, a check box control is CHECKBOX, and so on.

Because all controls in Windows are actually windows themselves, class names identify the type of control and the behavior associated with that control. For example, while a check box and a command button expect to be clicked, it doesn't make sense for that to happen for a static control. All controls are simply windows and therefore need to have class names associated with them so that it can be determined what type of window they are and how they can be expected to act.

To find out the class name associated with a given control, use the Window Information utility (also known as *Winfo*), which is discussed in Chapter 6.

Returning to the Open dialog box, shown in Figure 5-2, we can click the Open or Cancel buttons by using these statements:

```
wButtonClick("Open")
wButtonClick("Cancel")
```

Pretty simple. If you look up wButtonClick in the online help, you'll see there is a second, optional parameter that can be used as part of the statement. This tells the statement how long to look for the button it wants to click, before giving up and generating an error saying the control can't be found. This time-out parameter is usually only provided in circumstances where a dialog box containing the button might take longer than usual to display. If the parameter isn't provided, the default wait time specified by the SetDefaultWaitTimeout function is used.

Control without a Caption

Working with controls that have captions is pretty easy and straightforward. Where things become more interesting is when working with controls that don't have a caption as part of their configuration.

Combo boxes, edit controls, and toolbars don't have captions. Instead, they usually have another Windows control sitting next to them, called a *static control* or *label*, that acts as a caption. A static control is simply a control whose only purpose is to provide text next to a captionless control, to help the user identify the purpose of the control.

In the case of Visual Test, the static control serves another purpose: to provide a place for the Test language's routines to begin searching for a particular control. In the case of the edit control in the Open dialog box, where the name of a file is typed in, the static control associated with it has the caption "File name:" as seen in Figure 5-3. The text of the static control is used to specify which edit control is to be typed into.

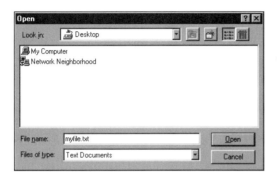

Figure 5-3: Notepad's Open dialog box with a file name typed into the edit control – and with the static control next to it.

An example of using the edit control by using the static control is shown in the next line of code. It results in the Open dialog box appearing (as in Figure 5-3), with MYFILE.TXT in the edit control:

```
wEditSetText("File name:","myfile.txt")
```

The first parameter of wEditSetText() is the name of the static control. The second argument is the text to be placed into that control. An optional third parameter is the amount of time to wait for the control to appear. As we discussed when we were working with a button, the time-out parameter can be typed in to do one of two things. Either it can explicitly control how long this specific line of code will wait for the control to appear, or the optional parameter can be excluded. This second option results in the wEditSetText statement waiting for the amount of time specified by the SetDefaultWaitTimeout function.

The captions and labels used to identify a control are not *case sensitive*. Therefore, the string supplied to the function or statement could be in capital letters, even though the label or caption might be lowercase. Also, to specify the underlined character in a label or caption, the ampersand (&) can be placed just before the letter to be underlined. This is not required, however, and if it isn't used, the control will still be found if the caption is spelled correctly. If the ampersand is used, it must be associated with the correct letter in the caption or label; otherwise, the control will not be found. Also, remember to include any punctuation marks found in the caption such as single quotes or ellipses (…).

Not Using a Caption or Label

In some cases controls don't have a caption or static control label associated with them, making it impossible to type in a descriptive text string to identify the control. In these situations, there are three good ways the control can be accessed:

✦ Ordinal value

✦ ID number

✦ Handle

Ordinals

An ordinal value is most easily described as the tab-position of the control. This isn't really what the ordinal is, but it's close enough.

When controls are added to a dialog box they are all on individual layers, commonly referred to as the *z-order*. These layers can be used to identify the control. With ordinals, the z-order is specifically relative to the number of the type of control in the dialog box. That is, if there are ten buttons and one edit control, the ordinal value associated with the edit control would have nothing to do with the ordinal values of the other ten buttons. Instead, in the case of a single edit control, its ordinal value would be 1.

Note   About Z-order: X is across the screen, Y is down the screen, and Z is *out* the screen. Microsoft Visual Basic does some sort of layers with controls on forms. All visible windows do fall somewhere in the Z-order, but creation order is probably the more likely candidate here.

Previously, an example was given using the `wEditSetText` statement to set the text of the edit control shown in Figure 5-3. Because this is the only edit control in the Open dialog box, the same goal could have been accomplished using an ordinal instead of the static control. An ordinal is a string value identified by an @ symbol preceding a number. If you pass this in place of a caption, the control's ordinal position will be used. Therefore, the following two statements, when working with the dialog box shown in Figure 5-3, accomplish exactly the same result:

```
wEditSetText("File name:","myfile.txt")
wEditSetText("@1","myfile.txt")
```

One benefit of using ordinals instead of captions is that, should the caption in the button ever change, as would be the case when localizing a product for another language, the script continues to function. This is because it's working with the ordinal value of the control instead of the text associated with it. The downfall is that ordinals change as controls of the same type are added or removed from a dialog box. Thus, using ordinals can be difficult when a product's user interface (UI) hasn't yet been frozen.

Note If you are localizing your product for an international market, you should read the "Automated Testing of Localized Products" section in Chapter 13, written by Bill Hodghead, an automation engineer at Microsoft Corporation who has written his share of flexible automated scripts.

The ordinal position of a control can be determined through hit-and-miss testing, by typing in different values and seeing if the correct control is affected. Another way is to use the Window Information utility (discussed in Chapter 6).

Tip If you find yourself writing a script—such as with a FOR/NEXT loop—where you're keeping an ordinal value as a number instead of a string, you'll probably find yourself writing a conversion to turn your ordinal number into a string and append the @ symbol. It would probably look like this (where iNum is the ordinal number):

```
wEditSetText("@"+trim$(str$(iNum)),"myfile.txt")
```

Because of a new macro introduced in version 4.0 you can cut down on some of this coding. The macro is called _ord() and will cause the preceding line of code to look cleaner, like this:

```
wEditSetText(_ord(iNum),"myfile.txt")
```

Similar macros are available for *window* handles (_hwnd()) and IDs (_id()).

Control ID numbers

Working with the ID number of a control is similar to working with the ordinal position of a control. Instead of using the @ symbol, you use the # symbol. This designates that you're passing the ID value of a control in place of a caption. Because I used the Winfo utility, I know that the ID number associated with the edit control in Figure 5-3 is 1152. I also know that it can be used to place text into that same edit control with this statement:

```
wEditSetText("#1152","myfile.txt")
```

The ID number of a control is assigned when the Windows programmer creates the control in the dialog box. These ID numbers are used by Windows programmers to affect a control or to determine which control is being acted upon by the user. This same ID number can be used by Visual Test programmers to identify a control, should the ordinal or caption value of the control not be a preferable means of identification.

The same perils are faced when using an ID number as when using an ordinal. Should a control be removed and then replaced, there is no guarantee that the ID number will be the same. As a matter of fact, much of the ID numbering is hidden from the Windows developer by placing those values into constants and then automatically changing those constants when the dialog box is modified.

The best way to work with a Windows control is to use its caption or associated label. Place the label into a constant and then use the constant every time that control is acted upon by one of the Test language's functions or statements. Then, should the product ever be localized for another language, the constant's value can be altered, effectively changing every place the caption was used throughout the script.

Tip   If you are localizing your product and don't want to have to modify your constants *and* you know that the order of the controls won't change, using the ordinal position of a control is a very good way to keep your scripts flexible so that little modification is required between different language versions of your product under test.

Using handles

Every window and control in the Windows operating system has a handle. A *handle* is a value that is associated with an item that is created by Windows so that it can be referred to by its handle value.

Using a handle is very similar to using ordinals and ID numbers. The biggest difference is that a handle changes each time a program is run, whereas ID numbers and ordinals only change if the program has been modified and recompiled. A handle to a control is used with the equal sign (=) in front of the value of the handle. For example:

```
hBtn = wEditFind("@1") 'Handle values must be gotten at runtime
strhBtn = "=" + trim$(str$(hBtn))
wEditSetText(strhBtn, "myfile.txt")
```

Control Pitfalls

There are several pitfalls to using controls. You need to be aware of these, so we'll take a look at them here. We'll cover three problems, those associated with:

- ✦ Nonstandard class names
- ✦ Labels not working
- ✦ Controls that aren't controls

Nonstandard class names

Sometimes a control won't have the class name you expect. In Windows a programmer can modify the behavior of a standard control so that it inherits some or all of the standard behavior but has some additional behavior added to it. When this is done, the correct thing for that Windows programmer to do is to give the control a nonstandard name so that it will not be confused with standard controls used in Windows. This is common practice, especially when the control's behavior has been modified so that it no longer observes standard Windows behavior. It is known as *subclassing* a control. In the case of Visual Basic buttons, they are known as `ThunderCommandButtons`, because the code name for Visual Basic when it first came out was Thunder. Therefore, Visual Basic's controls have Thunder as a prefix to their typical class names.

Visual Test is aware of the class names of Visual Basic's controls and will automatically recognize them. In the case of other applications, however, you'll have to inform Visual Test that a control isn't using a common class name. Use the Winfo utility to determine the control's class name and use the `W*SetClass` statement (where the asterisk (*) is replaced by the type of control). In the case of a button with the `MyButton` class name, the `wButton*` routines can be informed of it with this line of source code:

```
wButtonSetClass("MyButton\Button\ThunderCommandButton")
```

Using any of the `wButton*` routines will now result in those routines looking for controls with class names of `ThunderCommandButton`, `Button`, and `MyButton`.

Labels stop working

Static text controls, also known as labels, are typically placed next to a control that doesn't have a caption (such as an edit control). You can use these labels in different Test language routines to work with their associated controls.

Sometimes you'll find that the labels don't work, even though they're next to the control they should act upon. In these situations, it's possible the label isn't in the layer or z-order preceding its associated control.

A Visual Test routine, when working with a label, looks for the control just after the label in the z-order. The z-order is controlled by the dialog box editor the Windows developer uses when she creates a dialog box. If the developer first created a label, then some other controls, followed by the control associated with the label, it's possible the Test language routines won't find the control next to the label.

There are two possible fixes for situations such as these. The first is to work with the control's ordinal or ID values instead of the label or caption. Alternatively, you can work closely with the developer, so that she can reedit the dialog box and reorder the layering of the controls.

The controls are bitmaps

There are some situations where an application appears to have buttons, edit controls, combo boxes, list boxes, and so on, but Visual Test isn't able to recognize them. Even when you attempt to determine their class name by using the Winfo utility, the utility doesn't show any information.

In situations like these it's likely that the controls really don't exist and are simply bitmaps being manipulated by the program to look like Windows controls. An example would be any program created with Asymetrix's ToolBook development product. These applications look like they were created using true Windows controls, but they're bogus. ToolBook fakes the controls by supplying and manipulating bitmaps, in order to make the development of products easier and to provide specialized handling of controls. Borland's Delphi product also has fake controls. And some of the controls created through the Microsoft Foundation Classes (MFCs) are fake (or virtual) as well.

Until recently, the only solution in situations like these was to go to a very basic form of automation. You need to determine and use the specific coordinates of those controls on the screen, so that the mouse can be moved by Visual Test to those coordinates and told to click or drag. Now, as the prevalence of Microsoft Active Accessibility (MSAA) grows, the tester has another possible way to view and manipulate these "drawn" controls. MSAA makes it possible for window controls, even fake ones, to communicate information about themselves to the system. VT 6.0 now provides MSAA functions. Drawn controls written to support MSAA on an MSAA-enabled system are now available to Visual Test programmers. MSAA support is discussed in Chapter 13.

Note   Working with mouse and keyboard events is discussed later in this chapter, in the section "Mouse and Keyboard Events."

The Remaining Controls

The rest of the controls that can be manipulated through the Test language are shown in Table 5-3. The two main things to consider when working with any kind of control are:

✦ Do the controls have a caption or label associated with them?

✦ Do they need to be accessed using ordinals and control IDs?

This table will tell you where to look for the specifics of functions and statements available for each control. Refer also to Appendix A in this book, then look up information via online help for the specifics on each function or statement. Now that you understand the basics from the examples of working with buttons and edit controls, you're set for working with the other control types.

Table 5-3
Controls Used by Visual Test

Type of Control	Beginning of Function Name
MSAA controls	aa*()
Check box button	wCheck*()
Column header	wHeader*()
Combo box	wCombo*()
Command button	wButton*()
Custom control	wCustom*()
Date/Time Picker	wPicker*()
Desktop items	wDesktop*()
Desktop taskbar	wTaskbar*()
Edit box	wEdit*()
Web page controls	Web*()
List box	wList*()
Listview control	wView*()
Month Calendar control	wMonthCal*()
Option (radio) button	wOption*()
Progress box	wProgress*()
Rebar control	wRebar*()
Scroll bar	wScroll*()
Slider bar	wSlider*()
Spinner control	wSpin*()
Static label	wLabel*()
Static text	wStatic*()
Status bar	wStatus*()
Tab control	wTab*()
Toolbar control	wToolbar*()
Tooltips	wTips*()
Treeview control	wTree*()

Note New control support introduced in Visual Test 6.0 provides these new routines: wMonthCal*(), wPicker*(), wRebar*(), aa*(), and Web*().

Phasing Out Routines

Some of the routines you look up will give you the following warning when displayed in online help:

> **Important:** The **<old>** statement has been replaced by the **<new>** statement in Visual Test. **<old>** will still run if you use the MSTEST.INC include file in the test case.

(Where **<old>** and **<new>** represent the previous and newer versions of the statements, respectively.)

Many of these routines were subroutines that required an empty variable or buffer to be passed. The statement would fill it with the value the Test programmer wanted. The Visual Test team realized that the same thing could be done by using a function and assigning the return value to the variable that was once passed as a buffer. It removes one argument from the parameter list and makes it one less routine for the Visual Test team to maintain.

For backward compatibility the function will still work for old Test scripts if the MSTEST.INC file is included at the top of the test case file.

Working with Menus

Working with menus is very simple in Visual Test. Two types of menus may be available in an applications window:

✦ The first is a typical menu bar that goes across the top of the window, just under its caption.

✦ The second is the system menu in the upper left-hand corner of the window, on the caption bar.

Caution If you find that the wMenu* commands aren't working, you should use the Winfo utility (discussed in Chapter 6) to verify that the menu really is a menu. In some of the newer applications people are finding that a menu is really a toolbar after all. The result is that the wToolbar* routines need to be used instead.

The Menu Bar

When working with the menu bar, you have access to a number of functions and subroutines through the Test language, all of which start with `wMenu*`. Here is an example of how to pop down the File menu of an application:

```
wMenuSelect("File")
```

The `wMenuSelect` statement works in a similar way to accessing files in a directory structure. A path to the menu item is specified in the string passed to the statement. So to access the Open... menu item (usually found under the File menu), this line of source code is used:

```
wMenuSelect("File\Open...")
```

In the event that the program has cascading or hierarchical menus, where a menu item has its own submenu items, the path simply continues by using backslashes (\) to instruct `wMenuSelect()` how to reach the menu item.

The ellipsis (...) needs to be included, since it's part of the actual text of the menu item. However, any accelerator keys (such as Ctrl+O) don't need to be included. Also, if you want to specify the underlined character, an ampersand is placed in front of the letter that's underlined in the menu listing. (For example, "`&File\&Open...`" could be passed as the string, instead of simply "`File\Open....`")

If the direct-access method (DAM) keys are used, they must be used correctly. If the ampersand is included, it must be in the appropriate position. If it isn't in the correct location, then the `wMenuSelect` statement won't find the menu item and an error will be given.

Tip   Once displayed, context, or pop-up, menus can be treated just like regular menu bar menus. Playing the keyboard Shift+F10 or the special context menu key, if it's available, will display a control or window's context menu, as will simulating a right mouse-click. See the coverage of mouse and keyboard events later.

The System Menu

The system menu is very similar to the normal menu bar, except that the `wSysMenu*` functions and statements are used instead of `wMenu*`. The system menu sometimes doesn't appear on the window's caption bar; it depends on the style of window the programmer used. Typically, the system menu contains menu items to control the minimization, maximization, and restoration of a window. It also allows for moving and resizing the window.

Mouse and Keyboard Events

Even with all the different functions and statements in Visual Test that allow for the manipulation of Windows applications, certain situations arise in which it's necessary to manipulate an application through less sophisticated methods.

Two examples are:

✦ When working with fake, or virtual, controls that are simply bitmaps that act as Windows controls but go unrecognized by Visual Test.

✦ Occasions when it is necessary to emulate a user typing characters on the keyboard.

Fake Controls

In the first example, fake controls, I can cite two companies that widely use them. The first is Asymetrix Learning Systems (formerly Asymetrix Corporation). It makes an excellent Windows development tool called ToolBook. All applications created with this product have bitmaps in place of actual Windows controls, which makes them more difficult to automate.

The other company is Microsoft Corporation, which has dialog boxes in Microsoft Excel, Microsoft Word, and other applications. These dialog boxes are referred to as SDM (Simple Dialog Manager) dialog boxes. They have only one or two actual controls; the rest are bitmap simulated controls.

Other companies and situations have virtual controls, which is why the PLAY statement has been provided in Visual Test.

Note The PLAY statement allows for both keyboard and mouse simulation. When we designed the test suite for Notepad, PLAY() had to be used to place text into the Notepad editor, instead of wEditSetText(). When wEditSetText() was used, sections of Notepad were unaware that text had been placed in the editor. For example, it allowed you to exit the application without asking you to save changes. Using PLAY(), however, provided the expected results.

Keyboard Events

The PLAY statement is straightforward when it is used for keyboard events. It passes a string with the characters to be typed, and those characters are then sent to the active window. They generate the same Windows messages as if someone were actually typing at the keyboard.

Caution Since no one is actually typing at the keyboard or using the mouse, no hardware interrupt is actually generated. As a result, screen savers often become active during the running of an automated test. It's a good idea to turn them off before running lengthy automated tests.

Using keystrokes

Listing 5-11 is an example of a script using the PLAY statement. It pops down the File menu, clicks the Open… menu item, types in a filename, and then selects the Cancel button, all through keyboard strokes (based on Notepad's UI).

Listing 5-11: An example of a script written entirely using the PLAY statement

```
play "%fo"              'Pop down the File menu and select Open
play "%n"               'Select the "File &name:" edit control
play "myfile.txt"       'Type in a filename
play "{TAB 3}"          'Tab three times to the Cancel button
play " "                'Press the Spacebar to click the button
```

We see a number of things going on in this example. The first line of code shows that, to select the Alt key, the percent sign (%) must be placed next to the key letter (for example, "%f" is like hitting Alt+F). This results in the File menu popping down. Type in the letter O, in the case of Notepad, to select the Open… menu item. So far, so good.

Assume the Open dialog box is displayed. As the DAM key for the "File Name" edit control in our piece of source code is the letter N, send an Alt+N by supplying the play statement with the string "%n".

Now, assume that the focus is in the correct edit control and the text myfile.txt has been typed. You need to use two separate statements: a special symbol ({TAB}), along with the number 3 (to specify that three tabs are to be sent which positions the focus on the Cancel button). A single space simulates a use of the keyboard Spacebar, which clicks the Cancel button.

This shows how we can manipulate a dialog box without true Windows controls. Again, I can't stress enough how important it is to use control functions and statements such as wButton* and wEdit* before turning to the PLAY statement. It's very easy for a script to get out of sync. Because you're only sending keyboard strokes, instead of looking for specific controls, the script will continue on its merry way, spewing keystrokes into whatever application or window happens to be active. The PLAY statement is very much a last resort.

Use the PLAY Statement Sparingly

Because functions and subroutines provide a level of error-trapping when dealing with spe-cific Windows controls that the PLAY statement cannot, PLAY() should be used only as a last resort. An example is if you wanted to use the PLAY statement to access menu items. If the following command is issued through the Test language and a menu doesn't exist, the PLAY statement will send the keystrokes regardless:

```
play "%fo"
```

Whereas, if the wMenuSelect function is used, and a menu doesn't exist, an error stating that the menu cannot be found is given, helping to avoid a runaway script.

Special keys

While the PLAY statement does fine with normal text, it requires special characters to designate specific keys. As we've already seen, an Alt key is specified by using the percent sign (%). The Control and Shift keys are also available with PLAY() and are signified by the caret (^) and plus (+) signs, respectively. If you want to work with other types of keyboard keys, they can be simulated by placing braces ({ }) around specific keywords that map to those keys, as was done for the Tab key in our example. Refer to Table 5-4 for a list of these other keyboard keys.

Table 5-4
Special Strings Used with play() to Simulate Keyboard Keys

Keyboard Key	PLAY() *equivalent*
Enter key	"{ENTER}" or "~"
Escape key	"{ESC}"
Up arrow	"{UP}"
Down arrow	"{DOWN}"
Left arrow	"{LEFT}"
Right arrow	"{RIGHT}"
End key	"{END}"
Page-up key	"{PGUP}"
Page-down key	"{PGDN}"
Insert key	"{INSERT}"
Delete key	"{DELETE}"

Keyboard Key	PLAY() *equivalent*
Home key	"{HOME}"
Tab key	"{TAB}"
Backspace key	"{BS}"
F1 key	"{F1}", ... on to ...
F16 key	"{F16}"
Right Alt key	"{R_ALT}"

One situation that had me scratching my head for a good twenty minutes when I first used Microsoft Test was working with the DOKEYS statement in Test 1.0—this is an old statement that the PLAY statement now replaces. I was trying to test the accelerator keys to make sure they performed the appropriate menu actions. For example, Ctrl+O is in the File menu as the shortcut for displaying the Open dialog box. I knew I wanted to display the Open dialog box in Microsoft Word and so I used this line of code, which has been converted to the PLAY statement's equivalent:

```
play "^O"
```

The menu clearly shows Ctrl+O as the keystrokes to be used to activate the Open... menu item. What didn't occur to me until later was that, by using an uppercase O, I was actually sending a Ctrl+Shift+o. The PLAY statement had to use the Shift key in order to provide the uppercase O. Since Shift wasn't part of the keystroke that needed to be used, the accelerator wouldn't activate. When I changed the letter O to lowercase, it worked as expected.

Characters can be used in conjunction with one another to combine keystrokes. For example, I passed "^+o" to PLAY() to send a Ctrl+Shift+O. If I had wanted a key to act on multiple letters, I would have simply enclosed those letters in parentheses: "+(hello)" results in typing out "HELLO."

Mouse Events

The mouse events functionality of the PLAY statement allows you to move the mouse, click specific coordinates, click and drag, and release the mouse button. If the optional first parameter of the PLAY statement is provided with the handle to a window, the coordinates provided to the statement are relative to the upper left-hand corner of the specified window. Otherwise, the coordinates are relative to the upper left-hand corner of the desktop. Table 5-5 details the mouse action codes.

Table 5-5
Mouse Action Codes Recognized by the PLAY Statement

Action to Complete	Action Code
Click a mouse button down	BTNDOWN
Release a mouse button	BTNUP
Click at a specific location	CLICK
Double-click at a location	DBLCLICK
Drag to a location	DRAGTO
Move mouse to a location	MOVETO

These actions can also be affected by using the coordinate modifiers CURPOS and SCREEN. The CURPOS modifier causes the mouse to be moved, based on its current position. The SCREEN modifier overrides a window handle, if one's been provided, and bases the coordinates on the upper-left corner of the desktop. Listing 5-12 demonstrates some of these action codes and modifiers.

Listing 5-12: An example of controlling the mouse with the play statement

```
'Screen-relative coordinates to the paintbrush
const TOOL_BRUSH = "SCREEN+44,SCREEN+130"
const MAX_WAIT   = 5     'Wait max. 5 seconds

dim hWnd as long

hWnd = wFndWnd("Paint",FW_PART OR FW_ALL, MAX_WAIT)
if (hWnd = 0) then
    if (RUN("pbrush.exe") <> 0) then
        pause "Error running Paintbrush."
        stop
    else
        hWnd = wGetActWnd(0)
    endif
endif

'Maximize that window
wSysMenu(hWnd)
wMenuSelect("Maximize")

'Maximize the canvas
```

```
wMenuSelect("Image\Attributes...")
wEditSetText("Width:","400")
wEditSetText("Height:","250")
wButtonClick("OK")

'Select the paintbrush tool
play "{CLICK "+TOOL_BRUSH+"}"

'Letter K
play hWnd,"{MOVETO 130,130}{DRAGTO 130,220,LEFT}"
play hWnd,"{MOVETO 170,130}{DRAGTO 130,175,LEFT}"
play hWnd,"{DRAGTO 170,220,LEFT}"

'Letter I
play hWnd,"{MOVETO 180,130}{DRAGTO 180,220,LEFT}"

'Letter L
play hWnd,"{MOVETO 190,130}{DRAGTO 190,220,LEFT}"
play hWnd,"{DRAGTO 230,220}"

'Letter R
play hWnd,"{MOVETO 240,130}{DRAGTO 260,130,LEFT}"
play hWnd,"{DRAGTO 280,150,LEFT}"
play hWnd,"{DRAGTO 280,170,LEFT}"
play hWnd,"{DRAGTO 260,190,LEFT}"
play hWnd,"{DRAGTO 240,190,LEFT}"
play hWnd,"{MOVETO 240,130}{DRAGTO 240,220,LEFT}"
play hWnd,"{MOVETO 250,190}{DRAGTO 280,220,LEFT}"

'Letter O
play hWnd,"{MOVETO 290,130}{DRAGTO 290,220,LEFT}"
play hWnd,"{DRAGTO 330,220,LEFT}"
play hWnd,"{DRAGTO 330,130,LEFT}"
play hWnd,"{DRAGTO 290,130,LEFT}"

'Letter Y
play hWnd,"{MOVETO 340,130}{DRAGTO 360,190,LEFT}"
play hWnd,"{DRAGTO 380,130,LEFT}"
play hWnd,"{MOVETO 360,190}{DRAGTO 360,220,LEFT}"
end
```

The Screen Utility

The *screen utility* is made up of capture and comparison routines that take and compare snapshots of a selected window. The comparisons are done through bitmap comparisons. This results in a highly effective process for detecting whether a screen exactly matches a previously captured version of it. The utility can detect any changes, even a single pixel, in a screen that has been captured. Therefore, it's very effective in verifying that a dialog box or window has not changed from the last time the tests were run.

However, this utility has shortcomings relating to:

✦ The amount of disk space

✦ The time it takes for a comparison

✦ The number of captures that may be required for a single application

The size of a single bitmap can be quite large, depending on the resolution and number of colors displayed on the screen. Because of this, comparisons can take a significant amount of time. And if the comparisons are to be done at multiple screen resolutions, you need multiple capture files, since a captured bitmap at one resolution cannot be compared with a screen at another resolution.

The comparison and capture routines typically use a single capture file that can hold multiple bitmaps. These files, designated by an .SCN file extension, allow for easy encapsulation of multiple screens, so there aren't too many files floating around on your machine.

Instead, you need to have a flexible approach to these routines. Make sure you have a subroutine that accepts:

✦ The name of a screen being captured or compared

✦ The name of the .SCN file to store the captured screen in, or from which to draw for a comparison

✦ The handle to the window that is being captured or compared

You can control whether a capture or comparison is performed by using a global variable or constant. This can be set prior to the test's execution to ensure the screen comparisons are done or, if the variable is set for capture mode, that the capture files are rebuilt automatically. The latter approach requires you to verify by hand that the captures were performed correctly, as is discussed in Chapter 6. See Listing 5-13 for an example of how to use these routines. You can use the example code shown here to flexibly handle captures and comparisons of windows and dialog boxes.

Listing 5-13: **An example of a capture/comparison routine**

```
const NO_ERROR = 0   '0 means no error occurred
global gfCompare as integer
```

```
gfCompare = FALSE    'Results in window being captured

sub CompScreen(strScnName$, strScnFile$, hWnd&)
    dim ret as integer
    static iIndexErr as integer


    'If set to compare, then compare the screens
    if (gfCompare) then
        ret = ScnCompWindow(strScnFile, strScnName, hWnd,0,0)

        if (ret <> NO_ERROR) then
            iIndexErr = iIndexErr + 1
            ScnCaptureWindow("err.scn","err"+ _
                        str$(iIndexErr),hWnd,0)
            log "Comparison error. Check err.scn file at "+ _
                "screen err"+str$(iIndexErr)+" for capture."
        endif

    else    'Otherwise, capture the screen
        ScnCaptureWindow(strScnFile,strScnName,hWnd,0)
    endif
end sub 'CompScreen
```

Note   In the event that a comparison fails, this example subroutine automatically writes out a capture of the problem screen, logs the error information, and allows the script to continue its execution. By writing your routines to do this, you can return to the log files later and verify what exactly went wrong by looking at the captured window that was in error.

Simple Input/Output

You can read in and write out information through the Test language in a number of ways. The easiest are discussed here, to get you started quickly. The more advanced approaches are discussed in Chapter 13.

Visual Test 4.0 added a number of statements to make logging out information very easy for you. These continue to exist in version 6.0. The first is the LOG statement. This writes information out to the Viewport, as a text file or a database-compatible file, depending on how the test script is run. When the test script is executed through the Developer Studio, all output from the log statement goes into the Viewport section of the Output window. If, however, the script is run using the Suite Manager, the user has some options as to where to place the output. The output is directed by settings in the Suite Manager's Options dialog box (for more information on using the Suite Manager, refer to Chapter 6). Listing 5-14 is an example of how the LOG statement can be used.

> Listing 5-14: **The LOG statement provides an easy way to output information**

```
log "Now is the time for all good testers to come to"
log "the aid of their program manager."
log #10,"Extra information that can be printed out."
```

The first two lines are printed out at all times. The third line, however, is printed out only when the script is executed by the Suite Manager, and only if the Options dialog box has the detail level set to 10 or higher. The effect of this is that you can have LOG statements all over the place, but the level of detail is controllable through the Suite Manager.

Summary

This chapter covers what is available in the Test language in pretty broad strokes. There is much more to learn by looking through the online help, but this information will get you started on writing the simple scripts you need to start writing. Once you feel more comfortable with the language, explore what other options are available by working your way through the help file. Also, refer to the later chapters in this book for some more advanced examples.

The next chapter looks at the standalone utilities that accompany the Visual Test product. Then, Chapter 7 takes a look at a simple test case file and dissects it section by section.

✦ ✦ ✦

Visual Test Utilities

The purpose here is not to offer you an exhaustive description of utilities. Instead, we'll be looking at each of the utilities covered in this chapter briefly, to understand when and how they might be used during the development of test scripts.

All of these utilities can be found at the bottom of Visual Test's Test menu, on the Developer Studio toolbar, or in the Rational Visual Test program group (with one exception: the Scenario Recorder is not available in the Rational Visual Test program group). We will start by looking at the utility that helps build test scripts by recording a test engineer's actions: the Scenario Recorder.

The Scenario Recorder

The Scenario Recorder (also known as the Script Recorder in previous versions of Test) is one of the most misunderstood tools of Visual Test. As a matter of fact, while it most definitely helps sell the Visual Test product, it, and any automation tool that boasts a script recorder, does a disservice to the test engineers that use it because managers have misconceptions of its capabilities.

When activated, the Scenario Recorder tracks a user's actions and converts them to the Test language equivalent (see Figure 6-1). If the user clicks a button or selects a menu item, the recorder will generate the appropriate source code to repeat those actions.

From the sounds of it, the recorder is a powerful tool in building test scripts. In reality, however, the code generated is sequential and sometimes won't execute properly without modification. This isn't to say that the recorder is useless; it's simply a tool that can play a small part in automating a project but is not meant to be the main source for creating test scripts. The main source for creating flexible, reusable automated scripts is still the test engineer who writes those scripts.

Recording a Script

Let's take an example of recording a simple situation where a user turns the recorder on, performs some actions, then turns the recorder off again. In this example, we're going to have Microsoft Notepad up and running already, type some text into the editor, then save the contents of the editor to a file called TEST1.TXT.

We begin by displaying the Scenario Recorder. This is done by selecting the Scenario Recorder... menu item found under the Test menu, as shown in Figure 6-1.

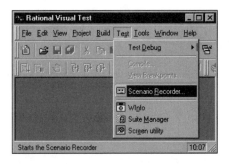

Figure 6-1: Selecting the Scenario Recorder tool from the Developer Studio's Test menu.

A simple dialog box is displayed offering the tester only a few options. These relate to how the script should be recorded. Figure 6-2 shows the settings used to generate the example script we'll be looking at in a moment.

Figure 6-2: The dialog box displayed when you select the Scenario Recorder tool from the Test menu.

Ordinals versus Captions

The Ordinals Only option brings up an interesting point. Why not use ordinals all the time, in place of literal strings that identify the buttons? There are pros and cons to both approaches, and it's up to you to decide what your needs are. One reason for using an ordinal is when an application will be tested in a number of different languages. The caption of the button will change, but the ordinal position of the button will remain the same.

In other situations, such as when the user interface (UI) is still in a state of flux and has yet to be frozen, other controls may be added to the dialog box, possibly causing the ordinal position of a button to change. If you use a caption instead of an ordinal value, the Visual Test routines will still find the button.

In both cases, either problem can be minimized by using proper programming techniques. In this case, the use of constants is warranted. We discuss them further in Chapter 8. Also, Bill Hodghead of Microsoft has written a section in Chapter 13 called "Automated Testing of Localized Products" that you should investigate.

The Ordinals Only check box makes the generated script more flexible by not relying solely on the labels associated with individual controls. For example, instead of clicking a button with the caption "Save" in the Save As dialog box, it would look for the tab order or *ordinal position* of the button in the dialog box. In our example, the Save button has an ordinal value of 1 (I'll show you how to determine this using the Window Information — Winfo — tool under "The Window Information Utility," later in this chapter). If we had clicked this check box, the recorder would have used `WButtonClick("@1")` instead of the `wButtonClick("&Save")` statement you see at the bottom of the listing in Figure 6-6 later in this chapter.

In this example we already have a blank, untitled instance of Notepad up and running. We've clicked the OK button in the Scenario Recorder dialog box, so the recorder is active.

We begin by typing a simple string into the editor, so that we can see what type of code will be generated (see Figure 6-3). A recurring theme, I use my old standby, "Now is the time…", for lack of a better idea. Oh, the strain of the creative process!

Figure 6-3: Type some text into Notepad and save it to the file TEST1.TXT.

After typing in the text, we select the Save menu item from the File menu, which saves the text we've entered. Right about here some of you should have a warning bell going off in your heads. It's not obvious right away, but it becomes so, once the script is executed. The problem is one that I mentioned at the beginning of this section: how generated scripts may not always work right away.

Once we finish recording this script and turn around to run it, a message box that wasn't displayed when the script was originally recorded will display "Replace existing file?" This is seen in Figure 6-4.

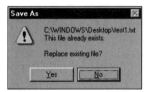

Figure 6-4: An example of how a script may not work when it is run right after it is recorded. When you record it the first time, the file may not exist. Playing the script back will result in a warning message that breaks your script, since it wasn't expecting this message box.

This is a simple example of how the recorder, while useful, isn't robust enough to catch events not encountered during the original recording. No script recorder is robust enough to catch things like this. Therefore, while the recorder offers a number of benefits, it's still necessary for you to go in and modify the scripts to handle the different events that can arise.

But we're a bit ahead of ourselves here. After completing the actions we wanted to record, we need to turn off the recorder. This is done by clicking its icon or entry in the taskbar. When doing so, you are prompted with another dialog box, shown in Figure 6-5.

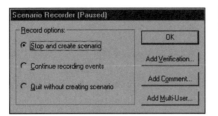

Figure 6-5: After deactivating the script recorder, you will see this dialog box.

A feature added to version 4.0 of Test that remains in Visual Test 6.0 is the Add Verification... button. This feature is pretty slick. It allows you to verify that the scenario or script you recorded ended up in the expected location of your application, that is, that a particular dialog box that was supposed to be displayed at the end of the execution of the script is actually displayed. It allows you to verify that you are in a given window or that a particular control exists before testing continues. It also lets you verify that the position of the window is as expected.

When you use this button, a `RecVerify*` function call (found in the RECORDER.INC include file) is placed in the source code generated by the recorder. In the sample script that we generated, the Add Verification... button wasn't used.

Note   There are a number of different flavors of the `RecVerify*` function, which is why there is an asterisk (*) signifying that the last part of the function call will depend upon exactly what is being verified.

Another button in this dialog box is Add Multi-User, which allows for the script to synchronize itself with other machines on a network. In Chapter 15 we discuss synchronizing scripts more fully. This option causes the script to insert a command that will communicate back to the controlling or *host* computer and await its signal to proceed.

When the OK button in the Scenario Recorder (Paused) dialog box (Figure 6-5) is clicked, the automatically generated script is placed into a source window in the Microsoft Developer Studio.

The script we created is shown in Figure 6-6. (The script you see might vary slightly from the figure, because of other actions you may have taken during the recording, such as selecting other menus, clicking text, working at a different screen resolution, using the keyboard for navigation instead of the mouse, and so on.)

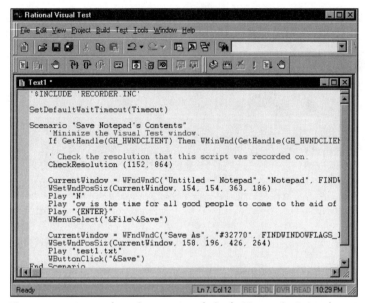

Figure 6-6: A sample script generated via the Scenario Recorder.

Realities of the Script Recorder

The Scenario Recorder is a helpful tool in automation but is not the only part of the automation equation. A common situation that testers new to automation encounter is similar to what happened to me when I first started using Microsoft Test 1.0: I was on a job where the Director of Development thought the recorder could do everything and that it didn't require any degree of intelligence to write automated scripts. Wrong.

Microsoft has made great improvements — and Rational has updated it to recognize newly supported controls — in the recorder since it was first introduced in version 1.0, but it doesn't replace the need for an automation engineer who knows and understands the Test language. Nor is it now Rational Software's intention to imply that using a script recorder is the end-all, be-all way to design your automated tests. Unfortunately, many people new to automation hear about the Scenario Recorder and assume it's a simple matter of just turning it on, recording a section of the product to be tested, and turning it off again. Sorry.

It's up to you to help correct the misconception that the script recorder is the silver bullet. Explain the pros and cons of the script recorder when the topic arises.

The Scenario Recorder is an excellent tool, especially when someone is first learning how to program in Rational Visual Test. As a matter of fact, I strongly recommend using it to record the testing of a given area when you aren't sure what commands to use for individual controls. As you grow to know the Test language better, though, you'll find yourself using the recorder less and less.

Tip The use of the recorder is implied in its name: Scenario Recorder. It's useful for recording short, individual tests or scenarios, not entire sections of an application. You can go in and cut out the sections of the autogenerated code you find useful and dispose of the rest. By using the script recorder in this fashion, you will quickly pick up on the syntax and common functions and statements that make up the Test language. Another good use of the recorder is to create a general skeleton of the area to be tested, allowing you to go in and fill in the more detailed sections of the test.

The Window Information Utility

The Window Information (Winfo) utility, also found under the Test menu, on the Developer Studio toolbar, and in the Rational Visual Test program group on the Start menu, is a very simple and straightforward tool. It's also a very necessary and valuable tool to have when automating scripts. It allows you to identify what would otherwise be hidden information about applications you are attempting to test.

Note The Winfo utility has undergone major enhancements for version 6. Now it not only provides information on windows, dialog boxes, and controls, it also provides information on ActiveX controls, MSAA (Microsoft Active Accessibility) applications, and HTML pages displayed in Internet Explorer 4.0 (or newer).

The General Tab

The General tab in the Window Information utility allows you to identify a window or control's type and how you can go about acting upon it through your test scripts. If you've done any Windows development, you'll find that the Winfo utility provides information similar to the Spy utility.

Drawn/virtual windows controls

As discussed in Chapter 5, the reality of Windows programs is that programmers don't always use *true* Windows controls. Sometimes they use bitmaps: fake/owner-drawn, or virtual, controls. Often, this is the only way for the programmers to provide the end user with a cool-looking interface that helps sell the product. The result is a nightmare for the Test programmer because Visual Test's routines only recognize Windows controls, or subclasses of those controls; they don't recognize a bitmap that looks and acts like a Windows control, such as a stylish-looking toolbar that was really drawn in a graphics editor.

Note   For details on subclassing in Windows, see "Subclassed Windows Controls" later in this chapter.

Let's look at Microsoft Paint as a simple example. When you have the main window of Paint up, you'll notice a palette to the left of the window that offers artists a number of tools with which to create their graphics. It looks like it's made up of a bunch of buttons with pictures of each individual tool (see Figure 6-7). It's really just a separate window, without a border, that contains a single bitmap or picture of controls instead of actual individual button controls. The developer who wrote the application simply checks the coordinates of where the user clicked the mouse to determine which tool becomes active. This is great for the end user, but how do you, as a test engineer, determine whether it's a grouping of controls or just a bitmap? This is where Winfo tab of the Window Information utility comes in handy (see Figure 6-8).

Figure 6-7: Microsoft Paint's tool palette.

After you select Winfo from the Test menu, the Window Information utility's window is displayed, as in Figure 6-8. With the Winfo tab selected, you can determine what types of controls you're dealing with. In this case, the control is a small, borderless window that holds a bitmap. Well, bummer . . .

Now you know you can't use the wToolBar* or wButton* statements that are part of the Test language. Instead, you'll have to resort to using the wMoveToWnd statement by determining the pixel coordinates of each control, relative to the application's window. Not a fun way to do things, but a situation that can be worked through.

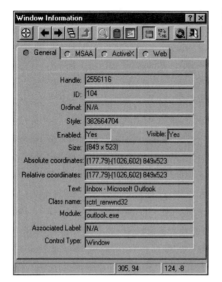

Figure 6-8: The Window Information (Winfo) utility window

Two other examples of nonstandard or fake Windows controls are the Open dialog boxes in Microsoft Word and Excel. If you display them and then move Winfo's Finder tool over the controls of the Open dialog box, you will notice that only some, not all, of the controls actually highlight. In most other Open dialog boxes, all the controls would highlight as the tool moved across them individually. So why does nothing happen in Word and Excel? Once again, this is an unpleasant situation for testers who are writing scripts to test those types of dialog boxes, because true Windows controls don't exist, only bitmaps of those controls.

Note   Refer to the "Mouse and Keyboard Events" section of Chapter 5 for more information on dealing with situations where *true* controls don't exist.

Fortunately, dialog boxes such as these aren't too common. I'm told that the reasons Microsoft Word and Excel have dialog boxes like these are two-fold:

✦ It cuts down on the number of resources used by the application.

✦ It makes porting the application to other platforms easier, since the developer is dealing with a bitmap of a control and the coordinates of where the user can click. Using a bitmap this way saves time, as it doesn't require the programmer to redesign the dialog box for another platform (such as the Apple Macintosh).

Subclassed windows controls

The Winfo tab also comes in handy when you're trying to act upon a Windows control and nothing is happening. Say, for example, that you try to click a button named "OK." The statement you'd use in your script would be `wButtonClick("OK")`. But you find yourself pulling your hair out because the control is clearly a button, its label is "OK," and yet for some reason Visual Test isn't clicking it.

It could be that it is a button and not a bitmap, but the `wButtonClick` statement doesn't recognize it. The routines in Visual Test that allow you to act upon a control determine which control they're looking for by its class name. Everything in Windows has a class name associated with it. For a typical button, the class name is `Button`. For an edit control, the class name is `Edit`. When you use the `wButton*` routines, the Test language looks for all of the objects in the active window that have `Button` as a class name. Then it searches through those objects, looking for the control that matches the caption you passed in that routine. If it doesn't find it, it reports an error back to you.

When a developer takes a Windows control and modifies its behavior to the point where it acts even a little differently than Microsoft intended, it's called *subclassing* the control. And because that control is a little bit different, it is given a different class name.

Now, remember that those routines in the Test language that act upon a control use those class names to ensure they are affecting the appropriate control. Therefore, in the example of the `wButtonClick` statement, if for some reason the button isn't being clicked, the Winfo tab in the Winfo utility can be used to determine the class name of that control.

Using the Finder tool (shaped like rifle scope's cross-hairs) on the Window Information utility's toolbar, you can select the troublesome control to get information about it. In the Class Name section of the window, you'll see the class associated with that control. If the control is indeed a subclassed button or simply behaves enough like a button for your purposes, then the `wButtonSetClass` statement can be used to tell the rest of the `wButton*` routines that the subclassed control should be considered a button.

Note   In addition to Chapter 5's section on mouse and keyboard events, refer to the "Testing Custom Controls" section in Chapter 13 for even more ideas on working with nonstandard controls.

The MSAA Tab

Microsoft has been working on computer accessibility since 1992 to help people with disabilities have easier access to computer programs. The MSAA (Microsoft Active Accessibility) software developer's kit (SDK) took the next big step in

Microsoft's strategy by creating native accessibility APIs so that all software development companies could make their products more accessible. Released in May 1997, this kit was a significant step because it marked the first time that a mainstream computer operating system provided this level of native support for accessibility. In short, a lot of the common busy work in creating accessibility support was done by Microsoft's MSAA SDK so that software developers had more time to innovate.

What does this all mean to Rational Visual Test users? Microsoft has described it this way: "Although built for the disability community, MSAA has many potential mainstream uses. Because the software can expose parts of the interface that are otherwise not accessible to the Windows developer, one of the most important uses could be in the area of automated testing. Many businesses could reduce the amount of manual testing, or get greater test coverage without additional resources by creating automated testing tools based upon MSAA." And Rational Software has done just that by adding support in Visual Test 6.0 for working with software applications that make use of MSAA.

The new MSAA tab on the Winfo utility automatically activates when the Finder tool — found on the Winfo toolbar — is dropped on an application that uses MSAA APIs, as shown in Figure 6-9. An example of how cool this is would be its effect when using Microsoft Word. In the past it was a major hassle to grab the text from the MS Word editor. Because Word is now MSAA-compliant, that information is exposed so that tools for the disabled can easily access that information (for example, a voice synthesizer program that "reads" the contents of a Word document to a computer user who is blind). Visual Test taps in to this capability, allowing greater flexibility in automation.

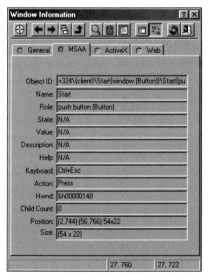

Figure 6-9: The MSAA tab in the Winfo utility provides information about MSAA-compliant applications. This tab activates when the Finder tool is dropped on an application using the MSAA SDK.

The ActiveX Tab

Testing OLE and ActiveX controls was possible with the version of Winfo provided in Visual Test 4.0 and earlier. In Visual Test 6.0 even more information is being provided about those controls, as can be seen in Figure 6-10. For more specific information on testing OLE/ActiveX controls refer to the section "Testing OLE Controls" found at the end of Chapter 13.

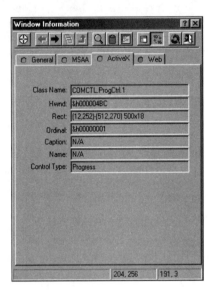

Figure 6-10: Even more information about an OLE or ActiveX control can be found when using the 6.0 version of Winfo and its ActiveX tab.

The Web Tab

Well over 100 functions were added to the Test language to support the testing of HTML documents — or Web pages — via Microsoft Internet Explorer 4.0 (and newer). This tab on the Winfo utility, shown in Figure 6-11, allows you to find out more specific information about an HTML document currently displayed in the Internet Explorer browser. The information includes the URL a link or image references and the type of tag a given section of text or object is using, as well as information about frames, forms and their elements, and so on. Use this section of Winfo to find more information about the pages you plan to automate with Visual Test.

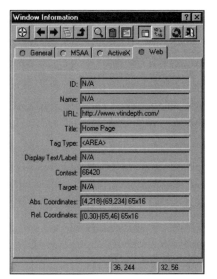

Figure 6-11: With over 100 functions added to support the testing of HTML documents, Winfo has been updated to help you decipher the contents of those pages.

The Visual Test Suite Manager

The Visual Test Suite Manager can be extremely useful, though you may well find yourself using it less as you become more familiar with Visual Test's language and tools. There are at least three key ways in which it is particularly useful:

✦ Managing multiple files

✦ Handling unexpected errors

✦ As an integrated tool

After examining each of these in detail, we shall briefly consider the developments in Test that led to the Suite Manager. The Suite Manager's main window can be seen in Figure 6-12.

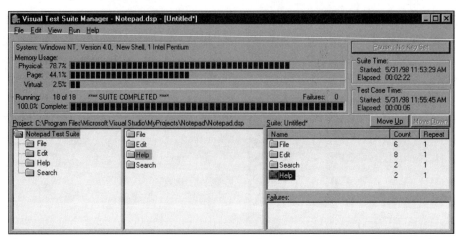

Figure 6-12: The Visual Test Suite Manager's main window. Here, it is displaying the contents of a test suite that tests the Notepad application.

Managing Multiple Files

When writing automated tests for a product, you will find that the number of files you have to test can become unwieldy. In the case of the suite displayed in Figure 6-12, there are only 18 files, broken down into four folders. While this is not a huge number, they can grow quickly, especially on a large project with multiple automation engineers.

The Suite Manager is designed to help manage all the test case files in a test suite. However, while it is fully functional and very capable in what it does, this doesn't mean you *must* use it. As a matter of fact, Visual Test provides you with the tools to create a driver of your own if you wish. (We look at a simple driver in Chapter 15.)

Information Displayed

While it may look complex at first glance, the Suite Manager is a fairly straightforward utility. At the top of its main window (see Figure 6-12) it displays information about the type of computer the test is running on, the version of Windows, memory usage, and the percentage of tests executed by the driver. Because this information can be helpful, the default option is for this information to continue to be displayed, even during the running of the tests.

While the Suite Manager falls to the background, it continues to monitor memory usage, how many test case files have been completed, the number that remain to be executed, and how many test scenarios in those test case files failed their tests. Figure 6-13 shows the default form the Suite Manager takes when running through its lists of test case files.

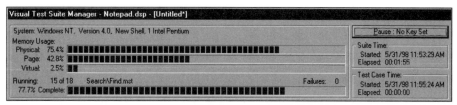

Figure 6-13: An example of the information the Visual Test Suite Manager can display while executing automated test cases. In this example, a total of 18 test case files are going to be run by the Suite Manager.

Handling Unexpected Errors

One of the nice options of the Suite Manager is its ability to detect an exception, or system error. This is typically known as a *general protection fault* or *access violation* (under Windows 3.*x* it was known as an *unrecoverable application error*). An example of an exception is when one program illegally attempts to access memory being used by Windows or another application. Other examples include *overflow*, *divide by zero,* and *illegal instruction* errors. Figure 6-14 shows the Options dialog box that allows you to handle exceptions.

In Figure 6-14, you'll also notice that the manager can be configured to look for windows that contain a particular caption. If this option is active, the Suite Manager will dismiss the window automatically and continue running the test case file. Therefore, you won't need to supply any code to deal with a window that contains the caption specified in this dialog box.

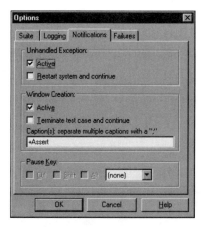

Figure 6-14: The Options dialog box allows you to configure how the Suite Manager logs out testing information and handles run-time errors.

An Integrated Tool

The Suite Manager is an integrated tool. It is very capable and provides you with the engine you need to run all your test case files. It works with the Developer Studio application and the .DSP (Developer Studio Project) file that is written to disk when a new Developer Studio project is created. This integration makes picking and choosing files from the project extremely simple. Once they are in the Suite Manager, the test case files (.MST files) can be dragged around to create different test suites based on which test case files are to be run. This list of test case files can be saved into a .VTS file (Visual Test Suite) so that many configurations can be saved and reloaded.

This utility was created using the Visual Test language and then compiled down to an executable form. This goes to show that if you don't care for the Suite Manager and would like to write your own, improved version of it, Visual Test's language and user interface editor make this a possibility. (See Chapter 15 for details.)

No Source Code

The Visual Test Suite Manager has undergone a number of changes over the years, as Microsoft Test has evolved to its current form in Rational Visual Test 6.0. Originally, it was a utility that came with Microsoft Test 2.0. Because it was written in the Test language, it served not only as a place to organize and run test case files, but also as an example of what you can create with the Test language and User Interface Editor.

In Visual Test 4.0 the Suite Manager took yet another step forward. It no longer included the Test language source code. But if you looked in the Visual Test installation directory, you would have seen that it had a .PCD file extension. In Visual Test 6.0 the result is the same except that the Suite Manager now sports the new .PC6 file extension. This is a Visual Test pseudocode file compiled using Visual Test, meaning it was written using the Test language.

I'm not sure why Microsoft originally chose not to include the source code for the driver in version 4.0 of Test, but Rational has continued this in version 6.0. My guess is either Microsoft found it too difficult to support (in other words, they didn't like to give *Introduction to Programming* lessons over their support line) or they were behind schedule in shipping the product and didn't have enough time to clean up the code.

Whatever the reason, this utility demonstrates the true power of Visual Test. It now has the capability to write a Windows application with the aid of a run-time engine to interpret the pseudocode file.

The Visual Test Screen Utility

The Visual Test Screen utility (see Figure 6-15) is used for capturing snapshots of anything that can be displayed on the Windows desktop. This can be a complete window, the entire desktop, or a specific rectangular region specified by the Test programmer using X and Y coordinates.

Figure 6-15: The main window of the Visual Test Screen utility.

Dare to Compare

The Visual Test Screen utility provides a means for you to compare a screen with a snapshot of the same screen made previously, perhaps on a completely different build or version of the product. For example, if a tester takes a snapshot of a dialog box for which the UI design has been frozen, you can compare that snapshot with future releases of the product from the development team.

During the development of a product, communication is crucial yet is not always as open between the programmers and tester engineers as it should be. A decision might be made to move a particular dialog box control (such as a button) without alerting the testers to this decision. While this is usually a fairly harmless adjustment, it is nonetheless necessary for the testing team to revisit this area of the product to verify that the dialog box still works as expected.

Three examples of what could happen when a dialog box is modified are:

✦ The tab order could change, causing the dialog box to no longer follow the common user interface design guidelines.

✦ The internal ID number of the control could change if the control was removed and re-added (possibly causing the programmer's source code to break if it depended upon that ID number).

✦ The documentation team could miss out on the opportunity to take a final screenshot of the dialog box, causing the documentation to be out-of-date with the final product.

While documentation and quality assurance don't necessarily communicate on issues such as these, this is yet another opportunity for the documentation team to be alerted, since two teams — the development and testing teams — now know of the modification.

Capturing Screens

The Visual Test Screen utility doesn't usually create the bulk of the screen capture files used by the automated test cases. Because the UI of a product tends to evolve as the development for that product matures, it's not practical to manually recapture screenshots (see Figure 6-16).

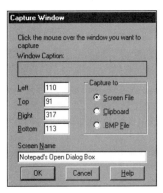

Figure 6-16: This dialog box is displayed when the user is capturing a window by hand.

The preferred method of capturing screens is programmatically. That is, design the comparison routines you'll need to write to serve a dual purpose:

✦ To compare a window with a previously captured screenshot of that window

✦ To make a screen shot of that window (if a switch has been turned on in the code base of the test suite, to cause the capturing to occur)

Note   We took a look at the Test language routines that perform these two tasks — capture and comparison — in "The Screen Utility" section of Chapter 5.

The utility allows a test engineer to step through the autogenerated capture files to verify that the captures were created as expected. This is known as creating a *gold capture file* or simply as *blessing* the capture files. It is necessary to bless them because, if an error in a dialog box exists during the capturing process (such as the misspelling of a label for a button), the later comparisons only serve to verify that the error still exists. Therefore, visually verifying the capture files is crucial each time they are regenerated.

The other use for the Visual Test Screen utility is to understand why a particular comparison failed. A good way to write the comparison function, which is discussed in Chapter 5, is to have it capture the window that fails the comparison and log out the fact that the comparison failed. The reason for this capture is so that, later, when you're running through your log files to determine which tests failed, you can use the Screen utility to compare the blessed capture of the window with the failed capture of the window, generated during the test run.

Example of a Failed Comparison

Figure 6-17 shows an example of how a comparison might look. A picture of Notepad's Open dialog box has been saved in the blessed screen capture file.

Figure 6-17: The screen capture of Notepad's Open dialog box will be the blessed capture, used for all present and future comparisons of Notepad's Open dialog box.

While the controls have maintained their positions and not changed as cited in a previous example of how the comparison utility can be helpful, something has changed and will cause the comparison to fail.

Figure 6-18 is the same dialog box with one difference: Its list box is displaying a list of drives available to the user, instead of the top-level view shown in Figure 6-17. In this example, the comparison fails and the comparison function saves a copy of the dialog box for later examination, to help determine the cause of the failure.

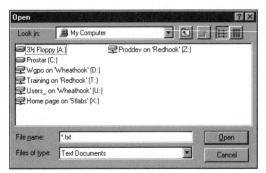

Figure 6-18: This is how Notepad's Open dialog box appeared during our supposed test run.

Your tests have been run, and you return to find that an error occurred during a comparison of one of the dialog boxes. Because you wrote your comparison function to make a capture of the dialog box in question, you can compare the failed dialog box against the approved capture of that dialog box.

Comparing the dialog boxes shown in Figures 6-17 and 6-18 using the Screen utility results in an XOR-ing of the two objects. That is, the Screen utility lays the two screenshots on top of each other, and any pixels that match up with each other or that have not changed will be canceled out. Those pixels that are different will show up in the comparison (see Figure 6-19).

Figure 6-19: Comparing the dialog boxes shown in Figures 6-17 and 6-18, using the Screen utility.

In the instance of text that existed in the same location of both captures, but that has changed in some way, that text will appear as a more garbled or fuzzy image in the comparison window.

Drawbacks

There are some drawbacks to using the Screen utility, however. For example, when you are working with any screen that has a flashing cursor or a value that can change (as in the previous example, where the contents of the list box changed), the result can be a failed comparison. Even a single pixel changing will cause a comparison to fail.

Another drawback occurs when performing comparisons at different resolutions. Screens captured at one resolution can't be used for comparisons at another resolution. If the testing is being performed at 640×480, 800×600, 1024×768, and so on, separate capture files will be needed for each resolution.

And there are more problems. If comparisons are being done at different color settings, such as 16 colors, 256 colors, and 16 million colors, separate screen comparison files will need to be kept for each of these color settings as well.

And, in the worst-case situation of performing captures and comparisons at 1024×768 pixels (or at a higher resolution) and at 16 million colors, the size of the capture file can grow large, quickly. And because the comparisons are done pixel by pixel, the time to compare each screenshot can grow as the resolution and bits per pixel (number of colors) grow.

If at all possible, keep things simple by picking one resolution and one color setting to be used for captures and comparisons. And keep the use of the screen comparisons to a minimum. Don't go nuts and do a screen comparison of every piece of UI in the product. Pick key areas that need to be monitored and use the screen comparison utility just for those.

Masking

The Microsoft Test team introduced the ability to mask regions of a captured image in version 3.0 of Test. This feature is still available in version 6.0 of Rational Visual Test.

The general idea of the masking feature is to specify a region to be ignored during the comparison of the two images. This is done using the Screen utility. The user opens the visually verified or *blessed* capture file and uses the mouse to draw a rectangle across the area to be ignored. This solves the problem mentioned previously, regarding values that can change between test runs. In Figure 6-20, we've masked out the areas shown in Figure 6-19 that changed and caused the comparison to fail.

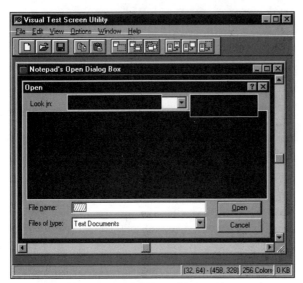

Figure 6-20: An example of masking out areas that can change between test runs.

Version 3.0 of Test didn't offer a way to set the exclude regions through the programming language. Fortunately, version 4.0 added a new function called ScnSetExcludeRects that allows for programmatically specifying such regions.

Summary

When I first sat down with Microsoft Test 1.0, I figured the product itself was an automated tool that built automated tests for me. How wrong I was! The tools that come with it can be helpful, but creating the test suite consists of a lot of script writing, learning how to deal with odd situations, maintaining the product as it evolves, and practicing patience as you move forward on tackling the task of automation.

No magic is involved in Visual Test. It's simply a programming language that contains some routines and tools to help you work with the Windows user interface. Dive in, move forward, and you'll find that, in no time, you'll have a large test suite helping you test your product. And you'll find automation getting easier as you progress.

While Microsoft has provided a number of utilities to make the job of automation easier on us, the bulk of the job still involves writing scripts by hand. The Scenario Recorder helps. It generates some simple test scenarios by recording a user's actions. However, these often require modification and ongoing maintenance. Use the recorder only when you're uncertain how to go about automating an area, or if you're trying to automate a product that uses controls you aren't familiar with. It may show up some commands you didn't know about previously.

The Suite Manager is very helpful in managing multiple files on a project and aids in handling error conditions. It also allows you to control how the results of your tests are logged: whether they go to a simple flat text file or into a database-compatible file format. It also allows you to control the number of times a test case file is run and tracks which of those files had failures.

The Winfo utility helps track down owner-drawn, or virtual, controls so that you know how you need to work with them. In many cases you'll find that such a control has simply been subclassed and requires the use of the `W*SetClass` statement. In other cases, you'll find that the control isn't recognized by Visual Test and will require you to provide X and Y coordinates to click a specific pixel location. New to this utility are the MSAA, ActiveX, and Web tabs that allow you to gather even more information on applications for which you plan to automate portions of your testing.

And finally, the Screen utility is helpful in verifying that a dialog box, a window, or the screen in general is exactly as it was when previously captured. It can become bulky, however, when working at high resolutions displaying a high number of colors. It can also be cumbersome when you need to keep screen comparisons of the product for multiple resolutions and color settings.

✦   ✦   ✦

Simple Coding Example

Now that we've had a chance to get an overview of Visual Test's user interface (UI), Test language, and accompanying utilities, let's take a look at what a typical first test script might look like.

In our example, we're going to use Microsoft Notepad, a simple text editor that ships with Windows NT 4.0 and 5.0 and Windows 95 and 98. We're using it both because it's a simple application to automate, so our first automation script will be easy, and because almost everyone who's ever used Windows is familiar with Notepad.

In Chapter 9 we take a closer look at how to decide on an overall approach to take. But as we're only automating a small piece of Notepad here, we won't be looking too closely at the overall approach just yet.

Note Remember that the compiler for the Test language is not case-sensitive. Therefore, the use of upper- and lowercase characters in my source listings is based only on my style; and that style can change from time to time, even though I've attempted to keep it consistent in this book.

The Sample Script

If you have a strong background in programming, you will notice I'm not using a lot of structure in this sample script. That is, I'm not focusing on constants, functions, macros, subroutines, or include files. The reason is simply so that this first script is easier to follow. Listing 7-1 is an example of a typical first test script.

Listing 7-1: A simple first script that tests Notepad's "New" menu item

```
'****************************************************************
'* This file contains a simple example of testing the "New"
'* menu item found under the File menu in the Windows Notepad
'* application.
'****************************************************************

dim strText$, hwndApp&

    'Make sure the viewport is cleared
    VIEWPORT CLEAR

    'Check to see if Notepad is already running. If not, run

    'it.
    hwndApp = wFndWnd("- Notepad", FW_ALL OR FW_EXIST OR

                                OR FW_PART OR FW_FOCUS OR _
                                FW_RESTORE)
    if (hwndApp = 0) then
        if (run("notepad.exe")) then
            print "Unable to run Notepad.exe"
            stop
        endif
        hwndApp = wGetActWnd(0)
    endif

    print
    print "Tests begun on: "+DATETIME$+" for "+NAME$
    print

    '
    'Test the "New" menu item, respond "no".
    '

    'Write out information about test to be performed
    print "Test #1: 'New' with text. Select 'No'."

    'Make sure there's text in the Notepad window.
    WEditSetText("@1","")   'Clears out the contents of editor
    play "Now is the time for all good..."

    'Select the "New" menu item
    WMenuSelect("File\New")

    If (GetText(NULL) = "Notepad") then '"Save Changes" DB?
```

```
    WButtonClick("No")                    'No, don't save changes

    'Notepad's main window is a big edit control.
    'We can give it the focus and check text, put text,

    'etc. just like any other edit control. We use "@1"

    'since it is the first and only edit control.
    If (EditText("@1") <> "") then
        'Write out error information: what went wrong?
        print "***Error: 'New' didn't clear window" + _

            "contents."
        print "Expected: <empty-window>"
        print "Received: "+EditText("@1")
        print
    EndIf
Else
    'Write out error information: what went wrong?
    print "***Error: 'New' with text didn't display "+ _
        "the 'Are you sure?' message box."
    print "Expected: Notepad"
    print "Received: "+GetText(NULL)
    print
EndIf

'
'Test the "New" menu item, respond "Yes".
'
print "Test #2: 'New' with text. Select 'Yes'."
play "Now is the time for all good..."
strText = EditText("@1")     'Get editor's contents.
WMenuSelect("File\New")

'Because there is unsaved text, the 'Save changes?

'message box should be displayed.
If (GetText(NULL) = "Notepad") then
    WButtonClick("Yes")
    If (GetText(NULL) = "Save As") then
        WButtonClick("Cancel")
    Else
        print "***Error: 'New' with 'Yes, save changes'"+ _
            " didn't display SaveAs DB."
        print "Expected: Save As"
        print "Received: "+GetText(NULL)
        print
    EndIf
Else
```

(continued)

Listing 7-1 *(continued)*

```
        print "***Error: 'New' with text didn't display "+ _
              "the 'Are you sure?' message box."
        print "Expected: Notepad"
        print "Received: "+GetText(NULL)
        print
EndIf

If (strText <> EditText("@1")) then
        print "***Error: Cancel out of SaveAs after 'New' "+ _
              "caused text change."
        print "Expected: "+strText
        print "Received: "+EditText("@1")
        print
EndIf

'
'Test the "New" menu item, respond "Cancel".
'
print "Test #3: 'New' with text. Select 'Cancel'."
strText = EditText("@1")
WMenuSelect("File\New")

'Because there is unsaved text, the Save changes?
'message box should be displayed.
If (GetText(NULL) = "Notepad") then
        WButtonClick("Cancel")
Else
        print "***Error: 'New' with text didn't display the"+ _
              " 'Are you sure?' message box."
        print "Expected: Notepad"
        print "Received: "+GetText(NULL)
        print
EndIf

'If the text changed even though cancel was used,
'an error occurred.
If (strText <> EditText("@1")) then
        print "***Error: Cancel out of 'New' caused " + _
              "text change."
        print "Expected: "+strText
        print "Received: "+EditText("@1")
        print
EndIf

print
print "*** Tests completed."

WMenuSelect("File\Exit")        'Exit the Notepad application
WButtonClick("No")              '"No" to "Save changes?"
END
```

The sample script can be broken up into four separate parts:

✦ Declarations

✦ Initialization

✦ Tests

✦ Clean-up

Each of these sections and the code that makes up these sections are discussed under the headings that follow.

Declarations

We begin our script by declaring the only two variables that are used:

```
'*****************************************************************
'* This file contains a simple example of testing the "New"
'* menu item found under the "File" menu in the Windows Notepad
'* application.
'*****************************************************************

dim strText$, hwndApp&
```

It is typical to have a declaration line shrink and grow as the script is first written and continues to evolve. As we discussed in Chapter 5, all variable declarations are made using the DIM, GLOBAL, or STATIC statements. strText$ is a variable of type string that holds a string of characters. HwndApp& is a variable of type LONG that holds a handle to an application's main window. This handle is used by other functions and statements to ensure that the proper application window is acted upon.

Just Jump In

Even though a finished script may be well organized and make sense upon examination, scripts don't start out that way. Don't look at this sample script as something that was written sequentially from start to finish. As when any program is first being written, the creative juices are flowing and the programmer is typically jumping back and forth between sections as the script unfolds. Only after a number of revisions have been made to a script does it start to resemble anything that looks somewhat organized.

The best way for you to create your own automated scripts is to jump in and start writing some automated tests. Don't worry if it's messy at first; you get better as you go along and you also get an idea of how you want to organize your overall automation task. As you continue to automate your tests, you find you do more planning—even if it's not on paper but just thinking something through in your head—before writing any actual code. If you're new to Visual Test, you're not at this stage, so just jump in. You'll get to where you can plan your automation with more forethought soon enough.

OR-ing

The `wFndWnd` function controls how it works by OR-ing together a number of constants known as *flags*. Those of you familiar with database queries shouldn't confuse this OR-ing with a typical database look-up. What is going on instead is a *bitwise-OR*, meaning it is taking the binary digits and adding them together. For this to work, the constant values are unique: They are all based on a power of 2, so that their binary representation is a single bit and unique from the other constants.

The main thing to understand is that the OR-ing going on in this function call has nothing to do with a "this or that" approach; it's more of a "this, and that, and that, and that" approach. By OR-ing the flags, we're actually adding the flags together, so that only one parameter needs to be passed to the `wFndWnd` function.

Getting Ready to Test — Initialization

The next few lines of code are used to initialize everything, so that the tests can begin:

```
'Make sure the viewport is cleared
VIEWPORT CLEAR

'Check to see if Notepad is already running. If not, run it.
hwndApp = wFndWnd("- Notepad", FW_ALL OR FW_EXIST OR FW_PART _
                        OR FW_FOCUS OR FW_RESTORE)
```

The first thing that occurs is a `VIEWPORT CLEAR` statement. This clears the window where all the output is placed. Any time the `print` statement is used, the output is placed in the Viewport (except in the situations when you are working with file input and output [I/O]).

After clearing the Viewport, the script uses the `wFndWnd` function to determine whether or not an application with the partial caption of "- Notepad" is up and running. Note that I said *partial caption*. `WFndWnd()` is configurable in how it works. This is controlled through OR-ing together a number of *flags* that are available to be used with this function.

The flags I've chosen to use in this circumstance are `FW_ALL`, `FW_EXIST`, `FW_PART`, `FW_FOCUS`, and `FW_RESTORE`. These tell `wFndWnd()` to search all windows, return a handle to the window if it exists, search partial captions to see if any of them contain the caption passed as the first parameter of the function call, give the window the focus (activate it) once it is found, and restore the window so that it is in normal mode — neither minimized nor maximized.

In the event that the window isn't found, zero (0) is returned, letting us know that a valid window handle couldn't be supplied. In this situation, we know Notepad isn't up and running, so we need to take appropriate steps to make it so.

We can get Notepad running by using Visual Test's run statement. Now, this routine comes in two flavors: function or statement. If we use the statement form, it attempts to run the specified program. If it fails, however, we may not find out until we try to test the application later. So in this situation, I prefer to use the functional form:

```
if (hwndApp = 0) then
    if (run("notepad.exe")) then
        print "Unable to run Notepad.exe"
        stop
    endif
    hwndApp = wGetActWnd(0)
endif
```

The functional form returns a number to us (whereas the statement form does not), letting us know whether or not it succeeded. Here's the counter-intuitive part of it, though. If it does succeed, it returns a zero (0) — a value commonly associated with FALSE, or something failure-related.

Microsoft (remember, Microsoft originally created what we now know as Rational Visual Test) designed this function this way with good reason: This way Visual Test can communicate exactly why it failed to run the program by returning any number of values that are documented in the online help to explain the cause of the failure.

In this case, however, we don't care why it failed. We just want to know if Notepad successfully ran. If anything other than zero (0) is returned, we step into the next line of code, which prints out an error message and stops the execution of the script.

Caution   A test for success is important, because if a script ever gets into a situation where the application you're testing isn't up and running, it'll usually keep running — possibly causing unexpected results as it performs operations on whatever application does happen to be up and running.

If we successfully run the application, we can use wGetActWnd() to give us the handle to its window, so we can refer to it later:

```
hwndApp = wGetActWnd(0)
```

Finally, we print out the beginning information. This informs you, as you stare at the Viewport bleary-eyed, exactly when the tests commenced:

```
print
print "Tests begun on: "+DATETIME$+" for "+NAME$
print
```

It could be argued that the "Test started" line could be placed where the tests actually begin, but as you see in later chapters, we turn this initialization code into a reusable module that all of our test cases will use. Therefore, we want the beginning test information printed in the initialization section. This is so that if changes need to be made later, they can be done in this one module, rather than by revisiting each test case or test file in turn.

The Tests

In this example, there are only three separate situations we're looking for when testing the New menu item. In all three, we are testing that the Save Changes? message box is being displayed. To do this, we need to make sure we have new, unsaved text in the editor. Then we select the New menu item.

Test One

An interesting factoid about Notepad is that its main window is one large edit control. This makes testing it simpler, since we can use the wEdit*() routines to retrieve information about the text it is displaying. We start by making sure we have a clean slate and that no text exists in Notepad's main window. We do this with the wEditSetText function:

```
'
'Test the "New" menu item, respond "no".
'

'Write out information about test to be performed
print "Test #1: 'New' with text. Select 'No'."

'Make sure there's text in the Notepad window.
WEditSetText("@1","")   'Clears out the contents of editor
play "Now is the time for all good..."
```

WEditSetText() requires two parameters. The first identifies the edit control we're working with. In our example, we use an *ordinal* ("@1") to identify the first and only edit control found in the main window of Notepad. The second parameter identifies the text to be placed in the control. By passing a *null* string (such as ""), we effectively clear the contents of the window, allowing us to place our own sample text into the editor. In this case, our test string is "Now is the time for all good . . . " Figure 7-1 shows Notepad being tested.

Figure 7-1: In initializing this test, we cleared any existing text from the Notepad editor and then placed new text into that editor using the Play statement.

We begin the first test by selecting the New menu item from the File menu. This is to verify that when we say "No" to save changes, the text is indeed cleared out of the editor's main window. We do it with the wMenuSelect statement. Because we've entered new text into Notepad, we're prompted to save changes. Listing 7-2 shows how we work with this situation.

Listing 7-2: Selecting the New menu item and handling the Save Changes? message box

```
'Select the "New" menu item
   WMenuSelect("File\New")

   If (GetText(NULL) = "Notepad") then '"Save Changes" DB?

       WButtonClick("No")                  'No, don't save changes

       'Notepad's main window is a big edit control.
       'We can give it the focus and check text, put text,

       'etc. just like any other edit control. We use "@1"

       'since it is the first and only edit control.
       If (EditText("@1") <> "") then
           'Write out error information: what went wrong?
           print "***Error: 'New' didn't clear window " + _
               "contents."
           print "Expected: <empty-window>"
           print "Received: "+EditText("@1")
           print
       EndIf
   Else
       'Write out error information: what went wrong?
       print "***Error: 'New' with text didn't display "+ _
           "the 'Are you sure?' message box."
```

(continued)

Listing 7-2 *(continued)*

```
        print "Expected: Notepad"
        print "Received: "+GetText(NULL)
        print
    EndIf
```

We use the `wButtonClick` statement to click the No button. Immediately afterward, we employ the `EditText` function to determine exactly whether any text is in the main window. If there is still text in it, something has gone wrong. Clicking No to save changes after selecting the New menu item should have cleared the contents of the window.

In the event that text is left over that shouldn't have been, the section of script that prints out an error message to the Viewport is executed.

If the Save Changes? message box wasn't found in the first place, all the source code for this test would be skipped and an error message would be printed to inform us of the problem.

Test Two

The second test begins on the assumption that the first test finished cleanly and that whether the test passed or failed, the error was handled:

```
'
'Test the "New" menu item, respond "Yes".
'
print "Test #2: 'New' with text. Select 'Yes'."
play "Now is the time for all good..."
strText = EditText("@1")    'Get editor's contents.
WMenuSelect("File\New")
```

A new text string is added to Notepad to set the editor's *dirty bit* so that, when the New menu item is selected, it verifies whether or not changes should be saved. For this test the contents of the editor are grabbed and saved in a variable called `strText`. This way, we can click Yes on the message box and verify later that the text remains unchanged. This can be seen in Listing 7-3.

Listing 7-3: **Verifying that the Save Changes? message box is displayed. If not, an error exists.**

```
'Because there is unsaved text, the 'Save changes/Are you sure?
'message box should be displayed.
If (GetText(NULL) = "Notepad") then
    WButtonClick("Yes")
    If (GetText(NULL) = "Save As") then
        WButtonClick("Cancel")
    Else
        print "***Error: 'New' with 'Yes, save changes' "+ _
            "didn't display SaveAs DB."
        print "Expected: Save As"
        print "Received: "+GetText(NULL)
        print
    EndIf
Else
    print "***Error: 'New' with text didn't display "+ _
        "the 'Are you sure?' message box."
    print "Expected: Notepad"
    print "Received: "+GetText(NULL)
    print
EndIf
```

The GetText function is used to determine the caption of the currently active window. It turns out that the expected message box has the same caption as the main application: "Notepad" (without the leading hyphen, in this case). If the message box isn't displayed as expected, the Else branch of the statement is exercised and an error message is printed to the Viewport.

Most likely, the message box will be displayed as expected and we can successfully click the Yes button. The application will then display the Save As dialog box prompting the user to type in a filename (see Figure 7-2).

Figure 7-2: The Save As dialog box is displayed when our script clicks the Yes button in the Save Changes? message box.

Caution   Windows NT users using a version prior to 4.0 or 5.0 of Windows NT will find that a script that does click the Save button, shown in Figure 7-2, will need to be modified to click the OK button instead. Windows NT 4.0 and 5.0 eliminate this problem, since they have UIs similar to Windows 95 and 98.

Because my intent was only to see what happened when we selected New from the File menu and clicked Yes as one of the three options in the Save Changes? message box, it's not my intention to use the Save As dialog box at this time. Therefore, I clicked the Cancel button in the dialog box instead.

Tip   If the Save As dialog box, shown in Figure 7-2, hadn't appeared in the last piece of code, the matching `Else` branch of the `If` statement that checked to see whether the dialog box appeared would be executed. This would cause an error message telling us that the dialog box didn't appear as expected.

The last part of our program is designed to verify that, after doing everything — clicking Yes to save changes, displaying the Save As dialog box, and then canceling out of that dialog box to return to the main window — our text remains unchanged:

```
If (strText <> EditText("@1")) then
    print "***Error: Cancel out of SaveAs after 'New' "+ _
          "caused text change."
    print "Expected: "+strText
    print "Received: "+EditText("@1")
    print
EndIf
```

So it seems that a number of tests were actually going on in our second test. First, we checked to make sure the Save Changes? message box was displayed. It was, so we moved on from there to see whether or not the Save As dialog box appeared as expected. We chose to stop there and return to Notepad's main window and verify that the text in the editor when the test began was still there and unchanged.

The Reality of Automation

An unfortunate reality of test automation programming is that all error conditions need to be checked. That is, if you expect a dialog box to appear, you should enter the necessary code to verify whether or not it did appear. Otherwise, if an expected window or dialog box doesn't appear, the script will continue to execute, most likely on an unintended section of the program. This can result in many errors being reported that don't actually exist, simply because the script is trying to run itself in the wrong context. Remember that test automation is its own separate development project and that it takes time to write, maintain, and constantly improve the scripts.

So why did Test Two only get counted as one test? Because that was the style I chose to follow. I had one main objective that I wanted to achieve: verifying that the Yes button worked and didn't change my editor's text. Some testers would have printed out the subtests that resulted (perhaps as Test 2.1, Test 2.2, and so on). It just depends on how you and your team choose to go about testing; there's no one right way to do it. The trick is to pick a method and move forward.

On the CD-ROM

There are many theories about how to effectively provide good test coverage. The scope of this book is to show you *how* to use Visual Test; it is not to go in detail on the different test coverage theories. I recommend you look at a book by Dr. Cem Kaner called *Testing Computer Software*, and also check out books by Boris Beizer. You might also read some of the articles provided by ST Labs, Inc., which are found on this book's CD-ROM.

Test Three

The final test, shown in Listing 7-4, is similar to Test Two. It too verifies that the text in the editor is unchanged after the tests have completed:

Listing 7-4: The third and final test in our example of checking the Save Changes? message box

```
'
'Test the "New" menu item, respond "Cancel".
'
print "Test #3: 'New' with text. Select 'Cancel'."
strText = EditText("@1")
WMenuSelect("File\New")

'Because there is unsaved text, the Save changes/Are you sure?
```

(continued)

Listing 7-4 *(continued)*

```
'message box should be displayed.
If (GetText(NULL) = "Notepad") then
    WButtonClick("Cancel")
Else
    print "***Error: 'New' with text didn't display the "+ _
         "'Are you sure?' message box."
    print "Expected: Notepad"
    print "Received: "+GetText(NULL)
    print
EndIf
'If the text changed even though cancel was used,
'an error occurred.
If (strText <> EditText("@1")) then
    print "***Error: Cancel out of 'New' caused text change."
    print "Expected: "+strText
    print "Received: "+EditText("@1")
    print
EndIf
```

This test verifies that the last of the three buttons works when selecting New from the File menu, when there is unsaved text in the editor.

As a matter of style, one of the things I like to include in my error messages — you've probably noticed it already — is the *expected* and *received* information. In addition to the actual error, I like to print out what the expected results of the tests are, and then what the actual results were that caused the error to occur. The final output found in the Viewport at the completion of the test script can be seen in Figure 7-3.

Figure 7-3: Output found in the Viewport at the completion of the sample test script

The Clean-Up

The last section of the sample script focuses on printing out final information and returning the application that was being tested to a known state:

```
print
print "*** Tests completed."

WMenuSelect("File\Exit")        'Exit the Notepad application
WButtonClick("No")              '"No" to "Save changes?"
END
```

In this case, we shut down Notepad. In other situations you might choose to have Notepad stay up and the contents cleared from its main window, so that the next test case that runs starts from a clean state. Shutting down the application is one way of achieving this. Your team will need to decide which it prefers. If you really want to keep things flexible, then you might consider using an .INI file or a Registry setting to control how your scripts execute. We look at some examples of this later in this book.

Summary

This first script should have given you some ideas on how to begin your automation testing. The key message I want you to take with you when you walk away from this chapter is that you need to just go ahead, dive in, and start writing code. Follow this script as an example as you begin writing your tests; meanwhile, keep in mind that there isn't any one way to automate something, so be open to experimentation.

In the next chapters, we get into writing more flexible scripts so that when the inevitable need for changes arises, you'll take less of a hit when it comes to revamping your scripts.

✦   ✦   ✦

Building a Test Suite

Common Coding Guidelines

Whenever a group of people engage in any given project, they bring all kinds of styles to the table. These styles apply to anything from ways to manage people, to how to draft a document, to how to program a piece of code.

This chapter's purpose is to give you some suggestions on standards that you may want to consider applying to your automation project. They are only suggestions and a starting point for those new to writing any kind of code. They are part of my style but are in no way the definitive way to do things. If you don't have your own style yet, however, they are a very good place to start.

When working on a project where more than one person is writing code, it is very important to define up front what types of standards or conventions are to be followed. You will appreciate the importance of this even more as common code is written that is shared between individuals on the team. It's also helpful to have a common style defined, so that when it becomes necessary to enter someone else's code, you'll have an idea of which file to look in and in which section of that file to find whatever problem exists.

This is such an important concept that many companies have their own document (many times simply titled *Common Coding Guidelines*) on coding practices to be followed by all of the programmers on the development team. This type of document is just as important when writing test scripts because these are code and can be just as complex as the source code that makes up the product you are testing. I suggest you ask around to see if any such document exists at your company, so that you can take it and tailor it to your automation team's needs.

By sitting down and building consensus among all of the testers who will be writing and maintaining the automated scripts, you can avoid many problems down the road. It is here that everyone's experiences and styles can come into play to help make a solid style that can be adhered to by everyone on the team. It's also key in getting new testers coming into a project up to speed quickly.

Coding Style

Let's take an example of a simple C program. I've been witness to a number of heated discussions between developers when it came to coding style. One such case was about where to place the curly braces ({ }) in relation to a conditional branch. For example:

An opening brace on the same line as the `if` statement:

```
if (strX == "Hello") {
    printf("Hello World!");
}
```

An opening brace on a line by itself, lined up with the closing brace:

```
if (strX == "Hello")
{
    printf("Hello World!");
}
```

The (optional) opening or closing braces aren't used at all:

```
if (strX == "Hello")
    printf("Hello World!");
```

In the C programming language, all three of these examples do precisely the same thing. The first is typical of programmers who follow Brian W. Kernighan and Dennis M. Ritchie's book, *The C Programming Language*, to the letter. This is characteristic of the true C programmers, who many times come from the UNIX operating system world.

The second example is also used and defended because it is easy to count the opening and closing braces, especially in a particularly hairy piece of code that is made up of multiple conditional branches (such as IF, ELSE, and WHILE); it's arguably easier to read that code when the braces are aligned. And the final example is legal because there is only one line of code relating to that conditional branch.

Many programmers tend to standardize on the second example, or a variation thereof, because of the increased readability of the code. Some people go so far as to advocate having the braces, even around a single line of code for that conditional branch. The reasoning for this is that, should it become necessary to add another line of code to that conditional branch, the braces are already in place and it lowers the odds that the developer will forget to add them, were they not already there. For example, if we add a line of code to the `if` statement (braces are forgotten):

```
if (strX == "Hello")
    printf("Hello World!");
    printf("How are you today?");
```

Here, the second `printf` is indented, but in fact it falls outside the `if` statement and will be executed every single time, which was not the intent of the programmer. To fix it, the braces would need to be added around both lines. The corrected code for the last example should be:

```
if (strX == "Hello")
{
    printf("Hello World!");
    printf("How are you today?");
}
```

When you're in a hurry to find an error in your code and you throw fatigue and stress into the mix, this is the type of error that will stare you in the face for a while, before you finally track it down.

Here's a list of some of the areas that are part of the topic of coding style. We discuss each of these in turn. They are

- ✦ Comments for yourself and others
- ✦ Templates for defining a style for others to follow
- ✦ Variable and function naming conventions
- ✦ Uses and abuses of unconditional branching
- ✦ Source code file types and what source code goes where
- ✦ The idea of a file hierarchy for sharing source code
- ✦ Encapsulation of common sections of code
- ✦ Creation of *wrapper* functions for future flexibility

Comments

A *comment* is information found in a source code file that exists solely for the benefit of the programmer. When a piece of code is compiled into a form usable by the computer and unreadable to an average programmer, the comments are stripped, since they serve no purpose in the final form of that file (in other words, the file is in a form preferable to a computer, not a human).

The use of comments varies and depends on the style of each programmer. I've been through code that is completely uncommented, and I've been through other code that has a comment on each and every line of the source code file. Neither extreme is preferable; it's up to you and/or your team to decide to what degree a file should be commented.

There are two main reasons why anyone comments code. The first is for yourself, so that when you return to a section of code later, sometimes months or years after you wrote it originally, you can understand the code more quickly than you would had the comments not been included. I can recall situations in college where I was up all night banging out some final code on a project that was due the next day. I'd take a two-hour nap and come back later only to try to figure out what the heck I'd done. Sometimes my code would be really well thought out and I was impressed as to how much I was in the groove when I was writing it. Other times (these were more common) I'd come back and try to figure out why I'd written it a certain way when it was now obvious that there was a much easier way to do it. Had I included comments, which would have explained my reasoning at the time of writing the particular section of code, I would have saved myself time and realized what I was thinking at the time of its writing.

The other reason for using comments is for other people. If you write routines that are useful to your team and therefore the company for which you work, most likely your routines will outlive the job position you're in. That is to say, you might move on to other groups or higher positions, and your code will stay behind. When someone else is supposed to pick up where you left off, or see if they can cut and paste helpful sections of your code into their code, it's easier for them to do this if there are clear comments describing how things are set up and what they do.

Another time that others would be looking at your code is when you are on a team and sharing that code. For example, if you've created a utility that is helpful and generic enough for others to use, then you'll want to share it and cut down on the support time you'd otherwise have to provide, by having plenty of comments describing how to use the routine.

When I was at Asymetrix Corporation (now Asymetrix Learning Systems), I came across a section of code that had what some people refer to as a *magic number* or *magic cookie*. It's referred to this way because the number simply exists in the code but no one, sometimes not even the original programmer, remembers how they arrived at that number. Therefore, it's a magic number. When I went to the programmer to ask him how he came up with it, he couldn't remember. He had to sit down with pencil and paper again to figure out how he came up with it to make his routine work. This is an example of a perfect place where a comment would be added to the source code. Had the programmer placed a comment describing how the number was derived, I wouldn't have had to track him down and then get him to work through the formulas again.

In Rational Visual Test, a comment is any line that has, as the first item on that text line, the letters REM or the single quote ('). REM is short for *remark,* and the single quote is an abbreviation for the REM designator. The following code shows an example of a function that has some comments in it:

```
function tnSaveFile(tnstrDir$, tnstrFilter$) as STRING
   dim ofnFile as OPENFILENAME
   dim strFileChoice as STRING * TN_MAXPATH
   dim ret%

   tnCmnGetSaveOps (ofnFile, (tnstrDir), (tnstrFilter))
   ofnFile.lpstrFile = cptr(varptr(strFileChoice))    'Info
buffer
   ofnFile.nMaxFile  = LEN(strFileChoice)             'Size of
buffer
   ofnFile.Flags     = OFN_OVERWRITEPROMPT OR _       'Warn if
exists
                       OFN_HIDEREADONLY   OR  _       'No Chkbox
                       OFN_PATHMUSTEXIST              'Warn: bad
path
   'Pass the struct on to the routine for final
   'processing and return a legal filename or
   'an empty string.

   if GetSaveFileName(ofnFile) then                   'Get file info
      tnSaveFile = trim$(trim$(strFileChoice,0))      'Return file
info
   else
      tnSaveFile = ""                                 'Return empty
string
   endif
end function 'tnSaveFile
```

My style is to put my comment on the same line as the code, if it will fit. Otherwise, I put comments just above the code, so that the person reading through the list understands what the next section of code is about to do.

I even go so far as to have a comment right after the end of the function block. That is, END FUNCTION 'tnSaveFile. I do this so that, if the function grows into something larger than it currently is, it'll be easier to tell when it ends. Otherwise, if my code has `END FUNCTION` a bunch of times, you have to scroll back up through the code to find the beginning of the function to figure out which function block you're looking at.

I admit that I'm a commenting fool. I'd rather take the time to comment my stuff so that it helps others than to have them throw my old code away because it was uncommented. Don't worry about making it pretty by lining things up, just make sure you have some kind of comments in your code, so that others will have an easier time deciphering your work.

Templates

Templates play a big role in setting up the style you want everyone on the team to follow. A template takes much of what the team has agreed upon and lays it out in a format to be used by everyone. Much of a template is made up of commented information (see Listing 8-1).

A sample include file template

There are two main source code file types in Visual Test. The first is the *include file* (.INC file extension), and the second is the *test case file* (.MST file extension). Include files and their uses are described more thoroughly when we look at the test case files next. Listing 8-1 is a sample template that might be used by a test automation team.

On the CD-ROM

This source code and all other source code found in this book have been placed on this book's CD-ROM.

Listing 8-1: A template for a typical include file

```
'********************** <filename.inc> **********************
'*
'* Purpose:
'*
'* Author:
'*
'* Revision History:
'*
'* [ 0]  da-mon-year   email  : action
'*
'**************************************************************

'$IFNDEF <AREA>_INCLUDED
'$DEFINE <AREA>_INCLUDED


'**************************************************************
```

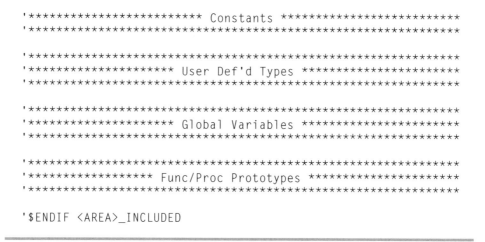

```
'************************** Constants ************************
'**********************************************************

'**********************************************************
'******************* User Def'd Types *******************
'**********************************************************

'**********************************************************
'******************* Global Variables *******************
'**********************************************************

'**********************************************************
'***************** Func/Proc Prototypes ******************
'**********************************************************

'$ENDIF <AREA>_INCLUDED
```

A sample template is shown in this listing. Six sections make up this template example.

The main comment block

The first section is the front comment block that describes what the file is to be used for and provides any special instructions on how to use that file. For example: Does it rely on other files being included already? Is it a standalone file that doesn't need to be included with anything else? Are separate data files required to be in particular directories?

This section also displays the name of the person who wrote the file. Having the name of the person handy makes it easier to track down whomever you need to answer any pressing questions about the use of the file.

And finally, the last section of the first block is the *Revision* section. This section's purpose is to provide information about the changes made to the file over its lifetime. Some people consider this "Big Brother"–ish, but the fact is that it makes it easier to resolve problems if another person should make changes to the file. What appears to be a simple change could in fact break other sections of the code base downstream. In the event that a situation like this occurs, the person who made the change can be contacted so that the situation can be resolved to everyone's benefit.

Conditional compilation

The next section of the template is in place to help save time tracking down problems.

The '$IFNDEF statement checks to see if the file has already been included. Say, for example, there is a file that contains common declarations for the entire project — perhaps a constant that holds the caption of the main window of the application being tested. Instead of having that constant defined for every test file that exists in your suite, it would be moved up to a common include file that everyone can add to their test files by using the '$INCLUDE metacommand. The result is, you only have to go to one file to make changes, instead of visiting multiple files.

In the event that there are more common files that rely on yet other common files, things can turn messy in a hurry. One common compilation error that occurs in any language is a *redeclaration error,* which is the compiler's way of saying, "Hey, you've already got a variable, function, or whatever named this!" If an include file — sometimes referred to as a header file — is accidentally included multiple times, this is typically the error that is encountered.

The conditional compilation is a way to avoid this error. True, it allows the testing team to be a little sloppier in their programming (because it won't complain if a file is included multiple times), but it saves time and avoids the nightmare of having to track down exactly which file is including another file a second time.

Here's how it works: When a test file is run, it needs to compile all the source code into a form understandable by the Visual Test interpreter. Some of these files are "including" information from other files, for reasons previously mentioned (that is, sharing common declarations instead of having multiple declarations for the same thing scattered throughout).

What's really going on underneath is that the *pre-compiler* is assembling all the files into one big file to be checked for syntax, and then compiled to its tokenized form (commonly referred to as *pseudocode*). When a '$INCLUDE metacommand is encountered, the contents of the file it references are inserted at the location of that '$INCLUDE command. The result: one big file that the compiler can finally crunch into pseudocode.

When a file is included a second time, the redeclaration error is usually encountered. This is where the conditional compilation comes in handy. The '$IFNDEF (if not defined) command checks to see if a particular *symbol* has already been defined. Now, in this case, a symbol can be any string or word. Visual Test's defined symbols don't hold an assigned value. Instead, the symbol is placed into a table letting the compiler know that it has been defined. The first time the pre-compiler brings in the file that contains the '$IFNDEF command, it checks to see if the symbol it refers to has been defined or not.

If it is the first time the file is being included, then most likely the symbol hasn't been defined (unless someone else is already using a symbol of the same name in some source code that you've included). The compiler then moves to the next line because the '$IFNDEF evaluates to true, since that particular symbol isn't yet defined.

So referring back to Listing 8-1, the next line is '$DEFINE. This is where the symbol is actually defined and then all the rest of the lines below it are included.

Let's look at this from another angle: the second time the file is included. The symbol has already been defined. When the '$IFNDEF metacommand is encountered, it finds that out. The result is just like any other if not() conditional branch: It doesn't enter that section of code. Instead, it drops out to the '$ENDIF command at the bottom of the file. As a result, the declarations in that file are totally skipped and any redeclaration error messages are avoided.

It turns out that, in Visual Test 4.0, Microsoft put in a check to make things easier for us. It decided that, if the constant, variable, or whatever has already been declared, the compiler doesn't care if the file is included for a second time, as long as the type (for example, INTEGER or STRING) or value hasn't changed. The reason this is being brought up in this book is that the redeclaration errors can still be encountered in Rational Visual Test 6.0, especially if your code is written to work with Microsoft Test 3.0 for 16-bit application testing (because Test 3.0 will still complain when a file is included more than once).

Constants

The next section in the template shown in Listing 8-1 is where *constants* are placed. Constants are basically variables that have values that never change and will cause an error to be generated if an attempt is made during the running of the script (*run time*) to change a constant's value. This protects us as Test programmers from accidentally modifying a value that should never change (the example used previously is the caption of the main window of the application whose testing is being automated). In the event the value does need to change while the script is running, then it shouldn't be a constant.

Using a constant throughout an entire code base makes it easy to change a value without having to edit multiple files because of the change. Let's say we're testing a program and the caption being used is "Notepad." Then, one day, someone decides it needs to be "Notepad -" with a hyphen, so that the name of the file currently being viewed can be appended to that name. Consider having 20 test case files that test the application and having to search through each of those files looking for and replacing every instance of "Notepad" with "Notepad -"! That's why you want to use constants, and be comfortable in the knowledge that the value can't be changed, except at the one place in which that value is declared. Making the change in one place — where it is declared — propagates that change to whatever script is using that constant.

Declaration Placement

Placement of declarations is critical when declaring constants, variables, and user-defined types. Visual Test uses what is known as a *one-pass compiler*. This means that it goes through a file one time as it does its compilation, usually from top to bottom. If it encounters a reference to something that has not yet been declared, a compiler error is encountered. If you used a constant when declaring a user-defined type, but it was declared lower in the file, you will encounter a sequence of errors similar to this:

```
Error VTC4317: Constant expression expected before 'mytype'
Error VTC4308: '<end of line>' expected before 'type'
```

These two errors were given simply because the declaration wasn't placed properly.

A rule of thumb for using constants is that, whenever a value is used more than once, and it's a value that shouldn't change during the running of the script, you should turn it into a constant. Not all constants necessarily go into one overall include file placed at the top of the shared file hierarchy (more on the hierarchy later). They might be placed down in the hierarchy near the test file that is using it, if that is the only place it is used. Otherwise, if a value is used only once, type that actual value into the program (this is known as a *literal*) and place comments next to it explaining how the value was derived, if it's not obvious already. (Remember, however, what may be obvious to you and your fellow Test programmers may not be obvious to those who later inherit your code.)

The names of constants usually appear in uppercase letters so that it is easy to determine what is a constant and what is a variable. The Visual Test editor and compiler are *not* case-sensitive, so even if the programmer declares a constant using uppercase letters, it can be referred to in lowercase. Thus, it's up to the Test programmers on the team to adhere to the style, even though Visual Test allows for sloppiness.

User-defined types

A *user-defined type* is a type not common enough to have already been defined in the programming language. An INTEGER is a basic type that shows up in all languages. If it's preferable to have all of the information about a test kept in one variable, or in an array, for example, it is then that a user-defined type needs to be used. Once that type has been declared by a Test programmer, a variable of that type can be declared and used for tracking the information about a test or whatever that programmer has decided to track. (See Chapter 5 to learn how to declare a user-defined type.)

Because constants can be used to make up a user-defined type, the section where constants are declared is above the area for the declarations of user-defined types.

Global variables

A *global variable* is a variable that is available, or *in scope*, every place in the test script. Unlike in the C language, where a global variable's scope can be limited to a particular file, in the Test language it is global no matter where you are in the overall code base, as long as the file is included directly or indirectly by the test case file. This is true, for example, wherever in a subroutine or function the global variable can be referenced and changed. (This is the same for constants, except constants' values can't be changed.)

Global variables should be used sparingly. It is usually considered poor programming style when they are overused. There are a number of reasons for this, one of the more important being that of dependencies. If a test suite is broken up into many parts to keep it modular, that modularity is undermined if it has to depend on a global variable declared someplace else. When possible, use variables that are local to the piece of code using that value.

The other reason not to use global variables is because they take up more memory. Local variables allocate memory only when they are being used. For example, memory is allocated for a local variable declared in a given function only when that function is being executed. At the end of its execution, its locally declared variable is freed from memory.

Sometimes, however, a global variable is the only way to go because the information stored in it is used by everyone. At other times, speed is a factor and avoiding the (albeit small) amount of time for allowing the interpreter to allocate the memory for a local variable saves crucial time. This is more the exception than the norm, however.

An example of a variable that you might consider keeping as a global would be a running counter that keeps track of the number of errors that have occurred during the running of your tests.

Function and subroutine prototypes

Known both as a *forward declaration* and a *prototype*, the act of declaring a function or subroutine and the values it uses is necessary to keep your code compatible with version 3.0 of Test. Just as a constant or user-defined type can't be used before it's declared, the same goes for a function or subroutine.

If the function Foo is declared first, and in that function it calls another function Bar, declared further down in the source code, compilation errors will result when that code is compiled under versions of Test previous to 4.0. However, versions 4.0 and 6.0 let you get away with more, and it is no longer necessary to prototype a function or subroutine, except when referring to functions stored in dynamic linked libraries (DLLs).

Caution   In Rational Visual Test 6.0, if a function Foo is defined and calls a function Bar that occurs lower in the code base, it will find Bar and run as expected. This isn't the case for older versions of Microsoft Test (versions 1.0 through 3.0). Keep this in mind if you intend to use your scripts in both Rational Visual Test 6.0 and older versions of Microsoft Test (you'd only use these older versions if you are still testing 16-bit applications).

A typical test case file template

A simple test case file was shown to you in Chapter 7. However, in order to offer clear demonstration of a test case file, it didn't use some of the common coding guidelines (such as constants). Listing 8-2 is an example of a template that might be used by a test automation team.

Listing 8-2: A template for a typical test case file

```
'***************************************************************
*
'* Filename:
'*
'* Purpose:
'*
'* Revision History:
'*
'*  [ 0]   da-mon-year     email   : action
'*
'***************************************************************
*
'*********************** INCLUDES
****************************
'$include '<>.inc'  'Bring in your consts, prototypes, macros,
...

'****************** GLOBALS INITIALIZED
***********************

'********************** Main Tests
****************************

'************* Your functions & subroutines
********************

'***************************************************************
*
'* Subroutine:  <name>
'* Purpose:
'*
'* Parameters:
```

```
'*
'****************************************************************
*

'****************************************************************
*
'* Function:     <name>
'* Purpose:
'*
'* Parameters:
'*
'* Returns:
'*
'****************************************************************
*
```

Naming Conventions

My first programming experience was on my Apple II Plus computer, back in 1982. I followed the tutorial that came with it and also bought a couple of books that had some games for the TRS-80 computer, which I had to convert to Applesoft Basic.

The variable names used in those days, and even today, were simple and didn't necessarily convey much information. For example, some programmers would start naming variables by working their way down the alphabet. The result was single-character epithets that didn't mean anything to someone looking through a printout of the program, unless they familiarized themselves with where they were declared and how they were used. Others would come up with slightly longer (two- or three-character) names for their variables, which attempted to give some kind of hint as to their use. In the end, it became a detective game to track down where the variable was used, to determine what type of value it held, and to understand its purpose.

Then along came a Microsoft developer who wrote his thesis on a naming convention that was termed the *Hungarian Notation*. This naming convention is now used by Microsoft and almost all developers who write applications for Microsoft Windows. It's a convention you might want to add to your *Common Coding Guidelines* document.

It's a fairly simple concept that became necessary as more powerful programming languages became available. Imagine being able to look at a piece of code and, without searching for the place it was declared, knowing what type of value that variable held. This is the idea.

The best way to explain the Hungarian Notation is to show you some examples. Table 8-1 gives a list.

Table 8-1: Sample Variables Following the Hungarian Notation Naming Convention.	
Variable	*How Declared in Visual Test*
strDescription	strDescription AS STRING
iDescription	iDescription AS INTEGER
iCount	iCount AS INTEGER
lTimer	lTimer AS LONG
pstrTestType	pstrTestType AS POINTER TO STRING * 10
rectWindow	rectWindow AS RECT
strfParse	FUNCTION strfParse (strX AS STRING) AS STRING

The first variable in Table 8-1 hints to the casual observer that it holds a description of some kind, and that the description is of type STRING. The second variable is also a description of some kind, but its type is an INTEGER. Perhaps it is an index into an array of strings? Unfortunately, to figure this out we'd need to dig deeper into the code; we can't tell from the name alone, but at least we have an idea.

The next two variables, iCount and lTimer, are an INTEGER and a LONG, respectively. iCount is most likely an index into a FOR-NEXT loop or a counter used within a WHILE loop. And lTimer is perhaps used to keep track of a clock's time for benchmarking purposes. Since some functions dealing with a computer's clock return the number of seconds since the computer was turned on, this is typically a large number requiring a LONG (four-byte) variable.

In the case of rectWindow, this is a situation where a standard type hasn't been used. Instead, a user-defined type has been created and a variable declared of that type. The RECT type is standard to Visual Test and is used to define the boundaries of a rectangular region (such as a window). In this example, it's most likely used to track the dimensions of a window, perhaps to verify that it is displayed at the appropriate size.

When it comes to naming conventions for functions, some programmers go to the level of including the return type of that function as part of its name. In the case of `strfParse`, this is a function that supposedly performs some kind of parsing on a value passed to it. That function then returns a `STRING` to the line of code that called the function. In the example, the `f` implies it is a function and not a typical variable. The `str` implies that the value returned by the function is of type `STRING`.

These examples should give you an idea of how helpful naming conventions can be. Whether you use Hungarian Notation or not, always keep in mind that you need to create descriptive variable names both for yourself and for anyone who eventually inherits your source code.

Unconditional Branching

Computer Science classes often downplay the idea of using a `GOTO` statement when programming. This is for a good reason; a `GOTO` is an *unconditional branch* that leads to *spaghetti code* and shows very poor programming practices. I stuck to this philosophy, and I still do to this day. I avoid `GOTO`s like the plague. However, I know of at least one computer company that allows for them in their Common Coding Guidelines document, but only for certain situations. And it turns out that these are, in fact, reasonable situations.

Immediate exiting

One situation in which the company allows and even encourages the use of `GOTO`s is when you're working in a deeply embedded conditional structure and you need to exit that structure immediately (for example, if an unrecoverable error occurs).

In this case, there is a section of code at the end of the function that the programmer can jump to using a `GOTO` and thus making a quick, clean exit. But the company has strict rules for when this is allowed:

1. First and foremost, avoid `GOTO`s if at all possible.

2. The `GOTO` must always jump down/forward in the code. This helps avoid endless loops and spaghetti code.

3. The section of code jumped to should be at the end of the routine containing the `GOTO`.

4. It is preferable that this section of code is always passed through when exiting the routine, whether the `GOTO` was used or not. This way, all clean-up code can be kept in one place for a given function.

ON ERROR GOTO

Other than this rare case, you normally avoid using this type of branching. However, Visual Test does have at least one circumstance where you have no choice, and that's when using the `ON ERROR GOTO` command. We get into this more when we discuss run-time errors in Chapter 13.

Test Language Source Code File Types

Two main source code file types are used in Rational Visual Test. These are standards, or conventions, that are encouraged but don't necessarily have to be adhered to. The source code files are simple text files, and the extension associated with these files used to be inconsequential. While it is still possible to make up your own file types by using a different three-letter extension (in lieu of .INC or .MST), the Microsoft Developer Studio 6.0 editor used by Rational Visual Test 6.0 may require you to take extra steps in doing so. And if you do decide to make up and use different file types for your source code, common guidelines need to be agreed upon and followed — or hopeless confusion will result.

Include files

As explained in a previous chapter, an *include* or *header file* is a text file that contains source code depended upon by another file to make itself complete. Usually it contains either generic, reusable information that is placed into a separate file so that other files can include it too, or it contains a bunch of the up-front declarations for the main test case file that are moved into the separate include file to help cut down on clutter, making the test case file more readable.

In Rational Visual Test, include files have .INC as their file extension. It's worth noting that include files are only text, and even though the standard is to use .INC as the file extension, any three-letter extension can be used.

Versions 1.0 to 3.0 of Microsoft Test used MSTEST.INC to include function and subroutine prototypes that linked into the DLLs that accompanied the product, constants to be used with the different functions, macros, and global variable declarations. It was included just as any other include file is incorporated into a test case file, by using the '$INCLUDE metacommand:

```
'$include 'mstest.inc'
```

Customarily, declarations for constants, macros, and function and subroutine prototypes for linking into DLLs go into an include file. Sometimes, reusable functions and subroutines (the actual definition code that controls the behavior of the routine, not just the declaration prototypes) are included as well.

Frequently, more than one include file is used in a test automation project. Listing 8-3 is an example of an include file that contains declarations common enough to be used by everyone on the testing team. Specifically, this file is for a test suite that tests sections of the Microsoft Windows Notepad program. Later we'll see include files specific to individual areas of the Notepad program that is being tested.

Listing 8-3: **NOTEMAIN.INC: The main include file that holds common declarations used throughout the notepad test suite**

```
'*********************** NOTEMAIN.INC ***********************
'*
'* PURPOSE: All decls global to all Notepad tests and utils.
'*
'****************************************************************

'$ifndef NOTEMAIN_INCLUDED  'If NOTEMAIN.INC hasn't been
included,
'$define NOTEMAIN_INCLUDED  'include it and define a symbol to
make
                            'sure it doesn't get brought in
again.
                            '(This avoids redeclaration errors)


'****************************************************************
'*********************** CONSTANTS ***********************
'****************************************************************

'*************** Name of Application Being Tested ***********
const APP_TARGET$   = "Notepad.exe"
const MAINWINDOW$   = "@1"  'Notepad editor window

'***************** Name of Temporary Files *****************
const TEMPFILE1$    = "TEMP1.TXT"
const TEMPFILE2$    = "TEMP2.TXT"

'****************** Test Data String *******************
const TEST_DATA1$   = "Now is the time for all good people."
const TEST_DATA2$   = "We, the people of the United States."

'Test_Data3 is a long string of text of word wrapping tests.
const TEST_DATA3$   = "Congress shall make no law respecting "
+ _
                      "an establishment of religion, or "
+ _
                      "prohibiting the free exercise thereof;"
+ _
                      " or abridging the freedom of speech, "
+ _
                      "or of the press..."

'*********************** Captions ***************************
```

(continued)

Listing 8-3 *(continued)*

```
const CAP_TARGETAPP$ = "Notepad"   'Main title bar & gen. msg
boxes

'********************** Button Captions **********************
const BTN_NO$         = "No"
const BTN_YES$        = "Yes"
const BTN_OK$         = "Ok"
const BTN_CANCEL$     = "Cancel"
const BTN_SAVE$       = "Save"
const BTN_OPEN$       = "Open"

'********************** Menu Bar Constants *******************
'***** File Menu
const MNU_FILE_NEW$        = "File\New"
const MNU_FILE_OPEN$       = "File\Open..."
const MNU_FILE_SAVE$       = "File\Save"
const MNU_FILE_SAVEAS$     = "File\Save As..."
const MNU_FILE_PRINT$      = "File\Print"
const MNU_FILE_PAGESETUP$  = "File\Page Setup..."
const MNU_FILE_PRINTSETUP$ = "File\Print Setup..."
const MNU_FILE_EXIT$       = "File\Exit"

'***** Edit Menu
const MNU_EDIT_UNDO$       = "Edit\Undo"
const MNU_EDIT_CUT$        = "Edit\Cut"
const MNU_EDIT_COPY$       = "Edit\Copy"
const MNU_EDIT_PASTE$      = "Edit\Paste"
const MNU_EDIT_DELETE$     = "Edit\Delete"
const MNU_EDIT_SELECTALL$  = "Edit\Select All"
const MNU_EDIT_TIMEDATE$   = "Edit\Time/Date"
const MNU_EDIT_WORDWRAP$   = "Edit\Word Wrap"

'***** Search Menu
const MNU_SEARCH_FIND$     = "Search\Find..."
const MNU_SEARCH_FINDNEXT$ = "Search\Find Next"

'***** Help Menu
const MNU_HELP_TOPICS$     = "Help\Help Topics"
const MNU_HELP_ABOUT$      = "Help\About Notepad"

'***********************************************************
'********************** User Def'd Types *******************
'***********************************************************


'***********************************************************
'********************** Global Variables *******************
'***********************************************************
'***********************************************************
```

```
'****************** Func/Proc Prototypes ***********************
'***************************************************************

'$endif NOTEMAIN_INCLUDED
```

When looking at Listing 8-3, you'll notice that the declarations are fairly high-level. That is, they are general enough to be used by almost any test case. If, for example, a test is written for the Find... menu item, the tester will most likely need to access the Search menu. In this case the test script should use the constant `MNU_SEARCH_FIND` for the Search menu and the Find... menu item. Listing 8-4 is an example of an include file that contains less common information.

Constant Affirmation

This section reaffirms the need for using constants. In it, I mention using a constant for a menu and one of its menu items. Now, suppose that other tests use that same menu and menu item, perhaps to set up a situation for yet another test. Perhaps there's a sample data file being used to test another feature, maybe the Delete key, but it needs to search to a particular section in the text file. The Find... menu item would be used. Since it's possible that other tests will need to use this menu item, the declaration statement for this constant should be placed in a common file accessed by all of the test case files, namely NOTEMAIN.INC.

Now let's further suppose that later in the development cycle the development team decides that Locate... is a better name for that menu item. If constants were used, the testers on the automation project would only need to go to the one file, in this case NOTEMAIN.INC, and change the value of that constant. Every place in the entire automation project where that menu item was used would change to the new value.

The only time this breaks down is when someone on the team doesn't use the constant and uses a *literal* string. Not every place would get updated, and an error will occur when that tester's test file is run, because the name of the menu item has been changed. In short, use constants to make it easier to update your test scripts.

Listing 8-4 is an include file that holds less common information. Specifically, it's holding information relative to one area of the Notepad application that many test case files will rely upon. However, the rest of the files that make up the test suite for the product don't require this information.

Listing 8-4: **FILE.INC: The include file for test cases that test the File menu in Notepad**

```
'*********************** FILE.INC ***********************
'*
'* PURPOSE: Decls for the File menu tests.
'*
'*********************************************************************

'$ifndef FILE_INCLUDED
'$define FILE_INCLUDED

'*********************************************************************
'*********************** CONSTANTS ***********************
'*********************************************************************

'***** Dialog Control Names
const DCN_FILENAME$          = "File Name:"
const DCN_SPECIFICPRINTER$   = "Specific Printer:"
const DCN_OUTPUTFILENAME$    = "Output File Name:"


'***** Captions
const CAP_SAVEAS$            = "Save As"         'Save As Common
DB
const CAP_OPEN$             = "Open"            'Open Common DB
const CAP_SAVE$             = "Save"            'Save Common DB
const CAP_PRINTTOFILE$      = "Print To File"   'print to file
DB
const CAP_PAGESETUP$        = "Page Setup"      'page setup DB
const CAP_PRINTSETUP$       = "Print Setup"     'print setup DB

'***** Misc
const MAX_COUNT             = 15

'*********************************************************************
'********************* User Def'd Types ***********************
'*********************************************************************


'*********************************************************************
'********************* Global Variables ***********************
'*********************************************************************
```

```
'*************************************************************
'****************** Func/Proc Prototypes *********************
'*************************************************************

'$endif FILE_INCLUDED
```

Note   Notice that not necessarily all of the sections in the template for this include file are used. Yet the comments are left in place so that if declarations need to be added to the template later in the project, an outline or template still exists that prompts you on where to place your declarations. For example, there aren't currently any user-defined types; however, a placeholder remains in the event user-defined types are required later in the project.

Another strong reason for using include files arises when you are working on a product that is to be localized to a foreign market. If separate include files exist that hold the strings or text associated with each menu, menu item, dialog box control, window caption, and so on, the international testing teams can make copies of the files created by the domestic testing team and localize them to the foreign language on which they're testing. The result is that the actual test code stays the same; only the include files are updated with the new foreign language values for captions, menu items, and so on.

Test case files

A *test case file* is a file that contains individual testing tasks or *scenarios*. Each individual test is considered a scenario and a group of related scenarios is considered a *test case*. An example of a test case is given in Chapter 7, when we look at our first sample test script. That test case has three scenarios for testing the New menu item found under the File menu. Had we continued with that example and created test cases for the rest of the File menu and other menus in Notepad, we would have created a *test suite* composed of those test cases.

Test case files have the .MST file extension, which is recognized by the Developer Studio editor and the Suite Manager, both tools discussed in Part II. These test case files merge in the include files (.INC files) to get the declarations, common functions, and subroutines needed to complete their testing tasks. As mentioned before, this merging or inserting is done by using the '$INCLUDE metacommand.

To help clarify what goes into a .MST file and to demonstrate some of the common coding guidelines we've discussed so far, the sample test case file shown in Listing 7-1 in Chapter 7 has been placed into the template shown in Listing 8-2 (it appeared earlier in this chapter). Look at the listing that follows, and the differences between Listings 7-1 and 8-5 will then be explored.

Listing 8-5: Sample code from Listing 7-1 placed into the .MST template. NEW.MST tests the New menu item

```
'*****************************************************************
*
'* Filename: new.mst
'*
'* Purpose:  Test scenarios for the New menu item.
'*
'* Revision History:
'*
'*  [ 0]   da-mon-year     email   : action
'*  [ 1]   19-Jun-1998     TomA    : created first version
'*
'*****************************************************************
*

'********************* INCLUDES
*****************************
'$include 'notemain.inc'    'Common decls used by all test
cases
'$include 'noteutil.inc'    'Common utils used by all test
cases
'$include 'file.inc'        'Decls used by File menu test cases

'***************** GLOBALS INITIALIZED
***********************

'********************* Main Tests
*****************************
TestsBegin
    dim strText$, hwndApp&

    '
    'Test the "New" menu item, respond "no".
    '
    scenario "Test #1: 'New' with text.  Select 'No'."
        ResetApp

        'Make sure there's text in the Notepad window.
        PutString "Now is the time for all good...", 10, 10

        'Select the "New" menu item
        SelMenu(MNU_FILE_NEW)

        '"Save Changes" DB display?
        If (GetText(NULL) = "Notepad") then
            WButtonClick(BTN_NO)  'No, don't save changes
```

```
                    'Notepad's main window is a big edit control.
                    'We can give it the focus and check text, put text,
                    'etc., just like any other edit control.  We use
     "@1"
                    ' since it is the first and only edit control.
                    If (EditText("@1") <> "") then
                        'Write out error information describing
        problem.
                        LogErr "'New' didn't clear window contents.", _
                            "", EditText("@1")
                    EndIf
            Else
                'Write out error info describing what went wrong.
                LogErr "'New' with text didn't display the 'Are "+
     _
                        "you sure?' message box.", "Notepad", _
                        GetText(NULL)
            EndIf
        end scenario

        'Only the first test from Listing 7-1 is used in this
    example
    TestsEnd
```

Comparing this listing to the first version of this test in Listing 7-1 shows a number of marked differences. Let's take these one at a time.

Include files

The first difference you notice is that we are now including a number of .INC files at the top of this .MST file. The first file, NOTEMAIN.INC, provides a number of declarations for common constants that many of the test cases will be using to test Notepad. An example is the BTN_NO constant, used to click on the No button in the Save changes? message box. This is a common button caption that will most likely be used by other test cases that make up the overall test suite, and therefore it is placed in the main include file called NOTEMAIN.INC. (A full listing of NOTEMAIN.INC was shown in Listing 8-3.)

The next include file is NOTEUTIL.INC. This file contains a number of utilities that were created during the development of the test suite. As functions and subroutines were written, if they were determined to be of use to the other test case files, they were moved into this separate .INC file, so that all .MST files had access to this common code. Some of the routines contained in NOTEUTIL.INC are used by the NEW.MST file, including TestsBegin(), ResetApp(), PutString(), SelMenu(), and LogErr(). Each of these is discussed in Chapter 11. SelMenu() is discussed in the *Encapsulation* section of this chapter.

The third include file is FILE.INC. This .INC file has declarations specific to the File menu; it was shown in Listing 8-4. Since the New menu item is in the File menu, NEW.MST needs to include FILE.INC. At first it might make sense that, as an example, the `MNU_FILE_NEW` constant would be placed into the FILE.INC include file. Once more test cases are created, however, you'll find you need this menu item when testing other areas of the product. Therefore, the declaration of `MNU_FILE_NEW` is placed at the top of the file hierarchy into NOTEMAIN.INC. This arrangement can be seen in Figure 8-1.

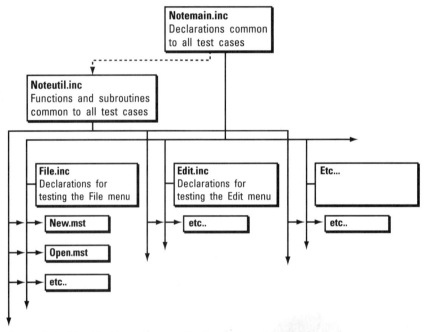

Figure 8-1: The file hierarchy used by the Notepad test suite

Reusable routines

Another difference between Listings 7-1 and 8-5 is that the latter has some routines that don't exist in the standard Test language. These were helpful enough to make available to the other test cases, so they were placed in the test suite's NOTEUTIL.INC file, so they could be shared.

Although Chapter 11 goes into more detail about the routines included in our sample suite's NOTEUTIL.INC file, to help further demonstrate the differences between Listings 7-1 and 8-5, the functionality of `TestsBegin()`, `ResetApp()`, `PutString()`, `SelMenu()`, and `TestsEnd()` — subroutines used in Listing 8-5 — are briefly described in this chapter.

As you'll recall from Chapter 7, four sections make up a test case file: declarations, initialization, tests, and clean-up. The declarations were mostly taken care of by including the separate .INC files. Any remaining variables that needed to be declared were done locally in the .MST file itself.

The initialization is carried out by the `TestsBegin()` subroutine, whose source code can be found in `NOTEUTIL.INC`. `TestsBegin()` focuses on preparing Notepad to be tested and setting up dependencies relied upon by the rest of the test case. Examples of such dependencies include opening text files to be used as logs for tests executed and allocating memory required by the tests.

`ResetApp()`, `PutString()`, and `SelMenu()` are routines that help with the third part of the test case file: test scenarios. `ResetApp()` was written to reset Notepad to a known state. It's a simple routine that selects the New menu item to clear the contents of Notepad and deals with any dialog boxes encountered during the resetting of the application (such as the Save Changes? message box). `PutString()` was constructed on the assumption that the tester might want to be able to control the column and row position of the text placed in the editor. And finally, `SelMenu()` is a *wrapper* around the Test language's `wMenuSelect` statement, allowing for more flexibility in the future (more on this in the "Wrapper" section, later in this chapter).

So, Briefly, What Goes into a .MST File?

So what really goes into a .MST file? The answer is, "Whatever you and your team decide to put into it." As I've pointed out, they are only text files with extensions to help clarify what a particular file's purpose is. If your team decides to follow Rational's conventions, then an .INC file holds declarations and reusable functions and subroutines, and a .MST file holds local declarations to that file and specific test scenarios.

Many people don't follow Rational's lead on this, however. Some with C programming backgrounds look at the .INC file as a .H file, and the .MST file as a .C file. So, what about the shared libraries that C uses (.LIB)? What's comparable to those in Visual Test?

Well, you could associate them with a .DLL file, but if you're looking at them strictly from the Visual Test point of view, such a file type doesn't exist. Rational suggests you use the .INC file for holding reusable/library routines in addition to declarations.

The limit to two source code file types in Visual Test has prompted many people to come up with their own third type of source code file that holds the sharable and reusable routines. Some people use .UTL (for utilities), others use .LIB (for libraries, but this can be confusing, especially if a C compiler is installed on the same machine), and still others figure that all executing source code (in other words, nondeclarations) should go into .MST files. As this can result in .MST files including other .MST files, it can get confusing.

(continued)

(continued)

As much as people may not agree with Rational's two-file-type approach to Test language source code, it's a style that has been suggested by the documentation for all five versions of its product and is being used by the majority of Visual Test automators today. It comes back to keeping things simple, so that those who inherit your code can understand it without too much effort. While a third type of Test language file called a .UTL is tempting, to avoid confusion it's a good idea to use Rational's approach of putting reusable code into .INC files. Plus, the Microsoft Developer Studio 6.0 editor used by Visual Test relies on there being only two file types: .MST and .INC files. Making up other types may require you to jump through extra hoops.

The last part of a test case file is clean-up. This is accomplished by the `TestsEnd()` subroutine. This returns Notepad to a known state, or perhaps even shuts the application down, depending on what the tester prefers and how the routine was written. It also does other clean-up tasks, such as closing any text files that were opened for logging of tests and freeing up any memory that might have been allocated during testing.

Constants

The last difference that you'll notice about Listing 8-5 is that it is now using constants. The value of these has already been mentioned a number of times. Remember the flexibility that constants provide — both for your team and potentially for the internationalization team — should your company choose to localize your product to foreign markets.

The File Hierarchy

Figure 8-2 shows the file hierarchy that we briefly looked at in Figure 8-1. The idea of this hierarchy is simple: Move anything that is useful to other test case files up the hierarchy so that it can be easily shared. Anything specific to a particular area of the test suite that isn't used by all of the other test cases should be moved down the hierarchy.

The theory is, why force another test case to include source code it won't use? Sometimes, however, this can't be avoided, because not all of your routines will be used by every test case file. Weigh the costs and benefits at the time. On a small project, you'll typically have a single UTIL.INC file (in this example, NOTEUTIL.INC), which is shared by all of the test cases.

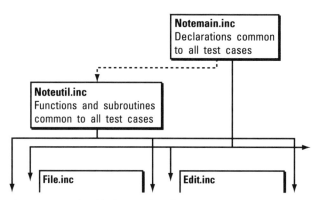

Figure 8-2: The file hierarchy allows you to move sharable source code to the top so that all files have access. The two top-level, commonly shared files are NOTEMAIN.INC and NOTEUTIL.INC.

In Figure 8-2, NOTEMAIN.INC is the main include file for the entire test suite on the Notepad editor. Anything that will most likely be needed by the majority of the test cases should be placed in this include file. Then all test case files should include NOTEMAIN.INC to acquire all those macros, constants, global variables, and function prototypes that link to DLLs.

FILE.INC, EDIT.INC, and so on, are the declarations relating to the menu areas being tested. In our example, a menu-based approach has been taken to cover the functionality of the product. Each menu is considered an area, and each area holds the common declarations for the test cases that test it.

Following this example, NEW.MST, OPEN.MST, and the other files shown in Figure 8-1 would fall into the File menu area of testing and would need to include FILE.INC to get the declarations they require. You could take this as far as having an .INC file for each test case. But going to this degree probably isn't necessary, and the declarations at the lower level of the hierarchy can be placed into the .MST file.

Notice that in this diagram NOTEMAIN.INC gets included twice. The first time is by NOTEUTIL.INC. NOTEUTIL.INC includes NOTEMAIN.INC because there are constants its utilities need to use. But then, all of the test cases include NOTEMAIN.INC and NOTEUTIL.INC, so it appears that NOTEMAIN.INC is being brought in multiple times.

The automation engineer could look at this and surmise that NOTEMAIN.INC will always be included, since NOTEUTIL.INC is always included by each test case. So why have the test case include NOTEMAIN.INC, too? This is done so that a file's dependencies can be determined simply by looking at the files it includes. If it ever became necessary to move one of the test case files, it would be easier to determine which files, or copies of those files, needed to go with it. If this explicit approach isn't taken, the tester would need to look through each separate include file to make sure the files it relies upon are being included. This can get really messy and confusing. Therefore, I suggest going ahead and letting files be included multiple times, just to make it easier down the line to determine which files rely upon which other files.

Refer to the section "Conditional Compilation" earlier in this chapter on how to avoid errors that can be generated when including a file multiple times.

Note   Even though we're referring to this as a file hierarchy, it doesn't necessarily mean that we're using a hierarchical directory structure. All these files can be in a single directory yet still maintain a hierarchical association with each other, as shown in Figures 8-1 and 8-2.

Encapsulation

The idea of encapsulation was broached when we briefly looked at the subroutines `TestsBegin()`, `TestsEnd()`, `ResetApp()`, `SelMenu()`, and `PutString()`. If you've already been through a C or Pascal programming class, or you've done any programming in Visual Basic or any other structured programming language, you are already aware of the importance of encapsulating source code.

This topic is being discussed here only because there have been many occasions when I've gone into a company using Visual Test and seen that the person writing the scripts is writing one long sequential piece of code. When he or she finds a section of code that acts as it should, and wants the same thing to happen in another section of the automation scripts, the author copies and pastes that code into that other area.

Whenever you have a piece of code that needs to be used more than once, it needs to be placed into either a function or a subroutine. These are blocks of code or subprograms that can be executed simply by placing the name of the routine where you want its code to execute.

Subroutines and functions are very much like constants. You should create them when a piece of code is used in more than one place, so that all you need to do to modify it is to alter the function or subroutine in question.

If working with functions and subroutines is completely new to you, I strongly suggest you take a beginning programming class in C, Pascal, or any other structured programming language, including Visual Basic.

The Wrapper

A *wrapper* function or subroutine is a routine that's been created around another function, statement, or subroutine. This is done so that extra features can be added to how the standard routine operates. Often, they contribute to the flexibility of the test suite when it becomes necessary to add new features to the test scenarios' capabilities.

The example I'll use for a wrapper is the `SelMenu()` subroutine mentioned earlier in this chapter. `SelMenu()` is a routine that I created and placed into the NOTEUTIL.INC file, to be used by all test cases when selecting a menu. If you are familiar with the `wMenuSelect` statement, then you're probably scratching your head wondering why I would try to recreate functionality that already exists.

The reason for doing this is based on my past experience of requests from my clients. On one project I used the `wMenuSelect` statement to select menus throughout all my test scripts. After writing hundreds of tests, I had a client come back to me and ask me to have Visual Test print out each menu as it was selected.

Unfortunately, `wMenuSelect` doesn't have this capability, so I would have had to revisit each test script and find where `wMenuSelect` was used and put a `PRINT` statement after it. Either that or get fancy and write some kind of Windows utility that would look for a message telling me a menu had popped up or a menu item had been selected.

In fact, I chose to do neither. Instead, I created a new function that I placed in my util file (in this case `NOTEUTIL.INC`), called `SelMenu()`. `SelMenu()` did exactly the same thing that `wMenuSelect` did.

I went through all my scripts and replaced `wMenuSelect` with `SelMenu()`, then I went into `SelMenu()` and placed a print statement right after the `wMenuSelect` statement. Did it pay off? Yes, it most certainly did, because later that week the client requested a way to turn printing the menu information on and off. Instead of revisiting a couple hundred test files, I was able instead to update my `SelMenu()` subroutine to check whether a global variable had been set to `TRUE` or `FALSE`. It took me less than two minutes to implement the new functionality, instead of a couple of hours.

This is a simple yet effective example of how helpful wrappers can be. As you are writing your tests, think of other wrappers you can create to save yourself time. If you find yourself always putting a `PRINT` statement after performing a particular action, this is a prime place to create a wrapper of some kind.

Summary

This chapter focused on common coding guidelines that should be created and followed by a single automation programmer or a team of programmers. By achieving consensus on styles and guidelines up front, you can avoid many problems as a project matures. The common coding guidelines should continue to grow throughout the project, so that a well-polished document is available when the next project begins.

As utilities are created on a project, you'll find that some are generic and helpful enough to be sharable with other teams. I encourage you or your team to follow Microsoft's example of sharing common utilities by making others in your company or others in your QA community aware of what utilities you've created in Visual Test. By sharing this information, teams can see what others who are using Visual Test have accomplished, which will help them support the direction they are headed in, or get ideas on other directions to explore. It's also an opportunity to swap these utilities so that each programmer's test automation arsenal grows stronger and more capable. Find time at the end of your project to document your creation—both in the code and in a separate document—so that it's easier for others to pick up and understand.

✦   ✦   ✦

Defining an Approach

When given a product to automate, the first thing you need to do is define the approach you're going to take. You do this by taking time out to explore and understand the application fully.

Looking through the user interface (UI) will give you an idea as to whether or not the product relies heavily on menus, dialog boxes, toolbars, floating palettes, or other, perhaps specially designed, UI elements.

A clear understanding from the customer, or the person requesting the automation, is necessary to ensure you don't spike too deeply into any given area, especially if it's of little or no interest to the overall automation of the product or portions of a product. Through constant communication, clear goals need to be set and understood in order to verify that the automation effort is on track.

Once goals are set, you'll have a better idea of how to approach and lay out the design of your automated tests, such as how many test cases and suites will need to be created, the directory structure you'll use, and how files will relate to each other.

Exploring the Application

While looking through the product, have Visual Test's Window Information (Winfo) utility up and running, so you can check to see if the controls are standard Windows controls, or if they are controls Visual Test might not recognize. This will give you an idea of the difficulty of the automation to be carried out (see Figure 9-1).

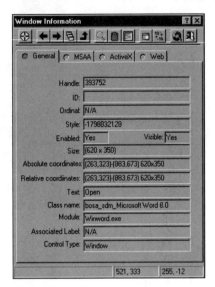

Figure 9-1: The Window Information (Winfo) utility

Tip   See Chapter 6 for more information on the Window Information utility and non-standard control types.

Continuing with Notepad as our sample application, we find it is an application with a user interface made up solely of menus and dialog boxes that are accessed through its menus. This makes our job as Test programmers easier, since Visual Test can work with menus by using its wMenuSelect statement. But what about the dialog boxes that are displayed?

It turns out that, as we bring up each dialog box and select a few controls in each of them using Winfo, we find that Notepad uses standard Windows controls. Even if it had subclassed controls, we'd still be able to work with them by using the w*SetClass statement that is available for every control type recognized by the Test language (for example: wButtonSetClass, wEditSetClass, wCheckSetClass, and so on).

Our attention then turns to Notepad's main window and the editor where the user will be typing in the text. By once again using Winfo, we find that Notepad's editing area is actually a separate window of class Edit. This means that Notepad's editor is actually a large edit control, which allows us to use Visual Test's wEdit* commands. Thus, Notepad doesn't have any nasty surprises. As we can see in Figure 9-2, its window controls are standard, and the text area is a large edit control that will allow us greater control over the manipulation of the text.

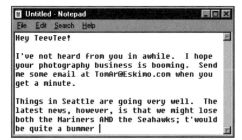

Figure 9-2: Fortunately for us Notepad doesn't hold any surprises.

After taking this tour through Notepad, we have an idea of the level of difficulty we will run into when writing scripts. Because Notepad uses common Windows controls, the automation process won't be too daunting.

Choosing an Approach

There isn't any one approach to take when it comes to automation. It depends on the type of UI the application makes available to the user. In the case of Notepad, most of its functionality is available via the menus, as shown in Figure 9-3. Therefore, we'll structure our tests around those menus and menu items.

Figure 9-3: Most of Notepad's functionality is available through its menus.

In the case of Notepad, since everything is accessible through its menus, the approach we'll be taking is a *menu-based* approach. This means our test case files will be organized around Notepad's menus and that our file and directory structure will follow this same type of organizational approach.

Another approach we could take with Notepad is a *dialog-centric* one. The idea of this is to have all testing originate from individual dialog boxes and for testing of the product to spread from that starting point. The menu-based approach is more straightforward in the case of Notepad, so it's the method we'll follow throughout this book when using the Notepad example. An example of Notepad's Find dialog box is shown in Figure 9-4.

Figure 9-4: Although Notepad definitely has its dialog boxes, they are simple instead of complex.

In the event that an application consists of a number of toolbars and not as many menus or dialog boxes, or that the center of attention for the application is its toolbars, a *toolbar-based* approach can be taken. This approach is similar to the menu-based and dialog-centric approaches, in that all testing centers around that aspect of the product and originates from this UI component.

What's more likely to happen, especially in a complex application that employs all of these and other types of user interfaces, is to have a combination of all three approaches. The tests that focus on the menus will go so far as to display the dialog boxes and test that each dialog box's controls perform some action, but will then stop testing at that point.

The testing of the effect of using a dialog box control would then be handled by the dialog-centric test case files, to verify that each control is acting as expected. The test case files would then follow the toolbar-based approach to verify that each toolbar is functional. This is known as taking a *component and functionality* approach to automation. Although following this combination method involves some overlap, an effort is made to keep this to a minimum. Figure 9-5 gives an example of an application that has menus, dialog boxes, and toolbars/tool palettes. In the case of Adobe Photoshop 5.0, a combination of approaches would be taken to fully automate the product.

Whatever approach you decide to take, don't be too concerned if you find later that it seems to make more sense to take a different approach. It's difficult to plan out exactly how to approach the task of automation. The only sound advice anyone can give is to pick an approach, move forward, and make adjustments along the way.

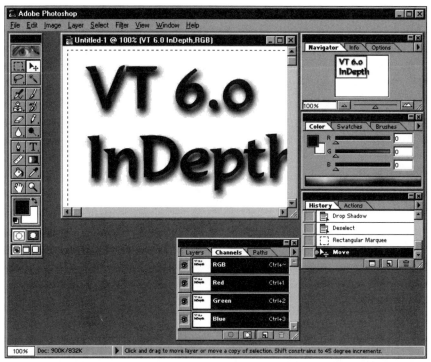

Figure 9-5: Adobe's Photoshop 5.0 is an example of an application that has menus, dialog boxes, and toolbars/tool palettes. It would be a formidable product to automate.

Defining What's to Be Tested

It's not uncommon to be on a project where the person running it comes in and says, "We want to automate the testing on our product so that it will be released with higher quality in a shorter period of time." A great sentiment, but when it comes down to the bottom line (time and money), the attitude can quickly change to, "This is costing us a fortune and the end is nowhere in sight!"

A realistic understanding and commitment to supplying whatever resources are needed must meet the requirements set for the automation team. Visual Test and other automation tools don't replace a mature and methodical approach to software quality assurance. If the company's goal is to increase the quality of the product with test automation as one of the tools to help in this effort, clear definitions need to be made and understood up front, so that larger frustrations can be avoided down the road.

When finding yourself in this situation, where the management team has heard wonderful things about test automation but doesn't necessarily understand the true commitment it requires of people and time, it's important to be as up-front and factual about the situation as possible. This is especially important if the testing team is new to automation and doesn't have previous war stories or metrics to help anecdotally explain or demonstrate automation.

Work Together

Begin by working with your manager to help define exactly what is to be automated. A typical response that I've received from clients is, "Automate everything!" You, too, might run into this response. In these situations, I explain how test automation is a tool to help software test engineers in their work, not to replace testers on a project.

A simple example I use is the Open dialog box that almost every Windows program has. Would the manager prefer that the programmer spend a day writing exhaustive test scenarios to test for all the possibilities they can think of for the Open dialog box (such as legal filenames, illegal filenames, names for files that don't exist, long paths to reach a file, opening network files, opening an illegal file type, and opening a file under low memory)? Or would he or she prefer that the programmer focus on a few key tests to make sure that, for the most part, the dialog box is functioning as expected (that it can open an existing file, and give an error message if the file is not found), leaving the exhaustive testing for later, when it can be done quickly though manual methods at key milestones in the project cycle?

Simply put, you don't want to spend time automating something that will take less time to test by hand.

By taking an exhaustive approach, you ensure that tests will be written that go deep into the functionality of a specific area of the product, but also that the testing team will run out of time in automating the entire product — that is, unless there is a very large team of automation programmers. You don't want to spend time automating something that will take less time to test by hand.

Break down your automation process into a couple of steps:

1. Pick an area of the product that you would like to have automated.

2. Set up a broad automation of the entire product.

Pick one area

First and foremost, pick an area of the product that you *and your manager* would like to have automated. (Refer to Chapters 10 and 11 for coding examples.) Spend a day or two automating that area to give yourself an idea of what's involved in putting a script together. Two things are happening when you do this:

✦ First, you're getting an idea of how long it takes to automate a feature of the product. This will help in future "educated guesses" on how long it will take to automate other features.

✦ Second, this will be an education for your manager on exactly what is involved in automating a feature of the product. Show her your source code, so she can see how much programming is required to test a simple feature of the product.

This is a great exercise because you are working with your manager instead of against her. You're explaining in a factual manner what the realities of automation are and helping her understand the time that will be needed to automate an entire product. This will help both of you estimate your time and resource requirements to complete your goals.

Design a skeleton

The next step is to set up a broad automation of the entire product. Determine the approach you're going to take and write some simple tests that basically touch each top-level feature of the product.

I always start with the menus, because they are simple to access and it's clear what I need to write code-wise to touch each menu item. This is known as a *breadth-first* layout: It stretches broadly across the top level of the product instead of diving deeply into individual areas or features. A *depth-first* layout focuses on one area at a time, going as deep as it can into that area before moving on to the next one. On a short time line with only one or two critical features to automate, the depth-first layout is the way to go. However, the breadth-first method offers more flexibility and room to grow. In the case of testing Notepad, following the menu-based approach and setting up a project in Visual Test results in the project tree shown in Figure 9-6.

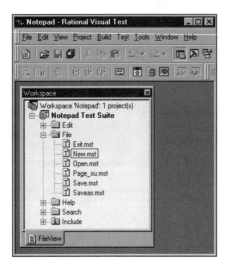

Figure 9-6: The project tree resulting from a menu-based approach

The result of the breadth-first method is a broad outline or *skeleton* of the automation project you are putting together. Once you have this set up, you can return to your manager with a list of each of the top-level areas you are touching through your automated scripts. Use this list to get direction from your manager on what features he or she feels are most important to focus on first. As these features are automated, you can work your way out to the less-critical features. Remember to use automation where automation makes sense. That is, if you can test something quickly by hand and it only needs to be tested by hand at critical milestones in the project, why automate it?

Avoid a False Sense of Security

As your test cases grow in number, guard against being lulled into the assumption that all test cases are thorough and complete. Just because a test case exists for a given feature of the product doesn't mean that it has been completed by an experienced tester or that the tester involved in writing the test case file had the necessary amount of time to complete a thorough list of scenarios. Keep records of which areas are being thoroughly tested through manual and automated tests so that future testing teams have a clear picture of the status of the testing effort. Having a lot of tests doesn't mean that they are relevant or that holes don't exist. Avoid getting lulled into a false sense of security just because some of your tests are automated.

Another benefit in setting up a skeleton as one of the first steps in your automation project is that your team now has a structure to follow for their test scenarios and regression tests. There is a file for each area, which your teammates can access and modify with their test scripts.

It also serves as a *smoke test* or quick verification that can be used whenever a new build is received from the development team. By running this framework, you can quickly and effectively determine which areas of the product have become unstable between builds.

If you want to be really fancy, you can set up your tests to check for a global variable's setting. This would determine whether you need to run the scenarios that will eventually be placed into a given file, or to simply touch the feature and then drop out from the test case file. This way, when your test case files grow, you can run smoke tests by simply setting a global value.

Once the skeleton has been set up, the team can then prioritize the areas that are to be automated. Once these goals are established, the team has a clear understanding of how much time should be spent on any given area and how deep it should go into automating a feature of the product.

Set Clear Goals

Goals are important. They enable the status of the project to be determined more easily. Also, by identifying areas of concern up front, you can adjust timelines to be more accurate and realistic.

Goals need to be adjusted throughout the automation test development cycle to reflect where the team is and whether or not it's falling behind or getting ahead of schedule. Reassessing these goals will help determine whether the focus is too deep or too shallow and whether more people need to be added to the automation project (see Figure 9-7). The goals of writing benchmark, full pass, smoke, and regression tests are all attainable. It's important to figure out where to focus attention first, however; otherwise the testing team might try to tackle all of the goals at once, resulting in a lot of work being done on a little of each goal.

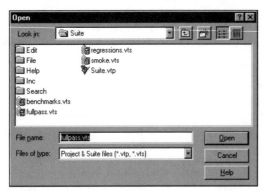

Figure 9-7: Once created, the test suite files (.VTS file extension) can then be run one at a time or in combination by using the Visual Test Suite Manager.

Make sure you understand exactly what it is your manager would like you to accomplish. Don't let her get away with simply saying that she wants the product to be tested quickly, while ensuring higher quality through test automation. It's clear from what I've said before that there's so much more to automation than taking a "just do it and I'll be back later to check on you" approach. Taking a lax approach leads to all parties making assumptions that will most likely be wrong.

Here are a couple of goals, my comments about those goals, and the requirements I see to help the testing team reach them. They are just a few to get you started in the many discussions your team will need to have regarding the project you're embarking upon.

Goal 1: *Use automated tests every time a new release of the product is given to the testing team by development.*

Comments: This is a very good use of automated tests, because it allows testers to get a feel for whether anything has broken or not. A break in a key feature may make it impossible to write any further automation for a new build of the product.

Requirements: The development group will need to fix the problems and compile another version for the testers. Management will need to support the testing team's decision to refuse a build, even in time-critical situations. Otherwise, the risk is that more time will be lost when the automation group modifies its scripts to skip testing on unstable areas.

Goal 2: *Use the automated tests for regressing known or reported bugs in the product.*

Comments: Another reasonable use of test automation. The testers can take the bugs found in the bug list and write automated tests that verify that they don't return in future builds. It will not be possible to automate 100 percent of the reported bugs because often they are found in special machine configurations or low memory situations. Sometimes it is easier and more efficient to attempt to reproduce a bug by hand than to attempt to automate it.

Regarding where to put regression tests, some people intermingle them with their existing test scenarios, while others keep them in separate test case files. I prefer a separate test case file so that, should a number of bugs that are being regressed still exist, the regression tests can be skipped, allowing the rest of the tests to run. It also allows me to pick what types of tests I'll be running: smoke, regression, full pass, benchmark, or whatever.

Requirements: Enough testers need to be available to write the automated regression tests. In the event that not enough are available, it must be understood that, while testing focuses on writing automated tests — for regressing bugs or testing features in general — the number of bugs reported by the testing team will drop. Sometimes the number of bugs filed is used as a measure to determine the stability of the product. In this situation, it's a false indicator because testing is focused on writing scripts instead of manually testing the product.

Tip
I suggest having at least one person who focuses solely on test automation who can drive the effort and direct other automators as they are brought in at peak times.

Goal 3: The entire product is to be automated, taking a breadth-first approach.

Comments: It sounds all well and good to tell you about setting up the breadth-first, or skeleton, layout, but the problem you're going to face, especially early in the development cycle, is the stability of the product. This instability, both in the fatal errors encountered in the product and the unfrozen nature of the user interface, makes automation challenging, to say the least. Many times you will find yourself having to rewrite sections of code because a decision has been made to redesign all of the dialog boxes, for whatever reason. Your time is best spent creating a general framework of common utilities. Pick one or two features to automate and take your time by building common utilities (such as the ones discussed in Chapter 11) that these beginning tests will use, and that future test case files will most likely use.

Requirements: Management needs to keep these issues in mind so that when design changes are made, it is understood that the testing team (and the documentation team) will take a hit in productivity. However, this should not be the deciding factor as to whether or not a feature should be changed in the product. It is only to say that managers should understand that these changes will break test scripts and require a maintenance pass to fix the test scripts.

Something very helpful is to create a mock application, specifically in Visual Basic, because of Test's ability to work with VB controls. Once the UI design is frozen based on this mock-up, the mock application can be handed over to testing for them to set up their testing structure. Or if the product is beyond a 1.0 version, the testing team should have access to the previous version of the product for writing its scripts. Then when the actual product becomes stable, the scripts will be further along and can be moved off the mock-up and onto the true build of the product.

Goal 4: *Visual Test is to be used to benchmark critical areas of the product.*

Comments: I would suggest creating a totally separate test suite, simply because of the nature of benchmarking. To arrive at accurate results, it's typical for actions to be run multiple times so that an average time can be calculated. This necessary repetition of tests makes the timing of events more accurate but can result in the tests taking a very long time to complete.

Requirement: The area to be benchmarked should be code complete and in a stable state.

In conclusion, the benefit you gain from involving your manager in the definition and goal-setting process is your manager's support and understanding of the process. This helps her explain the realities of automation to her managers as well.

Although it may seem strange to you to have company politics discussed in this book, it really is a necessary part of the automation process, because of the hype given to automating tests and general misconceptions held by those who have never been involved in the process. By setting clear goals, including them in your overall *test plan* for the project you're on, and educating your manager along the way, you will greatly reduce the frustrations experienced by others new to automation who don't take this approach.

Determine a Layout

You need to determine a layout to:

✦ Organize the files that make up your test suite
✦ Set the directory structure that will house your files

Suite Organization

Just because we've decided to take a menu-based approach with Notepad doesn't mean we need to break up our files and directory structure to follow that approach.

I've suggested you break up your files, but that isn't mandatory. The approach we're taking with Notepad is to step methodically through each menu item under each of Notepad's menus.

Now that we know how we'll step through and test Notepad, let's look at our options for creating our test case files. We have several.

Single file

One approach to a test case file is to use a single file to house all of Notepad's test scenarios. The benefit in doing this is that the Test programmer need only work with one file. Everything is in one place, and the Test programmer doesn't need to go searching high and low to find the source code she wants to edit. You can do this by placing each scenario into a separate function that returns a Boolean (TRUE or FALSE) value, letting the main program know whether or not the test scenario passed.

There are a number of downsides to this approach. The first is that, because everything is kept in one file, sharing common routines with other testing teams becomes difficult. Sure, the other teams can cut and paste the code they want to use out of the single file, but then there'll be two copies of those routines floating around, causing the source code to instantly be out of sync. Any advances the other team makes with the source code taken from the single automation file will need to be reintegrated, if there is any benefit to be gained.

Another problem is that, if there are a number of Test programmers on the team, it becomes very difficult to merge everyone's changes and modifications into a single file. If one team member modifies a common utility, such as a logging routine, and another member modifies that same routine, merging those changes gets ugly very quickly.

In the event of a feature in the product breaking from one build to the next, resulting in a general protection fault (GPF), the tester running the automated suite will need to go into the source code and comment out the problem area, so that the rest of the tests can execute. Then that tester will need to remember to uncomment the test for future passes on the product.

Using a single test suite file is an approach I've seen many companies take when they first start automating. This is usually because there is only one test automation programmer on the project, and that programmer is new to automation. After getting further into the details of automating the product, the programmer soon breaks the single file into multiple files for the reasons previously mentioned.

While you can start out with a single file, keep these problems in the back of your mind and be ready to move to multiple files once you have a handle on exactly how you want to approach the automation.

Area test case files

Another approach that many first-time Test programmers take is to break their tests up into multiple files based on the areas of the product being tested. In the case of Notepad, this would mean having a single test case file for the File menu, another one for the Edit menu, and so on. This isn't a bad approach to take, but you can still run into the problems mentioned previously. If, in the example of Notepad, selecting the New menu item under the File menu caused a GPF, the rest of the test scenarios in that file would go unexecuted unless the tester went in and placed comments around the line of code causing the error.

Functionality test case files

This last approach follows the method of breaking the test case files up into specific features of a product. An example would be to have a test case file for the New menu item under the File menu. So basically, we've taken things one step further by breaking them down into their most basic form and representing them as test case files.

According to this method, the File menu in Notepad would have seven test case files — a file for each menu item — made up of a number of scenarios. Figure 9-8 shows how a separate .MST file, or test case file, exists for each menu item under the File menu.

Note   Visual Test's defaults assume the approach shown in Figure 9-8, where multiple scenarios are placed into a test case file.

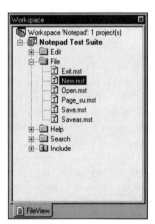

Figure 9-8: A separate test case file exists for each menu item under the File menu.

This is the approach I like to take because I can easily control which feature of a product I want to test. There is yet another level, however, that one can go to in organizing test files: into test scenarios.

Test scenario files

I've seen some companies, some (but not all) groups in Microsoft in particular, take the organization of their files one step further; and that is, to have a separate file for each test scenario.

To refresh your memory, a *test scenario* is a specific test on a feature. For example, testing that the appropriate error message is given when an illegal filename is supplied in the Open dialog box is a scenario. Testing that an error is given when you attempt to read the wrong type of file into the program is another scenario. A test case is a grouping of scenarios for a particular area.

Breaking down a test program into tests by scenarios may lead to hundreds — and very possibly thousands — of files to deal with. However, it allows individuals on a testing team to add their own individual scenarios to the hopper for testing. A driver like the Visual Test Suite Manager can be used to run those test files, or a separate driver can be written that pulls in all files from a specific directory and runs those tests individually.

In my opinion, this approach leads to too much structure. Each test scenario file needs to set up the application to a known state, so that it doesn't rely on the test scenario file that ran before it. Each file is also expected to clean up after itself when it completes its testing task. While this isn't an approach I've taken, many teams at Microsoft seem to do well with this method.

The result will mean you have a project structure resembling that in Figure 9-9.

Note   As a project's structure is constructed using Visual Test, a directory structure is built to map directly to the structure represented in the FileView (as shown in the FileView window in Figure 9-9).

Tip   When a file or folder is deleted from the FileView window, such as the window shown in Figure 9-9, that file or folder is not actually deleted from your disk drive. To permanently remove these files and/or directories, you will need to do this outside of the Developer Studio.

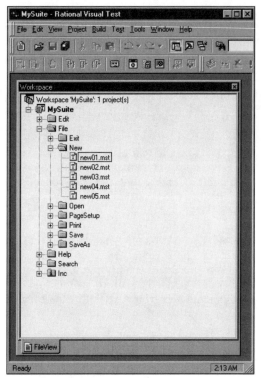

Figure 9-9: This is an example of putting one individual test scenario into a test case file.

A Word on Version Control

With all of these files in an automation project, you'll need to be concerned with keeping files — specifically shared files — in sync. When working on a team where people are modifying their own test scripts, shared utilities, and header files, it is very easy for two or more people to be working on the same file at the same time. The danger is that one person makes changes to a file just before another person saves changes back to the shared directory. The result is that the file on the server in the shared directory doesn't have all of the changes it should have because one person just wiped out another person's work.

As in the case of large development projects done in C/C++, tools such as Microsoft Visual Source Safe or Rational ClearCase can be used for version control and project file management. Because Visual Test is using Microsoft C++ Developer Studio as its development environment, it inherits the ability to integrate with Visual Source Safe. ClearCase has also been integrated with the product.

Use Visual Source Safe or ClearCase to keep your source files backed up on a server and in a project where only one person can work on a given file at a time. Or these tools can even be configured to allow for merging of changes so that multiple people can work on the same file at the same time.

Not only do you get the benefits of keeping your files in sync, you also get the benefit of being able to back out modifications that were made that proved detrimental. Source code version control tools are essential on projects that have two or more people. They're even helpful on single-developer projects.

File Sharing

As test scenarios are written, you'll create functions and subroutines common enough to be used by other test scenarios and test case files. These common routines usually find their way into separate files, so that sharing those routines is a simpler process.

Visual Test provides a special folder for those files that need to be included by test case files in different sections of the project. This is an *include folder* and shows up at the bottom of both Figures 9-8 and 9-9.

Files common to other areas of the project are placed in this folder. Examples include the main include file and the main utility file. The main include file holds common declarations, such as constants for menu items and captions of windows, that are broad enough to be made available to all test scenarios. The main utility include file holds function and subroutine utilities, such as log file routines, test initialization, and clean-up, that are likely to be used by test scenarios.

Summary

When we build our first scenarios in Chapter 10, the logic of creating common utilities and moving them into a sharable file and location will become much clearer, especially in our first scenario. We'll build the functionality that we need and later find that it's useful enough to move into a higher section of the project hierarchy, thereby making it available to everyone.

As I have said frequently throughout this book, I encourage you to dive in on the first couple of test case files and scenarios to get your feet wet and better understand what's available in the Test language. By jumping in and learning first, you will be able to write a more thorough description of how you are going to approach the automated testing on your project when it comes time to write your overall test plan, or to add information about the automation process to an existing test plan.

It is essential to take the time to define your approach to testing a product. You should first explore the product, checking to see what it consists of, how it functions, and what its features are. Then you need to decide on the approach to take, though this can change as you go along. It can be either menu-based, dialog-centric, toolbar-based, or based on functionality. Then you and your manager need to define what is to be tested and set clear goals.

Once your goals are defined, you need to determine a layout: How will you organize the files that make up your test suite, and set the directory structure that will house your files? You can take one of four possible approaches: single file, area test files, functionality test files, or test scenario files. But always bear in mind the need to share your files and update them.

✦　　✦　　✦

Writing Simple Test Cases

A *test case* is a group of tests, or test scenarios, that focus on a particular area or feature of a product that is being tested. A *test scenario* is a specific test that is performed on an area or feature of a product. This chapter focuses on creating the first simple test cases. To be able to create these test cases, however, we must first create the scenarios of which a test case is composed.

In Chapter 9, we talked about picking an approach to take with our automation on the product we're testing. Throughout this book we've been looking at Notepad as our test subject, and we shall continue to use it in this chapter. We determined in Chapter 9 that the basis of our approach with testing Notepad would be menu-based, because Notepad's functionality is all reachable through its menus: There aren't any toolbars, tool palettes, or separate windows that add to Notepad's functionality.

We also discussed in Chapter 9 how to determine which layout to use. Visual Test supports the concept of functionality test case files, where each automated test case file is for a specific feature of the product and contains a number of scenarios for that feature. This is opposed to a single test suite file that holds all tests, or a separate file for each test scenario, both extremes.

Following the menu-based approach and organizing our testing into test case files that contain scenarios for one feature of the product at a time means we need to create an .MST file (test case file) for each menu item.

The First Test Scenario

We'll start off with the New menu item found under the File menu (see Figure 10-1). Our goal with writing our first, simple test cases is just to get something down "on paper," so that we have some content to the overall structure we're building. We can add to it later; it's just there to give us a feel and provide others with examples, so that it's easier to add content to each test case file later.

Figure 10-1: The New menu item found under Notepad's File menu is the first feature we're going to test.

As we walk through the Notepad application and use the New menu item, we find there are three beginning situations relating to it that we could set up for our initial test scenarios. All of them center around Notepad having text in its window that has not yet been saved, which results in the Save Changes? message box, shown in Figure 10-2, being displayed. It contains three options: Yes, No, and Cancel.

Our first test case is going to center around these three options. Again, these three initial test scenarios are tests that will eventually need to be created, and since they're the most obvious, we choose to create them now, so they can provide some substance to the overall structure we're creating.

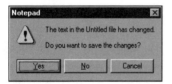

Figure 10-2: This message box is displayed when the New menu item is selected and unsaved text is in the Notepad editor. It has three options: Yes, No, and Cancel.

As we create these three key scenarios, we'll find that other scenarios come to mind. It's common to have other ideas for tests come to us as we move toward our set of goals. Because of this, we'll end up with more than just the three scenarios we mention here by the time we get to writing the first test case.

Version One

Because these are the very first lines of code, we're going to write a very simple beginning script to:

1. Run Notepad.

2. Put some text into the window.

3. Select the New menu item.

Here is our first script:

```
run "notepad.exe", nowait
play "Now is the time for all good people..."
wMenuSelect("File\New")
```

If the script runs as expected, when the script completes, Notepad should be up and running, "Now is the time for all good people . . ." should be in its main window, and the message box shown in Figure 10-2 should be displayed.

The RUN statement in the first line is a simple Test language statement that runs another program. The NOWAIT parameter, which is the second argument, tells the statement to run the program and not wait for the program to terminate before continuing with the script. Without the NOWAIT option, Visual Test would run Notepad and then wait until Notepad was exited before continuing with the script.

The second line, which contains the PLAY statement, causes Visual Test to type text into a window that has focus. This is a helpful command, but it can be a nuisance if it's not used cautiously. For example, if Notepad didn't run because of low memory or because the program wasn't found, the PLAY command would continue on its merry way and just spew text into whatever window had the focus.

The wMenuSelect statement on the third line causes Visual Test to select the New menu item found under the File menu. Note that if the New menu item had three dots or ellipses as part of its name, those ellipses would need to be included in the text (for example, wMenuSelect "File\New..."). If it had an accelerator or shortcut key, such as Ctrl+N, this would *not* be included as part of the text used by wMenuSelect.

Continuing with this first version of our script, we now need to verify that the message box was displayed as expected. If it wasn't, we need to report an error somehow, so we can track what error occurred. And as our last task, we'll go ahead and dismiss the message box by clicking the Cancel button. The continuation of our script is shown in the next piece of code:

```
run "notepad.exe", nowait
play "Now is the time for all good people..."
wMenuSelect("File\New")

if GetText(NULL) <> "Notepad" then
    print "Error: Message box not found."
else
    wButtonClick("Cancel")
endif
```

Tip

For this edition of the Visual Test book I've added an appendix (Appendix A) that is a language reference. It shows only the names of the Test language functions and subroutines, along with some other helpful information. It's mostly there to give you an idea of what's in the language so that you can look for more detailed information in the online help included with Rational Visual Test.

The GetText() function returns the text in the window's caption specified by the parameter passed to it. In this case, NULL is passed, which, according to the online help, tells the function to grab the text out of the active window. In this case, the message box should be the active window. And as shown in Figure 10-2, its caption is "Notepad."

How Could I Know?

One of the first and most common frustrations about any programming language is the question How would I know to use a particular statement, for example, the GetText and wButtonClick statements we used in the first and second versions of this beginning test case file? I didn't even know they existed until a few minutes ago!

By reading this book you will pick up on the most common statements and functions you'll need to write automated tests. What you need to do, though, is explore the online help that comes with Visual Test to pick up on the more obscure routines available. There's really no other way to do it. As you write your automated scripts and look at others' scripts, you'll begin to pick it up. No matter how good you get, however, you'll always be referring back to the online help to make sure that you're using many of the commands correctly. Don't get too frustrated; it's all a part of programming!

If the caption of Notepad's main window were also "Notepad," we'd have to find another way to verify that the message box was displayed, since we couldn't determine which window's caption we were receiving from the call to GetText(). Fortunately, the caption in Notepad's main window includes the name of the file that it is viewing, or "Untitled" if no file is being viewed.

The PRINT statement is employed to communicate that the message box wasn't found. Whenever this statement is used, and is not in conjunction with writing out to a file, the output is placed into the Output window, viewable when the Viewport tab is selected, as shown in Figure 10-3.

Figure 10-3: The PRINT statement places text into the Output window, specifically under the Viewport tab.

The wButtonClick statement looks for a button control with the specified caption as the first parameter for this statement. If it finds the button, it clicks it. If it doesn't find the button, it gives a run-time error message saying that it couldn't find it. (We'll discuss run-time errors in Chapter 13, "Beyond the Basics.")

In a nutshell, that's our first scenario. We ran the Notepad application, put some text into its main window so that we could set Notepad's dirty-bit (letting it know there was something in the main window that had not yet been saved), and selected the New menu item to display the message box, which then prompted us to save changes; we then clicked the Cancel button to dismiss the message box.

We could and probably should add some code to this script so that it verifies that the text remains unchanged. We can do this easily by using an edit control function to return the contents of Notepad's main window. (Remember that in Chapter 9 we discovered, by using the Window Information utility, that the text entry portion of Notepad's main window is really an edit control.) This results in the final first version of our script, shown here:

```
run "notepad.exe", nowait
play "Now is the time for all good people..."
wMenuSelect "File\New"

if GetText(NULL) <> "Notepad" then
    print "Error: Message box not found."
else
```

```
        wButtonClick "Cancel"
endif

if EditText("@1") = "Now is the time for all good people..."
then
        print "Test passed."
endif

END
```

We mentioned the use of ordinals back in Chapter 5 when working with controls. Because Notepad's text entry area is one big edit control, and because it doesn't have a caption associated with it, we can refer to it by using the "@1", since it is the only edit control available.

This first version works well and is a good outline with which to move forward. We can take this scenario and refine it so that it is even more flexible and capable, as you'll see in the second version of this script.

Version Two

The second version of our first script for the New menu item uses the SCENARIO statement, which was new to Visual Test 4.0 and is now in Visual Test 6.0. This statement allows us to break up our scripts into distinct sections for each test that is to be executed. Within the block of the test, or scenario, we are also able to control cleaning up any effects of the test, which allows us to return the application being tested to a known state.

This script accomplishes the same results as the last script except that we have now given it more structure by using the SCENARIO and END SCENARIO statements:

```
'** Initialize the test case **

viewport clear      'Clean the contents of the Viewport
                    'tab in the Output window.


'Get test application up and running. If it can't be run
'for whatever reason, print an error message and stop
'the execution of the script.

if run("notepad.exe") then
    print "Error: Unable to run notepad.exe"
    stop
endif


'** Beginning of the test scenarios **
```

```
scenario "Test that 'Save changes' message box is displayed."
    play "Now is the time for all good people..."
    wMenuSelect("File\New")

    if GetText(NULL) <> "Notepad" then
        fail "Error: Message box not found."
    endif

scenario cleanup
    if not(failed) then
        wButtonClick("Cancel")
    endif
end scenario

scenario "Verify that the original text remains unchanged."
    if EditText("@1")<>"Now is the time for all good people..."
then
fail "Original test text changed."
    endif
end scenario

'** Clean-up before the test case file ends **
wMenuSelect("File\Exit")     'Shut down Notepad application

if GetText(NULL) = "Notepad" then
    wButtonClick("No")       'Click 'No' to "Save changes?"
endif

END
```

In this second version you'll notice a new command called VIEWPORT CLEAR. This command causes the contents of the Viewport in the Output window to be cleared so that running a script again won't add to the contents. I use this option especially when designing new scripts because it is less confusing, since you then need only deal with the output from the latest run.

The STOP statement terminates the execution of the test case and is used in this script only in the event Notepad isn't able to be run. Optionally, the END statement could have been used in place of STOP, but what happens in that situation is that any ON END commands that have been set up will then be executed before terminating the test case.

Being Sensitive to a Character's Case

Many compilers for other languages, such as C, Fortran, and Pascal, are *case-sensitive*, meaning that lowercase and uppercase characters are treated as separate entities. In these situations it would be possible, although confusing, to have an x variable and an X variable that had no relation to one another.

In Visual Test, however, the Test language *isn't* case-sensitive. For all the compiler cares, your scripts could be typed all in uppercase or all in lowercase. My style varies in capitalization, and I've been asked many times in class whether capitalization matters. It doesn't, as far as the compiler is concerned. It may matter in terms of how your team defines its programming style (for example, whether constants are usually declared and used with all capital letters). Refer to Chapter 8, "Common Coding Guidelines," for more discussion on style.

This case-insensitivity does not apply, however, to literal strings, that is, text that appears in quotes. A quoted string of "ABCD" is not equal to "abcd."

Another difference between this script and the first version is that the FAIL statement is now used in place of the PRINT statement. It is to be used only in a scenario block; otherwise, an error is generated when encountered during script execution (run time). The FAIL statement causes the current scenario block to mark itself as a failed test scenario. The result is that script execution jumps to the END SCENARIO statement, except in the situation where a SCENARIO CLEANUP section of a test scenario exists.

In the scenario cleanup section of the first test scenario, you may have noticed this IF statement:

```
if not(failed) then
```

The FAILED identifier in this IF statement is actually a function call. It determines the state of the current test scenario and returns TRUE if the test scenario is considered to have failed, and FALSE if it is considered to have passed. This function is used in this script to determine whether or not it should click the Cancel button. If the scenario failed, then the message box can't have been displayed, and therefore it should not attempt to click the message box's Cancel button in the clean-up portion of the test scenario.

The last section of the latest version of this script has some final clean-up and shutdown code that wasn't in the first version. This clean-up code, shown in the next piece of code, is used to shut down the Notepad application. It's up to you whether or not you want to have something like this in your test case files. The reason I put it in mine is so that the application is more easily placed back into a known state for the next test case. If it's shut down and then rerun by the next test case file, it's back to a known condition.

```
'** Clean-up before the test case file ends **

wMenuSelect("File\Exit")      'Shut down Notepad application

if GetText(NULL) = "Notepad" then
    wButtonClick("No")        'Click 'No' to "Save changes?"
endif

END
```

The other reason I include shutdown code in my test case files is so that, if I'm using the Visual Test Suite Manager to run my test case files, and I pick and choose the files in no particular order, I'm certain Notepad is being closed down and multiple instances of Notepad won't be up and running. Because each test case file "shuts the lights off before it leaves," you ensure that the entire test suite is cleaning up after itself.

Final Version

After starting with a very simple script in Version One and moving to a more structured script in Version Two, we move to the final version of this script. This removes the code from this test case file that will be needed by other test case files and places it into a NOTEUTIL.INC file that can be included if needed. Constants are put into place as well for some of the values that are sharable between other tests. Those constants and other declarations are placed into a NOTEMAIN.INC file.

Not only does moving this code make things more sharable, it also makes the code less cluttered. The sections of code you need can be brought in with the '$INCLUDE metacommand, which causes the file to be placed at the same location as the '$INCLUDE line during compilation. So finally, we have our full testing version. It is presented in Listing 10-1.

Listing 10-1: **A final version of NEW.MST**

```
'***********************************************************
*
'* Filename:    NEW.MST
'*
'* Purpose:     Tests the New menu item for the File menu in
'*              Notepad's main window.
'*
```

(continued)

Listing 10-1 *(continued)*

```
'* Revision History:
'*
'*  [ 0]   da-mon-year   email    : action
'*  [ 1]   28-MAY-1998   TomAr     First few scenarios for the
"New"
'*                                 menu item to give some
'*                                 structure.
'*  [ 2]   29-MAY-1998   TVT       Created common constants, etc.
'*                                 and moved to notemain.inc. Made
'*                                 common subs and funcs and moved
'*                                 to noteutil.inc.
'*
'*****************************************************************
*


'*********************** INCLUDES
*****************************
'$include 'notemain.inc'
'$include 'noteutil.inc'

'****************** GLOBALS INITIALIZED
***********************

'******************* LOCALS DECLARED
************************

TestBegin()              'Initialize the test case

    '** Beginning of the test scenarios **
    scenario strTestNum()+"Test that 'Save changes' message
box"+ _
                        " is displayed."
        play DATA_TESTSTRING1

        SelMenu(MNU_FILE_NEW)

        if (GetText(NULL) <> CAP_SAVECHANGES) then
            fail strFailNum()+"Error: Message box not found."
        endif

    scenario cleanup
        if not(failed) then
            wButtonClick(BTN_CANCEL)
        endif
    end scenario
```

```
        scenario strTestNum()+"Verify that the original text
remains"+ _
                          " unchanged."
            if EditText(EDIT_NOTEPAD) <> DATA_TESTSTRING1 then
                fail strFailNum()+"Original test string changed."
            endif
        end scenario

TestEnd()
END
```

Listing 10-1 and the listings from the other chapters are available on the CD-ROM in the back of this book.

Template

A number of things have changed between Version Two and the Final Version. Looking through this listing, the first thing you'll notice is that comments have been added to make the code more informed and readable. These were taken from the templates mentioned in Chapter 8.

Include files

The '$INCLUDE metacommand is used in the last version to bring in two separate files that contain source code needed by this test case file. The order in which these files are brought in can be important, especially if the second file relies upon another file being included first.

It turns out that I've set up these include files so that they will include any files that they rely upon. In the event that a Test programmer doesn't realize what other files are needed, the files they bring in will include what they need. The include files have also been set up with *conditional compilation* commands to avoid any kind of recompilation errors should a file accidentally be included multiple times (such as, if they were included once explicitly by the test case file that needs a particular file, then included again by another include file used by the test case).

Remember that when you use the '$INCLUDE command, it is basically inserting the contents of the file at the location of the '$INCLUDE line. Depending on how your team sets up its include files, the order in which these files are included might be important.

New functions

A number of new subroutines and functions have been added to this latest version of our script. The first one is TestBegin(), which replaces the initialization code for starting up the application. That initialization code was moved to the

NOTEUTIL.INC file and placed into the new `TestBegin()` subroutine. Our code looks cleaner, and it's a function that all the other test cases can use.

The next routine added to this script is `strTestNum()`. When called, it increments a counter and returns a text string with that counter in it. You'll notice that `strTestNum()` is being used with the `SCENARIO` statement. By using it in this way, we arrange that the output for each of our scenarios not only contains a description of the scenario but also of the current test number. Furthermore, if other test scenarios are added later, also using `strTestNum()` alongside the text in the `SCENARIO` statement, the test count will be bumped up without requiring you to step through the code and change the numbers by hand. This is especially the case when a new test scenario is inserted between other scenarios. The exact same idea follows for the `strFailNum()` function that is called with the `FAIL` statement.

The `SelMenu()` subroutine was created to replace the `wMenuSelect` statement. It functions exactly like the `wMenuSelect` statement we used in the previous versions of this script, except it is now more flexible. `SelMenu()` takes the extra step of making sure no other menus are already displayed, before using the `wMenuSelect` statement. It also uses the `LOG` statement to write out information about which menus are selected during the test run. Coolest of all, the logging of this menu information is controllable through the Visual Test Suite Manager. You can turn it on and off, depending on the level of detail you want in your log files.

The last new subroutine is `TestEnd()`, which is placed at the very end of the test case file. `TestEnd()` replaces the clean-up and shutdown source code that was added in the second version of this script. It too can be found in the NOTEUTIL.INC file, making it available to all other test case files.

As the test automation project evolves, other needs will become apparent, and because many of these routines have been encapsulated and made sharable between test case files, there is less likelihood that small adjustments will require you to revisit every test case file to make those adjustments uniform. Instead, these common routines can be tweaked for any special needs that arise.

For example, if it later became apparent that it was necessary to log out memory information consistently, the Test programmer could either place `PRINT` or `LOG` statements that provide this information throughout each test case file or go to one or two of the commonly used routines and add the code there. A prime place for such a modification would be in the `SelMenu()` subroutine. You might also modify the `TestBegin()` and `TestEnd()` subroutines to log out beginning and ending memory information.

Global variable

A global variable was also added to make the handle to the Notepad application available to anyone who includes the NOTEMAIN.INC and NOTEUTIL.INC files. The variable is called `ghWndNotepad`. It is declared in the NOTEMAIN.INC file and initialized by the `TestBegin()` subroutine found in NOTEUTIL.INC. So many functions and statements in Visual Test require the handle to the main window that this is the easiest way to make it available.

There is a danger with using this global variable, especially on large teams. What happens if the variable gets modified somewhere deep in the source code? It's a variable, just like any other variable, except that it's global and many test case files will rely upon it.

This could easily happen if a Test programmer isn't aware of how the global variable should be used and simply employs it any way he or she sees fit. One way around this dilemma is to make the variable accessible only through a function call. That is, create the global variable but don't make mention of it anywhere in any documentation. Instead, create a function that simply returns the value of that variable. This approach is what's known as *data hiding*, which is something that can't be done as effectively in Visual Test as in other languages, such as C++. However, setting up a mechanism such as the function just mentioned helps to some degree.

Constants

The last change you may notice in the final version of the script is that it now uses constants where once there were text strings and numbers. These constants are declared in the NOTEMAIN.INC file and are generic enough that other test case files will make use of them. A common style to follow with constants is to capitalize them. This makes it obvious that they are values that cannot be changed during run time. Creating these constants and using them in all the test case files has one particular advantage. Should it later be necessary to change the name of a menu, the text of the test string, or the caption of a button from "Yes" to "Oui," it can be done in one place, resulting in all the test case files automatically being updated, since they include the NOTEMAIN.INC file and use the constants.

Preliminary Results

The preliminary results from running the final version of this test case file are shown in Figure 10-4. I say "preliminary" because our work is not yet done. All the subroutines, functions, constants, and files that have been created came from the one scenario we wrote. I broke it into two scenarios because it seemed to make most sense, but we've still only tested one situation although we set out at the beginning of this chapter to test three: Yes, No, and Cancel. The Cancel button has undergone its first tests. Now it's the turn of the Yes and No buttons.

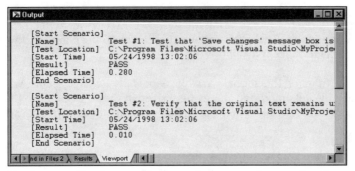

Figure 10-4: The Output window as it appears after running the final version of the NEW.MST test case file.

Again, the goal is to get a few simple test scenarios written and placed into the test case file. After this has been done, focus can shift to the next menu item and its test scenarios. After all the menus have had at least one or two tests, a structure exists that can be modified from there, depending on the goals of the automation team. Our file structure can be seen in Figure 10-5. It shows what Visual Test's Developer Studio Workspace looks like with the current test case and its associated files. As the number of test case files grows, so will the project and its structure.

Figure 10-5: Visual Test's representation of the files that have been created so far.

The Resulting Test Case

The last two scenarios took no time at all to write because the bulk of the support routines, which are discussed more fully in Chapter 11, were written with the first test scenario. The result is a total of four test scenarios. They test the three buttons on the Save Changes? message box and whether or not the text remains unchanged when the Cancel button is selected. The code for this is in Listing 10-2.

Listing 10-2: Our initial task of creating at least three tests for the Save Changes message box is complete.

```
'*****************************************************************
*
'* Filename:    NEW.MST
'*
'* Purpose:     Tests the New menu item for the File menu in
'*              Notepad's main window.
'*
'* Revision History:
'*
'*   [ 0]   da-mon-year   email   : action
'*   [ 1]   28-MAY-1998   TomAr   First few scenarios for the
"New"
'*                                menu item to give some
'*                                structure.
'*   [ 2]   29-MAY-1998   TVT     Created common constants, etc.
'*                                and moved to notemain.inc. Made
'*                                common subs and funcs and moved
'*                                to noteutil.inc.
'*   [ 3]   01-JUN-1998   TomAr   Added some final test scenarios
'*                                to fill in this first test
case.
'*
'*****************************************************************
*


'********************** INCLUDES
******************************
'$include 'notemain.inc'
'$include 'noteutil.inc'

'***************** GLOBALS INITIALIZED
***********************

'******************** LOCALS DECLARED
************************

TestBegin()            'Initialize the test case

    '** Beginning of the test scenarios **
    scenario strTestNum()+"Test that 'Save changes' message
box"+ _
                        " is displayed."
        play DATA_TESTSTRING1
```

(continued)

Listing 10-2 *(continued)*

```
        SelMenu(MNU_FILE_NEW)

        if (GetText(NULL) <> CAP_SAVECHANGES) then
            fail strFailNum()+"Error: Message box not found."
        endif

    scenario cleanup
        if not(failed) then
            wButtonClick(BTN_CANCEL)
        endif

    end scenario


    scenario strTestNum()+"Verify that the original text
remains"+ _
                        " unchanged after clicking Cancel."
        if EditText(EDIT_NOTEPAD) <> DATA_TESTSTRING1 then
            fail strFailNum()+"Original test string changed."
        endif
    end scenario

    ResetApp      'Clear contents of Notepad to get to known
state

scenario strTestNum()+"Click 'No' to 'Save Changes?' msg"
        play DATA_TESTSTRING1
        SelMenu(MNU_FILE_NEW)
        wButtonClick(BTN_NO)
        if EditText(EDIT_NOTEPAD) <> "" then
            fail strFailNum()+"Text was not cleared as
expected."
        endif
    scenario cleanup
        ResetApp
    end scenario


    scenario strTestNum()+"Click 'Yes' to 'Save changes?' msg"
        play DATA_TESTSTRING1

        SelMenu(MNU_FILE_NEW)
        wButtonClick(BTN_YES)    'Yes to save changes

        if (GetText(NULL) <> CAP_SAVEAS) then
            fail strFailNum()+"Save As dialog box not
displayed."
        else
```

```
                    'We don't want to test the Save As dialog box,
                    'just make sure it displays. We can determine
                    'how we want to test it later.
                    wButtonClick(BTN_CANCEL)
                endif
            scenario cleanup
                ResetApp
            end scenario

    TestEnd()
    END
```

Only three new constants and one subroutine were created. The three constants are BTN_YES, BTN_NO, and CAP_SAVEAS. This gives us support for clicking the Yes and No buttons, and for verifying the caption of the Save As dialog box. The one subroutine that was created is ResetApp(). The purpose of this subroutine is to place Notepad back into a known condition or *base state* by clearing the contents of its editor.

Note   Notice that in these last scenarios we're not checking for the existence of the message box before attempting to click the Yes or No buttons. In the event that the message box isn't displayed and the script attempts to click a button that won't be there without the message box, the scenario encounters a run-time error, marks the test scenario as a failure, and then moves on to the next test scenario (unless there is a scenario cleanup statement, when it runs through the clean-up code before moving on).

Summary

When focusing on an area to automate, the toughest part is writing that first line of code. The trick to it is to write something, anything, and move forward with more and more revisions to the work you've done. You're in a position very similar to that of a writer with writer's block; you're not sure what to write, and perhaps you're overwhelmed with the task ahead. But if you sit down and start typing, you'll eventually hit upon something that looks like it's worth keeping. So, you keep it, move forward, refine, adjust, and eventually you have something that looks like it will work.

This chapter covered the development of one single test case file but demonstrated how a number of utilities fall out of the beginning development. As more test cases are created, more utilities become necessary and are written to help support the testing on a product. Keep adding them to the separate utilities file, which in our case is NOTEUTIL.INC, and you'll soon have an admirable arsenal available to you and perhaps other teams at your company.

The remaining test case files that test the rest of the menu items in Notepad can be found in Appendix H, "Listings of All Test Cases." The final version of NOTEMAIN.INC is in Appendix F, "Listing for Notemain.inc," and the final version of the NOTEUTIL.INC file is in Appendix G, "Listing for Noteutil.inc." Look them over, take what you find useful, and keep the rest for later, in the event that you might need them. The source code is also available on the CD-ROM in the back of this book.

This chapter ran through a simple group of test scenarios using Notepad. It walked through three versions of the test, gradually getting more complex. It dealt with the problems you might encounter and how to deal with them. It discussed include files, new functions, global variables, and constants. Finally, it looked at the results of the test examples.

✦   ✦   ✦

Common Utilities and Routines

While developing the test case file in Chapter 10, we
ended up creating a couple of extra files that now
accompany the test case file and will be used by future test
case files. These two files are NOTEMAIN.INC and
NOTEUTIL.INC; they are the subject of discussion in this
chapter.

NOTEMAIN.INC

One of the two files we found that we needed to create when
writing the test case file in Chapter 10 was the NOTEMAIN.INC
file. This file holds all the declarations most likely needed by
other test case files. It will constantly change as the project
grows, and you'll find yourself moving pieces of
NOTEMAIN.INC to other include files specific to a given area of
the product, and other pieces of code from files lower in the
hierarchy up to NOTEMAIN.INC if they are common enough to
be used by multiple test case files. This file is written out in
Listing 11-1.

On the
CD-ROM

Remember that any listing in this chapter — or in any other
chapter — is available on the CD-ROM at the back of this book.

Listing 11-1: **NOTEMAIN.INC: The main include file**

```
'*********************** NOTEMAIN.INC ************************
'*
'* Purpose: Holds common declarations to be used by all test
'*          case files. Anything not common enough to be
'*          used by the majority of the test case files should
'*          be moved to an include file lower in the hierarchy
'*          specific to the area it concerns.
'*
'* Author:  Tom Arnold
'*
'* Revision History:
'*
'* [ 0]  da-mon-year     email    action
'* [ 1]  29-MAY-1998     TomAr    Created notemain.inc to hold
'*                                common declarations.
'* [ 2]  29-MAY-1998     TVT      Moved in some common constants.
'*************************************************************

'$IFNDEF NOTEMAIN_INCLUDED
'$DEFINE NOTEMAIN_INCLUDED


'*************************************************************
'*********************** Constants ************************
'*************************************************************

'********** General Application Info
const TEST_APP$          = "NOTEPAD.EXE" 'Exe file name

'********** Window captions/class names
const CAP_NOTEPAD$       = "- Notepad"   'Partial capt.: main
window
const CAP_SAVECHANGES$   = "Notepad"     'Caption of SaveChngs
msgbox
const CAP_SAVEAS         = "Save As"     'Caption of SaveAs
dialog
const TEST_APP_CLASS$    = "Notepad"     'Classname of app's
main win

'********** Logging Detail Settings
const LVL_MENUINFO%      = 10            'Menu info if Detail >
10
const LVL_VERBOSE%       = 100           'All calls to LOG
enabled

'********** Edit control captions
const EDIT_NOTEPAD$      = "@1"          'Notepad's main edit
window
```

```
'********** Button control captions
const BTN_NO$           = "No"          'Caption for No button
const BTN_YES$          = "Yes"         'Caption for Yes button
const BTN_CANCEL$       = "Cancel"      'Caption for Cancel
button

'********** Menu Bar and Menu Item captions
'***** Menu items for the File menu
const MNU_FILE_NEW$     = "File\New"
const MNU_FILE_OPEN$    = "File\Open..."
const MNU_FILE_SAVE$    = "File\Save"
const MNU_FILE_SAVEAS$  = "File\Save As..."
const MNU_FILE_PGSETUP$ = "File\Page Setup..."
const MNU_FILE_PRINT$   = "File\Print"
const MNU_FILE_EXIT$    = "File\Exit"

'***** Menu items for the Edit menu
const MNU_EDIT_UNDO$    = "Edit\Undo"
const MNU_EDIT_CUT$     = "Edit\Cut"
const MNU_EDIT_COPY$    = "Edit\Copy"
const MNU_EDIT_PASTE$   = "Edit\Paste"
const MNU_EDIT_DELETE$  = "Edit\Delete"
const MNU_EDIT_SELALL$  = "Edit\Select All"
const MNU_EDIT_TIMEDATE$= "Edit\Time/Date"
const MNU_EDIT_WRDWRAP$ = "Edit\Word Wrap"

'***** Menu items for the Search menu
const MNU_SEARCH_FIND$  = "Search\Find..."
const MNU_SEARCH_FNEXT$ = "Search\Find Next"

'***** Menu items for the Help menu
const MNU_HELP_TOPICS   = "Help\Help Topics"
const MNU_HELP_ABOUT    = "Help\About Notepad"

'********** Other constants
const MAX_WAIT%         = 5 '# of secs to search for window
const DATA_TESTSTRING1$ = "Now is the time for all good
people..."
const FW_NOTEPAD&       = FW_PART OR FW_ALL OR FW_FOCUS OR _
                          FW_RESTORE OR FW_EXIST
                          'Search criteria for Notepad


'*************************************************************
'********************** User Def'd Types *********************
'*************************************************************


'*************************************************************
'********************** Global Variables *********************
```

(continued)

Listing 11-1 *(continued)*

```
'****************************************************************

global ghWndNotepad&      'Global handle to Notepad's main window

'****************************************************************
'****************** Func/Proc Prototypes *********************
'****************************************************************

'$ENDIF NOTEMAIN_INCLUDED
```

Let's dissect this listing.

Conditional Compilation

A technique that can be used, and that is especially helpful for large teams, is the *conditional compilation* commands. These commands are referred to as *metacommands* in Visual Test; they provide instructions to the Test precompiler, telling it to perform certain actions before actually trying to compile the code.

This is the conditional compilation portion of NOTEMAIN.INC. Use this to avoid including source code multiple times:

```
'$IFNDEF NOTEMAIN_INCLUDED
'$DEFINE NOTEMAIN_INCLUDED
    :
... more code ...
    :
'$ENDIF NOTEMAIN_INCLUDED
```

The first two lines appear before any actual source code in the NOTEMAIN.INC file. The '$IFNDEF command checks to see if the NOTEMAIN_INCLUDED symbol has already been defined. If it has not, as in the case where the file is being included for the first time, it continues to the next line of code, where it then defines the symbol NOTEMAIN_INCLUDED. The rest of the source code in the NOTEMAIN.INC file is then included for compilation.

Note   In the case of Visual Test, a symbol declared using the '$DEFINE metacommand has no value. It is simply placed into a table internal to the Test language's compiler. Other metacommands can be used to determine whether or not a particular symbol has been defined, such as '$IFNDEF (if not defined), '$IFDEF (if defined), and so on.

If other source code files also include the NOTEMAIN.INC file, the `'$IFNDEF` metacommand will determine that `NOTEMAIN_INCLUDED` is already defined the second time the file is included, perhaps by a utility .INC file or the test case file itself. The compiler will jump down to the last line shown in the preceding code fragment and thereby not include any of the source code for a second time.

If source code is included more than once, a *redeclaration error* can occur, as shown in Figure 11-1. In the event of such an error, it is up to the Test programmer to determine how a variable is being reused or redeclared. Sometimes this is simply because someone else is already using the same variable name, which will require the Test programmer to change the name of their variable. At other times, it's because some source code from a file is being included multiple times, requiring the programmer to determine which file is being included multiple times and how that's happening.

Figure 11-1: An error occurs because a declaration for a global variable is causing a compilation error the second time the file is included.

Note   Note that in the case demonstrated in the figure, the error shows itself as something other than a redeclaration error, but the error is indeed being generated because the global declaration is being encountered a second time.

In a small source code base it isn't difficult to find out why a file is being included multiple times, because the programmer can simply search through the files in the project one at a time.

On a larger code base a multitiered hierarchy may exist to make code sharing easier, but this makes tracking down redeclaration errors more complex. Searching through a large number of files to determine which ones are being included and by which files can be time-consuming and frustrating. This is why the conditional compilation is so important. While it does lead to laxness in regulating how files are shared and included, on a time-critical project where frustrations are already high, it can pay off to set up the code base with this type of conditional compilation.

Figure 11-2 shows another type of redeclaration error. One of the frustrations of redeclaration errors is that they can be caused by including a file more than once without using conditional compilation to protect against the errors. The error won't be as exact as to say that you've included the file twice. Instead it will give you a symptom of the problem, relying on you to figure out what's causing it.

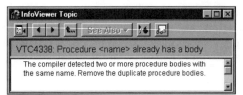

Figure 11-2: Another example of a redeclaration error.

Tip   Visual Test 6.0 has somewhat simplified the problem of redeclaration errors. If a declaration for a constant is encountered multiple times, for example, and its value or declaration hasn't changed, the 6.0 compiler will not report the error. However, if you are writing your scripts to work with previous versions of Test (3.0 or older) for testing in a 16-bit environment, you will need to use previous versions of Test that aren't as forgiving as version 6.0. Save yourself time by building in the conditional compilation up front.

Constants

The largest section of the NOTEMAIN.INC file is the Constants section. This holds values that will be used more than once and by multiple test case and utility files. If it becomes necessary to change any of the values, it can be done by editing this file. As a result, anywhere those constants were used, they're always updated to use the latest value. Listing 11-2 shows the section of code containing the constants.

Listing 11-2: The Constants section of NOTEMAIN.INC makes up the lion's share of the file.

```
'**************************************************************
'************************ Constants ***************************
'**************************************************************

'********** General Application Info
const TEST_APP$        = "NOTEPAD.EXE" 'Exe filename

'********** Window captions/class names
const CAP_NOTEPAD$     = "- Notepad"   'Partial capt.: main
window
const CAP_SAVECHANGES$ = "Notepad"     'Caption of SaveChngs
msgbox
const CAP_SAVEAS       = "Save As"     'Caption of SaveAs
dialog
const TEST_APP_CLASS$  = "Notepad"     'Classname of app's
main win
```

```
'********** Logging Detail Settings
const LVL_MENUINFO%     = 10            'Menu info if Detail >
10
const LVL_VERBOSE%      = 100           'All calls to LOG
enabled

'********** Edit control captions
const EDIT_NOTEPAD$     = "@1"          'Notepad's main edit
window

'********** Button control captions
const BTN_NO$           = "No"          'Caption for No button
const BTN_YES$          = "Yes"         'Caption for Yes button
const BTN_CANCEL$       = "Cancel"      'Caption for Cancel
button

'********** Menu Bar and Menu Item captions
'***** Menu items for the File menu
const MNU_FILE_NEW$      = "File\New"
const MNU_FILE_OPEN$     = "File\Open..."
const MNU_FILE_SAVE$     = "File\Save"
const MNU_FILE_SAVEAS$   = "File\Save As..."
const MNU_FILE_PGSETUP$  = "File\Page Setup..."
const MNU_FILE_PRINT$    = "File\Print"
const MNU_FILE_EXIT$     = "File\Exit"

'***** Menu items for the Edit menu
const MNU_EDIT_UNDO$     = "Edit\Undo"
const MNU_EDIT_CUT$      = "Edit\Cut"
const MNU_EDIT_COPY$     = "Edit\Copy"
const MNU_EDIT_PASTE$    = "Edit\Paste"
const MNU_EDIT_DELETE$   = "Edit\Delete"
const MNU_EDIT_SELALL$   = "Edit\Select All"
const MNU_EDIT_TIMEDATE$ = "Edit\Time/Date"
const MNU_EDIT_WRDWRAP$  = "Edit\Word Wrap"

'***** Menu items for the Search menu
const MNU_SEARCH_FIND$   = "Search\Find..."
const MNU_SEARCH_FNEXT$  = "Search\Find Next"

'***** Menu items for the Help menu
const MNU_HELP_TOPICS    = "Help\Help Topics"
const MNU_HELP_ABOUT     = "Help\About Notepad"

'********** Other constants
const MAX_WAIT%          = 5 '# of secs to search for window
const DATA_TESTSTRING1$ = "Now is the time for all good
people..."
```

(continued)

Listing 11-2 *(continued)*

```
const FW_NOTEPAD&      = FW_PART OR FW_ALL OR FW_FOCUS OR _
                         FW_RESTORE OR FW_EXIST
                         'Search criteria for Notepad
```

General constants

The first grouping of constants in NOTEMAIN.INC is the General and Window Captions constants. This grouping provides the test case files with information on the application that is being tested. This includes the name of the application and the captions of the main windows, dialog boxes, and message boxes that make up this application.

The naming conventions used for these constants roughly follow the idea of *Hungarian Notation* (see the "Naming Conventions" section of Chapter 8 for more information on Hungarian Notation). I've chosen to use CAP_ as the prefix to any constant that refers to a window caption, whether it's a top-level window, message box, or dialog box window. The TEST_APP_CLASS constant is a special case in that it isn't actually a caption but the class name of Notepad's main window. It seemed to fit best in the caption section of this file.

Logging detail

The Logging Detail Settings section of the include file, shown in the next code excerpt, was created specifically for use with the Visual Test Suite Manager. The Suite Manager has a dialog box, shown in Figure 11-3, that allows the tester to control the level at which the Test language's log statement will write out information. By setting up our tests to use the log statement with the constants we've created, we can have a number of levels at which information is logged out.

```
'********** Logging Detail Settings
const LVL_MENUINFO%    = 10                'Menu info if Detail >
10
const LVL_VERBOSE%     = 100               'All calls to LOG
enabled
```

The log statement has a number associated with it that tells that statement only to log out information when the details setting is higher than the number used by a given log line of code.

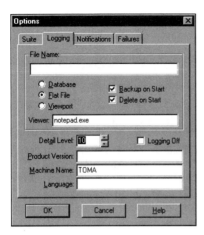

Figure 11-3: The Visual Test Suite Manager's dialog box. It allows the tester to specify at what level of detail information should be logged.

These levels are defined and controlled by the Test programmer. The levels shown in the last piece of code were created as a starting point. It is certain that more LVL_-type constants will be created as the project matures, and possibly it will become necessary to change the actual values of those constants. This is simply a place to start. LVL_VERBOSE was defined as 100 because it's assumed that other levels will fall in the range of 0 to 99. The verbose setting is meant to be a catchall way of getting as much detail out of the overall test suite as possible.

The log statement will be discussed and demonstrated more thoroughly when we look at the contents of NOTEUTIL.INC later in this chapter.

Control captions

The next section in this initial version of NOTEMAIN.INC declares constants that hold the values for commonly encountered captions in Windows controls. The first captions used by NEW.MST, in Chapter 10, are moved into the NOTEMAIN.INC file and made constants. The naming conventions for these constants use the type of control as the prefix to the name:

```
'********** Edit control captions
const EDIT_NOTEPAD$     = "@1"              'Notepad's main edit
window

'********** Button control captions
const BTN_NO$           = "No"             'Caption for No button
const BTN_YES$          = "Yes"            'Caption for Yes button
const BTN_CANCEL$       = "Cancel"         'Caption for Cancel
button
```

Remember that Notepad's main window, where text is typed in, is actually a large edit control. Because no label or caption is visibly associated with it, it's necessary to use the ordinal value to identify the control when using the wEdit* routines. Because this is the only edit control on the main window, the ordinal position is 1. This translates to "@1" so that the wEdit* routines know they are dealing with an ordinal and not a caption of "1."

Buttons with captions of Yes, No, and Cancel will be encountered throughout Notepad. Therefore, the constants for these controls are kept in NOTEMAIN.INC, the topmost portion of the file-sharing hierarchy. If this product is localized to the French, German, or Japanese markets, these commonly used button captions can be changed at this level. If this process were not followed when tests were written for different sections of Notepad, then other constants — or worse yet, no constants and just literal strings — would be used for these values. This would mean the testing team would have to visit multiple files to make a single caption change.

Menu constants

Even though NEW.MST, the first test case file created for this automation project, only used the New and Exit menu items found under the File menu, I took it upon myself to declare the rest of the constants that we'll eventually need to use as we continue setting up our overall automation structure for Notepad:

```
'********** Menu Bar and Menu Item captions
'***** Menu items for the File menu
const MNU_FILE_NEW$     = "File\New"
const MNU_FILE_OPEN$    = "File\Open..."
const MNU_FILE_SAVE$    = "File\Save"
const MNU_FILE_SAVEAS$  = "File\Save As..."
const MNU_FILE_PGSETUP$ = "File\Page Setup..."
const MNU_FILE_PRINT$   = "File\Print"
const MNU_FILE_EXIT$    = "File\Exit"

'***** Menu items for the Edit menu
const MNU_EDIT_UNDO$    = "Edit\Undo"
const MNU_EDIT_CUT$     = "Edit\Cut"
const MNU_EDIT_COPY$    = "Edit\Copy"
const MNU_EDIT_PASTE$   = "Edit\Paste"
const MNU_EDIT_DELETE$  = "Edit\Delete"
const MNU_EDIT_SELALL$  = "Edit\Select All"
const MNU_EDIT_TIMEDATE$= "Edit\Time/Date"
const MNU_EDIT_WRDWRAP$ = "Edit\Word Wrap"

'***** Menu items for the Search menu
const MNU_SEARCH_FIND$  = "Search\Find..."
const MNU_SEARCH_FNEXT$ = "Search\Find Next"
```

```
'***** Menu items for the Help menu
const MNU_HELP_TOPICS   = "Help\Help Topics"
const MNU_HELP_ABOUT    = "Help\About Notepad"
```

The MNU_ prefix was used for the menus. It's important to note that this is only the naming convention that I chose and that it could have been anything, as long as it was a unique and legal name that the compiler would understand, and preferably something that showed a sense of organization. You'll also notice that the equal signs line up in this listing. This is the degree to which I go so that the code is a little more readable. There's no reason for you to go to this degree, unless you want your scripts to appear ordered, maintained, and easy to read.

Other constants

The last section for the constants declared in NOTEMAIN.INC is for the three constants that don't yet fit into their own category. Therefore, they've been moved into a generic category. As the project matures, this will most likely change and they will be moved around into more clearly defined declaration blocks:

```
'********** Other constants
const MAX_WAIT%         = 5 '# of secs to search for window
const DATA_TESTSTRING1$ = "Now is the time for all good
people..."
const FW_NOTEPAD&       = FW_PART OR FW_ALL OR FW_FOCUS OR _
                          FW_RESTORE OR FW_EXIST
                          'Search criteria for Notepad
```

The first two constants are easily enough understood. The first is a default time used by a number of the Test language routines to determine how long the routine should wait for a control to appear before giving an error message or continuing on. The second is a generic test string that gets typed into the Notepad window for testing purposes.

The third and final constant is FW_NOTEPAD. This is unique in that it doesn't appear to be assigned one value. Instead, it uses other constants that are defined *intrinsically* to Visual Test (in other words, they aren't declared anyplace, they are already a part of the Test language). These values are being OR-ed together and assigned back to the FW_NOTEPAD constant.

The FW_ prefix stands for Find Window and was used in the FW_NOTEPAD name because it is basically a subset or specific definition of the other FW_ constants. These constants are used by the wFndWnd() and wFndWndC() functions to find a window or control. I wanted to control exactly how I search for a window and didn't want to have to type in all the other FW_ constants every time I performed such a search. Therefore, the FW_NOTEPAD constant was created.

> **Tip** Even though the `FW_` constants are being `OR`-ed together, this is not the same as a database type of `OR`-ing. In a database language this would be communicating that the search was looking for <this> value `OR` <that> value `OR` <this other> value. This isn't the case in this situation. What is actually going on is a bitwise `OR`-ing causing the binary digit values of each `FW_` constant to be merged or added together. It is done this way so that a single value can be passed to the `wFndWnd*` routine that contains the `OR`-ed results, instead of requiring `wFndWnd()` to take many more parameters that would need to be passed. This keeps the parameter list small, by requiring that only one value be passed to tell the `wFndWnd()` routine how to work.

Other Sections of NOTEMAIN.INC

The other sections of the NOTEMAIN.INC file are for the declarations of user-defined types, global variables, and function prototypes. The user-defined types section is placed after the constant declarations, since constants can be used as part of the declaration of a user-defined type.

The Visual Test compiler requires constants, types, and variable declarations to be declared prior to where they're used. Therefore, if a constant is used as part of a user-defined type declaration, that constant must appear before the type declaration in the source code listing.

```
'***************************************************************
'********************* User Def'd Types *********************
'***************************************************************

'***************************************************************
'********************* Global Variables *********************
'***************************************************************

global ghWndNotepad&     'Global handle to Notepad's main window

'***************************************************************
'****************** Func/Proc Prototypes *********************
'***************************************************************
```

At this stage, there aren't any user-defined types for the automation project. There is, however, a global variable declaration: `ghWndNotepad`. This variable is assigned the value of Notepad's main window handle by the `TestBegin()` subroutine found in the NOTEUTIL.INC include file. By making this variable global, we ensure that any time that the handle to Notepad's main window needs to be used as part of a function call (a common occurrence), the Test programmer has access to it.

In addition, the function prototype section is not yet being used. This section is meant for linking into libraries outside Rational Visual Test. An example would be linking into a dynamic-link library (DLL) that you or someone else may have written using Visual C/C++. Another example is linking into one of Windows' main libraries to use a Windows routine, such as a common dialog box or something to help track memory usage. Linking into external libraries is discussed later in this book in the "Linking to Windows APIs" section of Chapter 13.

NOTEUTIL.INC

The term *utilities* does not refer to actual standalone applications in the case of our automated test suite. Instead, it is referring to functions and subroutines that provide the test cases in our test suite with useful code, encapsulated into a function or subroutine, and made available by sharing it through a common include file; in this case, it's shared through NOTEUTIL.INC, as shown in Listing 11-3.

Listing 11-3: **We created this version of *NOTEUTIL.INC* to write a single test case to test the File menu's New menu item.**

```
'*********************** NOTEUTIL.INC ***********************
'*
'* Purpose: Common functions and subroutines useful to other
'*          test case files are placed into this file for
'*          our Notepad project. As this file grows, other
'*          testing teams might be interested in using this
'*          file to get a head start on their automation.
'*
'* Author:  Tom Arnold
'*
'* Revision History:
'*
'* [ 0]  da-mon-year    email    action
'* [ 1]  28-MAY-1998    TomAr    Created NOTEUTIL.INC to hold
'*                               common functions & subroutines.
'* [ 2]  29-MAY-1998    TVT      Moved in some common funcs.
'*********************************************************************

'$IFNDEF NOTEUTIL_INCLUDED
'$DEFINE NOTEUTIL_INCLUDED

'********************* INCLUDES
*****************************
'$include 'notemain.inc'
```

(continued)

Listing 11-3 *(continued)*

```
'****************************************************************
*
'* Subroutine:   PutString
'* Purpose:      Places a string into the Notepad editor at a
'*               specified line and character position. If the
'*               line or character doesn't exist, this routine
adds
'*               the necessary carriage returns and spaces.
'*
'* Parameters:   strOut$  String to be written to the editor
'*               iLine%   Line at which string is to be written
'*               iChar%   Character/column position to place
string
'*
'****************************************************************
*

sub PutString (strOut$, iLine%, iChar%)
    dim iCurrLine%      'Keeps track of what line the cursor is
on
    dim iCurrChar%      'Tracks which column the cursor is in
    dim iLoop%          'Used as index to for loop
    dim iLoopLimit%     'Used to determine end value of for
loop
    dim strDirection$   'Set to which keystroke should be used
'Get the current line and cursor position
    iCurrLine = wEditLine(EDIT_NOTEPAD)

    'Determine which direction to move based on
    'current position and desired position.
    if (iCurrLine < iLine) then
        iLoopLimit = (iLine - iCurrLine)
        strDirection = "{DOWN}"                  'We need to move
down
    else
        iLoopLimit = (iCurrLine - iLine)
        strDirection = "{UP}"                    'We need to move up
    endif

'Move to the desired position, adding lines if necessary.
    for iLoop = 1 to iLoopLimit
        if (wEditLine(EDIT_NOTEPAD) < wEditLines(EDIT_NOTEPAD))
then
            Play strDirection
        elseif (strDirection = "{DOWN}") then
            Play "{END}"
            Play "{ENTER}"
        else
```

```
                Play strDirection
        endif
    next iLoop

    'Get the current character position
    iCurrChar = wEditPos(EDIT_NOTEPAD)

    'Based on the current position, determine which
    'direction to move.
    if (iCurrChar < iChar) then
        iLoopLimit = (iChar - iCurrChar)
        strDirection = "{RIGHT}"
    else
        iLoopLimit = (iCurrChar - iChar)
        strDirection = "{LEFT}"
    endif

    'Move to the desired position adding spaces if needed.
for iLoop = 1 to iLoopLimit
        if (wEditPos(EDIT_NOTEPAD) < _
            wEditLineLen(EDIT_NOTEPAD,wEditLine(EDIT_NOTEPAD)))
then
            Play strDirection
        elseif (strDirection = "{RIGHT}") then
            Play " "
        else
            Play strDirection
        endif
    next iLoop

    Play strOut    'Type the string at the
                   'current location
end sub 'PutString()

'*****************************************************************
*
'* Subroutine:   ResetApp
'* Purpose:      Attempts to reset the application to a known
'*               state. This routine will likely grow in
'*               complexity as strange circumstances are
'*               discovered where it isn't able to reset the
'*               application.
'*
'*****************************************************************
*

sub ResetApp()
    WMenuEnd
```

(continued)

Listing 11-3 *(continued)*

```
    SelMenu(MNU_FILE_NEW)

    if (GetText(NULL) = CAP_SAVECHANGES) then
        wButtonClick(BTN_NO)
    endif
end sub 'ResetApp()


'***************************************************************
*
'* Subroutine:  SelMenu
'* Purpose:      This is a wrapper around the wMenuSelect
'*               statement, allowing us a level of detailed
'*               information if requested.
'*
'* Parameters:  STRING  A wMenuSelect-compatible string.
'*
'***************************************************************
*

sub SelMenu(strMenu$)
    WMenuEnd                    'Verify a menu isn't already popped
down
    wMenuSelect(strMenu)     'Select the menu item

    'The detail level represented by the LVL_MENUINFO constant
is
    'controlled from the Options dialog box in the Suite
Manager.
    'If the level specified in the Suite Manager is greater
than
    'the level specified by LVL_MENUINFO (below) then the info
    'will be logged out. Otherwise, the information isn't
logged.
    'This is a way to control the level/detail of information
    'provided.
    Log #LVL_MENUINFO, "Selected menu: "+strMenu$
end sub 'SelMenu()


'***************************************************************
*
'* Function:    strFailNum
'* Purpose:      Keeps a counter of the total number of failures
'*               that have occurred using the fail command for
'*               the current test case file. For this to work,
'*               it must be called for each failure and is
'*               therefore designed to work with the fail
```

```
'*                 statement.
'*
'* Parameters:  NONE
'*
'* Returns:     STRING  The string that is returned is
formatted
'*                      to fit in front of the text being
'*                      included in the fail statement.
'*
'* Format
'* returned:    "Fail #<num>: "
'*
'* Use:         FAIL strFailNum()+"<descrip-of-failure>"
'*
'****************************************************************
*

function strFailNum() as string
    static iCount%

    iCount = iCount + 1
    strFailNum = "Fail #"+trim$(str$(iCount))+": "
end function 'strFailNum()


'****************************************************************
*
'* Function:    strTestNum
'* Purpose:     Keeps a counter of the total number of tests
'*              that have been executed for the current test
'*              case file. For this to work, it must be
'*              called for each test. It is designed to work
'*              with the scenario statement. This is why it
'*              returns a string.
'*
'* Parameters:  NONE
'*
'* Returns:     STRING  The string that is returned is
formatted
'*                      to fit in front of the text being
'*                      included in the scenario statement.
'*
'* Format
'* returned:    "Test #<num>: "
'*
'* Use:         SCENARIO strTestNum()+"<descrip-of-test>"
'*
```

(continued)

Listing 11-3 *(continued)*

```
'****************************************************************
*
function strTestNum() as string
    static iCount%

    iCount = iCount + 1
    strTestNum = "Test #"+trim$(str$(iCount))+": "
end function 'strTestNum()

'****************************************************************
*
'* Subroutine:  TestBegin
'* Purpose:     All initialization code that needs to be run
'*              before the scenarios of a test case are
'*              executed should be placed in this subroutine.
'*              This subroutine needs to be called first by
'*              each test case.
'*
'* Parameters:  NONE
'*
'****************************************************************
*

sub TestBegin()
    log #LVL_VERBOSE, "Initializing Test Case and attempting
to"
    log #LVL_VERBOSE, "find or run ";TEST_APP;" application."

    viewport clear      'Clean the contents of the Viewport tab
                        'in the Output window.

    'Get test application up and running. If it can be run
    'for whatever reason, print an error message and stop
    'the execution of the script.

    ghWndNotepad = wFndWndC(CAP_NOTEPAD, TEST_APP_CLASS, _
                        FW_NOTEPAD, MAX_WAIT)

    if (ghWndNotepad = 0) then
        log #LVL_VERBOSE, "Unable to find ";TEST_APP;"."
        if run(TEST_APP) then
            fail "Error: Unable to run notepad.exe"
        else
            ghWndNotepad = wFndWnd(CAP_NOTEPAD, FW_NOTEPAD, _
                            MAX_WAIT)
            log #LVL_VERBOSE, "Successfully ran ";TEST_APP
        endif
```

```
        else
            log #LVL_VERBOSE, "Found ";TEST_APP;" already running."
            ResetApp()
        endif

        'Note: A call to the fail statement will generate
        'a run-time error, since it is not in a scenario block.
        'The result is an error message box, if you are in
        'Microsoft Developer Studio. If you are in the Visual
        'Test Suite Manager the Suite Manager will move on to the
        'next test case file. This, which is what you would want,
since
        'it doesn't make sense for the rest of the tests to run,
        'because the test application can't be brought up.
end sub 'TestBegin()


'*****************************************************************
*
'* Subroutine:   TestEnd
'* Purpose:      Clean-up code that needs to be executed after
'*               all scenarios for a given test case file have
'*               been executed.
'*
'* Parameters:   NONE
'*
'*****************************************************************
*

sub TestEnd()
    '** Clean-up before the test case file ends **

    wMenuSelect(MNU_FILE_EXIT)     'Shut down Notepad
application

    if (GetText(NULL) = CAP_SAVECHANGES) then
        wButtonClick(BTN_NO)       'Click 'No' to "Save
changes?"
    endif
end sub 'TestEnd()


'*****************************************************************
*
'* Subroutine:   <name>
'* Purpose:
'*
'* Parameters:
'*
```

(continued)

```
'*****************************************************************
*

'*****************************************************************
*
'* Function:     <name>
'* Purpose:
'*
'* Parameters:
'*
'* Returns:
'*
'*****************************************************************
*

'$ENDIF NOTEUTIL_INCLUDED
```

The NOTEUTIL.INC include file consists of seven functions and subroutines. They range from counters, to keep track of the number of tests and failures that occur, to test initialization and clean-up routines. Because this is the first version of this file, and it will grow as more test cases are added to the project, we'll take the opportunity to step through these first functions.

Why NOTEUTIL.INC Includes NOTEMAIN.INC

NOTEUTIL.INC includes NOTEMAIN.INC, the overall header file for the project, even though it's likely that a test case file would have already included NOTEMAIN.INC.

By having every file in the automation project include the files it needs, even in cases where it might cause a file to be included multiple times, you make determining file dependencies later a much simpler task. If someone should come along in a year or so and wish to remove sections of the automation project for use on another project, having these explicit declarations means the person knows exactly what files are needed for his test to run correctly.

A New Level of Retentiveness? You'd Think So... at First

You may or may not have noticed that the functions and subroutines in this file have been arranged into alphabetical order. A friend showed me this one time, and I thought it was a good idea. (I made fun of him at first, and then I saw the value in it, when he explained the idea further.)

The idea of organizing your routines like this doesn't make sense when you are working within an editor, and even less if the number of routines is low. However, as the file gets bigger in size—and one day you'll find yourself working from a printout of the utility file— you'll then see the benefit of this approach, since you'll know in which direction to search through your reams of paper. Just something to keep in mind.

One of the first lines of the NOTEUTIL.INC file is the metacommand to include our project's main header file. This command, shown in the following code, is in the NOTEUTIL.INC file because the NOTEUTIL.INC file relies upon declarations found in NOTEMAIN.INC. This is purely a matter of style, and it's arguable whether this style should be followed or not. I do it this way because I've set up my include files so that they don't cause a redeclaration error by using conditional compilation commands. This way, each file can include exactly what it needs to function correctly.

```
'*********************** INCLUDES
****************************
'$include 'notemain.inc'
```

PutString()

The `PutString()` subroutine was written because there might come a time when you need a test scenario to check whether certain text exists at a particular location. Perhaps this might occur when testing cut-and-paste functionality, or when typing text in the middle of a string and verifying that the word wrapping is working as expected. Whatever the case, this routine was written to provide everyone on our fictitious testing team a way to insert text at a specific line and character position. As Listing 11-4 shows, the `PutString()` subroutine takes three arguments. The first argument is the string to be placed into Notepad's editor, the second is the line position, and the third is the character position at which to place the string.

Listing 11-4: The PutString() subroutine takes three arguments.

```
'*****************************************************************
*
'* Subroutine:   PutString
'* Purpose:      Places a string into the Notepad editor at a
'*               specified line and character position. If the
'*               line or character doesn't exist, this routine
adds
'*               the necessary carriage returns and spaces.
'*
'* Parameters:   strOut$ String to be written to the editor
'*               iLine%  Line at which string is to be written
'*               iChar%  Character/column position to place
string
'*
'*****************************************************************
*
sub PutString (strOut$, iLine%, iChar%)
    dim iCurrLine%       'Keeps track of what line the cursor is
on
    dim iCurrChar%       'Tracks which column cursor is in
    dim iLoop%           'Used as index to for loop
    dim iLoopLimit%      'Used to determine end value of for
loop
    dim strDirection$    'Set to which keystroke should be used

    'Get the current line and cursor position
    iCurrLine = wEditLine(EDIT_NOTEPAD)

    'Determine which direction to move based on
    'current position and desired position.
    if (iCurrLine < iLine) then
        iLoopLimit = (iLine - iCurrLine)
        strDirection = "{DOWN}"               'We need to move
down
    else
        iLoopLimit = (iCurrLine - iLine)
        strDirection = "{UP}"                 'We need to move up
    endif

    'Move to the desired position, adding lines if necessary.
    for iLoop = 1 to iLoopLimit
        if (wEditLine(EDIT_NOTEPAD) < wEditLines(EDIT_NOTEPAD))
then
            Play strDirection
        elseif (strDirection = "{DOWN}") then
            Play "{END}"
```

```
                Play "{ENTER}"
            else
                Play strDirection
            endif
        next iLoop

        'Get the current character position
        iCurrChar = wEditPos(EDIT_NOTEPAD)

        'Based on the current position, determine which
        'direction to move.
        if (iCurrChar < iChar) then
            iLoopLimit = (iChar - iCurrChar)
            strDirection = "{RIGHT}"
        else
            iLoopLimit = (iCurrChar - iChar)
            strDirection = "{LEFT}"
        endif

        'Move to the desired position adding spaces if needed.
    for iLoop = 1 to iLoopLimit
            if (wEditPos(EDIT_NOTEPAD) < _
                wEditLineLen(EDIT_NOTEPAD,wEditLine(EDIT_NOTEPAD)))
    then
                Play strDirection
            elseif (strDirection = "{RIGHT}") then
                Play " "
            else
                Play strDirection
            endif
        next iLoop

        Play strOut     'Type the string at the
                        'current location
    end sub 'PutString()
```

Instead of stepping through each of these functions line by line, I'll just point out key things about each one. The main feature of PutString() is that it's basically an improved version of the PLAY statement, when it comes to working with keystrokes and Notepad. The user can easily specify where to place a line of text, and the routine will automatically add carriage returns and spaces to get to the appropriate line and character position in the editor.

ResetApp()

The ResetApp() routine was written so that the state of Notepad can be returned to a known starting point at any time during the running of an automated test (see the next piece of code). This routine is just a starting point and only considers the situations in which a menu might already be displayed or the Save changes? message box is displayed and must be dealt with. Notice also that ResetApp() is using another routine we've written, called SelMenu(), to select a menu item. Not only should the routines that you write be used by your test cases, they should be used by the utility routines themselves.

```
'***************************************************************
*
'* Subroutine:  ResetApp
'* Purpose:      Attempts to reset the application to a known
'*               state. This routine will likely grow in
'*               complexity as strange circumstances are
'*               discovered where this routine isn't able to
'*               reset the application.
'*
'***************************************************************
*
sub ResetApp()
    WMenuEnd
    SelMenu(MNU_FILE_NEW)
    if (GetText(NULL) = CAP_SAVECHANGES) then
        wButtonClick(BTN_NO)
    endif
end sub 'ResetApp()
```

There's always room for improvement when it comes to routines like this. The most obvious addition would be to deal with any dialog box that might be displayed when it is called. Other helpful clean-up tasks could be added to this and other commonly called routines. An example in the case of ResetApp() would be a routine to back up the current log file every time the routine is called. Another would be to dump out the current state of memory available.

Not only do routines like ResetApp() serve their obvious purpose, they also provide hooks into the automated scripts so that you can include other special routines for housekeeping and other reasons.

SelMenu()

SelMenu() is another simple subroutine whose true purpose is to provide an easy place for us to insert other routines. It provides a structure from which we can hang or insert status tracking routines. In its current form it first verifies that a menu isn't already displayed and then selects the menu item passed to it by using Visual Test's wMenuSelect statement. This can be seen in this block of code:

```
'****************************************************************
*
'* Subroutine:   SelMenu
'* Purpose:       This is a wrapper around the wMenuSelect
'*                statement, allowing us a level of detailed
'*                information if requested.
'*
'* Parameters:    STRING  A wMenuSelect-compatible string.
'*
'****************************************************************
*

sub SelMenu(strMenu$)
    WMenuEnd                    'Verify a menu isn't already popped
down
    wMenuSelect(strMenu)    'Select the menu item

    'The detail level represented by the LVL_MENUINFO constant
is
    'controlled from the Options dialog box in the Suite
Manager.
    'If the level specified in the Suite Manager is greater
than
    'the level specified by LVL_MENUINFO (below) then the info
    'will be logged out. Otherwise, the information isn't
logged.
    'This is a way to control the level/detail of information
    'provided.

    Log #LVL_MENUINFO, "Selected menu: "+strMenu$
end sub 'SelMenu()
```

The LOG statement was mentioned earlier in this chapter when we looked at the constants defined for the Visual Test Suite Manager. The last line before the end of the SelMenu() subroutine shows how this statement is used with one of the constants declared in NOTEMAIN.INC. If the level of detail set in the Suite Manager is greater than the level represented by the LVL_MENUINFO constant, then the information provided with this LOG statement will be written to the Viewport or log file, whichever is specified in the Suite Manager.

strFailNum() and strTestNum()

The SCENARIO and FAIL statements provided in the Test language are great for writing out information about the tests and any errors encountered by them.

However, they lack a counter to keep track of the number of tests and errors that occur.

One of the things that managers like to see is numbers, so that they have a feel for the status of a project. A typical figure that supervisors like to have available to them is the number of tests being run on a given area of the product. While this is somewhat silly, since the number of tests doesn't communicate the quality of those tests, it's a metric that people nonetheless like to hear. The same goes for the number of errors encountered for a given test case.

This is where strFailNum() and strTestNum() come in. Their source code is virtually the same. StrFailNum() returns the number of times it has been called; it is meant to be used with the FAIL statement. StrTestNum() is similar, except that it is used with the SCENARIO statement:

```
'****************************************************************
*
'* Function:     strFailNum
'* Purpose:      Keeps a counter of the total number of failures
'*               that have occurred using the fail command for
'*               the current test case file. For this to work,
'*               it must be called for each failure and is
'*               therefore designed to work with the fail
'*               statement.
'*
'* Parameters:   NONE
'*
'* Returns:      STRING  The string that is returned is
formatted
'*                       to fit in front of the text being
'*                       included in the fail statement.
'*
'* Format
'* returned:     "Fail #<num>: "
'*
'* Use:          FAIL strFailNum()+"<descrip-of-failure>"
'*
'****************************************************************
*

function strFailNum() as string
    static iCount%

    iCount = iCount + 1
    strFailNum = "Fail #"+trim$(str$(iCount))+": "
end function 'strFailNum()
```

These two routines are different than those we've already looked at. Instead of being subroutines, they're functions. They return a value back to the point at which the function call was placed.

The first thing you'll notice is that the comment block is somewhat different because it contains information about the return value. Also included is an example of how the function is to be used. This is so that, when my teammates go to use the function, they'll use it correctly the first time.

The next thing you'll notice is that a *static* variable is used. This is similar to a global variable in that it retains its value from function call to function call. However, static variables can only be accessed by the function. This way, the value can't be accidentally changed by another Test programmer. If you later decide to check how many failures have occurred without bumping the counter, the variable may need to be changed to a global variable.

Every time these functions are called, they bump their static counter variables by one and then return a string with the number in it. Because a STRING and an INTEGER are two different types, the number needs to be changed with a call to STR$()—a function built into the Test language.

The TRIM$() function trims off any leading or trailing spaces that might be a part of the number conversion. For example, a leading space is left when converting a number to a STRING. The STR$() function leaves room for a minus sign in the event that the number is negative.

TestBegin()

TestBegin() is the first subroutine called by every test case file in the entire test suite. This happens because our imaginary testing team has decided it's the way everyone will write their code. When a decision like this is made, it's a good idea to include it in the template used by the testing team, so that everyone remembers to start putting their code after the TestBegin() call.

The purpose of TestBegin() is to do whatever is necessary to set up the application to make it ready for testing. This includes locating an instance of Notepad that is already up and running, or running the application if it can't be found. Another thing that needs to be done is to assign the handle of the application's main window to a variable, so that it can be used later:

```
'*******************************************************************
*
'* Subroutine:  TestBegin
'* Purpose:     All initialization code that needs to be run
'*              before the scenarios of a test case are
'*              executed should be placed in this subroutine.
```

```
'*               This subroutine needs to be called first by
'*               each test case.
'*
'* Parameters:  NONE
'*
'***************************************************************
*
sub TestBegin()
    log #LVL_VERBOSE, "Initializing Test Case and attempting
to"
    log #LVL_VERBOSE, "find or run ";TEST_APP;" application."

    viewport clear         'Clean the contents of the Viewport tab
                           'in the Output window.

    'Get test application up and running. If it can be run
    'for whatever reason, print an error message and stop
    'the execution of the script.

    ghWndNotepad = wFndWndC(CAP_NOTEPAD, TEST_APP_CLASS, _
                            FW_NOTEPAD, MAX_WAIT)

    if (ghWndNotepad = 0) then
        log #LVL_VERBOSE, "Unable to find ";TEST_APP;"."
        if run(TEST_APP) then
            fail "Error: Unable to run notepad.exe"
        else
            ghWndNotepad = wFndWnd(CAP_NOTEPAD, FW_NOTEPAD, _
                            MAX_WAIT)
            log #LVL_VERBOSE, "Successfully ran ";TEST_APP
        endif
    else
        log #LVL_VERBOSE, "Found ";TEST_APP;" already running."
        ResetApp()
    endif

    'Note: Having a call to the Fail statement will generate
    'a run-time error, since it is not in a SCENARIO block.
    'The result is an error message box being given if you
    'are in Microsoft Developer Studio. If you are in the
    'Visual Test Suite Manager, the result will be the Suite
    'Manager moving on to the next test case file, which is
    'what you would want, since it doesn't make sense for the
    'rest of the tests to run since the test application
    'can't be brought up.

end sub 'TestBegin()
```

If the tests are being run by the Suite Manager and the level of detail is set to a value higher than `LVL_VERBOSE`, some initial information will be logged out at the beginning of the test suite.

Some of the initial setup is also handled by the Suite Manager. For example, I used to put code in this routine to delete or back up my log files. Since the Suite Manager in Visual Test 6.0 does this for me, the code is no longer included in my routines.

The `wFndWndC()` function is used to find an instance of Notepad that is already up and running. If one isn't found, then zero (0) is returned instead of a handle to a window.

Now here's something quirky about Visual Test that catches everyone at some point. It concerns the `NOT` operator. In the section of code after attempting to find an instance of Notepad is this line:

```
if (ghWndNotepad = 0) then
```

Most of you are looking at this and asking why the line of code shown in the next fragment wasn't used instead. The reason is because the `NOT` operator is a *bitwise* operator, not a *logical* operator. Therefore, it flips each digit in the binary representation of a number to its opposite value (1 goes to 0, 0 goes to 1).

```
if not(ghWndNotepad) then
```

Theoretically, at least in C and Pascal, these two pieces of code should behave exactly the same. Not so in Visual Test's language.

The intent of the line is to cause the code in the `IF` statement to execute in the event `ghWndNotepad` is equal to zero (0). In this case, both lines will behave in exactly the same way. In the situation where `ghWndNotepad` is set to a window handle, however, the first example will skip the code in the `IF` statement, as intended, but the second will move into the `IF` statement, which is not the desired behavior.

The reason is that the `NOT` operator flips the bits of the value stored in the `ghWndNotepad` variable, resulting in a value that still isn't zero (0, `FALSE`). If the value is nonzero, then it is considered to evaluate to `TRUE` and will continue into the `IF` statement. When the value is –1, however, it won't step into the `IF` statement. The binary representation of –1 in Visual Test is all of the binary digits set to 1, meaning that they all flip to 0 when the `NOT` operator is used. So stick to the explicit version when checking if a variable is zero (0) or not, unless you're truly dealing with `FALSE` and `TRUE` values, as defined by the Test language.

The rest of the routine is self-explanatory. The comment about the FAIL statement at the end of the subroutine points out that if it is used outside a scenario block it will generate a run-time error. If the Suite Manager is running, it stops execution on the current test case file and the Suite Manager moves on to the next test case file.

TestEnd()

TestEnd() is the same idea as TestBegin(), except that it cleans up after the testing is done. In its current form, it doesn't do much, but it will grow in complexity as more test cases are added to the suite:

```
'***************************************************************
*
'* Subroutine:   TestEnd
'* Purpose:      Clean-up code that needs to be executed after
'*               all scenarios for a given test case file have
'*               been executed.
'*
'* Parameters:   NONE
'*
'***************************************************************
*

sub TestEnd()
    '** Clean-up before the test case file ends **
    wMenuSelect(MNU_FILE_EXIT)    'Shut down Notepad
application

    if (GetText(NULL) = CAP_SAVECHANGES) then
        wButtonClick(BTN_NO)      'Click 'No' to "Save
changes?"
    endif
end sub 'TestEnd()
```

A different way to write this script is to have it call the ResetApp() subroutine and then call SelMenu() to select the Exit menu item. Don't be surprised if this is the case in the final version of this subroutine.

Final Comments

It's incredible how much support code can be written after setting up the first test case. The trick is to write that first test case and then cut out the sections of code that look as if they'll be needed by other test case files. Throw that code into subroutines and put them into a separate file, so that they're easy to share.

As your list of utilities grows, share them with other testing teams if you work at a big company. Or share them at discussion groups with others who are writing test automation. I know it's hard to share your code because you might be worried about other's opinions, but you'd be surprised how many beginners are out there who don't have a clue as to where to start. You can help both them and those who are more experienced—and who are often good enough to share their routines with you, so you can assimilate them into your existing code base.

Tip Refer to Appendix B, take a look at this book's CD-ROM, or check out `www.` `vtindepth.com` for information on how to subscribe to the MT_Info group. I created MT_Info originally to allow students in my hands-on Visual Test classes to be able to network and support each other after the classes were over. It has since grown to over 700 active subscribers and is one of the best sources of information about Visual Test. (Rational Software even uses it as one of their main methods to communicate with Visual Test users about what new features to add to future versions.)

One of the main themes of this section of the book, if you've not picked up on it already, is to keep your scripts as clean and as flexible as possible. Make your job and your teammates' jobs easy by using constants for common values and placing reusable code into files where they're accessible.

Summary

This chapter discusses two files: NOTEMAIN.INC and NOTEUTIL.INC.

NOTEMAIN.INC holds all the declarations that are most likely to be needed by other test case files. It deals with conditional compilation commands (also known as metacommands), constants, logging, control captions, declarations of user-defined types, global variables, and function prototypes.

NOTEUTIL.INC contains all the functions and subroutines that provide the test cases in our test suite with useful code, encapsulated into a function or subroutine, and made available by sharing it through a common include file—including NOTEMAIN.INC. These functions and subroutines are discussed in detail.

✦   ✦   ✦

Overview of the Final Test Suite

◆ ◆ ◆ ◆

In This Chapter:

Determining and
building a structure

Reviewing utilities
added to the suite

Running the final
test suite

Reviewing the results

◆ ◆ ◆ ◆

The previous two chapters, Chapters 10 and 11, have focused on building a test case file for Notepad's New menu item. The idea behind that exercise was to demonstrate exactly how much initial coding goes into creating the first couple of tests. Now that we have an understanding of what it took to write a single test case file, I've gone ahead and written the rest of the test cases to create a skeleton or structure that can be added to by other testers. The purpose of this chapter is to explore what effect the addition of these test cases has on the original files created in Chapters 10 and 11. Additionally, we'll explore how to run all of the test cases that have been created.

Developing a Structure

Before sitting down to write this chapter, I developed the structure that will be used as more tests are added to automate the testing of the Notepad application. I created a few tests for each feature of the product, so that they are all at least touched upon, albeit briefly. This was done based on the same idea followed for writing the tests for the New menu item found under the File menu. Figure 12-1 shows what the project looks like when viewed in Microsoft Visual Studio.

Now that the rest of the structure is in place, along with a few tests for each of Notepad's features, we can see what additional utilities have been created and placed into the NOTEUTIL.INC file (the main function and subroutine utilities shared by all test case files).

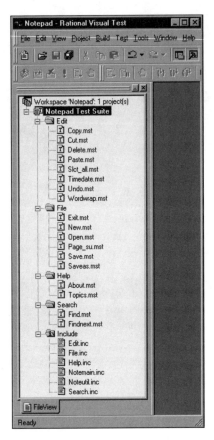

Figure 12-1: The Project Workspace window for the Notepad test suite, as it appears in the Microsoft Developer Studio 6.0.

After looking briefly at the new utilities we added as the structure filled out, we'll see how the test case files work with the Rational Visual Test Suite Manager. This includes seeing how logging is controlled using the Suite Manager's different settings.

Additional Utilities

The NOTEUTIL.INC file is a living and breathing component of the Notepad test suite. As tests are added to the suite, other utilities that are useful and generic enough to be used by other test case files become apparent and migrate to the NOTEUTIL.INC file.

The full versions of these scripts are available on the CD-ROM included with this book.

iFailCount() and iTestCount()

Two other functions that were added to make a Test programmer's life easier are iFailCount() and iTestCount(). These are very simple but critical to protect a variable from being changed. iFailCount() returns the total number of failures that have occurred during the running of a test case file:

```
'***************************************************************
*
'* Function:     iFailCount
* Purpose:       Returns current number of failures for the
                 current ' test case file. This only works if
'*               the test scenarios are using strFailNum()
'*               in conjunction with calls to the fail
'*               statement. It is done this way to avoid
'*               Test programmers directly accessing
'*               the giFailCount global variable.
'*
'* Parameters:   NONE
'*
'* Returns:      INTEGER Current value of giFailCount, which
'*                       is a global value incremented every
'*                       time strFailNum is called.
'*
'***************************************************************
*

function iFailCount() as integer
    iFailCount = giFailCount
end function 'iFailCount
```

Note Because iFailCount() **and** iTestCount() **are very similar, only the function** iFailCount() **is shown.**

The source code that makes up iFailCount() is extremely simple. All it does is return the value currently held in the giFailCount global INTEGER variable by assigning it to the function's name. As mentioned briefly in Chapter 8, this is a simple form of *data hiding*. The idea is to get the entire Test programming team to use the function instead of the actual variable when retrieving information about how many tests have been executed and how many of them have failed.

If Test programmers new to the team want to retrieve the current number of tests or failures, they need only refer to iTestCount() or iFailCount(). As a result, the odds of someone accidentally modifying the global variables that hold this information decrease.

The idea of data hiding isn't meant as a security measure, at least not in this situation. It's intended to cut down on the number of logical bugs that can be created because someone on the programming team modified a variable they shouldn't have. The goal in our example is to modify the value of giFailCount through the use of the strFailNum() function, which will be discussed shortly. To retrieve that value, iFailCount() is used, resulting in the global variable being modified indirectly at all times.

strFailNum() and strTestNum()

The Visual Test language provides a means to log out information as a test case is running. What it lacks, however, is a counter so that a running total of the number of tests and failures that have occurred can be tracked. strFailNum() and strTestNum() are my attempt to fill in this missing functionality and to provide more helpful information:

```
'*****************************************************************
'*  Function:     strFailNum
'*  Purpose:      Keeps a counter of the total number of
'*                failures that have occurred using the FAIL
'*                command for the current test case file.
'*                For this to work, it must be called for
'*                each FAILure and is therefore designed to
'*                work with the FAIL statement.
'*
'*  Parameters:   NONE
'*
'*  Returns:      STRING  The string that is returned is
'*                        formatted to fit in front of the
'*                        text being included in the FAIL
'*                        statement.
'*
'*  Format
'*  returned:     "Fail #<num>: "
'*
'*  Use:          FAIL strFailNum()+"<descrip-of-failure>"
'*
'*****************************************************************

function strFailNum() as string
    giFailCount = giFailCount + 1
    strFailNum = "Fail #"+trim$(str$(giFailCount))+": "
end function 'strFailNum()
```

Tracking the Numbers of Tests and Failures

All four functions—`strFailNum()`, `strTestNum()`, `iFailCount()`, and `iTestCount()`—work together to provide information about how many tests and failures have occurred for a given test case file.

Some people take a different approach, however, by hard-coding the test and fail numbers so that they don't change when new tests are added. On one project I was on, it was critical to cross-verify the automated tests with those described in the overall test plan. In this case, it was necessary to type in a unique test number of each test, thereby hard-coding that information into each test case file.

Usually this isn't required, at least not for most software companies. Therefore, the typical approach is to create functions similar to these four, so that when a test is moved or placed in front of another test, it isn't necessary to go through and renumber the hard-coded test information by hand. When the test case file completes, you have a count as to how many tests passed and how many failed.

`strFailNum()` is yet another simple function, but it is powerful in what it contributes to the overall test suite. When it is called, it increments a global counter variable, `giFailCount`, that keeps track of how many times `strFailNum()` is called. It is designed to work specifically with the Test language's `FAIL` statement. It returns a string that can be prepended to the text outputted by the `FAIL` statement.

This function is very similar to the one created in Chapter 11. It has since evolved, however, which is why it is being shown again. Now instead of using a static variable, it is using a global variable so that the current number of failures and tests can be retrieved more easily. The `giFailCount` global variable is the same one used by `iFailCount()`. The object is to get information about a test case file without adding to the potential for other bugs. Therefore, the `iFailCount()` function is provided so that you never need to interact directly with the global variable. Also, should the requirements change for how the global variable gets incremented, it's much easier to modify the guts of a function than to search through all existing scripts for a global variable and then change how it is used.

TestEnd()

The `TestEnd()` subroutine isn't a new routine added as the test suite grew. It did evolve, however, into a routine that provides more information at the end of the execution of each test case. `TestEnd()` now prints out summary information about

how many tests were executed and how many failures were encountered. This
listing provides more information than the original version shown in Chapter 11:

```
'*****************************************************************
*
'* Subroutine:   TestEnd
'* Purpose:      Clean-up code that needs to be executed after
'*               all scenarios for a given test case file have
'*               been executed.
'*
'* Parameters:   NONE
'*
'*****************************************************************
*

sub TestEnd()
    dim iPPass%              'Percent passed
    dim strMetrix$           'Misc metrics

    '** Clean-up before the test case file ends **

    wMenuSelect(MNU_FILE_EXIT)      'Shut down Notepad
                                    'application

    if GetText(NULL) = CAP_SAVECHANGES then
        wButtonClick(BTN_NO)        'Click 'No' to
                                    '"Save changes?"
    endif

    'Set up info to be logged out
    iPPass = ((iTestCount - iFailCount) / iTestCount) * 100
    strMetrix = "Scenarios: "+trim$(str$(iTestCount)) + _
            SPACE$(MAX_GAP) + "Errors:
"+trim$(str$(iFailCount)) _
            +SPACE$(MAX_GAP) + "Passed: " _
            +trim$(str$(iPPass))+"%"

    'Log out final information for the test case file
    'When doing the LEFT$() stuff a bunch of spaces are added
    'for padding and then are cropped off so that the max size
    'of the line being written out is 70 characters. By
cropping
    'like this the info can adjust its size and still have the
    'right-hand border of the box remain in line.
    log #LVL_SUMMARY,"************************* Test Case "+ _
                    "Results *************************"
    log #LVL_SUMMARY,"*"+space$(68)+"*"
    log #LVL_SUMMARY,"* Test Case: "+(left$(NAME$(0)+ _
                    space$(70),56))+"*"
    log #LVL_SUMMARY,"*"+space$(68)+"*"
    log #LVL_SUMMARY,"* "+left$(strMetrix+space$(70),67)+"*"
    log #LVL_SUMMARY,"*"+space$(68)+"*"
```

```
       log #LVL_SUMMARY,"* Test case completed testing at "+ _
                        left$(datetime$+space$(70),36)+"*"
       log #LVL_SUMMARY,"*"+space$(68)+"*"
       log #LVL_SUMMARY,STRING$(70,"*")
    end sub 'TestEnd()
```

TestBegin() and TestEnd() both assume that each test case calls them, respectively, before running any test scenarios, and after all the test scenarios have been completed for a given test case file. By operating on these assumptions, by building these subroutines into our Test templates, and by educating new programmers as they come onto the scene, we gain the flexibility to provide initialization and clean-up code for each test case file.

TestEnd() has evolved from the first version shown in Chapter 11. It now provides summary information about how many tests were run and how many failures were encountered. It also takes those numbers and comes up with a percentage of how many of the tests passed for the given test case file. As the project matures, so will the NOTEUTIL.INC file, and all the functions and subroutines it contains.

Documenting NOTEUTIL.INC

Because we created a template for subroutine and function comment blocks early on, as described in Chapter 8, the project is now at a state where documentation can be constructed so that newcomers can come up to speed quickly.

Each comment block in the NOTEUTIL.INC file can be copied and pasted into a document to be used when writing test scripts. By doing this, we're creating our own documentation that is helpful not only to new Test programmers but to existing Test programmers. After all, they need to remember which parameters have to be passed to a function or subroutine, and what value will be returned by a given function.

If you really want to be cool, you can copy and paste the information into an online help document and compile it down to a .HLP file similar to the Help files provided with almost any Windows application, or the new .CHM files using the new Help engine used by Microsoft Visual Studio 6.0. On one project, my teammates and I went so far as to write a script in Visual Test to step through the .INC file and copy all pertinent comment blocks over to a separate file, so that it was easy to paste them into a separate document.

Tip

The .CHM file format is a new format for help files. It's a compiled form of the Hypertext Markup Language. Instead of using Microsoft's new help compiler, you could also save out your comment blocks into HTML documents using the free plug-in for Microsoft Word (available from the Microsoft Web site) or any other HTML converter. This way you can have your documentation online within your company's intranet with easy access for everyone.

The entire listing for NOTEUTIL.INC can be found on the CD-ROM included at the back of this book. It is also in hard copy form, so you can easily view it now. The hard copy printout can be found in Appendix G, "Listing for NOTEUTIL.INC."

Running the Test Suite

The overall structure or skeleton is now in place, since there exists a test case file for each of Notepad's features (for this test suite, each of Notepad's menu items was considered a feature).

Note   If you're a user of Visual Test 4.0 and you're scratching your head about the .VTP file types, those no longer exist. In Visual Test 4.0 the project was saved into a Visual Test Project file (hence the .VTP extension). Now, in this newer and braver world, a more generic extension of .DSP is used. (Developer Studio Project).

Rational Software thought things through well in this latest version of Test, when it comes to how the project file for a given test suite, in this case NOTEPAD.DSP, is shared between the Microsoft Visual Studio and the Rational Visual Test Suite Manager. As Figure 12-2 shows, the .DSP file type is used by both the Visual Studio and the Suite Manager. (Remember, because Developer Studio is an integrated development environment used by many programming languages, Visual Test is only one player. Hence the generic name for the project file's extension.)

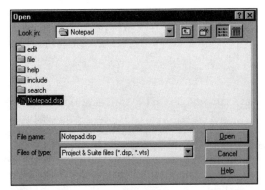

Figure 12-2: The .DSP file type is a Project file — in this case a Visual Test Project file — and is used by both Developer Studio 6.0 and the Suite Manager.

The .DSP file is created automatically whenever a new test suite is created and saved in Developer Studio. When you select the Suite Manager menu item from the Test menu in Developer Studio, the project that is currently open in Developer Studio is also opened in Suite Manager, as shown in Figure 12-3. Although the Suite Manager is a separate utility, they integrate seamlessly with each other, which makes the Test programmer's job that much less painstaking.

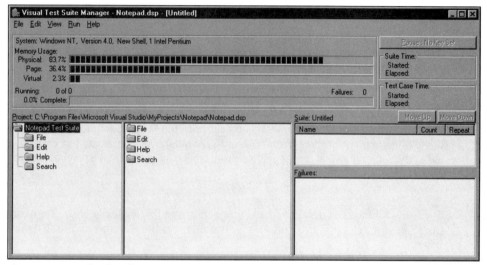

Figure 12-3: Selecting the Suite Manager menu item runs the separate driver utility, which results in opening the project currently being viewed in the Developer Studio.

Here's where all of the programming pays off. The test suite is now under the control of the Suite Manager, and the tests can be run all at once, one at a time, or even repeatedly. The Suite Manager is a *driver* that runs each script that shows up in its suite list.

Running the Tests

The first thing to do to get your tests up and running is to select which of the test cases you'd like to execute. To keep it simple, I'm going to have our example run all the tests in the Notepad project. By clicking each folder and dragging it over to the Suite: list box, I gradually build a suite of tests to run. Compare Figure 12-3 to Figure 12-4, to see the difference between a Suite Manager that has nothing to run, and a Suite Manager that has been configured to run all the tests found in the File, Edit, Search, and Help folders.

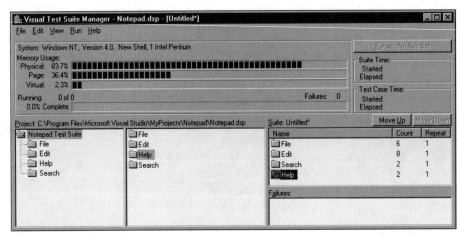

Figure 12-4: Folders have been dragged over from the Project: area to the Suite: area of the Suite Manager. Notice that the Count column shows how many test case files are in the folder and that the Repeat column can be used to cause a test case, or test cases, to be run multiple times.

The Suite Manager is now ready to run each of the test cases in turn. By pressing the F5 key or selecting the Run All menu item from the Run menu, the tests will begin.

Before we do this, however, I'd like to remind you of the LOG statements that we used throughout our test case files and utilities found in NOTEUTIL.INC. Recall that for each LOG statement, there was an associated level at which it would activate and write its information out to the Viewport, text file, or database-compatible file. The following code shows the section of constants declared in the NOTEMAIN.INC file, the main include file for the entire test suite. These constants were declared based on levels I defined, and they allow anyone running the test suite to adjust to the degree or level of detail he or she would like to see output:

```
'********** Logging Detail Settings
const LVL_SUMMARY%     = 5    'Summary info after each test
case
const LVL_MENUINFO%    = 10   'Give menu info if Detail > 10
const LVL_STATUSINFO   = 20   'General status info
const LVL_VERBOSE%     = 100  'Have all calls to LOG enabled
```

These levels used in the test case files by the LOG statement can now be controlled via the Logging section of the Options dialog box in the Suite Manager (see Figure 12-5).

Figure 12-5: The Logging section of the Options dialog box. The highest level of detail has been selected (100).

If the name of the log file isn't selected, a default file name will be created, based on the name of the suite (in this case it would be NOTEPAD.LOG).

Now that the final settings have been selected, the test suite is ready to be run. When the Run All menu item found under the Run menu is selected, the Suite Manager hides the lower portion of its window and keeps the upper portion active, behind the scenes. This is so that a quick glance will give the tester an idea as to where the test suite is in its execution (see Figure 12-6). Through the Options dialog box, shown in Figure 12-5, this behavior can be modified so that the Suite Manager's window disappears entirely if the test engineer so desires.

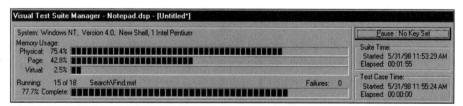

Figure 12-6: The upper portion of the Suite Manager stays visible and continuously updates itself, so that its status can be easily determined.

Note   For more information on the Visual Test Suite Manager, refer to Chapter 6, "Visual Test Utilities."

When the test suite has finished, any errors that were encountered during the run are shown in the Failures: section of the manager. In our example, an error didn't occur, so the Suite Manager returns to its previous full size. It shows the final results for the test suite just executed in the top portion of its window, as shown in Figure 12-7.

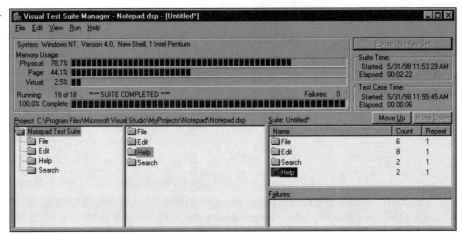

Figure 12-7: The summary results of the run for a test suite are shown in the top portion of the Suite Manager's window.

One of the key reasons to use the Suite Manager is that it takes care of many of the problems that can arise while running test case files. For example, if a compilation error occurs because someone didn't check their source code for typos, or a run-time error occurs because a control can't be found, or a memory access violation occurs, the Suite Manager will handle the situation and act accordingly.

Creating Other Test Suites

When we dragged the folders containing the test case files into the Suite: section of the Suite Manager, they defined a test suite. To avoid having to drag them around in the future, this suite can be saved to a separate file known as a suite file that has a .VTS extension (Visual Test Suite).

Even though a single project file exists for Notepad's test cases, multiple suite files can be defined, depending on what exactly it is that the test engineer wishes to accomplish. For example, this test suite could be saved under the name of FULLPASS.VTS, since it runs all of the tests that make up the Notepad project.

Another example is setting the numbers in the Repeat column to greater than 1, so that each test case is run multiple times. In this example, the test suite could be saved under the name of STRESS.VTS, signifying a stress test, since each test is run many times instead of just once.

A setting is available in the Options dialog box that allows you to specify that any test case files with a test scenario that fails should be placed into a separate test suite file, constructed automatically by the Suite Manager (see Figure 12-8). This way you can easily rerun the test case files that found problems. This can be very helpful and less time-consuming when tracking down the specific failures.

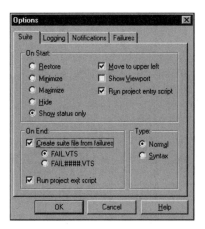

Figure 12-8: The Suite Manager can be configured to automatically create a test suite based on test case files that contain test scenarios that failed during the execution of the test suite.

Test Results

After the test suite has completed its run, if the logging setting wasn't turned off, then a log file exists in the same directory as your project. The entire log file for all of Notepad's test case files is available in Appendix I, "A Log File Generated from a Run of the Notepad Test Suite."

Closing Comments

The key to getting a structure for a test suite designed is to jump in, try out some ideas, make some mistakes, and adjust your approach from there. By focusing on one area of the product first and automating it, you will end up writing many of the key support utilities that the rest of the test case files will rely upon.

Do your best to keep things as flexible as possible. It's not easy to look forward and predict what requests your manager will have for output from the test cases. Nor to predict what might change in the product as a result of changes to the test suite.

By staying as flexible as possible, through using common coding guidelines, sharable utilities, and common sense, you will arrive at a test suite that will make maintenance less of a daunting task. Keep moving forward, and don't concern yourself so much with whether you're doing things right, so that you are constantly second-guessing yourself. You'll find the automation will get easier with time as you continue to practice this fine art.

Summary

In this chapter, we reviewed the structure for our beginning test suite. We then looked at those utilities that were modified or added to the NOTEUTIL.INC file: the `iFailCount()`, `iTestCount()`, `strFailNum()`, `strTestNum()`, and `TestEnd()` functions, as well as at documenting NOTEUTIL.INC. We then considered how to run a test suite, using the Suite Manager and the Project Workspace window. Before we ran the tests, we configured the Suite Manager to run all our tests, and we made use of the `LOG` statements we sprinkled throughout our test scripts. Finally, all the errors encountered were returned by the Suite Manager. Rather than having to create a new test suite each time, we found that we can save them in a suite file for a later test program.

✦   ✦   ✦

Advanced Topics

Beyond the Basics

All the previous chapters in this book have looked at the information needed to get started quickly on automating the testing of a product. In this chapter, we'll take a closer look at some of the features you'll find yourself needing as you get deeper into the building of your test suite.

We start by looking at how to work with files, so you can write and retrieve information using any of three separate access methods. Moving on to performance issues, we will focus on writing benchmarks for an application using Visual Test. Then we'll take a brief look at how pointers work in Visual Test, along with how to allocate and free up memory through the Test language. Next, we discuss how to link into the dynamic-linked libraries (DLLs) available to us in Windows. After that, we address the issue of trapping special run-time information using the tools built into Visual Test, including Rational Software's family of instrumentation tools: Purify, Quantify, and Coverage.

We look at how to compile scripts into distributable pseudocode (*p-code*) files that can be used with the Visual Test run-time engine. We get some tips from Bill Hodghead, of Microsoft, and Dan Hodge, a Visual Test trainer for the STA Group, both of whom have been on the front lines and have much wisdom to share. Finally, we'll ask Joe Benner, of the Visual Test 6.0 development team, to explain the relevant points of Microsoft-developed Active Accessibility (MSAA).

Note This chapter is serving as a catch-all for those topics that I consider "Beyond the Basics." Because of this, a section may not necessarily relate to the previous section or the one that follows it. I've placed contributions by other Visual Test users at the end of this chapter.

File Input/Output

Even though the Visual Test product has routines that help you write information out to database files and text files through the use of the SCENARIO, LOG, and FAIL statements, sometimes you will need to control exactly how the information is written out to or read in from a particular file.

An example of how capable Visual Test is in its file input/output (I/O) support is the Digger utility, which is included free on the CD-ROM in this book. Digger has the ability to read in the resources from a 16-bit executable file (sorry, the creators never updated it to read in 32-bit file formats before discontinuing the product), so that a template can be created with that resource information. It steps through the binary .EXE file, finds the table that holds the information about the application's menus and dialog boxes, and pulls that information into Digger so it can be converted to Test-compatible code. This entire utility was written using the Visual Test language; no special C or C++ had to be written or DLLs created to help with Digger's file I/O.

Note   Even though the Digger 1.0 utility only reads in 16-bit file formats, the Window Grabber tool in the main window of Digger supplies the same functionality by allowing you to click a window from which you want to extract resources. That is, for an executable file that is in the 32-bit file format, use Digger's Window Grabber tool to get resource information. Look for the Digger utility in the ST Labs folder on this book's CD-ROM.

Three types of file access can be done through Visual Test, other than using the SCENARIO, LOG, and FAIL statements. These types of access are *sequential*, *binary*, and *random*. Each of these types of access is controlled using the Test language's OPEN statement.

The OPEN Statement

Microsoft Visual Test's syntax for the OPEN statement is:

```
OPEN filename$ [FOR mode] AS [#] filenumber% [LEN = reclength%]
```

The square brackets show which sections of the OPEN statement are either optional or dependent on the *mode* that's being used.

A *file number* must be used when opening a file with the OPEN statement. Subsequent lines of code that work with the file use that file number when identifying which file to write to or read from. Only 20 file numbers are available, so this limited resource must be used in a flexible manner if you're not to step on other team members' use of file I/O through Visual Test.

Most programmers new to the OPEN statement just type any number between 1 and 20 in the place where the file number is required. While this works in the short term, if the routine that performs the I/O operations is placed into a location where it can be used and shared with others, problems can occur when another section of code attempts to use the same file number.

To avoid this problem, Visual Test has a function called FREEFILE to return the next available file number. When a file's I/O is terminated using the CLOSE statement, the file number associated with that file is placed back into the pool of free file numbers.

Before opening a file, make sure a variable is set to the return value of a FREEFILE function call and that the variable is then used to open the file and write to or read from it. Also use the variable to close the file. By taking this simple approach to working with files, you will find that tracking down error messages like the one shown in Figure 13-1 is no longer necessary.

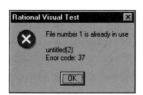

Figure 13-1: This error occurs when the same file number is used by two separate files. It can be avoided using the FREEFILE statement.

The individual modes that a file can be opened with are APPEND, BINARY, INPUT, OUTPUT, and RANDOM. We'll start by looking at the input, output, and append modes. They are associated with accessing a sequential file.

Sequential Access

A sequential file is typically the same thing as a text file; it is used in situations such as keeping track of a test case file's status by writing out information as each test case is performed. While this use has been replaced by the LOG statement (introduced in Visual Test 4.0), it's still useful when you need to write any other kind of information out to a text file. It's also the easiest of the three file I/O access methods to use.

The OPEN statement has three different modes for working with sequential files:

   ✦ APPEND: Using the append mode will cause the file pointer (an internal variable managed by the operating system that keeps track of where we are in the text file) to move to the end of the file, so that any information written to the file using the PRINT statement will be placed at the end of that file.

✦ INPUT: Using the input mode causes the file to be opened and ready for reading in information using the INPUT statement.

✦ OUTPUT: The output mode is similar to the append mode, except that it begins writing information out at the beginning of the file, effectively writing over the top of any information previously stored in that file.

Listing 13-1 shows an example of writing out to a text file and then reading information back in from that file and printing it to the Output window's Viewport tab.

Listing 13-1: **How to write out a file, read it back in, and print the results**

```
CONST FILENAME$ = "test.txt"
dim iFileNum%, strLineIn$

    viewport clear  'Clear contents of the Output window

    'Get Visual Test to give us an available file number
    iFileNum = FREEFILE

    'Open the file for output so we can write information
    open FILENAME$ for output as #iFileNum

    'Use the #<file-number> to write to the file
    print #iFileNum, "This is an example of writing text to"
    print #iFileNum, "a sequential file. This text was"
    print #iFileNum, "written on ";DATETIME$

    'Close the file and free the file number for
    'others to use.
    close #iFileNum

    'Prove that it wrote something out by reading it
    'back in and printing it to the Output window
    iFileNum = FREEFILE

    open FILENAME$ for input as #iFileNum
    print "Output of file ";FILENAME$;":"
    while not(EOF(iFileNum))
        line input #iFileNum, strLineIn
        print strLineIn
    wend
    close #iFileNum
end
```

The PRINT and LINE INPUT statements are used to place or get text to or from a sequential (text) file. The PRINT command, along with a # symbol and the number of the file, places the text associated with it into the file. A LINE INPUT command, which also uses the # symbol and the file number, pulls text from the sequential file one line at a time.

Note

As implied by its name, a sequential file can only be read from or written to in a sequential manner. That is, you can't jump around in the file to write out or read in information. Also, a file cannot be opened both for reading and for writing at the same time; it must be one or the other.

Because each file has a unique file number associated with it, up to 20 files can be open at any one time. They can all be read from or written to through the Test language.

Tip

The FREEFILE function doesn't consider a file number to be in use until the file is actually opened. Therefore, if you plan on having multiple files open at the same time, get a freefile number to a file, open it, and then get the next freefile number. Otherwise, doing all of the freefiles at one time will result in the same number being returned.

Also note that the CLOSE statement can either be used by itself, closing all files at once, or it can be used with specific file numbers to close individual files. Take the extra time to close each file individually. That way, if the code is ever shared with others, it won't end up closing other programmers' open files, which may be lurking behind the scenes in the same code base.

The EOF() function was also used in that chunk of code. This function returns a TRUE value if the end of the file has been reached. Reading past the end of a file will generate a run-time error with the error message "Input past end of file." This error is easily avoided by using the EOF() function before attempting to read in anything from the data file.

Binary Files

Accessing a binary file isn't any more difficult than working with a sequential text file. The only difference is that more effort is required to keep track of where you are in the file, and you must know the file format.

Listing 13-2 is an example of reading in the header of a Windows 16-bit executable file.

Listing 13-2: Working with binary files looks nasty at first but can be a fun challenge.

```
type EXEHEADER
    exSignature      as short
    exExtraBytes     as short
    exPages          as short
    exRelocItems     as short
    exHeaderSize     as short
    exMinAlloc       as short
    exMaxAlloc       as short
    exInitSS         as short
    exInitSP         as short
    exCheckSum       as short
    exInitIP         as short
    exInitCS         as short
    exRelocTable     as short 'if val >= &h40 it's a Win app
    exOverlay        as short
    reserved         as long
end type 'EXEHEADER

type OLDHEADER
    msdosHeader      as EXEHEADER
    breserved        as string * 28
    winInfoOffset    as short
    wreserved        as short
    msdosStub        as string * 1
end type 'OLDHEADER

dim ohHeader as OLDHEADER
dim strApp$, hFile%

    strApp = inputbox("Enter the full path name of " + _
            "an EXE file:")

if EXISTS(strApp) then
        hFile = FREEFILE                   'get a file number
        open strApp for BINARY as #hFile   'open the file
        get #hFile, 1, ohHeader            'read byte 1 into
                                           'the variable

                                           'ohHeader
        close hFile                        'close the file
    endif
end
```

Admittedly, this looks a little hairy at first, but really it's not. It's made up of everything you've already learned about Visual Test. The first part consists of user-defined types based on the file formats I found in a book called *Inside Windows File Formats* by Tom Swan.

All I did was convert the C structures that he listed in his book to Visual Test–compatible structures. And again, that was just experimentation to figure out what seemed to work best. The most important part of the conversion was making sure I had the right number of bytes for each element in the user-defined types. While it's simple to provide a variable of a particular type for Visual Test to fill with information from a given file, it's another matter to make sure you're getting what you really intended.

According to Swan's book, and as is commented in the code we've written, if the exRelocTab field has a value equal to or greater than hex 40 (which is decimal 64), then the executable file is, by definition, a Windows program (as opposed to a DOS executable file).

By checking a couple of other key values to make sure I've read everything in correctly, such as looking at the contents of the variable in the Developer Studio's Test Locals window, as shown in Figure 13-2, I can move on and read in the rest of the information I need. The previous section of code is just a simple example of reading in the first few bytes of information, but it demonstrates the process we need to go through. A structure is created, a variable of that structure or user-defined type is declared, and then that variable is passed to the GET command associated with the BINARY mode of input. The Test programmer then needs to verify through the Test Locals window in the Developer Studio that the values are as expected.

This form of I/O is the most painstaking because you're not dealing with a single user-defined type, you're dealing with many user-defined types that are reading in information from a file. And you also need access to documentation or books like Tom Swan's *Inside Windows File Formats*.

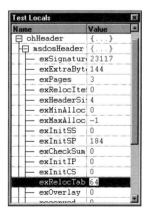

Figure 13-2: The Test Locals window shows the values read into the ohHeader variable by the GET statement.

Random Access I/O

If the sequential access method is the easiest one to work with, the binary mode is at the other extreme, because it requires attention to detail and access to file format information. The random mode, for working with random access files, is in between in regard to ease of use.

A random access file is constructed using a specific file structure used throughout that file. By using a single structure (user-defined type), or record, it's easy to randomly pick a record in the file and quickly read it in. This is because the location of a record can be determined simply by looking at the size of a single record and multiplying it by the position of the record you want to get out of the file, minus one record. Also, keep in mind that unlike a standard array in Visual Test, a random access file's contents are 1-based instead of 0-based. That is, to access the first record in a file, you don't access record 0, you access record 1.

In the example shown in Listing 13-3, a type has been created with the intent of tracking statistics on test scenarios. Only generic, meaningless data is used in this example to show how to write to a file and read information back out of it.

Listing 13-3: **Writing records out to a file requires the use of a user-defined type.**

```
const MAX_STRING = 40
const FILENAME$  = "test.tst"

type SCENARIOINFO
    iTestID     as integer
    strTestDesc as string * MAX_STRING
    strResExp   as string * MAX_STRING
    strResRec   as string * MAX_STRING
    fPassed     as integer
end type 'SCENARIOINFO

dim iLoop%, iFileNum%, iRecSize%
dim siRecord as SCENARIOINFO

    viewport clear

    'LEN() isn't just for lengths of strings, it
    'returns how many bytes types take up in memory.
    iRecSize = len(SCENARIOINFO)

    'Notice that LEN= is now used with the open
    'statement. Only for RANDOM mode, though.
    iFileNum = FREEFILE
```

```
open FILENAME for random as iFileNum len=iRecSize

'Write out some sample records just so we have
'something to play with. fPassed will flip between
'TRUE and FALSE just for fun.
for iLoop = 1 to 10
    'Fill with test info
    siRecord.iTestID    = iLoop
    siRecord.strTestDesc= "Desc for test #"+str$(iLoop)
    siRecord.strResExp  = "Results for #"+str$(iLoop)
    siRecord.strResRec  = "Received for #"+str$(iLoop)
    siRecord.fPassed    = ((iLoop mod 2) = 0)

    put #iFileNum, iLoop, siRecord
next iLoop

'Let's grab the 5th record from the file and
'print it to the Output window's Viewport tab.
get #iFileNum, 5, siRecord
print siRecord.iTestID
print siRecord.strTestDesc
print siRecord.strResExp
print siRecord.strResRec

close #iFileNum
end
```

Because a single record is used for each random access file, when a section of code requests a specific record out of the file, the access time is quick and the retrieval, simple, since the location of the record can be calculated by the size of the records.

Notice that in the user-defined type SCENARIOINFO a *fixed-length string* was used. Because records can't stray from a fixed size when working with a random-mode file, the only way to guarantee that the strings will be the correct size is to use fixed-length strings. Attempting to use a variable-length string will result in this error message: "error VTC4456: Illegal variable type for random file I/O."

Even though much of the information in each record is text, it can't be cleanly viewed using a text editor because not all the values are text values. Take, for example, the iTestID field in the SCENARIOINFO type. When it has the value of 1, that's not the same as a string with the number 1 in it. Instead, it's written out as a 1 that, when read into a text editor, is interpreted as Ctrl+A (CHR$(1)). This is why you see garbage (unprintable characters) mixed in with text when you attempt to open a nontext file.

Notice that the `LEN()` function is used to determine the size of the `SCENARI-OINFO` structure. Many Test programmers only think of using `LEN()` to determine the length of a string. By using it instead of calculating the size of a structure by hand, you're saving yourself time and making your code flexible should the fields in the user-defined type ever be modified or removed.

Benchmark Testing

Benchmark tests for software are created to assess the performance of key sections of source code or user interface components. By running benchmarks for this type of verification, the testing team can track whether or not a given feature or features are remaining within the guidelines set by the product specification for performance.

A typical example of using benchmarks is in intensive operations such as searches and sorts, whether they're performed in the computer's memory or on a disk drive. One of the more difficult goals of benchmarking is keeping the results as precise and error-free as possible. If, for example, you were tracking the performance of a search or sort that is disk-drive intensive, the results could have a high degree of error because the disk drive's performance is affected by a number of variables: disk fragmentation, the amount of data on the disk, and the position of the drive head when the tests began. Seek time and disk latency are timing averages made by the drive manufacturer and also add to the range of the error that can occur in the test results.

Part of the job of benchmarking is to make sure that results reported on performance are accurate and relevant. If a task is reported to have taken 5.4723 seconds, perhaps a second faster than previously reported, and the error is plus or minus 1.35 seconds, it should not necessarily be reported as a performance increase. Such a favorable gain might turn out to be lost the following week when a new build comes out from the development group. Given a ±1.35 second error, you are setting yourself up for a thumping by the development staff for drawing unnecessary attention from upper management for a supposed performance loss.

Therefore, it's critical to cut down on the *noise*, or errors, that creep into a benchmark's results by measuring only the precise section of code or user interface component that is of concern.

One way to help cut back on these errors is to run a test multiple times, so that an average time can be taken and a more accurate set of numbers communicated to others. Both favorable and unfavorable information must be communicated, but some thought must be put into it; otherwise, there is an increased risk of losing faith in the results of the benchmarks.

Listing 13-4 shows a simple example of a benchmark test that calculates the average time it takes the Open dialog box to display. (Note the included .INC files.)

Listing 13-4: A simple example of a benchmark script that uses pieces of code you've already written

```
'$include 'notemain.inc'
'$include 'noteutil.inc'
'$include 'file.inc'
'$include 'winapi.inc'

const BENCH_ITERS = 20   'Number of bench iterations

TestBegin
    dim lTimeStart as long, lTimeStop as long
    dim lAvgTime as long, iLoop as integer

    viewport clear

    wMenuSelect(MNU_FILE_OPEN)
    wButtonClick(BTN_CANCEL)

    dTimeStart = GetTickCount()
    for iLoop = 1 to BENCH_ITERS
        wMenuSelect(MNU_FILE_OPEN)

        if (GetText(NULL) = CAP_OPEN) then
            wButtonClick(BTN_CANCEL)
        endif
    next iLoop
    dTimeStop = GetTickCount()

    dAvgTime = (dTimeStop - dTimeStart) / BENCH_ITERS

    log "Average time to display the "+CAP_OPEN
    log "dialog box = ";dAvgTime;" seconds."
TestEnd
```

A number of things going on here need to be pointed out. As this continues the testing of Notepad, we've created a new folder in the Project Workspace named Benchmarks (see Figure 13-3). Because it's in the same hierarchy as the rest of the test case files, it has access to the following four files:

- ✦ NOTEMAIN.INC: This has all the main declarations for the Notepad application; it was included so that the `MNU_FILE_OPEN` and `BTN_CANCEL` constants could be used.

- ✦ NOTEUTIL.INC: This has all of the common utilities; it was included so that the `TestBegin()` and `TestEnd()` subroutines could be used.

- ✦ FILE.INC: This has the File menu–specific declarations; it was included so that the `CAP_OPEN` constant could be used.

- ✦ WINAPI.INC: This is a file we've not yet explored; it has declarations for working with the Windows libraries and was included so that the `GetTickCount()` function could be used to track how many milliseconds it took to open and close the dialog box (accurate to increments of 55 milliseconds).

Figure 13-3: A new folder has been added to the Project Workspace that holds benchmark tests. Because this folder is a part of the project, it has access to the same include files that the rest of the test case files have.

The `Timer` function, which is intrinsic to the Test language, could also have been used. It would have required the use of variables declared as `DOUBLE`s instead of `LONG`s. There isn't any noticeable difference between the two, other than that the `Timer` function returns the results in seconds instead of milliseconds. (Subtracting the two values of `GetTickCount()` returned 955 milliseconds, whereas the use of the `Timer` function resulted in .955031967 seconds.) By using `Timer()`, however, you avoid having to include `WINAPI.INC`, and a good deal of compile time is saved by not including it.

Note   Benchmark times are dependent on the machine and its configuration. You could even go so far as to have the SIMMs (the single in-line memory modules that serve as the computer's RAM or main memory) in each test machine the same speed to cut back on errors in accuracy. If benchmarks are important to your company's product, take care to use the same machine in the same configuration each time benchmarks are generated.

Notice also that before the benchmarks were executed, the dialog box was brought up and dismissed once. The reason for this is that the first time a dialog box is displayed, Windows needs to load in the resources for it. Assuming that the results sought for displaying the dialog box are based on subsequent accesses to the dialog box, a good deal of error is reduced in the timing calculations by getting the loading of resources out of the way before the benchmarks begin. This way the tests are measuring only the time to display the dialog box instead of timing how long it takes to load in the resources as well.

Working with Pointers

Simply put, a *pointer* is a variable that holds a memory address. Sometimes it's the memory location of another variable, and at other times it's the address of the first chunk of memory in a block of allocated memory. Everyone has a hard time when they first start working with pointers, so don't feel like it's beyond you if you're new to them. They are crucial when working beyond the basics of Visual Test, however, especially when working with Windows APIs (discussed in the section "Linking to Windows APIs" later in this chapter). If you are new to pointers, I strongly suggest you purchase a book on beginning to advanced programming, because this book assumes you have a general knowledge of programming, including programming with pointers. Even so, we'll take some simple examples of pointers.

Pointer Types

Pointers in Visual Test can be of almost any type. You can have a pointer to an INTEGER, a LONG, a STRING, and even other pointers. You can also have pointers to user-defined types. To get the address of a variable, so that it can be assigned to a pointer, the VarPtr() function is used. The variable whose address needs to be obtained is placed as the parameter in the VarPtr() call, with the return value assigned to the pointer variable. VarPtr() plays the equivalent role to the C language's ampersand (&) operator in getting a variable's address. To dereference a pointer so that the value it is pointing to can be determined, the square brackets are used with a zero (0) as an index. For example, ptrX[0] is a dereference of the pointer variable called ptrX. Listing 13-5 is an example of using VarPtr() to get the address of a variable.

> ### Listing 13-5: **In the Test language, VarPtr() is used to get the address of a variable.**

```
dim ptrX as pointer to integer
dim y as integer
    y = 7
    ptrX = VarPtr(y)      'Get address of y
    print ptrX            'Address of y is printed
    print ptrX[0]         '7 is printed
end
```

Dereferencing a pointer in the Test language is similar to doing so in other languages but uses its own notation, as shown in Table 13-1.

Table 13-1
Examples of How the Test, C, and Pascal Languages Dereference a Pointer

Language	Dereference
Visual Test	ptrX[0]
C	*ptrX
Pascal	ptrX^

When using pointers with user-defined types with fields, the comparisons shown in Table 13-2 can be made.

Table 13-2
Examples of How the Test, C, and Pascal Languages Dereference a Variable Pointing to a User-Defined Type

Language	Dereference
Visual Test	ptrX[0].
C language #1:	(*ptrX).
C language #2:	ptrX->
Pascal	ptrX^.

Dynamic Memory

In addition to creating variables that point to other variables' memory addresses, you can allocate blocks of memory for whatever use you might have.

To do this, use the ALLOCATE statement. When you've finished using the block of memory, free it up with the DEALLOCATE statement. Listing 13-6 shows an example of using both statements.

Listing 13-6: Each ALLOCATE has a matching DEALLOCATE so that memory is freed after use.

```
dim iLoop as integer
dim ptrA as pointer to long
    allocate ptrA, 10      'Because ptrA is pointing to a LONG,
                           '40 bytes are allocated because each
                           'LONG value takes up 4 bytes.

    for iLoop = 0 to 9
        ptrA[iLoop] = iLoop * iLoop
    next iLoop

    for iLoop = 0 to 9
        print ptrA[iLoop]
    next iLoop

    deallocate ptrA
end
```

This source code could have been written using an array, so it seems kind of silly to go through the extra steps of allocating and deallocating memory. But this was just a simple example to get us started. Now, the next example is a little more fun; it demonstrates how a linked list can be created using the Test language. It allocates memory one node at a time and then uses a recursive subroutine to free up the allocated memory, as shown in Listing 13-7.

Listing 13-7: **A recursive subroutine is a great way to free allocated memory.**

```
'Simple example of a singly linked list
const MAX_NODES = 20

type CTRLNODE
    strDesc as string
    pcnNext as pointer to CTRLNODE
end type 'CTRLNODE

dim cnHead as CTRLNODE
dim pcnTemp as pointer to CTRLNODE
dim iLoop as integer

    viewport clear
    iLoop = 0
    cnHead.strDesc = "Node # 0"

    'pcnTemp is a temporary pointer that steps through
    'the list of all of the records, setting the values
    'of each one's strDesc field.
    pcnTemp = varptr(cnHead)

    'Allocate one node at a time
    do
        iLoop = iLoop + 1
        allocate pcnTemp[0].pcnNext, 1
        pcnTemp = pcnTemp[0].pcnNext
        pcnTemp[0].strDesc = "Node #"+str$(iLoop)
    loop until  (iLoop >= MAX_NODES)

    'Print the nodes out
    pcnTemp = varptr(cnHead)
    while (pcnTemp <> NULL)
        print pcnTemp[0].strDesc
        pcnTemp = pcnTemp[0].pcnNext
    wend

    FreeNodes(varptr(cnHead))
end

'Easiest way to free up a singly linked list
'is recursively.
sub FreeNodes(pcnNode as pointer to CTRLNODE)
    if (pcnNode <> NULL) then
        FreeNodes(pcnNode[0].pcnNext)
        deallocate pcnNode
    endif
end sub 'FreeNodes
```

A Short Story

On one project I had a feature that I had to test each time I progressed another level deeper in the product. That feature allowed me to escape back to the very top of the menu hierarchy, no matter how deep I was into the program's menu tree. No big deal, right?

Well, the trick was being able to work my way back down to where I was, so that I could continue where I left off. The only way to do this cleanly, without a lot of repeated code, was to build a linked list that kept track of my menu selections as I stepped deeper into the program. When I popped back to the top of the structure, all I had to do was walk the linked list using the menu selections it had recorded on my way down, to return to where I was. By using a linked list that allocated memory only as it was needed, I didn't need to use an array that would sit around taking up memory even when it wasn't being used. The linked list grew and shrank depending on how deep I was in the menu structure.

Visual Test's language really is a very capable and fully functional programming language. I've wondered why the Microsoft Visual Basic team didn't follow Visual Test's lead and make pointers available so that linked lists, open-ended hash tables, binary trees, directed graphs, and other basic data structures could be created. This could be especially useful in automated testing when tracking paths that have been taken.

Linking to Windows APIs

One of the great features of Visual Test is its ability to link into Windows APIs and other dynamic-link libraries (DLLs). This functionality makes the Visual Test language extensible; if you have a DLL that has functionality you want to access from Visual Test, odds are you'll be able to link into it without any trouble.

A Simple Example

To link into a DLL, you must type in a declaration or *prototype* for linking into that library. The easiest way to explain this is with an example, as shown in Listing 13-8.

Listing 13-8: Linking into a DLL requires a declaration from the Test language to the DLL's function.

```
declare function MessageBox lib "user32.dll" _
        alias "MessageBoxA" (hWnd&, lpText$, lpCaption$, _

        uType&) as long


MessageBox(NULL, "This is our test message box", _
        "Test Caption", MB_OK OR MB_ICONSTOP)
```

This is yet another piece of source code that looks kind of hairy, right? Again, it's not as bad as it looks. It looks especially weird because the lines were so long that continuation marks (_) were used to make the code more easy to read.

The first line declares that a function called MessageBox() is going to be based upon a function in the USER32.DLL called MessageBoxA(). Because linking into a DLL is case-sensitive, even though Visual Test's compiler is case-insensitive, the alias option has been provided so that the correct upper- and lowercase characters can be used for establishing the link with the DLL. It also provides a way for the Test programmer to use a function name different than the one used in the actual DLL.

Tip   Aliasing is also especially useful if the DLL has a function name that matches an intrinsic Test language function name.

Our example goes one step further in that MessageBox() is no longer available, as was the case in the 16-bit version of the DLLs. It is now called MessageBoxA(). Through this same aliasing technique, it's also possible to declare a function with a name to be used through the Test language that is different from the name of the actual function in the dynamic-link library. In our example, we linked to MessageBoxA() but will use the name MessageBox() when accessing the function through the Test language. Figure 13-4 shows the results of our labor.

Figure 13-4: Calling the MessageBoxA API function results in a simple message box with an OK button and a Stop icon.

That's all there is to establishing a link with a function in a DLL. Now, depending on the function itself, it can get a little more challenging and therefore a little more fun.

A More Complex Example

Let's take an example that's a little more involved and requires a little more attention to what's going on. Windows 3.1 introduced the concept of common dialog boxes, which made frequently used dialog boxes available to developers at a fraction of the time it would take to write comparable dialog boxes. At the same time, if developers used these common dialog boxes, they got a free ride whenever Microsoft made changes to those dialog boxes in future versions of Windows.

An example of a common dialog box is the Open dialog box. If a program is written and run under Windows 3.1*x*, the Open dialog box is an old-style dialog box associated with Windows 3.1*x*. When running that same program under Windows 95, without any changes to that program's source code, the dialog box that appears is the new and improved Windows 95, 98, or NT 4.0 or 5.0 dialog box, shown in Figure 13-5.

Figure 13-5: The Windows common Open dialog box as it appears in Windows 95

This is the power of the common dialog box. The code that manages the user's actions — clicking a button, filling the contents of a list box, verifying that a file exists, navigating up and down the directory tree, and so on — has been programmed and tested by Microsoft already. The only thing a Windows programmer needs to do is supply the initialization information so that the dialog box can display itself appropriately and then return information back to the program that invoked it.

Listing 13-9 is an example of a more challenging API call using the common Open dialog box. The API to display the Open dialog box is `GetOpenFilename()`.

Listing 13-9: **A more complex API found in the COMDLG32.DLL, which is linked to by the WINAPI.INC file**

```
'*** Include file ***
'$include 'winapi.inc'          'Contains link to COMDLG32.DLL's
                                'functions.


'*** My constants ***
const MAXPATH    = 128          'Max size path
const FILTDELIM = ","           'Filter delimeter
const NUL        = CHR$(0)      'A string NULL


'*** Main program ***
dim strFilter as string

    viewport clear
    strFilter = "Executable,*.exe,Text,*.txt,Word,*.doc"
    print strGetFile("C:\WINDOWS",strFilter)
END

'*** Function def ***
function strGetFile(strDir$, strFilter$) AS STRING
    dim iRet            AS INTEGER
    dim ofnFile         AS OPENFILENAME
    dim strFileChoice   AS STRING * MAXPATH
    dim strStartDir     AS STRING * MAXPATH
    dim strFileFilter   AS STRING * MAXPATH

    strStartDir = strDir+NUL   'Ensure this is null terminated

    'Replace all FILTDELIM characters with CHR$(0). Make sure
    'string is terminated with two nulls as required by
    'GetOpenFileName() API.
    iRet = INSTR(strFilter, FILTDELIM)
    while (iRet)
        MID$(strFilter, iRet, 1) = NUL
        iRet = INSTR(strFilter, FILTDELIM)
    wend
    strFileFilter = trim$(strFilter) + NUL + NUL

    'Initialize the structure before passing it
    ofnFile.lStructSize     = LEN(OPENFILENAME)
    ofnFile.hwndOwner       = wGetActWnd(0)
    ofnFile.lpstrFilter     = cptr(varptr(strFileFilter))
    ofnFile.nFilterIndex    = 1
    ofnFile.lpstrInitialDir = cptr(varptr(strStartDir))
    ofnFile.lpstrFile       = cptr(varptr(strFileChoice))
    ofnFile.nMaxFile        = LEN(strFileChoice)
```

```
        ofnFile.Flags          = OFN_FILEMUSTEXIST OR _
                                 OFN_HIDEREADONLY  OR _
                                 OFN_PATHMUSTEXIST

    if GetOpenFileName(ofnFile) then
        strGetFile = trim$(trim$(strFileChoice,0))
    else
        strGetFile = ""
    endif
end function 'strGetFile
```

Yet another gross-looking piece of code, you say? While there are a number of things going on that we need to look at, it's not all that bad, especially as it's broken down and explained step by step. In most cases, a function needs a lot of experimentation until it works correctly, and then it takes some hands-on testing to make sure it's working as expected.

The first part of coming up with a piece of code like this is to determine which API you'd like to use. This requires some hunting through the MSDN (Microsoft Developers Network) online help for working with WIN32 APIs. I found help on the common Open dialog box under the heading of "Common Dialog Box Functions" (see Figure 13-6).

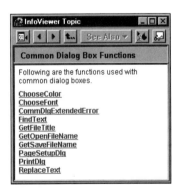

Figure 13-6: Tracking down a function that does what you want takes a lot of searching and persistence.

The only way you're going to know what's in the SDK's online help is to take some time to scroll through it to familiarize yourself with what's available. This is the same action you should take with the Visual Test online help.

Use the Options dialog box accessed through the Tools menu and Options menu item. This dialog box allows you to select which Help System to use (options vary depending on which development products you have installed). In the example shown in Figure 13-7 we've selected "Visual Test Help (4/3/98)" as the *preferred collection.*

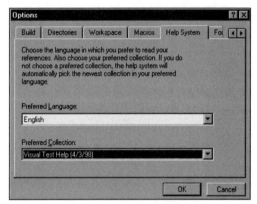

Figure 13-7: You can select which Help files are available to you for context-sensitive searching by going into the Options dialog box and selecting the Help System tab.

The Help System tab in the Options dialog box tells the editor which online help file to search when performing keyword lookups. That is, if you select MSDN help and search on the function name GetOpenFileName, the MSDN help file will be searched. An even better shortcut is to select the help file as just described, then type the function name into the Developer Studio editor, click the function name, and press the F1 key to invoke the context-sensitive help.

Once you've found the function you want to work with, read through the online documentation to see how it works. The first thing you'll notice is that it's all assuming that you're going to access the libraries through C or C++. Therefore, you're going to notice C and C++ types being used that you may not be familiar with. Again, sweat it out. C and C++ have the same base types as the Test language does. What Microsoft has done with their C language is to add some more types created from those base types.

In some cases, even though the online help for the main routine is found, deeper digging is required. In the case of GetOpenFileName(), as shown in Figure 13-8, a structure called OPENFILENAME is passed to the function.

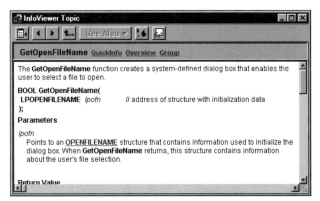

Figure 13-8: The `GetOpenFileName()` function's documentation is available in the MSDN online help.

Clicking the highlighted structure in the help file shows exactly what it looks like, as shown in Figure 13-9.

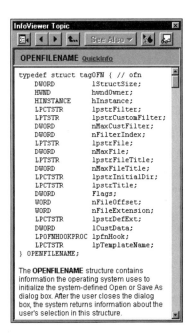

Figure 13-9: The `OPENFILENAME` structure is used by the `GetOpenFileName()` function. It needs to be initialized with data according to how you want it to be displayed.

By jumping to the OPENFILENAME topic in the online help, we've finally reached the meat of working with the GetOpenFileName function. Remember, though, that this help topic is based on the C language, and therefore some of the types are foreign to us as Test programmers. Fortunately, the Visual Test team created an include file for us called WINAPI.INC. The C structure shown in Figure 13-9 has a counterpart in the WINAPI.INC file with the same user-defined type name. The Test version of this structure, or user-defined type, is shown in Listing 13-10.

Listing 13-10: The OPENFILENAME structure as it is defined in the Test language and found in the WINAPI.INC file

```
type OPENFILENAME
    lStructSize       as long
    hwndOwner         as long
    hInstance         as long
    lpstrFilter       as pointer to string * 1
    lpstrCustomFilter as pointer to string * 1
    nMaxCustFilter    as long
    nFilterIndex      as long
    lpstrFile         as pointer to string * 1
    nMaxFile          as long
    lpstrFileTitle    as pointer to string * 1
    nMaxFileTitle     as long
    lpstrInitialDir   as pointer to string * 1
    lpstrTitle        as pointer to string * 1
    Flags             as long
    nFileOffset       as short
    nFileExtension    as short
    lpstrDefExt       as pointer to string * 1
    lCustData         as long
    lpfnHook          as dlgproc
    lpTemplateName    as pointer to string * 1
end type
```

Note The WINAPI.INC file provides function prototypes, sometimes referred to as links, for the same APIs used by Windows developers working in the C/C++ language. WINAPI.INC also provides the Test language user-defined types that match the C structures used by many of the APIs.

Referring to Table 13-3, you'll notice that any time a C type has anything to do with a WORD, it is a SHORT in the Test language. A LONG is a LONG; any kind of handle (such as HWND or HDC) is a LONG; and any pointer to a string in a user-defined type is a POINTER TO STRING * 1 in the Test language.

Table 13-3
Summary of Some of the Declarations Used by
C Programmers Who Write Windows Applications and the
Test Language Equivalent

Description	C Language	Visual Test Equivalent
16-bit Integer	WORD	SHORT
32-bit Integer (LONG)	DWORD	LONG
Handle to a window	HWND	LONG
Handle to an instance	HINSTANCE	LONG
Long pointer to constant string	LPCTSTR	POINTER TO STRING * 1
Long pointer to a string	LPTSTR	POINTER TO STRING * 1
Pointer to a function	LPFNHOOKPROC	DLGPROC
RGB color reference	COLORREF	LONG
Long parameter	LPARAM	LONG
Word parameter	WPARAM	SHORT
Generic handle	HANDLE	LONG
Handle to a device context	HDC	LONG

If you feel overwhelmed at first, don't worry about it; it'll make more sense as you use them more and more. Fortunately the WINAPI.INC file already has the Visual Test equivalents for most of the Windows APIs, with their structures and constants already defined for you. You'll really be tested on how well you understand this when you're working with someone else's DLLs. And even then, it's usually trial and error, so just press on until it falls into place and use the WINAPI.INC file as a handy reference for your conversions.

Here again is the first part of the code that brings in the WINAPI.INC file and tests our function strGetFile(), written to wrap around the GetOpenFileName API. (This is only a section of the complete listing. For the complete listing see Listing 13-9 found earlier in this chapter).

```
'*** Include file ***
'$include 'winapi.inc'

'*** My constants ***
const MAXPATH   = 128        'Max size path
const FILTDELIM = ","        'Filter delimeter
```

```
const NUL        = CHR$(0)    'A string NULL

'*** Main program ***
dim strFilter as string

    viewport clear
    strFilter = "Executable,*.exe,Text,*.txt,Word,*.doc"
    print strGetFile("C:\WINDOWS",strFilter)
END
```

This first section includes the WINAPI.INC file, making all of the declarations relating to the APIs available to use, and linking into those APIs. Next, it defines some constants that we'll be needing in our function to make it easier to adjust things later, should it become necessary. And finally, because we created a function of our own to call the Windows API that displays the Open dialog box (our function is called strGetFile), we need to call that function with some test data to get it to display the dialog box.

Note   When you read through the online help about the GetOpenFileName API, you'll see that the help identifies which fields in the user-defined type need to be filled and with what information. To make it simple, our function only requires two parameters—the starting directory and the filter used by the dialog box—to display the Open dialog box. The rest of the parameters are set within the function.

In the next piece of code, we've taken the front portion of the strGetFile function, to show you what the first steps of the function are. In the C language, most all of the functions that deal with strings expect a byte at the end of the string with a zero value.

This is called a null character and is represented in C by a "\0"; in Visual Test, however, it is represented by a CHR$(0) (not the NULL value, which is used with pointers). This is known as a *zero-terminated* or *null-terminated* string and is used by the C libraries to determine when they've reached the end of a string.

If the null termination is forgotten, many times the result is a *general protection fault*, because the function read past the end of the string into a section of memory that might be allocated by someone else. Therefore, you'll notice that a null (which, as you'll notice in the next-to-last piece of code, is a constant we created and set to CHR$(0)) is appended to the strDir parameter that specifies that directory to be used by the Open dialog box.

These are the first few lines of our function, which add the required null characters to the strings that were passed and also step through the filter string, formatting it to be compatible with the GetOpenFileName API's requirements. (This is only a section of the complete listing. For the complete listing see Listing 13-9 found earlier in this chapter.)

```
'*** Function def ***
function strGetFile(strDir$, strFilter$) AS STRING
    dim iRet            AS INTEGER
    dim ofnFile         AS OPENFILENAME
    dim strFileChoice   AS STRING * MAXPATH
    dim strStartDir     AS STRING * MAXPATH
    dim strFileFilter   AS STRING * MAXPATH

    strStartDir = strDir+NUL   'Ensure this is null terminated

    'Replace all FILTDELIM characters with CHR$(0). Make sure
    'string is terminated with two nulls as required by
    'GetOpenFileName() API.
    iRet = INSTR(strFilter, FILTDELIM)
    while (iRet)
        MID$(strFilter, iRet, 1) = NUL
        iRet = INSTR(strFilter, FILTDELIM)
    wend
    strFileFilter = trim$(strFilter) + NUL + NUL
```

Also in this piece of code, you'll notice that `strFilter` is being stepped through, so that the commas, specified by the `FILTDELIM` constant, can be removed and replaced with null characters. This is done because it's what the online documentation for the `OPENFILENAME` structure has told us to do. The filter string must be a description of the filter, a null character, and then the actual filter to be used, another null, then another filter description, a null, and the filter, and so on.

After all filter descriptions and filters have been supplied, two null characters must be placed at the end of the string. Again, this is according to the documentation on the API and how it wants the information to be provided to it. For example:

```
"Executable file<NULL>*.EXE<NULL>Text
file<NULL>*.TXT<NULL><NULL>"
```

where `<NULL>` is a `CHR$(0)`.

This step could have been avoided by requiring the user of our function to pass a string like this to our function:

```
"Executable file"+CHR$(0)+"*.EXE"+CHR$(0)+ _
"Text file"+CHR$(0)+"*.TXT"+CHR$(0)+CHR$(0)
```

Instead, to make a friendlier function, we only require a comma-separated string and then have our function replace the commas with the null characters.

The last part of our function simply assigns values to the variable ofnFile, which was declared of the type OPENFILENAME. A variable of OPENFILENAME is required by the GetOpenFileName API and is defined in the WINAPI.INC file provided by Visual Test. (This is only a section of the complete listing. For the complete listing see Listing 13-9 earlier in this chapter.)

```
'Initialize the structure before passing it
    ofnFile.lStructSize      = LEN(OPENFILENAME)
    ofnFile.hwndOwner        = wGetActWnd(0)
    ofnFile.lpstrFilter      = cptr(varptr(strFileFilter))
    ofnFile.nFilterIndex     = 1
    ofnFile.lpstrInitialDir  = cptr(varptr(strStartDir))
    ofnFile.lpstrFile        = cptr(varptr(strFileChoice))
    ofnFile.nMaxFile         = LEN(strFileChoice)
    ofnFile.Flags            = OFN_FILEMUSTEXIST OR _
                               OFN_HIDEREADONLY  OR _
                               OFN_PATHMUSTEXIST

    if GetOpenFileName(ofnFile) then
        strGetFile = trim$(trim$(strFileChoice,0))
    else
        strGetFile = ""
    endif
end function 'strGetFile
```

All that's left is to fill in the OPENFILENAME structure using the ofnFile variable, which was declared at the top of this function. The first field in the structure is lStructSize and needs to be set to the size of the structure. Instead of counting up how many bytes the structure uses, the quicker method is to use the LEN function, which is intrinsic to the Test language.

The hwndOwner field is set to wGetActWnd(0), which is also an intrinsic function of the Test language. By passing zero (0) to wGetActWnd(), it returns the handle to the currently active window and assigns it to hwndOwner. This tells the GetOpenFileName function who the parent of the Open dialog box is and won't allow the dialog box to fall behind its parent window, even when you click that parent.

Here's where things get a bit strange. The lpstrFilter field requires a pointer to a string that contains the list of filters to be used by the Open dialog box. Looking back four pieces of code, to the Listing 13-10, which shows the Test language version of the OPENFILENAME structure, you'll see that this field is declared as POINTER TO STRING * 1.

The problem is the strFileFilter, which is what lpstrFilter (actually ofnFile.lpstrFilter) is being set to, is a fixed-length string of size MAXPATH (our previously defined constant of 128 characters). We can get a pointer to our strFileFilter string by using the Test language's VARPTR(), but it will be a pointer to a string of size 128, and lpstrFilter only wants a string of size 1.

The way around this is to change the pointer returned by VARPTR() into an untyped, or VOID, pointer. This is done using the CPTR function, which is also part of the Test language. CPTR() makes the pointer generic, so that the Test compiler won't complain about a type mismatch (attempting to assign a 128-character string to a 1-character string).

Why did the Visual Test team members declare it as a pointer to a string of size 1 instead of 128? Because they didn't know what size string would be passed to it. Size 1 is the smallest string pointer that can be created, and therefore that is what was used.

The rest of the fields are initialized based on the requirements specified by the online help. This includes strFileChoice, which serves as a buffer that is filled when the call to GetOpenFileName() returns. Therefore, in the last part of the code, where the API is called and the structure passed, if you select a legal file from the Open dialog box, the API returns a nonzero value (interpreted as TRUE) and your function is assigned the value that was placed in the strFileChoice field before the API returned.

If you select the Cancel button in the dialog box or the API fails in some way, a FALSE (0) value is returned and we assign an empty string to be returned by our function.

Callback Functions

A *callback function* is a function that passes a pointer of itself to other functions so that the other functions can, in turn, dereference that pointer to call back the function referenced by the pointer. An example of a callback function is a window procedure, or winproc. A winproc is a function associated with a window that processes all messages sent to that window. Every single window in Windows has a winproc associated with it, so that it can deal with things like mouse movements or clicks to the window. A dialogproc is the same idea as a winproc, except that it focuses specifically on handling messages for dialog boxes.

A simple example of a callback function is working with the SetTimer API, which is declared in the MSDN as:

```
UINT SetTimer(HWND hwnd, UINT idTimer, UINT uTimeout, TIMERPROC
tmprc);
```

A UINT is an unsigned integer, meaning that the last bit in that integer isn't used to signify whether the number is positive or negative. Therefore, since that sign-bit is now ignored, it can allow for large positive integers. In Visual Test there's no such thing as an unsigned integer, and so really big numbers will still appear to Visual Test as negative numbers. This doesn't hurt anything, other than confusing the Test programmer now and then. There will be times when you are expecting a large positive number, but you find a negative number showing up in the Test Locals window. We already know from Table 13-3 that HWND is LONG.

Well, what about that TIMERPROC type then? As we look further down into the online help for the SetTimer API we find that TIMERPROC is declared as:

```
VOID CALLBACK TimerProc(HWND hwnd, UINT uMsg, _
                        UINT idEvent, DWORD dwTime);
```

So the TIMERPROC type is actually a pointer to the kind of function that needs to be supplied by the programmer.

The SetTimer API is a nifty little function that creates what is known as a timer, which, after a certain amount of time (specified when the timer was created), dereferences a pointer to a function and calls it with the parameters shown in the TimerProc declaration. It's up to the programmer to fill in the details of what TimerProc does when it's called: to define the TimerProc() function.

Listing 13-11 is an example of a callback function using the SetTimer API. By providing a pointer to a function we've written called aTest to the SetTimer API, aTest() will be called whenever one second elapses.

Listing 13-11: Callback functions can be used in Visual Test 4.0 and 6.0. This wasn't done as easily in previous versions.

```
'$include 'winapi.inc'

global giCount%
dim iTimerID%
dim pfnaTest as TIMERPROC

    viewport clear
    pfnaTest = varptr(aTest)
    iTimerID = SetTimer(0,0,1000,pfnaTest)

    giCount = 0
    while (giCount < 10)
        sleep .1
```

```
        print "Waiting for timer"
    wend

    KillTimer(0,iTimerID)
end

sub aTest(hWnd&, iMsg&, iEvent&, dwTime&)
    giCount = giCount + 1
    print "Callback #";giCount
end sub 'aTest
```

When you look at this code, you'll probably do a double-take when you see the WHILE statement. That statement loops until the variable giCount is equal to or greater than 10; yet nowhere in the loop does it increment that counter. It appears to be an endless loop.

Because a timer was created using the SetTimer API, a timer delay of 1,000 milliseconds (1 second) was specified, and a pointer to the function aTest() was passed. Even while the program is looping, when the timer calls back aTest() it's as if a function call to aTest() were inserted at the next line of code to execute. The function completes its task of incrementing the giCount global variable, and control returns back to where the execution left off before the interruption. Eventually the aTest function is called enough times, incrementing giCount each time, causing the loop to terminate.

Tip One problem with Visual Test that previous versions didn't have is that it doesn't yield often enough to allow the timer to perform the callback. Therefore, it's necessary to put in a delay, albeit a small one (such as SLEEP .1).

Capturing Information

The Visual Test language provides a number of ways to trap information during the execution of a test suite. The way these traps work is very similar to how a callback function works, except these are built into the language.

Trapping Run-Time Errors

A *run-time error* is an error that is generated through some action of the Test language that is illegal and occurs while the script is executing. The error isn't a syntax error or an error that could have been caught by the compiler, it's an error that could not have been determined to have existed until the script actually executed.

An example of a run-time error is having the script attempt to access an element of an array that doesn't exist, resulting in an out-of-bounds error. Another example of a run-time error is attempting to access a file that doesn't exist. In both of these examples, the compiler could not have determined that an error condition existed until the scripts were actually executed.

The script shown in Listing 13-12 starts by setting up a run-time error trap using the ON ERROR GOTO statement and then purposely causes an error by attempting to delete a nonexistent file, to demonstrate how error handling works.

Listing 13-12: Trapping run-time errors in the Test language is a simple task.

```
on error goto MyErrorHandler
dim i$

    viewport clear
    i$ = "thisisanerrorwaitingtohappen.txt"
    print i$
    kill(i$)     'The KILL statement deletes a file
end

MyErrorHandler:
    print "An error occurred."
```

The actual code for a run-time error handler is typically placed after the main code's final END statement. If it were placed before the end of the main code block, the error handler's code would be executed, since MyErrorHandler is only a label used by the GOTO statement and not a subroutine or function that only executes when called.

Options in an error handler

Once an error occurs, and execution jumps down into the error handling code, a number of options are available to the Test programmer. The first is to simply RESUME from the same line on which the error occurred. Perhaps the error handler fixes whatever the error condition is and allows the interpreter another shot at the same line of code.

Another option is to simply continue on with the next line of code in the test script. This can be done using the RESUME NEXT statement. Many people who want their scripts to continue no matter what, use this as their only form of error handling. The result is a script that trips along and, sometimes, recovers from the error. Other times the script just keeps tripping until the end of the script is reached. If at all possible, it's preferable to handle each error in some way, so that execution can continue as cleanly as possible.

Another option is to resume operation but at a different section of code. This can be accomplished using the RESUME <label> statement where <label> is a GOTO label that exists some place in the code base. Execution then moves to that section of code.

The final option was introduced in Visual Test 4.0 and allows for multiple error handlers in the same script. The RESUME ERROR statement communicates that it doesn't want to deal with the error, and that the error handler the next level up can deal with the problem. If no other error handler exists, the script's execution terminates and a message box describing the error is presented to the Test programmer.

Note   There can be only one global error handler to which local errors can be escalated. If a local error handler ignores an error using the RESUME ERROR statement, it is passed on to the global error handler. While there can only be one global error handler, it can be changed as the script is executing should the situation merit that a different catchall error trap be used.

Local error handlers

Visual Test has provided Test programmers with another level of run-time error handling. This is known as the local handler and is specified by using the keyword LOCAL in the ON ERROR GOTO statement.

This type of error handling allows the user to create error handlers within functions and subroutines that are specific only to those routines. Something of a hierarchy is set up by doing this, which is especially noticeable when the main section of code that has an error handler calls a function that has an error handler, which in turn calls another function or subroutine, which also has an error handler.

Each function or subroutine can attempt to process its own errors by using the ON LOCAL ERROR GOTO statement, and if things get too out of hand, the routine can use the RESUME ERROR statement, which bumps error handling up one level. The statement for setting up a local error trap must be inside the function or subroutine for which it is trapping errors.

A local error handler remains active as long as execution continues in the subroutine or function that contains it. Once the subroutine or function finishes execution, the error handler for that routine goes out of scope and is turned off.

To turn off an ON ERROR GOTO statement, you need only supply a zero (0) in place of a label (as in ON ERROR GOTO 0).

Information in an error handler

A few functions and a global variable are available to you specifically for getting information about the run-time error that occurred. The first function is ERF(), which returns the name of the file in which the error occurred. ERL() is similar to ERF(), except that it returns the line number on which the error was generated. And the ERR global variable has the error number associated with the error that most recently occurred. Used in conjunction with the ERROR$ function, passing ERR to ERROR$() will return an error string associated with the specified error.

With access to this type of information, you can write out the same information that would have otherwise been displayed in a message box had the error trap not been activated. And by writing code to handle specific error conditions that occur, you have a better chance of getting the script back on track by fixing the problem in the error handler.

Event Handling

One of the cool features of Visual Test is how it offers you the ability to detect certain events that can occur and to react to those events. In previous versions of Visual Test only a few events could be checked:

✦ KeyPress: Notifies the handler when a key on the keyboard was pressed. This allowed the Test programmer to put in code to provide that, in the event a specific key were pressed, a certain action would take place (such as stopping the script from executing).

✦ UnhandledException: Notifies the handler when an unrecoverable error is encountered. Unrecoverable application errors are system modal dialog boxes that can cause Visual Test to become inactive. When invoked, this handler allows Visual Test to preempt that error.

✦ WindowCreate: Notifies the handler when a window has been created.

✦ WindowDestroy: Notifies the handler when a window has been destroyed. (Note: closing a window does not necessarily destroy it; it could just hide it.)

These are cool events to look for, but this part of the Visual Test language was not used by most Visual Test programmers. And in many cases, only those who dove into the depths of the Test language knew about their existence.

Visual Test 4.0 saw the addition of a new type of event: BoundsCheckerNotify. This event allowed Visual Test to be used in conjunction with NuMega Technologies' BoundsChecker program. (See the "Special notification support" section later in this chapter.)

In Visual Test 6.0 this list has grown even longer, allowing similar support for Rational Software's family of testing products. Support has also been added for assistance in keeping tests synchronized when testing Web pages (discussed in Chapter 17):

✦ `CoverageNotify`

✦ `PurifyNotify`

✦ `QuantifyNotify`

✦ `WebLoadBegin`

✦ `WebLoadReady`

✦ `WebLoadComplete`

Note   Three of the new notifications that relate to the new Web functionality in Visual Test 6.0 — `WebLoadBegin`, `WebLoadReady`, and `WebLoadComplete` — are discussed in detail in Chapter 17.

Trapping notifications in Visual Test is done using the `ON. . .CALL` statement, which takes the form:

```
ON [LOCAL] <NotificationName> [(parameters)] CALL <handler>
```

The `ON...CALL` statement sets up a callback function (discussed earlier in this chapter) that allows you to look for a specific notification as provided by Visual Test. A subroutine — in this case called a *handler* — must be provided so that when the event is encountered that subroutine can immediately be called.

Note   Rational provides TOOLS.INC in the \VT6\INCLUDE installation directory. This acts as a template for integrating their other testing products into Visual Test.

Again, this is just like callback functions in the sense that no matter where your program is during its execution, when a notification is encountered for which a subroutine has been provided, execution will immediately jump into the handler routine. Execution will only resume from where it left off when that handler is exited. So as with callback functions, care should be taken *not* to change things that the previously executing script was relying upon. That includes not changing the current directory, not closing any data files, not dismissing dialog boxes, and so on.

Depending on the type of notification being called, different data can be passed. As a result, the handler routine takes a `VARIANT` data type as its only parameter. A handler takes the form:

```
sub MyHandler (vData as variant)
    '*** place Test language commands here
end sub
```

Note that in this example, `MyHandler` can be any subroutine name. Once you've created the handler routine, you can then invoke the event handler with the notification of your choice. In the case of `WindowCreate` that call would take the form:

```
ON WindowCreate CALL MyHandler
```

The result is that whenever a window is created in the Windows operating system, this handler will be called. This would be one busy little handler, so in the case of `WindowCreate` and `WindowDestroy`, you can actually provide more information in the optional parameter list. That would take the form:

```
ON WindowCreate ("Untitled - Notepad","Notepad") _
CALL MyHandler
```

In this example, the `MyHandler` handler routine will only be called when a new instance of Microsoft Notepad is created. The two parameters in this example are the window's caption and its class name. When `MyHandler` is called by the `WindowCreate` notification, the window's handle is passed as the single parameter to `MyHandler`.

A notification can be turned off simply by passing `NULL` as the name of the handler routine. For example:

```
ON WindowCreate CALL NULL
```

Special notification support

NuMega Technologies, Inc., and the Microsoft Visual Test 4.0 team put their heads together for Visual Test 4.0 to provide an additional way to gather as much information as possible during the running of a test suite. The result was NuMega's BoundsChecker technology.

Note You won't find any information about using BoundsChecker in the 6.0 version of Visual Test because it has been removed from all documentation. BoundsChecker is a competing product to Rational Software's Purify product. Although removed from documentation, it remains intact in the program to avoid backward-compatibility problems. It will only work, however, if a full installation of BoundsChecker exists and NuMega has made their setup program take appropriate actions when finding an existing installation of Visual Test.

In Visual Test 6.0, Rational Software built upon this idea by adding support for some of their tools as well: Purify, Quantify, and Coverage.

Rational added support for their tools

There are two ways these tools can be invoked in Visual Test. The first is to use BOUNDSCHECKER, PURIFY, QUANTIFY, or COVERAGE as a parameter with the RUN statement (for example, RUN "NOTEPAD.EXE", PURIFY). This approach results in the generation of a run-time error when Rational Software's Purify tool detects any errors in the Notepad application. Or if a PurifyNotify statement has been put in place using the ON...CALL event handler (discussed earlier in this chapter), the subroutine specified as the handler for the PurifyNotify event will be called with more information about that error.

Listing 13-13 gives an example of a Purify notification event and handler. Just like an ON ERROR GOTO statement, the Purify notification can be invoked at the beginning of the script so that the entire script can make use of the Purify information.

Listing 13-13: It's now possible to make use of other Rational tools with Visual Test.

```
on PurifyNotify (NULL) call MyErrorHandler

    viewport clear
    run "notepad.exe", PURIFY        'In lieu of NOWAIT parameter

    'run all test scenarios

    wMenuSelect("File\Exit")
end

sub MyErrorHandler(vInfo as variant)
    print "A Purify notification occurred: ";vInfo
end sub
```

The vInfo parameter is a VARIANT type, meaning that any kind of value can be passed to it. Scripts written using QuantifyNotify, CoverageNotify, and BoundsCheckerNotify will look very similar to the example shown for PurifyNotify.

Flexible Error Handling

The error handling code needs to be placed in the upper hierarchy of the shared files so that it is automatically invoked when a test case file includes the main .INC files it needs. This is one method of making sure that the same error handling information is shared throughout the code base.

Another approach is to create a generic error handler that is at the top of the hierarchy for handling any error conditions that are ignored by the test case files. Then the error handling can be handled by the test case itself or ignored, so that the handler for the test suite can take a crack at it.

An approach that I used before this multitiered error handling was introduced was to create an include file called ERR_HDR.INC (error header) that held the front, initialization portion of the on-error handler and notifications. This was included with the rest of the include files.

Another file, called ERR_FTR.INC (error footer), was created and included right after the test case file's end statement. It held the meat of the error handling code that actually attempted to deal with the error.

The reasoning behind this approach was that the test case template — and therefore all test case files — would automatically include the error handling source code. If modifications needed to be made, only the ERR_HDR.INC and ERR_FTR.INC files themselves would need be updated, since they were automatically brought in by the test case files. This is a simple approach and is still valid, but it is not as flexible as using multiple levels of error handling.

Working with Compiled Scripts

Visual Test has a feature that allows you to compile your scripts down into a tokenized file known as a pseudocode file, or p-code. These files were denoted with the .PCD file extension in versions previous to Visual Test 6.0. In this latest release, however, the file extension has been changed to .PC6 to help avoid conflicts with older compiled Visual Test files and also file associations for some graphics programs.

So why would you want to compile your scripts into a p-code format? There are a number of reasons. The first is that when a script is in its raw, .MST form it must be compiled before execution. An .MST file can also be changed or edited by those who you may not want changing your scripts. And .MST files typically require many .INC files to be compiled and included before they can run. All of these potential disadvantages go away when using a compiled form of your scripts.

When you compile your scripts into a .PC6 file, running those scripts can be a quicker process in a number of ways. It is faster to start its execution because it skips the compilation step. By avoiding the compilation step, you avoid errors introduced by others editing the source .MST files. You also avoid missing source code file problems when moving your scripts from machine to machine. This last benefit is one of the best reasons to compile your scripts, especially if you're in a large company on a team that has many testers who need to run your scripts. You can distribute the Visual Test run-time files along with your p-code files, along with any other external files you rely upon (such as initialization files or log files), and you're set. There are no issues with paths to find your include files, no hassles with setting up the full version of Visual Test on others' machines.

Although there are many advantages to compiling your scripts, there are, of course, downsides. The first is that if your script is changed you will need to recompile your .PC6 files. So if you're doing a lot of editing on your source .MST and .INC files and you want to keep your pseudocode files updated, you're going to find yourself recompiling and resaving your .PC6 files frequently. Also, although these scripts are in compiled form, and although you save a lot of time by avoiding the compilation step, the execution time of a compiled Test script and uncompiled Test script are exactly the same. This is because Visual Test needs to compile your script into a temporary .PC6 file to execute anyway, so you're gaining no execution speed.

Compiling Your Scripts

Saving your scripts as .PC6 files is a piece of cake. If you can already run your scripts from the Developer Studio editor or from the Suite Manager, then clearly your scripts compile and the only step left is saving that compilation.

Figure 13-10 shows that the Compile menu item can be found under the Test menu. Select this menu item; the script window that is currently active will begin to compile, and when it finishes compiling you will be prompted with a Save P-Code dialog box. Here is where you can type in the filename you want to use for your compiled script.

Figure 13-10: Select the Compile menu item to compile the script in the currently active window.

Note Keep in mind that if you are using any conditional compilation symbols, the resulting compiled code is only code that was compiled based on those symbols. That is, if you have a metacommand that causes a different section of code to be conditionally included and compiled for Windows NT, and you then compile that script, moving to a Windows 98 machine will not cause the source code to be excluded. If you were running the .MST file, then this conditional compilation would take place. But with a compiled .PC6 file the symbols that are in effect when the p-code file is compiled determine how that file executes.

Running Compiled Scripts

When you have your file compiled and you're ready to distribute it to another machine that doesn't have Visual Test 6.0 installed, three files are required in addition to the p-code file itself (along with one optional file for displaying logged information):

✦ MSVCRT.DLL: the Microsoft C run-time library

✦ VTEST60.DLL: the Rational Software Visual Test run-time library

✦ MTVIEW.EXE: If your tests are logging output to the Viewport, this file is necessary. If not, then it is optional.

✦ MTRUN.EXE: the Visual Test run-time engine

Note A file was installed with Visual Test called NOREDIST.WRI. Locate that file for information on which files you cannot redistribute royalty free with your Visual Test compiled scripts. While it wasn't on the beta release of the software, there was talk of creating a REDIST.WRI file that would list the distributable files. Look for it on your Visual Test 6.0 CD or in your installation directory.

Once you've copied these files to the destination machine, placed MSVCRT.DLL in the SYSTEM directory of your Windows directory, and put the MTRUN.EXE file in the path, you're ready to put your compiled file to use. The easiest way to learn how to use this is to create a shortcut. To create a shortcut, right-click your desktop, select the New menu item, and select the Shortcut submenu item. You should see a dialog box similar to the one shown in Figure 13-11, after you've typed in the appropriate syntax for MTRUN.EXE, which is:

```
MTRUN.EXE FileName.PC6 [ /T TestModeString ][ /C CommandString
]
```

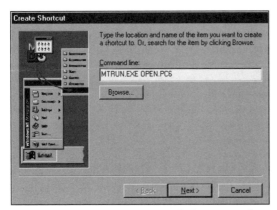

Figure 13-11: The MTRUN.EXE file has a simple syntax. In many cases you'll find yourself creating a shortcut to run your compiled script.

Command-Line Arguments

You'll notice that MTRUN.EXE takes two optional command line parameters. The first one is designated by "/T" and the second one, by "/C"; using either of these two parameters followed by a value will result in the global variables TESTMODE$ and COMMAND$ being set, respectively. This is one way for you to send information to your script so that it can act on this information. Perhaps you specify /T SMOKE, which results in the TESTMODE$ global variable being set to "SMOKE." Furthermore, perhaps you've set up your compiled script to look for this value in TESTMODE$; upon encountering it, your scripts move into a mode in which only a broad testing pass is performed. You get the idea. This is just a simple way to pass information to your scripts so that you can configure them to run in different ways depending on those arguments.

Tip   There is another file called MT.EXE in the Visual Test installation directory that works just like MTRUN.EXE, with one difference. MTRUN.EXE is used with compiled, .PC6 files, whereas MT.EXE is used with the original source, .MST files.

Front-Line Wisdom

Now that we've looked at some of Visual Test's features, let's turn to a couple of experts in the field for some advice. Bill Hodghead is a test engineer at Microsoft Corporation who uses Visual Test as one of the tools for helping to release high-quality products. Dan Hodge is a Visual Test trainer and consultant for ST Labs, Inc., and for his own company, The STA Group (Software Test Automation Group).

I asked Bill and Dan to give me a couple of tips and tricks from their experiences. Bill's response was to provide tips on writing scripts for testing localized products, killing a rogue program from inside Visual Test, and using ODBC from within this automation tool. Dan contributed information about how to work with and test OLE/ActiveX controls in Visual Test.

Note   You can find Bill Hodghead's sample code in the \SAMPLES\MICROSOFT directory on this book's CD-ROM.

Automated Testing of Localized Products

If your product is ever going to be sold in foreign markets, you should be prepared with test code that can be run on the product no matter what language it's in. The most common method of writing localizable tests is to put all your hotkeys and language-dependent strings into an include file as constants and to only use the constants in your code. This technique has a serious flaw — someone must correctly translate not just the product, but also the test include file, and then make sure they match. To do this is a lot of work.

To avoid extra translation work, here are some tips and functions that will allow you to write language-independent code that never needs translating.

Use ordinals or control IDs

The first tip is already built into Visual Test. Don't ever refer to a control on a dialog box by its caption or hotkey. The caption will be translated. Instead, always use the ordinal or control ID. In our experience, ordinals are slightly better then IDs because they change less often.

The ordinal is a number based on the tab order of each type of control. The first edit box is ordinal one; the second edit box is ordinal two, and so on. You can use Winfo to see the ordinals of each control. Each class of controls has a different numbering; thus, edit box one may be next to combo box one. As a side benefit, using numbers as constants instead of strings can take much less memory, as Visual Test simply replaces them when it compiles the code. Strings have to remain in memory. Here are two examples:

```
'The bad old way
Const BTNOK = "OK"
WButtonClick(BTNOK)

'The language independent way
Const BTNOK = 1
WButtonClick(_ord(BTNOK))
```

Using hotkeys with ordinals

A problem with calling functions like WButtonClick is that they are not really doing what a user would do. A user doesn't send a click message to a button. A user clicks with a mouse, presses a hotkey or tabs, and hits Enter or the spacebar.

Often, in application testing, clicking with the mouse works (the developer usually tries that), but pressing the hotkey is more likely to fail.

To test what the user really does, you can use the function ClickItem found in LOCALIZATION.INC on this book's CD-ROM. ClickItem takes the ordinal or caption of a control, finds the hotkey, and presses it. Not only is this a better test than WButtonClick, but it is language independent.

```
Const BTNHELP = 3
Const BTNOK = 1

'ClickItem also works with menus
Const MNUFILEOPEN = "@1/@2"'

'click on the button with the mouse
ClickItem(BTNOK, V_BUTTON, CI_MOUSECLICK)'

'press the hotkey of the button
ClickItem(BTNHELP, V_BUTTON)'

'press Alt+F, O for file open.
ClickItem(MNUFILEOPEN, V_MENU)'
```

Getting resource strings

Not everything can be done with ordinals. If you want to check for a dialog box, you will probably have to look for its caption. Rather than placing the caption in the include file as a constant, you can get the caption on the fly from the resource table to the application.

```
'The bad old way
Const MYAPPCAPTION = "Notepad"
if WfndWnd(MYAPPCAPTION,FW_DEFAULT or FW_PART _
          or FW_FOCUS) > 0 then

'The language independent way
Const MYAPPCAPTIONID = 12
Const APPEXE = "Notepad.exe"
dim strCaption$
strCaption = strGetResourceString(Environ("windir") + "\" + _
             APPEXE, MYAPPCAPTIONID)
if WfndWnd(strCaption,FW_DEFAULT or FW_PART _
          or FW_FOCUS) > 0 then
```

The new method uses a function `strGetResourceString` that you can find on the CD in LOCALIZATION.INC. It takes the executable file's name and the ID of the string in the application's string table.

To see the string table, just choose File ➪ Open to open the EXE in Visual Test. Expand and double-click the application's string table. These are all the strings that may be changed when the application is translated. You can stay perfectly in synch with the translation if you load the string from this table by the string's ID number.

Not all applications store their strings in the EXE string table. Some put the strings in the string table of a DLL that the application calls. You may need to hunt a bit or ask the developer to find the string you are looking for. If the string is not in the table and the developer has hard-coded it, then this is a bug — it can't be easily translated.

Note   A common error occurs when using `strGetResourceString`. When you use the function repeatedly, after one or more successful calls it fails to open the EXE or DLL to get the string. This is caused by a bug in the EXE that occurs because the developers are not releasing everything they allocated when the EXE loaded. This is a very poor coding practice and should be stamped out.

Getting a file's language

If you need to log the language an application was translated for, you can use the function `strAppLanguage` provided in LOCALIZATION.INC. For example:

```
strLanguage = strAppLanguage(Environ("windir") + _
              "\notepad.exe")
```

If you need to write special case code for each language, then you won't want to use the language string as it changes. Under English NT, your German application will be called "German," but under German NT, it will return "Deutsche." To get a language-independent value, get the language ID using `nFileGetLangCode`. For example:

```
select case str(nFileGetLangCode (Environ("windir") + _
"\notepad.exe"))
```

Killing an Application

One of the most important parts of automated testing is error recovery. If you run a lot of tests, you must be sure that errors in one test don't destroy the later tests. To do this, you need to be able to set the test application back to a known state at the start of each test. If an unexpected error occurs, however, a test may not be able to go back to a known state using the UI. Therefore, you need to be able to kill the test application and restart it.

On the CD-ROM is source code that has been provided by Microsoft and Bill Hodghead. This code makes it easier for you to kill a program that has become unresponsive through the user interface.

While VT provides functions to run applications, it doesn't provide any functions for killing the application. On the CD that comes with this book, we provide the function bKillProcess, which finds and terminates an application. To use this function, include KILLPROCESS.INC. For example:

```
if bKillProcess("Notepad.exe") then
    LOG "Notepad was found and terminated."
Endif
```

Using ODBC with Visual Test

The Open Database Connectivity (ODBC) specification is standard for retrieving data. Most database suppliers provide an ODBC driver to allow applications to access their database products.

Open database connectivity is one of the most popular methods for working with databases under Windows. Common database manipulation routines are wrapped into these ODBC libraries, making it easier for you to work with databases. In this section Bill tells you how to make use of the ODBC-related code that's been provided on this CD-ROM.

ODBC uses SQL (Structured Query Language) to send requests to the database and get results back. SQL is another standard that is implemented by most databases today. An example SQL statement might be select name from employees where dept = 4101. This query searches the employee table and returns the names of all the employees in the correct department.

It's beyond the scope of what I'm writing to explain how to create SQL queries; however, many applications will create SQL queries for you. For instance, Microsoft Access shows the SQL version of any query. If you are creating Visual Test ODBC code to connect to Access, you can create and test the SQL query in Access and then cut and paste it into your Visual Test code.

Visual Test doesn't come with ODBC functions predefined for you, so we provide them on the CD that comes with this book. These functions are designed for use with Microsoft SQL Server, Oracle, and Microsoft Access, but they can easily be modified for other databases (just modify tODBCConnectToServer).

The following files are found on the CD-ROM in the \SAMPLES\MICROSOFT directory:

✦ ODBC.INC: This contains the ODBC function declarations and definitions. Include this file to get ODBC functionality.

✦ ODBCSERVERS.INI: The ODBC functions in ODBC.INC use an INI file to describe how to connect to different servers. Edit this file to add your local server or database information, and save the file in your Windows directory.

✦ ODBCEXAMPLE.MST: This is an example of how to use the ODBC functions.

✦ UNICODE.INC: (Optional) Uncomment the include statement for UNICODE.INC if you want to access data sources that support Unicode datatypes such as Microsoft SQL Server 7.0.

Using the ODBC functions

This section discusses how to use the ODBC functions we've provided on this book's CD-ROM. The ODBC functions make use of two primary concepts: a server connection and a query handle.

The database server connection establishes communication with the database. Calling tODBCConnectToServer makes a connection. This returns a structure with connection information that is used by many other functions. When you are done with the database server, always call ODBCDisconnectFromServer to release the connection.

Each query has a unique query handle. Open the query with hODBCOpenQuery or hODBCExecuteWithMessages. When you are done with the query handle, close it with ODBCCloseQuery. Some databases allow a user to have multiple queries active at the same time, but not all of them do. It's best to have only one query active at a time on any database connection.

To get data from a query, pass your query handle to functions like vODBCGetValue, bODBCNextRow, or bODBCMatchingResult. See the sample code in ODBCEXAMPLE.MST for more on how to use these functions.

Additional ODBC function tips

Most databases only allow forward movement through the data. If hODBCOpenQuery returns any rows, then you are at the first row of the data. Use bODBCNextRow to move through the rows of the result. If a message is returned, then hODBCOpenQuery will not retrieve the data so that you have a chance to retrieve the message first with strODBCDiagnostic (getting the data destroys the message) before calling bODBCNextRow to move to the first row of the data. hODBCExecuteWithMessages does this for you and returns both the messages and a query handle that points to the data.

Many databases can handle several queries at once. If you do send multiple queries in the same query string, then the results will come back in separate result sets. hODBCOpenQuery returns a handle to the first result set that contains either data or a message. You can move forward through result sets with bODBCFetchNextResultSet. As with fetching rows, you can only move forward to the next result set. To get previous results or rows, you have to close and reopen the query.

It's a good idea to check to see if data was returned from a query before you try to read it. Check the fRowsExist flag returned by hODBCOpenQuery to be sure something came back from the server before calling functions like vODBCGetValue to read the data.

Testing Custom Controls

Often when writing test code, you come across controls that are not part of the standard Windows set. For some reason the developers wrote their own grid control or date edit field to do something that Windows wouldn't allow them to do. When you run into these controls, Visual Test can't directly find out much information about the state of the control—nor can it do much to manipulate it. If the control is an important part of your application, you may need more than Visual Test can give directly. You need test hooks into the controls.

Note Anyone who has done any automation testing under Microsoft Windows has encountered the dreaded *custom control*. These controls aren't standard Windows controls and are therefore not easily recognized—and in some cases are not recognized at all—by Visual Test.

A *test hook* is code you have to get the developer to add to the control just for testing purposes. Developers can add hooks that allow you to send a message to the control asking for information or telling the control to take some action.

Deciding what you need from the developer

Naturally, developers are busy. You will probably only have a chance to add test hooks early in the project's life cycle, and you'd better know what you want. Make a list of the information you will need from the control. Keep it short and eliminate any duplicate information. Remember that Visual Test's WCustom functions can give you some information. Add to your list any actions you need to perform on the control that you can't do in any other way. Keep these to a few simple actions.

Note Custom controls are different from testing OCXs. For more information on testing OLE controls, refer to the "Testing OLE Controls" section found in this chapter.

Talk with your developers about the list and what they can give you. Some of what you are asking for may be too hard to do, or it may be easier to provide information in a different format that matches the internal format the control uses. Be clear with the developer on the following points. Test automation is a separate process from the test application, so it doesn't have access to any of the application's internal strings or structures. To communicate with the control, you have one basic technique available to you. You can send a message to the application and get a number back (a LONG), or you can send a message and ask for a file in memory back.

Simple hooks

Where possible, always design the test hooks to return information in the form of a LONG. These are the easiest hooks to write. Use the Windows API SendMessage to send a WM_USER message to the control. The developer modifies the control to respond to that particular message by returning a number or executing an action. Most of your test function is devoted to getting the handle of the control.

WM_USER messages are a range of messages that Windows sets aside for just this sort of thing. You and the developer must agree on the message number to add to the constant WM_USER. Include the WINAPI.INC or DECLARES.INC files when using hooks to get the SendMessage declaration (see Listing 13-14).

> ### Listing 13-14: **An example of a hook and how Visual Test makes use of it**

```
Const DATECTLDATE    = "DimensionDateCtlClass" 'Date ctrls
Const WM_DATECTL_GET = (WM_USER + 4505)
'*****************************************************************
'* Function: strGetDate
'*
'* Description: strGetDate works with a custom date control
'*
'* Parameters:
'*   lDateOrd - the ordinal of the date control
'*
'* Returns: the current "YYYYMMDD" in the control,
'*          regardless of locale set in the control panel
'*
'* Example: if strGetDate (1) = "19980516" then
'*
'* Author: Bill Hodghead
'*****************************************************************
Function strGetDate$(lDateOrd& = 1)
dim lDate&, hWnd&
    'use WCustomFind to get the hWnd of the date control
```

```
      WCustomSetClass(DATECTLDATE)
      hWnd = WCustomFind(_ord(lDateOrd))
      WCustomSetClass(Null)
      if hWnd = 0 then
         Fail "strGetDate: Unable"+ _
         " to find date control, ordinal = " + str(lDateOrd)
      endif

      'send the message to get the date value.
      lDate = SendMessage(hWnd,WM_DATECTL_GET,0,0)
      strGetDate = str(lDate)
   end function
```

Complex hooks

More complex custom control hooks are required when you need a string or a structure back from the control. Creating a complex hook is initially the same as creating a simple hook: First get the handle to the control, and then send the WM_USER message. When the custom control receives the message, it has to open a file shared in memory and put the string or other data in it. You open this file in your code and read the information out. The Windows APIs used here are the file mapping APIs that are used for interprocess communication. The APIs are not quite like file APIs in that they just return a pointer to a block of memory. You and the developer of the custom control have to agree on the name of the file, its maximum size, and the format of the data in the file. If the format is not something simple, like a string, you will have to define a structure that matches the format. Listing 13-15 shows an example of a more complex hook.

Listing 13-15: A more complex hook than the one shown in Listing 13-14

```
CONST GRAPHCLASS = "GraphManagerClass"
CONST MAPFILE = "GutsDebugMappingObject"
CONST WM_GRAPH_GETBAR_VALUES_DBG = (WM_USER+4809)

'Structure to hold the series' for each bar in the graph
'database
type GRAPHBARVALUE
   iLegend as integer 'DB Index number
   lValue as long      'Actual value for the series for this bar
end type
```

(continued)

Listing 13-15 *(continued)*

```
Const MAX_BAR_NAME = 256

'Structure to hold a record for each bar
type GRAPHBAR
    szBarName as string * MAX_BAR_NAME  'Bar name
    iValues as integer                  'Number of series
    pValues as pointer to GRAPHBARVALUE 'Pointer to BAR_VALUE
end type

'***************************************************************
'* Function:    strGraphBarName
'*
'* Description: Gets the label associated with the bar of
'*              the custom graph control
'*
'* Parameters:
'*  nGraphOrd - optional, the ordinal number of the graph
'*              control.
'*  lBarNumber - required, the number of the bar to get the
'*              name of the label of the graph bar
'*
'* Returns:  the label of the graph bar
'*
'* Example:  if strGraphBarName(1) = strCaption then
'*
'* Author: Bill Hodghead
'***************************************************************
Function strGraphBarName$(lBarNumber&, nGraphORD&=1)
dim hMapFile&  'the shared file handle
dim pMapAddress as pointer to GRAPHBAR 'a pointer to the file
                                       'defined in the struct-
                                       'ure of the file data
dim strTemp$
dim hWndGraph& 'the handle to the control

    'get the handle of the graph control
    WCustomSetClass(GRAPHCLASS)
    hWndGraph = WCustomFind(_ord(nGraphORD))

    if hWndGraph = NULL then FAIL " strGraphBarName: "+ _
        " the Graph Control could not be found."

    'open the shared file, 1024 bytes in size
    hMapFile = CreateFileMapping(&HFFFFFFFF&,NULL, _
            PAGE_READWRITE,0,1024,MAPFILE)

    if (hMapFile= NULL) then FAIL "strGraphBarName: "+ _
                                  "Unable to open map file."
```

```
'get a pointer to the first byte of the shared file
pMapAddress = CPtr(MapViewOfFile(hMapFile, _
            FILE_MAP_ALL_ACCESS,0,0,0))
if (pMapAddress=NULL) then
   CloseHandle(hMapFile)
   FAIL "strGraphBarName: Unable to "+ _
         "open View of map file."
endif

'send a message asking the graph control to fill the
'file with information
SendMessage(hWndGraph,WM_GRAPH_GETBAR_VALUES_DBG, _
            lBarNumber,0)

strTemp = pMapAddress[0].szBarName
strGraphBarName = ConvertSZ(strTemp) 'ConvertSZ is defined
                                     'in ODBC.inc.

'It returns the characters up to the first null

UnmapViewOfFile(pMapAddress)   'Release the pointer
                               'to the file
   CloseHandle(hMapFile)       'Close the file
end function
```

Testing OLE Controls

Before we jump in with both feet, let's first get some terminology out of the way. Visual Test can manipulate both ActiveX and OLE custom controls. (In case you're not aware of it, these are the same.) Microsoft originally created what we know as the OLE custom control for the Windows environment. "OLE custom control" is a mouthful, so of course an acronym was created for it: OCX. You may have heard the term *OCX,* especially if you've done much Visual Basic programming.

The usefulness of OCXs goes beyond applications. The Internet has grown immensely, and so has the creative aspect of Web pages. We all like to see Web pages that have cool animations and allow us to interact with them. Web page developers can accomplish this in several ways. You're probably familiar with Java, but another means is ActiveX controls. Yes, Microsoft has adapted the OCX control to the Web. Rather than use the somewhat blah names of OCX or OLE control, it's much more interesting to call it an ActiveX control; nonetheless, it's all the same. Chances are that if you look in your WINDOWS\SYSTEM directory, you'll find many files with the extension .OCX. These are the ActiveX/OLE controls on your system.

So what exactly is an OCX? We'll keep the description simple, since getting into the specifics can be quite technical. An OCX is a simply a "canned" program that performs some kind of function that developers plug into their own applications. This saves developers the time and effort of developing the functionality themselves. Think of them as reusable plug-in modules. ActiveX controls can come in any flavor and do just about anything — from implementing a special type of control to allowing an application to browse the Web. There are literally thousands of these controls that individuals and companies have created and that can be bought or found on the Internet. Their popularity continues to climb because they're so easy for developers to use. If you haven't encountered one yet in your testing, you probably will in the future.

Some assembly required

Because OCXs are not standard Windows controls like buttons or check boxes, they're not as straightforward to test. Before you can use Visual Test to automate testing of an OCX, three conditions must be met. All three of these conditions are briefly mentioned in the online help, and meeting these conditions may require the assistance of a developer.

Meeting the first condition

When you install Visual Test, a file named VTEST.OCX is installed in the WINDOWS\SYSTEM directory. You should recognize this file as an OLE control by its extension. The purpose of this control is to allow the scripts you write to communicate with the OCXs in an application by acting as a kind of intermediary. This means that VTEST.OCX must be placed on every window in the application containing an OCX. The developer would typically do this. Figure 13-12 shows VTEST.OCX being placed on a form in a Visual Basic application. It is only visible at design time. A grid OLE Control is shown to its left.

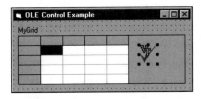

Figure 13-12: The VTEST.OCX file must be added to every window containing an OCX in the application.

To some, requiring an additional control on the application is an invasive approach to testing. What happens when testing is finished and the control is removed? Will it affect the application and possibly cause bugs? While there have not been any reports of adverse reactions to removing the control, the VTEST.OCX is freely distributable. Thus, if you feel uncomfortable removing the control once testing is completed, you are free to leave it on the application and ship the control as well.

Meeting the second and third conditions

To meet the next two requirements, we once again bring up some technical terminology. OLE controls are held in *containers*. If a Visual Basic application contains an OCX, then we say that Visual Basic is the container. To keep it simple, you can think of the application itself as the container. For Visual Test to communicate with an OCX, the container (application) must support the IOleContainer Interface. Through this interface Visual Test can "talk" to OCXs contained in the application. The best method for determining if the interface is supported by your application, short of trial and error, is to ask the developer.

The third condition states that the IOleContainer Interface support the EnumObjects method. Think of a method as just a function; the application must have a function that Visual Test can call to enumerate each OCX. You may wish to ask the developer of the application whether the EnumObjects method is supported.

OLE control properties

Most OCX automation testing is accomplished by getting or setting the values of properties associated with an OLE Control. Visual Basic programmers are familiar with the idea of control properties. Those of you who are not should read on.

Any given OCX has properties associated with it. The properties of an OCX are determined by its purpose. The creators of an OCX can give it any properties they desire. Though different OCXs may share a few common properties, they will most likely have many different properties.

As an example, let's consider a standard pushbutton like an OK button found on a dialog box. Even though it's not an OCX, it does have properties. One property is its caption. So we can say the caption property of the button is "OK." Another property of the button would be its color, which might be gray. Other properties would be its height, width, and position on the dialog box. All of these properties would have some value. By using Visual Test procedures like GetText() and wGetInfo(), we can obtain some of these properties. If the button were an OCX, we might even be able to set them. However, it's important to recognize that not all properties of an OCX can always be set and retrieved.

Knowing the properties of an OCX is a requirement if testing consists of getting and setting them. There are a number of ways to find out what properties are associated with an OCX:

   ✦ Winfo

   ✦ A Visual Test script

   ✦ Third-party utilities similar to Winfo

   ✦ The developer

   ✦ Documentation for the control

The best method is to obtain the documentation for the control. While WInfo and other similar utilities provide you with a list of properties, that may not be enough. Besides knowing the properties, you must know their purpose. You can make educated guesses about some, but others can be cryptic.

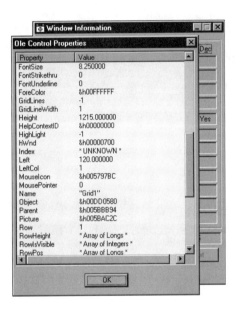

Figure 13-13: The OLE Properties window, showing the properties associated with the Grid OLE control

WInfo will display the properties for an OCX if the three conditions previously mentioned are met. Simply drag the Finder tool over the OCX and release the mouse button. The Properties window shown in Figure 13-13 will appear. In addition, we can get this same information by writing a script. The script to accomplish this can be found at the end of this topic.

OLE control procedures

You can use a number of Visual Test procedures to manipulate OLE controls. The procedures have the prefix of `OleCtl` and can easily be found in the online help by typing the prefix in the Search dialog box.

Many of the procedures are similar to those for standard controls. For instance, there is the `OleCtlClick()` procedure to click an OLE Control. Two commonly used procedures are `OleCtlSetProperty()` and `OleCtlGetProperty()`, which allow you to set and retrieve the properties of an OCX. But before we put these procedures to use, we need to find out how to identify an OCX.

Identifying OLE controls

Recall that when we use the Visual Test procedures for standard controls, we must identify the control by its caption, ordinal, ID, or handle. Though we still must identify OLE controls when referring to them in our script, we no longer use all of the same methods we use for standard controls. OLE controls can be identified by one of four methods:

- ✦ Caption
- ✦ Ordinal
- ✦ Name
- ✦ IUnknown Interface Pointer

Captions and ordinals work the same. If you're using ordinal values, remember to preface the value with an "@" character. The following example demonstrates using a caption and an ordinal value to click an OCX.

```
OleCtlClick("MyControl")
OleCtlClick("@1")
```

Even though you don't use IDs and Handles to identify OLE controls, the Name property and IUnknown Interface Pointer are very similar. The name of a control is one of the many properties of the control. A common mistake is to confuse the name with the caption. The caption property is actually viewable when the application is run. The name only exists as a property of the control and cannot be viewed.

If you refer back to Figure 13-13, you'll see the Name property listed for the grid example. The name is Grid1. The developer can assign the name of an OCX in the same way he assigns an ID to a button. The two are used the same way. The difference is that an ID is a number and the name is usually a string. Because these two are so similar, when identifying an OCX by its name property, you use the "#" sign as you do for IDs.

```
OleCtlClick("#Grid1")
```

The IUnknown Interface pointer is yet another way for Visual Test to access individual OCXs within the application. While it's not truly a handle, it might be easiest to think of it as one. Like a handle, the pointer is dynamic, so it cannot be hard-coded within your script. If you choose this method of identifying an OCX, use OleCtlFind() to return the correct pointer. The procedure returns a long value that must be converted to a string and prefaced with an "=" character. Sound familiar? This is how the procedures for working with standard controls such as wButtonFind() work. The code that follows demonstrates how to use the IUnknown Interface pointer to identify the grid control in Figure 13-12.

```
Dim pGrid As Long

'Obtain the pointer using the Name property
PGrid = OleCtlFind("#Grid1")

'Convert pGrid to a string and preface it with an "="
OleCtlClick("=" + trim$(str$(pGrid)))
```

Note that in order to retrieve the IUnknown Interface pointer, the Name property is used. Since we're looking for the pointer, we first have to use a different method to obtain it.

Having to convert pGrid to a string and then preface it with an "=" looks a little messy within the OleCtlClick procedure. The _ctl() function can do all of this for you and make your code cleaner. The function takes a LONG value, converts it to a STRING, and automatically prefaces the string with the "=" character. The following two lines perform the same task:

```
OleCtlClick("=" + str$(pGrid))
OleCtlClick(_ctl(pGrid))
```

Note   Though the IUnknown interface is similar to handles, it does not share the same unique ability that handles have. Handles allow you to identify a control that is not on the active window. The IUnknown interface pointer requires the window containing the OCX to have the focus.

Putting it to use

Here is the code to get and set the text of a cell in the grid example. Row and Col are two properties of the OCX. These properties can be set or queried. Setting the values of either of these two properties moves the focus to a different cell in the grid. The Text property can also be set or queried. Setting this property sets the text of the cell having the focus. Note the use of the Name property as the method to identify the control. Figure 13-14 shows the result of running this snippet of code. Also, notice that VTEST.OCX is not visible when the application is run.

```
'Move to column 3 row 2
OleCtlSetProperty("#Grid1", "Col", 3)
OleCtlSetProperty("#Grid1","Row",2)
'Set the text of the cell
OleCtlSetProperty("#Grid1","Text","Cool!")
'Retrieve the text and print it out
Print OleCtlGetProperty("#Grid1","Text")
```

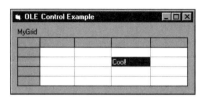

Figure 13-14: Setting the contents of a cell within the OLE Grid control

Earlier in the chapter I mentioned that there was a way to obtain the properties associated with an OCX though the use of a script. Listing 13-16 uses the OleCtlPropertyList() procedure to obtain the properties and their values and print them to the Viewport.

Listing 13-16: **An example of working with OLE controls**

```
'Create record to hold property and value
Type OLECTL_PROPERTY
    PropName As String
    PropValue As Variant
End Type

'An array of size 1 is created to hold the properties.
'Visual Test redimensions this array to the number of
'properties associated with the control
Dim aCtlProps(1) As OLECTL_PROPERTY
Dim iNumItems As Integer
Dim iLoop As Integer

'Make call to get the properties
iNumItems = OleCtlPropertyList ( "#MSFlexGrid1", _
          aCtlProps)

'iNumItems contains the number of properties associated
'with the control
PRINT "Number of properties:";iNumItems

'Print the properties array.  The array is 0 based so
'subtract one from the number of property items.
For iLoop = 0 to iNumItems-1
    Print "The property '" + aCtlProps(iLoop).PropName + _
    "' is equal to: ", aCtlProps(iLoop).PropValue
Next iLoop
```

Understanding Microsoft Active Accessibility

Microsoft developed Active Accessibility (MSAA) in response to a very real need: to make computers more accessible to people with disabilities. I worked for quite a few years at a college where I had the opportunity to help blind, deaf, and physically disabled students use computers. Audible cues for blind people, visible cues for deaf people, and more controllable input devices for the physically challenged are a rarity. Microsoft is meeting this need by creating a standard way for programs to expose information about themselves, such as caption text information, to any application that's interested.

Note   This section on MSAA was written by Joe Benner, who was a part of the Visual Test 6.0 development team. He was responsible for creating MSAA support in the Test language. Because Joe knows this area so intimately, I asked him to write this section on MSAA.

MSAA enables a conversation between an MSAA server and an MSAA client through COM (common object model) automation. MSAA is COM-based. An MSAA-enabled server application can describe what is being pointed to on the screen, what the next item is in a navigational sequence, the role of the thing being pointed to, and a fair number of its other standard characteristics. An MSAA-enabled client application can both request and respond to this information and use it to provide screen reading utilities, navigational utilities, alternate input devices, or more control over existing input devices.

A Peek at the Internals

In general terms, MSAA will generate a message (WM_GETOBJECT); if an MSAA-enabled server application responds appropriately, an MSAA client will be able to interact with the application (through an exposed IAccessible or IDispatch interface). This makes a number of MSAA methods and properties available to the client. The value of the Name property, for example, can be gotten or set through get_accName and set_accName methods.

Some of the standard MSAA properties are:

✦ Name: The user-friendly name by which the user would refer to this object, such as a window's caption, a control's label, or the ToolTip shown for a toolbar button.

✦ Role: A value describing the nature of this object, such as whether the user perceives and interacts with it as a pushbutton, a text field, or any of a number of other standard object types.

✦ Location: The screen coordinates occupied by this object.

✦ Value: The current setting for an edit box, slider, or similar control.

✦ State: An array of flags indicating common attributes, such as whether the object is hidden, unavailable, checked, and so forth.

✦ Description: A string that describes the visual appearance of a graphic object, similar to the ALT text used in documents on the World Wide Web. This is important for users who are blind or accessing their computer in other "eyes-free" environments.

✦ Navigate: Used to determine the spatial or logical ordering of objects, such as icons in a folder or controls in a dialog box.

Achieving Standard Support for MSAA

MSAA is not available on all Microsoft operating systems. Currently it can be added to Windows 95, and it ships with Windows 98. The first NT version that will ship with MSAA is 5.0. For more information about MSAA contact Microsoft or search for "Active Accessibility" on their Web site. There, among the descriptions of MSAA's strengths, you'll find the claim that MSAA is expected to make automation tools much more robust because the tool will be able to actively gather data from the application being tested. MSAA provides a very granular representation of the screen, making those "fake" dialog boxes (mentioned in Chapter 5) accessible to automation on MSAA-enabled applications, and it provides a wide range of descriptive text about the application at run time.

To get a general sense of what sort of information an MSAA-enabled application exposes, get the MSAA SDK from Microsoft and take a look at some of the tools that come with it, or use Visual Test's Window Information utility. To add MSAA to a Windows 95 machine, you'll need to get the MSAA SDK from Microsoft.

If you know that MSAA is enabled on your system and aaIsEnabled reports that it is not, you might need to register Visual Test's MSAA client DLL. Its name is VTAA.DLL, and it can be found in the VT6\BIN directory of your installation.

Taking Testing to a New Level

If MSAA did nothing more than help make computers more accessible to disabled people, it would be enough. At its core, MSAA enables applications to reveal a considerable amount of information about themselves to whatever client is interested. Visual Test, working as an MSAA client, takes what an MSAA server exposes and makes it available to Visual Test programmers.

Currently, Windows common controls (and some uncommon ones, too, I suppose) support MSAA in a rudimentary way. So even if the application you're testing is not MSAA-enabled yet, on an MSAA-enabled system you'll be able to get additional information to use in your test cases.

The degree of granularity of information you get from MSAA objects is probably greater than you're accustomed to. The more information an MSAA client has about the screen, the better chance it will have to make the application more accessible. The kind of information you get might very well change the way you "look" at the screen. A list box, for example, exposed through Visual Test's wList functions, provides familiar information about the list box as well as mouse and keyboard simulation. On an MSAA-enabled system, each element of the list box, the text items in it, the parts of the scrollbar, and the list box window itself are described. The states of these items (selected, selectable, focus, focusable), the roles of these items (list item, window, button, scroll, background), the next default action (via MSAA), and the values of appropriate items (list item text) are exposed.

With MSAA you can still perform the familiar actions on standard controls that you could with the regular Visual Test functions. And those w* functions are, of course, still available, but MSAA takes testing to a new level.

Using the MSAA Functions

Since MSAA is not available on all systems, the first thing you'll probably want to do is check to see if it's enabled on your test system (see Listing 13-17). If it isn't, you can't proceed. Because of the possibility that MSAA won't be available, it's probably useful to group your MSAA-based tests together and terminate before any other MSAA-dependent scenarios are run.

Listing 13-17: Checking to see if MSAA is enabled on your test system

```
scenario "Check to see if MSAA is enabled on this system"
    if not aaIsEnabled then
        fail "MSAA is not enabled: Terminating script."
    endif

    log "MSAA is enabled."

scenario cleanup
    if failed then end
end scenario
'Proceed with MSAA enabled scenarios
```

If that's not appropriate, probably the next best thing to do is to check for MSAA availability as needed either with a call to aaIsEnabled or with a Global flag you set once.

The MSAA recognition string

Just as windows have a system-unique identifier — the window handle — so do MSAA objects. And just as you might expect, the unique MSAA identifier exposes more information. Generally you'll use an MSAA recognition string (or *cookie*) as transparently as you do a window handle. That is, you'll call aaFndWnd, keep the return value in a string variable, and use whatever is in that string for subsequent aa function calls dealing with that object.

Not all MSAA objects are window-based. The Visual Test function name, aaFndWnd, is modeled after the familiar wFndWnd. The search criteria match for the most part, but the return value is significantly different. In MSAA, a menu item, for example, is a distinct MSAA object. There is no Windows-equivalent view of a menu item. In Windows, a menu is a menu. To MSAA, a menu is an MSAA object that has the role of "menu" and contains other MSAA objects with the role of "menu item." Those "menu item" objects have the default action of "click."

MSAA levels the playing field. Every MSAA-enabled thing in the system exposes itself in a uniform way. To get a sense of this uniformity and take a peek at the recognition strings, give Listing 13-18 a whirl on an MSAA-enabled system. It will print out the first ten MSAA objects that Visual Test 6.0 finds.

Listing 13-18: **Print out the first 10 MSAA objects that Visual Test 6.0 finds**

```
dim strAA as string
dim iLoop as long

viewport clear

if not aaIsEnabled then
    print "MSAA is not enabled. Terminating."
    end
end if

for iLoop = 1 to 10
    print aaFndWnd(_ord(iLoop))
next
```

MSAA in action

In Windows systems without Active Desktop installed, the menu that appears when the Start button is clicked is actually a menu — the wMenu functions work on it once you've exposed it with wTaskbarStartClk. They are owner-draw menus though, which don't have strings of their own. So you can't access them through Visual Test by caption—only by ordinal. Otherwise it's most likely a normal menu.

In Windows with Active Desktop installed, that's no longer a menu at all: It's a toolbar. After a wTaskbarStartClk call, wToolbar functions work on them.

The start "menu" is exposed through MSAA, however, and there it has an assigned role of {menu}, and the items in it have assigned roles of {menu item}.

Here's a little sample I wrote for the README.WRI file that ships with Visual Test (see Listing 13-19). It takes a standard Visual Test menu description, "Programs\Rational Visual Test 6.0\Rational Visual Test," and breaks it up on the "\" character. Then it builds an MSAA recognition string for a {menu item} with that caption and clicks the MSAA object for that recognition string.

Listing 13-19: A sample of using MSAA

```
const STR_MENU_DELIM = "\"
const STR_START_PATH = "\"
const STR_MENUITEM = "{menu item}"

'************************
'sub aaStartMenuSelect
'   Shows the Start button then...
'   Splits a STR_MENU_DELIM delimited string and consecutively
'   calls aaClkWnd with the substrings as parameters
'   strMenu - [in] VT menu path string
'
sub aaStartMenuSelect(strMenu as string)
dim strLocal as string
dim strItem as string
dim iPos as long

    strLocal = strMenu

    iPos = instr(strLocal, STR_MENU_DELIM)
    while iPos > 0 and len(strLocal) > 0
        strItem = left(strLocal, iPos - 1)
        strLocal = right(strLocal, len(strLocal) - iPos)

        aaClkWnd(STR_START_PATH + strItem + STR_MENUITEM)

        iPos = instr(strLocal, STR_MENU_DELIM)
    wend

    aaClkWnd(STR_START_PATH + strLocal + STR_MENUITEM)

end sub
```

Since MSAA isn't interested in what Windows thinks the Start "menu" is, this function will choose the specified Start menu item whether or not Active Desktop is installed, because the MSAA objects are exposed as {menu items}.

MSAA's Future

MSAA-enabled applications are just beginning to catch on — and for good reason: Computers need to be made more accessible to more people. A side effect of this is that test automation writers now have more tools available because of MSAA. The goal of MSAA is to make applications more accessible. And it does. For now, MSAA is probably useful in test automation for solving strange problems like the system menu and Active Desktop problem just described. As MSAA-enabled applications grow in numbers, MSAA could conceivably open up a whole new level of software testing by enabling the automation tool to actively get feedback about the application it's running from the application itself.

Summary

Visual Test is a very capable programming language and can actually be used to create a Windows application if one wishes to use it as that kind of tool. That's not the true purpose of the language, however. Its creators have attempted to provide as much flexibility as possible so that a Test programmer is not hindered by the tool. The original Microsoft Visual Test team succeeded in creating a powerful automation tool, and Rational Software has continued to grow it in this 6.0 version. If you're interested in learning more about Windows programming, you'll probably want to check out one of the many good books available on the subject.

This chapter has looked at a number of advanced topics, which aren't necessarily closely related. It began with how to work with files and moves on to performance issues, such as writing benchmarks. It continued with pointers, and allocating and freeing up memory. It also covered dynamic-linked libraries (DLLs), how to link into Windows application programmer interfaces (APIs), and how to trap special run-time information using the tools built into Visual Test, including Rational Software's line of testing tools. From those topics, the chapter moved on to how to compile your scripts for easy distribution. It also included some tips and tricks from those currently in the thick of automation at Microsoft and abroad. And finally, it covered one of the new features in Visual Test 6.0, MSAA.

✦   ✦   ✦

Black Box Monkey Testing

◆   ◆   ◆   ◆

In This Chapter

Testing software with "monkeys"

Understanding code-based smart monkeys

Understanding the differences between smart and dumb monkeys

Introducing Freddie: a sample monkey

Facing potential problems with monkeys

◆   ◆   ◆   ◆

As you have seen so far in this book, there are many ways to go about testing a software application through the use of automation tools like Visual Test 6.0.

In this chapter we look at several different kinds of testing tools called "monkeys." We'll see how they can help you test applications, and we'll do some experiments with the monkey tools on the CD-ROM included with this book. The Visual Test tricks and Win32 API calls needed to make an effective Windows GUI test monkey may be useful to you, even if you decide not to use monkeys to test your applications.

Note This chapter was written by Noel Nyman, who works in Microsoft's Semantics Platform Test, Distributed Applications Platform Division. Noel is a seasoned test engineer who is well-qualified to explain the concept, as well as the creation, of automated monkeys.

Note The source code listings in this chapter highlight some of the features of Freddie, the automated monkey I describe. Rather than taking up a lot of space here with all the code related to Freddie's care and feeding, I've chosen to devote Appendix E to that purpose. Take a look at Appendix E if you're interested in learning more about Freddie's source code.

Can We Really Test Software with Monkeys?

"Six monkeys pounding on six typewriters at random for a million years will recreate all the works of Isaac Asimov." You've undoubtedly heard some variation of this aphorism about monkeys creating well-known literary works.

Of course, the monkeys would find typewriters boring after just a few seconds, and very little keyboarding would get done. Instead they'd spend their time doing other monkey things. Yet the idea of monkeys diligently typing lots of gibberish, and occasionally reproducing great works of literature, is appealing. And there's nothing wrong with the theory. It *would* work, given enough time, typewriters, and monkeys. You'd need a human support staff as well, and we'll come back to that.

It's easy to imagine the monkeys doing things with software on computers instead of using paper in typewriters. If we could keep them from throwing the mice at each other, the monkeys would eventually do everything with a software application that can possibly be done, and in every possible sequence. It follows that, in the process of doing *every* thing in *every* way, they'd stumble across all the bugs in the application.

Obviously we can't test software using real monkeys. Our test cycles are too short and we don't have a budget for monkey chow. We could use "virtual monkeys," though. The essence of monkeys testing software is their selection of random inputs without the bias about "the right thing to do next" that humans might have. We can simulate that primate random input talent with software to create dedicated "monkey" test tools. We solve several problems that way. Software doesn't eat, it stays focused on the task at hand, and it's cheap to reproduce. We could have many, many copies of a software monkey running during the limited time of our real test cycle, and they *might* find *some* bugs. There's still that support staff problem, though.

Note　Some testers prefer the term "stochastic" testing to "monkey" testing. It does sound more technical, but we like the warm and simian feeling we get from "monkey."

The monkeys replicating Dr. Asimov's work produce typed copy, but they can't read it. We need humans to review the monkeys' output and compare it with Asimov's prolific writings to determine which pages are pure Asimov and which are just garbage. In testing terms, we need an "oracle." Creating software monkeys and oracles, and setting up the hardware to run them, is expensive. Can we really find enough bugs with monkeys to justify that cost?

Although some experts question their value, test monkeys are useful and cost-effective tools for some kinds of tests:

✦ **Load and stress testing:** Tools that present randomly varying loads to servers are test monkeys.

✦ **Resource leak testing:** Monkeys will keep doing different things to your system for as long as you want.

✦ **Event-driven environment/timing problems testing:** Even careful code reviews and traditional test techniques can miss bugs exposed in multithreaded applications running in event-driven operating systems that allow multiple simultaneous processes. Monkeys can help recreate and test "random" environment events.

✦ **Early testing:** The dumb monkey we'll look at later can start testing your application while the developers are still changing the interface.

✦ **Cheap testing:** If you can create a simple, limited test monkey quickly, you can set her up on an old, slow machine none of your human testers wants to use. She can test your application all day, every day. And if she stumbles across just one new bug, it will be one of the cheapest bugs you find.

We should pay some attention to the warnings of the testing gurus, though. No application can be adequately tested using *only* monkeys. Monkeys may find bugs sooner and cheaper than traditional tests might, or they may not. Well-selected combinations of formal requirements tests and code-based tests will find more bugs than monkeys do, and the bugs they find will be easier to log and fix. Like any tool, monkeys have weaknesses and strengths. Use them wisely to augment all your other testing techniques.

 Note Boris Beizer suggests that test monkeys aren't very useful for testing today's "professionally created software." The analysis in his book *Black-Box Testing* (John Wiley and Sons, 1995) concludes that the use of good testing practices will find more bugs than "keyboard-scrabbling or Rachmaninoff testing."

Code-Based Smart Monkeys (*Pongidae Codec Sapiens*)

Like biological primates, there are several similar but different genera of test monkeys. Monkeys that test API functions without using a GUI interface are called "code-based smart monkeys." They're usually cheap to create and easy to understand. We'll use a code-based monkey to test a simplified version of the classic triangle program problem.

 Note Glenford Myers presents the triangle problem in the preface to *The Art of Software Testing* (John Wiley & Sons, 1979), and Paul Jorgensen describes many different formal ways to test Triangle code in *Software Testing: A Craftsman's Approach* (CRC Press, 1995).

Our version of the Triangle program accepts three integers in the range 1– inclusive and returns one of four results:

1. The integers can form an Equilateral triangle (all sides are equal).

2. The integers can form an Isosceles triangle (two sides are equal, but it's not an Equilateral triangle).

3. The integers can form a Scalene triangle (no sides the same length).

4. The integers cannot form a triangle.

We often see this problem used in interviews and software testing classes. Usually the range of integers is much larger and the goal is to produce the minimum set of test cases that will "satisfactorily" test a Triangle program. For our purposes, the integer range is limited, so we can use a brute-force technique to test *all* the possible valid inputs and, in theory, find *all* the bugs. To keep the discussion simple, we'll also ignore the many possible tests using invalid inputs such as nonintegers and integers outside the 1–10 range.

The program function we'll test, `TriangleType()`, is part of the file TRIANGLE.DLL located in the \MONKEY\TRIANGLE folder on the CD-ROM that comes with this book. (See Figure 14-1 for a diagram of this test script.) We've used a DLL to make this true black box testing. You can't examine the function code itself (at least not easily). You must rely entirely on inputs and outputs to find bugs. There is at least one bug to be found.

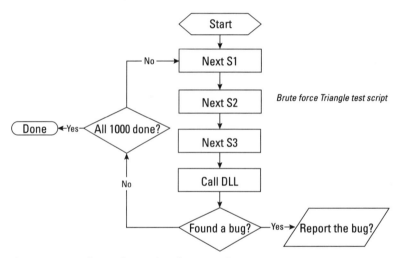

Figure 14-1: A brute force triangle test script.

Note   Teachers of beginning electronics classes test students by building simple circuits inside black metal or plastic boxes. The students can't see the parts and wiring inside the boxes. Using only switches and lights on the outside of the boxes, the students must figure out what the circuits inside the boxes do. *Black box software testing* treats a function or an entire application like one of those sealed boxes. You, the tester, can't see the code that makes the application work, and even if you do have access to the code, you don't look at it. Black box testers are just like users. The only part of the application they can see is the interface.

A Traditional or Conventional Triangle Test Program

The Visual Test script All_Values_DLLTest.mst, also located in the \MONKEY\TRIANGLE folder on the CD-ROM that comes with this book, is a brute force test tool for the Triangle application. It uses a set of three nested `For-Next` loops to generate all 1,000 permutations of the three integers. A support script, Triangle_Test_Routines.inc, contains Test routines that call the DLL function being tested with each set of integers and then compare the DLL output with an oracle. When you run the All Values test, it finds no bugs, even though it tests *all* the possible valid inputs.

Creating a Test Monkey for the Triangle Program

The test monkey we created for this problem is Monkey DLLTest.mst; and she uses the same support script (see Figure 14-2). She's different from the brute force tests because she generates each input randomly from the range of valid values. Like any test monkey, she may repeat the same three inputs in the same sequence many times. She may also fail to test some input permutations at all. She doesn't use `For-Next` loops, so there's no inherent way to tell when she's "done" testing. We've told this monkey to stop testing either when she finds a bug or after testing for a specific amount of time.

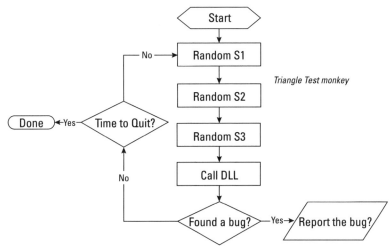

Figure 14-2: The triangle test monkey.

When you run the monkey, she'll find a bug in the Triangle function. Our 1,000 "comprehensive" brute force tests miss this bug. On a 133 MHz machine running Microsoft Windows NT 4.0, the monkey averaged 32 seconds to find the bug, about 15 times longer than the brute force tests run on the same machine. Monkeys usually take longer to find bugs than well-designed "conventional tests" because monkeys are inherently inefficient. Of course, the brute force tests don't find this bug, so the faster run time wasn't very helpful.

Looking at the Test Monkey's Results

The All Values brute force test uses every test case that Myers, Jorgensen, and several others suggest, and about 850 additional tests as well. Suppose that the Triangle function is part of your application: You may run all 1,000 tests, or some subset of them, every test cycle. You will find no bugs and feel confident about your application. When you finally release your application, some users *will* find the bug. This bug returns an Isosceles triangle code for three integers that don't make a valid triangle.

Perhaps your human user will spot the error and work around it. Or maybe the user isn't a human but another software application that's not smart enough to spot your bugs. What if, instead of triangle codes, your application supplies tax return values, or data on prescription drug interactions, or commands to an automobile braking system?

This experiment demonstrates that monkey testing, or even enough human "ad hoc" testing, can find bugs missed by traditional, formal, well-designed black box test plans. Why did the monkey find a bug after we'd already tested every input permutation? To be fair, this is a somewhat artificial bug that was contrived to make a point. Even a cursory review of the code would quickly find this bug, and it would probably be fixed before you could do any black box testing. (That's *if* the code is ever actually reviewed. Many functions in real applications are tested only with black box techniques.)

For readers who like to find solutions to problems like this on their own, rather than read them, we won't spoil your fun by describing the nature of the bug in this chapter. We do give you the bug details in the file DON'T READ THIS YET.TXT located in the \MONKEY\TRIANGLE folder on the CD-ROM that comes with this book.

Note   Testers use "ad hoc" (literally "to this" in Latin) differently than other disciplines. Ad hoc testing is usually testing without a specific plan or purpose. The tester just starts the application and does things with it. Some professionals frown on this. Without a plan, how can you know that you've tested everything you should? Others use terms like "directed ad hoc testing" and "exploratory testing" to describe tests that have a direction or purpose, even if they don't follow some pre-determined outline.

The "Smart" Part of the Smart Monkey

Our Triangle testing monkey is "smart" because she knows what inputs the `TriangleType` function uses. She also knows what values `TriangleType` should return for each set of integers. She has an *oracle*. In this example, the oracle is an algorithm for the triangle problem implemented in Visual Test code. Because the oracle is program code, it could have bugs. We need to test the oracle before we can rely on it to accurately verify results from the function.

The Triangle function is relatively simple, so we can quickly create and debug an oracle for it. Most monkeys aren't so fortunate. Real functions are often too complex to use an algorithmic oracle or have no underlying algorithm at all. Many functions and applications use a list or table of results instead of an algorithm. In those cases the monkey also uses a list or table as an oracle. Table oracles are even more bug-prone than algorithms. A bug in algorithm code will likely cause a whole set of related errors. By contrast, a single table entry can contain a bug that does not affect any other table entry. Good oracles are expensive to create and maintain, for both monkeys and traditional test tools.

GUI Smart Monkeys (Pongidae GUIus Sapiens)

Monkeys that use automation tools like Visual Test to operate directly on the GUI interface of Windows applications are called *GUI monkeys*. Most of them are "smart" because they have a list or table of things to do and the results to expect from the application. We often use the term *state* to describe the application's condition before and after the monkey performs each test. The oracle for most GUI smart monkeys is a list of the application's states, a *state table*.

Note State has a specific technical meaning to many testers, and they can discuss at great length the fine points of what is and what is not a state. For this chapter we'll use the term in a colloquial, fuzzy sense, with apologies to the experts.

Testing a Sample Word Processor

Imagine you're testing a word processor. A document is open, and the application is waiting for you to either edit something or choose a command. You can think of this condition as a state. Your test monkey's state table would list all the valid commands she could execute from this state. "Save the file" is probably a valid command now, while "Close the Help dialog box" is not (assuming Help is not open).

When the monkey tests "Save the file," she'll do what's needed to execute that command. Choosing Save on the File menu or pressing Ctrl+S would execute the Save command in many Windows applications. The application's state will change to a new state (at least it should), perhaps one with the Save dialog box open. The monkey's commands are more limited from the new Save dialog state. Menu commands won't work, for example, since the Save dialog box has focus, and it doesn't have menus. Make a list of all the other states you can think of, add all the valid ways to leave each state and go to another, and you have a state table for the application.

Well, you have the start of one, anyway. A problem with black box testing GUI applications is that we can't always tell the differences among several states just by looking at the screen. In the Save example, our initial state could be one of at least four states:

1. If this is a new document and you haven't entered any text, many word processors will display an error dialog box when you choose Save. The application won't save "empty" documents.

2. If you've entered text and you choose Save for the first time, the Save As dialog box should come up instead of Save. You need to enter a name and location to save the document the first time.

3. If you haven't changed anything since the last Save command, the document isn't "dirty." For most word processors, nothing happens...at least nothing the user or the monkey can see.

4. Once you've saved the document in some word processors, additional Save commands make no change in the current GUI state, and no Save dialog box appears.

Using State Tables

Each of these examples represents a separate state. The application knows what state it's in using internal, hidden values and flags. This state-of-the-state data is sometimes called the *state attributes*. For a monkey or a human tester to tell what state the application is in, they must have the same "hidden" information the application does. It may be hard to query the application about the hidden attributes. So monkeys and humans usually keep track of the state attributes on their own. If they use the wrong attributes, or forget them, they may report false bugs or miss real ones.

The state table is also the monkey's oracle. When the monkey picks a command in state "A" but the command can't be executed, she's found a bug. If the command works, but the monkey either reaches state "X" or she encounters a state she doesn't recognize, she's found a bug. If the bug isn't too serious and the monkey is robust, she can log all the information she can find about the error and then return to a known base state and continue testing.

State tables can be kept in any format that's convenient for the tester and the monkey. Some formats can provide additional data as well as act as a testing oracle. With a Markov chain state table you can generate a wealth of mathematical analysis such as MTTF (mean time to failure). You can even "certify" the application by predicting the likelihood of remaining bugs given a specific set of tests. Other state table formats include Petri nets, directed graphs, and data flow graphs.

All state table formats share one common characteristic. They grow geometrically as new features are added to the application. Even using automated techniques, adding a single new state to the tables for nontrivial applications requires days of fast computer time.

 Tip Dr. James Whittaker is a preeminent authority on using Markov state tables for monkey testing. Visit his Web site at `http://www.cs.fit.edu/~jw/` for a list of related publications.

State table complexity has limited the number of GUI smart monkeys in actual use. Many test groups find their testing time is better spent on more traditional test techniques. GUI smart monkeys are effective for testing small applications or isolated features in larger applications where state tables are small enough to build and maintain at reasonable cost. The state table maintenance problem for large applications leads directly to the next genus of test monkeys.

Dumb GUI Monkeys (Pongidae GUIus Ignorantis)

For many years, the author was part of the Windows NT Applications Test team. That team tests the NT operating system (OS) using commercial applications as their testing engines. They use programs that run bug free (mostly) on the OSs they were designed for. The team tests those programs on *new* versions of NT and looks for bugs. Any errors they see should be in the new version of NT, not the released application. We call this "double black box" testing. Because we have no source code for a retail application, it's black box #1. We aren't sure just what OS functions the application will call or what parameters it will use. Looking at the OS source code is useless until we actually find a bug. The operating system is black box #2.

There are thousands of applications that could be used as OS test engines. We only have the time and the resources to create traditional tests for a few hundred of them. We catch all the OS bugs those several hundred applications expose. But we'd also like to do some testing with the other applications.

In NT Test, we decided to use monkeys to test those "other" applications. Windows applications use the menus, windows, and controls the OS supplies to do their work. And it's bugs in those OS-provided resources we're looking for. We designed monkeys to test just the GUI features that are common to most Windows apps. The monkeys could do their testing without a state table for each application. A monkey with no state table is "dumb" instead of smart. ("Ignorant" is more accurate, and some purists prefer "stateless." But "dumb monkey" was the first name used for this genus, and it's still the most popular.)

But what can we use as an oracle if we don't have a state? Without a list of valid or "known" states, *all* states will look like bugs to a dumb monkey. There are at least two solutions, and we've used both. The first solution is to define several "generic" states. We'll take a look at this in more detail later. The second solution is to run both the application and OS under a debugger. We're looking for the most egregious bugs with dumb monkeys: access violations, in-page errors, and the blue-screen-of-death. All those bugs will break to a debugger. The debugger acts as the oracle and gives developers immediate access to the problem with all the machine-level esoterica that developers like to have when debugging systems. Both solutions are easier to implement and cheaper to use than a state table oracle.

Dumb Monkeys Find Different Bugs

Before we look in detail at Freddie, the simple dumb monkey on the CD-ROM accompanying this book, we should examine the implications of dumb monkey testing. What kinds of bugs can we expect to find compared with using either smart monkeys or more traditional testing tools?

The large oval in the diagram in Figure 14-3 represents all the bugs in your application. Most of them, the smaller gray oval, are bugs you can find with black box tests: menu options that don't work, poorly drawn dialog boxes, clipped text, access violations, and so on. These are the kinds of bugs lots of your users will find if you don't. Anyone who uses the feature or sees the error dialog box will be plagued with the bug. The remaining bugs, the white part of the bug space oval, are code faults that you're unlikely to find with black box tests: unexpected boundaries in what should be equivalence classes, error checking code that misses one or two errors, and memory leaks.

Note   An *equivalence class* is a set of inputs that we expect will all be handled in the same way by a program under test. The English language alphabet should be an equivalence class to a word processor. If typing the letter "a" doesn't crash the application, typing the letters "b," "c," or "d" probably won't crash it either, and there's no point in wasting resources testing them. Of course, there may be hidden boundaries that make some values *not* part of the equivalence class. The date September 9, 1999, is such a hidden boundary for some programs because a few programmers years ago used "9999" as a special code flag, never thinking their work would still be in use on 9-9-99.

When a bug is exposed by just one of millions of possible values, you need luck, not skill, to find it with black box tests. Those bugs are best found by looking at the code and creating tests based on the code structure…white box bugs. White box bugs are much easier for testers to miss than black box bugs. Fortunately most end users aren't likely to find them, either. Unfortunately, they're often really nasty bugs that destroy data and lose customers.

Note   Testing software without looking at the source code is called *black box testing*. So we often call testing that specifically looks at the source code *white box testing*. A better term is *clear box,* since even a white box is usually opaque and you couldn't see the code through its sides. Both terms are used, but *white box* is more common.

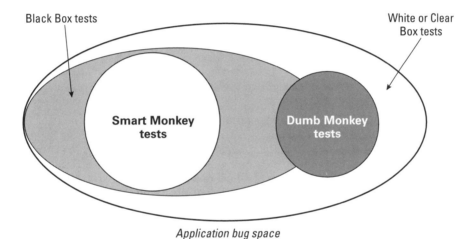

Application bug space

Figure 14-3: Smart and dumb monkey tests find different kinds of bugs.

Finding Bugs Through Trial and Error

As an example, imagine that the application you're testing is intended to import .ZZZ graphics files. To create traditional black box tests, or a state table for a smart monkey, you'd review the specifications for the application and write a test case that imports a "typical" .ZZZ graphic you found somewhere or created yourself. You'd add a test case for each method available to activate the import option for .ZZZ files. If you think boundary testing might find bugs, you'd import the smallest possible .ZZZ file. There may be no maximum size .ZZZ, so you'd just use a very, very large one. If you feel guerilla testing is important, you might use one or more "bad" or "broken" .ZZZ files, other graphic file types that are mislabeled with the .ZZZ extension, and even files that aren't graphics at all. That's quite a few test cases, and you'd be justified in feeling confident that you'd thoroughly tested the .ZZZ import option.

Note   Testing that tries to "break" a product by stressing it beyond all reason or just doing very nasty things to it is called *guerilla testing.* You may see people use the term "gorilla" testing, instead. Usually they've heard someone talk about guerilla testing, but haven't seen the word spelled. "Gorilla" almost never refers to any kind of test monkey.

Hiding from you, the black box tester, is a bug in the .ZZZ import handling algorithm. Your application will crash if you import a .ZZZ file that's *exactly* 2,048 bytes (2KB) long. Larger and smaller files are no problem. Your application's developers used a library routine that, at one time long ago, handled 2KB buffers as a special case. The buffer size issues have been resolved for years. The code that handled them is gone, but a stray pointer to the 2KB handler was accidentally left in the library. The pointer to that missing code is never initialized for .ZZZ imports and your application gets very confused when it tries to use the pointer with a 2KB file. As a black box tester you have no reason to specifically choose a 2KB .ZZZ file from the many different size files available for your tests. All reasonable size .ZZZ files should form one equivalence class, and testing *any one* of them should be sufficient.

This bug is so specific that neither you nor your customers may ever find it. If a few users do see it, they and your technical support staff may assume that the individual .ZZZ files are "bad," a guess that's reinforced because all the user's other .ZZZ graphics can be imported bug free. Or you may be unlucky, and your most important account's new logo just happens to be a 2KB .ZZZ file, which your competitor's product can import without a problem. The bug in our Triangle DLL has the same lurking malevolence. Most users will never see it. Traditional black box testing probably won't find it. Both the .ZZZ file bug and the Triangle bug are best found by white or clear box tests.

Uncovering Bugs with Dumb Monkeys

Smart GUI monkeys that use a state table may do things at random, but they always make their input choices from the same set of things. If you let a smart GUI monkey use random data values in spreadsheet cells or type random text in a document, she could set up different state attributes for each random value. If you ignore those additional state attributes, the monkey will start reporting false errors because she'll quickly wind up in a "wrong" state. When you allow a state table monkey to use random data, your state table explodes from merely huge to nearly infinite. For example, if you allow the monkey to enter sets of one to forty random characters from the printable ANSI character set (0032–0255), you've created 2.53×10^{92} separate states.

To keep smart monkey state table sizes reasonable, you need to limit the monkey to using just a few specific data values. Early in your product cycle the smart monkey will find unexpected paths to states and states that aren't coded properly...black box bugs. She may find an occasional white box bug, but only if you're lucky enough to pick *exactly* the single data value that exposes the bug. Late in your product cycle, most smart monkey and other black box tests are regression tests. They find no new bugs, but running them gives you confidence in the quality of the product.

Dumb GUI monkey test space is different from the domain of smart GUI monkeys. The dumb monkey doesn't know what the "right" state should be when he runs a test, so it's hard for him to recognize a "wrong" state. When most dumb monkeys enter random values in the spreadsheet or type random text into a document, they'll dismiss any error dialog boxes that appear. You tell them to do that because they'll trigger error dialog boxes with nearly every test they make. Reporting every error dialog box as a bug wastes the time of the humans who must sift through them. We call those "monkey noise" bugs, and they're common with dumb monkeys.

On the other hand, the dumb monkey's penchant for random input values may find that uninitialized 2KB .ZZZ import pointer. Because he's using random values, he's more likely to expose new memory leaks. He'll find the kinds of pesky, dirty bugs a good "ad hoc" or guerilla human tester would find. He's just a dumb monkey, so he doesn't have a talented tester's instincts for where bugs might be lurking. But he's probably faster than the human tester, and he doesn't get tired or bored. So he'll do more tests and may find more of those nasty crash-type bugs than the human.

Understanding the fundamental differences between smart and dumb monkeys will help you accurately set your expectations for using each of them.

Smart monkeys

- Find good black box bugs, especially in the early stages of a project
- Are expensive to create and maintain if they are broad coverage smart monkeys

Dumb monkeys

- Are relatively cheap to use.
- Find fewer bugs than smart monkeys, and they usually find white/clear box bugs. Dumb monkeys may generate a lot of monkey noise bugs, too. But the *good* bugs they uncover are the most evil bugs: crashes and hangs that can lead to data loss.

All testing is a trade-off, and monkey testing is no exception.

Freddie: A Lite Dumb Monkey

To give you an idea of what dumb monkeys can do, we've included Freddie on the CD-ROM accompanying this book. Freddie isn't very knowledgeable about Windows applications yet. He will test just about anything, though. Simple as he is, he found one bug in an application while we were developing him for this chapter. You can add code to Freddie and make him as clever as you want. Just remember that the law of diminishing returns applies to dumb monkey creation. Even a very clever dumb monkey will still find only a few good bugs, mostly of the white box variety.

What Makes Freddie Tick

Freddie uses a simple model to test any application (see Figure 14-4). First he starts the application and makes a list of all the menu items he can find. He only makes the menu list once on each test run. Then he chooses either one of the menu items at random or any additional tests we've taught him to do. If the test caused a new dialog box to appear in the application, Freddie looks for edit boxes in the dialog box and enters some random text characters in them. Then he randomly clicks inside the dialog box a few times. He may change the state of some controls when he does that. After he's done testing the new dialog box, Freddie tries to close it. He knows several ways to do that, and we'll look at them in more detail later.

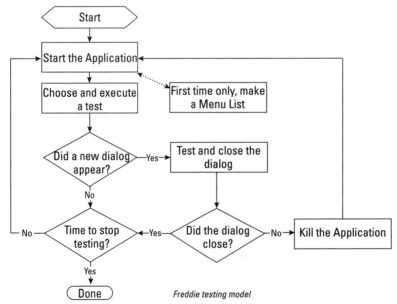

Figure 14-4: The Freddie testing model.

If the new dialog box goes away, Freddie randomly chooses another test and repeats the cycle again, unless it's time for the test run to end. Sometimes Freddie can't close the dialog box, often because he entered an "illegal" value in one of the edit boxes. When he's exhausted all his dialog closing tricks, Freddie does what any frustrated monkey would do. He kills the application by terminating the application process. When the application dies, it takes all its dialogs with it. Then Freddie restarts the application and begins testing again as if nothing nasty happened.

Two methods for using oracles

We use the two methods we discussed earlier to act as the oracles to identify any bugs Freddie finds. First, we've taught Freddie a few "generic" states:

- ✦ State 1: The application to be tested is *not* running.
- ✦ State 2: The application is in its base state, ready to be tested.
- ✦ State 3: A new dialog box has appeared (after a test).
- ✦ State 4: The new dialog box has edit boxes to test.
- ✦ State 5: The new dialog box has gone away.

Freddie knows how to deal with each of those states. None of them represents an error to Freddie, although they might expose bugs to us humans or a smart(er) monkey. The one and only error state as far as Freddie's concerned is "everything else." That usually means a new dialog box didn't close for him. When he sees this "everything else" error state, he kills the application and tells us about it in his log. That log entry is his "bug report," and the log may be filled with mostly monkey noise bugs. You can cut down on the noise by teaching Freddie how to deal with the common error dialog boxes in your application.

The second bug-identifying method is more reliable and finds better bugs. We use a debugger to monitor the application Freddie is testing. When something really nasty happens, the debugger stops Freddie and makes the system available for us to examine.

In the final part of this chapter we'll look at a few of the interesting sections of the Visual Test scripts that let Freddie test and kill applications. Even if you decide not to create monkey test tools, you may find parts of Freddie useful in your test automation. If you'd like to start using Freddie right away without looking at the gory details of Freddie's innards, skip to the "How to Test with Freddie" section at the end of the chapter.

The essential Freddie

The Freddie monkey is a single Visual Test script (.MST) with several support (.INC) files. Assembling Freddie as code modules makes him, like any other programming project, easier to create and maintain.

> **Tip**   Even if you decide not to create monkey test tools, you may find parts of the source code useful. Take a few minutes to look it over.

Here's a list of Freddie's parts and what they do:

✦ FREDDIE.MST: The main Freddie script. Everything starts here.

✦ FREDDIE_INCLUDES.INC: Lists all the .INC files to compile along with FREDDIE.MST.

✦ FREDDIE_VARIABLES_AND_CONSTANTS.INC: Declares the constants, variables, and macros Freddie uses.

✦ FREDDIE_START_KILL_APP.INC: Includes functions Freddie uses to start and kill test applications.

✦ FREDDIE_TESTS.INC: Includes routines that choose and execute the tests Freddie knows how to perform in applications.

✦ FREDDIE_LOG_ROUTINES.INC: Includes code that customizes how, where, and what data Freddie logs for you as he tests.

✦ FREDDIE_GENERAL_ROUTINES.INC: Includes all the Freddie code that didn't fit in the other categories.

✦ APPLICATION_STRINGS.INC: Includes information specific to your application that helps Freddie do more tests. You may have several of these files for localized versions of your application (versions in languages of other countries).

✦ *<APPLICATION>*.INI: Tells Freddie how to identify your application and how many minutes to test it. You might use several of these for different versions of the test application or for several different applications.

The benefits of planning ahead

Freddie is a test tool, not a commercial application. Using many different .INC files may seem like overkill, but it's not. Planning ahead a bit and keeping your code in separate modules will save you time in the long run, even if you are the only person who ever uses and maintains the project. If you're part of a larger team and everyone will use the test tool, you may need to take even more time with the structure of the project and adhere to standards everyone understands.

As we said earlier, testing is a trade-off. There's never enough time to do everything. You can spend your time making test tools that meet the highest commercial code quality standards but that still don't find you any more bugs than sloppily coded versions. You can also write quick-and-dirty, but effective, tools in a casual style and then waste extra time a few weeks later trying to figure out how to make changes in the spaghetti code. Either way your testing resources are used up on your tools instead of finding bugs.

Try for a balance. Maximize both your bug-finding time and the effectiveness of your test tools by using just enough structure to make maintenance easy. Software quality assurance expert James Bach suggests that the most efficacious software isn't perfect but "good enough" to get the job done. Apply the same standard to Freddie and your other test tools.

Tip Look for "The Challenge of 'Good Enough' Software" and other articles by James Bach in the Article Archives section on ST Labs' Web site at http://www.stlabs.com/testnet.htm.

How Freddie Reads and Writes .INI Files from Visual Test Scripts

Freddie can't be totally dumb. He needs to know how to start your application and how to recognize its parent window, the base state. You can use constants or strings in the Freddie scripts for that information, but we find .INI files more convenient. They're easy to edit because the .INI extension is associated with Notepad in Windows. If you use a dumb monkey to test several applications in a single run, as we do, it's easier to use several .INI files than an array of strings with application-specific information.

The .INI files are plain text, and you could read and parse them with Test's `Input` and string commands. The Win32 API has special "Private Profile" functions that work with .INI files to make things much easier. An example is shown in Listing 14-1.

Listing 14-1: Using GetPrivateProfileString() to access .INI settings

```
Function fnReadApplicationSectionKey(strKeyName _
        as String)   as String
  Dim strKeyBuffer    as String
  Dim lProfileReturn  as Long

  strKeyBuffer  = Space$(1024)
  lProfileReturn = GetPrivateProfileString("Application",_
                strKeyName, "", strKeyBuffer, 1024,   _
                gstrAppIniFile)
  fnReadApplicationSectionKey = Left$(strKeyBuffer, _
                        lProfileReturn)
End Function
```

This function in FREDDIE_GENERAL_ROUTINES.INC uses the Win32 function `GetPrivateProfileString` to read a key directly from the .INI file, no parsing required. The .INI file is shown in Listing 14-2.

Listing 14-2: **What Freddie's .INI file looks like**

```
[Application]
Exe=notepad.exe
PathToExe=C:\WINNT\system32\
ParentCaption=Notepad
ParentClass=Notepad
```

The string inside the brackets is the "section" name, and each of the lines under it is a "key." To read the value of a key, we pass the name of the key, the name of the section it's stored in, and the name of the .INI file to `GetPrivateProfileString()`. We also need to pass a pointer to a buffer to hold the value from the key. Freddie uses a global variable for the .INI filename. His .INI files have only one section, so we've "hard coded" that name in this Test function.

If you add other sections, you can create similar functions for them. The Win32 API call requires a pointer to the buffer that will receive the key value. We only need to pass the name of the buffer, and Test will convert it into a pointer for us. The API call returns the length of the key value. We use that with Test's `Left$` command to make sure we don't get any residual garbage that might be in the buffer. (Test does that for us here, but that won't always be the case, and it's a good idea to make sure your data is clean.) There's a complimentary `WritePrivateProfileString` API call so that you can change a key value or even create a new key. We'll examine that when we talk about Freddie's logging routine.

Freddie Gets Assertive

The error trap in FREDDIE.MST gives two "FREDDIE_" error values special treatment. Test uses positive integers for its trappable errors; the numbers that appear in the reserved ERR variable. You can generate any of those errors yourself using the `Error` command followed by an integer. Test allows you to use a negative integer for ERR. Test itself uses only positive ERR values, so you can use negative integers for your own private errors.

```
Const FREDDIE_ASSERT_ERROR = -1

Sub FreddieAssert(lIsTrue as Long)
If (False = lIsTrue) Then
    gstrFreddieError = "False statement at " + Name$(2)
    Error FREDDIE_ASSERT_ERROR
  EndIf
End Sub
```

C and C++ programmers use an error function called "assert." They can "assert" that something is true. If the something *is* True when the program runs, life is good, and the program continues. If the something is False, the program breaks to an error routine. The `FreddieAssert` function gives us the same feature in Visual Test. Any statement that isn't True creates a trappable error. `FreddieAssert` adds the output from `Name$(2)` to a global error string so that the error trap can print the name of the script and the line number where the False statement was `FreddieAsserted`.

I'm using a constant for the `FREDDIE_ASSERT_VALUE` so that I don't have to change it in more than one place. I'd like the constant to be defined inside the `FreddieAssert` routine, just to keep everything together in case I want to copy-and-paste this code in Freddie II. Test doesn't allow constant definitions inside functions, so I have to put it just outside as shown.

Tom Arnold prefers all constants for a program to be in the same place. That makes sense. If they're all together, you know where to find them and it's easier to see what values are already used when you add a new error constant. I still like having this error value next to the function. Neither approach is right or wrong. It's a matter of style. Use whichever system you prefer, or make one of your own. But try to have a good reason for doing it whichever way and be consistent. If you're developing tools that will be used by everyone in your group, use the group coding standards instead. If your group doesn't have any standards, call a meeting and get them to adopt yours.

Freddie's Macros

Macros are often elegant alternatives to functions in Visual Test. Freddie uses two macros, defined in FREDDIE_VARIABLES_AND_CONSTANTS.INC. This macro converts a numeric value to a string and trims off any extra leading and trailing spaces in the process:

```
Macro _trm(NumericValue) = Trim$(Str$(NumericValue))
```

You could use the `Trim$` and `Str$` functions directly in your code, but `_trm` is cleaner and faster to type.

In the same .INC file you'll find the definition for the macro _RndBetween, which takes two integers and returns a random integer between them, inclusively. (Freddie uses the _RndBetween macro a lot.) For example, _RndBetween(1, 3) will return 1, 2, or 3 with about equal frequency. The integers must be in "low, high" order for this macro to work properly.

I copied _RndBetween from another project where the integers might not always be in "low, high" order. So the macro uses extra code to swap the integers if necessary (see Figure 14-3). There are comments explaining how that works if you're interested. If you understand immediately how the integers are swapped without reading the comments, you've spent far too much time programming in BASIC. Get a life!

Listing 14-3: Part of TestDialog in FREDDIE_TESTS.INC.

```
iCount = 1
While WEditExists(_ord(iCount))
    strTextBuffer = ""
    For iCount1 = 1 to 100
        strTextBuffer = strTextBuffer + _
                          chr(_RndBetween(32, 255))
    Next
    WEditSetText(_ord(iCount), strTextBuffer)
    iCount = iCount + 1
WEnd
```

Each Edit control has an "ordinal" value in sequence, beginning with 1. The Test _ord macro converts an integer to the proper ordinal format for us. Using the While loop and incrementing the ordinal counter, Freddie looks for any/all Edit controls. When he finds one, he uses _RndBetween to put 100 random printable text characters into it. Almost always that's not a string the application expects. Freddie often gets error dialog boxes in the application after doing this, such as "Not a valid file name" or "Number between 0 and 256 required." He also occasionally finds bugs when the application tries to make good values from garbage and fails, but he uses the garbage anyway.

How Freddie Closes Dialog Boxes

We don't teach Freddie details about any dialog boxes in the test application. *You* could, but be careful not to waste time trying to make Freddie into a smart monkey. If you need to do smart monkey testing, building a good state table tool from the start will be a better use of your time.

Since Freddie can't recognize any specific dialog boxes, he uses some generic closing methods, one at a time, until one works or he decides to kill the application. The code starts on line 262 of TestDialog in FREDDIE_TESTS.INC. Freddie tries these steps in sequence:

1. **Click the OK button, if there is one:** Since Freddie has done stuff in this dialog box, clicking OK may change your application's state. That's good. You get more complex tests that way, and complex tests find more bugs than simple tests.

Tip

Brian Marick taught us this effective strategy of using complex tests rather than simple tests whenever possible. Look for links to Marick's publications in "Marick's Corner" in the "QA on the Web" section at the ST Labs Web site (http://www.stlabs.com/testnet.htm).

2. **Click the Cancel button, if there is one:** We could try Yes or No buttons, too. But which means what? We may not want Freddie to ever click Yes in a "Do you really want to format your hard drive" dialog box. We told Freddie to ignore Yes, No, Ignore, and Retry. You can add them if you want to.

3. **Press the ESC key:** This closes some dialog boxes, whether they have buttons or not.

4. **Post a WM_CLOSE message to the dialog box:** When the user does something in a dialog box that's supposed to close it, Windows posts a WM_CLOSE message to the dialog box's message queue. Doing it with Freddie simulates what the user might be able to do, even though Freddie doesn't understand exactly what that might be. If you feel brave and reckless, you can use a WM_DESTROY message instead.

5. **Click the window:** Some splash screen type dialogs have no controls and don't respond even to WM_CLOSE in their message queues. They ignore everything except a mouse click. We try to click in an "innocent" location on the background of the dialog box.

6. **Press Ctrl+F4:** Sometimes this works when everything else has failed.

There are other ways to close dialog boxes. If dialog boxes in your application use them, add them to this list in TestDialog.

Why So Many of These Commands?

You'll see quite a few sets of these commands in Freddie:

```
SetForegroundWindow(hWnd)
WSetActWnd(hWnd)
```

The Test command `WSetActWnd(hWnd)` makes the window with handle `hWnd` the "active" window. The active window is the one with focus. Keyboard entries are sent to it, and menu commands operate on it. `SetForegroundWindow(hWnd)` is a Win32 API call that brings the `hWnd` window to the foreground and gives it focus. The two commands seem to have identical results, and often they do. Unfortunately, we've found that sometimes one or the other fails to make `hWnd` active. Using both is good insurance.

Using Other Visual Test Routines in Freddie

We had to do some elegant, strange, and occasionally ugly things to get Freddie to test a wide variety of applications. You may find some of these routines useful. All are commented:

✦ `MakeMenuList` **in FREDDIE_START_KILL_APP.INC:** When Freddie first starts an application, he makes a list of all the menu items. To do that, he drops the top-level menus, adds the menu item strings (or ordinals) to a global array, and follows menus with pop-ups to get the submenu items. He grows the global array as he finds menus, so it's always just the right size. This used to be pretty clean-looking code until some top-level menus became what look like toolbars to Test. There's some added stuff now to let Freddie see the `MsoCommandBar` class menus some applications use.

✦ `ExecuteATest` **in FREDDIE_TEST.INC:** We've added some word-processor-type tests to Freddie, in addition to the menu tests he can do on his own. This routine uses `_RndBetween` to choose among them on a weighted basis. Freddie does 60 percent menu tests and splits the other 40 percent among four other tests. You can change the percentages or add more tests here.

✦ `fnRandomChar` **in FREDDIE_TEST.INC:** The `Play` command in Test reserves a few special keys, such as % and +. When Freddie wants to enter them in an application, he has to surround them with braces, { and }. This routine does that automatically.

✦ `SetNewFont` **in FREDDIE_TEST.INC:** This test opens the Font dialog box in Windows Notepad and WordPad, the two applications we use to demonstrate Freddie. This test is especially dramatic in Notepad because changing the font immediately makes all the text look different. At least that's what happens in the Windows NT Notepad. The version of Notepad in Windows 95 doesn't have a Font dialog box. We need a way to tell Freddie to skip this test for

Notepad on Windows 95, and this routine uses the Win32 API call `GetVersionEx` to find out what version of Windows Freddie is running on. As written, Freddie thinks Windows 98 is Windows 95. To change that, you'll have to add some code that uses the `MajorVersion` part of the `OSVERSIONINFO` structure `GetVersionEx` returns.

Killing Applications with Freddie

Freddie only kills the application when he can't close a dialog box. That usually means he can't simply close the application by choosing Exit on the File menu, either. There's no easy way to kill an application with Visual Test commands, so we have to use Win32 API calls instead.

The code Freddie uses is in the function `KillAnyRunningAppProcesses` in FREDDIE_START_KILL_APP.INC. We can kill the application process using `TerminateProcess` (almost too logical). The problem is that `TerminateProcess` requires an `hProcess` (the handle to a process), and all we get from Test is an `hWnd` (the handle to the application's parent window). Getting from `hWnd` to `hProcess` takes two steps:

1. First we call `GetWindowThreadProcessID` using the application's `hWnd`. That gives us a process `ID`.

2. Using the process `ID`, we can open an `hProcess` using the `PROCESS_TERMINATE` flag. We defined that flag as part of Freddie's code. It's not defined in the Visual Test WINAPI.INC file.

Once we have the `hProcess`, `TerminateProcess` will terminate the process and the application. We need to close the `hProcess` we opened, or Freddie will leak some resources.

Using a Callback to Look for New Dialog Boxes

After Freddie chooses a menu item, he looks for a new dialog to appear. This task sounds relatively simple, but it actually requires some of the most complex code in the Freddie scripts. We don't know what the caption or class of the dialog box will be, so we can't get much help from the Visual Test `WFndWndC` command. The active window `WGetActWnd` finds may have nothing to do with our application, or it may be a window that was around before we did the menu test. We can use the `WGetActWnd` command to locate a new dialog box, but we need to give it some help.

The method we've found that works best requires six steps:

1. Before doing a test, make a list of all the current windows that belong to our application.

2. Do the test and wait a bit.

3. Use `WGetActWnd` to get the active window.

4. Make sure it's *not* on the list of "old" windows from step 1.

5. Make sure it's *not* the parent window of our application.

6. Make sure it's a child window of our application's parent.

When the active window meets all our requirements, it's a new dialog box that Freddie should test.

The complex part is making a list of, or *enumerating,* the child windows. That's done using two routines, `EnumerateChildrenToArray` and `fnWndEnumProc_GetHWNDS`. Both of them are in FREDDIE_GENERAL_ROUTINES.INC. We use Win32 API calls to do the actual enumerating, and they require two parameters, the handle of the parent whose child windows we want to enumerate and a function of our own that the operating system will "call back" to when it finds each of the children. (There are actually three parameters, but the third one is always zero.)

`fnWndEnumProc_GetHWNDS` is Freddie's callback function. When Windows finds a child window, it calls back to this function and passes it the handle of the child window. It may also send us a value in `lParam`, but we don't use that. (See Listing 14-4.)

Listing 14-4: Freddie's callback function that is called when Windows finds a child window

```
Function fnWndEnumProc_GetHWNDS(hWnd as Long, _
          lParam as Long) as Long

  fnWndEnumProc_GetHWNDS = True

  If hWnd Then
    Redim Preserve ghWndChildren(0 _
          to Ubound(ghWndChildren) + 1) as HWND
    ghWndChildren(UBound(ghWndChildren)) = hWnd
  Else
    fnWndEnumProc_GetHWNDS = False
  EndIf
End Function
```

If the hWnd is null (zero), Windows has enumerated all the children. In that case, we return False so that Windows knows we've finished our work and Windows can terminate its enumeration loop. Some callbacks in other situations might return False to quit before all the windows have been enumerated.

If the hWnd is not null, it's the handle of a child window, and the callback routine adds that handle to a global array ghWndChildren. So when Windows has finished enumerating the child windows, we have a list of their handles in the array that any Freddie routine can look at.

Applications in Windows 95 and 98 and Windows NT can be multithreaded, and a test Freddie chooses can pop up a dialog box from any of those threads. So the first thing we have to do is make a list of the top level windows of each of the threads:

```
pfnWndEnumProc = VarPtr(fnWndEnumProc_GetHWNDS)
lThreadId = GetWindowThreadProcessId(hWnd, Null)
EnumThreadWindows(lThreadId, pfnWndEnumProc, 0)
```

As shown in the preceding code, we start by putting the address of our callback function in a pointer variable. Then we get the thread ID of the application parent window hWnd. The Windows function EnumThreadWindows uses the thread ID to enumerate all the thread windows, calling the callback function with each handle. When EnumThreadWindows is finished, all the thread top-level window handles are stored in the global array.

We need copies of those handles in a separate array because we need to enumerate their children, too. The following code from EnumerateChildrenToArray creates the copy:

```
lArrayUBound = UBound(ghWndChildren)
Redim Preserve hWndThreadWnds(0 to lArrayUBound) as HWND
For lIndex = 1 to lArrayUBound
  hWndThreadWnds(lIndex) = ghWndChildren(lIndex)
Next lIndex
```

In the For-Next loop shown here the handles of the top-level windows in each thread are passed, one by one, to EnumChildWindows and the children's handles are added to the array:

```
For lIndex = 1 to lArrayUBound
  EnumChildWindows(hWndThreadWnds(lIndex), _
                   pfnWndEnumProc, 0)
Next lIndex
```

We have the handles of all the parent window's threads' children in the global array, but we don't have the children of the parent itself. This last line passes the handle of the parent, `hWnd`, to `EnumChildWindows`, and its children's handles are added to the array:

```
EnumChildWindows(hWnd, pfnWndEnumProc, 0)
```

Now we have the handle of every window, dialog, toolbar, control, and static label that belongs to our application for its current state. After Freddie performs his next test, he waits a bit and then uses `WGetActWnd` to get the handle of whichever window is the "active" one. If its handle is in the array, it's not a "new" window and Freddie can ignore it.

Code in `LookForAndTestDialog` in FREDDIE_TESTS.INC does the rest of the work. If the handle is *not* in the array, Freddie makes sure the window isn't the parent itself and uses the Windows function `GetParent` to make sure the new window *is* a child of our application. It might be a dialog box from another application, such as Help, or Windows itself, and we only want Freddie to test and close windows that belong to our application.

How to Test with Freddie

We've created an application .INI file to use with Freddie for the Windows Notepad application. To show how little you need to change in Freddie when your application's GUI changes, we'll also use Windows WordPad as a "new version" of Notepad and test that.

First create a folder on your hard drive to hold Freddie and his support files, we'll assume C:\FREDDIE. Copy all the files from the \FREDDIE folder on the compact disc included with this book to C:\FREDDIE.

To test Notepad with Freddie:

1. Open OURAPP BUILD1.INI and change the value of this key to point to NOTEPAD.EXE on your system. Save the changed .INI file with the same name:

   ```
   PathToExe=C:\WINNT\system32\
   ```

2. Open FREDDIE_VARIABLES_AND_CONSTANTS.INC and make sure the value for this constant points to the location of OURAPP BUILD1.INI on your machine, then save the .INC file:

   ```
   Const APP_INI_FILE = "c:\freddie\OurApp Build1.ini"
   ```

3. Open APPLICATION_STRINGS.INC and make sure the strings are remarked and unremarked as shown. We have to make this change because Notepad and WordPad use different menu commands to open the Font dialog box. Save the .INC file when you're done:

```
'UnREM this line for testing Notepad
Const MENU_FONT = "Edit\~Set Font"
'UnREM this line for testing Wordpad
REM Const MENU_FONT = "Format\~Font"
```

4. Open and run FREDDIE.MST.

5. When Freddie completes his test run, examine the OURAPPLOG.LOG file in your \FREDDIE folder.

6. You can change the time Freddie runs by changing the value of the `TimeToTest` key in the .INI file.

To test WordPad with Freddie:

1. Open OURAPP BUILD2.INI and change the value of this key to point to NOTEPAD.EXE on your system. Save the changed .INI file with the same name:

   ```
   PathToExe=C:\WINNT\system32\
   ```

2. Open FREDDIE_VARIABLES_AND_CONSTANTS.INC and make sure the value for this constant points to the location of OURAPP BUILD1.INI on your machine, then save the .INC file:

   ```
   Const APP_INI_FILE = "c:\freddie\OurApp Build2.ini"
   ```

3. Open APPLICATION_STRINGS.INC and make sure the strings are remarked and unremarked as shown. We have to make this change because Notepad and WordPad use different menu commands to open the Font dialog box. Save the .INC file when you're done:

   ```
   'UnREM this line for testing Notepad
   REM Const MENU_FONT = "Edit\~Set Font"
   'UnREM this line for testing Wordpad
   Const MENU_FONT = "Format\~Font"
   ```

4. Open and run FREDDIE.MST.

5. When Freddie completes his test run, examine the OURAPPLOG.LOG file in your \FREDDIE folder.

With the minor changes shown here, Freddie will test both Notepad and WordPad on Windows NT. He'll also test Notepad successfully on Windows 95 and 98, but you may see some problems with WordPad. Freddie kills the application process when he can't close a dialog box. That's a pretty drastic step. It doesn't allow the application or its DLLs to "clean up" as they might when they are closed in the normal way.

In the case of most applications we've tested with dumb monkeys like Freddie, killing their processes seems to have no serious side effects. Most important for us as testers, it doesn't seem to result in "false" bugs. WordPad on Windows 95 and 98 is an exception. When we kill the process after we've opened our test file, and restart WordPad, it doesn't let us open that same file again. There are at least two ways to deal with this problem. You can either skip opening the test file completely, or you can teach Freddie how to deal with the WordPad error dialog box so he doesn't have to kill WordPad.

Moving on with Freddie

Freddie is a simple dumb monkey. Even so, he can do quite a bit of testing on any application, and he's likely to find you some bugs early in your product cycle, long before your GUI is stable enough to spend time creating traditional automated tests. With some additions, he may find even more bugs. Adding features to Freddie, or creating your own dumb monkey using Freddie as a model, will cost you test time you could use in other ways. Testing is a trade-off.

Here are some ideas you may want to consider if you decide that making Freddie "smarter" is a good way to find more bugs.

✦ **Logging:** Monkeys are most useful when you can reproduce the bugs they find by testing things in the same ways they did. You can have the monkey log each test he does along with the random values he uses, so you can manually do the same things. That's tedious for human testers. With Freddie we seed Test's random number generator with the system tick count for the first test. Freddie writes that seed to the application .INI file as the `LastRandomSeedValue` using the Windows function `WritePrivateProfileString`. If you want Freddie to do the same tests over again with the same "random" values, copy the saved value to the `RandomSeedValue` in the .INI file and rerun Freddie.

Caution   Rerunning tests in this manner only works if Freddie can start your application from *exactly* the same state every time he starts a test run!

✦ **Custom tests:** Freddie does a good job testing menus. He doesn't even see toolbars or custom controls. If your application uses those controls, you'll get broader testing from Freddie if you teach him how to test them. If you already have routines in your regular Visual Test automation that use the controls, you can probably add them to Freddie easily and quickly.

✦ **Sophisticated edit box tests:** Freddie pumps random garbage into every edit box, and that brings up a lot of error messages. If you teach Freddie to recognize some edit boxes (by label or ordinal) and enter a more realistic set of values in them, you'll have better test control and reduce the "monkey noise" bug count. Don't completely eliminate the random characters, though. They sometimes find really good bugs.

✦ **Broader coverage on dialog controls:** Freddie only knows about Edit controls. You can add some interesting tests if you teach him how to recognize and manipulate scrollbars and spin boxes. Visual Test has a robust set of commands for those controls. Combo boxes, option buttons, check boxes, and all the other standard Windows controls are additional opportunities for new Freddie features. It's easy to create very elegant and sophisticated code for more controls that don't find any more bugs, though. Testing is a trade-off.

✦ **Skip some menu items:** Testing Exit probably won't find any bugs and just wastes the time Freddie needs to restart the application. Windows Help is a separate process from your application. Freddie won't test it, and its windows may get in his way. Any menu item that starts Help is another candidate for a menu skip routine. You may also want to avoid menu options that hide toolbars and menus. We'll leave implementing this feature to your imagination.

Warning: Monkeys Do the Darnedest Things

Sometimes those wacky things they do are really cute. Other times they can cost you, big time. You might want to take these precautions on your monkey testing machine:

✦ **Connect your printer to a null port:** Freddie will eventually try to print something, unless you've implemented a "don't test these menu items" routine. He may produce quite a lot of hard copy (paper) in the process.

✦ **Turn off the sound:** Freddie opens lots of error dialog boxes. They are often accompanied by beeps, dings, or blats…lots and lots of noise. We remove the sound board and unplug the internal speaker on machines we use for monkey testing.

✦ **Put blank formatted disks in floppy drives:** You get "noise" errors if Freddie tests the combo box in common dialog boxes, and Windows finds no disks in the drives.

✦ **Back up your hard drives:** Freddie will seldom stumble on the right combination of commands to actually format your hard drive. Once is one too many times, though. Remember, given enough time, Freddie will do *everything*.

✦ **Consider disconnecting the monkey machine from the network:** If Freddie can format your local hard drive, he can do the same thing to your manager's machine on the network. Because many applications these days interface with a Web browser, Freddie may also start visiting inappropriate Web sites, and you'll never convince anyone it was Freddie's idea to go there!.

✦ **Uninstall mail:** If you decide not to disconnect the network, at least consider disabling your mail program. Applications often have a "send mail" option. Eventually Freddie will find it and his e-mail messages to "everyone" won't win you many friends, even if the text is only garbage.

One pitfall to avoid is adding too many features to your test monkey. Monkeys are really cool, especially when they start testing the application in ways you didn't expect. Monkeys provide you with the opportunity to create fancy logging, elaborate front-end drivers, and elegant tests for your custom Windows controls. It's all really neat stuff, but it may *not* find you *one more bug*. Keep a close eye on the cost of monkey development versus the payback in bugs found, and be willing to stop adding features when those costs get too high.

Regardless of how you decide to use monkeys, make sure they won't be the only "testers" on your test team. If you start your test plan by implementing monkeys and the test budget is suddenly cut, you may not have enough resources left to create "conventional" tests. In that unhappy situation, you'll be worse off than having no automated tests at all.

Summary

You can use the ideas presented in this chapter to add smart or dumb monkeys to your kit of tools to test applications. Over the years we've seen many different smart monkeys, and a few dumb ones, implemented on product test teams. All the monkeys found bugs, and a few monkeys that were used early in product cycles found over 25 percent of the bugs on their projects. That's because the monkeys got to the bugs sooner, and more cheaply, than the human testers, who certainly would have found the majority of the bugs with "conventional" tests. More often monkeys found resource leaks because they could run for days or weeks without stopping. A few monkeys found esoteric bugs that had been missed by other testing for years over several versions of a product.

✦   ✦   ✦

Working with Resources

Versions 2.0 and 3.0 of Microsoft Test offered the ability to add menus, dialog boxes, and a special icon bar to test scripts. The same capability is available in this latest version of Visual Test. As with Visual Test 4.0, the 6.0 version uses the User Interface Editor that comes with the Microsoft Developer Studio. The icon bar and `sysMenu` functionalities, however, were removed in version 4.0. The abilities to work with string tables, bitmaps, icons, and cursors were added in 4.0 and remain in Rational Visual Test 6.0.

Visual Test Resource Files

Visual Test scripts can make use of *resources* — interface elements providing a means of communication between the program and the user — through the use of a Visual Test Resource (.VTR) file. All the different types of resources that can be created for use by Visual Test can be stored in one file so as to avoid multiple files lying around on the Test programmer's machine.

In previous versions of Test, a separate include (.INC) file was needed to keep track of the information needed to work with the resources stored in a .RES file. In Visual Test 4.0 and 6.0, however, these two files have been combined into the single .VTR file to make things less complex. And the Visual Test team has gone one step further. Now the .VTR file can be combined with a pseudocode (.PCD) file that is created when compiling and saving a Test language source code file. No longer is it necessary to track multiple files when distributing compiled test cases to other machines. Now the .VTR file can be a part of the compiled script file.

Creating a Resource File

A Visual Test Resource file can be created in the Developer Studio by selecting the New menu item under the File menu, clicking the Files tab, and then selecting the Visual Test Resource File item from the dialog box, as shown in Figure 15-1.

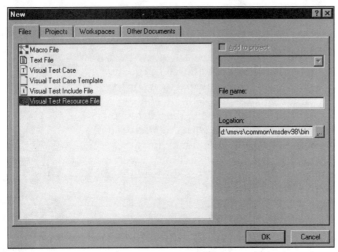

Figure 15-1: The Test programmer is given the option of what type of new item to create. To create a .VTR file, select the Visual Test Resource File item in the New dialog box's list box — under the Files tab.

Tip   If you right-click the Developer Studio's toolbar, you will see a pop-up menu listing the different kinds of toolbars available to you. Select Resource, and the Resource toolbar will be displayed, allowing you to easily add new resources to the current resource file.

When a new resource file is first created, it looks similar to the screen shown in Figure 15-2. No resources exist yet, but they can be added easily by selecting the Resource menu item from the Developer Studio's Insert menu.

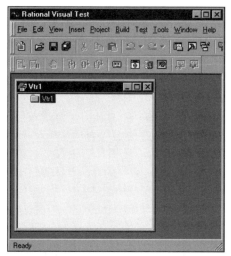

Figure 15-2: A new resource file has been created showing nothing more than a folder named Vtr1.

Note

Notice that the menu bar will adjust itself according to which window is currently active. That is, when the new resource file is created as shown in Figure 15-2, the Insert menu becomes available. When you are creating a specific resource, such as a dialog box, the Insert menu will disappear and the Layout menu will be displayed. For a bitmap resource, the Image menu will be added. The menu bar will adjust itself to the currently active resource window, and the menu will depend on the type of resource being viewed. Different palettes will also be displayed depending on the resource type.

When creating a new resource via the Insert menu or through the appropriate toolbar icon, you have 10 types of resources from which to choose, as shown in Figure 15-3. The main types of resources that Test programmers find themselves creating are menus, string tables, and dialog boxes. The remainder of the resources can be used individually, or as part of the design for menus and dialog boxes (for example, icons and bitmaps can be added to a dialog box, and accelerator tables can work with menus).

Tip

As an optional shortcut, you can also right-click the TestRes1 folder to insert items — much as you can when creating items in a Test project.

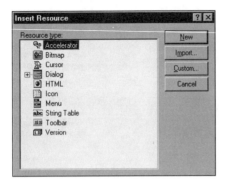

Figure 15-3: Ten kinds of resources can be created in the Developer Studio and saved into a Visual Test Resource (.VTR) file.

Each type of resource has a folder associated with it. As more resources are created for a .VTR file, they are automatically placed into the appropriate folder. For a large project that is using a number of different types of resources, you may find that the resource file is using many or all of the different types of resources. Figure 15-4 shows what a typical resource file might look like in this situation.

Figure 15-4: As more of the 10 types of resources are added, the .VTR file's graphical depiction will look similar to this.

The Resource Editors

When creating any kind of resource for a Visual Test Resource file, you can access the *properties* (or settings) associated with each resource via the Properties dialog box, shown in Figure 15-5. The contents of this dialog box change depending on the individual resource whose settings are being modified. The Properties dialog box for the Accelerator Editor shows the simplicity of this type of resource. It allows the Test programmer to determine which key and modifier to use to invoke an action. Also, the ID setting is used to associate an accelerator with a menu item.

Tip　Use the pushpin button in the upper-left corner of the Properties dialog box (see Figure 15-5) to force the dialog box to remain visible as you work with any of the editors.

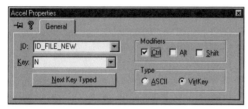

Figure 15-5: The *properties* (or settings) associated with each resource are accessible via the Properties dialog box.

Note　Although 10 types of resources can be created in the Developer Studio, only seven of those types can be utilized by Visual Test. Those resource types are dialog boxes, string tables, bitmaps, icons, cursors, menus, and accelerator tables. The HTML, toolbar, and version resources aren't supported by the Test language.

The Accelerator Editor

The Accelerator Editor allows for associating a shortcut or accelerator key with a menu item or specific action. This editor is used to create an accelerator key associated with a given menu item. When you create a new resource for an accelerator key or keys and type the key for which an accelerator is to be created, you are prompted with the Properties dialog box associated with accelerator keys. You then define exactly which keystrokes are to be used to invoke the action and to which menu item it is associated. (When we look at creating a menu later in this chapter, we will use the Accelerator Editor to create shortcuts.)

The Binary Editor

The Binary Editor is what the Developer Studio uses when it is asked to open a nontext file that is not recognized as any of the resource types supported by the Developer Studio (for example: bitmap, icon, cursor). It is an editor that is not for the faint of heart. Specifically, it allows for the manipulation of data at the binary level so that individual bytes can be modified. Changing these types of values can result in a file being interpreted as corrupt and may cause a program reading the modified file to act unexpectedly. Only use this editor if you know what you're doing at the byte level in a binary file. Figure 15-6 shows what a wave file looks like when opened in the Developer Studio.

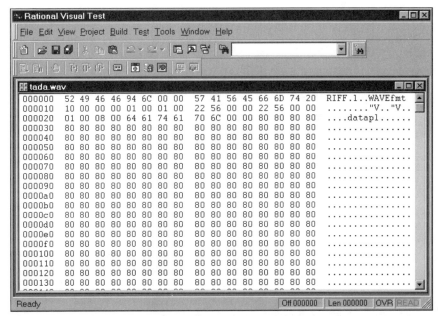

Figure 15-6: This is an example of a binary file that was opened by the Developer Studio but not recognized as a resource it supports. It is a wave file, as can be seen in the right-hand column where the ASCII representation of the data is displayed. The left side is the hexadecimal values of the bytes in the file.

The Graphic Editor

The Graphic Editor (see Figure 15-7) is used for creating bitmaps, cursors, and icons, which are all resource types supported by the Developer Studio and available to Visual Test. This editor closely resembles a painting program but is integrated into the studio and saves out to the different resource types.

Figure 15-7: A bitmap file has been opened, causing the Graphic zEditor and its associated toolbars to be displayed.

The Dialog Editor

The Dialog Editor (see Figure 15-8) resembles a drawing program and has two toolbars (Dialog and Controls) that appear when the editor is active. The Dialog palette allows for aligning, resizing, and testing the current state of the dialog box and its controls. The Controls palette allows you to place different types of controls onto the dialog box for designing the dialog box.

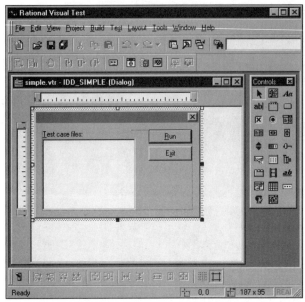

Figure 15-8: The Dialog Editor allows the Test programmer to design a dialog box simply by drawing the controls onto the dialog box window.

The Menu Editor

The Menu Editor is created simply by typing the names of the menus and their menu items. The Properties dialog box (shown in Figure 15-9 along with the Menu Editor) allows for controlling the name of the menus, their menu items, the IDs associated with the menus and menu items, and the way that each item should appear.

Figure 15-9: The Menu Editor and its Properties dialog box are used to create a menu bar by typing the name of the menu and its menu items.

The String Editor

The String Editor (see Figure 15-10) allows for the creation of string tables that can be accessed from the Test language using the RES$ function. The editor can be used to create commonly used strings that must be loaded as a test case file is run. While some Test programmers use constants to hold values, in the event Visual Test's memory space runs low, a string table can be used instead, thus allowing only required strings to be loaded individually.

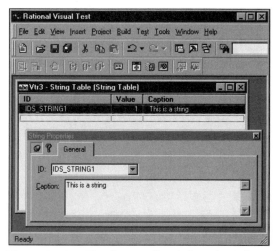

Figure 15-10: Simply type directly into the String Editor (which looks similar to the Accelerator Editor) to add to and edit its contents.

The result is that instead of having separate .INC files (depending upon which language the tests are being run in), a separate .VTR file can be used. This separate file holds menus, dialog boxes, string tables, and so on that are for a specific language, should you choose to take that approach.

Working with Dialog Boxes

The way to work with dialog boxes in Visual Test 6.0 isn't always the most intuitive approach. It's a holdover from Visual Test 4.0's implementation. However, it does result in a number of files being encapsulated and is, therefore, a little cleaner in its implementation.

Dialog boxes in Visual Test can take two forms: simple and complex. In versions 2.0 and 3.0 of Test, these two styles of dialog boxes were invoked by using the DlgBox and DlgBoxEx functions. Things were simplified in version 4.0 and remain this way in 6.0 with the use of a single function called Dialog.

Creating a Dialog Box

Before discussing the two separate types of dialog boxes, let's first create a dialog box that is to be used by the Test language. In this example, we will create a resource file called SIMPLE.VTR that will allow us to create and work with a beginning dialog box.

The resource file is created by selecting New from the File menu and selecting the Test Resource item displayed in the subsequent dialog box (see Figure 15-1). By then selecting the Resource... menu item from the Developer Studio's Insert menu, a Test programmer can select Dialog from the Insert Resource dialog box. After selecting Save from the File menu and typing **simple.vtr**, you will see the newly created resource file shown in Figure 15-11.

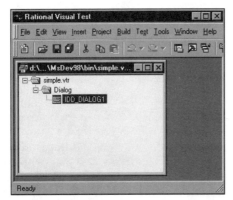

Figure 15-11: After creating a new resource file, inserting a dialog box resource, and saving the file, you will see the resource window as shown here.

As mentioned earlier in this chapter, the editor used to create a dialog box is very similar to a drawing program. Instead of having lines, rectangles, ellipses, and other shapes on a toolbar, you can place controls directly on the mock dialog box that appears in the editor. A simple dialog box is shown in Figure 15-12.

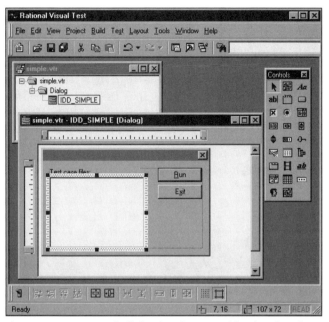

Figure 15-12: A mock dialog box is created by drawing the desired controls onto the dialog box shown in the editor.

As each control is created on the dialog box, its properties can be set to help manage how each control appears or behaves. To access the Properties dialog box, right-click the object and select Properties from the pop-up menu. Or double-click the object, and the Properties dialog box will appear. As an example, Figure 15-13 shows the properties associated with a list box control. Remember that you can press the F1 key to obtain specific descriptions of each option in a dialog box, including each of the controls in the Properties dialog box.

Figure 15-13: The properties for a control can be viewed by double-clicking the control. This is also where the names of the constants that are associated with a control and used by the Test language can be modified.

Double-clicking the dialog box itself also allows for adjusting how the dialog box appears and behaves. In each of these properties dialog boxes for each control, the constant associated with the control can be modified. It is this constant that is used in the Test language to identify the dialog box and its controls.

After drawing the desired controls onto the dialog box, you can test and modify them within the editor. To test the dialog box, either click the toolbar item that looks like a light switch or select the Test menu item under the Layout menu (see Figure 15-14).

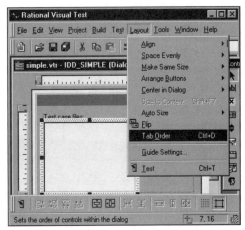

Figure 15-14: The Layout menu appears when working with the Dialog Editor. Many of the menu items on this menu are available through the toolbars that appear when the editor appears.

Also available in the Layout menu is the Tab Order menu item, which allows you to specify which control has the focus when the dialog box first appears, and in what order the controls are cycled through when the Tab key is pressed. Selecting the Tab Order menu item shown in Figure 15-14 causes the dialog box in the editor to have numbers placed by each control, indicating their tab positions (see Figure 15-15). Clicking each control, one at a time, in the order in which the tabbing should occur, results in those numbers adjusting themselves.

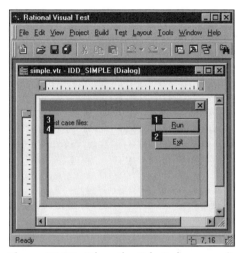

Figure 15-15: When the Tab Order menu item is selected from the Layout menu, numbers appear next to each control in the dialog box that is being edited. Click the controls in the order to which they should be tabbed to adjust those tab values.

A Simple Dialog Box

A *simple* dialog box is employed to communicate between the program and the user when it doesn't need to interact with the user by updating items in its list box, process the selection of menu items, or activate gray controls depending on its settings. A simple dialog box, as implied by its name, is an easy-to-construct-and-implement interface that allows simple communication between the user and the program that is executing. When a simple dialog box is displayed, however, the script controlling the dialog box comes to a halt until the user dismisses the dialog box or performs some action to cause the dialog box to dismiss itself.

We're now going to put to use the dialog box that we just created. The purpose is to provide an easy interface to a tester, allowing the tester to see a list of test case files and choose whether to run each of them in turn, or to exit the program that is driving the running of the test cases one by one.

Three steps must be followed to make the newly created dialog resource available to the script we are about to create. The first step is to include the .VTR file, previously named SIMPLE.VTR, into a sample project we'll call *Simple Dialog*. The resource is added to the project just as any other file is — by clicking the project in the workspace and selecting Import Test Project Items... under the Add To Project submenu found in the Project menu.

The second step is to create a script that will use the resource file. In this case, we will create our own simple driver that runs the test case files in the Notepad test suite one at a time. We'll create a new test case file that won't necessarily hold any test cases but will contain a script to act as a driver. Keeping it simple, we'll name it SIMPLE_DRIVER.MST.

These files can be found on the CD-ROM included in the back of this book. The path to those files is \SAMPLES\SUITE\SIMPLE.

The third and final step is to include the Visual Test Resource (.VTR) file into the source code file itself. This is the same idea as including an include (.INC) file, except that, in this case, it is a file holding resources. Instead of using the '$INCLUDE metacommand, we'll use the '$RESOURCE metacommand.

The Notepad project window and the resulting SIMPLE_DRIVER.MST script appear as shown in Figure 15-16 after the SIMPLE.VTR resource file has been added to the project and the new .MST file has been created.

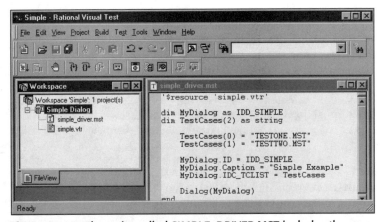

Figure 15-16: The script called SIMPLE_DRIVER.MST includes the resource file, initializes the structure associated with the dialog box, and then displays the dialog box by passing the structure to the dialog function.

When a dialog box is created and saved into a .VTR file, an internal type is created that is associated with that dialog box and its controls. The simple form of working with a dialog box (see Figure 15-16) consists of creating a variable of that internal type, initializing the members or elements of that type, and then passing the variable to the dialog function. The result of running the script shown in Figure 15-16 is the dialog box shown in Figure 15-17. This dialog box, created earlier in this chapter, is accessed by saving it as part of a .VTR file and including it into a Test Project. Including the .VTR file into the script, initializing a variable of a type created when the dialog box was created, and passing that variable to the dialog function causes the dialog box to appear when the script is executed. No actual guts to the driver have been provided yet; this is simply an example of how to get the dialog box to display itself.

Figure 15-17: Access this dialog box by saving it as part of a .VTR file and including it into a Test Project.

In most cases, when dealing with the simple form of a dialog box, the constant values won't be used, other than the one that identifies the ID number of the dialog box to be displayed. The only thing the user must do is determine which user-defined type to use, declare a variable of that type, initialize the fields in the type that are of interest to the Test programmer, and then pass that type to the dialog function along with the ID number or constant for the dialog box to be displayed.

When the dialog function completes its task (which is when the user clicks one of the command buttons), the variable that was initialized and passed to dialog() has been reset to reflect any changes to the controls of the dialog box made by the user. In the example shown in Figure 15-16, the return value for the dialog function is ignored. If it weren't ignored, the function would have returned the ID number of the button that was used to dismiss the dialog box. This way, the user could determine which button caused the dialog box to be dismissed.

Determining Types and Constants

In Microsoft Test 2.0 and 3.0, determining the type was a simple exercise. When the dialog box was saved, it was placed into a .RES file. An .INC file that held the type and constant declarations associated with the dialog box and its controls was created at the same time the .RES file was created. It was a matter of including the .INC file to get access to the user-defined type and then specifying the name of the

.RES file in the call to `DlgBox()`. In Visual Test 4.0 and 6.0, however, the .INC and .RES files are combined into the single .VTR file, and the `dialog` function is used instead of `DlgBox()`. While I think this is a very cool way to handle the problem of multiple files, my concern is that the user-defined type and its constants are now somewhat hidden unless you know the method to finding those types. Trying to track down this information for the first time can be frustrating when stepping through all of the online documentation.

To display the type and constants associated with the dialog box, you must include the .VTR file into a project. Once they are included in the project, you can then right-click the .VTR file (in this case, SIMPLE.VTR) and select a menu item that wasn't available previously: Display Declarations. Selecting this pop-up menu item causes all of the constants and types associated with dialog boxes, bitmaps, icons, and every other kind of resource stored in the .VTR file to be dumped to the Output window under the Viewport tab, as shown in Figure 15-18. Unlike in Test 2.0 and 3.0, where a separate .INC file was automatically generated that held this kind of information, this information is now all kept in a single .VTR file. Using the Output window is now the preferred way to access information about the declarations.

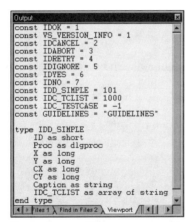

Figure 15-18: The constant and type declarations for a given .VTR file can be dumped to the Output window.

A Complex Dialog Box

The *complex* dialog box, which we'll use to complete the driver described earlier in this chapter, is a bit more challenging than the *simple* dialog box. It involves an approach to programming similar to straight Windows programming using the C language. Because of this, there is a fine line between discussing the complex dialog box and moving into Windows programming topics. We'll end up blurring that line a little bit to get you started as an advanced Test programmer, but you will need to continue learning on your own by looking through the Windows APIs.

When you must process events that occur while a dialog box is up and displayed to a user, you must use a complex dialog box. The simple dialog box works by filling a structure and getting the user's selections returned in that structure when the dialog box is dismissed. The complex dialog box, which also gets the final settings of the controls in the dialog box, allows another level of control such that the Test program can interact with the dialog box while it is displayed.

For this example, the DRIVER.MST file has been created to work with a complex dialog box. Also, the DRIVER.VTR file is being used in lieu of the SIMPLE.VTR file used in the previous example. And all of it has been added to the Notepad project that has been created over the course of this book. This new and improved dialog box is shown in Figure 15-19. It is in a file called DRIVER.VTR and has been added to the Notepad project. (The two types of dialog boxes can coexist in the same resource file if the Test programmer so chooses.)

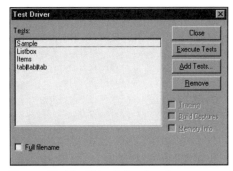

Figure 15-19: This dialog box is a new and improved version over the simple dialog box we looked at previously.

When working with a complex dialog box, you must declare a variable of the type that was (automatically) created when the dialog box was saved into the .VTR file. The only element of the type that must be initialized, however, is the proc field, as shown in Listing 15-1.

On the CD-ROM

The full listing for DRIVER.MST can be found in the \SAMPLES\SUITE directory on the CD-ROM found in the back of this book.

Listing 15-1: **A partial listing of DRIVER.MST**

```
'(Some initial comments and code removed

    dlgTestDriver.proc = VARPTR(DriverProc)
    Dialog(dlgTestDriver)
end

'***************************************************************
'* Function:    DriverProc
'* Purpose:
'*              Main procedure for the driver.
'*
'* Parameters:
'*          hWnd&
'*                  Handle to the parent window
'*          msg&
'*                  Message that's being sent to the dialog
'*          wParam&
'*                  Word parameter associated with msg%
'*          lParam&
'*                  Long parameter associated with msg%
'*
'* Returns:
'*              INTEGER
'*                  TRUE if this proc handled the msg.
'*                  FALSE if windows default should occur.
'*
'***************************************************************

function DriverProc (hWnd&, msg&, wParam&, lParam&) as long
    dim ret%
    dim strTemp as string * MAX_FILENAME
    dim iSel%
    dim index%

    select case msg
        case WM_INITDIALOG
            InitDriver(hWnd)     'Init dialog box w/ .INI

            LoadList (hWnd)      'Load in list of test suites

            'execScripts = 0 we know we are ready to execute
            'execScripts = 1 we know we are executing scripts
            'execScripts = 2 we just clicked the stop button

            execScripts = 0 'Initialize execScripts
        case WM_COMMAND
            select case wParam
                case IDCANCEL
```

```
            if execScripts = 0 then
                SaveDriver (hWnd)           'Save settings
                EndDialog (hWnd, wParam)'Close dialog
                DriverProc = TRUE
            else
                execScripts = 2
            end if

    case BTN_ADD
        strTemp=strGetFile("", FILTERSTRING)

        if (strTemp <> "") then
            '* increment the tail
            TestListTail  = TestListTail + 1
            '* write the new one.
            TestList(TestListTail) = strTemp

            if fDisplayPath then
                ret=SendMessage(GetDlgItem(hwnd, _
                    LB_TESTS),LB_ADDSTRING, _
                    0,strTemp)
            else
                ret=SendMessage(GetDlgItem(hwnd, _
                    LB_TESTS),LB_ADDSTRING,0, _
                    strGetFilename(strTemp))
            end if
        endif
        DriverProc = TRUE

    case BTN_REMOVE
        iSel = SendMessage(GetDlgItem(hwnd, _
            LB_TESTS), _
            LB_GETCURSEL,0,0)
        if (iSel <> LB_ERR) then
            ret=SendMessage(GetDlgItem(hwnd, _
                LB_TESTS), LB_DELETESTRING,
                iSel, 0)

            'Keep selection when removing items
            ret=SendMessage(GetDlgItem(hwnd,_
                LB_TESTS), _
                LB_GETCOUNT, 0, 0)
            if (iSel > (ret-1)) then
                ret=SendMessage(GetDlgItem(hwnd, _

                    LB_TESTS), LB_SETCURSEL, _
                    (ret-1), 0)
            else
                ret=SendMessage(GetDlgItem(hwnd, _
```

(continued)

Listing 15-1 *(continued)*

```
                            LB_TESTS), LB_SETCURSEL, _
                            iSel, 0)
                endif

                'Synch listbox with TestList array
                for index = iSel to TestListTail - 1
                    '* bump everything up 1.
                    TestList(index) = TestList(index _
                                        + 1)
                next index
                TestListTail = TestListTail -1
            endif
            DriverProc = TRUE

        case BTN_EXEC
            SaveDriver(hWnd) 'Save before run
            execScripts = 1
    enableWindow(GetDlgItem(hwnd,BTN_EXEC),FALSE)
    enableWindow(GetDlgItem(hwnd,BTN_ADD),FALSE)
    enableWindow(GetDlgItem(hwnd,BTN_REMOVE),FALSE)
            SetDlgItemText (hwnd,IDCANCEL,"Stop")
            RunTests(hWnd) 'Run tests
            ret = ShowWindow(hwnd, SW_SHOW)
            DriverProc = TRUE

        case CB_FULLNAME
            ret = SendMessage(GetDlgItem(hwnd, _
                LB_TESTS),LB_RESETCONTENT, 0,0)
            if wCheckState("Full Filename")=CHECKED then
                '* TestList array is 0 based, thus ...
                for index = 0 to TestListTail
                    ret = SendMessage(GetDlgItem(hwnd, _
                        LB_TESTS),LB_ADDSTRING,  _
                        0,trim$(TestList(index)))
                next index
                fDisplayPath = TRUE
            else
                for index = 0 to TestListTail
                    ret = SendMessage(GetDlgItem(hWnd, _
                        LB_TESTS),LB_ADDSTRING, 0, _

    strGetFilename(TestList(index)))
                next index
                fDisplayPath = FALSE
            end if
        case else
            DriverProc = FALSE
    end select
```

```
     case else
          DriverProc = FALSE
     end select
end function 'DriverProc
```

A number of the functions that `DriverProc()` calls are in the remainder of the DRIVER.MST file. Many of the others, however, are Windows API calls that are the same calls that Windows programmers use when writing Windows applications.

A *proc* (pronounced "prock") is a procedure that handles all the messages for a window in the Windows 95 or Windows NT operating system. When a mouse is moved across a window, the proc is called with a message letting it know something is happening. When a control is clicked, the proc is called with the message, the ID number of the control, and other information. When a dialog box is about to be displayed, the proc is notified by sending a `WM_INITDIALOG` message.

Windows messages begin with the `WM_` prefix, and all procs are sent four arguments when they're called. Those arguments are a handle to the window receiving the message, the message that is being sent, and two parameters (`wParam` and `lParam`) whose values depend on the type of message being sent. Looking up a message in the *MSDN* online help will explain what information is passed to the `wParam` and `lParam` parameters depending on the Windows message.

When a message is sent to a proc, it can be either processed or ignored. If it is processed by the proc, the proc must return a nonzero value, letting Windows know that the message was not ignored. If the message is ignored, returning a 0 (`FALSE`) informs Windows that it should go ahead and handle the message in the default manner (in many cases, Windows' default response is to do nothing).

When a control is clicked, a `WM_COMMAND` message is sent. All messages in a proc are typically handled in a `CASE` statement structure. It is up to yet another `CASE` statement to deal with determining which control was clicked and what to do for that control. In the case of a `WM_COMMAND`, the `wParam` parameter holds the ID number of the control that was clicked. This secondary case statement can then respond, based on which control was selected.

Something to keep in mind when dealing with a proc is that tons of messages are being sent over and over again to the proc. It is necessary to keep track of the state that the dialog box is in. In our proc, we have a global variable called `execScripts` that tracks whether the driver is in the process of stepping through and running each test case one at a time, and whether the dialog box is idling, awaiting the user's command, or the Stop button has been clicked to cause the execution of the scripts to halt. Because the proc is called by Windows itself, extra parameters cannot be added to the parameter list for the proc. Therefore, many times it is necessary to use global variables to make data available to the proc, although this is not necessarily the preferable way to pass data around in a program.

Note Missing from the top of Listing 15-1 is the statement for including the WINAPI.INC file discussed in Chapter 13. When working with Windows APIs, including the WINAPI.INC file automatically links into a number of the APIs and provides declarations for constants and user-defined types associated with those APIs. For more information on working with Windows APIs or the WINAPI.INC file, refer to Chapter 13.

Working with Menus

Figure 15-20 shows an example of a menu that has been created for the example test case driver shown earlier in this chapter. This figure shows the Menu Editor and its Properties dialog box. Again, it is here, in the Properties dialog box, that the names of the constants can be set.

Tip To add a *direct access method* (DAM) key to a menu item, use the ampersand in front of the letter to be underlined. Want to actually have the ampersand displayed instead of causing a menu's letter to be underlined? Enter it twice (&&). Do not confuse a DAM key with an accelerator or shortcut key. The DAM key is for use with the Alt key.

Once a menu has been added to a resource file, that menu can be used through the Test language's SetMenu statement. This function takes the handle to the window as the first parameter and the menu ID as the second.

Caution If you're still using Visual Test 4.0 and its documentation, note that the Visual Test 4.0 documentation said that SetMenu took three parameters instead of just the two, and the order of the parameters was reversed.

The SetMenu function call can be placed in the WM_INITDIALOG section of the proc, and the IDs associated with the menu items can be intermingled with the existing IDs found in the case statement under the WM_COMMAND section. Excerpts of the modified dialog proc are shown in Listing 15-2. Adding a menu requires a call to SetMenu() with the handle of the window to add the menu to, the ID number of the resource, and then modifications to the proc so that selecting menu items results in something happening.

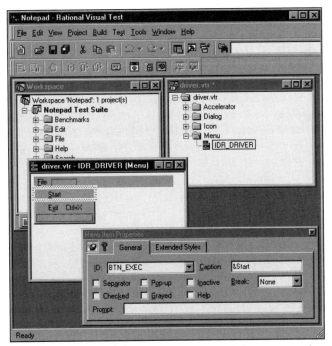

Figure 15-20: IDR_DRIVER is the name of the constant that represents the menu for the sample driver stored in the DRIVER.VTR resource file. Adding menus and menu items is as simple as typing the names directly into the editor.

The menu is successfully integrated by adding the SetMenu function call to the WM_INITDIALOG section of the CASE statement. Also, the constants associated with the menu IDs (ID_FILE_EXIT and ID_FILE_START) are added to the same section of the case statement as the IDCANCEL for the Close button, and BTN_EXEC for the Execute Tests button, as shown in Listing 15-2. Another way to attach a menu to a dialog box is via the Properties dialog box in the dialog box editor. Through this UI approach you can select the menu to associate with the dialog box.

Listing 15-2: Excerpts of the modified dialog proc

```
(... code above this section is not shown ...)
select case msg
    case WM_INITDIALOG
        SetMenu(hWnd,IDR_DRIVER) 'Add menu to the dialog window
        InitDriver(hWnd)          'Init dialog box via .INI

        LoadList (hWnd)           'Load in list of test suites

(... some code removed ...)

case WM_COMMAND
    select case wParam
        case IDCANCEL,ID_FILE_EXIT
            if execScripts = 0 then
                SaveDriver (hWnd)        'Save settings
                EndDialog (hWnd, wParam)'Close dialog
                DriverProc = TRUE
            else
                execScripts = 2
            end if

        case BTN_EXEC, ID_FILE_START
            SaveDriver (hWnd)       'Save settings before running
            execScripts = 1
            enableWindow (GetDlgItem(hwnd, BTN_EXEC),FALSE)
            enableWindow (GetDlgItem(hwnd, BTN_ADD),FALSE)
            enableWindow (GetDlgItem(hwnd, BTN_REMOVE),FALSE)
            SetDlgItemText (hwnd,IDCANCEL,"Stop")
            RunTests (hWnd)         'Run tests
            ret = ShowWindow(hwnd, SW_SHOW)
            DriverProc = TRUE

(... code continues ...)
```

Accelerator Keys

Adding an accelerator key is as simple as typing the key into the Accelerator Editor and selecting which modifier (that is, Ctrl, Alt, or Shift) key to use with the chosen letter. Once this has been done, the accelerator can then be associated with the ID of a menu item that should already have been created.

The Visual Test documentation states that the description of the accelerator key will automatically be added to the menu, but I couldn't get this to work. Therefore, if it does not work for you either, you can type the accelerator key in next to the name of the menu item and separate the two descriptions with a tab. To separate with a tab, use the \t escape sequence as part of the string. For example, to create a menu item named Exit that has its letter "x" marked as the DAM key and Ctrl+X identified as the accelerator key, type **E&xit\tCtrl+X** into the menu item's Properties dialog box.

Caution Accelerator keys do not work with menus that have been attached to dialog boxes. I couldn't find this mentioned in the Visual Test 4.0 or 6.0 online help, but this was the case and was stated in the Test 2.0 and 3.0 documentation.

The Remaining Resources

The remaining resources are easy and straightforward to use. These resources are the icon, bitmap, cursor, and string table.

The Icon Resource

Icons are basically 32×32 pixel-sized bitmaps that can be used in dialog boxes or painted into windows (or device contexts). Icons can also be used with list view controls. To load an icon out of a resource file, first include the .VTR file (as it was in the listings shown earlier in this chapter) by using the $RESOURCE metacommand. The Icon function loads the icon in the resource file by specifying the ID number or name of the icon. A handle is returned that can later be used with other functions and statements.

Note Icons can also be 16×16 and 48×48.

To draw an icon to a window or device context, use the DrawIcon statement. Once an icon has been loaded by using the Icon function, it remains in memory until either the script terminates or the DestroyIcon statement is called.

One of the more interesting uses of icons is with the list view control in a dialog box. While we didn't look at a list view control, it is very similar to a list box control. To load an icon and associate it with the text being displayed in a list view control, use the ImageIcon function. When you prepend the return value of the ImageIcon function to the text that is to be displayed in the list view control, the icon appears in that control with the text.

The Bitmap Resource

Working with a bitmap resource is also straightforward. Its only function is to be used as an object in a dialog box or to be drawn to a window using the `DrawBitmap` statement.

Like the icon resource, the bitmap resource can be manipulated by using the `Bitmap` function to load a bitmap, the `DrawBitmap` statement to display a bitmap in a given window, and the `DestroyBitmap` statement to remove the resource from memory.

Referring to the `DrawBitmap` section of the online help, the Test programmer will find that the bitmap can be drawn in a number of ways, including drawing the bitmap as expected, or merging it with the graphics that already exist at the specified location.

The Cursor Resource

Similar to the other resources, a cursor can be loaded into memory (`Cursor` function), drawn to a window (`DrawCursor` statement), and destroyed or removed from memory (`DestroyCursor` statement). You can also change the current mouse pointer by using the `SetCursor` command.

The String Table Resource

The string table resource is a nice addition to Visual Test (made available in version 4.0) because it allows for text strings to be implemented in a flexible fashion.

An approach to keeping several strings around to be used as a part of testing is to replace individual string constants with a string table. When only a few strings are used, this may not be worthwhile. However, when many strings are needed to refer to all text in an application (including text strings that must be used to provide test data to the application), the amount of memory used in Visual Test's stack can grow quite high.

In these situations, you may opt to use disk space to store strings instead of using Visual Test's limited stack segment of memory. To do so, place the strings into a string table and then load the individual strings as they are needed. This solution, however, is at the expense of speed, since the string must be loaded in from the disk and placed into a variable. This doesn't consume a huge amount of time, but it is slower than when working with conventional random-access memory.

As with any resource, the items defined in the resource are accessed by IDs. By calling the RES$ function with an ID, the function returns the string associated with that ID. Because the same variable can be used again for another string, the value previously stored in the variable is freed from memory. There is no need to worry about freeing strings loaded in from a string table.

Summary

By providing access to resources from the Visual Test language, Microsoft and Rational Software have made Visual Test a very capable tool for testing and adding UI components to your test scripts to make them easier to use. Simple dialog boxes provide an easy way to communicate with the user of the test script, whereas a complex dialog box approaches the level of Windows development by working with the Windows APIs.

Although this is an area of Visual Test that isn't used as often as other sections of the product, it is nice to know that it has these capabilities that allow for future modifications to automated tests.

✦   ✦   ✦

Testing Across a Network

One of the more interesting aspects of Visual Test is its support for distributing tests across a NetBIOS-compatible network. NetBIOS is an application programmer interface (API) that activates network operations on IBM PC compatibles running under a Microsoft operating system. NetBIOS is the main protocol on which Microsoft applications depend.

With this support for distributing tests, a number of possibilities are opened to the Test programmer when automating testing on an application. Two possibilities, for example, are running the same tests on different computer configurations, and running tests to test database access from multiple stations. When it comes to running tests on multiple machines, there are, of course, other possibilities that are too numerous to list here. Because of the support that Visual Test provides, many of these scenarios can be accomplished through the use of the *Visual Test Network Distribution Procedures*.

Note   The network functionality was changed in Visual Test 4.0 from the support that was provided in previous versions of Test. These changes helped simplify the entire process, thus making it easier to learn, use, and understand. Any scripts that were written previous to Visual Test 4.0 must be updated to follow the new Test language functions. Between versions 4.0 and 6.0 of Visual Test no new functionality has been added.

Roles and Responsibilities

Two roles must be filled in order for Visual Test's network routines to work. The first role is that of the *host*, whose duty it is to find available stations, pass tasks to those stations, and then collect data from those stations.

The second role is that of the *station*, whose job it is to contact a host, notify the host that it is willing to take on tasks, run those tasks, and then report the results back to the host.

For a station to be able to work on a network, there must first be a host. For a host to be effective, it must have a station or stations with which to work. While the host generally manages the stations by assigning tasks and collecting results, it is not in control of the station. The station, depending on how its script has been written, can disconnect from the host at any time. Therefore, it is a cooperative effort and the scripts must be written in a particular way to allow the communication and cooperation to occur.

Figure 16-1 shows a common model of working with a host and station. In this example, a single host exists that is working with one or more stations. The host first establishes itself as a host and then checks the network for any stations that have declared themselves as available to a host. Tasks are distributed to the station (or stations), and results are collected.

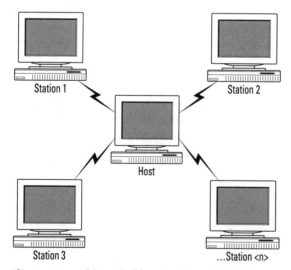

Figure 16-1: This typical host/station relationship model is used when working with the Visual Test Network Distribution Procedures.

Capabilities of the Host

A computer that acts as a host is any computer running Visual Test that declares itself to be a host on the network. Therefore, a computer that acted as a station in one situation can be a host in another.

The host has specific duties for which it is responsible when acting as a host. The first is to establish itself on the network as a host, so that any available stations can locate it and make themselves known as being available for processing tasks. The second is to locate available stations and initiate a session with one or more of the available stations. Third, the host must monitor the status of the station so that it knows if it is idling, passing back information, or no longer available to the host. Fourth, it must assign tasks to the stations (based on the host's needs). Receiving data back from the stations is the fifth responsibility of the host machine. The host is also responsible for handling any special situations that arise on the host's side (such as run-time errors). Finally, the host is responsible for cleaning up after itself and terminating the sessions with the stations. These responsibilities are shown in Figure 16-2.

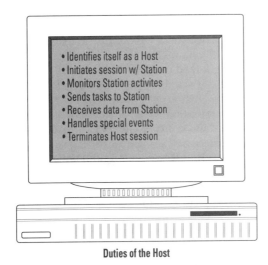

• Identifies itself as a Host
• Initiates session w/ Station
• Monitors Station activites
• Sends tasks to Station
• Receives data from Station
• Handles special events
• Terminates Host session

Duties of the Host

Figure 16-2: The host is responsible for identifying itself as a host, managing the selected stations and itself, and terminating testing sessions when the final tasks have been completed.

Identifying a Host

To avoid the "chicken-and-the-egg" scenario, the host is obligated to start the host/station relationship by identifying itself on the network as a host. This is done by using the `TalkCreateHost` function. This function requires a name to be passed to it, which will be used to identify the host, along with a pointer to a subroutine that will process all messages sent to the host. This function takes this form:

```
TalkCreateHost(strHostName$, varptr(AHostMsgHandler))
```

In the documentation, it looks confusing and it's difficult to understand how the second parameter (in this case, `AHostMsgHandler`) is supposed to be used. This is yet another situation where things look weird at first but really are not too bad once you've had a chance to read through everything. The unfortunate reality of online help is that it makes it difficult to locate information; many times it is necessary to jump to multiple topics instead of finding all information in one place. Once the general concepts are understood, however, the online help is an excellent tool.

The first parameter to `TalkCreateHost()` is a 15-character, alphanumeric string that uniquely identifies the host on the network. So type in any name that you know isn't in use. Use only letters and numbers to identify your host on the network. The second parameter is a pointer to a subroutine. This pointer is being passed to `TalkCreateHost()` so that when an event occurs of which the host should be aware, the host can be notified automatically no matter what it is otherwise doing. This is known as a callback routine. As discussed in Chapter 13, a callback routine is used for events that can occur at any time (also known as *asynchronous* events).

It is up to you, the Test programmer, to create the routine that will be called automatically by Visual Test when an event occurs that affects the host. I used `AHostMsgHandler` in the previous example just to show how the name of the callback routine isn't important. The values that it takes are important, however. When the callback is made by Visual Test, it expects to be able to pass a certain number and certain types of parameters to the callback routine. These parameters are defined in the online help. They result in the Test programmer having to define a subroutine similar to this:

```
sub AHostMsgHandler(iMsg%, hHost&, iStation%, lType&, _
                vData as VARIANT)

    … guts of the subroutine go here …

end sub 'AHostMsgHandler
```

The result is a subroutine that takes five parameters of type SHORT, LONG, SHORT, LONG, and VARIANT, where VARIANT allows for any type of value to be passed.

Note The online help uses the SHORT data type instead of the INTEGER type when speaking about the callback function that works with a host script. Because the SHORT and INTEGER data types are virtually the same, I'm using the shorthand notation for an INTEGER declaration (%) instead of SHORT. This will work without any ill effects.

By calling TalkCreateHost(), your code has established a handler for all messages sent to the host by the station (or by Visual Test) because of an action taken by a station. No matter which line of code the host is currently executing when a message comes in, the host will act as if a call to AHostMsgHandler() has been placed on the very next line of code to be executed. Execution will jump into the message handler and, upon completion, return control back to the host where it was interrupted.

Caution Because a callback can occur at any time, no matter what the host script is doing, it is important to not have any code in the callback routine that adjusts or affects the state of an application that is potentially being manipulated by the host. For example, if the host is clicking items in a dialog box and a callback occurs, the callback routine should not dismiss the dialog box, because, when control returns to the main script, the dialog box will no longer be available and will result in errors, since the script tries to continue from where it was interrupted. This same situation applies to adjusting the current directory or active disk drive.

The return value of TalkCreateHost() is a number or *handle* that identifies the host. Because multiple host sessions can be running on the network, and even in a single script, the handle to the host is very important in identifying exactly which host is making requests to the stations on the network.

Assuming a host script with a callback routine called AHostMsgHandler, the identification process required by a host script would look something like this:

```
dim hHost&
    hHost = TalkCreateHost("MainHost",varptr(AHostMsgHandler))
    '…more source code follows…
end
```

The Host's Callback Routine

When a host is identified by using the TalkCreateHost function, a pointer to a callback function must be provided. A typical callback function that processes messages sent to the host would take a form similar to Listing 16-1.

Listing 16-1: **This callback routine processes messages sent to the host.**

```
Sub AHostMsgHandler(iMsg%, hHost&, iStation%, lType&, _
                 vData AS VARIANT)
    Dim strStationName AS STRING

    strStationName = TalkGetStationName(hHost, iStation)

    Print "Station ["+strStationName+"] has ";
    Select Case(iMsg)
        Case TALK_CONNECT
            Print "connected."

        Case TALK_HUNGUP
            Print "disconnected."

        Case TALK_DATA
            Print "sent data."
            'Use another SELECT CASE statement to
            'determine the data type and what to do
            'with the data that has been passed.

        Case TALK_SYNC
            Print "notified it is ready to synchronize."

        Case Else
         'Unexpected message has been sent
    End Select
end sub 'AHostMsgHandler
```

This script is only a beginning shell to a typical handler for processing a host's messages. It is up to you as the Test programmer to provide the reactions to the different messages that can be sent using the network procedures.

As you will see later in this chapter, the callback routine used by the station is nearly the same. Both a host and a station must have a callback routine, so that they can process incoming messages as they occur. The callback routine provides for working with these asynchronous events.

Locating Stations

A host locates stations that are available on the network by using the `TalkGetStationCount` function. The host passes its handle to this function along with a Boolean (`TRUE` or `FALSE`) value that determines whether the number of active stations (or active and inactive stations) is returned. Typically, the second parameter will be set to `TRUE`, so that `TalkGetStationCount()` returns the number of active stations on the network.

As the host finds stations on the network via its call to `TalkGetStationCount()`, it assigns values to each station it encounters, beginning with 1. If a station deactivates or disconnects itself from the host, it is considered inactive, and the host maintains its unique identifying number should the station reactivate. As new stations become available, they are given the next highest number in the existing list of stations. The number returned by `TalkGetStationCount()` is considered the last ID number of the available stations. Therefore, the numbers from 1 to whatever value was returned by `TalkGetStationCount()` are all ID numbers of available stations on the network. The numbers correspond to an internal station list that was built by Visual Test when stations identified themselves on the network and the `TalkGetStationCount` function was called. This list is automatically maintained by Visual Test and accessible only by using the ID numbers associated with each station.

Monitoring a Station

Once the host has ascertained how many connections exist for stations on the network through the use of `TalkGetStationCount()`, the host can then begin querying information about those stations. The first function available to the host for extracting information is `TalkGetStationName()`. By passing one of the station ID numbers to this function, a string is returned that is the network name of the computer. This information can be helpful in logging information about tests run on a specific machine. Because the ID number of a station depends on the order in which stations registered themselves on the network as being available to a host, the ID number changes from session to session, making the station name the only static information available (unless the owner of the station changes the network name of the computer).

As a host hands out tasks to the available stations, it should first verify that each station is still active. This can be done through the use of the `TalkStationActive` function, which returns a `TRUE` or a `FALSE` value depending on the status of the station. If a station is inactive and the host attempts to send information, an error will result, notifying the host that the station is no longer available.

The last way of monitoring a station's activity is an inactive approach on the side of the host. That is, a callback function was established when the host first identified itself to the network. Should the stations take any actions that could affect the host, the host will be notified. The two previously mentioned functions are an active approach to gathering information on and monitoring a station. The latter form of using the callback function helps to monitor the station, but it is more of an involuntary reflex than a voluntary one.

The code shown in Listing 16-2 is an example of pulling together what I've shown you so far. This script identifies the computer it is running on as a host on the network. It will then look for any computers that are running a script that identifies those computers as stations. Then, it will step through the list of stations, one by one, and print out the name of each of those stations. (Note: This is assuming that a station script is running on a computer somewhere on the network.)

Listing 16-2: A simple script that demonstrates how the host finds stations on a network

```
dim hHost&, iStationCount%, iLoop%

    hHost = TalkCreateHost("MainHost",varptr(AHostMsgHandler))
    iStationCount = TalkGetStationCount(hHost, TRUE)

    for iLoop = 1 to iStationCount
        print "Station #";iLoop;" = [" + _
            TalkGetStationName(hHost,iLoop) + "]"
    next iLoop
end

'***
'* Simple message handler for messages sent to the Host
'***
Sub AHostMsgHandler(iMsg%, hHost&, iStation%, lType&, _
                    vData AS VARIANT)
    dim strStationName AS STRING

    strStationName = TalkGetStationName(hHost, iStation)

    print "Station ["+strStationName+"] has ";
    select case(iMsg)
        case TALK_CONNECT
            print "connected."

        case TALK_HUNGUP
            print "disconnected."

        case TALK_DATA
```

```
        print "sent data."
        'Place another select case statement here based on
        'the lType parameter to determine the type of data
        'sent and how to deal with it.

      case TALK_SYNC
        print "notified it is ready to synchronize "+ _
            "testing."

      case else
        'Unexpected message has been sent. Print an error
        'message or just ignore it.
    end select
  end sub 'AHostMsgHandler
```

Sending and Receiving Data

Once the host has identified itself, has set up a callback function for processing
messages sent by the station, and has set up a session with available stations on
the network, it can then begin sending tasks to a station or stations. This is done
through the use of the `TalkSendData` function, which takes this form:

```
TalkSendData (hHost&, iStation%, lDataType&, vData AS VARIANT)
```

The `hHost` parameter is the handle of the host sending the data. This is the value
that is returned by `TalkCreateHost()` and is used to identify which host session is
sending the information. The `iStation` parameter is the ID number of the station
that is to receive the data. If 0 is sent instead of a specific ID number, then the data
is sent to all the stations currently active. The `lDataType` parameter is a value that
informs the station what kind of data is being sent in the `vData` parameter. This can
be any string or number, and the `lDataType` value is defined by the Test
programmer, depending on the different types of data being sent.

A piece of functionality that was lost when moving to Visual Test 4.0 is the ability to
copy a file across the network from one machine to another. In Test 2.0 and 3.0, a
function called `GetDataFile` would pull a file across the network to the station.
Because this is no longer available, it is up to those of us using Visual Test 4.0 and
6.0 who are running the host and station scripts to define how we will provide
access to different types of files. One example is to use a common, shared directory
on the network. By passing the path to that file in that directory, the host or station
can then use the Test language's copy statement to bring the file across. Another
(less appealing) method would be to read in a text file one line at a time and pass it
across to the station, allowing it to reassemble the file on the other side by writing
the lines back out one at a time. Two examples of situations in which it is necessary
to pass files back and forth across the network are when a script file must be
executed on another machine and when a log file must be sent back to a host.

The `TalkSendData` statement is used both by the host and the station whenever information must be sent back and forth. The station, however, provides a 0 for the `iStation` parameter. I'll go into this a little further when I introduce you to the station side of the network routines.

Terminating a Session

The final responsibility of a host script is to terminate the session it has with the other stations. Fortunately, this is a simple task accomplished by using the `TalkHangUp` statement. By calling this statement and providing the handle to the host that is hanging up, you ensure that all of the stations are automatically notified that the host has severed connections. An example of what this might look like is:

```
TalkHangUp(hHost)  'Where hHost is a handle to the host
```

Note   Hosts and stations are responsible for handling unexpected events. What is specifically being referred to in this sense is dealing with run-time errors (a station or host that has disconnected, among other things). This is no different than any other test script. It should do its best to robustly handle unexpected situations.

The Station's Role

The station uses much of the same functionality as the host. Figure 16-3 shows some of the duties of the station.

In order for a station session to begin on a network, there must first be a host script running somewhere on that same network. If there is a host session available, the station can connect by using the `TalkCallHost` function. The station must know the name of the host session that is running, and pass that as the first parameter to `TalkCallHost()`. Like the host session, the station must also provide a pointer to a callback function so that messages sent to the station by the host (or because of actions taken by the host) can be processed by the station:

```
dim hHost&
    hHost = TalkCallHost("MainHost",varptr(AStationMsgHandler))
```

The `TalkCallHost` function returns a `LONG` value that is the handle to the host session. This handle is used when the station is working with the host (by sending it information), or when disconnecting from a host session.

The Station's Callback Routine

The station's callback routine is very similar to the style of routine used by the host. It takes the same parameters and processes the messages in the same fashion. However, the station can receive only two types of messages from the host: `TALK_DATA` and `TALK_HUNGUP`. A simple station script is shown in Listing 16-3.

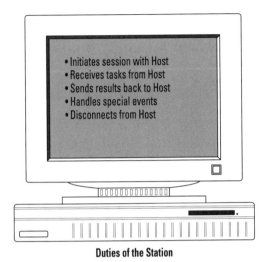

Duties of the Station

Figure 16-3: The station is responsible for contacting the host, receiving tasks from the host and carrying out those tasks, and returning results back to the host. It must also cleanly disconnect and terminate when the host severs the connection.

Listing 16-3: An example of the message handler for a station. This processes messages from the host.

```
sub AStationMsgHandler(iMsg%, hHost&, iStation%, lType&, _
                       vData AS VARIANT)
    print "Host #";hHost;" has ";
    select case(iMsg)
        case TALK_HUNGUP
            print "disconnected."
        case TALK_DATA
            print "sent data."
            'Extra code should be added here to determine the
            'type of data being sent and how to process that
            'data.
        case else
            'Unexpected message has been sent
    end select
end sub 'AStationMsgHandler
```

The `iMsg` parameter is one of the `TALK_` messages. The `hHost` parameter identifies from which host the information is coming (a station can connect to multiple hosts if it wants to). The `iStation` parameter is unused in this situation, since it is the station that is receiving the information. The `lType` parameter is a value defined and agreed upon by the host and station scripts. It identifies the type of data being sent. The `vData` parameter is the actual data that was sent by the host.

Some examples of constants that one might create for the `lType` variable are:

```
const DT_DISPLAY = 1    'Print the data sent in vData
const DT_TYPE    = 2    'Use the PLAY statement to type
const DT_FNAME   = 3    'vData contains a filename
const DT_NETLOC  = 4    'vData holds a network path
const DT_SENDLOG = 5    'Send current log file. (vData unused)
```

I used `DT_` to stand for data type, and also in part because Visual Test already has at least one constant relating to this that is defined in the language: `DT_NO_DATA` (which is equal to 0). The last constant in the example could be used as a request to the station by the host asking that the current log file be sent to it. In this example, `vData` isn't used. However, it might make sense to use `vData` to hold the network location where the host would like the log file placed. The point is that this is a flexible situation, where it is necessary for the host and station script writers to work together and agree upon a standard set of messages. Typically, a second `SELECT CASE` statement is used to process these different types of data, just as the `SELECT CASE` statement is used to process the different messages that can be sent.

Hanging Up

When a station has completed its tasks or is in a situation where it is decided that it should sever communications with the host, the `TalkHangUp` statement is used. When this statement is called by the station and the handle to a host is passed as the first and only parameter, the host with which the station was communicating receives a `TALK_HUNGUP` message, and the station is marked as inactive in the internal list kept by Visual Test. Any calls to the `TalkStationActive` function made by the host for a station that has hung up result in `FALSE` being returned, signifying that the station is no longer available.

The station can reconnect with a host session whenever it wants. When this happens, the station is assigned the same ID number it was using before, and the host can continue working with that station. Reconnecting with the station is accomplished through the same process as when originally connecting. The host will receive a `TALK_CONNECT` message, letting it know that a station is sending it a message, and the message is that it is available for processing tasks.

Waiting for Messages

Even though a station or host can be working on other tasks while it is awaiting messages from its counterpart, oftentimes the scripts for a station or host are much simpler — simpler in the sense that all they want to do is sit there and process messages from one another, assigning tasks when they can, and sending results back from those tasks.

In this situation, a method that can be used is putting the script to sleep until a message is received. This can be done using the SLEEP statement. Using this statement without a number after it will put the script to sleep indefinitely, awaking only when it receives a message. The result is that the only functioning portion of the host or station script is in the callback function. In the case of the station script, it might remain asleep or performing tasks until it receives a TALK_HUNGUP message. Upon receiving this message, it understands that the host is no longer available and that it can terminate its execution by using the END statement.

The host is less likely to be a script that will sleep. It will most likely be sending tasks off to any station that will make itself available, and then processing the results of those tasks as they come back. However, in the event of times when there is nothing for the host to do, it too can make use of the SLEEP statement.

Tip Some programmers prefer to check for other things while awaiting a call to the callback function. In these cases, they typically use a WHILE statement and simply loop, looking for whatever situation it is that they're looking for and awaiting a callback. In some situations the WHILE loop is executing so fast that a callback can't occur or interrupt the script. Therefore, in these situations it is a good idea to use a SLEEP .1 in the loop, so that it at least pauses for a fraction of a second. This was done in Chapter 13, when the SetTimer function was demonstrated for callback functions.

Synchronizing Scripts

One option available through the Talk routines is the ability for the stations to be synchronized by a host so that the tasks passed to the stations begin execution at roughly the same time. An example of when this might be useful in testing is in verifying database access and verifying that critical sections (such as record locking) are working as expected.

For synchronizing to work, the host must be informed by each station as to when it is ready and waiting for the signal from the host. This is done by each station calling the `TalkWaitSync` function. The result is the host receiving a `TALK_SYNC` message informing it as each station is awaiting the signal from the host. Another way for the host to determine how many stations are ready is for it to call the `TalkGetSyncCount` function. This function returns the number of stations that are awaiting the signal to begin the processing of the task.

Once the stations are all awaiting the signal, the host releases the stations from waiting, allowing each station to begin processing the tasks, by calling `TalkReleaseSync()`. The `TalkReleaseSync` function causes the `TalkWaitSync` function, which was called by each station, to return from the function call. If the result of the function call is `TRUE`, the station knows to move forward. If `FALSE` is returned, then the synchronization most likely timed-out or the host passed a `FALSE` to the `TalkReleaseSync` function notifying the station to abort. The station is free to attempt a resynchronization with the host if it so chooses.

Network Protocols

Windows 95 and 98 and Windows NT 4.0 and 5.0 support NetBEUI as their main NetBIOS-compatible protocols. NetBEUI (which stands for NetBIOS Extended User Interface) is the standard Windows protocol and is basically a superset of NetBIOS.

Another protocol available in Windows (and also considered the de facto standard in the UNIX world) is TCP/IP (Transmission Control Protocol over Internet Protocol)—two protocols at different layers working together across a network.

For information on installing these protocols and others that support NetBIOS, refer to your Windows documentation. Visual Test does support these protocols.

Note
The network routines that were available in previous versions of Visual Test were somewhat flaky and difficult to get to work when moving from network to network. Scripts that friends and I wrote worked perfectly on our standard Windows 3.1 network but failed when moving to a classroom that had the exact same simple network installed. Unfortunately, the versions of these routines introduced in Visual Test 4.0 (and unchanged in Visual Test 6.0) have inherited some of that flakiness and require some tweaking, experimentation, and patience to get some of the scripts to work. The latest version of the network routines are nonetheless more reliable and much easier to use.

Summary

The network procedures offer another level of automated testing such that the tester can run scripts on multiple machines at the same time. This is helpful when running the same scripts on multiple machine configurations for compatibility testing, and it is also helpful for simulating multiple users on a given application (for example, database access).

Two roles, that of the station and that of the host, are played to allow for running the different tasks, and for managing the tasks that are being passed to the multiple machines. Through this coordination, tasks can be dispatched and results collected from multiple machines running asynchronously. It is also possible to closely synchronize the tasks on multiple machines for the testing of mutual-exclusion situations, semaphores, and critical sections.

While capable and fairly straightforward to use, these procedures can be twitchy when moving from network to network. While they may run on one network protocol that supports NetBIOS, they may react differently on another protocol that also purports to support NetBIOS. While the situation can get frustrating, the feeling of accomplishment is very gratifying when the host and station scripts finally run and perform as expected.

✦   ✦   ✦

Testing Web Pages

The virtual world of the Internet is a huge place that allows for all kinds of possibilities in commerce, self-education, research, general sharing of information, and many other possibilities. I use the Internet daily and feel at a loss when I can't jump on the Internet.

The Internet has become an important part of communication for those of us in the software industry. It's become huge for those not in the software industry, too. Take the publisher of this book, for example. Because of the Internet, we were able to create this book without having to print out the manuscript. I would write a chapter, pack it and its figures into a compressed file, and e-mail it off to the editor. From there it would bounce around between the different reviewers until I got it back for a last look, without a single sheet of paper being printed. Incredible!

Another example is the medical industry, which is spending billions of dollars to move much of their information to the Internet so that many of their databases can be searched by the common user. Billions of dollars! They, like many others, are advertising their services by moving brochure-type information to Web servers.

With all kinds of companies and government agencies moving to the Internet, the need to create and test Web pages has exploded. Because of the huge number of Web sites on the Internet, and with the amount of information that is changing daily, the process is dynamic and *ongoing*. Concerns with the World Wide Web (WWW) have progressed beyond the simple problem of a broken link that causes a Web page not to be found. New kinds of controls that can be added to a Web page require testing, not to mention the forms that can be created and processed behind the scenes by the Web page's server. These are all aspects of testing Web pages that go beyond the simple HTML scripting and require a closer look by software quality assurance experts.

Web pages have changed from simple, formatted documents to more complicated pages that are as complex as many of the software products available from software development companies today. The complexities now found on Web sites require the same kinds of testing used on conventional software products (as well as coverage of a few new issues specific to the Internet).

As a result of the complexities of the Web, more than 140 new functions have been added to the Visual Test language. These new functions allow you to work with components on everything from the simplest Web pages on up to the more complex sites that support forms that process information entered by the person surfing the Web. These can range from entering an address to request a catalog to placing an order for a product from a company such as Amazon.com. These functions also allow you to test Microsoft ActiveX controls that have extended the capabilities — and thereby increased the testing complexities — of Web pages. The functions in the Test language that allow the user to work with these components and address these complexities are discussed in this chapter.

Along with new functionality comes new challenges. One of the biggest challenges when working with the Internet is the delay that may be encountered when accessing a site. This can be caused by a slow connection on the user's side, a slow server on the main Internet service provider's (ISP) site, or a slow link between the ISP and the server holding the Web pages being accessed. It is because of these latency issues that extra synchronization support needed to be provided. This support will be discussed in this chapter.

Tip   For a complete list of the Visual Test Web functions refer to Appendix A. Tables in the second part of this chapter list some of the functions relevant to this discussion.

A Question of Browsers

Rational Software had to make an important decision when it came to adding to Visual Test the new functionality that supports working with Web pages and their components. Should a generic approach be taken, allowing any browser to be used in the testing of HTML documents, or should a specific browser be chosen?

While the obvious answer might at first seem to be "generic browser," taking that approach would not have provided the developers of Visual Test the flexibility and control they would have if they relied on the functionality of a specific browser. Working closely with a browser's own object model — the way the browser tracks a Web page's information "under the hood" — the developers of Visual Test were able to provide more capable functionality. As a Test programmer, you benefit by this close link to a specific browser. Rational chose to work with Microsoft Internet Explorer 4.0 (IE 4.0) and above, most likely because of their close ties with Microsoft development teams.

Hypertext Markup Language

The Hypertext Markup Language (HTML) is a growing and evolving language. Attempts have been made to standardize HTML as much as possible through the formation of the World Wide Web Consortium (W3C), a global organization based in the United States at MIT (the Massachusetts Institute of Technology), in France at INRIA (Institut National de Recherche en Informatique et en Automatique), and in Japan at the Keio Research Institute. Despite the push to standardize, Microsoft and Netscape — the two biggest players in the world of browsers — have added their own spins to the language. Visual Test works with the general HTML 4.0 specification as documented at the W3C Web site (www.w3c.org). Because Visual Test works so closely with the innards of Microsoft Internet Explorer, Rational's tool can support some of Microsoft's browser-specific behaviors and functionality, such as working with ActiveX controls that are found on many Web sites today.

Note This chapter assumes that you have a general knowledge of HTML. This section gives a quick overview of the HTML language.

A Simple Page

Let's take a look at a simple HTML document as an example so that we can all be sure we're all on the same page. Figure 17-1 shows a fictitious Company Picnic Web announcement as it would be displayed in IE 4.0. This could be a page that appears on the company's internal *intranet* or on an external site visible to all who use the Internet.

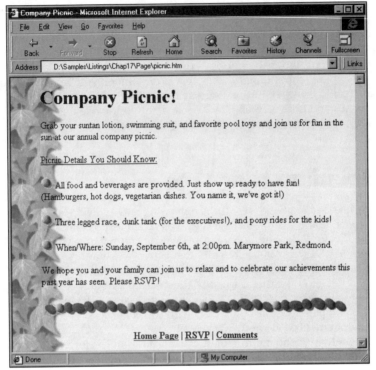

Figure 17-1: A simple example of a Web page

The source code that was used to create the Web page is shown in Listing 17-1. This is a good example of what many of the Web pages on the Internet look like. They contain a few graphics, a couple of links, and simple formatting that makes it easy to read.

Listing 17-1: **Source code for the Web page shown in Figure 17-1**

```
<HTML>

<HEAD>
<TITLE>Company Picnic</TITLE>
</HEAD>

<BODY LINK="#0000ff" BACKGROUND="Image1.gif">
<DIR>
```

```
<H1>Company Picnic!</H1>

<P>
Grab your suntan lotion, swimming suit, and favorite
pool toys and join us for fun in the sun at our annual
company picnic.
<P>
<U>Picnic Details You Should Know:</U>
<P>
<IMG SRC="Image2.gif" WIDTH=20 HEIGHT=19> All
food and beverages are provided. Just show up ready to
have fun! (Hamburgers, hot dogs, vegetarian dishes. You
name it, we've got it!)
<P>
<IMG SRC="Image2.gif" WIDTH=20 HEIGHT=19> Three
legged race, dunk tank (for the executives!), and
pony rides for the kids!
<P>
<IMG SRC="Image2.gif" WIDTH=20 HEIGHT=19> When/Where:
Sunday, September 6th, at 2:00pm. Marymore Park, Redmond.
<P>
We hope you and your family can join us to relax and to
celebrate our achievements this past year has seen. Please
RSVP!
<P>
<IMG SRC="Image3.gif" WIDTH=528 HEIGHT=30>
<P>
</DIR>

<CENTER>
<B><a href="http://www.vtindepth.com">Home Page</a>
 | <a href="mailto:lorin@inproduction.com">RSVP</a>
 | <a href="mailto:feedback@inproduction.com">Comments</a></B>
</CENTER>

</BODY>
</HTML>
```

This Web page and its accompanying graphics files (GIF files) can be found on the CD-ROM in \SAMPLES\LISTINGS\CHAP17\PAGE.

A (Very) Brief Look at HTML

A listing like the one shown in Listing 17-1 can be a bit intimidating to anyone who is new to HTML. As it turns out, HTML scripting is no big deal; it's just a matter of learning and remembering the elements that define HTML.

An HTML document is simply a text file that is interpreted by a program known as a *browser*. Browsers look through this text file and pick out HTML *elements* that help it understand how the author of the text file wanted the document displayed. These elements are defined by *tags*. Typically an element has start and end tags, but this isn't always the case, as will be shown later in the chapter.

One example of an element in Listing 17-1 is the *underline* tag. If the HTML script writer wanted a word or words to appear underlined, the code would resemble this:

```
<U>Picnic Details You Should Know:</U>
```

In this example, the *start tag* is the `<U>` and the *end tag* is the `</U>`. Together they define the *underline* or `<U>` *element*. The result is the following text displayed in the browser:

Picnic Details You Should Know:

Required elements

A browser knows that it is reading an HTML document when it encounters the `<HTML>` tag in the text file it is attempting to display. This tag surrounds the entire contents of the document, which means that the end tag—`</HTML>`—is the last line of the document.

Note   Hardcore HTML script writers will tell you that all HTML documents should begin with a `<!DOCTYPE>` indicator. This is what should be used when following strict HTML programming guidelines as defined by the W3C. I'm attempting to give a quick overview of HTML. I suggest that if you want to know HTML intimately, you should visit the W3C Web site at `www.w3c.org` or purchase an HTML reference.

The next element in an HTML document is the `<HEAD>` element, which is the top of the document. In addition to the title of the document (the title typically appears in the caption bar of the browser), other supplementary information can be defined with this element as well. In Listing 17-1 I've used the `<TITLE>` element to determine what appears in my browser's caption bar.

The next element is the `<BODY>`, which defines the beginning of the bulk of the HTML script that defines the document. The `<BODY>` start tag has a complementary end tag, which is `</BODY>`. In Listing 17-1 the `<BODY>` element has additional *attributes* as part of its start tag. The attributes help define how the element will affect the contents found between its start and end tags. In this example, it has `LINK="#0000ff"` and `BACKGROUND="Image1.gif"` as the only attributes. The `LINK` attribute defines what color an *anchor* or link to another HTML component or document should be. In this case it will be blue, since `0000ff` is the hexadecimal representation for blue in the RGB (red, green, blue) coloring scheme. The `BACKGROUND` attribute causes the graphic in the IMAGE1.GIF file to be displayed underneath any text found in the body of the document.

Caution   HTML is not WYSIWYG (What You See Is What You Get). It's what some people jok-ingly refer to as WYGIWYG (What You Get Is What You Get). A document that looks one way displayed in Microsoft Internet Explorer may look very different when dis-played in another browser, such as Netscape Navigator. When designing a Web page to be displayed to the masses, it's worth taking the time to view it in the products of the two most popular browser makers on the market—Microsoft and Netscape.

Other elements

Found toward the end of the document in Listing 17-1 is an element known as an *anchor,* or link. This element has a start tag of <A> and, as you may have guessed, an end tag of </A>. This element is used to navigate to another section of the current document or to jump to a completely new page. It can also be used to invoke other commands, such as initiating a file transfer session or sending electronic mail.

Note   While most elements have both start and end tags, a number of elements require only a single tag. For more details on exactly what all of those elements are, refer to the W3C Web page for the HTML definition document or purchase an HTML ref-erence from your local bookstore.

In Listing 17-1 the paragraph, or <P>, element optionally takes an end tag (</P>). There aren't many elements for which the end tag can be ignored without causing the entire document to be affected. For example, if the end tag is forgotten for the <B> element, the majority of the document, after the <B> tag, will appear in bold.

The image element allows graphics to be inserted into a document. It requires a single tag (<IMG>). It also takes additional attributes that identify the filename, width, and height of the image to be displayed.

Common attributes

As you will see when you look at an HTML reference, all kinds of attributes can be used with a given element. Note, though, that these attributes vary as widely as the elements that they affect and that not all attributes can be used within all elements.

There is a core set of attributes that are common to all elements and their tags. These are ID, CLASS, STYLE, and TITLE. While ID makes using the Visual Test Web functions much easier, the ID attribute isn't commonly used by HTML script writers. TITLE is used in some cases so that additional text is displayed (for example, on a graphic that is displayed in an HTML document), but it isn't always used consistently either. The CLASS and STYLE attributes aren't really useful when working with the new Web functions.

Note   This is a simplistic introduction to HTML that is aimed at making sure we are all using the same terms when working with the Visual Test functions. The key terms, again, are *element, tag,* and *attribute*.

Visual Test Web Functions

Visual Test's Web functionality can be broken up into three distinct components: general browser-related functions, element-specific functions, and generic functions. The element-specific functions make up the largest portion of the Visual Test Web functions. Before we dive into the specific functions, however, the concept of *context* needs to be addressed.

 Note   It is not my intention in this chapter to go through every single function that makes up the new Web functionality in Visual Test 6.0. The goal is to familiarize you with how they work in general in order to give you a base from which to explore further. Appendix A lists every single Web function, along with most of the other functions found in Visual Test. If you see something that promises to meet your needs, visit the Visual Test online documentation for specific details about it.

The Concept of Context

Every window in the Microsoft Windows operating system has a value associated with it so that the window can be referred to easily. This value is known as a *handle* and is the starting point used when working with a window or control. A similar concept exists for working with Web pages, and the term used in this case is *context*. The context helps the Web functions understand to which Web page a given action applies. This Web page can be displayed in a browser or in a frame within a browser.

Unlike the other Visual Test functions that assume that the currently active window is the implied handle, the Web functions require that the context be provided in each function call. Because there is no concept of focus in the world of Web pages — a fact that is especially noticeable in the case of a page with multiple frames — it is necessary to pass the context for each function call.

General Functions

The general functions listed here don't really fall into any single category. They are functions that allow for retrieving a context associated with a browser or frame, affecting navigation much as the controls on the IE 4.0 toolbar do. The general functions allow for starting or finding a browser and getting an identifier or *context* to that browser. These functions also allow for simple navigation from one Web page to another.

Getting a context

The first thing that must be done when working with Web pages is to identify which page is to be operated upon by the functions. This requires the acquisition of a context, which can be achieved in a number of ways.

The most frequently used method is through a call to the WebExplore function. This function takes a URL (universal resource locator) that identifies which Web page is to be displayed in a new instance of IE 4.0. An initial script that calls this function will look something like this:

```
dim strContext$
    strContext = WebExplore("http://www.visualtest.com")
```

Notice that a context is returned by the WebExplore function in the form of a string. This is what is then passed as the first parameter for all of the other Web functions. (If a call to WebExplore fails, however, an empty string [""] is returned.)

Another method for obtaining a context is to search for an existing browser or frame. This can be done through the WebFndBrowser and WebFndFrame functions. For example, let's assume that there is a browser already up and running (in this example it is displaying Rational Software's Web site), as shown in Figure 17-2.

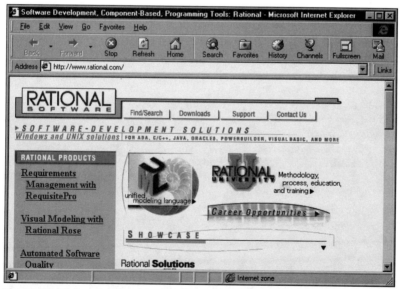

Figure 17-2: A context can be obtained from a browser that is already up and running, as shown in this example of a typical Web page.

Searching for a browser that is already up and running is very similar to searching for a window using the wFndWnd function. However, while wFndWnd returns a handle, WebFndBrowser returns a context:

```
dim strContext$
    strContext = WebFndBrowser("+Rational")
```

Tip   Working with IE 4.0–compliant *embedded* browsers requires an extra step. For the Web functions to work with an embedded browser, that browser must first load in the IEPAGE.HTM document that was copied to \VT6\SAMPLES\WEB when you installed Visual Test 6.0. Either that or place the following text into your Web page:

```
<OBJECT ID="IEH1prObj"
CLASSID="CLSID:CE7C3CF0-4B15-11D1-ABED-
709549C10000"></OBJECT>
```

The IEHELPER.DLL file must already be registered and available on your machine, which is done for you when Visual Test is installed. Using IEPAGE.HTM is not a required step for a standalone instance of IE 4.0. Because an embedded browser is surrounded by another program, Visual Test needs assistance in locating that browser. This <OBJECT> element provides that assistance.

Searching for Web Components

Searching for elements or objects on a Web page, or searching for a browser or frame, is done using methods very similar to the methods already used by other Visual Test routines when searching for a window or control. A control can be searched for by its full caption or partial caption, and the same holds true when working with the new Web functions. That is, searching for a browser that has "Software" as the prefix text (as is the case in Figure 17-2) is done by passing a tilde (~) as part of the string (as in, "~Software"). When searching for partial text, where a word or phrase must be a part of the caption, the plus (+) is used (as in, "+Rational"). Furthermore, a Web browser, frame, form, or element can be found using its ordinal position. For example, if the third anchor or link element (<A></A>) is to be clicked upon by the WebLinkClick function, the string "@3" would be passed as one of the parameters to the function. Dialog box controls all have a unique identifier (ID), and this can also be the case with HTML elements. That means that if an element is using the "ID=" attribute in the HTML script, this ID can be referred to when working with the Web functions. For example, if a link's HTML script had the following form:

```
<a href="http://www.rational.com/index.html" ID="Home">Main
page</a>
```

the Web function for clicking on that link would look like:

```
WebLinkClick(strContext, "#Home")
```

If you've read the previous chapters of this book regarding working with windows controls, you'll notice that the Web functions have adopted that same behavior. The main difference with IDs, however, is that IDs can be text when working with Web pages as opposed to numbers when working with windows controls.

Note

For a summary of how to control your search when working with the Web functions, type in the keywords **Search Summary** under the Search tab of the online help. You'll see such topics as WebActiveX Search Summary, WebFndBrowser Search Summary, WebForm Search Summary, and WebFormElement Search Summary, among others.

Similar to the WFndWnd function, the WebFndBrowser function has a class of flags that can be OR-ed together to control how the search takes place. For example, the WFndWnd function can be passed a flag called FW_FOCUS that will cause the window, when found, to activate. The WebFndBrowser function has a similar flag called FWEB_ACTIVATE, which will cause the same thing to happen to a browser.

Tip

It is still possible to use the WFndWnd function when searching for a browser. Remember, however, that WFndWnd returns a handle (number) to the window it finds. If you require a context to be returned, then you will need to use the WebFndBrowser function, which will return a context (string) instead of a handle.

A frame inside of a browser is found by using a function called WebFndFrame. This function requires that a context already be known for the browser in which the frame is displayed. In the instance of finding the second frame in a browser, the code will look something like this:

```
dim strContext$, strFrameContext$
    strContext = WebExplore("http://www.stlabs.com/testnet.htm")
    strFrameContext = WebFndFrame(strContext, "@2")
```

The return value for WebFndFrame is another context that is to be used specifically when working with frames.

Note

In the previous script example, if you were to print strContext and strFrameContext, you'd notice that the only difference in their values is that strFrameContext has ,@2 appended to the browser's context.

Caution

The context string is an internal Visual Test construct and does not have a documented format for public consumption. If you end up building your own context strings instead of using the functions provided, you could find your scripts breaking if Rational were to update how context strings are built.

Simple navigation

Now that you've got the context to the browser, you're ready to move forward and start having some fun. These first functions allow for simple navigation and are comparable to the Back and Forward buttons found on the IE 4.0 toolbar. There is also a function that allows you to specify a URL and is comparable to the Address line in IE 4.0 that allows the browser to be moved from one page to another.

WebNavigate takes a context so that it knows which browser it is working with, and a URL so that it knows where it is supposed to navigate to. The function takes the following form:

```
dim strContext$
    strContext = WebExplore("http://www.rational.com")
    WebNavigate(strContext, "http://www.vtindepth.com")
    WebNavigate(strContext, "http://www.stlabs.com")
```

Once you have moved from one site to another, the other two functions become useful. WebBack and WebForward also take a context and will, by default, move one step in the appropriate direction. They both have optional parameters that allow for specifying how many steps backward or forward the function should take. Continuing where the previous script left off, this would look like:

```
WebBack(strContext, 2)      'Moves back two steps
WebForward(strContext)      'Moves forward 1 step
WebForward(strContext, 1)   'Also moves forward 1 step
```

The final function in this section is WebQuit. I'm not sure if it's really considered a navigational function in any way other than that it puts an end to your navigating. WebQuit is what is called when you have finished working with a browser. Just as you should be tidy in closing down any programs you open during testing, or closing files you have opened, you should use similar care when working with instances of IE 4.0:

```
dim strContext$
    strContext = WebExplore("http://www.visualtest.com")
    'add your tests here
    WebQuit(strContext)
END
```

It's all in the timing

Working with Web pages is not very different from working with a very slow Windows application. Unless you're testing with local HTML documents, there tends to be a noticeable lag or *latency*. Because of this, there is a built-in timer allowing the Web functions enough time to locate a browser, frame, form, or element before giving an error that reflects the Test language's inability to find the requested item.

This is similar to the way the other Visual Test routines work in that there is a default timeout. In working with normal Windows controls, this is controlled by a call to the SetDefaultWaitTimeout function. In working with Web pages, a function called WebSetDefaultWaitTimeout provides similar control over how long Visual Test waits before reporting that it cannot find something. The default timeout is 10 seconds when working with the Web functions.

All of the Web functions have an optional `timeout` parameter, which is the last parameter in each function. It is there so that if the Test programmer wishes to override the timeout for a specific function, it can be done by supplying the timeout (in seconds) for that particular function call. If it isn't provided, it defaults to using 10 seconds, or whatever value was set via a call to `WebSetDefaultWaitTimeout`.

Tip There are occasions when the control is in sight and the Test language moves forward and begins clicking on an object. However, moving too fast can cause Internet Explorer problems and can result in an object not reflecting the expected results. If you find yourself having problems with controls not being selected as you'd expect, inserting a `SLEEP 1` statement just prior to the command will probably fix the problem. (You may want to experiment with the delay. One second may be too long in most situations.)

Element-Specific Functions

Each of the Web functions works with the start tag in a given element. Therefore these functions are sometimes referred to in the online documentation as *tag functions*. Most of the Hypertext Markup Language is represented in these functions. The program's designers did this because many of the HTML tags map directly to the Internet Explorer object model and allow Visual Test to return exactly what Internet Explorer is tracking beneath the surface of the application.

Let's look at the `WebLink*` functions as an example of element-specific Web functions. Table 17-1 lists all of the `WebLink*` functions and their parameters.

Planning for the Future

Rational was thinking ahead when it designed its Web functions and decided that, since it is HTML's nature to continue to grow, they needed to be ready to grow with it. The result is a set of generic functions that will work with existing elements and any new elements or tags introduced down the road. It's worth noting that although the generic functions can be used instead of the element-specific versions, you might actually see different results when comparing the two. As mentioned earlier, this is because the element-specific functions return what the IE 4.0 object model sees, and the generic functions use a more conservative approach to returning information so that they can be as flexible as possible.

The moral of this story is this: If the Test language has a function specific to the type of element with which you'd like to work, use it. Otherwise use the generic functions. (Of course, it's always worth trying both if you're not getting the behavior you really want.) Generic functions are discussed in the next section.

Table 17-1
The WebLink* Functions in the Test Language

Routine Name	Parameter List	Returns
WebLinkCount	(strContext$, timeout& = DEF_WAIT)	long
WebLinkExists	(strContext$, strLink$, timeout& = DEF_WAIT)	long
WebLinkInnerText	(strContext$, strLink$, timeout& = DEF_WAIT)	string
WebLinkTitle	(strContext$, strLink$, timeout& = DEF_WAIT)	string
WebLinkSetTitle	(strContext$, strLink$, strIn$, timeout& = DEF_WAIT)	
WebLinkHREF	(strContext$, strLink$, timeout& = DEF_WAIT)	string
WebLinkTarget	(strContext$, strLink$, timeout& = DEF_WAIT)	string
WebLinkClick	(strContext$, strLink$, timeout& = DEF_WAIT)	

Note   The term *link* is synonymous with what HTML calls an *anchor* (<A></A>) element.

Figure 17-3 shows another snapshot of the Rational Software Web site. Along the left side of its page are a number of links identified by the underlined words and sentences. Whether something is a link can be determined manually by moving the mouse over the words suspected to be links. In IE 4.0, if the mouse cursor changes from a cursor to a hand, you know you're over a link. This can also be determined by looking at the page's source and looking for all uses of the anchor element with the HREF attribute. For example:

```
<a href="/products/visualtest/">Rational Visual Test</a>
```

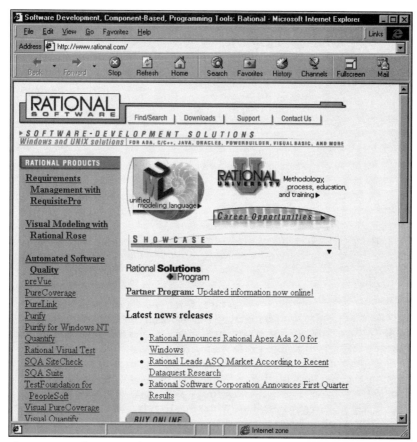

Figure 17-3: The Rational Software Web site is an example of a site with many links.

You can see all of the links on a given page programmatically by using the Test language. The script shown in Listing 17-2 begins by clearing the Developer Studio output window, grabs a context to the browser that is already running (shown in Figure 17-3), gets a count of how many links are on the page, and then steps through and prints each link individually, as shown in Figure 17-4.

Listing 17-2: Stepping through a page's links and printing them one by one

```
dim iLoop%, iCount%, strContext$, strText$
    viewport clear
    strContext = WebFndBrowser("+Rational", FWEB_ACTIVATE)

    iCount = WebLinkCount(strContext)

    for iLoop = 1 to iCount
        strText = WebLinkInnerText(strContext,_ord(iLoop))

        if (strText <> "") then
            print strText
        endif
    next iLoop
END
```

A number of things are worth noting about Listing 17-2. The first is that the WebLinkInnerText function—a function that returns the text between the <A> and </A> anchor tags, or the *inner text*—is making use of an *ordinal* to find each link. As is done with controls in a dialog box or menu items in a menu in other parts of the Test language, ordinals can also be used when locating a specific element on a Web page. If you're not familiar with the _ord macro, you may want to note that it is performing a "@"+trim$(str$(iLoop)) operation that converts the iLoop variable from a number to a string, trims off any extra white space, and prepends the '@' symbol, which is what, to Visual Test, identifies the number as an ordinal value.

Figure 17-4: Results of Listing 17-2 and printing out the inner text of each link on the Web page

Another notable thing about Listing 17-2 is that we're checking to make sure WebLinkInnerText has returned a string before attempting to print it. This is because some links are graphic images that don't have inner text associated with them.

Some But Not All

Something that can be confusing at first—but that you come to appreciate once you get the gist of it—is that there isn't a function call for every attribute of an element. Continuing along the lines of the WebLink* functions, we notice that there is a function for grabbing the TITLE attribute of a link. For example, the following HTML code is a link using the TITLE attribute:

```
<a href="http://www.vtindepth.com" title="VT InDepth">Visual
Test</a>
```

Assuming we have a legal context assigned to strContext, and assuming further that this is the first link on a page (and it therefore has an ordinal value of 1), this attribute can be retrieved via the Test language by using:

```
print WebLinkTitle(strContext, "@1")
```

But what about the other attributes such as HREF, NAME, ID, DIR, TARGET, and some of the other attributes an anchor element can have in its start tag? Well, some of them are provided, such as WebLinkHref and WebLinkTarget, for example. However, there are *not* functions called WebLinkName, WebLinkID, WebLinkDir, and so on.

Rational's approach to the question of whether to have a function for each attribute is a, well, *rational* approach. It comes back to the evolving nature of HTML. Rational made an educated guess, based on feedback from Beta users, as to which attributes were used most often. These were then turned into functions, and the rest of the attributes were left to be polled through the use of the more generic functions: the WebTag* functions. Grabbing the ID attribute from the <A> start tag, if the ID attribute exists, would be done like so:

```
print WebTagProperty(strContext, "@1", "A", "ID")
```

The concepts shown using the WebLink* functions are similar to the rest of the Web functions found in the Test language. The specific details of each function can be found in the online help. Table 17-2 shows the names of the element-specific functions. Appendix A lists every single function, including its parameter list and return value.

In Table 17-2 you'll notice that not all of the functions rely specifically on the start tag; some of them rely on the TYPE attribute. This happens specifically with the <INPUT> tag, which is an approach the creators of HTML took to working with controls on forms. I'm not really sure why they didn't just go ahead and create separate tags called <CHECKBOX>, <RADIO>, and so on, and instead overloaded the <INPUT> tag.

Table 17-2
Element-Specific Functions

Name	Purpose	Element
WebActiveX	ActiveX/OLE controls	<OBJECT>
WebCheckbox	Check box controls	<INPUT TYPE=CHECKBOX>
WebForm	Form tags	<FORM>
WebHidden	Hidden control	<INPUT TYPE=HIDDEN>
WebImage	Image tags	<IMG>
WebInputImage	Input image	<INPUT TYPE=IMAGE>
WebInputText	Text control	<INPUT TYPE=TEXT>
WebLabel	Label tags	<LABEL>
WebLink	Anchor or link tags	<A>
WebPassword	Password control	<INPUT TYPE=PASSWORD>
WebRadio	Radio/option buttons	<INPUT TYPE=RADIO>
WebReset	Form Reset button	<INPUT TYPE=RESET>
WebSelect	Select tag	<SELECT>
WebSelectOption	Options in a select tag	<OPTION>
WebSubmit	Form Submit button	<INPUT TYPE=SUBMIT>
WebTable	Tables, rows, and cells	<TABLE>
WebTextArea	Multiline Textbox	<TEXTAREA>

I'm guessing that's what happens when you have a language that continues to evolve. You find these inconsistencies. Take the <TEXTAREA> element, for example. Why does HTML have a separate tag for that type of control on a Web page instead of having TEXTAREA as yet another TYPE used in the <INPUT> tag?

Generic Functions

The final set of functions act as a catch-all for attributes or properties of an element or tag not supported directly through the Web functions. They also provide forward compatibility as HTML continues to evolve. Each of the generic functions begins with WebTag*, and all of them are listed in Table 17-3. Generic functions can be used for tags that don't have functions specific to a given element type.

Table 17-3
Generic Functions Used for Tags

Name	Purpose
WebTagCount	Determines how many of the specified tag exist on the page.
WEBTagExists	Determines whether a particular tag type exists on the page.
WebTagHTML	Returns the HTML tag for an end-all, be-all way to grab information.
WebTagInnerText	Returns the text found between the start and end tags.
WebTagMoveTo	Moves the mouse cursor over the top of the specified tag.
WebTagProperty	Gets the specified attribute's value from a given tag.
WebTagSetHTML	Allows the HTML of a tag to be set.
WebTagSetInnerText	Sets the text found between the start and end tags.
WebTagSetProperty	Sets (if it can be set) the specified attribute's value for a given tag. (Whether or not an attribute can be set is controlled by IE 4.0.)

Note In addition to getting the values of attributes in the start tag, it is also possible to set the values of some of those attributes. Doing so will only change the values in the page as it is displayed in your browser. Navigating to another page or reloading the current page will cause the browser to be refreshed and any setting changes you have made to be lost.

Similar to the functions having to do with elements on a form, there are generic functions for existing and future controls. These are shown in Table 17-4.

Note When working with elements on a form, note that an extra parameter exists for identifying which form the element exists on. The identifier for the form is similar to how other elements of a Web page are identified. This can be done by ordinal position, by NAME attribute, or by the ID attribute, which must be a part of the <FORM> start tag.

Table 17-4
Generic Functions for Working with Controls on a Form

Name	Purpose
WebInputElementClick	Clicks on the specified element (actually generates a click message as opposed to just setting its attribute).
WebInputElementEnabled	Determines whether the element is grayed or available for input.
WEBInputElementExists	Returns TRUE if the element exists, FALSE if not.
WebInputElementProperty	Allows an attribute in a form element to be gotten.
WebInputElementSetEnabled	Sets the element to enabled or disabled.
WebInputElementSetProperty	Allows setting an attribute in a form element.
WebInputElementSetState	Allows the check box or radio button to be set to on or off (different from a click).
WebInputElementState	For check boxes and radio buttons, returns whether the button is on or off.
WebInputElementTitle	Returns the title of the specified element, if any.
WebInputElementType	Returns the type of the specified form element.
WebInputElementValue	Returns the value held by the element, if any.

Synchronizing Events

Although the Web functions themselves synchronize clicking on the elements of a Web page to a certain degree, you may need to be a little more certain as to whether a Web page is ready for testing.

The current functions will first attempt to find a control for up to the default value of 10 seconds, or whatever time limit has been set through the use of the WebSetDefaultWaitTimeout function. If the control appears before the 10 seconds have elapsed, the function carries out its action and the execution of the Test script continues. If the control isn't found within the waiting period, however, a run-time error message will be generated explaining that the object could not be found.

In the event the standard approach to synchronizing your Web functions with the currently loaded page, or a page that is in the process of being loaded, can't be used, there are three events by which you can be notified: WEBLOADBEGIN, WEBLOADCOMPLETE, WEBLOADREADY:

✦ WEBLOADBEGIN is a notification that is sent to a Visual Test script if it was enabled using the ON CALL statement. This notification occurs when the IE 4.0 browser begins to load a new Web page.

✦ WEBLOADREADY is a notification that is sent when the browser has loaded enough of the page that it can be acted upon. An example is when loading a Web page with a lot of large graphics files. While the graphics themselves may not have completed loading, the other links on the page can be clicked upon.

✦ WEBLOADCOMPLETE is sent when the page has fully loaded into the browser, including any large graphics on it.

These notifications are exactly like the notifications discussed in Chapter 13. Listing 17-3 is an example of a script using the ON CALL statement with the WEBLOADCOMPLETE notification.

Listing 17-3: Using the WEBLOAD* notifications is simple

```
dim strContext$
on webloadcomplete (strContext) call PageLoaded

    strContext = WebExplore("http://www.rational.com")
    sleep
END

sub PageLoaded (notification_data as variant)
    pause "Page loaded!"
    print "Data: "+notification_data
end sub
```

In Listing 17-3 the notification is started through a call to the ON CALL statement using the WEBLOADCOMPLETE notification name. In this case, I'm supplying strContext so that the notification occurs only for the browser I run via the WebExplore function. If I didn't supply the strContext, then the notification would occur for every browser that I had running on my system.

The next line in Listing 17-3 is the SLEEP statement. Because there isn't a value provided after the SLEEP statement, it will pause the script until the script is stopped by the user. From then on, every time the browser navigates to another page, the PageLoaded function is called. This occurs only when the page has completely loaded itself. When the PageLoaded function does get called, it displays a simple message box that says "Page loaded!" and then writes out the data that was sent to the function by the notification. The value that is sent back is the URL for the page that is currently loaded and displayed.

Note For more information on using notification handlers refer to Chapter 13.

Summary

In this chapter we took a quick look at the Hypertext Markup Language and how the new Web functions in Visual Test can be used for testing Web pages. This chapter assumes that you have a knowledge of HTML scripting and further assumes you have experience in using all other aspects of the Visual Test language.

The Web functions were listed in three major categories: General, element-specific, and generic functions. The general functions allow for starting or finding a browser and getting an identifier or *context* to that browser. These functions also allow for simple navigation from one Web page to another. The element-specific functions allow for working with specific start tags in the HTML language along with some of their most common attributes. The generic functions allow for getting (and setting) other attributes in known tags and in working with future elements introduced in the HTML language.

The last section of this chapter looked at using notifications for determining when a Web page begins loading, is ready to be utilized, or has completed its loading process. Although the Web functions have synchronization code built into them, it may be necessary to have more information as to when a page is ready for testing. These notifications provide that kind of information.

✦   ✦   ✦

Visual Test Language Reference

The purpose of this language reference appendix is not to list all of the details of the Visual Test language that you can find in the online help. It is meant to give you a quick reference to the language keywords and their syntax. If you're unfamiliar with exactly what they do, type the function/statement name into a new or existing Visual Test file in the Developer Studio editor, click on that keyword, and press the F1 key to access context-sensitive help. This will give you more detailed information.

Consider this a high-level view that you can turn to when you know what the function does but you can't remember the order of the parameters. Or when you're not really sure what's in the language and need a list of keywords to look through to help you find what you're looking for, this is the place to come as well.

This appendix is broken into two sections. The "Core Test Language" section lists the basic routines and components that make up the BASIC-like language of Visual Test. The "Control APIs" section lists those parts of the language that work specifically with the interface components of an application.

Core Test Language

The Test Language consists of operators, constants, variable types, predefined structures, control structures, and simple statements.

Operators

These operators are used in the Test language for arithmetic, bitwise, and Boolean operations.

	Table A-1 **Test Language Operators**	
Type of Operator	*Operator*	*Description*
Arithmetic	–	Subtraction (or negates the number)
Arithmetic	*	Multiplication
Arithmetic	/	Floating-point division
Arithmetic	\	Integer division
Arithmetic	+	Adds numbers or concatenates strings
Arithmetic	mod	Modulus (integer)
Bitwise	AND	Bits set to 1 and AND-ed with 1 will result in 1 result
Bitwise	NOT	Bits toggled from 0 to 1 or vice versa
Bitwise	OR	Results in 1 if either of the compared bits is a 1.
Bitwise	XOR	Similar to OR. Two 1s compared result in 0, however.
Logical	AND	Values on each side of the AND must result in TRUE to result in a final result of TRUE.
Logical	NOT	Binary operator that negates the Boolean value. If FALSE, using NOT changes it to TRUE.
Logical	OR	Either one of the values on either side of the OR must result in TRUE to cause a final TRUE result.
Relational	<	Less than
Relational	<=	Less than or equal to
Relational	<>	Not equal
Relational	=	Equal
Relational	>	Greater than
Relational	>=	Greater than or equal to

Constants

These constants are predefined in the Test language for use with the Test language's intrinsic functions.

Note Numbers shown with "&h" preceding the value denote a hexidecimal value.

Caution Those values designated as "(undocumented)" should be used with caution. If a constant is undocumented, then it may very possibly disappear in future versions of Visual Test.

Table A-2 Timeout Values		
Constant	**Value**	**Description**
DEF_WAIT	-2	Timeout: Causes the control API to wait the default wait timeout. Not providing a value in the optional parameter causes this to happen anyway. This is probably why it's undocumented. **(Undocumented.)**
FOREVER	-1	Timeout: Causes the function to wait forever. Each control function can take an optional parameter that determines how long the function waits before giving an error if the control can't be found. **(Undocumented.)**

Table A-3 Checkbox States		
Constant	**Value**	**Description**
CHECKED	1	Value used with functions for setting a checkbox state or in determining the current state of a checkbox control
GRAYED	2	Value used with functions for setting a checkbox state or in determining the current state of a checkbox control
UNCHECKED	0	Value used with functions for setting a checkbox state or in determining the current state of a checkbox control

Table A-4
Coordinate and Size Parameters (wDesktop*, wTreeClk, and wViewClk Functions)

Constant	Value	Description
W_CENTER	&h7FFFFFFE	Center of the control
W_DEFAULT	&h7FFFFFFD	No change in the size parameter
W_SPACE	&h7FFFFFFF	Dead space in treeview and listview controls

Table A-5
Display Flags for wDisplayInfo and wMenuDisplayInfo

Constant	Value	Description
DI_CLIPBOARD	8	Display flags for wDisplayInfo and wMenuDisplayInfo
DI_DIALOG	1	Display flags for wDisplayInfo and wMenuDisplayInfo
DI_VIEWPORT	4	Display flags for wDisplayInfo and wMenuDisplayInfo

Table A-6
Flags for the wFndWnd* Functions

Constant	Value	Description
FW_ACTIVE	&h00000008	Searches through the active window's children.
FW_ACTIVE_ONLY	&h00008000	Searches only for the active window.
FW_ALL	&h00000000	Searches through all windows. (Default.)
FW_AMPERSAND	&h00000000	Ampersands in the caption are not optional and must be included as part of the search string. (This is different from how other functions work in that they ignore the ampersand, which usually specifies a direct access method key.) (Default.)
FW_AMPERSANDOPT	&h00000100	Allows the ampersand not to be included as part of the search string.

Constant	Value	Description
FW_CASE	&h00000004	The search string's upper- and lowercase characters must match exactly those in the caption.
FW_CHILDNOTOK	&h00000020	Only top-level windows are included in the search.
FW_CHILDOK	&h00000000	Looks through all windows including MDI (multiple document interface), child, and top-level windows. **(Default.)**
FW_DEFAULT	&h00000000	Using this flag by itself is the same as not passing a value in optional *flag* parameter in the wFndWnd* functions. Essentially FW_DEFAULT is equal to all flags that have a 0 value (FW_NOERROR, FWDIALOGOK, FW_NOIGNOREFILE, FW_AMPERSAND, FW_EXIST, FW_CHILDOK, FW_HIDDENNOTOK, FW_ALL, FW_NOCASE, FW_FULL, FW_NOFOCUS).
FW_DIALOG	&h00001000	Finds only those dialog boxes with the #32770 class (a "true" windows dialog box).
FW_DIALOGOK	&h00000000	Dialog boxes are included in the search for windows. **(Default.)**
FW_ERROR	&h00002000	Will cause a run-time error to be generated if the window isn't found.
FW_EXIST	&h00000000	Causes the function to search until the timeout (default or user-specified) time is reached or the window is found. **(Default.)**
FW_FI	(see notes)	Combination of FW_FOCUS and FW_IGNOREFILE flags. **(Undocumented.)**
FW_FOCUS	&h00000001	Causes the window, when found, to receive the focus.
FW_FP	(see notes)	Combination of FW_FOCUS and FW_PART functionality. **(Undocumented.)**
FW_FULL	&h00000000	Requires a full match on the caption in order to result in the window being found. **(Default.)**
FW_HIDDENNOTOK	&h00000000	Invisible/hidden windows are excluded from the search. **(Default.)**

(continued)

Table A-6 (continued)

Constant	Value	Description
FW_HIDDENOK	&h00000010	Includes hidden/invisible windows in the search.
FW_IGNOREFILE	&h00000200	Allows the search to exclude the filename portion of the caption.
FW_IGNOREFILE_LEFT	&h00010000	Causes the left portion of the caption to be ignored in the search (useful in situations such as those where programs have a hyphen "-" that separates the window caption from the filename that is displayed as part of that caption).
FW_IGNOREFILE_RIGHT	(see notes)	Same value as FW_IGNOREFILE (assumes filename appears to the right of the hyphen character "-").
FW_MAXIMIZE	&h00000800	If the window is found, it will be maximized.
FW_MINIMIZE	&h00000400	If the window is found, it will be minimized.
FW_NOCASE	&h00000000	The search is case-insensitive. **(Default.)**
FW_NOERROR	&h00000000	A run-time error will not be generated if the window isn't found. **(Default.)**
FW_NOEXIST	&h00000040	Causes the function to wait until the timeout (default or user-specified) interval is reached or the window ceases to exist.
FW_NOFOCUS	&h00000000	If no flag is specified, it is assumed that no focus should be given to the window when it is found. **(Default.)**
FW_NOIGNOREFILE	&h00000000	Causes the entire window caption to be part of the search, even if it includes the filename in that caption's text. **(Default.)**
FW_PART	&h00000002	Allows for a partial caption match to result in the window being found.
FW_PREFIX	&h00004000	Causes the search to look for a caption with a prefix specified by the function's search string.
FW_RESTORE	&h00000080	Causes the window to be restored from a maximized or iconized state.
FW_RESTOREICON	(see notes)	Same value as FW_RESTORE

Table A-7
Values for wGetWndPos* Functions

Constant	Value	Description
W_ABSOLUTE	FALSE	Causes use of the screen as the upper-left origin.
W_RELATIVE	TRUE	Causes the use of coordinates relative to the parent window's upper-left corner.

Table A-8
Listview Control Display Mode Values

Constant	Value	Description
LVS_ICON	0	WviewMode: Value returned by wViewMode representing the the Listview control's display mode. 0 means that it is in icon format.
LVS_LIST	3	WviewMode : Value returned by wViewMode representing the the Listview control's display mode. 3 means that it is in a list format.
LVS_REPORT	1	WviewMode: Value returned by wViewMode representing the the Listview control's display mode. 1 means that it is in a report format.
LVS_SMALLICON	2	WviewMode: Value returned by wViewMode representing the the Listview control's display mode. 2 means that it is in a small icon format.

Table A-9
Mouse Button Specifiers

Constant	Value	Description
VK_LBUTTON	1	Specifies the *left* mouse button in functions that allow the Test programmer to identify which button is to be used during the click.
VK_MBUTTON	4	Specifies the *middle* mouse button in functions that allow the Test programmer to identify which button is to be used during the click.
VK_RBUTTON	2	Specifies the *right* mouse button in functions that allow the Test programmer to identify which button is to be used during the click.

Table A-10
MSAA Constants

Constant	Value	Description
FAA_SELFLAG_ADDSELECTION	&h00000008	Object will take input focus and become the selection anchor.
FAA_SELFLAG_DEFAULT	(see notes)	FAA_SELFLAG_TAKEFOCUS and FAA_SELFLAG_TAKESELECTION combined.
FAA_SELFLAG_EXTENDSELECTION	&h00000004	To include the object, the current selection will be logically extended.
FAA_SELFLAG_NONE	&h00000000	Same result as if no flags are passed at all **(Default.)**
FAA_SELFLAG_REMOVESELECTION	&h00000010	Current object will be removed from the selection.
FAA_SELFLAG_TAKEFOCUS	&h00000001	Object will take the input focus and become the selection anchor.
FAA_SELFLAG_TAKESELECTION	&h00000002	Object becomes the only selected object.

Table A-11
Option (Radio) Button States

Constant	Value	Description
NOTSELECTED	0	Option button (also known as radio button) value
SELECTED	1	Option button (also known as radio button) value

Table A-12
Treeview Control Expansion States

Constant	Value	Description
COLLAPSED	0	Tree view item expansion states
EXPANDED	1	Tree view item expansion states
EXPANDEDPARTIAL	2	Tree view item expansion states

<table>
<tr><td colspan="3" align="center">Table A-13
WebFndBrowser Constants</td></tr>
<tr><td>Constant</td><td>Value</td><td>Description</td></tr>
<tr><td>FWEB_ACTIVATE</td><td>&h00000001</td><td>If the browser is found, it will be made active.</td></tr>
<tr><td>FWEB_CASE</td><td>&h00000004</td><td>The search done on the browser's caption is case-sensitive.</td></tr>
<tr><td>FWEB_DEFAULT</td><td>&h00000000</td><td>When passed with no other flags, the default settings are used. (Default.)</td></tr>
<tr><td>FWEB_ERROR</td><td>&h00002000</td><td>Instructs the function to return a run-time error if the browser is not found.</td></tr>
<tr><td>FWEB_EXIST</td><td>&h00000000</td><td>Searches for the existence of a browser. If one isn't found, it will wait up to the default wait timeout. (Default.)</td></tr>
<tr><td>FWEB_FULL</td><td>&h00000000</td><td>Requires a full match on the caption in order to result in the window being found. (Default.)</td></tr>
<tr><td>FWEB_MAXIMIZE</td><td>&h00000800</td><td>If the window is found, it will be maximized.</td></tr>
<tr><td>FWEB_MINIMIZE</td><td>&h00000400</td><td>If the window is found, it will be minimized.</td></tr>
<tr><td>FWEB_NOACTIVATE</td><td>&h00000000</td><td>If specified, it is assumed that the browser should not be activated if found. (Default.)</td></tr>
<tr><td>FWEB_NOCASE</td><td>&h00000000</td><td>The search is case-insensitive. (Default)</td></tr>
<tr><td>FWEB_NOERROR</td><td>&h00000000</td><td>A run-time error will not be generated if the window isn't found. (Default.)</td></tr>
<tr><td>FWEB_NOEXIST</td><td>&h00000040</td><td>Causes the function to wait until the timeout (default or user-specified) time is reached or the window ceases to exist.</td></tr>
<tr><td>FWEB_NONAME</td><td>&h00040000</td><td>Search does not include the <name> tag.</td></tr>
<tr><td>FWEB_NOTITLE</td><td>&h00020000</td><td>Search does not include the <title> tag.</td></tr>
<tr><td>FWEB_PART</td><td>&h00000002</td><td>A partial match of the caption is allowed.</td></tr>
<tr><td>FWEB_PREFIX</td><td>&h00004000</td><td>Causes the search to look for a caption with a prefix specified by the function's search string.</td></tr>
<tr><td>FWEB_RESTORE</td><td>&h00000080</td><td>If the browser is iconized, the window is restored when found.</td></tr>
</table>

Variables

All computer languages require the use of variables: containers that hold a value that can change during the course of the execution of a program. This section identifies the types of variables that can be declared in Visual Test along with how to carry out those declarations.

Table A-14
The Basic Types in the Test Language

Type	Description
CALLBACK	Stores an address of a function. (Refer to the advanced chapters of this book for examples on how to use POINTERs and CALLBACKs.)
DOUBLE	Positive or negative floating-point number (has fractional part). 64 bits (8 bytes) in size, a DOUBLE can range from -1.7×10^{308} to 1.7×10^{308}. DOUBLEs are accurate to approximately 15 decimal places.
INTEGER	Positive or negative whole number. 16 bits (2 bytes) in size, an INTEGER can range from $-32{,}768$ to $32{,}767$. Has no fractional part.
LONG	Positive or negative INTEGER that is 32 bits (4 bytes) in size. Can hold values ranging from $-2{,}147{,}483{,}648$ to $2{,}147{,}483{,}647$.
POINTER	Stores an address to another data type. POINTERs are 4 bytes in size.
SHORT	Same as type INTEGER.
SINGLE	Positive or negative floating-point number (has fractional part). 32 bits (4 bytes) in size, a SINGLE can range from -3.4×10^{308} to 3.4×10^{308}. SINGLEs are accurate to approximately 7 decimal places.
STRING	Stores a variable-length sequence of ASCII characters. This variable type will automatically adjust its size depending on the size of the sequence (string) of characters.
STRING *	Similar to a STRING type, except the size is permanently set.
VARIANT	Variable type that is initially undetermined (empty) and assumes the type of the value assigned to it. The variable can retype itself as different types of values are assigned to it.

Note The SHORT data type is a leftover from the Microsoft Test 3.0 days when Test 3.0 ran on both 16- and 32-bit operating systems. An INTEGER type would fluctuate in size depending on the operating system Microsoft Test was being run on. A SHORT was guaranteed to stay at 16 bits.

Declaring variables

Variables can be declared using the DIM statement. It uses the following syntax:

```
DIM variable [(subscripts)][ AS type][, variable
[(subscripts)][ AS type]] …
```

where variable is the name of a variable being defined. The subscripts define the size (dimension) of an array of variables.

Table A-15
Shorthand Notation for Declaring Variables

Type	Shorthand	Example
DOUBLE	#	dim Y#, Z#
INTEGER	%	dim M%
LONG	&	dim N&
POINTER	n/a	dim ptrNum as POINTER to INTEGER
SHORT	%	dim X%
SINGLE	!	dim avgVal!
STRING	$	dim strName$
STRING *	n/a	dim strAddr as STRING * 20
VARIANT	n/a	dim valUnknown as VARIANT

A longhand form of declaration can also be used for INTEGER, SHORT, LONG, SINGLE, DOUBLE, and STRING, such as:

```
Dim M as INTEGER
```

User-defined types

A user-defined type is created using the base set of types provided in the Test language.

```
TYPE user-defined-type-name
    declaration-list
END TYPE
```

Example:

```
'Defining the user-defined type
TYPE TESTINFO
    strTestDescr as STRING * 25
    iPassed as INTEGER
END TYPE

'Declaring an array of 10 elements of type TESTINFO
DIM tiTests(10) as TESTINFO

'Using the user-defined type
tiTests(1).strTestDescr="Verify boundary cases"
tiClass(1).iPassed=FALSE
'And so on…
```

Predefined structures

Visual Test contains some of its own predefined, user-defined data structures.

Window Size and Position Structures

```
type WNDPOS
    wLeft    as long
    wTop     as long
end type

type WNDSIZ
    wWidth   as long
    wHeight  as long
end type

type WNDPOSSIZ
    wLeft    as long
    wTop     as long
    wWidth   as long
    wHeight  as long
end type
```

wMenuGetInfo Structure

```
type MENUINFO
    nID          as long
    nIndex       as long
    nStyle       as long
    nPopup       as long
    fEnabled     as long
    fGrayed      as long
    fChecked     as long
    fString      as long
    fBitmap      as long
    FullText     as string
    Text         as string
    Accelerator  as string
end type
```

wDisplayInfo Structure

```
type INFO
    hwnd    as long
    Id      as long
    ALeft   as long
    ATop    as long
    ARight  as long
    ABottom as long
    RLeft   as long
    RTop    as long
    RRight  as long
    RBottom as long
    wWidth  as long
    wHeight as long
    Style   as long
    Ordinal as long
    Visible as long
    Enabled as long
    Text    as string
    Class   as string
    Module  as string
    Label   as string
    VTClass as string
end type
```

aaDisplayInfo Structure

```
type AAINFO
    ObjectId    as string
    ObjName     as string
    Role        as string
    State       as string
    Value       as string
    Desc        as string
    Help        as string
    Shortcut    as string
    Action      as string
    hwnd        as long
    ChildCount  as long
    ObjPosition as WNDPOS
    ObjSize     as WNDSIZ
end type
```

OleCtlDisplayInfo Structures

```
type OLECTL_HITTEST
    pt         as POINT
    rc         as RECT
    ctlName    as string
    ctlClass   as string
    ctlCaption as string
    ctlOrdinal as long
    ctlVTClass as string
end type

type OLECTL_PROPERTY
    propName   as string
    propValue  as variant
end type
```

WebGetInfo Structure

```
type WEBINFO
    Id            as string
    NameAttribute as string
    URL           as string
    Title         as string
    Tag           as string
    Ordinal       as string
```

```
      Label         as string
      Target        as string
      Context       as string
      AbsCoord      as string
      RelCoords     as string
end type
```

Control Structures

A control structure lets you control the flow of the program as it executes. This can be done with conditional branching, as with the IF/THEN statement, or through looping using WHILE, DO/UNTIL, and FOR/NEXT. GOTO is an unconditional way to control the flow of a program.

DO ... LOOP Statement

```
DO [WHILE|UNTIL] condition
[one-or-more-statements]
LOOP
```

FOR ... NEXT Statement

```
FOR index=begin TO end [STEP increment]
[one-or-more-statements]
[EXIT FOR]
NEXT [index]
```

FOR ... IN FILELIST ... NEXT Statement

```
FOR filename [,attributes] IN FILELIST [SORTED BY [NAME |
EXTENSION]]
[one-or-more-statements]
[EXIT FOR]
NEXT [filename]
```

GOTO Statement

```
GOTO label
```

IF ... THEN Statement

```
IF condition THEN
    one-or-more-statements
[ELSEIF condition THEN
    one-or-more-statements
...]
[ELSE
    one-or-more-statements]
ENDIF
```

SELECT CASE Statement

```
SELECT CASE condition
[CASE expression
[one-or-more-statements]
...]
[CASE ELSE
[one-or-more-statements]
]
END SELECT
```

WHILE ... WEND Statement

```
WHILE condition
[one-or-more-statements]
WEND
```

File Commands

```
EXISTS(filespec$ [,attributes$])
FILELIST [ADD|REMOVE] filename$ [,attributes$][, RECURSIVE]
FILELIST CLEAR
FILELIST REFRESH
KILL filename$
MKDIR pathname$
NAME currentname$ AS newname$
RMDIR pathname$
RUN(filename$)
RUN filename$[,NOWAIT[,showcommand]][PURIFY|QUANTIFY|COVERAGE]
SHELL commandline$
SPLITPATH filepath$,drive$,directory$,filename$,extension$
```

File I/O

```
EOF(filenumber%)
GET [#]filenumber%,[recordnum%], varname
LINE INPUT #filenumber%, varname$
LOC(filenumber%)
LOF(filenumber%)
OPEN filename$ [FOR mode] AS [#]filenumber% [LEN=record-
length%]
PRINT #filenumber%,[expression[;|,][expression[;|,]]…]
PUT [#]filenumber%,[recordnum%],varname
SEEK(filenumber%)
SEEK filenumber%,position%
```

Output

```
ECHO [ON|OFF]
PRINT [expression[;|,][expression[;|,]]…]
```

Math Functions

Visual Test's language has a number of math-related intrinsic functions.

Table A-16	
Math-Related Functions Intrinsic to the Test Language	
Function	*Description*
ABS	Returns an absolute value.
ATN	Returns the arc-tangent value.
CDBL	Converts a number to a type DOUBLE.
CINT	Converts a number to a type INTEGER.
CLNG	Converts a number to a type LONG.
COS	Returns the cosine of an angle.
CSNG	Converts a number to a type SINGLE.
EXP	Returns natural logarithm e raised to the power specified.
LOG	Returns the natural log.
SIN	Returns the sine of an angle.
SQR	Returns the square root.
TAN	Returns the tangent of an angle.

Syntax for User-Defined Subroutines and Functions

When a section of your Test script is used more than once, you typically place it in a subroutine or function instead of just copying and pasting the block of code over and over again. Functions return a value (that can be ignored), and subroutines don't return a value.

Subroutine and function declarations

Before a function or subroutine can be used it must first be declared. This can be for a function written by the Test programmer, or it can link into a DLL ("LIB").

```
DECLARE SUB subname [STDCALL | CDECL | BASIC][LIB libname
[ALIAS "aliasname"]](parameter-list)]
DECLARE FUNCTION funcname [STDCALL | CDECL | BASIC][LIB libname
[ALIAS "aliasname"]](parameter-list)] AS datatype
```

Subroutine and function definitions

Once declared, if a function or subroutine is not being linked to in a DLL, it must be defined. The definition of a function or subroutine contains the actual code that gets executed when the routine is called.

```
[STATIC] SUB subname [(parameter-list)]
one-or-more-statements
END SUB

[STATIC] FUNCTION funcname [(parameter-list)] AS datatype
one-or-more-statements
END FUNCTION
```

Control APIs

Remember that this appendix is not here to replace online help; it is only meant to provide you with a list of those items that combine to create the Test language. If you're trying to recall the name of a function or perhaps the number and types of parameters it takes, this is the appendix to turn to. For more information on each of these functions or subroutines refer to the Rational Visual Test 6.0 online documentation.

Note Routines that show a return value (for example, "as long") at the end of the declaration are functions. Those that don't show a return value are subroutines.

Caution Routines that are undocumented may disappear from future versions of Visual Test. I have not had time to explore what many of these undocumented functions do. Proceed with caution.

Caution This section lists everything in the Test language, including those routines that have been marked as obsolete in the online documentation. Note that these routines may disappear in future versions of Visual Test.

Tip Many of the undocumented functions are undocumented for a reason. I figured I'd list them just because it's kind of cool to find hidden treasures like these. However, I strongly advise against bothering Rational Technical Support about them, since these functions aren't supported.

Table A-17
Miscellaneous Functions and Subroutines

Routine Name	Parameter List	Returns
_ctl	(pIUnknown&)	string
_hwnd	(hwnd&)	string
_id	(id&)	string
_idx	(idx&)	string
_ord	(ord&)	string
_url	(url$)	string
SetActiveTimeout	(timeout&)	long
SetDefaultWaitTimeout	(timeout&)	long
SetRetryInterval	(interval&)	long
SetSuspendedTimeout	(timeout&)	long
*Wmessage	(hWnd&, wMsg&)	
*WmessageL	(hWnd&, wMsg&, lp As Any)	
*WmessageW	(hWnd&, wMsg&, wp&)	
*WmessageWL	(hWnd&, wMsg&, wp&, lp as Any)	

* Undocumented language component

Tip

Functions that show a parameter equal to a value mean that the parameter has that value by default if a value for that parameter is not provided when the function is called. For example, WmenuExists has two parameters. The second parameter uses the default wait timeout as a default value if a value for that parameter is not provided by the Test programmer:

```
WMenuExists (strItem$, timeout&=DEF_WAIT) as long
```

Table A-18
Information Routines

Routine Name	Parameter List
AADisplayInfo	(strMSAAobj$, wDisplay&=DI_DIALOG)
AAGetInfo	(strMSAAobj $, AAInfo as AAINFO)
OleCtlDisplayInfo	(hWnd&, x&, y&, wDisplay&=DI_DIALOG)

Routine Name	Parameter List
OleCtlGetInfo	(hWnd&, OleCtlInfo as OLECTL_HITTEST)
WDisplayInfo	(hWnd&, wDisplay&=DI_DIALOG)
WebDisplayInfo	(strContext$, nIndex&, wDisplay&=DI_DIALOG)
WebGetInfo	(strContext$, nIndex&, WebGetInfo as WEBINFO)
WGetInfo	(hWnd&, Info as INFO)

Table A-19
General Window Routines

Routine Name	Parameter List	Returns
GetAltKeys	()	string
GetDupAltKeys	()	string
GetText	(hWnd&)	string
WAdjWndPos	(hWnd&, deltaLeft&=W_DEFAULT, deltaTop&=W_DEFAULT)	
WAdjWndPosSiz	(hWnd&, deltaLeft&=W_DEFAULT, deltaTop&=W_DEFAULT, deltaWidth&=W_DEFAULT, deltaHeight&=W_DEFAULT)	
WAdjWndSiz	(hWnd&, deltaWidth&=W_DEFAULT, deltaHeight&=W_DEFAULT)	
WClkWnd	(hWnd&, x&=W_CENTER, y&=W_CENTER, nBtn&=VK_LBUTTON)	
WCtrlClkWnd	(hWnd&, x&=W_CENTER, y&=W_CENTER, nBtn&=VK_LBUTTON)	
WCtrlDragToWnd	(hWnd&, x&=W_CENTER, y&=W_CENTER, nBtn&=VK_LBUTTON)	
WDblClkWnd	(hWnd&, x&=W_CENTER, y&=W_CENTER, nBtn&=VK_LBUTTON)	
WDragToWnd	(hWnd&, x&=W_CENTER, y&=W_CENTER, nBtn&=VK_LBUTTON)	

(continued)

Table A-19 *(continued)*

Routine Name	Parameter List	Returns
WFndWnd	(strCaption$, wFlags&=FW_DEFAULT, timeout&=DEF_WAIT)	long
WFndWndC	(strText$, strClass$, wFlags&=FW_DEFAULT, timeout&=DEF_WAIT)	long
WFndWndWait	(strCaption$, wFlags&=FW_DEFAULT, timeout&=DEF_WAIT)	long
WFndWndWaitC	(strText$, strClass$, wFlags&=FW_DEFAULT, timeout&=DEF_WAIT)	long
WGetActWnd	(hWnd&=0)	long
WGetFocus	()	long
WGetWndPos	(hWnd&, WndPos as WNDPOS, fRelative&=W_RELATIVE)	
WGetWndPosSiz	(hWnd&, WndPosSiz as WNDPOSSIZ, fRelative&=W_RELATIVE)	
WGetWndSiz	(hWnd&, WndSiz as WNDSIZ)	
WisMaximized	(hWnd&)	long
WisMinimized	(hWnd&)	long
WisVisible	(hWnd&)	long
WMaxWnd	(hWnd&)	
WMinWnd	(hWnd&)	
WMoveToWnd	(hWnd&, x&=W_CENTER, y&=W_CENTER)	
WNumAltKeys	()	long
WNumDupAltKeys	()	long
WResWnd	(hWnd&)	
WSetActWnd	(hWnd&)	
WSetText	(hWnd&, strText$)	
WSetWndPos	(hWnd&, wLeft&=W_DEFAULT, wTop&=W_DEFAULT)	

Routine Name	Parameter List	Returns
WSetWndPosSiz	(hWnd&, wLeft&=W_DEFAULT, wTop&=W_DEFAULT, wWidth&=W_DEFAULT, wHeight&=W_DEFAULT)	
WSetWndSiz	(hWnd&, wWidth&=W_DEFAULT, wHeight&=W_DEFAULT)	
WShftClkWnd	(hWnd&, x&=W_CENTER, y&=W_CENTER, nBtn&=VK_LBUTTON)	
WShftDragToWnd	(hWnd&, x&=W_CENTER, y&=W_CENTER, nBtn&=VK_LBUTTON)	
WTextLen	(hWnd&)	long

Table A-20
Button Routines, Parameter List, and Return Values

Routine Name	Parameter List	Returns
ButtonGetClass	()	string
WButtonClassLen	()	long
WButtonClick	(pszCtrl$, timeout&=DEF_WAIT)	
WButtonDefault	(pszCtrl$, timeout&=DEF_WAIT)	long
WButtonDefaults	()	long
WButtonEnabled	(pszCtrl$, timeout&=DEF_WAIT)	long
WButtonExists	(pszCtrl$, timeout&=DEF_WAIT)	long
WButtonFind	(pszCtrl$, timeout&=DEF_WAIT)	long
WButtonFocus	(pszCtrl$, timeout&=DEF_WAIT)	long
WButtonMoveTo	(pszCtrl$, x&=W_CENTER, y&=W_CENTER, timeout&=DEF_WAIT)	
WButtonSetClass	(pszClassName$)	
WButtonSetFocus	(pszCtrl$, timeout&=DEF_WAIT)	

Table A-21
Checkbox Routines, Parameters, and Return Values

Routine Name	Parameter List	Returns
WCheckSetClass	(strClassName$)	
CheckGetClass	()	string
WCheckClassLen	()	long
WCheckExists	(strCtrl$, timeout&=DEF_WAIT)	long
WCheckFind	(strCtrl$, timeout&=DEF_WAIT)	long
WCheckEnabled	(strCtrl$, timeout&=DEF_WAIT)	long
WCheckFocus	(strCtrl$, timeout&=DEF_WAIT)	long
WCheckState	(strCtrl$, timeout&=DEF_WAIT)	long
WCheckSetState	(strCtrl$, state&, timeout&=DEF_WAIT)	
WCheckClick	(strCtrl$, timeout&=DEF_WAIT)	
WCheckCheck	(strCtrl$, timeout&=DEF_WAIT)	
WCheckUnCheck	(strCtrl$, timeout&=DEF_WAIT)	
WCheckSetFocus	(strCtrl$, timeout&=DEF_WAIT)	
WCheckMoveTo	(strCtrl$, x&=W_CENTER, y&=W_CENTER, timeout&=DEF_WAIT)	

Table A-22
Combobox Routines, Parameters, and Return Values

Routine Name	Parameter List	Returns
ComboGetClass	()	string
ComboGetLBClass	()	string
ComboItemText	(strCtrl$, iItem&, timeout&=DEF_WAIT)	string
ComboSelText	(strCtrl$, timeout&=DEF_WAIT)	string
ComboText	(strCtrl$, timeout&=DEF_WAIT)	string
WComboClassLen	()	long
WComboCount	(strCtrl$, timeout&=DEF_WAIT)	long

Routine Name	Parameter List	Returns
WComboDragTo	(strCtrl$, x&=W_CENTER, y&=W_CENTER, nBtn&=VK_LBUTTON, timeout&=DEF_WAIT)	
WComboEnabled	(strCtrl$, timeout&=DEF_WAIT)	long
WComboExists	(strCtrl$, timeout&=DEF_WAIT)	long
WComboFind	(strCtrl$, timeout&=DEF_WAIT)	long
WComboFocus	(strCtrl$, timeout&=DEF_WAIT)	
WComboIndex	(strCtrl$, timeout&=DEF_WAIT)	long
WComboItemClk	(strCtrl$, strItem$, timeout&=DEF_WAIT)	
WComboItemDblClk	(strCtrl$, strItem$, timeout&=DEF_WAIT)	
WComboItemDragTo	(strCtrl$, strItem$, nBtn&=VK_LBUTTON, timeout&=DEF_WAIT)	
WComboItemExists	(strCtrl$, strItem$, timeout&=DEF_WAIT)	long
WComboItemIndent	(strCtrl$, strItem$, timeout&=DEF_WAIT)	long
WComboItemIndex	(strCtrl$, strItem$, timeout&=DEF_WAIT)	long
WComboItemLen	(strCtrl$, iItem&, timeout&=DEF_WAIT)	long
WComboItemMoveTo	(strCtrl$, strItem$, timeout&=DEF_WAIT)	
WComboLBClassLen	()	long
WComboLen	(strCtrl$, timeout&=DEF_WAIT)	long
WComboMoveTo	(strCtrl$, x&=W_CENTER, y&=W_CENTER, timeout&=DEF_WAIT)	
WComboSelLen	(strCtrl$, timeout&=DEF_WAIT)	long
WComboSelStart	(strCtrl$, timeout&=DEF_WAIT)	long
WComboSetClass	(strClass$)	
WComboSetFocus	(strCtrl$, timeout&=DEF_WAIT)	
WComboSetLBClass	(strClass$)	
WComboSetSel	(strCtrl$, lSelStart&, lSelLength&, timeout&=DEF_WAIT)	
WComboSetText	(strCtrl$, strText$, timeout&=DEF_WAIT)	

Table A-23
Custom Control Routines, Parameters, and Return Values

Routine Name	Parameter List	Returns
CustomGetClass	()	string
CustomGetText	(strCtrl$, timeout&=DEF_WAIT)	string
WCustomClassLen	()	long
WCustomClick	(strCtrl$, iBtn&=VK_LBUTTON, timeout&=DEF_WAIT)	
WCustomClickAt	(strCtrl$, x&=W_CENTER, y&=W_CENTER, iBtn&=VK_LBUTTON, timeout&=DEF_WAIT)	
WCustomCtrlDragTo	(strCtrl$, x&=W_CENTER, y&=W_CENTER, nBtn&=VK_LBUTTON, timeout&=DEF_WAIT)	
WCustomDblClk	(strCtrl$, iBtn&=VK_LBUTTON, timeout&=DEF_WAIT)	
WCustomDblClkAt	(strCtrl$, x&=W_CENTER, y&=W_CENTER, iBtn&=VK_LBUTTON, timeout&=DEF_WAIT)	
WCustomDragTo	(strCtrl$, x&=W_CENTER, y&=W_CENTER, nBtn&=VK_LBUTTON, timeout&=DEF_WAIT)	
WCustomEnabled	(strCtrl$, timeout&=DEF_WAIT)	long
WCustomExists	(strCtrl$, timeout&=DEF_WAIT)	long
WCustomFind	(strCtrl$, timeout&=DEF_WAIT)	long
WCustomFocus	(strCtrl$, timeout&=DEF_WAIT)	long
WCustomMoveTo	(strCtrl$, x&=W_CENTER, y&=W_CENTER, timeout&=DEF_WAIT)	
WCustomSetClass	(strClassName$)	
WCustomSetFocus	(strCtrl$, timeout&=DEF_WAIT)	
WCustomSetText	(strCtrl$, strText$, timeout&=DEF_WAIT)	
WCustomShftDragTo	(strCtrl$, x&=W_CENTER, y&=W_CENTER, nBtn&=VK_LBUTTON, timeout&=DEF_WAIT)	
WCustomTextLen	(strCtrl$, timeout&=DEF_WAIT)	long

Table A-24
Date/Time Picker Control Routines, Parameters, and Return Values

Routine Name	Parameter List	Returns
PickerGetClass	()	string
WPickerClassLen	()	long
WPickerCloseMonthCal	(strCtrl$, timeout&=DEF_WAIT)	
WPickerDateMode	(strCtrl$, timeout&=DEF_WAIT)	long
WPickerDisableEntry	(strCtrl$, timeout&=DEF_WAIT)	
WPickerEnabled	(strCtrl$, timeout&=DEF_WAIT)	long
WPickerEnableEntry	(strCtrl$, timeout&=DEF_WAIT)	
WPickerEntryEnabled	(strCtrl$, timeout&=DEF_WAIT)	long
WPickerExists	(strCtrl$, timeout&=DEF_WAIT)	long
WPickerFind	(strCtrl$, timeout&=DEF_WAIT)	long
WPickerFocus	(strCtrl$, timeout&=DEF_WAIT)	long
WPickerGetDay	(strCtrl$, timeout&=DEF_WAIT)	long
WPickerGetHour	(strCtrl$, timeout&=DEF_WAIT)	long
WPickerGetMinute	(strCtrl$, timeout&=DEF_WAIT)	long
WPickerGetMonth	(strCtrl$, timeout&=DEF_WAIT)	long
WPickerGetMonthCal	(strCtrl$, timeout&=DEF_WAIT)	long
WPickerGetSecond	(strCtrl$, timeout&=DEF_WAIT)	long
WPickerGetYear	(strCtrl$, timeout&=DEF_WAIT)	long
WPickerOpenMonthCal	(strCtrl$, timeout&=DEF_WAIT)	
WPickerSetClass	(strClassName$)	
WPickerSetDay	(strCtrl$, iDay& , timeout&=DEF_WAIT)	
WPickerSetFocus	(strCtrl$, timeout&=DEF_WAIT)	
WPickerSetHour	(strCtrl$, iHour& , timeout&=DEF_WAIT)	

(continued)

Table A-24 *(continued)*

Routine Name	Parameter List	Returns
WPickerSetMinute	(strCtrl$, iMinute&, timeout&=DEF_WAIT)	
WPickerSetMonth	(strCtrl$, iMonth& , timeout&=DEF_WAIT)	
WPickerSetSecond	(strCtrl$, iSecond&, timeout&=DEF_WAIT)	
WPickerSetYear	(strCtrl$, iYear& , timeout&=DEF_WAIT)	
WPickerTimeMode	(strCtrl$, timeout&=DEF_WAIT)	long

Table A-25
Desktop Control Routines, Parameters, and Return Values

Routine Name	Parameter List	Returns
DesktopItemText	(strItem$)	string
WDesktopClk	(x&=W_SPACE, y&=W_SPACE, nBtn&=VK_RBUTTON)	
WDesktopCount	()	long
WDesktopCtrlDragTo	(x&=W_SPACE, y&=W_SPACE, nBtn&=VK_LBUTTON)	
WDesktopDragTo	(x&=W_SPACE, y&=W_SPACE, nBtn&=VK_LBUTTON)	
WDesktopFind	()	long
WDesktopItemClk	(strItem$, nBtn&=VK_LBUTTON)	
WDesktopItemCtrlClk	(strItem$, nBtn&=VK_LBUTTON)	
WDesktopItemCtrlDragTo	(strItem$, nBtn&=VK_LBUTTON)	
WDesktopItemDblClk	(strItem$, nBtn&=VK_LBUTTON)	
WDesktopItemDragTo	(strItem$, nBtn&=VK_LBUTTON)	
WDesktopItemExists	(strItem$)	long
WDesktopItemLabelClk	(strItem$, nBtn&=VK_LBUTTON)	

Routine Name	Parameter List	Returns
WDesktopItemLen	(strItem$)	long
WDesktopItemMoveTo	(strItem$)	
WDesktopItemShftClk	(strItem$, nBtn&=VK_LBUTTON)	
WDesktopItemShftDragTo	(strItem$, nBtn&=VK_LBUTTON)	
WDesktopMoveTo	(x&=W_SPACE, y&=W_SPACE)	
WDesktopSelCount	()	long
WDesktopSelItem	(strItem$)	long
WDesktopShftDragTo	(x&=W_SPACE, y&=W_SPACE, nBtn&=VK_LBUTTON)	

Table A-26
Edit Box Routines, Parameters, and Return Values

Routine Name	Parameter List	Returns
EditGetClass	()	string
EditLineText	(strCtrl$, lIndex&, timeout&=DEF_WAIT)	string
EditSelText	(strCtrl$, timeout&=DEF_WAIT)	string
EditText	(strCtrl$, timeout&=DEF_WAIT)	string
WEditChar	(strCtrl$, timeout&=DEF_WAIT)	long
WEditClassLen	()	long
WEditClick	(strCtrl$, timeout&=DEF_WAIT)	
WEditCtrlDragTo	(strCtrl$, x&=W_CENTER, y&=W_CENTER, nBtn&=VK_LBUTTON, timeout&=DEF_WAIT)	
WEditDragTo	(strCtrl$, x&=W_CENTER, y&=W_CENTER, nBtn&=VK_LBUTTON, timeout&=DEF_WAIT)	
WEditEnabled	(strCtrl$, timeout&=DEF_WAIT)	long
WEditExists	(strCtrl$, timeout&=DEF_WAIT)	long
WEditFind	(strCtrl$, timeout&=DEF_WAIT)	long
WEditFirst	(strCtrl$, timeout&=DEF_WAIT)	long

(continued)

Table A-26 *(continued)*

Routine Name	Parameter List	Returns
WEditFocus	(strCtrl$, timeout&=DEF_WAIT)	
WEditLen	(strCtrl$, timeout&=DEF_WAIT)	long
WEditLine	(strCtrl$, timeout&=DEF_WAIT)	long
WEditLineLen	(strCtrl$, lIndex&, timeout&=DEF_WAIT)	long
WEditLines	(strCtrl$, timeout&=DEF_WAIT)	long
WEditMoveTo	(strCtrl$, x&=W_CENTER, y&=W_CENTER, timeout&=DEF_WAIT)	
WEditPos	(strCtrl$, timeout&=DEF_WAIT)	long
WEditSelLen	(strCtrl$, timeout&=DEF_WAIT)	long
WEditSelStart	(strCtrl$, timeout&=DEF_WAIT)	long
WEditSetClass	(strClass$)	
WEditSetFocus	(strCtrl$, timeout&=DEF_WAIT)	
WEditSetSel	(strCtrl$, lSelStart&, lSelLength&, timeout&=DEF_WAIT)	
WEditSetText	(strCtrl$, strBuffer$, timeout&=DEF_WAIT)	
WEditShftDragTo	(strCtrl$, x&=W_CENTER, y&=W_CENTER, nBtn&=VK_LBUTTON, timeout&=DEF_WAIT)	

Table A-27
Gupta SQL Window Table Routines, Parameters, and Return Values

Routine Name	Parameter List	Returns
GuptaTableCellText	(strCtrl$, nRow&, Col as variant, timeout&=DEF_WAIT)	string
GuptaTableClick	(strCtrl$, x&=W_CENTER, y&=W_CENTER, nBtn&=VK_LBUTTON, timeout&=DEF_WAIT)	
GuptaTableColumns	(strCtrl$, timeout&=DEF_WAIT)	long

Routine Name	Parameter List	Returns
GuptaTableDblClk	(strCtrl$, x&=W_CENTER, y&=W_CENTER, nBtn&=VK_LBUTTON, timeout&=DEF_WAIT)	
GuptaTableDragTo	(strCtrl$, x&=W_CENTER, y&=W_CENTER, nBtn&=VK_LBUTTON, timeout&=DEF_WAIT)	
GuptaTableExists	(strCtrl$, timeout&=DEF_WAIT)	long
GuptaTableFind	(strCtrl$, timeout&=DEF_WAIT)	long
GuptaTableGetClass	()	string
GuptaTableMoveTo	(strCtrl$, x&=W_CENTER, y&=W_CENTER, timeout&=DEF_WAIT)	
GuptaTableRows	(strCtrl$, timeout&=DEF_WAIT)	long
GuptaTableSave	(strCtrl$, strFile$, timeout&=DEF_WAIT)	
GuptaTableSetClass	(strClassName$)	

Table A-28
Header Control Routines, Parameters, and Return Values

Routine Name	Parameter List	Returns
HeaderGetClass	()	string
HeaderItemText	(strCtrl$, strItem$, timeout&=DEF_WAIT)	string
WHeaderClassLen	()	long
WHeaderCount	(strCtrl$, timeout&=DEF_WAIT)	long
WHeaderEnabled	(strCtrl$, timeout&=DEF_WAIT)	long
WHeaderExists	(strCtrl$, timeout&=DEF_WAIT)	long
WHeaderFind	(strCtrl$, timeout&=DEF_WAIT)	long
WHeaderItemClk	(strCtrl$, strItem$, nBtn&=VK_LBUTTON, timeout&=DEF_WAIT)	
WHeaderItemExists	(strCtrl$, strItem$, timeout&=DEF_WAIT)	long

(continued)

Table A-28 *(continued)*

Routine Name	Parameter List	Returns
WHeaderItemLen	(strCtrl$, strItem$, timeout&=DEF_WAIT)	long
WHeaderItemMoveTo	(strCtrl$, strItem$, timeout&=DEF_WAIT)	
WHeaderMoveTo	(strCtrl$, x&=W_CENTER, y&=W_CENTER, timeout&=DEF_WAIT)	
WHeaderSetClass	(strClassName$)	

Table A-29
Listbox Routines, Parameters, and Return Values

Routine Name	Parameter List	Returns
ListGetClass	()	string
ListItemText	(strCtrl$, iItem&, timeout&=DEF_WAIT)	string
ListText	(strCtrl$, timeout&=DEF_WAIT)	string
WListClassLen	()	long
WListCount	(strCtrl$, timeout&=DEF_WAIT)	long
WListCtrlDragTo	(strCtrl$, x&=W_CENTER, y&=W_CENTER, nBtn&=VK_LBUTTON, timeout&=DEF_WAIT)	
WListDragTo	(strCtrl$, x&=W_CENTER, y&=W_CENTER, nBtn&=VK_LBUTTON, timeout&=DEF_WAIT)	
WListEnabled	(strCtrl$, timeout&=DEF_WAIT)	long
WListExists	(strCtrl$, timeout&=DEF_WAIT)	long
WListFind	(strCtrl$, timeout&=DEF_WAIT)	long
WListFocus	(strCtrl$, timeout&=DEF_WAIT)	
WListIndex	(strCtrl$, timeout&=DEF_WAIT)	long
WListItemClk	(strCtrl$, strItem$, timeout&=DEF_WAIT)	
WListItemClkEx	(strCtrl$, strItem$, ixOffset&, timeout&=DEF_WAIT)	
WListItemCtrlClk	(strCtrl$, strItem$, timeout&=DEF_WAIT)	

Routine Name	Parameter List	Returns
WListItemCtrlClkEx	(strCtrl$, strItem$, ixOffset&, timeout&=DEF_WAIT)	
WListItemCtrlDragTo	(strCtrl$, strItem$, nBtn&=VK_LBUTTON, timeout&=DEF_WAIT)	
WListItemDblClk	(strCtrl$, strItem$, timeout&=DEF_WAIT)	
WListItemDblClkEx	(strCtrl$, strItem$, ixOffset&, timeout&=DEF_WAIT)	
WListItemDragTo	(strCtrl$, strItem$, nBtn&=VK_LBUTTON, timeout&=DEF_WAIT)	
WListItemExists	(strCtrl$, strItem$, timeout&=DEF_WAIT)	long
WListItemIndex	(strCtrl$, strItem$, timeout&=DEF_WAIT)	long
WListItemLen	(strCtrl$, iItem&, timeout&=DEF_WAIT)	long
WListItemMoveTo	(strCtrl$, strItem$, timeout&=DEF_WAIT)	
WListItemShftClk	(strCtrl$, strItem$, timeout&=DEF_WAIT)	
WListItemShftClkEx	(strCtrl$, strItem$, ixOffset&, timeout&=DEF_WAIT)	
WListItemShftDragTo	(strCtrl$, strItem$, nBtn&=VK_LBUTTON, timeout&=DEF_WAIT)	
WListLen	(strCtrl$, timeout&=DEF_WAIT)	long
WListMoveTo	(strCtrl$, x&=W_CENTER, y&=W_CENTER, timeout&=DEF_WAIT)	
WListSelCount	(strCtrl$, timeout&=DEF_WAIT)	long
WListSelItems	(strCtrl$, lpIntArray As Pointer To Long, timeout&=DEF_WAIT)	
WListSetClass	(strClass$)	
WListSetFocus	(strCtrl$, timeout&=DEF_WAIT)	
WListShftDragTo	(strCtrl$, x&=W_CENTER, y&=W_CENTER, nBtn&=VK_LBUTTON, timeout&=DEF_WAIT)	
WListTopIndex	(strCtrl$, timeout&=DEF_WAIT)	long

Table A-30
ListView Control Routines, Parameters, and Return Values

Routine Name	Parameter List	Returns
ViewGetClass	()	string
ViewHeaderText	(strCtrl$, strHdr$, timeout&=DEF_WAIT)	string
ViewItemText	(strCtrl$, strItem$, strSubItem$="", timeout&=DEF_WAIT)	string
WViewClassLen	()	long
WViewClk	(strCtrl$, x&=W_CENTER, y&=W_CENTER, nBtn&=VK_LBUTTON, timeout&=DEF_WAIT)	
WViewCount	(strCtrl$, timeout&=DEF_WAIT)	long
WViewCtrlDragTo	(strCtrl$, x&=W_CENTER, y&=W_CENTER, nBtn&=VK_LBUTTON, timeout&=DEF_WAIT)	
WViewDragTo	(strCtrl$, x&=W_CENTER, y&=W_CENTER, nBtn&=VK_LBUTTON, timeout&=DEF_WAIT)	
WViewEnabled	(strCtrl$, timeout&=DEF_WAIT)	long
WViewExists	(strCtrl$, timeout&=DEF_WAIT)	long
WViewFind	(strCtrl$, timeout&=DEF_WAIT)	long
WViewFocus	(strCtrl$, timeout&=DEF_WAIT)	long
WViewHeaderClk	(strCtrl$, strHdr$, nBtn&=VK_LBUTTON, timeout&=DEF_WAIT)	
WViewHeaderCount	(strCtrl$, timeout&=DEF_WAIT)	long
WViewHeaderExists	(strCtrl$, strHdr$, timeout&=DEF_WAIT)	long
WViewHeaderLen	(strCtrl$, strHdr$, timeout&=DEF_WAIT)	long
WViewHeaderMoveTo	(strCtrl$, strHdr$, timeout&=DEF_WAIT)	
WViewItemClk	(strCtrl$, strItem$, nBtn&=VK_LBUTTON, timeout&=DEF_WAIT)	
WViewItemCtrlClk	(strCtrl$, strItem$, nBtn&=VK_LBUTTON, timeout&=DEF_WAIT)	

Routine Name	Parameter List	Returns
WViewItemCtrlDragTo	(strCtrl$, strItem$, nBtn&=VK_LBUTTON, timeout&=DEF_WAIT)	
WViewItemDblClk	(strCtrl$, strItem$, nBtn&=VK_LBUTTON, timeout&=DEF_WAIT)	
WViewItemDragTo	(strCtrl$, strItem$, nBtn&=VK_LBUTTON, timeout&=DEF_WAIT)	
WViewItemExists	(strCtrl$, strItem$, timeout&=DEF_WAIT)	long
WViewItemGetCheck	(strCtrl$, strItem$, timeout&=DEF_WAIT)	long
WViewItemIndent	(strCtrl$, strItem$, timeout&=DEF_WAIT)	long
WViewItemIndex	(strCtrl$, strItem$, timeout&=DEF_WAIT)	long
WViewItemLabelClk	(strCtrl$, strItem$, nBtn&=VK_LBUTTON, timeout&=DEF_WAIT)	
WViewItemLen	(strCtrl$, strItem$, strSubItem$="", timeout&=DEF_WAIT)	long
WViewItemMoveTo	(strCtrl$, strItem$, timeout&=DEF_WAIT)	
WViewItemSelected	(strCtrl$, strItem$, timeout&=DEF_WAIT)	long
WViewItemSetCheck	(strCtrl$, strItem$, bVal&, timeout&=DEF_WAIT)	long
WViewItemShftClk	(strCtrl$, strItem$, nBtn&=VK_LBUTTON, timeout&=DEF_WAIT)	
WViewItemShftDragTo	(strCtrl$, strItem$, nBtn&=VK_LBUTTON, timeout&=DEF_WAIT)	
WViewMode	(strCtrl$, timeout&=DEF_WAIT)	long
WViewMoveTo	(strCtrl$, x&=W_CENTER, y&=W_CENTER, timeout&=DEF_WAIT)	
WViewSelCount	(strCtrl$, timeout&=DEF_WAIT)	long
WViewSelItem	(strCtrl$, strItem$, timeout&=DEF_WAIT)	long
WViewSetClass	(strClassName$)	
WViewSetFocus	(strCtrl$, timeout&=DEF_WAIT)	
WViewShftDragTo	(strCtrl$, x&=W_CENTER, y&=W_CENTER, nBtn&=VK_LBUTTON, timeout&=DEF_WAIT)	

Table A-31
Functions for Working with Menus

Routine Name	Parameter List	Returns
MenuFullText	(strItem$, timeout&=DEF_WAIT)	string
MenuGetAltKeys	(timeout&=DEF_WAIT)	string
MenuGetDupAltKeys	(timeout&=DEF_WAIT)	string
MenuText	(strItem$, timeout&=DEF_WAIT)	string
Wmenu	(strItem$, ...)	
WmenuChecked	(strItem$, timeout&=DEF_WAIT)	long
WmenuCount	(timeout&=DEF_WAIT)	long
WmenuDisplayInfo	(strItem$, flags&=DI_DIALOG, timeout&=DEF_WAIT)	
WmenuEnabled	(strItem$, timeout&=DEF_WAIT)	long
WmenuEnd	()	
WmenuEx	(strItem$, ...)	
WmenuExists	(strItem$, timeout&=DEF_WAIT)	long
WmenuFullLen	(strItem$, timeout&=DEF_WAIT)	long
WmenuGetInfo	(strItem$, mi as MENUINFO, timeout&=DEF_WAIT)	
WmenuGrayed	(strItem$, timeout&=DEF_WAIT)	long
WmenuHasPopup	(strItem$, timeout&=DEF_WAIT)	long
WmenuLen	(strItem$, timeout&=DEF_WAIT)	long
WmenuNumAltKeys	(timeout&=DEF_WAIT)	long
WmenuNumDupAltKeys	(timeout&=DEF_WAIT)	long
WmenuSelect	(strItem$, timeout&=DEF_WAIT)	
WmenuSeparator	(nIndex&, timeout&=DEF_WAIT)	long
WsysMenu	(hWnd&)	
WsysMenuExists	(hWnd&)	long

Table A-32
Month/Calendar Control Routines, Parameters, and Return Values

Routine Name	Parameter List	Returns
MonthCalGetClass	()	string
WMonthCalClassLen	()	long
WMonthCalClickAt	(strCtrl$, x&=W_CENTER, y&=W_CENTER, iBtn&=VK_LBUTTON, timeout&=DEF_WAIT)	
WMonthCalDisplayMonths	(strCtrl$, timeout&=DEF_WAIT)	long
WMonthCalDragTo	(strCtrl$, x&=W_CENTER, y&=W_CENTER, nBtn&=VK_LBUTTON, timeout&=DEF_WAIT)	
WMonthCalEnabled	(strCtrl$, timeout&=DEF_WAIT)	long
WMonthCalExists	(strCtrl$, timeout&=DEF_WAIT)	long
WMonthCalFind	(strCtrl$, timeout&=DEF_WAIT)	long
WMonthCalFirstMonth	(strCtrl$, timeout&=DEF_WAIT)	long
WMonthCalFirstYear	(strCtrl$, timeout&=DEF_WAIT)	long
WMonthCalFocus	(strCtrl$, timeout&=DEF_WAIT)	long
WMonthCalGetDay	(strCtrl$, timeout&=DEF_WAIT)	long
WMonthCalGetDayCount	(strCtrl$, timeout&=DEF_WAIT)	long
WMonthCalGetMonth	(strCtrl$, timeout&=DEF_WAIT)	long
WMonthCalGetYear	(strCtrl$, timeout&=DEF_WAIT)	long
WMonthCalMoveTo	(strCtrl$, x&=W_CENTER, y&=W_CENTER, timeout&=DEF_WAIT)	
WMonthCalNext	(strCtrl$, timeout&=DEF_WAIT)	
WMonthCalPrev	(strCtrl$, timeout&=DEF_WAIT)	
WMonthCalSetClass	(strClassName$)	
WMonthCalSetDay	(strCtrl$, iDay& , timeout&=DEF_WAIT)	
WMonthCalSetDayCount	(strCtrl$, iDays& , timeout&=DEF_WAIT)	

(continued)

Table A-32 *(continued)*

Routine Name	Parameter List	Returns
WMonthCalSetFocus	(strCtrl$, timeout&=DEF_WAIT)	
WMonthCalSetMonth	(strCtrl$, iMonth&, timeout&=DEF_WAIT)	
WMonthCalSetYear	(strCtrl$, iYear& , timeout&=DEF_WAIT)	

Table A-33
MSAA Routines, Parameters, and Return Values

Routine Name	Parameter List	Returns
AAClkWnd	(strObj$, x&=W_CENTER, y&=W_CENTER, nBtn&=VK_LBUTTON, timeout&=DEF_WAIT)	
AACompareState	(strObj$, strState$, timeout&=DEF_WAIT)	integer
AACtrlClkWnd	(strObj$, x&=W_CENTER, y&=W_CENTER, nBtn&=VK_LBUTTON, timeout&=DEF_WAIT)	
AADblClkWnd	(strObj$, x&=W_CENTER, y&=W_CENTER, nBtn&=VK_LBUTTON, timeout&=DEF_WAIT)	
AADoAction	(strObj$, timeout&=DEF_WAIT)	
AAFndChildByPos	(strObj$, pos&, timeout&=DEF_WAIT)	string
AAFndNextSibling	(strObj$, timeout&=DEF_WAIT)	string
AAFndParent	(strObj$, timeout&=DEF_WAIT)	string
AAFndPrevSibling	(strObj$, timeout&=DEF_WAIT)	string
AAFndWnd	(strName$, strStartObj$="", wFlags&=FW_DEFAULT, timeout&=DEF_WAIT)	string
AAFndWndC	(strName$, strRole$, strStartObj$="", wFlags&=FW_DEFAULT, timeout&=DEF_WAIT)	string
AAFndWndFromPt	(x&, y&, wFlags&=FW_DEFAULT, timeout&=DEF_WAIT)	string
AAGetAction	(strObj$, timeout&=DEF_WAIT)	string
AAGetChildCount	(strObj$, timeout&=DEF_WAIT)	integer
AAGetDescription	(strObj$, timeout&=DEF_WAIT)	string

Routine Name	Parameter List	Returns
AAGetHelpString	(strObj$, timeout&=DEF_WAIT)	string
AAGetHwnd	(strObj$, timeout&=DEF_WAIT)	long
AAGetName	(strObj$, timeout&=DEF_WAIT)	string
AAGetRole	(strObj$, timeout&=DEF_WAIT)	string
AAGetShortKey	(strObj$, timeout&=DEF_WAIT)	string
AAGetState	(strObj$, timeout&=DEF_WAIT)	string
AAGetValue	(strObj$, timeout&=DEF_WAIT)	string
AAGetWndPos	(strObj$, lpWndPos As WNDPOS, timeout&=DEF_WAIT)	
AAGetWndPosSiz	(strObj$, lpWndPosSiz As WNDPOSSIZ, timeout&=DEF_WAIT)	
AAGetWndSiz	(strObj$, lpWndSiz As WNDSIZ, timeout&=DEF_WAIT)	
AAIsEnabled	()	long
AASetName	(strObj$, strName$, timeout&=DEF_WAIT)	
AASetSelection	(strObj$, wFlags&=FAA_SELFLAG_DEFAULT, timeout&=DEF_WAIT)	
AASetValue	(strObj$, strValue$, timeout&=DEF_WAIT)	
AAShftClkWnd	(strObj$, x&=W_CENTER, y&=W_CENTER, nBtn&=VK_LBUTTON, timeout&=DEF_WAIT)	

Table A-34
OLE/OCX Control Routines, Parameters, and Return Values

Routine Name	Parameter List	Returns
OleCtlExists	(strCtrl$, timeout&=DEF_WAIT)	long
OleCtlFind	(strCtrl$, timeout&=DEF_WAIT)	long
OleCtlGetProperty	(strCtrl$, strProp$, timeout&=DEF_WAIT)	variant

(continued)

Table A-34 *(continued)*

Routine Name	Parameter List	Returns
OleCtlSetProperty	(strCtrl$, strProp$, pVar as VARIANT, timeout&=DEF_WAIT)	
OleCtlHasProperty	(strCtrl$, strProp$, timeout&=DEF_WAIT)	long
OleCtlMoveTo	(strCtrl$, x&=W_CENTER, y&=W_CENTER, timeout&=DEF_WAIT)	
OleCtlDragTo	(strCtrl$, strKey$="", nBtn&=VK_LBUTTON, x&=W_CENTER, y&=W_CENTER, timeout&=DEF_WAIT)	
OleCtlClick	(strCtrl$, strKey$="", nBtn&=VK_LBUTTON, x&=W_CENTER, y&=W_CENTER, timeout&=DEF_WAIT)	
OleCtlDblClk	(strCtrl$, strKey$="", nBtn&=VK_LBUTTON, x&=W_CENTER, y&=W_CENTER, timeout&=DEF_WAIT)	
OleCtlSetClass	(strClass$)	
OleCtlGetClass	()	string
OleCtlHitTest	(hwnd&, ht as OLECTL_HITTEST)	long
OleCtlPropertyList	(strCtrl$, propList as array of OLECTL_PROPERTY, timeout&=DEF_WAIT)	long
OleCtlGetItem	(strCtrl$, strProp$, pItem as VARIANT, timeout&=DEF_WAIT)	variant

Table A-35
Option Button Routines, Parameters, and Return Values

Routine Name	Parameter List	Returns
OptionGetClass	()	string
WOptionClassLen	()	long
WOptionClick	(strCtrl$, timeout&=DEF_WAIT)	
WOptionEnabled	(strCtrl$, timeout&=DEF_WAIT)	long
WOptionExists	(strCtrl$, timeout&=DEF_WAIT)	long

Routine Name	Parameter List	Returns
WOptionFind	(strCtrl$, timeout&=DEF_WAIT)	long
WOptionFocus	(strCtrl$, timeout&=DEF_WAIT)	long
WOptionMoveTo	(strCtrl$, x&=W_CENTER, y&=W_CENTER, timeout&=DEF_WAIT)	
WOptionSelect	(strCtrl$, timeout&=DEF_WAIT)	
WOptionSetClass	(strClassName$)	
WOptionSetFocus	(strCtrl$, timeout&=DEF_WAIT)	
WOptionState	(strCtrl$, timeout&=DEF_WAIT)	long

Table A-36
PowerSoft Data Window Routines, Parameters, and Return Values

Routine Name	Parameter List	Returns
PBDataWindowCellText	(strCtrl$, nRow&, Col as variant, timeout&=DEF_WAIT)	string
PBDataWindowClick	(strCtrl$, x&=W_CENTER, y&=W_CENTER, nBtn&=VK_LBUTTON, timeout&=DEF_WAIT)	
PBDataWindowColumns	(strCtrl$, tim&=DEF_WAIT)	long
PBDataWindowDblClk	(strCtrl$, x&=W_CENTER, y&=W_CENTER, nBtn&=VK_LBUTTON, timeout&=DEF_WAIT)	
PBDataWindowDragTo	(strCtrl$, x&=W_CENTER, y&=W_CENTER, nBtn&=VK_LBUTTON, timeout&=DEF_WAIT)	
PBDataWindowExists	(strCtrl$, timeout&=DEF_WAIT)	long
PBDataWindowFind	(strCtrl$, timeout&=DEF_WAIT)	long
PBDataWindowGetClass	()	string
PBDataWindowMoveTo	(strCtrl$, x&=W_CENTER, y&=W_CENTER, timeout&=DEF_WAIT)	
PBDataWindowRows	(strCtrl$, timeout&=DEF_WAIT)	long
PBDataWindowSave	(strCtrl$, strFile$, timeout&=DEF_WAIT)	
PBDataWindowSetClass	(strClassName$)	

Table A-37
Progress Control Routines, Parameters, and Return Values

Routine Name	Parameter List	Returns
ProgressGetClass	()	string
WProgressClassLen	()	long
WProgressExists	(strCtrl$, timeout&=DEF_WAIT)	long
WProgressFind	(strCtrl$, timeout&=DEF_WAIT)	long
WProgressMoveTo	(strCtrl$, x&=W_CENTER, y&=W_CENTER, timeout&=DEF_WAIT)	
WProgressSetClass	(strClassName$)	

Table A-38
Rebar Control Routines, Parameters, and Return Values

Routine Name	Parameter List	Returns
RebarGetClass	()	string
WRebarBandLen	(strCtrl$, iBand&, timeout&=DEF_WAIT)	long
WRebarBandText	(strCtrl$, iBand&, timeout&=DEF_WAIT)	string
WRebarClassLen	()	long
WRebarClickAt	(strCtrl$, x&=W_CENTER, y&=W_CENTER, iBtn&=VK_LBUTTON, timeout&=DEF_WAIT)	
WRebarDragTo	(strCtrl$, x&=W_CENTER, y&=W_CENTER, nBtn&=VK_LBUTTON, timeout&=DEF_WAIT)	
WRebarEnabled	(strCtrl$, timeout&=DEF_WAIT)	long
WRebarExists	(strCtrl$, timeout&=DEF_WAIT)	long
WRebarFind	(strCtrl$, timeout&=DEF_WAIT)	long
WRebarFocus	(strCtrl$, timeout&=DEF_WAIT)	long
WRebarGetBandCount	(strCtrl$, timeout&=DEF_WAIT)	long
WRebarGetBandWidth	(strCtrl$, iBand& ,timeout&=DEF_WAIT)	long
WRebarGetRowCount	(strCtrl$, timeout&=DEF_WAIT)	long
WRebarGetRowHeight	(strCtrl$, iRow& ,timeout&=DEF_WAIT)	long
WRebarMoveTo	(strCtrl$, x&=W_CENTER, y&=W_CENTER, timeout&=DEF_WAIT)	

Routine Name	Parameter List	Returns
WRebarSetClass	(strClassName$)	
WRebarSetFocus	(strCtrl$, timeout&=DEF_WAIT)	

Table A-39
Registry Routines, Parameters, and Return Values

Routine Name	Parameter List	Returns
RegistryClose	(RegKey&)	
RegistryCompareFile	(strRegFile$)	long
RegistryCompareKeys	(RegKey1 as variant, RegKey2 as variant)	long
RegistryCopyKey	(RegKeySrc as variant, RegKeyDest as variant)	
RegistryCreateKey	(RegKey as variant, strSubKey$)	
RegistryDeleteKey	(RegKey as variant, strSubKey$)	
RegistryDeleteValue	(RegKey as variant, strValueName$)	
RegistryGetSubkeyCount	(RegKey as variant)	long
RegistryGetSubkeyName	(RegKey as variant, nIndex&)	string
RegistryGetValue	(RegKey as variant, strValueName$)	variant
RegistryGetValueCount	(RegKey as variant)	long
RegistryGetValueName	(RegKey as variant, nIndex&)	string
RegistryGetValueType	(RegKey as variant, strValueName$)	string
RegistryKeyExists	(strKey$)	long
RegistryOpen	(strKey$)	long
RegistryOpenSubkey	(RegKey as variant, strSubKey$)	long
RegistryRestoreKey	(strFile$)	
RegistrySaveKey	(strKey$, strFile$)	
RegistrySetValue	(RegKey as variant, strValueName$, Value as variant)	
RegistryValueExists	(RegKey as variant, strValueName$)	long

Table A-40
Scrollbar Control Routines, Parameters, and Return Values

Routine Name	Parameter List	Returns
ScrollGetClass	()	string
WScrollClassLen	()	long
WScrollEnabled	(strCtrl$, timeout&=DEF_WAIT)	long
WScrollEnd	(strCtrl$, timeout&=DEF_WAIT)	
WScrollExists	(strCtrl$, timeout&=DEF_WAIT)	long
WScrollFind	(strCtrl$, timeout&=DEF_WAIT)	long
WScrollFocus	(strCtrl$, timeout&=DEF_WAIT)	long
WScrollHome	(strCtrl$, timeout&=DEF_WAIT)	
WScrollLine	(strCtrl$, iLines&, timeout&=DEF_WAIT)	
WScrollMax	(strCtrl$, timeout&=DEF_WAIT)	long
WScrollMin	(strCtrl$, timeout&=DEF_WAIT)	long
WScrollMoveTo	(strCtrl$, x&=W_CENTER, y&=W_CENTER, timeout&=DEF_WAIT)	
WScrollPage	(strCtrl$, iPages&, timeout&=DEF_WAIT)	
WScrollPos	(strCtrl$, timeout&=DEF_WAIT)	long
WScrollSetClass	(strClass$)	
WScrollSetFocus	(strCtrl$, timeout&=DEF_WAIT)	
WScrollSetPos	(strCtrl$, iPos&, timeout&=DEF_WAIT)	

Table A-41
Slider Control Routines, Parameters, and Return Values

Routine Name	Parameter List	Returns
SliderGetClass	()	string
WSliderBy	(strCtrl$, nTicks&, timeout&=DEF_WAIT)	
WSliderByLine	(strCtrl$, nLines&, timeout&=DEF_WAIT)	
WSliderByPage	(strCtrl$, nPages&, timeout&=DEF_WAIT)	
WSliderClassLen	()	long

Routine Name	Parameter List	Returns
WSliderEnabled	(strCtrl$, timeout&=DEF_WAIT)	long
WSliderExists	(strCtrl$, timeout&=DEF_WAIT)	long
WSliderFind	(strCtrl$, timeout&=DEF_WAIT)	long
WSliderFocus	(strCtrl$, timeout&=DEF_WAIT)	long
WSliderLine	(strCtrl$, timeout&=DEF_WAIT)	long
WSliderMax	(strCtrl$, timeout&=DEF_WAIT)	long
WSliderMin	(strCtrl$, timeout&=DEF_WAIT)	long
WSliderMoveTo	(strCtrl$, x&=W_CENTER, y&=W_CENTER, timeout&=DEF_WAIT)	
WSliderPage	(strCtrl$, timeout&=DEF_WAIT)	long
WSliderPos	(strCtrl$, timeout&=DEF_WAIT)	long
WSliderSelMax	(strCtrl$, timeout&=DEF_WAIT)	long
WSliderSelMin	(strCtrl$, timeout&=DEF_WAIT)	long
WSliderSetClass	(strClassName$)	
WSliderSetFocus	(strCtrl$, timeout&=DEF_WAIT)	
WSliderToMax	(strCtrl$, timeout&=DEF_WAIT)	
WSliderToMin	(strCtrl$, timeout&=DEF_WAIT)	
WSliderToPos	(strCtrl$, nPos&, timeout&=DEF_WAIT)	
WSliderToSelMax	(strCtrl$, timeout&=DEF_WAIT)	
WSliderToSelMin	(strCtrl$, timeout&=DEF_WAIT)	

Table A-42
Spin Control Routines, Parameters, and Return Values

Routine Name	Parameter List	Returns
SpinGetClass	()	string
WSpinBy	(strCtrl$, nTicks&, timeout&=DEF_WAIT)	
WSpinClassLen	()	long
WSpinEnabled	(strCtrl$, timeout&=DEF_WAIT)	long
WSpinExists	(strCtrl$, timeout&=DEF_WAIT)	long

(continued)

Table A-42 *(continued)*

Routine Name	Parameter List	Returns
WSpinFind	(strCtrl$, timeout&=DEF_WAIT)	long
WSpinFocus	(strCtrl$, timeout&=DEF_WAIT)	long
WSpinMax	(strCtrl$, timeout&=DEF_WAIT)	long
WSpinMin	(strCtrl$, timeout&=DEF_WAIT)	long
WSpinMoveTo	(strCtrl$, x&=W_CENTER, y&=W_CENTER, timeout&=DEF_WAIT)	
WSpinPos	(strCtrl$, timeout&=DEF_WAIT)	long
WSpinSetClass	(strClassName$)	
WSpinSetFocus	(strCtrl$, timeout&=DEF_WAIT)	
WSpinToMax	(strCtrl$, timeout&=DEF_WAIT)	
WSpinToMin	(strCtrl$, timeout&=DEF_WAIT)	
WSpinToPos	(strCtrl$, nPos&, timeout&=DEF_WAIT)	

Table A-43
Static Control Routines, Parameters, and Return Values

Routine Name	Parameter List	Returns
LabelText	(hwnd&)	string
StaticGetClass	()	string
StaticText	(strText$, timeout&=DEF_WAIT)	string
WLabelLen	(hwnd&)	long
WResetClasses	()	
WStaticClassLen	()	long
WStaticExists	(strText$, timeout&=DEF_WAIT)	long
WStaticFind	(strText$, timeout&=DEF_WAIT)	long
WStaticLen	(strText$, timeout&=DEF_WAIT)	long
WStaticMoveTo	(strCtrl$, x&=W_CENTER, y&=W_CENTER, timeout&=DEF_WAIT)	
WStaticSetClass	(strClassName$)	

Table A-44
Statusbar Control Routines, Parameters, and Return Values

Routine Name	Parameter List	Returns
StatusGetClass	()	string
StatusItemText	(strCtrl$, strItem$, timeout&=DEF_WAIT)	string
WStatusClassLen	()	long
WStatusCount	(strCtrl$, timeout&=DEF_WAIT)	long
WStatusExists	(strCtrl$, timeout&=DEF_WAIT)	long
WStatusFind	(strCtrl$, timeout&=DEF_WAIT)	long
WStatusItemExists	(strCtrl$, strItem$, timeout&=DEF_WAIT)	long
WStatusItemIndex	(strCtrl$, strItem$, timeout&=DEF_WAIT)	long
WStatusItemLen	(strCtrl$, strItem$, timeout&=DEF_WAIT)	long
WStatusItemMoveTo	(strCtrl$, strItem$, timeout&=DEF_WAIT)	
WStatusMoveTo	(strCtrl$, x&=W_CENTER, y&=W_CENTER, timeout&=DEF_WAIT)	
WStatusSetClass	(strClassName$)	

Table A-45
TabView Control Routines, Parameters, and Return Values

Routine Name	Parameter List	Returns
TabGetClass	()	string
TabItemText	(strCtrl$, strItem$, timeout&=DEF_WAIT)	string
WTabClassLen	()	long
WTabCount	(strCtrl$, timeout&=DEF_WAIT)	long
WTabExists	(strCtrl$, timeout&=DEF_WAIT)	long

(continued)

Table A-45 *(continued)*

Routine Name	Parameter List	Returns
WTabFind	(strCtrl$, timeout&=DEF_WAIT)	long
WTabFocus	(strCtrl$, timeout&=DEF_WAIT)	long
WTabItemClk	(strCtrl$, strItem$, timeout&=DEF_WAIT)	
WTabItemExists	(strCtrl$, strItem$, timeout&=DEF_WAIT)	long
WTabItemIndex	(strCtrl$, strItem$, timeout&=DEF_WAIT)	long
WTabItemLen	(strCtrl$, strItem$, timeout&=DEF_WAIT)	long
WTabItemMoveTo	(strCtrl$, strItem$, timeout&=DEF_WAIT)	
WTabItemSelected	(strCtrl$, strItem$, timeout&=DEF_WAIT)	long
WTabSetClass	(strClassName$)	
WTabSetFocus	(strCtrl$, timeout&=DEF_WAIT)	

Table A-46
Taskbar Control Routines, Parameters, and Return Values

Routine Name	Parameter List	Returns
WTaskbarClk	(nBtn&=VK_RBUTTON)	
WTaskbarClockClk	(nBtn&=VK_LBUTTON)	
WTaskbarClockDblClk	(nBtn&=VK_LBUTTON)	
WTaskbarClockMoveTo	()	
WTaskbarCount	()	long
WTaskbarFind	()	long
WTaskbarFocus	()	long
WTaskbarIconClk	(nIcon&, nBtn&=VK_LBUTTON)	
WTaskbarIconCount	()	long
WTaskbarIconDblClk	(nIcon&, nBtn&=VK_LBUTTON)	
WTaskbarIconMoveTo	(nIcon&)	
WTaskbarItemClk	(strItem$, nBtn&=VK_LBUTTON)	
WTaskbarItemExists	(strItem$)	long

Routine Name	Parameter List	Returns
WTaskbarItemIndex	(strItem$)	long
WTaskbarItemMoveTo	(strItem$)	
WTaskbarItemSelected	(strItem$)	long
WTaskbarSetFocus	()	
WTaskbarStartClk	(nBtn&=VK_LBUTTON)	
WTaskbarStartMoveTo	()	

Table A-47
Toolbar Control Routines, Parameters, and Return Values

Routine Name	Parameter List	Returns
ToolbarButtonText	(strCtrl$, strBtn$, timeout&=DEF_WAIT)	string
ToolbarGetClass	()	string
WToolbarButtonChecked	(strCtrl$, strBtn$, timeout&=DEF_WAIT)	long
WToolbarButtonClk	(strCtrl$, strBtn$, timeout&=DEF_WAIT)	
WToolbarButtonCmdId	(strCtrl$, strBtn$, timeout&=DEF_WAIT)	long
WToolbarButtonEnabled	(strCtrl$, strBtn$, timeout&=DEF_WAIT)	long
WToolbarButtonExists	(strCtrl$, strBtn$, timeout&=DEF_WAIT)	long
WToolbarButtonIndex	(strCtrl$, strBtn$, timeout&=DEF_WAIT)	long
WToolbarButtonLen	(strCtrl$, strBtn$, timeout&=DEF_WAIT)	long
WToolbarButtonMoveTo	(strCtrl$, strBtn$, timeout&=DEF_WAIT)	
WToolbarButtonPressed	(strCtrl$, strBtn$, timeout&=DEF_WAIT)	long

(continued)

Table A-47 *(continued)*

Routine Name	Parameter List	Returns
WToolbarClassLen	()	long
WToolbarCount	(strCtrl$, timeout&=DEF_WAIT)	long
WToolbarExists	(strCtrl$, timeout&=DEF_WAIT)	long
WToolbarFind	(strCtrl$, timeout&=DEF_WAIT)	long
WToolbarMoveTo	(strCtrl$, x&=W_CENTER, y&=W_CENTER, timeout&=DEF_WAIT)	
WToolbarSetClass	(strClassName$)	

Table A-48
Tooltips Control Routines, Parameters, and Return Values

Routine Name	Parameter List	Returns
TipsGetClass	()	string
TipsText	(strCtrl$, timeout&=DEF_WAIT)	string
WTipsClassLen	()	long
WTipsExists	(strCtrl$, timeout&=DEF_WAIT)	long
WTipsFind	(strCtrl$, timeout&=DEF_WAIT)	long
WTipsLen	(strCtrl$, timeout&=DEF_WAIT)	long
WTipsSetClass	(strClassName$)	

Table A-49
TreeView Control Routines, Parameters, and Return Values

Routine Name	Parameter List	Returns
TreeGetClass	()	string
TreeGetPathChar	()	string
TreeItemPath	(strCtrl$, strItem$, timeout&=DEF_WAIT)	string
TreeItemText	(strCtrl$, strItem$, timeout&=DEF_WAIT)	string
WTreeClassLen	()	long

Routine Name	Parameter List	Returns
WTreeClk	(strCtrl$, x&=W_CENTER, y&=W_CENTER, nBtn&=VK_LBUTTON, timeout&=DEF_WAIT)	
WTreeCount	(strCtrl$, timeout&=DEF_WAIT)	long
WTreeCtrlDragTo	(strCtrl$, x&=W_CENTER, y&=W_CENTER, nBtn&=VK_LBUTTON, timeout&=DEF_WAIT)	
WTreeDragTo	(strCtrl$, x&=W_CENTER, y&=W_CENTER, nBtn&=VK_LBUTTON, timeout&=DEF_WAIT)	
WTreeEnabled	(strCtrl$, timeout&=DEF_WAIT)	long
WTreeExists	(strCtrl$, timeout&=DEF_WAIT)	long
WTreeFind	(strCtrl$, timeout&=DEF_WAIT)	long
WTreeFocus	(strCtrl$, timeout&=DEF_WAIT)	long
WTreeItemClk	(strCtrl$, strItem$, nBtn&=VK_LBUTTON, timeout&=DEF_WAIT)	
WTreeItemCollapse	(strCtrl$, strItem$, timeout&=DEF_WAIT)	
WTreeItemCount	(strCtrl$, strItem$, timeout&=DEF_WAIT)	long
WTreeItemCtrlDragTo	(strCtrl$, strItem$, nBtn&=VK_LBUTTON, timeout&=DEF_WAIT)	
WTreeItemDblClk	(strCtrl$, strItem$, nBtn&=VK_LBUTTON, timeout&=DEF_WAIT)	
WTreeItemDragTo	(strCtrl$, strItem$, nBtn&=VK_LBUTTON, timeout&=DEF_WAIT)	
WTreeItemExists	(strCtrl$, strItem$, timeout&=DEF_WAIT)	long
WTreeItemExpand	(strCtrl$, strItem$, timeout&=DEF_WAIT)	
WTreeItemExpanded	(strCtrl$, strItem$, timeout&=DEF_WAIT)	long

(continued)

Table A-49 (continued)		
Routine Name	**Parameter List**	**Returns**
WTreeItemExpandState	(strCtrl$, strItem$, timeout&=DEF_WAIT)	long
WTreeItemIndex	(strCtrl$, strItem$, timeout&=DEF_WAIT)	long
WTreeItemLen	(strCtrl$, strItem$, timeout&=DEF_WAIT)	long
WTreeItemMoveTo	(strCtrl$, strItem$, timeout&=DEF_WAIT)	
WTreeItemPathLen	(strCtrl$, strItem$, timeout&=DEF_WAIT)	long
WTreeItemSelected	(strCtrl$, strItem$, timeout&=DEF_WAIT)	long
WTreeItemShftDragTo	(strCtrl$, strItem$, nBtn&=VK_LBUTTON, timeout&=DEF_WAIT)	
WTreeMoveTo	(strCtrl$, x&=W_CENTER, y&=W_CENTER, timeout&=DEF_WAIT)	
WTreeSetClass	(strClassName$)	
WTreeSetFocus	(strCtrl$, timeout&=DEF_WAIT)	
WTreeSetPathChar	(strChar$)	
WTreeShftDragTo	(strCtrl$, x&=W_CENTER, y&=W_CENTER, nBtn&=VK_LBUTTON, timeout&=DEF_WAIT)	

Table A-50 Web ActiveX Routines, Parameters, and Return Values		
Routine Name	**Parameter List**	**Returns**
WebActiveXClick	(strContext$, strCtrl$, strKey$="", nBtn&=VK_LBUTTON, x&=W_CENTER, y&=W_CENTER, timeout&=DEF_WAIT)	
WebActiveXCount	(strContext$, timeout& =DEF_WAIT)	long

Routine Name	Parameter List	Returns
WebActiveXDblClk	(strContext$, strCtrl$, strKey$="", nBtn&=VK_LBUTTON, x&=W_CENTER, y&=W_CENTER, timeout&=DEF_WAIT)	
WebActiveXDragTo	(strContext$, strCtrl$, strKey$="", nBtn&=VK_LBUTTON, x&=W_CENTER, y&=W_CENTER, timeout&=DEF_WAIT)	
WebActiveXExists	(strContext$, strCtrl$, timeout& =DEF_WAIT)	long
WebActiveXGetItem	(strContext$, strCtrl$, strProp$, pItem as variant, timeout&=DEF_WAIT)	variant
WebActiveXGetProperty	(strContext$, strCtrl$, strProp$, timeout& =DEF_WAIT)	variant
WebActiveXHasProperty	(strContext$, strCtrl$, strProp$, timeout& =DEF_WAIT)	long
WebActiveXMethod	(strContext$, strCtrl$, strProp$, Args as array of variant)	variant
WebActiveXMoveTo	(strContext$, strCtrl$, x&=W_CENTER, y&=W_CENTER, timeout&=DEF_WAIT)	
WebActiveXPropertyList	(strContext$, strCtrl$, propList as array of OLECTL_PROPERTY, timeout&=DEF_WAIT)	long
WebActiveXSetProperty	(strContext$, strCtrl$, strProp$, pVar as variant, timeout& =DEF_WAIT)	

Table A-51
Web General Routines, Parameters, and Return Values

Routine Name	Parameter List	Returns
WebBack	(strContext$, Distance%=1, timeout&=DEF_WAIT)	
WebBrowserActivate	(strContext$, timeout& =DEF_WAIT)	
WebBrowserCount	(timeout& =DEF_WAIT)	long
WebBrowserExists	(strContext$, timeout& =DEF_WAIT)	long
WebBrowserInnerText	(strContext$, timeout& =DEF_WAIT)	string
WebBrowserTitle	(strContext$, timeout& =DEF_WAIT)	string
WebBrowserUpdate	()	
WebBrowserURL	(strContext$, timeout& =DEF_WAIT)	string
WebCheckboxClick	(strContext$, pForm$, pInputElement$, timeout&=DEF_WAIT)	
WebCheckboxExists	(strContext$, strForm$, strInputElement$, timeout&=DEF_WAIT)	long
WebCheckboxSetState	(strContext$, strForm$, strInputElement$, l&, timeout&=DEF_WAIT)	
WebCheckboxState	(strContext$, strForm$, strInputElement$, timeout&=DEF_WAIT)	long
WebExplore	(strURL$, timeout&=DEF_WAIT)	string
WebFndBrowser	(strBrowser$, dwFlags&=FWEB_DEFAULT, timeout&=DEF_WAIT)	string
WebFndFrame	(strContext$, strFrame$, dwFlags&=FWEB_DEFAULT, timeout&=DEF_WAIT)	string
WebFormAction	(strContext$, strForm$, timeout&=DEF_WAIT)	string
WebFormCount	(strContext$, timeout&=DEF_WAIT)	long

Routine Name	*Parameter List*	*Returns*
WebFormEncoding	(strContext$, strForm$, timeout&=DEF_WAIT)	string
WebFormExists	(strContext$, strForm$, timeout&=DEF_WAIT)	long
WebFormMethod	(strContext$, strForm$, timeout&=DEF_WAIT)	string
WebFormSetTarget	(strContext$, strForm$, strIN$, timeout&=DEF_WAIT)	
WebFormTarget	(strContext$, strForm$, timeout&=DEF_WAIT)	string
WebForward	(strContext$, Distance%=1, timeout&=DEF_WAIT)	
WebFrameCount	(strContext$, timeout&=DEF_WAIT)	long
WebFrameExists	(strContext$, strFrame$, timeout&=DEF_WAIT)	long
WebFrameProperty	(strContext$, pstrFrame$, pstrProp$, timeout&=DEF_WAIT)	variant
WebFrameSetProperty	(strContext$, pstrFrame$, pstrProp$, pVar as VARIANT, timeout&=DEF_WAIT)	
WebFrameSrc	(strContext$, strFrame$, timeout&=DEF_WAIT)	string
WebFrameTitle	(strContext$, strFrame$, timeout& =DEF_WAIT)	string
WebHiddenExists	(strContext$, strForm$, strInputElement$, timeout&=DEF_WAIT)	long
WebImageAlt	(strContext$, strImage$, timeout& =DEF_WAIT)	string
WebImageClick	(strContext$, strImage$, key&=VK_LBUTTON, x&=W_CENTER, y&=W_CENTER, timeout&=DEF_WAIT)	

(continued)

Table A-51 *(continued)*		
Routine Name	**Parameter List**	**Returns**
WebImageCount	(strContext$, timeout& =DEF_WAIT)	long
WebImageExists	(strContext$, strImage$, timeout&=DEF_WAIT)	long
WebImageISMAP	(strContext$, strImage$, timeout& =DEF_WAIT)	long
WebImageMapAreaCoords	(strContext$, strImage$, nIndex&, timeout& =DEF_WAIT)	string
WebImageMapAreaCount	(strContext$, strImage$, timeout& =DEF_WAIT)	long
WebImageMapAreaHref	(strContext$, strImage$, nIndex&, timeout&=DEF_WAIT)	string
WebImageMapAreaShape	(strContext$, strImage$, nIndex&, timeout&=DEF_WAIT)	string
WebImageRect	(strContext$, strImage$, rc as RECT, timeout&=DEF_WAIT)	
WebImageSetTitle	(strContext$, strImage$, strIN$, timeout& =DEF_WAIT)	
WebImageSrc	(strContext$, strImage$, timeout& =DEF_WAIT)	string
WebImageTitle	(strContext$, strImage$, timeout& =DEF_WAIT)	string
WebImageUSEMAP	(strContext$, strImage$, timeout& =DEF_WAIT)	string
WebInputElementClick	(strContext$, pForm$, pInputElement$, pType$, timeout&=DEF_WAIT)	
WebInputElementCount	(strContext$, strForm$, strType$, timeout& =DEF_WAIT)	long
WebInputElementEnabled	(strContext$, strForm$, strInputElement$, strType$, timeout&=DEF_WAIT)	long

Routine Name	*Parameter List*	*Returns*
WebInputElementExists	(strContext$, strForm$, strInputElement$, strType$, timeout&=DEF_WAIT)	long
WebInputElementProperty	(strContext$, strForm$, strInputElement$, strType$, pstrProp$, timeout&=DEF_WAIT)	variant
WebInputElement SetEnabled	(strContext$, strForm$, strInputElement$, strType$, l&, timeout&=DEF_WAIT)	
WebInputElement SetProperty	(strContext$, strForm$, strInputElement$, strType$, pstrProp$, pVar as VARIANT, timeout&=DEF_WAIT)	
WebInputElement SetState	(strContext$, strForm$, strInputElement$, strType$, l&, timeout& =DEF_WAIT)	
WebInputElementState	(strContext$, strForm$, strInputElement$, strType$, timeout& =DEF_WAIT)	long
WebInputElementTitle	(strContext$, strForm$, strInputElement$, strType$, timeout& =DEF_WAIT)	string
WebInputElementType	(strContext$, strForm$, strInputElement$, timeout& =DEF_WAIT)	string
WebInputElementValue	(strContext$, strForm$, strInputElement$, strType$, timeout&=DEF_WAIT)	string
WebInputImageClick	(strContext$, pForm$, pInputElement$, timeout& =DEF_WAIT)	
WebInputImageExists	(strContext$, strForm$, strInputElement$, timeout& =DEF_WAIT)	long
WebInputImageSrc	(strContext$, strForm$, strInputElement$, timeout& =DEF_WAIT)	string

(continued)

Table A-51 *(continued)*		
Routine Name	*Parameter List*	*Returns*
WebInputTextClick	(strContext$, pForm$, pInputElement$, timeout& =DEF_WAIT)	
WebInputTextExists	(strContext$, strForm$, strInputElement$, timeout& =DEF_WAIT)	long
WebInputTextMaxLength	(strContext$, strForm$, strInputElement$, timeout& =DEF_WAIT)	long
WebInputTextSize	(strContext$, strForm$, strInputElement$, timeout& =DEF_WAIT)	long
WebInputTextValue	(strContext$, strForm$, strInputElement$, timeout& =DEF_WAIT)	string
WebLabelCount	(strContext$, strForm$, timeout& =DEF_WAIT)	long
WebLabelFor	(strContext$, strForm$, strLabel$, timeout&= DEF_WAIT)	string
WebLabelInnerText	(strContext$, strForm$, strLabel$, timeout&= DEF_WAIT)	string
WebLinkClick	(strContext$, strLink$, timeout&=DEF_WAIT)	
WebLinkCount	(strContext$, timeout& =DEF_WAIT)	long
WebLinkExists	(strContext$, strLink$, timeout&=DEF_WAIT)	long
WebLinkHref	(strContext$, strLink$, timeout&=DEF_WAIT)	string
WebLinkInnerText	(strContext$, strLink$, timeout&=DEF_WAIT)	string
WebLinkSetTitle	(strContext$, strLink$, strIN$, timeout&=DEF_WAIT)	

Routine Name	Parameter List	Returns
WebLinkTarget	(strContext$, strLink$, timeout&=DEF_WAIT)	string
WebLinkTitle	(strContext$, strLink$, timeout&=DEF_WAIT)	string
WebNavigate	(strContext$, strURL$, timeout&=DEF_WAIT)	
WebPasswordClick	(strContext$, pForm$, pInputElement$, timeout& =DEF_WAIT)	
WebPasswordExists	(strContext$, strForm$, strInputElement$, timeout& =DEF_WAIT)	long
WebPasswordMaxLength	(strContext$, strForm$, strInputElement$, timeout& =DEF_WAIT)	long
WebPasswordSize	(strContext$, strForm$, strInputElement$, timeout& =DEF_WAIT)	long
WebPasswordValue	(strContext$, strForm$, strInputElement$, timeout& =DEF_WAIT)	string
WebQuit	(strContext$, timeout& =DEF_WAIT)	
WebRadioClick	(strContext$, pForm$, pInputElement$, timeout& =DEF_WAIT)	
WebRadioExists	(strContext$, strForm$, strInputElement$, timeout& =DEF_WAIT)	long
WebRadioSetState	(strContext$, strForm$, strInputElement$, l&, timeout&=DEF_WAIT)	
WebRadioState	(strContext$, strForm$, strInputElement$, timeout& =DEF_WAIT)	long

(continued)

Table A-51 *(continued)*		
Routine Name	*Parameter List*	*Returns*
WebResetClick	(strContext$, pForm$, pInputElement$, timeout& =DEF_WAIT)	
WebResetExists	(strContext$, strForm$, strInputElement$, timeout& =DEF_WAIT)	long
WebSelectCount	(strContext$, strForm$, timeout&=DEF_WAIT)	long
WebSelectEnabled	(strContext$, strForm$, strInputElement$, timeout& =DEF_WAIT)	long
WebSelectExists	(strContext$, strForm$, strInputElement$, timeout& =DEF_WAIT)	long
WebSelectOptionClick	(strContext$, strForm$, strInputElement$, strOption$, timeout&=DEF_WAIT)	
WebSelectOptionCount	(strContext$, strForm$, strInputElement$, timeout& =DEF_WAIT)	long
WebSelectOptionExists	(strContext$, strForm$, strInputElement$, strOption$, timeout&=DEF_WAIT)	long
WebSelectOption InnerText	(strContext$, strForm$, strInputElement$, strOption$, timeout&=DEF_WAIT)	string
WebSelectOptionProperty	(strContext$, strForm$, strInputElement$, strOption$, pstrProp$, timeout&=DEF_WAIT)	variant
WebSelectOption SetProperty	(strContext$, strForm$, strInputElement$, strOption$, pstrProp$, pVar as VARIANT, timeout&=DEF_WAIT)	
WebSelectOptionSetState	(strContext$, strForm$, strInputElement$, strOption$, l&, timeout&=DEF_WAIT)	

Routine Name	Parameter List	Returns
WebSelectOptionSetText	(strContext$, strForm$, strInputElement$, strOption$, strText$, timeout&=DEF_WAIT)	
WebSelectOptionState	(strContext$, strForm$, strInputElement$, strOption$, timeout&=DEF_WAIT)	long
WebSelectSize	(strContext$, strForm$, strInputElement$, timeout& =DEF_WAIT)	long
WebSetDefault WaitTimeout	(timeout&)	
WebSubmitClick	(strContext$, pForm$, pInputElement$, timeout& =DEF_WAIT)	
WebSubmitExists	(strContext$, strForm$, strInputElement$, timeout& =DEF_WAIT)	long
WebTableCellCount	(strContext$, strTable$, timeout&=DEF_WAIT)	long
WebTableCellExists	(strContext$, strTable$, strCell$, timeout&=DEF_WAIT)	long
WebTableCellInnerText	(strContext$, strTable$, strCell$, timeout&=DEF_WAIT)	string
WebTableCellProperty	(strContext$, strTable$, strCell$, pstrProp$, timeout& =DEF_WAIT)	variant
WebTableCellSetProperty	(strContext$, strTable$, strCell$, pstrProp$, pVar as VARIANT, timeout&=DEF_WAIT)	
WebTableCellTitle	(strContext$, strTable$, strCell$, timeout&=DEF_WAIT)	string
WebTableColumns	(strContext$, strTable$, timeout&=DEF_WAIT)	long
WebTableCount	(strContext$, timeout&=DEF_WAIT)	long

(continued)

Table A-51 *(continued)*

Routine Name	Parameter List	Returns
WebTableExists	(strContext$, strTable$, timeout&=DEF_WAIT)	long
WebTableRows	(strContext$, strTable$, timeout&=DEF_WAIT)	long
WebTagCount	(strContext$, strType$, timeout&=DEF_WAIT)	long
WebTagExists	(strContext$, strTag$, strType$, timeout&=DEF_WAIT)	long
WebTagHTML	(strContext$, strTag$, strType$, timeout&=DEF_WAIT)	string
WebTagInnerText	(strContext$, strTag$, strType$, timeout&=DEF_WAIT)	string
WebTagMoveTo	(strContext$, strTag$, strType$, x&=W_CENTER, y& =W_CENTER, timeout&=DEF_WAIT)	
WebTagProperty	(strContext$, pTag$, pType$, pstrProp$, timeout&=DEF_WAIT)	variant
WebTagSetHTML	(strContext$, strTag$, strType$, strIN$, timeout&=DEF_WAIT)	
WebTagSetInnerText	(strContext$, strTag$, strType$, strIN$, timeout&=DEF_WAIT)	
WebTagSetProperty	(strContext$, pTag$, pstrProp$, pType$, pVar as VARIANT, timeout&=DEF_WAIT)	
WebTextAreaClick	(strContext$, pForm$, pInputElement$, timeout& =DEF_WAIT)	
WebTextAreaCols	(strContext$, strForm$, pInputElement$, timeout& =DEF_WAIT)	long
WebTextAreaCount	(strContext$, strForm$, timeout&=DEF_WAIT)	long
WebTextAreaEnabled	(strContext$, strForm$, strInputElement$, timeout& =DEF_WAIT)	long

Routine Name	Parameter List	Returns
WebTextAreaExists	(strContext$, strForm$, strInputElement$, timeout& =DEF_WAIT)	long
WebTextAreaProperty	(strContext$, strForm$, strInputElement$, pstrProp$, timeout&=DEF_WAIT)	variant
WebTextAreaRows	(strContext$, strForm$, pInputElement$, timeout& =DEF_WAIT)	long
WebTextAreaSetProperty	(strContext$, strForm$, strInputElement$, pstrProp$, pVar as VARIANT, timeout& =DEF_WAIT)	
WebTextAreaValue	(strContext$, strForm$, strInputElement$, timeout& =DEF_WAIT)	string

Tip Like any good software product on the market, Visual Test has an *Easter egg*. Create a new Visual Test document in the Developer Studio and type in the following function call to see information about the Visual Test team:

```
VisualTestCredits
```

✦   ✦   ✦

Visual Test Products and Services

This appendix points you to companies and individuals offering products and services — for profit or otherwise — related to Visual Test.

The `www.vtindepth.com` Web site's purpose is to provide this same information, updated in a timely manner. For *up-to-date* information on hands-on training, video tapes, add-on products, and general freebie-type stuff, visit this Web site. It's the one-stop site for your Visual Test needs.

Videotapes

Currently, only one company is developing a set of training videos on Visual Test 6: InDepth Productions, Inc.

VT6 InDepth

The name of this new video series is *VT6 InDepth*. I'm the host of this new video series and will do my best to *show* you how to get started quickly using Visual Test.

What's in the video series

This video series is broken up into five (5) volumes (there are 2 VHS video tapes per volume):

+ Volume 1: The Tool, The Legend
+ Volume 2: Learning the Environment, Utilities, and Language

- ✦ Volume 3: Building a Powerful Test Suite
- ✦ Volume 4: Blowing Past the Basics
- ✦ Volume 5: Breaking Out 6.0's New Features

Note Also included throughout these volumes are interviews with people behind the scenes of the development of Visual Test. You'll hear what the programmers, test engineers, and other team members have to say about the creation of this awesome tool.

My unique opportunity to be a part of the development of Visual Test 6.0 allowed me to understand exactly what went into the product and why. I hope you find these videos helpful whether you're a beginner to Visual Test or a seasoned professional looking for ideas on how to improve upon your automation efforts.

Tip Detailed information on these videos can be found in the ad in the back of this book. Information on hands-on classes can be found later in this appendix.

Video pricing

Here is the pricing information for the Visual Test materials:

- ✦ *Visual Test 6 Bible* with CD-ROM: $49
- ✦ Any *VT6 InDepth* volume (2 tapes): $199
- ✦ All five volumes (10 video tapes) plus book with CD: $899

For more information call 425-644-9827 or e-mail info@inproduction.com.

Instruction and Consulting

There are only a few companies currently offering hands-on training on Visual Test: InDepth Productions, STA Group, and ST Labs. ST Labs has been offering Visual Test classes the longest. InDepth Productions is a newcomer that I'll be providing classes for. The STA Group is the newest company—just now arriving on the scene.

InDepth Productions

I'm personally going to be teaching the hands-on classes for InDepth Productions and hope that you will consider them when looking for help on learning Visual Test 6.0. For information on class times and dates, or to arrange a class at your company's site, visit InDepth Productions, Inc., on the Web at www.vtindepth.com/classes.htm. You can also call 425-644-9827, fax 425-747-9164, or e-mail info@inproduction.com for more information.

On the CD-ROM you'll find some of the interviews that were taped and edited by InDepth Productions for ST Labs. These are in RealVideo format. You'll need to download the RealNetworks RealPlayer from `www.real.com` and install it on your computer so that you can view these clips.

STA Group

The STA Group (Software Test Automation Group) offers Visual Test instruction and consulting. You can also contact them at 425-788-8015, fax 425-788-9073, or e-mail `info@stagroup.com`.

Refer to the information earlier in this appendix about training videos.

ST Labs

The software quality assurance services offered by ST Labs include creating a test plan, testing for hardware and software compatibility, providing short- or long-term consultants on site, or creating a full test team in its facilities for your testing project. Their hands-on classes are available in two forms: on site (at your company's location) and off site, in open enrollment classes they schedule monthly. Their hands-on three-day classes are around $1,500 per student. Visit them on the Web at `www.stlabs.com`. You can also call 800-STLLAB1 (785-5221), fax 425-974-0150, or e-mail `training@stlabs.com` for more information.

Information on ST Labs' hands-on classes can be found in their ad in the back of this book.

A few of ST Labs' articles on software quality assurance are on the CD-ROM. Make sure that you check these out from the main INDEX.HTM page found at the root of the CD.

A Free Online VT Book

A free book on Visual Test is available only in electronic form. Written by Richard Wartner and a number of contributors, this book is free for the taking. Source code is included and can be used in your testing projects. Although it is free, the authors of this book still maintain its copyright. For the latest version of this book, visit Mr. Wartner's Web site at `members.aol.com/rwvtest/index.htm`. (If this link isn't working, as can happen on the Web, visit `www.vtindepth.com` for the latest link.)

Richard also provides consulting on Visual Test, so if you're looking for an automation expert, visit his Web site or e-mail him at RWartner@aol.com for more information.

Richard Wartner was kind enough to allow me to include on the CD-ROM the latest version of his book that was available at the time of this writing. It can be found in the \RWARTNER directory (MAVBK05.EXE, version 1.05, May 30, 1998).

As I mentioned earlier, an "end-all and be-all" Web site has been created to point you to more sources of information about Visual Test. If you're looking for freebies, add-on tools, training, or just general information on Visual Test, visit www.vtindepth.com.

If you know of other companies or individuals offering services, freebies, or information, please visit this site and fill out the feedback form. This helps the site's managers keep it up to date with helpful, Visual Test–related information.

✦   ✦   ✦

James Bach's "Useful Features of a Test Automation System"

This appendix offers some insights into how an experienced professional software tester approaches the job. You may find that many of the concepts described will help you organize your own testing situations.

James Bach

James Bach has been in the software quality assurance industry for 13 years. An experienced tester for Apple Computer and a QA Manager at Borland International (renamed to Inprise Corporation), James most recently worked with ST Labs, Inc., as their Chief Scientist. He has since moved on to work on a book with Dr. Cem Kaner about software quality assurance.

Over the past couple of years, James has been compiling a list of useful features of automated tests. That list is provided here for your perusal. "Useful Features of a Test Automation System" is reprinted with permission from Software Testing Laboratories, Inc. (copyright 1995–1998, ST Labs, Inc.).

Useful Features of a Test Automation System

"I've run test teams at Apple and Borland. We tried to automate our tests. We had some success with it, but mostly we failed. Test automation for modern GUI software is very challenging. Along the way, though, I've collected this list of useful features and caveats that you might want to consider in doing your automation." — James Bach

1. **Suite is structured to support team development.** Break large monolithic source files down into smaller, cohesive units. Put the system under source control to prevent team members from overwriting each other's work. Naturally, this applies only if the suite is being developed jointly, but beware of those small projects that become big projects: It might be worthwhile to plan ahead.

2. **Suite can be distributed across a network of test execution systems.** As your test suite grows in size, and as your organization gains more test suites and products to test, you will find it increasingly difficult to make efficient use of your test machines.

   One way of maximizing efficiency is to centralize a group of test machines (at Borland there is a lab with 50 or more identical, centrally controlled systems) and create test suites that can be distributed to a number of machines at once. This can substantially reduce the time needed for a test cycle and eliminate the possibility that a problem with one machine will stop the whole suite from running.

   Another idea is to make the suite distributable to machines that are not otherwise dedicated to testing, such as computers normally used in development or administration. There are obvious risks to this strategy (such as the possibility of an automated test destroying a programmer's hard disk), but if your company has very few computers and a big need to test, it's useful to have the option of borrowing a few systems and getting each of them to run part of the test cycle.

3. **Suite can execute tests individually or by group.** You might design the suite such that it can run an individual test, a set of specific tests, a group of related tests, all tests, all tests except specific tests or groups of tests, or only tests that failed the last time through. Also, allow the order of tests to be modified. You get the idea—the suite should provide flexibility in test execution.

4. **Suite inter-operates with bug tracking system (bugs and tests are linkable).** Depending on the kind of testing that you do, enabling the test suite to record a failure directly into your bug tracking system (whether that system is a flat-file database or something more elaborate) may save time and effort. It may also waste time, if a high percentage of failures are due to automation problems and not defects in the product.

Another possible linkage might be the ability of the test automation to look in the bug tracking system for all fixed bugs and verify that they are still fixed. This requires that each bug report is accompanied by an automated test. Similar to that is the idea of marking a test as a "known failure until bug #3453 is fixed" and design the suite to execute that test, but ignore the failure until the associated bug is marked as fixed in the database.

The most feasible linkage I can think of is the ability to navigate directly from a bug in the tracking system to the part of the test suite that relates to it, and vice versa.

5. Suite can perform hardware reset of test machines in case of system crashes. It's common for test machines to crash during testing, so you want some way to restart the hardware if that happens. In one project, we used a software-controllable power strip attached to each test machine, and used another computer to monitor the status of each test machine. If a crash was detected, the monitoring computer would cycle the power on that system.

With modern O/S's, it's sometimes possible to monitor the status of one process from within another process on the same computer. That may be easier and cheaper to arrange than the hardware reset.

6. Suite can execute unattended. While a test suite that must be continually monitored can still be a lot better than manual testing, it's often more valuable to design it to run to completion without any help.

7. Suite execution can be restarted from the point of interruption in case of catastrophic failure (for example, power loss). The more tests that you automate, the less you want your tests to start all over again from the beginning if the suite is halted in the middle of execution. This isn't as easy as it may sound, if your test drivers are dependent on variables and structures stored in memory.

By designing the system to write checkpoints out to disk, and to have an automatic start process that activates on reboot, and to have a means of resynchronizing to any other systems that it is connected to (such as file servers, which typically take longer to reset after the power goes out), you ensure that your suite will survive a power outage and still be kicking.

8. Suite can be paused, single-stepped, and resumed. In debugging the suite, or monitoring it for any reason, it's often important to be able to stop it or slow it down, perhaps to diagnose a problem or adjust a test, and then set it going again from where it left off.

9. Suite can be executed remotely. Unless you live with your test machines, as some do, it's nice to be able to send a command from your workstation and get the test machines to wake up and start testing. Otherwise, you do a lot of walking to the lab. It's especially nice if you can query the status of a suite, start it, stop it, or adjust it over the phone. Even from home, you'd be able to get those machines cracking.

10. Suite is executable on a variety of system configurations to support compatibility testing. Automated suites should be designed with a minimum of assumptions about the configuration of the test machine. Since compatibility testing is so important, try to parameterize and centralize all configuration details, so that you can make the suite run on a variety of test machines.

11. Suite architecture is modular for maximum flexibility. This is as true for testware as it is for software. You will reuse your testware. You will maintain and enhance it. So build it such that you can replace or improve one part of it, say the test reporting mechanism, without having to rewrite every test.

> Remember: *testware is software.*
>
> Just as software requires careful thought and design, you will discover that testware requires the same. Another aspect of good structure is to centralize all suite configuration parameters in one place. Here are some factors that might be controlled by a configurations file:
>
> • Whether or not to log every navigational step taken during the test
>
> • Whether or not to write out memory info before/after each test
>
> • Where output is directed: common I/O, log file, debug monitor, nowhere
>
> • Whether to perform screen comparisons or to rebuild capture files instead
>
> • Which directory in which to place log files
>
> • Which directories in which to read/write binary (capture) files

12. Suite can reset test machine(s) to known state prior to each test. There are good reasons to reset the test machine to a clean, known state, and there are also good reasons not to do that. Resetting helps in the process of investigating a problem, but not resetting is a more realistic test, since presumably your users will not be rebooting their computers between opening a file and printing it! A good idea is to make it a selectable option, so the tests can run either way.

13. Suite execution and analysis take less time and trouble than hand-testing. I know, it sounds pretty obvious. Alas, it needs to be said. Too many testers and managers approach test automation for its own sake. Instead, look critically at how much time and effort you are heaping on your automation. In the beginning automation costs more, yes, but too often even after a couple of years it still takes more effort to manage the automation than it would just to do the same thing by hand.

> The most common problems, in my experience, are false fails. Every time the test suite reports a fail that turned out to be a problem with the suite itself, or a trivial misalignment between the test and the latest conception of the product, all the time needed to solve that problem is pure automation cost. Generally speaking, keep the suite architecture as simple as possible, to keep maintenance costs down.

14. Suite creates summary, coverage, result, debug, and performance logs.

> A summary log is an overview of the results of the test suite: how many tests were executed, how many passed, failed, are unknown, and so on.

> A coverage log shows what features were tested. You can achieve this by maintaining an electronic test outline that is associated with the test suite. If you have the appropriate tool, a coverage log should also report on code-level coverage.

> A result log records the outcome of each test.

> A debug log contains messages that track the progress of the test suite. Each entry should be time-stamped. This helps in locating problems with the suite when it mysteriously stops working.

> A performance log tracks how long each test took to execute. This helps in spotting absolute performance problems, as well as unexpected changes in relative performance.

15. Suite creates global (suite-wide) and local (test-specific) logs. Except for the summary log, all the logs should have global and local versions. The local versions of the logs should be cumulative from test cycle to test cycle. Each local log pertains to a single test and is stored next to that test. They form a history of the execution of that test. Global logs should be reinitialized at every test cycle, and they should include information about all of the tests.

16. Suite logs are accessible and readable. Logs ought to be both machine readable and human readable. I also recommend that they be tied into an icon or some other convenient front end, so that they are easy to get to.

17. Tests can be selectively activated or deactivated. There should be a mechanism (other than commenting out test code) to deactivate a test, such that it does not execute along with all the other tests. This is useful for when a test reveals a crash bug, and there is no reason to run it again until the bug is fixed.

18. Tests are easily reconfigured, replicated, or modified. An example of this is a functional test of a program with a graphical user interface that can be configured to simulate either mouse input or keyboard input. Rather than create different sets of tests to operate in different modes and contexts, design a single test with selectable behavior.

> Avoid hard-coding basic operations in a given test. Instead, engineer each test in layers and allow its behavior to be controlled from a central configuration file. Move sharable/reusable code into separate include files.

19. Tests are important and unique. You might think the best test suite is one with the best chance of finding a problem. Not so. Remember, you want to find a lot of important problems, and be productive in getting them reported and fixed. So in a well-designed test suite, for every significant bug in the product, one and only one test will fail. This is an ideal, of course, but we can come close to it.

In other words, if an enterprising developer changes the background color of the screen, or the spelling of a menu item, you don't want 500 tests to fail (I call it the "500 fail scenario," and it gives me chills). You want one test to fail, at most.

Whenever a test fails, you know that at least one thing went wrong, but you can't know if more than one thing went wrong until you investigate. If 500 tests fail, it would help you to budget your time if you were confident that 500 different and important problems had been detected. That way, even before your investigation began, you would have some idea of the quality of the product. Likewise, you don't want tests to fail on bugs so trivial that they won't be fixed, while great big whopper bugs go unnoticed.

Therefore, I suggest automating interesting and important tests before doing the trivial ones. Avoid full-screen snapshots, and use partial screen shots or pattern recognition instead. Maybe have one single test that takes a series of global snapshots, just to catch some of those annoying little UI bugs. Also, consider code inspection, instead of test automation, to test data-intensive functionality, like online help. It's a lot easier to read files than it is to manipulate screenshots.

20. Dependencies between tests can be specified. Tests that depend on other tests can be useful. Perhaps you know that if one particular test fails, there's no reason to run any other tests in a particular group. However, this should be explicitly specified to the test suite, so that it will skip dependent tests. Otherwise, many child tests will appear to fail due to one failure in a parent test.

21. Tests cover specific functionality without covering more than necessary. Narrowly defined tests help to focus on specific failures and avoid the 500 failure scenario. The downside is that overly narrow tests generally miss failures that occur on a system level. For that reason, specify a combination of narrow and broader tests. One way to do that is to create narrow tests that do individual functions, then create a few broad tests, dependent on the narrow ones, that perform the same functions in various combinations.

22. Tests can be executed on a similar product or a new version of the product without major modification. Consider that the test suite will need to evolve as the software that it tests evolves. It's common for software to be extended, ported, or unbundled into smaller applications. Consider how your suite will accommodate that.

One example is localization. If you are called upon to test a French version of the software, will that require a complete rewrite of each and every test? This desirable attribute of test automation can be achieved, but may lead to very complex test suites. Be careful not to trade a simple suite that can be quickly thrown out and rewritten for a super-complex suite that is theoretically flexible but also full of bugs.

23. Test programs are reviewable. Tests must be maintained, and that means they must be revisited. Reviewability is how easy it is to come back to a test and understand it.

24. Test programs are easily added to the suite. In some suites I've seen, it's major surgery just to add a new test. Make it easy and the suite will grow more quickly.

25. Tests are rapidly accessible. I once saw a test management system where it took more than 30 seconds to navigate to a single test from the top level of the system. That's awful. It discouraged test review and test development. Design the system such that you can access a given test in no more than a few seconds. Also, make sure the tests are accessible by anyone on the team.

26. Tests are traceable to a test outline. To some it's obvious, for me it was a lesson that came the hard way: Do not automate tests that can't already be executed by hand. That way, when the automation breaks, you will still be able to get your testing done. Furthermore, if your automated tests are connected to a test outline, you can theoretically assess functional test coverage in real time. The challenge is to keep the outline in sync with both the product and the tests.

27. Tests are reviewed, and their review status is documented in-line. This is especially important if several people are involved in writing the tests. Believe it or not, I have seen many examples of very poorly written tests that were overlooked for years. It's an unfortunate weakness (and most of us have it) that we will quickly assume that our test suite is full of useful tests, whether or not we personally wrote those tests. Many bad experiences have convinced me that it's dangerous to assume this!

    Test suites most often contain nonsense. *Review them!*

    In order to help manage the review process, I suggest recording the date of review within each test. That will enable you to periodically re-review tests that haven't been touched in a while. Also, review tests that never fail, and ones that fail very often. Review, especially, those tests that fail falsely.

28. Test hacks and temporary patches are documented in-line. Adopt a system for recording the assumptions behind the test design, and any hacks or workarounds that are built into the test code. This is important, as there are always hacks and temporary changes in the tests that are easy to forget about. I recommend creating a code to indicate hacks and notes, perhaps three asterisks, as in: `*** Disabled the 80387 switch until co-processor bug is fixed`. Periodically, you should search for triple-asterisk codes, in order not to forget about intentionally crippled tests.

29. Suite is well documented. You should be able to explain to someone else how to run the test suite. At Borland, I used the "Dave" test. When one of my testers claimed to have finished documenting how to run a suite, I'd send Dave, another one of the testers, to try to run it. That invariably flushed out problems.

✦   ✦   ✦

Other Materials Relating to Software Quality Assurance

This appendix points you to other sources of information that relate to the realm of software quality assurance.

The Internet

The Internet is a wealth of information for everyone, including those interested in quality assurance and test automation. Newsgroups, list servers, and Web sites are some of the most common ways to get information on areas of interest.

Newsgroups

The COMP.SOFTWARE.TESTING newsgroup covers all areas of software quality assurance, ranging from UNIX applications, to Macintosh applications, to Microsoft Windows applications. Use your favorite Internet provider — Microsoft Network (MSN), CompuServe, America Online (AOL), or a local provider — to get access to this newsgroup. If you're looking for a job in QA, have job openings in your group, want to know others' thoughts on a particular testing tool, or just want to share your opinion on testing methodologies, this is the place to come.

Also, since software testing is a subdiscipline of software engineering, you might find COMP.SOFTWARE-ENG helpful.

MT_Info

When a subject area isn't large enough to warrant a newsgroup, list servers are created. A list server is a large mailing list that people with Internet e-mail accounts can add themselves to. When someone sends a message to a given list server, that message is then broadcast to the members of that list.

I created one such list in January 1995 in the interest of providing a forum for the discussion of test automation using Microsoft Test, Visual Test, and now Rational Visual Test 6.0. This list has continued to grow and currently has over 700 members!

To join in on the discussion, or to just "lurk" and read what others write, subscribe to the list by sending e-mail to mt_info-request@eskimo.com with the word SUBSCRIBE in the Subject line of your message. Take care not to have any text in the body of your message, including any kind of auto-signature.

Should you want to remove yourself from this list, simply send e-mail to mt_info-request@eskimo.com again. This time, however, use the word UNSUBSCRIBE in the Subject line of your message (again ensuring that no text is in the body of your message).

You can also visit www.vtindepth.com, which has information about this listserver. There are plans to archive some of the listserver messages at this site as well.

The CD-ROM in the back of this book has information about the MT_Info listserver and the www.vtindepth.com Web site. Be sure to check it out.

Web Sites

A lot of Web sites have popped up just in the last two years—since this book was first published. To find relevant sites, I suggest going to a search engine like www.yahoo.com or any other engine that you might have as a favorite. Type in the keywords: **software quality assurance**. This will provide you with a wealth of Web sites. It is here that I will point out some of my favorites.

VT InDepth

This site is one that I help maintain, and hence I'm listing it first because it is my favorite of all of these Web sites ;-) . My goal is to make it *the end-all, be-all Visual Test Web site!* It will provide links to other Visual Test–related pages, information about services offered by other companies (such as hands-on training and consulting), products (such as video tapes and add-on tools), and free stuff to help you get the most effective use out of Visual Test. It will also point to the links listed in this appendix and to others as time goes on. Visit this Web site at www.vtindepth.com.

A link to this site and information about its video tapes are available on the CD-ROM in the back of this book.

Rational Web Pages

Rational Software has a number of helpful Web pages. Their main home page is at www.rational.com.

For general information about Visual Test, the Web site to visit is www.rational.com/products/visualtest/.

ST Labs' Visual Test Page

The following Web page provides tips on using Visual Test, and it has links to other Web pages relating to Visual Test. Here's the direct path to their Visual Test pages so that you can avoid their annoying sign-up screen (if they read this, this path may change. Visit www.vtindepth.com for the latest links): www.stlabs.com/testnet/docs/mst.htm.

ST Labs has provided some of their articles and white papers on the CD-ROM in the back of this book. If you don't have a current link to the Internet (are you reading this on an airplane right now?), then you can begin by reading these articles. The next time you have access to the Internet, be sure to visit their Web site—specifically their Testers Network—for more great articles.

Note that ST Labs updates their Web server frequently, so if this link suddenly becomes broken, go to their home page at www.stlabs.com and work your way down to the Testers Network.

Data Dimensions

Data Dimensions develops solutions and services to help organizations manage enterprise-wide system changes. Since 1991, Data Dimensions has helped over 200 clients address their Year 2000 issues. You can reach them at www.data-dimensions.com.

Marick's Corner

Brian Marick maintains the following Frequently Asked Questions (FAQs) lists and posts them periodically to the comp.software.testing newsgroup mentioned previously:

 ✦ Testing Contractors and Consultants

 ✦ Testing Courses

 ✦ Testing Tool Suppliers

These FAQs are also available at:

```
www.stlabs.com/marick/root.htm
ftp://cs.uiuc.edu/pub/testing/faqs/
```

Brian is working on getting his FAQs approved for `news.answers` and the standard repositories that go with it.

Mainsoft Corporation

Are you doing UNIX and Microsoft Windows NT application development? Are you planning on using Rational Visual Test? If so, you need to check these guys out because they are the ones who have an agreement with Microsoft at Rational Software to port versions of Visual Test over to the UNIX platform running X-Windows. You can reach them at `www.mainsoft.com`.

NuMega Technologies

NuMega Technologies brings QA into the beginning of the development cycle by helping developers find bugs before releasing a build to the testing team. This is accomplished through their SoftICE and BoundsChecker products. They were purchased in 1997 by Compuware Corporation and continue to provide some of the coolest tools on the market for helping you release high-quality products. Visit NuMega on the Web at `www.numega.com`.

Compuware Corporation

Compuware provides the whole enchilada. They have SQA products, services, and training. These guys focus on large scale IT projects helping with the design, develop, and deployment phases. Check 'em out at `www.compuware.com`.

STA Group

The STA Group (Software Test Automation Group) is an automation-specific instruction and consulting company that can help you get your test automation projects on track. If Visual Test automation is in your sights, this group may be able to help write scripts to get you started. Visit them at their Web site: `www.stagroup.com`.

Software Productivity Center

SPC is an industry-driven, nonprofit, technical resource center for software developers. Founded in 1992, it has more than 100 members and offers a wide range of courses, seminars, and products. Both products and services are offered nationally and internationally. The home page for the SPC is `www.spc.ca`.

Vericode, Inc.

These guys are like a small version of ST Labs, Inc. They provide outsourced testing services to software development organizations. Their automation skills focus on Rational Visual Test and SQA TeamTest. Visit them at `www.vericode.com`.

Publications

If you're the type who avoids surfing the Net and prefer materials provided to you in hard copy form, then you'll be interested in the following newsletters and books on the subject of testing software.

Newsletters

This section lists the publisher's name, newsletter title, and address for each newsletter.

Computing Trends

The Software Practitioner

350 Dalkeith Avenue

Los Angeles, CA 90049

Tel: 310-440-9982

Software Maintenance News Inc.

Software Maintenance News

B10, Suite 237

4546 El Camino Real

Los Altos, CA 94022

ST Labs, Inc.

STL Report

3535–128th Avenue SE

Sterling Plaza — Third Floor

Bellevue, WA, 98006

Tel: 425-974-0174 or 800-STLLAB1 (785-5221)

Fax: 425-974-0150

E-mail: Info@STLabs.com

TTN

Testing Techniques Newsletter

Tel: 415-957-1441 or 800-942-SOFT

Fax: 415-957-0730

E-mail: ttn@soft.com

Books

Arnold, Thomas. *Software Testing with Visual Test 4.0*. IDG Books Worldwide, 1996. ISBN 0-7645-8000-0.

Beizer, Boris. *Software System Testing and Quality Assurance*. New York: Von Nostrand Reinhold, 1984. ISBN 0-442-21306-9.

Beizer, Boris. *Software Testing Techniques*, Second Edition. New York: Von Nostrand Reinhold, 1990. ISBN 0-442-20672-0.

DeMillo, R.A., McCracken, W.M., Martin, R.J., and Passafiume, J.F. *Software Testing and Evaluation*. Menlo Park, CA: Benjamin/Cummings, 1987. ISBN 0-8053-2535-2.

Deutsch, M.S. *Software Verification and Validation — Realistic Project Approaches*. Englewood Cliffs, NJ: Prentice Hall, 1982. ISBN 0-13-822072-7.

Dunn, Robert H. *Software Quality: Concepts and Plans*. Englewood Cliffs, NJ: Prentice Hall, 1990. ISBN 0-13-820283-4.

Dustin, Elfriede, Paul, John, and Rashka, Jeff. *Automated Software Testing*. 1998 (or 1999. Not published as of the published date of this Visual Test 6 book. Hopefully their title and ISBN number that they gave me haven't changed). Addison-Wesley. ISBN 0-201-43287-0.

Friedman, Michael, and Voas, Jeffrey M. *Software Assessment: Reliability, Safety, Testability*. New York: Wiley Press, 1995. ISBN 0-471-01009-X.

Hetzel, B. *The Complete Guide to Software Testing*, Second Edition. Wellesley, MA: QED Information Sciences, 1988. ISBN 0-89435-242-3.

Ince, Darrel. *An Introduction to Software Quality Assurance and Its Implementation*. London, New York: McGraw Hill, 1994. ISBN 0-07-707924-8.

Kaner, Cem, Falk, J., and Nguyen, H.Q. *Testing Computer Software*, Second Edition. New York: Von Nostrand Reinhold, 1993. ISBN 0-442-01361-2.

Marick, Brian. *The Craft of Software Testing.* Englewood Cliffs, NJ: Prentice Hall, 1995. ISBN 0-13-177411-5.

Marks, D.M. *Testing Very Big Systems.* New York: McGraw Hill, 1992. ISBN 0-07-040433-X.

McConell, Steve. *Code Complete: A Practical Handbook of Software Construction.* Redmond, Washington: Microsoft Press, 1993. ISBN 1-55-615484-4.

Mosley, D.J. *The Handbook of MIS Application Software Testing.* Englewood Cliffs, NJ: Prentice Hall, 1993. ISBN 0-13-907007-9.

Myers, Glenford J. *The Art of Software Testing.* New York: John Wiley and Sons, 1979. ISBN 0-471-04328-1.

Ould, M.A., and Unwin, C., eds. *Testing in Software Development.* Cambridge: Cambridge University Press, 1986. ISBN 0-521-33786-0.

Parrington, Norman, and Roper, Marc. *Understanding Software Testing.* Ellis Horwood Limited, 1989. ISBN 0-7458-0533-7. (Also: Ellis Horwood Limited. ISBN 0-470-21462-7 [Halsted Press].)

Royer, T.C. *Software Testing Management—Life on the Critical Path.* Englewood Cliffs, NJ: Prentice Hall, 1993. ISBN 0-13-532987-6.

✦   ✦   ✦

Listing for the Automated Monkey

The following listings are from the monkey discussed in Chapter 14. The idea of the automated monkey is that it goes beyond a simple chimp that bangs on the keyboard. Instead it has some knowledge of how to deal with situations so that it can continue its testing. This source code was written by Noel Nyman of Microsoft Corporation, with some of the ideas provided by Brian Tervo and Rom Walton, also of Microsoft.

On the CD-ROM

The source code file for these listings can be found in the MONKEY folder on the CD-ROM included with this book.

Note

FREDDIE.MST

The FREDDIE.MST file is the main file that gets run by Visual Test to cause the
monkey tests to execute. You'll notice that it's fairly small to make it easily readable
and understandable. The bulk of the code can be found in its include files (which
are all included by a single main include file called FREDDIE_INCLUDES.INC).

```
'=========================================================
' Freddie.mst
'
' Purpose:
'    Demonstrate GUI stateless or "dumb" monkey testing
'    of Windows applications.
'
' Dependencies:
'    * Several .inc (include) files listed in
'      Freddie_Includes.inc
'    * An .ini (initialization) text file that lists
'      characteristics
'      of the application being tested
'
' Some of the best parts of Freddie are based on ideas from
' Brian Tervo and Rom Walton.
'=========================================================

On Error Goto ErrorTrap    'handles both VT trappable errors and
                           'some custom errors Freddie generates

'list of all .inc files Freddie uses
'$Include 'Freddie_Includes.inc'

InitializeFreddie    'fill variables and seed random number
                     'generator
StartApplication     'kill any instances and start the app

'Calculate time to stop testing
iStartTime = Int(Timer/60)
iTargetTime = iStartTime + giTimeToTest
giTestNumber = 0

'Keep testing until the test time is up
While (Int(Timer/60) < iTargetTime)
    'Restart the app if it's gone (perhaps we tested File\Exit)
    If fnWindowIsGone(ghWndExe, 1) Then
        StartApplication
    EndIf

    'Put something on the clipboard in case Freddie tests paste
    Clipboard "Freddie is testing at " + Time + " on " + Date
```

```
        'Add test numbers to the log
        giTestNumber = giTestNumber + 1
        FreddiePrint("")
        FreddiePrint("-- Test " + _trm(giTestNumber) + " --")
        'Test something
        ExecuteATest
WEnd

'Done, wrap it up
Pause "All done, closing the application."
FreddiePrint("")
FreddiePrint("*********************************************")
FreddiePrint("**** All done, closing the application *******")
FreddiePrint("****        Ended: " + Time)
FreddiePrint("*********************************************")

'Kill app at end of tests
KillAnyRunningAppProcesses

End

ErrorTrap:
 'Process Freddie's custom errors first
 If ERR = FREDDIE_GENERAL_ERROR Then
    FreddiePrint("*** ERROR: A general Freddie error
occurred")
    FreddiePrint("***          " + gstrFreddieError)
 ElseIf ERR = FREDDIE_ASSERT_ERROR Then
    FreddiePrint("*** ERROR: " + gstrFreddieError)

  'Everything left are VT errors
 Else
    FreddiePrint("*** ERROR: Something really nasty
happened!")
    FreddiePrint("*** #" + _trm(ERR) + ", " + _
                 Error$ + " at " _
                 + _trm(ERL) + " in " + ERF)
    FreddiePrint("***        Freddie will kill and restart" _
                 + " the application")
    StartApplication
 EndIf
```

FREDDIE_INCLUDES.INC

Noel took the approach of creating a master include file that includes all of the other necessary include files needed by FREDDIE.MST. This is a great approach to working with include files.

```
'============================================================
' Freddie_Includes.inc
'
' Purpose:
'     Support file for Freddie.mst
'============================================================
'$Include 'winapi.inc'
'$Include 'Freddie_Variables_And_Constants.inc'
'$Include 'Freddie_General_Routines.inc'
'$Include 'Application_Strings.inc'
'$Include 'Freddie_Start_Kill_App.inc'
'$Include 'Freddie_Tests.inc'
'$Include 'Freddie_Log_Routines.inc'
```

WINAPI.INC

The WINAPI.INC file is not listed here. It is a standard file that comes with Visual Test that allows for linking into the standard Windows interface. This not only provides the function declarations for providing those links, it also provides the declarations for user-defined data types. Go to the INCLUDE directory in the VT6 folder in the installed Visual Studio folder on your hard drive. That is where you can find and view the WINAPI.INC file (it's rather large).

FREDDIE_VARIABLES_AND_CONSTANTS.INC

The globally used variables and constants for the FREDDIE.MST file and its subroutines are found in this FREDDIE_VARIABLES_AND_CONSTANTS.INC file.

```
'============================================================
' Freddie_Variables_And_Constants.inc
'
' Purpose:
'     Support file for Freddie.mst
'     Declare/define constants, variables, macros and a type
'============================================================
'$IfNDef Freddie_Variables_And_Constants
'$Define Freddie_Variables_And_Constants

'Change this constant to point to the current app .ini file
Const APP_INI_FILE    = "c:\freddie\OurApp Build1.ini"
'Change this constant use a different name for the log file
Const APP_LOG_FILE    = "OurAppLog.log"

'Increase for slow machines, you may be able to reduce them
'on fast machines
```

```
Const SHORT_WAIT        = 5
Const AVERAGE_WAIT      = 10

'Saves typing for all those WFndWnd commands
Const EXIST             = FW_PART or FW_EXIST or FW_ERROR
Const NOEXIST           = FW_PART or FW_NOEXIST or FW_ERROR

'VT doesn't use negative error numbers, so we can use them
'for Freddie's "private" error codes and detect them in the
'error trap
Const FREDDIE_GENERAL_ERROR = -2

'Not defined in winapi.inc for some reason. We need this to
'use a callback to enumerate child window handles
Type WNDENUMPROC as Pointer to _
Function StdCall (hwnd&, lParam&) as Long


'-- Globals --
Global ghWndChildren(0 to 0)    as HWND
Global ghWndExe                 as HWND
Global giTestNumber             as Integer
Global giTimeToTest             as Integer
Global gstrApplicationCaption   as String
Global gstrApplicationClass     as String
Global gstrAppIniFile           as String
Global gstrExeName              as String
Global gstrExePath              as String
Global gstrFreddieError         as String
Global gstrMenus(0 to 0)        as String
Global gstrTestFileName         as String

'-- Macros --
    'Trim white space from numeric converted strings
Macro _trm(NumericValue) = Trim$(Str$(NumericValue))

    'Returns a random value between a and b inclusive
    '   Random algorithm:  Smaller + Int( Rnd * (Larger -
    '                       Smaller + 1 ))
    '
    '   To determine the smaller of and b:  -1 * b * (a > b)
    '                                       -1 * a * (a <= b)
    '       since (a > b) is either 0 or -1
    '   (The Mod call works around a Rnd bug in VT4)
Macro _RndBetween(a, b) = _
        -1 * b * (a > b) _
        -1 * a * (a <= b) _
        + Int((Rnd Mod 1) * ( _
        -1 * (b * (b > a) + a * (b <= a)) _
        + (b * (a > b) + a * (a <= b)) + 1 ))

'-- Main scope (not global) variables --
```

```
      Dim iStartTime      as Integer
      Dim iTargetTime     as Integer

      '$EndIf            'Freddie_Variables_And_Constants
```

FREDDIE_GENERAL_ROUTINES.INC

```
      '==========================================================
      ' Freddie_General_Routines.inc
      '
      ' Purpose:
      '    Support file for Freddie.mst
      '
      '    Functions used in several parts of Freddie
      '==========================================================
      '$IfNDef Freddie_General_Routines
      '$Define Freddie_General_Routines

      Declare Sub ClickAtRandom(hWnd as HWND)
      Declare Sub EnumerateChildrenToArray (hWnd as HWND)
      Declare Sub InitializeFreddie
      Declare Sub FreddieAssert(lIsTrue as Long)
      Declare Function fnReadApplicationSectionKey(strKeyName as _
      String) as String
      Declare Function fnThisIsANewWindow(hWndNewWindow as _
                       HWND) as Long
      Declare Function fnWindowIsGone(hWnd as HWND, iTimeToWait as _
      Integer) as Long
      Declare Function fnWndEnumProc_GetHWNDS(hWnd as Long, lParam _
      as Long) as Long
      Declare Sub FreddicAssert(lIsTrue as Long)
      Declare Sub InitializeFreddie


      '_____
      ' Sub ClickAtRandom(hWnd as HWND)
      '
      ' Click at random points in hWnd. May click on controls, drop
      ' lists, scroll bars, buttons, or nothing at all.
      ' Occasionally one of these clicks will dismiss the
      ' dialog (click on Cancel, for example) before all the
      ' clicks are done.
      '_____

      Sub ClickAtRandom(hWnd as HWND)
          Dim iCellWidth  as Integer
          Dim iCellHeight as Integer
          Dim iCount      as Integer
          Dim iXpos       as Integer
```

```
    Dim iYPos          as Integer
    Dim wInfo          as Info

    'Divide the hWnd client area into an imaginary
    '10x10 grid of "cells"
    WGetInfo(hWnd, wInfo)
    iCellWidth = Int(wInfo.wWidth/10)
    iCellHeight = Int(wInfo.wHeight/10)

    For iCount = 1 to 10
        'Pick a point inside one of the 100 "cells"
        iXPos = 5 + (_RndBetween(0, 9) * iCellWidth)
        iYPos = 5 + (_RndBetween(0, 9) * iCellHeight)

        'Click the chosen spot
        'make sure it's still a valid window
        '(they tend to vanish sometimes)
        If IsWindow(hWnd) Then
            Play hWnd, "{CLICK " + _trm(iXPos) + ", " +
_trm(iYPos) + "}"
        EndIf
        Sleep 0.5
    Next
End Sub


'_____
'
' EnumerateChildrenToArray(hWnd)
'
' Clears the global array ghWndChildren() and puts the
' handles of all of hWnd's children in the array.
'_____


Sub EnumerateChildrenToArray (hWnd as HWND)
    Dim pfnWndEnumProc   as WNDENUMPROC
    Dim hWndChild        as HWND
    Dim lThreadId        as Long
    Dim lIndex           as Long
    Dim lArrayUBound     as Long
    Dim hWndThreadWnds (0 to 0) as HWND

    'Enumerate all the top level windows of the hWnd main
    'thread to the global chidren array
    pfnWndEnumProc = VarPtr(fnWndEnumProc_GetHWNDS)
    lThreadId = GetWindowThreadProcessId(hWnd, Null)
    EnumThreadWindows(lThreadId, pfnWndEnumProc, 0)

    'Assemble an array of all the top level thread windows
    lArrayUBound = UBound(ghWndChildren)
    Redim Preserve hWndThreadWnds(0 to lArrayUBound) as HWND
    For lIndex = 1 to lArrayUBound
        hWndThreadWnds(lIndex) = ghWndChildren(lIndex)
```

```
        Next
        'Enumerate the children of all the top level windows of the
        'hWnd main thread to the global children array
        For lIndex = 1 to lArrayUBound

EnumChildWindows(hWndThreadWnds(lIndex),pfnWndEnumProc,0)
        Next

        'Enumerate the children of hWnd to the global
        'children array
        EnumChildWindows(hWnd, pfnWndEnumProc, 0)
End Sub


'_____

' FreddieAssert( IsTrue% )
'
' Accepts a statement that evaluates to True or False and
' "FreddieAsserts" it to be True. If the statement is True,
' FreddieAssert returns control to the calling routine. If the
' statement is False, a FREDDIE_ASSERT_ERROR is generated and
' trapped by the error trap.
'_____


Const FREDDIE_ASSERT_ERROR = -1

Sub FreddieAssert(lIsTrue as Long)
        'Don't use 'If Not IsTrue Then...' since it will
        'evaluate as True for any integer except -1. Using
        'Using 'IsTrue = 0' lets us evaluate positive
        ' integers (as returned by Instr()) as 'True'
    If (False = lIsTrue) Then
        gstrFreddieError="A false statement was " + _
                        "FreddieAsserted at " _
                        + Name$(2)
        Error FREDDIE_ASSERT_ERROR
    EndIf
End Sub


'_____

' InitializeFreddie
'
' Initialize global variables and other stuff we need to
' do when Freddie starts.
'_____


Sub InitializeFreddie
    Dim lRandomSeed as Long

        'Make sure the app .ini file exists, fail if we can't
        'find it
        gstrAppIniFile = APP_INI_FILE
```

```
If Not Exists(gstrAppIniFile) Then
    gstrFreddieError = "Could not locate the file '" _
                       + gstrAppIniFile + "'"
    Error FREDDIE_GENERAL_ERROR
EndIf

'Initialize variables using values in the .ini keys
gstrExeName = fnReadApplicationSectionKey("Exe")
gstrExePath = fnReadApplicationSectionKey("PathToExe")
gstrApplicationCaption = _
            fnReadApplicationSectionKey("ParentCaption")
gstrApplicationClass = _
            fnReadApplicationSectionKey("ParentClass")

'Get time Freddie should test the app from in the
'.ini file, quit if the time evaluates to zero
'minutes.
giTimeToTest =
Val(fnReadApplicationSectionKey("TimeToTest"))
If giTimeToTest = 0 Then
    gstrFreddieError="The value of the " + _
                     "'TimeToTest' key in '" _
                     + gstrAppIniFile + _
                     "' evaluates to zero."
    Error FREDDIE_GENERAL_ERROR
EndIf

'Get the test file Freddie should use from in the
'.ini file, quit if it's not in the current
'folder.
gstrTestFileName = CurDir + "\" + _

fnReadApplicationSectionKey("TestFileName")
If Not Exists(gstrTestFileName) Then
    gstrFreddieError = "Could not locate the file '" _
                       + gstrTestFileName + "'"
    Error FREDDIE_GENERAL_ERROR
EndIf

'Seed the random number generator with a seed from the .ini
'file (tends to do the same things over agai) or, if
'the .ini value evaluates to zero, use the current
'tick count to get a whole new random number series.

lRandomSeed=Val(fnReadApplicationSectionKey("RandomSeedValue"))
If lRandomSeed = 0 Then
    lRandomSeed = GetTickCount
    'Write the seed used to the .ini file for future
    'reference
  WritePrivateProfileString("Application", _
    "LastRandomSeedValue", _trm(lRandomSeed), _
```

```
            gstrAppIniFile)
        EndIf
        Randomize lRandomSeed
    End Sub


    '_____
    '
    ' fnReadApplicationSectionKey(strKeyName as String)
    '
    ' Returns the value of the key strKeyName in the
    ' [Application] of the "private" application .ini file
    ' gstrAppIniFile.
    '_____

    Function fnReadApplicationSectionKey(strKeyName$) as String
        Dim strKeyBuffer     as String
        Dim lProfileReturn   as Long

        strKeyBuffer = Space$(1024)
        lProfileReturn = GetPrivateProfileString("Application", _
                    strKeyName, "", strKeyBuffer, 1024,        _
                    gstrAppIniFile)
        fnReadApplicationSectionKey = Left$(strKeyBuffer, _
                                        lProfileReturn)
    End Function


    '_____
    '
    ' fnThisIsANewWindow(hWndNewWindow)
    '
    ' Tests the global array of child window handles
    ' ghWndChildren() to see if hWndNewWindow is in the
    ' array. If it is, fnThisIsANewWindow returns False
    ' because the window is not "new." The routine returns
    ' True if hWndNewWindow is not in the array.
    '_____

    Function fnThisIsANewWindow(hWndNewWindow as HWND) as Long
        Dim iCount  as Integer

        fnThisIsANewWindow = True
        For iCount = 1 to UBound(ghWndChildren)
            If hWndNewWindow = ghWndChildren(iCount) Then
                fnThisIsANewWindow = False
                Exit For
            EndIf
        Next
    End Function


    '_____
    '
    ' fnWindowIsGone(hWnd as HWND, iTimeToWait as Integer)
    '
    ' Similar to WFndWnd() with the FW_NOEXIST flag except it
```

```
' takes an hWnd to test for nonexistence. WFndWnd fails
' when with an error instead of returning True when an
' hWnd is used to specify the window.
'_____

Function fnWindowIsGone(hWnd as HWND, iTimeToWait as Integer)
    Dim iCount        as Integer

    fnWindowIsGone = False
    For iCount = 1 to iTimeToWait
        Sleep 1
        If (IsWindow(hWnd) = False) Then
            fnWindowIsGone = True
            Exit For
        EndIf
    Next
End Function


'_____
'
' fnWndEnumProc_GetHWNDS
'
' Callback routine used by EnumChildWindows() to add the
' hWnd to the global array of child window handles.
'_____


Function fnWndEnumProc_GetHWNDS(hWnd&, lParam&) as Long

    fnWndEnumProc_GetHWNDS = True

    If hWnd Then
        Redim Preserve ghWndChildren(0 to _
                    Ubound(ghWndChildren) _
                    + 1) as HWND
        ghWndChildren(UBound(ghWndChildren)) = hWnd
    Else
        fnWndEnumProc_GetHWNDS = False
    EndIf
End Function

'$EndIf   'Freddie_General_Routines
```

APPLICATON_STRINGS.INC

```
'=========================================================
' Application_Strings.inc
'
' Purpose:
'     Support file for Freddie.mst
```

```
'        Constants to represent strings in the app. This is
'        the file to change for localized versions of the
'        ap.
'=========================================================
'$IfNDef Application_Strings
'$Define Application_Strings

Const BUTTON_CANCEL                 = "Cancel"
Const BUTTON_OK                     = "OK"
Const BUTTON_OPEN                   = "Open"

Const CAPTION_OPEN_DIALOG           = "Open"
Const CAPTION_FONT_DIALOG           = "Font"

Const CTRL_PLUS_F4                  = "^({F4})"
Const ESCAPE_KEY                    = "{ESC}"

Const HOT_KEY_NAME_IN_OPEN_DIALOG   = "%(n)"

Const MENU_FILE_OPEN                = "File\~Open"

    'UnREM this line for testing Notepad
Const MENU_FONT                     = "Edit\~Set Font"
    'UnREM this line for testing Wordpad
'Const MENU_FONT                    = "Format\~Font"

'$EndIf            'Application_Strings
```

FREDDIE_START_KILL_APP.INC

```
'=========================================================
' Freddie_Start_Kill_App.inc
'
' Purpose:
'    Support file for Freddie.mst
'    Routines that start and kill the application and run
'    routines before and after starting the app, if
'    necessary
'=========================================================
'$IfNDef Freddie_Start_Kill_App
'$Define Freddie_Start_Kill_App

Declare Sub StartApplication  'this is the "main" routine in
                              'this file
Declare Sub AddMenuString(gstrMenustring as String)
Declare Sub DoThisAfterStartingExe
Declare Sub DoThisBeforeStartingExe
Declare Function fnParsedMenuNameForBackSlashes(strMenuName _
```

```
                         as String) as String
Declare Sub KillAnyRunningAppProcesses
Declare Sub StartExe

Sub StartApplication
    KillAnyRunningAppProcesses      'kill all instances of
                                    'the app before we
                                    'start testing
DoThisBeforeStartingExe             'to test some apps we
                                    'need to "log in" or
                                    'something
    StartExe                        'start the app to be tested
    DoThisAfterStartingExe          'for some apps we get more
                                    'tests if we do something
                                    'like open a document
                                    'in the app
    MakeMenuList                    'make a global list of
                                    'all the
                                    'menu items available
End Sub

'_____

' AddMenuString(gstrMenustring as String)
'
' Redimensions gstrMenus() and adds a new string at the
' new Ubound
'_____

Sub AddMenuString(gstrMenustring as String)
    Redim Preserve gstrMenus(0 to UBound(gstrMenus) + 1)_
                    as String
    gstrMenus(UBound(gstrMenus)) = gstrMenustring
End Sub

'_____

' DoThisAfterStartingExe
'
' For some apps, more tests become available if we do something
' like open a file.
'_____

Sub DoThisAfterStartingExe
    SetForegroundWindow(ghWndExe)
    WSetActWnd(ghWndExe)
        'Open file gstrTestFileName
    WMenuSelect(MENU_FILE_OPEN)
    WFndWnd(CAPTION_OPEN_DIALOG, FW_DIALOG or EXIST,
AVERAGE_WAIT)
    Play HOT_KEY_NAME_IN_OPEN_DIALOG
    Play gstrTestFileName
        'Close the open file dialog
    WButtonClick(BUTTON_OPEN)
```

```
        WFndWnd(CAPTION_OPEN_DIALOG, FW_DIALOG or NOEXIST, _
            AVERAGE_WAIT)
End Sub


'_____
'
' DoThisBeforeStartingExe
'
' For some apps, we need to dismiss a dialog, like a
' logon prompt, before the app's parent is available for
' testing.
'_____
Sub DoThisBeforeStartingExe
    'Add code here
End Sub


'_____
'
' fnParsedMenuNameForBackSlashes(strMenuName as String)
'
' Adds a second "\" to any menu string containing them,
' required by WSelectMenu.
'_____
Function fnParsedMenuNameForBackSlashes(strMenuName$) as String
    Dim iCount      as Integer
    Dim strTemp     as String

    strTemp = ""
    For iCount = 1 to Len(strMenuName)
        strTemp = strTemp + Mid$(strMenuName, iCount, 1)
        If Mid$(strMenuName, iCount, 1) = "\" Then
            strTemp = strTemp + "\"
        EndIf
    Next

    fnParsedMenuNameForBackSlashes = StrTemp
End Function



'_____
'
' KillAnyRunningAppProcesses
'
' Kills all instances of the app gstrApplicationCaption,
' gstrApplicationClass.
'_____
Const FREDDIE_PROCESS_TERMINATE = &H00000001&
'not defined in the VT4 version of winapi.inc

Sub KillAnyRunningAppProcesses
    Dim hWnd            as HWND
    Dim hProcess        as Long
    Dim lProcessId      as Long
    Dim lplProcessId    as Pointer to Long
```

```
        Do
        'Get the hWnd of a running process of our app (there
        'may be more than one)
            hWnd=WFndWndC(gstrApplicationCaption, _
                        gstrApplicationClass,FW_PART or _
                        FW_EXIST, SHORT_WAIT)

        If hWnd Then
                'Get the process ID for the hWnd
            lplProcessId = VarPtr(lProcessId)
            GetWindowThreadProcessId(hWnd, lplProcessId)
                'Terminate the process
            hProcess = OpenProcess(FREDDIE_PROCESS_TERMINATE,
                        FALSE, lProcessId)
            TerminateProcess(hProcess, 0)
            CloseHandle(hProcess)
                'Generate an error if the window is still there
                'after a suitable delay
            FreddieAssert(fnWindowIsGone(hWnd, AVERAGE_WAIT))
        EndIf
    Loop While hWnd
End Sub


'_____
'
' MakeMenuList
'
' Drop all top level menus in the app. Go down two more
' levels for menus with popups. Add each menu item found,
' even if disabled or grayed, to the global menu item
' array.
'_____
Sub MakeMenuList
    Dim iCount          as Integer
    Dim iCount2         as Integer
    Dim iCount3         as Integer
    Dim lMenuTop        as Long
    Dim lMenuIndex      as Long
    Dim strMenuText     as String
    Dim strMenuTop      as String
    Dim strMenuSecond   as String


    'Make a list of menu commands in the app, go three
    'levels down
    If UBound(gstrMenus) = 0 Then
        For iCount = 1 to wMenuCount
            If (WMenuExists(_ord(iCount))) and _
               (MenuText(_ord(iCount)) <> "") Then
                strMenuTop = MenuText(_ord(iCount))
                WMenuSelect(_ord(iCount))
```

```
For iCount2 = 1 to wMenuCount
    If WMenuExists(_ord(iCount2)) Then
    'Add the menu string to the global array,
    'use ordinals
    'if VT can't see the string text
        strMenuText = _
        Trim$(MenuText(_ord(iCount2)))

        If strMenuText = "" Then _
        StrMenuText = "@" + _trm(iCount2)

        AddMenuString(strMenuTop + "\" + _
fnParsedMenuNameForBackSlashes(strMenuText))
                'Deal with popups and add
                'them to the array
        If WMenuHasPopup(_ord(iCount2)) Then
            strMenuSecond = _
fnParsedMenuNameForBackSlashes(strMenuText)
            WMenuSelect(_ord(iCount2))
            For iCount3 = 1 to wMenuCount
                If WMenuExists(_ord(iCount3))
Then

                    strMenuText = _
                Trim$(MenuText(_ord(iCount3)))

                    If strMenuText = "" Then
                        StrMenuText = "@" + _
                                _trm(iCount3)
                    EndIf
                AddMenuString(strMenuTop + _
                "\" + strMenuSecond + "\" + _

fnParsedMenuNameForBackSlashes(strMenuText))
                EndIf
            Next
            Play ESCAPE_KEY
        EndIf
    EndIf
Next
WMenuEnd
EndIf
        Next
    EndIf
End Sub


'_____

' StartExe
'
' Start the app.
'_____

Sub StartExe
```

```
        Run gstrExePath + gstrExeName, NoWait
        ghWndExe = WFndWndC( gstrApplicationCaption, _
                    gstrApplicationClass, EXIST, AVERAGE_WAIT )
    End Sub

    '$EndIf          'Freddie_Start_Kill_App
```

FREDDIE_TESTS.INC

```
    '==========================================================
    ' Freddie_Tests.inc
    '
    ' Purpose:
    '     Support file for Freddie.mst
    '     Selects and executes tests
    '==========================================================
    '$IfNDef Freddie_Tests
    '$Define Freddie_Tests

    Declare Sub ExecuteATest
    'this is the "main" routine in this file

    Declare Sub DoMenuTest
    Declare Sub DoTextEntryTest
    Declare Function fnRandomChar as String
    Declare Sub InsertionPointToBottom
    Declare Sub InsertionPointToTop
    Declare Sub LookForAndTestDialog(iMenuIndex as Integer)
    Declare Sub SetNewFont
    Declare Sub TestDialog(hWnd)


    '_____
    '
    ' ExecuteATest
    '
    ' Pick a test at (weighted) random and execute it.
    '_____
    Sub ExecuteATest
        Dim iRandomNumber        as Integer

        iRandomNumber = _RndBetween(1, 100)

        Select Case iRandomNumber
            Case is < 60
                DoMenuTest 'Choose one of the menu items
            Case 61 to 70
                InsertionPointToTop 'Enter text at the top of
                DoTextEntryTest     'the document
            Case 71 to 80
```

```
            InsertionPointToBottom    'Enter text at the
                                      'end of the
            DoTextEntryTest           'document
        Case 81 to 90
            DoTextEntryTest           'Enter text at current
        Case Else                     'insertion point
            SetNewFont                'Pick a font from the Font
    End Select                        'dialog
End Sub


'_____
'
' DoMenuTest
'
' Keep choosing menu items until we find one that's
' enabled. Wait for a dialog to come up and test it if it
' does.
'_____

Sub DoMenuTest
    Dim iMenuIndex          as Integer
    Dim strMenuString       as String
    Dim bCurrentMenuStringIsEnabled     as BOOL

    SetForegroundWindow(ghWndExe)
    WSetActWnd(ghWndExe)
    bCurrentMenuStringIsEnabled = False

    While Not bCurrentMenuStringIsEnabled
        iMenuIndex = _RndBetween(1, UBound(gstrMenus))

        If gstrMenus(iMenuIndex) <> "" Then
        'Staggered If-Thens with WMenuEnd required for
        'Office '97 type menus
          WMenuEnd
          If WMenuExists(gstrMenus(iMenuIndex)) Then
              WMenuEnd
              If WMenuEnabled(gstrMenus(iMenuIndex)) Then
                WMenuEnd
                If Not WMenuGrayed(gstrMenus(iMenuIndex)) Then
                  WMenuEnd
                  bCurrentMenuStringIsEnabled = True
                EndIf
              EndIf
          EndIf
        EndIf
    WEnd
    LookForAndTestDialog(iMenuIndex)
End Sub


'_____

' DoTextEntryTest
'
```

```
' Enter 10 to 100 random characters at the current
' insertion point
'_____
Sub DoTextEntryTest
    Dim iNumberOfCharsToEnter    as Integer
    Dim iCount                   as Integer

    SetForegroundWindow(ghWndExe)
    WSetActWnd(ghWndExe)
    iNumberOfCharsToEnter = _RndBetween(10, 100)
    FreddiePrint("Entering " + _trm(iNumberOfCharsToEnter) + _
                " random characters")
    For iCount = 1 to iNumberOfCharsToEnter
        Play fnRandomChar
    Next
    Play "{ENTER}"
End Sub


'_____
' fnRandomChar
'
' On all calls return a random character between ANSI(0032) and
' ANSI(0255) inclusive. Add braces around characters Play
' interprets as special commands.
'_____

Function fnRandomChar as String
    Dim strOurChar as String

    strOurChar = Chr(_RndBetween(32, 255))
    Select Case strOurChar
        'Must surround VT "special" characters with braces
      Case "[","]","(",")","{","}","+","%","^","~"
        fnRandomChar = "{" + strOurChar + "}"
      Case else
        fnRandomChar = strOurChar
    End Select
End Function


'_____
' InsertionPointToBottom
'
' Move insertion point to bottom of current document
'_____

Sub InsertionPointToBottom
    SetForegroundWindow(ghWndExe)
    Play "^(+({END}))"            'Ctrl+Shift+End
End Sub

'_____
```

```
' InsertionPointToTop
'
' Move insertion point to top of current document
'_____
Sub InsertionPointToTop
    SetForegroundWindow(ghWndExe)
    Play "^(+({HOME}))"            'Ctrl+Shift+Home
End Sub


    '_____
' LookForAndTestDialog(iMenuIndex as Integer)
'
' Wait for a new child window to appear. If it does, call
' TestDialog.
'_____
Sub LookForAndTestDialog(iMenuIndex as Integer)
    Dim bWaitUntilIdleReturn          as BOOL
    Dim hWnd                          as HWND
    Dim iDialogWait                   as Integer
    Dim nTimerStart                   as Double
    Dim nTimerEnd                     as Double

        'Enumerate the current children of ghWndExe so we can
        'tell if a new one pops up
    Redim ghWndChildren(0 to 0) as HWND
    EnumerateChildrenToArray(ghWndExe)

    FreddiePrint("Choosing menu " + gstrMenus(iMenuIndex))
    WMenuSelect(gstrMenus(iMenuIndex))


        'Because WaitUntilIdle doesn't always do that
    Sleep 2
        'Wait until the app is idle
    SetNotIdle
    nTimerStart = Timer
    bWaitUntilIdleReturn = WaitUntilIdle (SHORT_WAIT)
    'Wait up to SHORT_WAIT seconds
    nTimerEnd = Timer
    iDialogWait = 1
    Do
        Sleep 1
        hWnd = WGetActWnd(0)
                'Make sure hWnd is not the app parent...

        If (hWnd <> ghWndExe) _
        '...and it's not Null
            and (hWnd <> 0) _
        '...and it's not a window that was around before
        '...this test
            and fnThisIsANewWindow(hWnd) _
```

```
        '...and it's a child of the app parent
            and (GetParent(hWnd) = ghWndExe) Then
        '...Then a new window has appeared. TestDialog() will
        '   test controls based on flags, then try to close
            TestDialog(hWnd)
            Exit Do
        EndIf
        iDialogWait = iDialogWait + 1
    Loop While iDialogWait < SHORT_WAIT

    WMenuEnd
End Sub


'_____
'
' SetNewFont
'
' Select a random font from the Font dialog. There is no Font
' dialog in Win9x Notepad (bummer), so skip the test on that
' platform.
'_____
Sub SetNewFont
    Dim osv as OSVERSIONINFO

    osv.dwOsVersionInfoSize = Len(osv)
    GetVersionEx(osv)

        'PlatformID = 1 (the enumerated constants aren't
        'defined in winapi.inc) means Win9x and its
        'Notepad doesn't have a Font dialog
    If osv.dwPlatformID <> 1 Then
        FreddiePrint("Choosing random font in Font dialog")
        SetForegroundWindow(ghWndExe)
        WSetActWnd(ghWndExe)
            'Open the Font dialog
        WMenuSelect(MENU_FONT)
        WFndWnd(CAPTION_FONT_DIALOG, FW_DIALOG or EXIST, _
            AVERAGE_WAIT)
            'Click on a random font name on the list
        WComboItemClk(_ord(1), _ord(_RndBetween(1, _
            WComboCount(_ord(1)))))
        WButtonClick(BUTTON_OK)
        WFndWnd(CAPTION_FONT_DIALOG, FW_DIALOG or NOEXIST, _
            AVERAGE_WAIT)
    Else
        FreddiePrint("Skipping Font dialog test on Windows 9x")
    EndIf
End Sub


'_____
'
' TestDialog(hWnd)
'
```

```
'      - Fill and edit boxes with random characters
'      - Click at random points in the dialog several times
'      - Try to close the dialog, kill the app if we can't
'_____
Sub TestDialog(hWnd)
    Dim wInfo as    INFO
    Dim iCount  as Integer
    Dim iCount1  as Integer
    Dim strTextBuffer    as String

    SetForegroundWindow(hWnd)
    WSetActWnd(hWnd)
    WGetInfo(hWnd, wInfo)
    FreddiePrint("Found dialog: " + wInfo.Text + ", class: " _
                + wInfo.Class)

        'If there are edit boxes, put 100 random characters
        '(0032-0255) into each one
    iCount = 1
    While WEditExists(_ord(iCount))
        strTextBuffer = ""
        For iCount1 = 1 to 100
            strTextBuffer = strTextBuffer _
                            + Chr(_RndBetween(32, 255))
        Next
        WEditSetText(_ord(iCount), strTextBuffer)
        iCount = iCount + 1
    WEnd

    ClickAtRandom(hWnd) 'click at random in the dialog,
                        'we may hit something

    '-- Try to close the dialog using several methods in order
    'Try the OK button first, if there is one
    If WButtonExists(BUTTON_OK) Then
        WButtonClick(BUTTON_OK)
            'See if the dialog closed when OK was clicked
        If fnWindowIsGone(hWnd, SHORT_WAIT) Then
            FreddiePrint("   Dialog closed with OK button")
            Exit Sub
        EndIf
    EndIf

        'Dialog still here, try Cancel
    If WButtonExists(BUTTON_CANCEL) Then
            WButtonClick(BUTTON_CANCEL)
                'See if the dialog closed when Cancel was
                'clicked
            If fnWindowIsGone(hWnd, SHORT_WAIT) Then
                FreddiePrint("Dialog closed with "+ _
                            "Cancel button")
```

```
        Exit Sub
    EndIf
EndIf

    'Dialog still here, try ESC
Play ESCAPE_KEY
    'See if the dialog closed when ESC was pressed
If fnWindowIsGone(hWnd, SHORT_WAIT) Then
    FreddiePrint("   Dialog closed pressing ESC key")
    Exit Sub
EndIf

    'Dialog is still here, try sending WM_ClOSE
PostMessage(hWnd, WM_CLOSE, 0, 0)
If fnWindowIsGone(hWnd, SHORT_WAIT) Then
    FreddiePrint("   Dialog closed by posting a WM_CLOSE")
    Exit Sub
EndIf

    'Dialog is still here try clicking on it
    '(near top center where there aren't likely to be
    'any buttons)
WClkWnd(hWnd, W_CENTER, 5)
If fnWindowIsGone(hWnd, SHORT_WAIT) Then
    FreddiePrint("   Dialog closed by clicking on it")
    Exit Sub
EndIf

    'Dialog still here, try Ctrl+F4
Play CTRL_PLUS_F4
If fnWindowIsGone(hWnd, SHORT_WAIT) Then
    FreddiePrint("   Dialog closed pressing Ctrl+F4")
    Exit Sub
EndIf

    'Can't close this dialog, kill app and restart
FreddiePrint("Can't close this dialog, Freddie will" _
            +" kill and restart the app")
StartApplication

End Sub

'$EndIf       'Freddie_Tests
```

FREDDIE_LOG_ROUTINES.INC

```
'===========================================================
' Freddie_Log_Routines.inc
'
' Purpose:
'     Support file for Freddie.mst
'     Create a simple log file for test comments and the error
'     trap strings
'===========================================================
'$IfNDef Freddie_Log_Routines
'$Define Freddie_Log_Routines

Sub FreddiePrint(strStringToPrintToLog as String)
    Static bLogFileHasBeenCreated    as BOOL
    Dim iFileNumber                  as Integer

    'Create a log file header the first time this routine
    'is called
    If Not bLogFileHasBeenCreated Then
        iFileNumber = FreeFile
        Open CurDir + "\" + _
        APP_LOG_FILE for Output as iFileNumber
        Print #iFileNumber, _
            "*********************************************"
        Print #iFileNumber, _
            "**** Test log for: " + gstrExePath + gstrExeName
        Print #iFileNumber, _
            "****         started: " + Time + " - " + Date
        Print #iFileNumber, _
            "*********************************************"
        Close iFileNumber
        bLogFileHasBeenCreated = True
    EndIf

        'Append strStringToPrintToLog to the log file
    iFileNumber = FreeFile
    Open CurDir + "\" + APP_LOG_FILE for Append as iFileNumber
    Print #iFileNumber, strStringToPrintToLog
    Close iFileNumber
End Sub

'$EndIf      'Freddie_Log_Routines
```

✦   ✦   ✦

Listing for NOTEMAIN.INC

The NOTEMAIN.INC file is the main declaration or *include* file for the sample test suite discussed throughout this book. Declarations of constants, user-defined types, prototypes, or links into external dynamic-link libraries (DLLs) and macros that are common enough to be used by most test case files in the project are placed into this top-level include file.

This file is a living file; it changes as more tests are added to the test suite. Sometimes declarations are moved to other include (.INC) files in the project if they only apply to a specific set of test cases. Other declarations find their way up to this top-level include file as it becomes apparent that the declarations are common enough to be applicable to many test case files in the test suite.

The source code file for this listing can be found on the CD-ROM included with this book under the name of NOTEMAIN.INC.

```
'*********************** NOTEMAIN.INC ***********************
'*
'* Purpose: Holds common declarations to be used by all test
'*          case files.  Anything not common enough to be
'*          used by the majority of the test case files should
'*          be moved to an include file lower in the hierarchy
'*          specific to the area it concerns.
'*
'* Author:  Tom Arnold
'*
'* Revision History:
'*
'* [ 0]  da-mon-year     email    action
'* [ 1]  29-MAY-1998     TomAr    Created NOTEMAIN.INC to hold
'*                                common declarations.
'* [ 2]  29-MAY-1998     TVT      Moved in some common constants.
'* [ 3]  06-JUN-1998     TomAr    Added consts for rest of suite.
'***************************************************************

'$IFNDEF NOTEMAIN_INCLUDED
'$DEFINE NOTEMAIN_INCLUDED


'***************************************************************
'*********************** Constants ***********************
'***************************************************************


'********** General Application Info
const TEST_APP$          = "NOTEPAD.EXE" 'Exe file name of
                                         'test subject

'********** Window captions/class names
const CAP_NOTEPAD$       = "- Notepad"   'Partial caption
                                         'of main window
const CAP_SAVECHANGES$   = "Notepad"     'Caption of Save Chngs
                                         'msg box
const TEST_APP_CLASS$    = "Notepad"     'Classname of app's
                                         'main window

'********** Logging Detail Settings
const LVL_SUMMARY%       = 5             'Summary info after
                                         'each test case
const LVL_MENUINFO%      = 10            'Give menu info if
                                         'Detail > 10
const LVL_STATUSINFO     = 20            'General status info
const LVL_VERBOSE%       = 100           'Have all calls to LOG
                                         'enabled

'********** Edit control captions
const EDIT_NOTEPAD$      = "@1"          'Notepad's main edit
                                         'window
```

```
'********** Button control captions
const BTN_NO$          = "No"       'Caption for No button
const BTN_YES$         = "Yes"      'Caption for Yes button
const BTN_CANCEL$      = "Cancel"   'Caption for Cancel
const BTN_SAVE$        = "Save"     'Caption for Save
const BTN_OK$          = "Ok"       'Caption for Ok button
const BTN_OPEN         = "Open"     'Caption for Open

'********** Menu Bar and Menu Item captions
'***** Menu items for the File menu
const MNU_FILE_NEW$    = "File\New"
const MNU_FILE_OPEN$   = "File\Open..."
const MNU_FILE_SAVE$   = "File\Save"
const MNU_FILE_SAVEAS$ = "File\Save As..."
const MNU_FILE_PGSETUP$ = "File\Page Setup..."
const MNU_FILE_PRINT$  = "File\Print"
const MNU_FILE_EXIT$   = "File\Exit"

'***** Menu items for the Edit menu
const MNU_EDIT_UNDO$   = "Edit\Undo"
const MNU_EDIT_CUT$    = "Edit\Cut"
const MNU_EDIT_COPY$   = "Edit\Copy"
const MNU_EDIT_PASTE$  = "Edit\Paste"
const MNU_EDIT_DELETE$ = "Edit\Delete"
const MNU_EDIT_SELALL$ = "Edit\Select All"
const MNU_EDIT_TIMEDATE$= "Edit\Time/Date"
const MNU_EDIT_WRDWRAP$ = "Edit\Word Wrap"

'***** Menu items for the Search menu
const MNU_SEARCH_FIND$ = "Search\Find..."
const MNU_SEARCH_FNEXT$ = "Search\Find Next"

'***** Menu items for the Help menu
const MNU_HELP_TOPICS  = "Help\Help Topics"
const MNU_HELP_ABOUT   = "Help\About Notepad"


'********** Name of Temporary Files
const TEMPFILE1$          = "TEMP1.TXT"
const TEMPFILE2$          = "TEMP2.TXT"


'********** Other constants
const MAX_WAIT%        = 5      '# of secs to search for window
const MAX_GAP%         = 10     '# spaces gap used in logging
const DATA_TESTSTRING1$ = "Now is the time for all good " + _
                          "people..."
const FW_NOTEPAD&         = FW_PART OR FW_ALL OR FW_FOCUS OR _
                          FW_RESTORE OR FW_EXIST
                          'Search criteria for Notepad
```

```
'****************************************************************
'********************** User Def'd Types ***********************
'****************************************************************


'****************************************************************
'********************** Global Variables ***********************
'****************************************************************

global ghWndNotepad&      'Handle to Notepad's main window
global giTestCount%       'Incr. by strTestNum()
global giFailCount%       'Incr. by strFailNum()

'****************************************************************
'***************** Func/Proc Prototypes ***********************
'****************************************************************


'$ENDIF NOTEMAIN_INCLUDED
```

Listing for NOTEUTIL.INC

The NOTEUTIL.INC file is the main set of function and subroutine utilities for the sample test suite discussed throughout this book. Functions and subroutines that are common enough to be used by most test case files in the project are placed into this top-level include file.

Similar to the NOTEMAIN.INC file shown in Appendix F, this file is also a living file; it changes as more tests are added to the test suite. Sometimes functions and subroutines are moved to test case (.MST) files in the project if they only apply to those specific test cases. Other functions and subroutines find their way up to this top-level include file as it becomes apparent that they are common enough to be applicable to many test case files in the test suite.

The source code file for this listing can be found on the disk included with this book under the name of NOTEUTIL.INC.

```
'********************** noteutil.inc **********************
'*
'* Purpose: Common functions and subroutines that are useful
'*          to other test case files are placed into this
'*          file for our Notepad project. As this file grows
'*          other testing teams might be interested in using
'*          this file to get a head-start on their automation.
'*
'* Author:  Tom Arnold
'*
'* Revision History:
'*
'* [ 0]  da-mon-year    email    action
'* [ 1]  28-MAY-1998    TomAr    Created noteutil.inc to hold
'*                               common functions & subroutines.
'* [ 2]  29-MAY-1998    TVT      Moved in some common funcs.
'* [ 3]  06-JUN-1998    TomAr    Fixed TVT's bugs, added more
'*                               support routines.
'**************************************************************

'$IFNDEF NOTEUTIL_INCLUDED
'$DEFINE NOTEUTIL_INCLUDED

'********************* INCLUDES **************************

'$include 'notemain.inc'


'**************************************************************
'* Function:    fGrayMenu
'* Purpose:     Returns true if the menu item is grayed, false
'*              if not.
'*
'* Parameters:  strMenuItem$
'*                      String compatible with the wMenuSelect
'*                      command for a menu and its menu item.
'*
'* Returns:     INTEGER A boolean flag value is returned.
'*
'**************************************************************

function fGrayMenu (strMenuItem$) as Integer
    dim strMenu$, strItem$

    'The backslash '\' separates the menu from the menu item.
    'This version of fGrayMenu doesn't currently work for
    'hierarchical menus.
    strMenu = left$(strMenuItem,instr(strMenuItem,"\")-1)
strItem = right$(strMenuItem,len(strMenuItem)- _
                    instr(strMenuItem,"\"))
```

```
        wMenuEnd                        'Pop-up any open menus
        wMenuSelect(strMenu)            'Pop-down chosen menu
        if wMenuGrayed(strItem) then    'Check menu item
            fGrayMenu = TRUE
        else                            'Set appropriate return value
            fGrayMenu = FALSE
        end if
        wMenuEnd                        'Pop-up open menu
end function 'GrayMenu



'*****************************************************************
'* Function:    iFailCount
'* Purpose:     Returns current number of failures for current
'*              test case file. This only works if the test
'*              scenarios are using strFailNum() in conjunction
'*              with calls to the fail statement. Done this
'*              way to avoid Test programmers directly
'*              accessing the giFailCount global variable.
'*
'* Parameters:  NONE
'*
'* Returns:     INTEGER Current value of giFailCount, which is
'*                      a global value incremented every time
'*                      strFailNum is called.
'*
'*****************************************************************

function iFailCount() as integer
    iFailCount = giFailCount
end function 'iFailCount



'*****************************************************************
'* Function:    iTestCount
'* Purpose:     Returns current number of test scenarios
'*              executed for current test case file. This
'*              only works if the test scenarios are using
'*              strTestNum() in conjunction with calls to the
'*              scenario statement. Done this way to
'*              avoid Test programmers directly accessing the
'*              giTestCount global variable.
'*
'* Parameters:  NONE
'*
'* Returns:     INTEGER Current value of giTestCount, which is
'*                      a global value incremented every time
'*                      strTestNum is called.
'*
'*****************************************************************
```

```
function iTestCount() as integer
    iTestCount = giTestCount
end function 'iTestCount


'****************************************************************
'* Subroutine:   PutString
'* Purpose:      Places a string into the Notepad editor at a
'*               specified line and character position. If the
'*               line or character doesn't exist, this routine
'*               adds the necessary carriage returns and spaces.
'*
'* Parameters:   strOut$ String to be written to the editor
'*               iLine%  Line at which string is to be written
'*               iChar%  Character/column pos to place string
'*
'****************************************************************

sub PutString (strOut$, iLine%, iChar%)
    dim iCurrLine%        'Keeps track of cursor position
    dim iCurrChar%        'Tracks which column cursor is in
    dim iLoop%            'Used as index to for-loop
    dim iLoopLimit%       'Used to determine end val of for-loop
    dim strDirection$     'Set to which keystroke should be used

    'Get the current line and cursor position
    iCurrLine = wEditLine(EDIT_NOTEPAD)

    'Determine which direction to move based on
    'current position and desired position.
    if (iCurrLine < iLine) then
        iLoopLimit = (iLine - iCurrLine)
        strDirection = "{DOWN}"          'We need to move down
    else
        iLoopLimit = (iCurrLine - iLine)
        strDirection = "{UP}"            'We need to move up
    endif

    'Move to the desired position, adding lines
    'if necessary.
    for iLoop = 1 to iLoopLimit
        if (wEditLine(EDIT_NOTEPAD) < _
            wEditLines(EDIT_NOTEPAD)) then
            Play strDirection
        elseif (strDirection = "{DOWN}") then
            Play "{END}"
            Play "{ENTER}"
        else
            Play strDirection
        endif
    next iLoop
```

```
    'Get the current character position
    iCurrChar = wEditPos(EDIT_NOTEPAD)

    'Based on the current position, determine which
    'direction to move.
    if (iCurrChar < iChar) then
        iLoopLimit = (iChar - iCurrChar)
        strDirection = "{RIGHT}"
    else
        iLoopLimit = (iCurrChar - iChar)
        strDirection = "{LEFT}"
    endif

    'Move to the desired position adding spaces if needed.
    for iLoop = 1 to iLoopLimit
        if (wEditPos(EDIT_NOTEPAD) < wEditLineLen(EDIT_NOTEPAD,

            wEditLine(EDIT_NOTEPAD))) then
            Play strDirection
        elseif (strDirection = "{RIGHT}") then
            Play " "
        else
            Play strDirection
        endif
    next iLoop

    Play strOut    'Type the string at the current location
end sub 'PutString()


'***************************************************************
'* Subroutine:    ResetApp
'* Purpose:       Attempts to reset the application to a known
'*                state. This routine will likely grow in
'*                complexity as strange circumstances are
'*                discovered where this routine isn't able to
'*                reset the application.
'*
'***************************************************************

sub ResetApp()
    wMenuEnd
    SelMenu(MNU_FILE_NEW)

    if (GetText(NULL) = CAP_SAVECHANGES) then
        wButtonClick(BTN_NO)
    endif
end sub 'ResetApp()
```

```
'****************************************************************
'* Subroutine:  SelMenu
'* Purpose:     This is a wrapper around the wMenuSelect
'*              statement, allowing us a level of detailed
'*              information if requested.
'*
'* Parameters:  STRING  A wMenuSelect-compatible string.
'*
'****************************************************************

sub SelMenu(strMenu$)
    wMenuEnd                  'Make sure a menu isn't already
                                'popped down
    wMenuSelect(strMenu) 'Select the menu item

    'The detail level represented by the LVL_MENUINFO constant
    'is controlled from the Options dialog box in the Suite
    'Manager. If the level specified in the Suite Manager is
    'greater than the level specified by LVL_MENUINFO (below)
    'then the information will be logged out. Otherwise, the
    'information isn't logged. This is a way to control the
    'level/detail of information provided.

    Log #LVL_MENUINFO, "Selected menu: "+strMenu$
end sub 'SelMenu()


'****************************************************************
'* Function:    strFailNum
'* Purpose:     Keeps a counter of the total number of failures
'*              that have occurred using the fail command for
'*              the current test case file. For this to work,
'*              it must be called for each failure and is
'*              therefore designed to work with the fail
'*              statement.
'*
'* Parameters:  NONE
'*
'* Returns:     STRING  The string that is returned is
formatted
'*                      to fit in front of the text being
'*                      included in the fail statement.
'*
'* Format
'* returned:    "Fail #<num>: "
'*
'* Use:         FAIL strFailNum()+"<descrip-of-failure>"
'*
'****************************************************************
```

```
function strFailNum() as string
    giFailCount = giFailCount + 1
    strFailNum = "Fail #"+trim$(str$(giFailCount))+": "
end function 'strFailNum()



'***************************************************************
'* Function:     strTestNum
'* Purpose:      Keeps a counter of the total number of tests
'*               that have been executed for the current test
'*               case file. For this to work, it must be
'*               called for each test. It is designed to work
'*               with the scenario statement. This is why it
'*               returns a string.
'*
'* Parameters:   NONE
'*
'* Returns:      STRING  The string that is returned is
'*                       formatted to fit in front of the text
'*                       being included in the scenario.
'*
'* Format
'* returned:     "Test #<num>: "
'*
'* Use:          SCENARIO strTestNum()+"<descrip-of-test>"
'*
'***************************************************************

function strTestNum() as string
    giTestCount = giTestCount + 1
    strTestNum = "Test #"+trim$(str$(giTestCount))+": "
end function 'strTestNum()



'***************************************************************
'* Subroutine:   TestBegin
'* Purpose:      All initialization code that needs to be run
'*               before the scenarios of a test case are
'*               executed should be placed in this subroutine.
'*               This subroutine needs to be called first by
'*               each test case.
'*
'* Parameters:   NONE
'*
'***************************************************************

sub TestBegin()
    log #LVL_VERBOSE, "Initializing Test Case and attempting "
    log #LVL_VERBOSE, "to find or run ";TEST_APP;" app."
```

```
    viewport clear        'Clean the contents of the Viewport
                          'tab in the Output window.

    'Get test application up and running. If it can be run
    'for whatever reason, print an error message and stop
    'the execution of the script.

    ghWndNotepad = wFndWndC(CAP_NOTEPAD, TEST_APP_CLASS, _
                              FW_NOTEPAD ,MAX_WAIT)

    if (ghWndNotepad = 0) then
        log #LVL_VERBOSE, "Unable to find ";TEST_APP;"."
        if run(TEST_APP) then
            fail "Error: Unable to run notepad.exe"
        else
            ghWndNotepad = wFndWnd(CAP_NOTEPAD, FW_NOTEPAD, _
                              MAX_WAIT)
            log #LVL_VERBOSE, "Successfully ran ";TEST_APP
        endif
    else
        log #LVL_VERBOSE, "Found ";TEST_APP;" already running."
        ResetApp()
    endif

    'Note: Having a call to the fail statement will generate
    'a run-time error since it is not in a scenario block.
    'As a result, an error message box will be given, if you
    'are in Microsoft Developer Studio. If you are in the
    'Visual Test Suite Manager, the result will be the Suite
    'Manager moving on to the next test case file. This is
    'what you would want, as it doesn't make sense for the
    'rest of the tests to run, since the test application
    'can't be brought up.

end sub 'TestBegin()


'*****************************************************************
*
'* Subroutine:  TestEnd
'* Purpose:     Clean-up code that needs to be executed after
'*              all scenarios for a given test case file have
'*              been executed.
'*
'* Parameters:  NONE
'*
'*****************************************************************
*
```

```
sub TestEnd()
    dim iPPass%             'Percent passed
    dim strMetrix$          'Misc metrics

    '** Clean-up before the test case file ends **

    wMenuSelect(MNU_FILE_EXIT)      'Shut down Notepad app

    if GetText(NULL) = CAP_SAVECHANGES then
        wButtonClick(BTN_NO)         'Click 'No' to msg box
    endif

    'Set up info to be logged out
    iPPass = ((iTestCount - iFailCount) / iTestCount) * 100
    strMetrix = "Scenarios: "+trim$(str$(iTestCount)) + _
                SPACE$(MAX_GAP) + "Errors: "+ _
                trim$(str$(iFailCount)) + _
                SPACE$(MAX_GAP) + "Passed: " + _
                trim$(str$(iPPass))+"%"

    'Log out final information for the test case file.
    'When doing the LEFT$() stuff a bunch of spaces are added
    'for padding and then are cropped off, so that the max size
    'of the line being written out is 70 characters. By
    'cropping like this the info can adjust its size and still
    'have the right-hand border of the box remain in line.
    log #LVL_SUMMARY,"*********************** Test Case "+ _
                     "Results " +
"***********************"
    log #LVL_SUMMARY,"*"+space$(68)+"*"
    log #LVL_SUMMARY,"* Test Case:
  "+(left$(NAME$(0)+space$(70)),56))+"*"
    log #LVL_SUMMARY,"*"+space$(68)+"*"
    log #LVL_SUMMARY,"* "+left$(strMetrix+space$(70),67)+"*"
    log #LVL_SUMMARY,"*"+space$(68)+"*"
    log #LVL_SUMMARY,"* Test case completed testing at "+ _
                     left$(datetime$+space$(70),36)+"*"
    log #LVL_SUMMARY,"*"+space$(68)+"*"
    log #LVL_SUMMARY,STRING$(70,"*")
end sub 'TestEnd()

'$ENDIF NOTEUTIL_INCLUDED
```

✦   ✦   ✦

Listings of All Test Cases

The following listings are the test case files that make up the Notepad test suite that is discussed throughout this book. The test scenarios that make up the test case files are just a beginning to provide some structure and examples. By creating this structure and some beginning scenarios, other Test programmers have examples to follow when setting out to create their own tests for the different features of the Notepad application.

Please note that should you want to cut and paste any of this source code, you can find it on the CD-ROM in the back of this book.

File Menu

The File menu is made up of seven menu items. These are New, Open, Save, Save As, Page Setup, Print, and Exit. Following this example (menu-based), the automated tests traverse the menus that make up the Notepad product.

Based on these seven menu items, eight files should be created for testing those menu items: FILE.INC, NEW.MST, OPEN.MST, SAVE.MST, SAVEAS.MST, PAGE_SU.MST, PRINT.MST, and EXIT.MST. In this example, PRINT.MST has not been included.

The FILE.INC include file holds declarations common to the menu items that make up the File menu. Any declarations that might be used by the other test case files should be placed into the FILE.INC include file. Declarations that are even more generic, and useful to other menus and menu items, should be moved up higher, into the NOTEMAIN.INC file.

FILE.INC

Any declarations that aren't generic enough to go into the main header file for the
Notepad test suite (NOTEMAIN.INC) and are specific to the test case files that
perform tests on the File menu are placed into this file.

```
'************************ FILE.INC ************************
'*
'* PURPOSE: Decls for the File menu tests.
'*
'*********************************************************

'$ifndef FILE_INCLUDED
'$define FILE_INCLUDED

'*********************************************************
'******************** CONSTANTS **************************
'*********************************************************

'***** Dialog Control Names

const DCN_FILENAME$          = "File Name:"
const DCN_SPECIFICPRINTER$   = "Specific Printer:"
const DCN_OUTPUTFILENAME$    = "Output File Name:"


'***** Captions

const CAP_SAVEAS$            = "Save As"
const CAP_OPEN$             = "Open"
const CAP_SAVE$             = "Save"
const CAP_PRINTTOFILE$      = "Print To File"
const CAP_PAGESETUP$        = "Page Setup"
const CAP_PRINTSETUP$       = "Print Setup"

'***** Misc

const MAX_COUNT             = 15


'*********************************************************
'***************** User Def'd Types **********************
'*********************************************************


'*********************************************************
'***************** Global Variables *********************
'*********************************************************
```

```
'*************************************************************
'*************** Func/Proc Prototypes ********************
'*************************************************************


'$endif FILE_INCLUDED
```

NEW.MST

```
'*************************************************************
'*  Filename:    NEW.MST
'*
'*  Purpose:     Tests the New menu item for the File menu in
'*               Notepad's main window.
'*
'*  Revision History:
'*
'*   [ 0]   da-mon-year   email    : action
'*   [ 1]   28-MAY-1998   TomAr    First few scenarios for the
'*                                 New menu item to give some
'*                                 structure.
'*   [ 2]   29-MAY-1998   TVT      Created common constants,
'*                                 etc. and moved to
'*                                 NOTEMAIN.INC. Made common
'*                                 subs common subs & funcs and
'*                                 moved to NOTEUTIL.INC.
'*   [ 3]   01-JUN-1998   TomAr    Added some final test
'*                                 scenarios to fill in this
'*                                 first test case.
'*   [ 4]   06-JUN-1998   TomAr    Moved File menu-specific
'*                                 consts to FILE.INC and out
'*                                 of NOTEMAIN.
'*
'*************************************************************
*


'********************** INCLUDES *************************
'$include 'notemain.inc' 'General common constants
'$include 'noteutil.inc' 'Utilities generic/sharable
'$include 'file.inc'     'Constants/utils generic to File


TestBegin()              'Initialize the test case

    '** Beginning of the test scenarios **
    scenario strTestNum()+"Test that 'Save changes' "+_
                    "message box is displayed."
        PutString(DATA_TESTSTRING1, 1, 1)

        SelMenu(MNU_FILE_NEW)
```

```
        if (GetText(NULL) <> CAP_SAVECHANGES) then
            fail strFailNum()+"Error: Message box"+_
                            " not found."
        endif
scenario cleanup
    LOG #LVL_VERBOSE, "Cleaning up for test "+_
                        "scenario #"+str$(iTestCount)
    if not(failed) then
        wButtonClick(BTN_CANCEL)
    endif
end scenario


scenario strTestNum()+"Verify that the original text"+_
                    " remains unchanged after "+_
                    "clicking Cancel."
    if EditText(EDIT_NOTEPAD) <> DATA_TESTSTRING1 then
        fail strFailNum()+_
            "Original test string changed."
    endif
end scenario

ResetApp      'Clear Notepad to get to known state


scenario strTestNum()+"Click 'No' to "+_
                    "'Save Changes?' msg"
    PutString(DATA_TESTSTRING1, 10, 10)

    SelMenu(MNU_FILE_NEW)
    wButtonClick(BTN_NO)
    if EditText(EDIT_NOTEPAD) <> "" then
        fail strFailNum()+"Text was not cleared "+_
                            "as expected."
    endif
scenario cleanup
    LOG #LVL_VERBOSE, "Cleaning up for test "+_
                        "scenario #"+str$(iTestCount)
    ResetApp
end scenario


scenario strTestNum()+"Click 'Yes' to 'Save changes?'"+_
                    " msg"
    PutString(DATA_TESTSTRING1, 10, 10)

    SelMenu(MNU_FILE_NEW)
    wButtonClick(BTN_YES)    'Yes to save changes

    if (GetText(NULL) <> CAP_SAVEAS) then
```

```
                        fail strFailNum()+"Save As dialog box not "+_
                                    "displayed."
            else
                'We don't want to test the Save As dialog box,
                'just make sure it displays.  We can determine
                'how we want to test it later.
                wButtonClick(BTN_CANCEL)
            endif
        scenario cleanup
            LOG #LVL_VERBOSE, "Cleaning up for test "+_
                                "scenario #"+str$(iTestCount)
            ResetApp
        end scenario

    TestEnd()
    END
```

OPEN.MST

```
'*************************************************************
'* Filename:    OPEN.MST
'*
'* Purpose:     Tests the Open menu item for the File menu
'*              in Notepad's main window.
'*
'* Revision History:
'*
'* [ 0]    da-mon-year  email    : action
'* [ 1]    06-JUN-1998  TomAr    First few scenarios to give
'*                                some general structure.
'*
'*************************************************************


'******************* INCLUDES ****************************
'$include 'notemain.inc'    'Common general constants
'$include 'noteutil.inc'    'Utilities generic/sharable
'$include 'file.inc'        'Constants/utils for File menu

TestBegin
    dim strText$

        '
        'Create a test file to use with the Open menu item.
        '
    LOG #LVL_STATUSINFO, "Creating temporary file to open."
    If not exists(TEMPFILE1) then
        PutString(DATA_TESTSTRING1,1,1)
        SelMenu(MNU_FILE_SAVEAS)
        WEditSetText(DCN_FILENAME,TEMPFILE1)
        WButtonClick(BTN_SAVE)
```

```
        EndIf


        '
        'Tests the "Open" menu item, dirty bit not set.
        '
        scenario strTestNum()+MNU_FILE_OPEN+" file when no "+_
                "text in editor exists."
            SelMenu(MNU_FILE_OPEN)  'Select menu item "Open".

            If(GetText(NULL) = CAP_OPEN) then
                WEditSetText(DCN_FILENAME,TEMPFILE1)
                WButtonClick(BTN_OPEN)

                'See If filename is in the caption.
                If INSTR(ucase$(GetText(NULL)),_
                    ucase$(TEMPFILE1)) = 0 then
                    fail strFailNum()+ TEMPFILE1 + _
                        " was not opened."
                EndIf
            Else
                fail strFailNum()+MNU_FILE_OPEN+ _
                    " without text didn't display dialog."
            EndIf
        end scenario


        '
        'Open menu item with text and click 'Cancel' to save
        '
        scenario strTestNum()+MNU_FILE_OPEN+" file and select "+_
                BTN_CANCEL+" to Save Changes prompt."
            PutString(DATA_TESTSTRING1, 2, 1)
            strText = EditText(EDIT_NOTEPAD)  'Grab contents
            SelMenu(MNU_FILE_OPEN)

            'Since text was added the Save Changes message box
            If (GetText(NULL) = CAP_SAVECHANGES) then
                WButtonClick(BTN_CANCEL)
            Else
                fail strFailNum()+MNU_FILE_OPEN+_
                    " w/ text didn't display Save Changes "+_
                    "msgbox."
            EndIf
        end scenario


        scenario strTestNum()+"Verify text didn't change "+_
                        "from previous scenario"
            If (strText <> EditText(EDIT_NOTEPAD)) then
                Fail strFailNum()+BTN_CANCEL+" to Save Changes."
```

```
        EndIf
end scenario


'
'Open menu item with text and clicking 'No' to msg box
'

scenario strTestNum()+"'Open' file and 'No' to Save"+_
                    " Changes msgbox."
    SelMenu(MNU_FILE_OPEN)

    If (GetText(NULL) = CAP_SAVECHANGES) then
        WButtonClick(BTN_NO)
        If(GetText(NULL) = CAP_OPEN) then
            WEditSetText(DCN_FILENAME,TEMPFILE1)
            WButtonClick(BTN_OPEN)

            'See If filename is in the caption.
            If INSTR(ucase$(GetText(NULL)),_
                ucase$(TEMPFILE1)) = 0 then
                fail strFailNum()+ TEMPFILE1 + _
                        " was not opened."
            EndIf
        Else
            fail strFailNum()+MNU_FILE_OPEN+ _
                " with text didn't display."
        EndIf
    Else
        fail strFailNum()+MNU_FILE_OPEN+" w/ text "+_
            "didn't give Save Changes msgbox."
    EndIf
end scenario
'
'Open menu item with text and clicking 'yes' to
'message box and click 'cancel' in save as db.
'
scenario strTestNum()+MNU_FILE_OPEN+" w/ text. "+ _
        BTN_YES+" to Save Changes, then "+ _
        BTN_CANCEL+" to Open dialog box."
    SelMenu(MNU_FILE_NEW)
    PutString(DATA_TESTSTRING1, 3, 1)
    strText = EditText(EDIT_NOTEPAD)
    SelMenu(MNU_FILE_OPEN)

    If (GetText(NULL) = CAP_SAVECHANGES) then
        WButtonClick(BTN_YES)
        If(GetText(NULL) = CAP_SAVEAS) then
            WButtonClick(BTN_CANCEL)
```

```
                            'Make sure text did not change.
                            If (strText <> EditText(EDIT_NOTEPAD)) then
                                fail strFailNum()+BTN_CANCEL+ _
                                    " out of 'SaveAs' caused text change."
                            EndIf
                    Else
                        fail strFailNum()+MNU_FILE_OPEN+" with "+_
                            BTN_YES+" to Save Changes didn't "+_
                            "display SaveAs DB."
                    EndIf
                Else
                    fail strFailNum()+MNU_FILE_OPEN+" w/ text "+_
                        "didn't give Save Changes msgbox."
                EndIf
        end scenario

        '
        'Open menu item with text and clicking 'Yes' to msg box
        'message box and saving the file before opening another.
        '
        scenario strTestNum()+MNU_FILE_OPEN+" w/o text. Press"+_
                BTN_YES+" then "+BTN_OK
            PutString(DATA_TESTSTRING1, 4, 1)
            SelMenu(MNU_FILE_OPEN)

            If (GetText(NULL) = CAP_SAVECHANGES) then
                WButtonClick(BTN_YES)
                If(GetText(NULL) = CAP_SAVEAS) then
                    WEditSetText(DCN_FILENAME,TEMPFILE2)
                    WButtonClick(BTN_SAVE)
                    If(GetText(NULL) = CAP_OPEN) then
                        WEditSetText(DCN_FILENAME,TEMPFILE1)
                        WButtonClick(BTN_OPEN)

                        'See if filename is in the caption.
                        If INSTR(ucase$(GetText(NULL)),_
                            ucase$(TEMPFILE1)) = 0 then
                                fail strFailNum()+TEMPFILE1 + _
                                    " was not opened."
                        EndIf
                    Else
                        fail strFailNum()+MNU_FILE_OPEN+ _
                            " with text didn't display."
                    EndIf
                Else
                    fail strFailNum()+MNU_FILE_OPEN+ _
                        ", click "+BTN_YES+ _
                        " to Save Changes didn't display "+_
                        "SaveAs"
                EndIf
            Else
```

```
                    fail strFailNum()+MNU_FILE_OPEN+_
                    " w/ new text didn't give Save Changes msgbox."
            EndIf
        scenario cleanup
            log #LVL_VERBOSE, "Removing temporary text files"+_
                " for test scenario #"+str$(iTestCount)
            kill TEMPFILE1
            kill TEMPFILE2
        end scenario
TestEnd
```

SAVE.MST

```
'************************************************************
'* Filename:    SAVE.MST
'*
'* Purpose:     Tests the Save menu item for the File menu
'*              in Notepad's main window.
'*
'* Revision History:
'*
'* [ 0]   da-mon-year   email    : action
'* [ 1]   06-JUN-1998   TomAr    First few scenarios to give
'*                                some general structure.
'*
'************************************************************

'***************** INCLUDES ***************************
'$include 'notemain.inc'    'General common constants
'$include 'noteutil.inc'    'Utilities generic/sharable
'$include 'file.inc'        'Constants/utils for File menu

TestBegin
    dim strText$

        '
        'Save with text untitled.
        '
    scenario strTestNum()+MNU_FILE_SAVE+" with text. "+_
            " Untitled instance"
        PutString(DATA_TESTSTRING1,1,1)
        strText = EditText(EDIT_NOTEPAD)
        SelMenu(MNU_FILE_SAVE)

        If (GetText(NULL) = CAP_SAVEAS) then
            WEditSetText(DCN_FILENAME, TEMPFILE2)
            WButtonClick(BTN_SAVE)

            'File already exists?
            if (GetText(NULL) = CAP_SAVEAS) then
```

```
                WButtonClick(BTN_YES)
        endif

        If (INSTR(ucase$(GetText(NULL)),_
            ucase$(TEMPFILE2)) <> 0) then
                If (strText <> EditText(EDIT_NOTEPAD)) then
                    fail strFailNum+"Saving the file "+_
                         "caused the text to change."
                EndIf
        Else
            fail strFailNum+TEMPFILE2+_
                 " was not Saved."
        EndIf
    Else
        fail strFailNum+MNU_FILE_SAVE+_
            " with text didn't display "+CAP_SAVEAS+_
            " dialog."
    EndIf
end scenario


'Save with text in saved instance.
'
scenario strTestNum()+MNU_FILE_SAVE+" with text.  "+_
        "Saved instance"
    PutString(DATA_TESTSTRING1, 2, 1)
    strText = EditText(EDIT_NOTEPAD)
    SelMenu(MNU_FILE_SAVE)

    If (WGetActWnd(0) <> ghWndNotepad) then
        fail strFailNum+MNU_FILE_SAVE+_
            " should not have displayed a dialog."
        Play("{Esc}")   'Dismiss the dialog.
    EndIf
scenario cleanup
    log #LVL_VERBOSE, "Cleaning up for test scenario #"+_
                      str$(iTestCount)
    ResetApp()
end scenario


'Verify text saved by opening file saved in previous
'scenario and comparing with text of previous scenario
'
scenario strTestNum()+"Verify text was saved to file."
    SelMenu(MNU_FILE_OPEN)  'Open up the saved file.
    WEditSetText(DCN_FILENAME,TEMPFILE2)
    WButtonClick(BTN_OPEN)
```

```
            If (strText <> EditText(EDIT_NOTEPAD)) then
                fail strFailNum+MNU_FILE_SAVE+_
                    " didn't save changes."
            EndIf
scenario cleanup
        log #LVL_VERBOSE, "Cleaning up for test scenario #"+_
                          str$(iTestCount)
        ResetApp()
end scenario



'
'Save to a file that already Exists.  Respond 'No'.
'
scenario strTestNum()+MNU_FILE_SAVE+_
            " to existing file. Click "+BTN_NO
        PutString(DATA_TESTSTRING1, 1, 1)
        strText = EditText(EDIT_NOTEPAD)
        SelMenu(MNU_FILE_SAVE)

        If (GetText(NULL) = CAP_SAVEAS) then
            WEditSetText(DCN_FILENAME, TEMPFILE2)
            WButtonClick(BTN_SAVE)
            If (GetText(NULL) = CAP_SAVEAS) then
                WButtonClick(BTN_NO)
                If (GetText(NULL) = CAP_SAVEAS) then
                    WButtonClick(BTN_CANCEL)
                    If (strText<>EditText(EDIT_NOTEPAD)) then
                        fail strFailNum+BTN_CANCEL+" "+_
                            MNU_FILE_SAVE+_
                            " caused text to change."
                    EndIf
                Else
                    fail strFailNum+BTN_NO+_
                        " to 'Replace?' didn't return to"+_
                        " Save As db."
                EndIf
            Else
                fail strFailNum+"'File Exists' message"+_
                    " box didn't appear."
            EndIf
        Else
            fail strFailNum+MNU_FILE_SAVE+" w/ text "+_
                "didn't give 'Save As' dialog."
        EndIf
scenario cleanup
        log #LVL_VERBOSE, "Cleaning up for test scenario #"+_
                          str$(iTestCount)
        ResetApp()
end scenario
```

```
'
'Save to existing file.  Respond 'Yes'.
'
scenario strTestNum()+("'Save' to an existing file. "+_
        " Respond 'Yes'.")
    PutString(DATA_TESTSTRING1, 1, 1)
    strText = EditText(EDIT_NOTEPAD)
    SelMenu(MNU_FILE_SAVE)

    If (GetText(NULL) = CAP_SAVEAS) then
        WEditSetText(DCN_FILENAME, TEMPFILE2)
        WButtonClick(BTN_SAVE)
        If (GetText(NULL) = CAP_SAVEAS) then
            WButtonClick(BTN_YES)
            If (WGetActWnd(0) = ghWndNotepad) then
                If INSTR(ucase$(GetText(NULL)),_
                    ucase$(TEMPFILE2)) = 0 then
                    fail strFailNum+TEMPFILE2+_
                        " was not Saved."
            EndIf
        Else
            fail strFailNum+BTN_YES+" to "+_
                "replace file did go back to "+_
                "main window."
        EndIf
    Else
        fail strFailNum+"File Exists msgbox "+_
            "didn't appear."
    EndIf
    Else
        fail strFailNum+MNU_FILE_SAVE+" with text "+_
            "didn't display "+CAP_SAVEAS+" dialog."
    EndIf
scenario cleanup
    log #LVL_VERBOSE,"Cleaning up for test scenario #"+_
        str$(iTestCount)
    ResetApp()
end scenario


'
'Check to make sure the file that was overwritten was
'truly overwritten.
'
scenario strTestNum()+"Verify file was actually "+_
        "replaced."
    SelMenu(MNU_FILE_OPEN)
    WEditSetText(DCN_FILENAME,TEMPFILE2)
    WButtonClick(BTN_OPEN)
```

```
            If (strText <> EditText(EDIT_NOTEPAD)) then
                fail strFailNum+"The file was not overwritten."
            EndIf
        scenario cleanup
            kill TEMPFILE2
        end scenario
TestEnd
```

SAVEAS.MST

```
'************************************************************
'* Filename:     SAVEAS.MST
'*
'* Purpose:      Tests the SaveAs menu item for the File menu
'*               in Notepad's main window.
'*
'* Revision History:
'*
'*  [ 0]   da-mon-year   email    : action
'*  [ 1]   06-JUN-1998   TomAr    First few scenarios to give
'*                                some general structure.
'*
'************************************************************

'****************** INCLUDES *****************************
'$include 'notemain.inc'    'General constants
'$include 'noteutil.inc'    'Utilities generic/sharable
'$include 'file.inc'        'Constants/utils File menu

TestBegin
    dim strText$

        '
        'SaveAs with text in an untitled instance
        '
    scenario strTestNum()+MNU_FILE_SAVEAS+" w/ text."+_
            " Untitled"
        ResetApp()
        PutString(DATA_TESTSTRING1, 1, 1)
        strText = EditText(EDIT_NOTEPAD)
        SelMenu(MNU_FILE_SAVEAS)

        If (GetText(NULL) = CAP_SAVEAS) then
            WEditSetText(DCN_FILENAME, TEMPFILE2)
            WButtonClick(BTN_SAVE)
            if (GetText(NULL) = CAP_SAVEAS) then
                WButtonClick(BTN_YES)
            endif

            'See If filename is in the caption
```

```
                    If INSTR(ucase$(GetText(NULL)),_
                        TEMPFILE2) = 0 then
                            fail strFailNum+TEMPFILE2+" was not Saved."
                    EndIf
            Else
                fail strFailNum+MNU_FILE_SAVEAS+ _
                " w/ text didn't display "+CAP_SAVEAS+" dialog."
            EndIf
    end scenario


    '
    'SaveAs with text in an already saved instance.
    '
    scenario strTestNum()+MNU_FILE_SAVEAS+" w/ text. "+_
            " Saved instance"
        PutString(DATA_TESTSTRING1, 2, 1)
        strText = EditText(EDIT_NOTEPAD)
        SelMenu(MNU_FILE_SAVEAS)

        If (GetText(NULL) = CAP_SAVEAS) then
            WEditSetText(DCN_FILENAME, TEMPFILE1)
            WButtonClick(BTN_SAVE)
            if (GetText(NULL) = CAP_SAVEAS) then
                WButtonClick(BTN_YES)
            endif
            If INSTR(ucase$(GetText(NULL)),TEMPFILE1)=0 then
                fail strFailNum+TEMPFILE1+" was not Saved."
            EndIf
        Else
            fail strFailNum+MNU_FILE_SAVEAS+_
                " w/ text didn't give "+CAP_SAVEAS+_
                " dialog box."
        EndIf
    scenario cleanup
        log #LVL_VERBOSE,"Cleaning up for test scenario #"+_
                        str$(iTestCount)
        ResetApp()
    end scenario


    '
    'Verify text saved in strText variable in previous scenario
    'matches the text in the saved file.  This verifies the
    'file was saved as reported.
    '
    scenario strTestNum()+"Verify text was saved."
        SelMenu(MNU_FILE_OPEN)
        WEditSetText(DCN_FILENAME,TEMPFILE1)
        WButtonClick(BTN_OPEN)
```

```
            If strText <> EditText(EDIT_NOTEPAD) then
                fail strFailNum+MNU_FILE_SAVEAS+_
                    " didn't save any changes."
            EndIf
        scenario cleanup
            log #LVL_VERBOSE,"Cleaning up for test scenario #"+_
                            str$(iTestCount)
            ResetApp()

            if exists(TEMPFILE1) then
                kill TEMPFILE1
            endif

            if exists(TEMPFILE2) then
                kill TEMPFILE2
            endif
        end scenario
TestEnd
```

PAGE_SU.MST

```
'****************************************************************
'* Filename:    PAGE_SU.MST
'*
'* Purpose:     Tests the Page Setup menu item for the File
'*              menu in Notepad's main window.
'*
'* Revision History:
'*
'*  [ 0]   da-mon-year   email    : action
'*  [ 1]   06-JUN-1998   TomAr    First few scenarios to give
'*                                some general structure.
'*
'****************************************************************

'$include 'notemain.inc'   'General constants
'$include 'noteutil.inc'   'Utilities generic/sharable
'$include 'file.inc'       'Constants/utils File menu

TestBegin
    dim strText$

    '
    'Bring up "PageSetup" with no text. Click "Cancel".
    '
    scenario strTestNum()+MNU_FILE_PGSETUP+" w/o text in "+_
            "editor, click "+BTN_CANCEL
        SelMenu(MNU_FILE_PGSETUP)

        'See If "PageSetup" DB appears.
```

```
         If (GetText(NULL) = CAP_PAGESETUP) then
             WButtonClick(BTN_CANCEL)
         Else
             fail strFailNum()+CAP_PAGESETUP+" dialog didn't"+_
                  " appear."
         EndIf
end scenario


    '
    'Bring up the "PageSetup" with no text. click "OK".
    '
    scenario strTestNum()+MNU_FILE_PGSETUP+_
             " w/o text in editor, click "+BTN_OK
         SelMenu(MNU_FILE_PGSETUP)

         'See If "PageSetup" DB appears.
         If (GetText(NULL) = CAP_PAGESETUP) then
             WButtonClick(BTN_OK)
         Else
             fail strFailNum+CAP_PAGESETUP+_
                  " dialog didn't appear."
         EndIf
end scenario


    '
    'Bring up the "PageSetup" DB with text. Click "Cancel".
    'Verify text in editor doesn't change.
    '
    scenario strTestNum()+MNU_FILE_PGSETUP+_
             " w/ text, click "+BTN_CANCEL
         PutString(DATA_TESTSTRING1, 1, 1)
         strText - EditText(EDIT_NOTEPAD)
         SelMenu(MNU_FILE_PGSETUP)

         If (GetText(NULL) = CAP_PAGESETUP) then
             WButtonClick(BTN_CANCEL)
         Else
             fail strFailNum()+CAP_PAGESETUP+_
                  " dialog didn't appear."
         EndIf

         If (strText <> EditText(EDIT_NOTEPAD)) then
             fail strFailNum()+BTN_CANCEL+CAP_PAGESETUP+_
                  " caused the text to change."
         EndIf
end scenario

    '
    'Bring up the "PageSetup" DB with text. Click "OK"
```

```
            'Verify text in editor doesn't change.
            '
            scenario strTestNum()+CAP_PAGESETUP+" w/ text. Click "+_
                    BTN_OK
                PutString(DATA_TESTSTRING1, 2, 1)
                strText = EditText(EDIT_NOTEPAD)
                SelMenu(MNU_FILE_PGSETUP)

                If (GetText(NULL) = CAP_PAGESETUP) then
                    WButtonClick(BTN_OK)
                Else
                    fail strFailNum()+CAP_PAGESETUP+_
                        " dialog didn't appear."
                EndIf

                If (strText <> EditText(EDIT_NOTEPAD)) then
                    fail strFailNum()+CAP_PAGESETUP+_
                        " dialog caused the text to change."
                EndIf
            end scenario
    TestEnd
```

EXIT.MST

```
    '*************************************************************
    '* Filename:      EXIT.MST
    '*
    '* Purpose:       Tests the Exit menu item for the File menu in
    '*                Notepad's main window.
    '*
    '* Revision History:
    '*
    '*  [ 0]   da-mon-year  email    : action
    '*  [ 1]   06-JUN-1998  TomAr    First few scenarios to give
    '*                                some general structure.
    '*
    '*************************************************************


    '****************** INCLUDES ***************************
    '$include 'notemain.inc'    'General constants
    '$include 'noteutil.inc'    'Utilities generic/sharable
    '$include 'file.inc'        'Constants/utils File menu


    TestBegin()
        dim strText$

        scenario strTestNum()+"'Exit' w/o text in editor"
            SelMenu(MNU_FILE_EXIT)
```

```
        sleep 1   'Give app time to shut down
      If (WGetActWnd(0) = ghWndNotepad) then
          fail strFailNum()+"'Exit' did not exit the app."
      endif
  scenario cleanup
      log #LVL_VERBOSE,"Cleaning up for test scenario #"+_
                      str$(iTestCount)
      if not(failed) then
          If (Run(TEST_APP) = 0) then
              ghWndNotepad = wGetActWnd(0)
          Else
              Fail strFailNum()+"Unable to rerun the app."
          EndIf
      EndIf
  end scenario


  scenario strTestNum()+"'Exit' with text.   "+_
          "Select 'Cancel'."
      PutString(DATA_TESTSTRING1, 1, 1)
      strText = EditText(EDIT_NOTEPAD)
      SelMenu(MNU_FILE_EXIT)

      If (GetText(NULL) = CAP_SAVECHANGES) then
          WButtonClick(BTN_CANCEL)
      Else
          fail "'Exit' didn't prompt to save changes."
          run TEST_APP
      EndIf
  end scenario


  scenario strTestNum()+"Verify text in editor "+_
          "didn't change."
      If (strText <> EditText(EDIT_NOTEPAD)) then
          fail "Cancel Exit caused the text to change."
      EndIf
  end scenario


  scenario strTestNum()+"'Exit' with text.   Select 'No'."
      PutString(DATA_TESTSTRING1, 2, 1)
      SelMenu(MNU_FILE_EXIT)

      If (GetText(NULL) = CAP_SAVECHANGES) then
          WButtonClick(BTN_NO)
      Else
          fail "'Exit' didn't prompt to save changes."
      EndIf

      if (wGetActWnd(0) = ghWndNotepad) then
```

```
                fail strFailNum()+"'Exit' did not exit the app"
        endif
scenario cleanup
    LOG #LVL_VERBOSE,"Cleaning up for test scenario #"+_
                    str$(iTestCount)
    if not(failed) then
        If (Run(TEST_APP) = 0) then
            ghWndNotepad = wGetActWnd(0)
        Else
            Fail strFailNum()+"Unable to rerun the app."
        EndIf
    EndIf
end scenario


scenario strTestNum()+"'Exit' w/ text. Select 'Yes'"+_
        " then 'Cancel'."
    PutString(DATA_TESTSTRING1, 3, 1)
    strText = EditText(EDIT_NOTEPAD)
    SelMenu(MNU_FILE_EXIT)

    If (GetText(NULL) = CAP_SAVECHANGES) then
        WButtonClick(BTN_YES)
        If (GetText(NULL) = CAP_SAVEAS) then
            WButtonClick(BTN_CANCEL)
            If (WGetActWnd(0) = ghWndNotepad) then
                If (strText<>EditText(EDIT_NOTEPAD)) then
                    fail strFailNum()+_
                        "Cancel Exit caused the text "+_
                        "to change."
                EndIf
            Else
                fail strFailNum()+"'Cancel' SaveAs "+_
                    "from Exit still exited app."
            EndIf
        Else
            fail strFailNum()+"'Yes' did not bring up"+_
                " a Save As dialog."
        EndIf
    Else
        fail strFailNum()+"'Exit' didn't prompt to "+_
            "save changes."
    EndIf
end scenario


scenario strTestNum()+"'Exit' with text.  Select "+_
        "'Yes' then 'OK'."
    PutString(DATA_TESTSTRING1, 4, 1)
    SelMenu(MNU_FILE_EXIT)
```

```
            If (GetText(NULL) = CAP_SAVECHANGES) then
                WButtonClick(BTN_YES)
                If (GetText(NULL) = CAP_SAVEAS) then
                    WEditSetText(DCN_FILENAME,TEMPFILE1)
                    WButtonClick(BTN_SAVE)
                    If (GetText(NULL) = CAP_SAVEAS) then
                        WButtonClick(BTN_YES)
                    EndIf
                    If (WGetActWnd(0) = ghWndNotepad) then
                        fail strFailNum+"App didn't shut down."
                    Else
                        If not exists(TEMPFILE1) then
                            fail strFailNum()+_
                            "Exiting did not save the file."
                        EndIf
                    EndIf
                Else
                    fail strFailNum()+"'Yes' did not bring "+_
                        "up a Save As DB."
                EndIf
            Else
                fail strFailNum()+"'Exit' didn't prompt to "+_
                    "save changes."
            EndIf
        scenario cleanup
            LOG #LVL_VERBOSE,"Cleaning up for test scenario #"_
                +str$(iTestCount)

            if exists(TEMPFILE1) then
                kill TEMPFILE1                'Delete test file
            endif

            if not(failed) then
                If (Run(TEST_APP) = 0) then
                    ghWndNotepad = wGetActWnd(0)
                Else
                    Fail strFailNum()+"Unable to rerun the app."
                EndIf
            EndIf
        end scenario
    TestEnd()
```

Edit Menu

The Edit menu is made up of eight menu items. These are Undo, Cut, Copy, Paste, Delete, Select All, Time/Date, and Word Wrap. Based on the approach that is being taken in this example (menu-based), the automated tests traverse the menus that make up the Notepad product.

Based on these eight menu items, nine files should be created for testing those menu items: EDIT.INC, UNDO.MST, CUT.MST, COPY.MST, PASTE.MST, DELETE.MST, SLCT_ALL.MST, TIMEDATE.MST, and WORDWRAP.MST.

The EDIT.INC include file holds declarations common to the menu items that make up the Edit menu. Any declarations that might be used by the other test case files should be placed into the EDIT.INC include file. Declarations that are even more generic, and useful to other menus and menu items, should be moved up higher, into the NOTEMAIN.INC file.

EDIT.INC

Any declarations that aren't generic enough to go into the main header file for the Notepad test suite (NOTEMAIN.INC) and are specific to the test case files that perform tests on the Edit menu are placed into this file.

```
'*********************** EDIT.INC **********************
'*
'* PURPOSE: Decls for the Edit menu tests.
'*
'************************************************************

'$ifndef EDIT_INCLUDED
'$define EDIT_INCLUDED

'************************************************************
'******************** CONSTANTS **************************
'************************************************************


'************************************************************
'*************** Dialog Control Names ******************
'************************************************************


'************************************************************
'****************** Captions ***************************
'************************************************************


'************************************************************
'**************** User Def'd Types ******************
'************************************************************



'************************************************************
'**************** Global Variables *******************
'************************************************************



'************************************************************
```

```
'*************** Func/Proc Prototypes **********************
'**********************************************************


'$endif EDIT_INCLUDED
```

UNDO.MST

```
'**********************************************************
'*  Filename:     UNDO.MST
'*
'*  Purpose:      Tests the Undo menu item for the Edit menu
'*                in Notepad's main window.
'*
'*  Revision History:
'*
'*  [ 0]   da-mon-year   email    : action
'*  [ 1]   06-JUN-1998   TomAr    First few scenarios to give
'*                                some general structure.
'*
'**********************************************************


'****************** INCLUDES **********************
'$include 'notemain.inc'        'Common declarations
'$include 'noteutil.inc'        'Common utilities
'$include 'edit.inc'            'Decls specific to Edit menu

TestBegin
    dim strText$


    '
    '"Undo" should be disabled when starting.
    '
    scenario strTestNum+MNU_EDIT_UNDO+_
            " is disabled after 'File/New'."
        if not fGrayMenu(MNU_EDIT_UNDO) then
            fail strFailNum()+MNU_EDIT_UNDO+_
                " menu item is not disabled."
        end if
    end scenario


    '
    '"Undo" should be enabled when you enter text.
    '
    scenario strTestNum+MNU_EDIT_UNDO+_
            " enabled after typing."
        PutString(DATA_TESTSTRING1, 1, 1)
        strText = EditText(EDIT_NOTEPAD)
        if fGrayMenu(MNU_EDIT_UNDO) then
```

```
              fail strFailNum()+MNU_EDIT_UNDO+_
                  " should be available after typing."
        end if
end scenario


'"Undo" after typing should leave editor blank.
'
scenario strTestNum+MNU_EDIT_UNDO+" typing in a string."
      SelMenu(MNU_EDIT_UNDO)
      if (EditText(EDIT_NOTEPAD) <> "") then
          fail strFailNum()+MNU_EDIT_UNDO+" did not clear."
      end if
end scenario



'"Undo" again should put the text back into the editor.
'
scenario strTestNum+MNU_EDIT_UNDO+" again should "+_
            "'REDO' the typing."
      SelMenu(MNU_EDIT_UNDO)
      if (EditText(EDIT_NOTEPAD) <> strText) then
          fail strFailNum()+MNU_EDIT_UNDO+_
                " a second time did not reenter the text."
      end if
end scenario
'
'"Cut" should be undoable.
'
scenario strTestNum+"Test "+MNU_EDIT_CUT+" is undoable."
      SelMenu(MNU_EDIT_CUT)

      if (EditText(EDIT_NOTEPAD) <> strText) then
          SelMenu(MNU_EDIT_UNDO)

          if (EditText(EDIT_NOTEPAD) <> strText) then
              fail strFailNum()+"Undoing a "+MNU_EDIT_CUT+_
                  " action changed the text."
          end if
      else
          fail strFailNum()+MNU_EDIT_CUT+_
                " did not remove the text."
      end if
end scenario
'
'"Copy" then "Undo" should redo the "Cut" operation.
'
scenario strTestNum+"Undoing a "+MNU_EDIT_COPY+_
```

```
                " action should redo the "+_
            MNU_EDIT_CUT+" action."
    CLIPBOARD CLEAR
    SelMenu(MNU_EDIT_COPY)
    if (CLIPBOARD$ = strText) then
        SelMenu(MNU_EDIT_UNDO)
        if (EditText(EDIT_NOTEPAD) <> "") then
            fail strFailNum()+MNU_EDIT_COPY+_
                " action changed the Undo buffer."
        end if
    else
        fail strFailNum()+MNU_EDIT_COPY+_
            " did not copy the text."
    end if
end scenario

'
'"Paste" should be undoable.
'
scenario strTestNum+"Test that "+MNU_EDIT_PASTE+_
        " is undoable."
    ResetApp()
    SelMenu(MNU_EDIT_PASTE)
    SelMenu(MNU_EDIT_UNDO)
    if (EditText(EDIT_NOTEPAD) <> "") then
        fail strFailNum()+"Undoing a "+MNU_EDIT_PASTE+_
            " action changed the text."
    end if
end scenario

'
'"Delete" should be undoable.
'
scenario strTestNum+"Test that "+MNU_EDIT_DELETE+_
        " is undoable."
    SelMenu(MNU_EDIT_DELETE)
    if (EditText(EDIT_NOTEPAD) = "") then
        SelMenu(MNU_EDIT_UNDO)
        if (EditText(EDIT_NOTEPAD) <> strText) then
            fail strFailNum()+"Undoing a "+_
                MNU_EDIT_DELETE+_
                " action changed the text."
        end if
    else
        fail strFailNum()+MNU_EDIT_DELETE+_
            " did not delete the text."
    end if
end scenario

'
'"Undo" again should "Redo" the delete action.
```

```
    scenario strTestNum+MNU_EDIT_UNDO+" again should "+_
            "'Redo' the delete"
        SelMenu(MNU_EDIT_UNDO)
        If (EditText(EDIT_NOTEPAD) <> "") then
            fail strFailNum()+MNU_EDIT_UNDO+_
                " a second time, did not 'Redo' the"+_
                " 'Delete action."
        end if
    end scenario


    'Time/Date stamp should disable the "Undo" menu item.
    '
    scenario strTestNum+"Test Time/Date action disables "+_
            "'Undo'."
        SelMenu(MNU_EDIT_TIMEDATE)
        if not fGrayMenu(MNU_EDIT_UNDO) then
            fail strFailNum()+MNU_EDIT_UNDO+_
                " menu item is not disabled."
        end if
    end scenario
TestEnd
```

CUT.MST

```
'*****************************************************************
'* Filename:    CUT.MST
'*
'* Purpose:     Tests the Cut menu item for the Edit menu in
'*              Notepad's main window.
'*
'* Revision History:
'*
'* [ 0]   da-mon-year  email     : action
'* [ 1]   06-JUN-1998  TomAr     First few scenarios to give
'*                               some general structure.
'*
'*****************************************************************


'****************** INCLUDES ****************************
'$include 'notemain.inc'        'Common declarations
'$include 'noteutil.inc'        'Common utilities
'$include 'edit.inc'            'Decls specific to Edit menu

TestBegin
    dim strText$

    '
    '"Cut" should be disabled when starting.
```

```
'
scenario strTestNum()+MNU_EDIT_CUT+_
        " is disabled after "+MNU_FILE_NEW
    if not fGrayMenu(MNU_EDIT_CUT) then
        fail strFailNum()+MNU_EDIT_CUT+_
            " menu item is not disabled."
    end if
end scenario

'
'"Cut" should be disabled After you enter text.
'
scenario strTestNum()+_
        "'Cut' still disabled after typing."
    PutString(DATA_TESTSTRING1, 1, 1)
    strText = EditText(EDIT_NOTEPAD)
    if not fGrayMenu(MNU_EDIT_CUT) then
        fail strFailNum()+MNU_EDIT_CUT+_
            " should be grayed."
    end if
end scenario

'
'"Cut" should be available after selecting text.
'
scenario strTestNum()+MNU_EDIT_CUT+_
        " available after selecting text."
    SelMenu(MNU_EDIT_SELALL)
    if fGrayMenu(MNU_EDIT_CUT) then
        fail strFailNum()+MNU_EDIT_CUT+_
            " should not be gray."
    end if
end scenario

'
'Text should be blank after "Cut".
'
scenario strTestNum()+MNU_EDIT_CUT+_
        " should remove the text."
    PutString(DATA_TESTSTRING1, 3, 10)
    strText = EditText(EDIT_NOTEPAD)
    SelMenu(MNU_EDIT_SELALL)
    SelMenu(MNU_EDIT_CUT)
    if (EditText(EDIT_NOTEPAD) <> "") then
        fail strFailNum()+MNU_EDIT_CUT+_
            " did not remove the text."
    end if
end scenario

'
'Test should be on clipboard
```

```
            scenario strTestNum()+MNU_EDIT_CUT+_
                    " should put text onto clipboard."
                if (CLIPBOARD$ <> strText) then
                    fail strFailNum()+MNU_EDIT_CUT+_
                            " did not put text onto clipboard."
                end if
            end scenario
    TestEnd
```

COPY.MST

```
    '****************************************************************
    '* Filename:    COPY.MST
    '*
    '* Purpose:     Tests the Copy menu item for the Edit menu
    '*              in Notepad's main window.
    '*
    '* Revision History:
    '*
    '*  [ 0]   da-mon-year   email   : action
    '*  [ 1]   06-JUN-1998   TomAr    First few scenarios to give
    '*                                some general structure.
    '*
    '****************************************************************

    '****************** INCLUDES ****************************
    '$include 'notemain.inc'        'Common declarations
    '$include 'noteutil.inc'        'Common utilities
    '$include 'edit.inc'            'Decls specific to Edit menu

    TestBegin
        dim strText$

        '
        '"Copy" should be disabled when starting.
        '
        scenario strTestNum()+MNU_EDIT_COPY+_
                " is disabled after "+MNU_FILE_NEW
            ResetApp()
            if not(fGrayMenu(MNU_EDIT_COPY)) then
                fail strFailNum()+MNU_EDIT_COPY+_
                        " menu item should be disabled."
            end if
        end scenario


        '
        '"Copy" should be disabled after you enter text.
        '
```

```
       scenario strTestNum()+MNU_EDIT_COPY+_
               " still disabled after typing."
           PutString(DATA_TESTSTRING1, 1, 1)
           strText = EditText(EDIT_NOTEPAD)
           if not fGrayMenu(MNU_EDIT_COPY) then
               fail strFailNum()+MNU_EDIT_COPY+_
                   " should be grayed."
           end if
       end scenario


       '
       '"Cut" should be available after selecting text.
       '
       scenario strTestNum()+MNU_EDIT_COPY+_
               " available after selecting text."
           SelMenu(MNU_EDIT_SELALL)
           if fGrayMenu(MNU_EDIT_COPY) then
               fail strFailNum()+MNU_EDIT_COPY+_
                   " should be available."
           end if
       end scenario


       '
       '"Copy" text to the clipboard
       '
       scenario strTestNum()+MNU_EDIT_COPY+" the selected text."
           SelMenu(MNU_EDIT_COPY)
           If (CLIPBOARD$ <> strText) then
               fail strFailNum()+MNU_EDIT_COPY+_
                   " did not copy the text to the clipboard."
           end if
       end scenario
   TestEnd
```

PASTE.MST

```
'*************************************************************
'* Filename:    PASTE.MST
'*
'* Purpose:     Tests the Paste menu item for the Edit menu
'*              in Notepad's main window.
'*
'* Revision History:
'*
'*  [ 0]   da-mon-year   email    : action
'*  [ 1]   06-JUN-1998   TomAr    First few scenarios to give
'*                                some general structure.
'*
```

```
'**********************************************************

'******************** INCLUDES ***************************
'$include 'notemain.inc'          'Common declarations
'$include 'noteutil.inc'          'Common utilities
'$include 'edit.inc'              'Decls specific to Edit menu

TestBegin
    dim strText$

    '
    '"Paste" should be disabled when clipboard is empty.
    '
    scenario strTestNum()+MNU_EDIT_PASTE+_
            " disabled when clipboard is empty."
        ClipBoard CLEAR
'clear contents of the clipboard.
        if not fGrayMenu(MNU_EDIT_PASTE) then
            fail strFailNum()+MNU_EDIT_PASTE+_
                " should be disabled."
        end if
    end scenario

    '
    'Typing text should keep Paste disabled.
    '
    scenario strTestNum()+"Typing should not affect "+_
            MNU_EDIT_PASTE
        PutString(DATA_TESTSTRING1, 1, 1)
        strText = EditText(EDIT_NOTEPAD)
        if not fGrayMenu(MNU_EDIT_PASTE) then
            fail strFailNum()+MNU_EDIT_PASTE+_
                " should be disabled."
        end if
    end scenario

    '
    'Cutting text should enabled "Paste".
    '
    scenario strTestNum()+MNU_EDIT_CUT+" enables "+_
            MNU_EDIT_PASTE
        SelMenu(MNU_EDIT_SELALL)
        SelMenu(MNU_EDIT_CUT)
        if (CLIPBOARD$ = strText) then
            if fGrayMenu(MNU_EDIT_PASTE) then
                fail strFailNum()+MNU_EDIT_PASTE+_
                    " should be enabled."
            end if
        else
            fail strFailNum()+MNU_EDIT_CUT+" did not work."
        end if
```

```
        end scenario

        '
        '"Paste" the text.
        '
        scenario strTestNum()+MNU_EDIT_PASTE+_
                " text into empty editor."
            SelMenu(MNU_EDIT_PASTE)
            if (EditText(EDIT_NOTEPAD) <> strText) then
                fail strFailNum()+MNU_EDIT_PASTE+_
                    " text did not match original text."
            end if
        end scenario

        '
        '"Paste" text after text of editor.
        '
        scenario strTestNum()+MNU_EDIT_PASTE+" text after text."
            'Add strText to strText for second paste.
            strText = strText+strText
            SelMenu(MNU_EDIT_PASTE)
            if (EditText(EDIT_NOTEPAD) <> strText) then
                fail strFailNum()+MNU_EDIT_PASTE+_
                    " text did not match."
            end if
        end scenario

        '
        '"Paste" text over selected text.
        '
        scenario strTestNum()+MNU_EDIT_PASTE+" before text."
            PutString("", 1, 1)
            strText = DATA_TESTSTRING1 + strText
            SelMenu(MNU_EDIT_PASTE)
            if (EditText(EDIT_NOTEPAD) <> strText) then
                fail strFailNum()+MNU_EDIT_PASTE+_
                    " before text did not match."
            end if
        end scenario

        '
        'Paste should not be affected by File/New.
        '
        scenario strTestNum()+MNU_FILE_NEW+" then try "+_
                MNU_EDIT_PASTE
            ResetApp()
            SelMenu(MNU_EDIT_PASTE)
            if (EditText(EDIT_NOTEPAD)<>DATA_TESTSTRING1) then
                fail strFailNum()+MNU_EDIT_PASTE+_
                    " text did not match."
            end if
        end scenario
TestEnd
```

DELETE.MST

```
'***************************************************************
'* Filename:     DELETE.MST
'*
'* Purpose:      Tests the Delete menu item for the Edit menu
'*               in Notepad's main window.
'*
'* Revision History:
'*
'*  [ 0]  da-mon-year  email    : action
'*  [ 1]  06-JUN-1998  TomAr    First few scenarios to give
'*                              some general structure.
'*
'***************************************************************

'****************** INCLUDES ***************************
'$include 'notemain.inc'        'Common declarations
'$include 'noteutil.inc'        'Common utilities
'$include 'edit.inc'            'Decls specific to Edit menu

TestBegin
    dim strText$

    '
    '"Delete" should be disabled in empty editor.
    '
    scenario strTestNum()+MNU_EDIT_DELETE+_
            " is disabled in empty editor."
        if not fGrayMenu(MNU_EDIT_DELETE) then
            fail strFailNum()+MNU_EDIT_DELETE+_
                " should be grayed."
        end if
    end scenario


    '
    '"Delete" should be disabled with no text selected
    '
    scenario strTestNum()+MNU_EDIT_DELETE+_
            " is disabled with no text selected."
        PutString(DATA_TESTSTRING1, 1, 1)
        if not fGrayMenu(MNU_EDIT_DELETE) then
            fail strFailNum()+MNU_EDIT_DELETE+_
                " should be grayed."
        end if
    end scenario


    '
```

```
        '"Delete" enabled with text selected."
        '
        scenario strTestNum()+MNU_EDIT_DELETE+_
                " is enabled with text selected."
            SelMenu(MNU_EDIT_SELALL)
            if fGrayMenu(MNU_EDIT_DELETE) then
                fail strFailNum()+MNU_EDIT_DELETE+_
                    " should be enabled."
            end if
        end scenario


        '
        '"Delete" should remove the text."
        '
        scenario strTestNum()+MNU_EDIT_DELETE+_
                " should clear the selected text."
            SelMenu(MNU_EDIT_DELETE)
            if (EditText(EDIT_NOTEPAD) <> "") then
                fail strFailNum()+MNU_EDIT_DELETE+_
                    " did not remove the text."
            end if
        end scenario


        '
        '"Delete first word of text."
        '
        scenario strTestNum()+MNU_EDIT_DELETE+_
                " first word of text."
            PutString(DATA_TESTSTRING1, 1, 1)

            'Jump to beginning of first line (CTRL+Home)
            'Ctrl+Shift+Right-arrow to select first word
            Play ghWndNotepad,"^{HOME}"
            Play ghWndNotepad,"^+{RIGHT}"

            SelMenu(MNU_EDIT_DELETE)
            strText = right$(DATA_TESTSTRING1,_
                    (len(DATA_TESTSTRING1) _
                    - instr(DATA_TESTSTRING1," ")))
            if (EditText(EDIT_NOTEPAD) <> strText) then
                fail strFailNum()+MNU_EDIT_DELETE+_
                    " did not delete first word."
            end if
        end scenario
    TestEnd
```

SLCT_ALL.MST

```
'***************************************************************
'* Filename:     SLCT_ALL.MST
'*
'* Purpose:      Tests the Select All menu item for the Edit
'*               menu in Notepad's main window.
'*
'* Revision History:
'*
'*  [ 0]   da-mon-year   email    : action
'*  [ 1]   06-JUN-1998   TomAr    First few scenarios to give
'*                                some general structure.
'*
'***************************************************************


'****************** INCLUDES ****************************
'$include 'notemain.inc'         'Common declarations
'$include 'noteutil.inc'         'Common utilities
'$include 'edit.inc'             'Decls specific to Edit menu

TestBegin

    '
    '"SelectAll" is enabled with no text.
    '
    scenario strTestNum()+ MNU_EDIT_SELALL+_
            " enabled with no text."
        if fGrayMenu(MNU_EDIT_SELALL) then
            fail strFailNum()+MNU_EDIT_SELALL+_
                " is not enabled."
        end if
    end scenario


    '
    '"SelectAll" is a no op with no text.
    '
    scenario strTestNum()+ MNU_EDIT_SELALL+_
            " is a no-op with no text."
        SelMenu(MNU_EDIT_SELALL)

        'Make sure a dialog or another window did not appear
        if (WGetActWnd(0) <> ghWndNotepad) then
            fail strFailNum()+MNU_EDIT_SELALL+_
                " with no text is not a no-op."
        end if
    end scenario


    '
    '"SelectAll" enabled with text.
```

```
        '
        scenario strTestNum()+ MNU_EDIT_SELALL+_
                " enabled with text."
            PutString(DATA_TESTSTRING1, 1, 1)
            if fGrayMenu(MNU_EDIT_SELALL) then
                fail strFailNum()+MNU_EDIT_SELALL+_
                    " is not enabled with text."
            end if
        end scenario

        '
        '"SelectAll" selects the text. 1 line.
        '
        scenario strTestNum()+ MNU_EDIT_SELALL+_
                " selects 1 line of text."
            SelMenu(MNU_EDIT_SELALL)
            SelMenu(MNU_EDIT_DELETE)
            if (EditText(EDIT_NOTEPAD) <> "") then
                fail strFailNum()+MNU_EDIT_SELALL+_
                    " did not select all the text."
            end if
        end scenario

        '
        '"SelectAll" selects the text 3 lines.
        '
        scenario strTestNum()+ MNU_EDIT_SELALL+_
                " selects 3 lines of text."
            PutString(DATA_TESTSTRING1, 1, 1)
            PutString(DATA_TESTSTRING1, 2, 1)
            PutString(DATA_TESTSTRING1, 3, 10)
            SelMenu(MNU_EDIT_SELALL)
            SelMenu(MNU_EDIT_DELETE)
            if (EditText(EDIT_NOTEPAD) <> "") then
                fail strFailNum()+MNU_EDIT_SELALL+_
                    " did not select all the text."
            end if
        end scenario
TestEnd
```

TIMEDATE.MST

```
'*************************************************************
'* Filename:    TIMEDATE.MST
'*
'* Purpose:     Tests the Time/Date menu item for the Edit
'*              menu in Notepad's main window.
'*
'* Revision History:
'*
```

```
'*  [ 0]   da-mon-year  email    : action
'*  [ 1]   06-JUN-1998  TomAr    First few scenarios to give
'*                                some general structure.
'*
'***************************************************************


'********************** INCLUDES *************************
'$include 'notemain.inc'          'Common declarations
'$include 'noteutil.inc'          'Common utilities
'$include 'edit.inc'              'Decls specific to Edit menu

TestBegin
    dim strText$


    '
    '"Time/Date" menu is enabled.
    '
    scenario strTestNum()+MNU_EDIT_TIMEDATE+_
            " menu is enabled."
        if fGrayMenu(MNU_EDIT_TIMEDATE) then
            fail strFailNum()+MNU_EDIT_TIMEDATE+_
                " menu should not be gray."
        end if
    end scenario


    '
    'Put "Time/Date" into an empty editor.
    '
    scenario strTestNum()+"Put "+MNU_EDIT_TIMEDATE+_
            " into an empty editor."
        SelMenu(MNU_EDIT_TIMEDATE)
        SelMenu(MNU_EDIT_SELALL)
        SelMenu(MNU_EDIT_CUT)
        SelMenu(MNU_EDIT_TIMEDATE)

        If (EditText(EDIT_NOTEPAD) <> CLIPBOARD$) then
            fail strFailNum()+MNU_EDIT_TIMEDATE+_
                " string differs."
        end if
    end scenario
TestEnd
```

WORDWRAP.MST

```
'***************************************************************
'* Filename:    WORDWRAP.MST
'*
'* Purpose:     Tests the Wordwrap menu item for the Edit
'*              menu in Notepad's main window.
'*
```

```
'* Revision History:
'*
'*  [ 0]   da-mon-year  email    : action
'*  [ 1]   06-JUN-1998  TomAr    First few scenarios to give
'*                               some general structure.
'*
'***************************************************************

'********************** INCLUDES **************************
'$include 'notemain.inc'        'Common declarations
'$include 'noteutil.inc'        'Common utilities
'$include 'edit.inc'            'Decls specific to Edit menu

TestBegin
    '
    'Type in long string with WordWrap off.
    '
    scenario strTestNum()+"Type text with WordWrap off."
        PutString(DATA_TESTSTRING1, 1, 1)    'Put in a lot
        PutString(DATA_TESTSTRING1, 1, 30)   'of test text.
        PutString(DATA_TESTSTRING1, 1, 60)

        if (WEditLines(EDIT_NOTEPAD) > 1) then
            fail strFailNum()+_
                "Text wrapped when it shouldn't."
        end if
    end scenario


    '
    '"WordWrap" on with existing text.
    '
    scenario strTestNum()+_
            "Turn 'WordWrap' on with existing text."
        SelMenu(MNU_EDIT_WRDWRAP)
        if (WEditLines(EDIT_NOTEPAD) < 2) then
            fail strFailNum()+MNU_EDIT_WRDWRAP+_
                " didn't wrap text."
        end if
    end scenario


    '
    'Type text with WordWrap on.
    '
    scenario strTestNum()+"Type text with WordWrap on."
        ResetApp()
        PutString(DATA_TESTSTRING1, 1, 1)
        PutString(DATA_TESTSTRING1, 1, 30)
        PutString(DATA_TESTSTRING1, 1, 60)

        if (WEditLines(EDIT_NOTEPAD) < 2) then
            fail strFailNum()+_
```

```
                    "Typing text with wordwrap on did not wrap."
            end if
      end scenario
   TestEnd
```

Search Menu

The Search menu is made up of two menu items. They are Find and Find Next. Based on the approach that is being taken in this example (menu-based), the automated tests traverse the menus that make up the Notepad product.

Based on these two menu items, three files should be created for testing those menu items: SEARCH.INC, FIND.MST, and FINDNEXT.MST.

The SEARCH.INC include file holds declarations common to the menu items that make up the Search menu. Any declarations that might be used by the other test case files should be placed into the SEARCH.INC include file. Declarations that are even more generic, and useful to other menus and menu items, should be moved up higher, into the NOTEMAIN.INC file.

SEARCH.INC

Any declarations that aren't generic enough to go into the main header file for the Notepad test suite (NOTEMAIN.INC), and are specific to the test case files that perform tests on the Search menu, are placed into this file.

```
'*********************** SEARCH.INC **********************
'*
'* PURPOSE: Decls for the Search tests.
'*
'***********************************************************

'$ifndef SEARCH_INCLUDED
'$define SEARCH_INCLUDED

'***********************************************************
'********************** CONSTANTS **************************
'***********************************************************

'***********************************************************
'**************** Dialog Control Names ********************
'***********************************************************
const DCN_FINDWHAT$        = "Find What:"

'***********************************************************
'******************** Captions ****************************
```

```
'****************************************************************
const CAP_FIND$          = "Find"
const CAP_NOTFOUND$      = "Notepad"

const BTN_DOWN           = "Down"        'Down button
const BTN_FINDNEXT$      = "Find Next"   'Find Next button


'****************************************************************
'***************** User Def'd Types *********************
'****************************************************************


'****************************************************************
'***************** Global Variables *********************
'****************************************************************


'****************************************************************
'*************** Func/Proc Prototypes *******************
'****************************************************************


'$endif SEARCH_INCLUDED
```

FIND.MST

```
'****************************************************************
'* Filename:     FIND.MST
'*
'* Purpose:      Tests the Find menu item for the Search menu
'*               in Notepad's main window.
'*
'* Revision History:
'*
'*  [ 0]   da-mon-year  email    : action
'*  [ 1]   06-JUN-1998  TomAr    First few scenarios to give
'*                               some general structure.
'*
'****************************************************************

'***************** INCLUDES ***************************
'$include 'notemain.inc'     'Common declarations
'$include 'noteutil.inc'     'Common utilities
'$include 'search.inc'       'Decls specific to Search

TestBegin
    dim strSearchText$

    '
    '"Find" menu should be enabled with no text.
    '
    scenario strTestNum()+MNU_SEARCH_FIND+_
             " menu enabled with no text."
```

```
            if fGrayMenu(MNU_SEARCH_FIND) then
                fail strFailNum()+MNU_SEARCH_FIND+_
                    " menu should not be grayed."
            end if
        end scenario


        '
        '"Find" menu item brings up Find DB.
        '
        scenario strTestNum()+MNU_SEARCH_FIND+_
                " brings up 'Find' DB with no text."
            SelMenu(MNU_SEARCH_FIND)
            if (GetText(NULL) <> CAP_FIND) then
                fail strFailNum()+MNU_SEARCH_FIND+_
                    " dialog did not appear."
            else
                WButtonClick(BTN_CANCEL)
            end if
        end scenario


        '
        '"Find" the first char of a string.
        '
        scenario strTestNum()+MNU_SEARCH_FIND+_
                " the first char of a string."
            strSearchText = MID$(DATA_TESTSTRING1,5,1)
            PutString(DATA_TESTSTRING1, 1, 1)
            PutString("", 0, 0)
            SelMenu(MNU_SEARCH_FIND)
            WEditSetText(DCN_FINDWHAT, strSearchText)
            WOptionClick(BTN_DOWN)
            WButtonClick(BTN_FINDNEXT)

            if (GetText(NULL) <> CAP_FIND) then
                fail strFailNum()+MNU_SEARCH_FIND+_
                    " DB did not stay up."
            end if
        end scenario


        '
        '"Find" next occurrence of strSearchText.
        '
        scenario strTestNum()+MNU_SEARCH_FIND+_
                " next occurrence of SearchText."
            WButtonClick(BTN_FINDNEXT)
            if (GetText(NULL) <> CAP_FIND) then
                fail strFailNum()+MNU_SEARCH_FIND+_
                    " did not find occurrence 2."
                wButtonClick(BTN_OK)
            end if
        end scenario
```

```
'
'"Find" next does not find anything.
'
scenario strTestNum()+MNU_SEARCH_FIND+_
        " again will not find anything."
    WButtonClick(BTN_FINDNEXT)
    if (GetText(NULL) <> CAP_NOTFOUND) then
        fail strFailNum()+MNU_SEARCH_FIND+_
            " did not display not Found msgbox."
    else
        WButtonClick(BTN_OK)          'Dismiss "Not Found"
        WButtonClick(BTN_CANCEL)      'Dismiss "Find" DB.
    end if
end scenario


'
'See if text found matches search text.
'
scenario strTestNum()+"Check that text found "+_
        "matches search text."
    if (LCASE$(EditSelText(EDIT_NOTEPAD))<> _
        LCASE$(strSearchText)) then
        fail strFailNum()+_
            "Found text did not match Search Text."
    end if
end scenario


'
'"Find" first word of string.
'
scenario strTestNum()+MNU_SEARCH_FIND+_
        " first word of a string."
    strSearchText = LEFT$(DATA_TESTSTRING1,3)
    PutString("", 0, 0)
    SelMenu(MNU_SEARCH_FIND)
    WEditSetText(DCN_FINDWHAT, strSearchText)
    WButtonClick(BTN_FINDNEXT)

    if (GetText(NULL) <> CAP_FIND) then
        fail strFailNum()+MNU_SEARCH_FIND+_
            " DB did not stay up."
    end if
end scenario


'
''Find Next' should display message.
'
scenario strTestNum()+MNU_SEARCH_FIND+_
        " again should display message box."
    WButtonClick(BTN_FINDNEXT)
```

```
        if (GetText(NULL) <> CAP_NOTFOUND) then
            fail strFailNum()+MNU_SEARCH_FNEXT+_
                " did not display not Found msg."
        else
            WButtonClick(BTN_OK)            'Dismiss "Not Found"
            wButtonClick(BTN_CANCEL)        'Dismiss "Find" DB.
        end if
end scenario

'
'See if text found matches search text.
'
scenario strTestNum()+"Check that text found"+_
        " matches search text."
    if (LCASE$(EditSelText(EDIT_NOTEPAD)) <> _
        LCASE$(strSearchText)) then
        fail strFailNum()+"Found text did not "+_
            "match Search Text."
    end if
end scenario

'
'"Find" last word of a string.
'
scenario strTestNum()+MNU_SEARCH_FIND+_
        " last word of a string."
    strSearchText = RIGHT$(DATA_TESTSTRING1,3)
    PutString("",0,0)
    SelMenu(MNU_SEARCH_FIND)
    WEditSetText(DCN_FINDWHAT, strSearchText)
    WButtonClick(BTN_FINDNEXT)

    if (GetText(NULL) <> CAP_FIND) then
        fail strFailNum()+MNU_SEARCH_FIND+_
            " DB did not stay up."
    end if
end scenario

'
'"Find" again will not find anything.
'
scenario strTestNum()+MNU_SEARCH_FIND+_
        " again will not find another occurrence."
    WButtonClick(BTN_FINDNEXT)
    if (GetText(NULL) <> CAP_NOTFOUND) then
        fail strFailNum()+MNU_SEARCH_FNEXT+_
            " did not display 'not found' msg."
    else
        WButtonClick(BTN_OK)            'Dismiss "Not Found"
        WButtonClick(BTN_CANCEL)        'Dismiss "Find" DB.
    end if
```

```
        end scenario

        '
        'See if text found matches search text.
        '
        scenario strTestNum()+"Check that text found "+_
                "matches search text."
            if (LCASE$(EditSelText(EDIT_NOTEPAD)) <> _
                LCASE$(strSearchText)) then
                fail strFailNum()+"Found text did not "+_
                    "match Search Text."
            end if
        end scenario
    TestEnd
```

FINDNEXT.MST

```
'*************************************************************
'* Filename:    FINDNEXT.MST
'*
'* Purpose:     Tests the Find Next menu item for the Search
'*              menu in Notepad's main window.
'*
'* Revision History:
'*
'* [ 0]   da-mon-year  email    : action
'* [ 1]   06-JUN-1998  TomAr    First few scenarios to give
'*                              some general structure.
'*
'*************************************************************

'****************** INCLUDES ***************************
'$include 'notemain.inc'         'Common declarations
'$include 'noteutil.inc'         'Common utilities
'$include 'search.inc'           'Decls specific to Search

TestBegin
    dim strSearchText$

        '
        '"Find Next" should display the "Find" DB.
        '
        scenario strTestNum()+MNU_SEARCH_FNEXT+" with 'Find'"+_
                " Buffer empty."
            SelMenu(MNU_SEARCH_FNEXT)
            if (GetText(NULL) <> CAP_FIND) then
                fail strFailNum()+MNU_SEARCH_FNEXT+_
                    " did not display."
            else
                WButtonClick(BTN_CANCEL)
```

```
        end if
end scenario

'
'"Find Next" with text.
'
scenario strTestNum()+MNU_SEARCH_FNEXT+_
        " with next but Find buffer empty."
    strSearchText = MID$(DATA_TESTSTRING1,5,1)
    PutString(DATA_TESTSTRING1, 1, 1)
    PutString("", 0, 0)
    SelMenu(MNU_SEARCH_FNEXT)

    if (GetText(NULL) = CAP_FIND) then
        WEditSetText(DCN_FINDWHAT, strSearchText)
        WButtonClick(BTN_FINDNEXT)
        If (GetText(NULL) <> CAP_FIND) then
            fail strFailNum()+_
                "'Find' DB did not stay up."
        end if
        WButtonClick(BTN_CANCEL)
    else
        fail strFailNum()+MNU_SEARCH_FNEXT+_
            " did not display."
    end if
end scenario

'
'See if text found matches search text.
'
scenario strTestNum()+"Check that text found "+_
        "matches search text."
    if (LCASE$(EditSelText(EDIT_NOTEPAD)) <> _
        LCASE$(strSearchText)) then
        fail strFailNum()+"Found text did not "+_
            "match Search Text."
    end if
end scenario


'
''Find Next' finds the next occurrence without display
'the DB.
'
scenario strTestNum()+MNU_SEARCH_FNEXT+_
        " with 'Find' buffer filled."
    SelMenu(MNU_SEARCH_FNEXT)
    if (WGetActWnd(0) <> ghWndNotepad) then
        fail strFailNum()+MNU_SEARCH_FNEXT+ _
            " did not find next occurrence."
    end if
```

```
       end scenario

       '
       'See if text found matches search text.
       '
       scenario strTestNum()+"Check that text found "+_
               "matches search text."
           if (LCASE$(EditSelText(EDIT_NOTEPAD)) <> _
               LCASE$(strSearchText)) then
               fail strFailNum()+"Found text did not "+_
                   "match Search Text."
           end if
       end scenario

       '
       ''Find Next' should display "not found" message box.
       '
       scenario strTestNum()+MNU_SEARCH_FNEXT+ _
               " should display 'Not Found' message box."
           SelMenu(MNU_SEARCH_FNEXT)
           if (GetText(NULL) <> CAP_NOTFOUND) then
               fail strFailNum()+MNU_SEARCH_FNEXT+_
                   " did not display."
           else
               WButtonClick(BTN_OK)
           end if
       end scenario

       '
       'See if text found matches search text.
       '
       scenario strTestNum()+"Check that text found "+_
               "matches search text."
           if (LCASE$(EditSelText(EDIT_NOTEPAD)) <> _
               LCASE$(strSearchText)) then
               fail strFailNum()+"Found text did not match "+_
                   "Search Text."
           end if
       end scenario
   TestEnd
```

Help Menu

The Help menu is made up of two menu items. They are Help Topics and About
Notepad. Based on the approach that is being taken in this example (menu-based),
the automated test traverses the menus that make up the Notepad product.

Based on these two menu items, three files should be created for testing those menu items: HELP.INC, TOPICS.MST, and ABOUT.MST.

The HELP.INC include file holds declarations common to the menu items that make up the Help menu. Any declarations that might be used by the other test case files should be placed into the HELP.INC include file. Declarations that are even more generic, and useful to other menus and menu items, should be moved up higher, into the NOTEMAIN.INC file.

HELP.INC

Any declarations that aren't generic enough to go into the main header file for the Notepad test suite (NOTEMAIN.INC), and are specific to the test case files that perform tests on the Help menu, are placed into this file.

```
'********************** HELP.INC ************************
'*
'* PURPOSE: Decls for the Help tests.
'*
'******************************************************

'$ifndef HELP_INCLUDED
'$define HELP_INCLUDED

'******************************************************
'******************** CONSTANTS ***********************
'******************************************************


'******************************************************
'****************** Captions **************************
'******************************************************
const CAP_TOPICS$           = "Help Topics: Notepad Help"
const CAP_ABOUT$            = "About Notepad"

'******************************************************
'***************** User Def'd Types *******************
'******************************************************


'******************************************************
'***************** Global Variables *******************
'******************************************************


'******************************************************
'************** Func/Proc Prototypes ******************
'******************************************************

'$endif HELP_INCLUDED
```

TOPICS.MST

```
'*************************************************************
'* Filename:    TOPICS.MST
'*
'* Purpose:     Tests the Help Topics menu item for the Help
'*              menu in Notepad's main window.
'*
'* Revision History:
'*
'*  [ 0]   da-mon-year   email    : action
'*  [ 1]   06-JUN-1998   TomAr    First few scenarios to give
'*                                some general structure.
'*
'*************************************************************

'****************** INCLUDES **************************
'$include 'notemain.inc'        'Common declarations
'$include 'noteutil.inc'        'Common utilities
'$include 'help.inc'            'Decls specific to Help menu

TestBegin
    '
    'Select the "Contents" menu item
    '
    scenario strTestNum()+"Select the "+MNU_HELP_TOPICS+_
            " menu item"
        SelMenu(MNU_HELP_TOPICS)
      wFndWnd(CAP_TOPICS, FW_ALL OR FW_FOCUS)
        If (GetText(NULL) = CAP_TOPICS) then
            WButtonClick(BTN_CANCEL)
        else
            fail MNU_HELP_TOPICS+" help did not open."
        end if
      wFndWnd(CAP_NOTEPAD, FW_ALL OR FW_FOCUS)
    end scenario
TestEnd
```

ABOUT.MST

```
'*************************************************************
'* Filename:    ABOUT.MST
'*
'* Purpose:     Tests the About menu item for the Help menu
'*              in Notepad's main window.
'*
'* Revision History:
'*
'*  [ 0]   da-mon-year   email    : action
```

```
'*  [ 1]   06-JUN-1998  TomAr   First few scenarios to give
'*                              some general structure.
'*
'***************************************************************

'****************** INCLUDES ****************************
'$include 'notemain.inc'      'Common declarations
'$include 'noteutil.inc'      'Common utilities
'$include 'help.inc'          'Decls specific to Help menu

TestBegin
    scenario strTestNum()+"Select the "+_
            MNU_HELP_ABOUT+" menu item."
        SelMenu(MNU_HELP_ABOUT)

        if (GetText(NULL) = CAP_ABOUT) then
            WButtonClick(BTN_OK)
        else
            fail CAP_ABOUT+" dialog did not appear."
        end if
    end scenario
TestEnd
```

✦   ✦   ✦

Log File Generated from Run of Notepad Test Suite

◆ ◆ ◆ ◆

The following log file was generated when the Notepad test script was run in its entirety. The detail level was set to zero (0) to show only the detail that Visual Test provides as a default. For more verbose information, refer to the different levels available as declared in the NOTEMAIN.INC file (for example, Detail Level 5 would provide summary information after each test case file had completed its test run).

A version of this log file that has its detail level set to 100 (that is, verbose) can be found on the CD-ROM in the SUITE directory.

Use this log file to compare the output for the source code for the test case files shown in Appendix H, *Listings of All Test Cases*.

```
[Start Suite Header]
[Suite Name]          Notepad Test Suite
[Machine]             CHIANTI
[Start Time]          05/31/1998 18:37:26
[End Suite Header]

   [Start Case Header]
[Case Name]           C:\Program Files\Microsoft
Visual
Studio\MyProjects\Notepad\File\New.mst
   [Product Version]  Windows NT 4.0
   [Language]         English
   [Machine]          CHIANTI
   [Start Time]       05/31/1998 18:37:26
```

```
    [End Case Header]

    [Start Scenario]
    [Name]              Test #1: Test that 'Save changes'
message box is displayed.
    [Test Location]  C:\Program Files\Microsoft Visual
Studio\MyProjects\Notepad\File\New.mst (32)
    [Start Time]     05/31/1998 18:37:33
    [Result]         PASS
    [Elapsed Time]   0.341
    [End Scenario]

    [Start Scenario]
    [Name]              Test #2: Verify that the original text
remains unchanged after clicking Cancel.
    [Test Location]  C:\Program Files\Microsoft Visual
Studio\MyProjects\Notepad\File\New.mst (49)
    [Start Time]     05/31/1998 18:37:33
    [Result]         PASS
    [Elapsed Time]   0.010
    [End Scenario]

    [Start Scenario]
    [Name]              Test #3: Click 'No' to 'Save Changes?' msg
    [Test Location]  C:\Program Files\Microsoft Visual
Studio\MyProjects\Notepad\File\New.mst (59)
    [Start Time]     05/31/1998 18:37:33
    [Result]         PASS
    [Elapsed Time]   0.651
    [End Scenario]

    [Start Scenario]
    [Name]              Test #4: Click 'Yes' to 'Save changes?'
msg
    [Test Location]  C:\Program Files\Microsoft Visual
Studio\MyProjects\Notepad\File\New.mst (73)
    [Start Time]     05/31/1998 18:37:34
    [Result]         PASS
    [Elapsed Time]   2.083
    [End Scenario]

  [Case Result]      PASS
  [Elapsed Time]     10.495
  [End Case]

  [Start Case Header]
  [Case Name]          C:\Program Files\Microsoft Visual
Studio\MyProjects\Notepad\File\Page_su.mst
  [Product Version]  Windows NT 4.0
  [Language]         English
  [Machine]          CHIANTI
```

```
    [Start Time]        05/31/1998 18:37:37
    [End Case Header]

    [Start Scenario]
    [Name]              Test #1: File\Page Setup... w/o text in
editor, click Cancel
    [Test Location]  C:\Program Files\Microsoft Visual
Studio\MyProjects\Notepad\File\Page_su.mst (31)
    [Start Time]        05/31/1998 18:37:42
    [Result]            PASS
    [Elapsed Time]   1.122
    [End Scenario]

    [Start Scenario]
    [Name]              Test #2: File\Page Setup... w/o text in
editor, click Ok
    [Test Location]  C:\Program Files\Microsoft Visual
Studio\MyProjects\Notepad\File\Page_su.mst (46)
    [Start Time]        05/31/1998 18:37:44
    [Result]            PASS
    [Elapsed Time]   0.481
    [End Scenario]

    [Start Scenario]
    [Name]              Test #3: File\Page Setup... w/ text, click
Cancel
    [Test Location]  C:\Program Files\Microsoft Visual
Studio\MyProjects\Notepad\File\Page_su.mst (62)
    [Start Time]        05/31/1998 18:37:44
    [Result]            PASS
    [Elapsed Time]   0.550
    [End Scenario]

    [Start Scenario]
    [Name]              Test #4: Page Setup w/ text. Click Ok
    [Test Location]  C:\Program Files\Microsoft Visual
Studio\MyProjects\Notepad\File\Page_su.mst (82)
    [Start Time]        05/31/1998 18:37:45
    [Result]            PASS
    [Elapsed Time]   0.561
    [End Scenario]

  [Case Result]        PASS
  [Elapsed Time]   9.033
  [End Case]

  [Start Case Header]
  [Case Name]          C:\Program Files\Microsoft Visual
Studio\MyProjects\Notepad\File\Save.mst
  [Product Version]  Windows NT 4.0
  [Language]           English
```

```
[Machine]            CHIANTI
[Start Time]         05/31/1998 18:37:46
[End Case Header]

    [Start Scenario]
    [Name]           Test #1: File\Save with text.  Untitled
instance
    [Test Location]  C:\Program Files\Microsoft Visual
Studio\MyProjects\Notepad\File\Save.mst (32)
    [Start Time]     05/31/1998 18:37:51
    [Result]         PASS
    [Elapsed Time]   0.621
    [End Scenario]

    [Start Scenario]
    [Name]           Test #2: File\Save with text.  Saved
instance
    [Test Location]  C:\Program Files\Microsoft Visual
Studio\MyProjects\Notepad\File\Save.mst (61)
    [Start Time]     05/31/1998 18:37:52
    [Result]         PASS
    [Elapsed Time]   0.391
    [End Scenario]

    [Start Scenario]
    [Name]           Test #3: Verify text was saved to file.
    [Test Location]  C:\Program Files\Microsoft Visual
Studio\MyProjects\Notepad\File\Save.mst (80)
    [Start Time]     05/31/1998 18:37:52
    [Result]         PASS
    [Elapsed Time]   0.520
    [End Scenario]

    [Start Scenario]
    [Name]           Test #4: File\Save to existing file. Click
No
    [Test Location]  C:\Program Files\Microsoft Visual
Studio\MyProjects\Notepad\File\Save.mst (97)
    [Start Time]     05/31/1998 18:37:53
    [Result]         PASS
    [Elapsed Time]   0.742
    [End Scenario]

    [Start Scenario]
    [Name]           Test #5: 'Save' to an existing file.
Respond 'Yes'.
    [Test Location]  C:\Program Files\Microsoft Visual
Studio\MyProjects\Notepad\File\Save.mst (130)
    [Start Time]     05/31/1998 18:37:54
    [Result]         PASS
    [Elapsed Time]   0.691
```

```
    [End Scenario]

    [Start Scenario]
    [Name]              Test #6: Verify file was actually
replaced.
    [Test Location]  C:\Program Files\Microsoft Visual
Studio\MyProjects\Notepad\File\Save.mst (163)
    [Start Time]     05/31/1998 18:37:54
    [Result]         PASS
    [Elapsed Time]   0.380
    [End Scenario]

  [Case Result]      PASS
  [Elapsed Time]     9.514
  [End Case]

  [Start Case Header]
  [Case Name]          C:\Program Files\Microsoft Visual
Studio\MyProjects\Notepad\File\Exit.mst
  [Product Version]  Windows NT 4.0
  [Language]         English
  [Machine]          CHIANTI
  [Start Time]       05/31/1998 18:37:55
  [End Case Header]

    [Start Scenario]
    [Name]              Test #1: 'Exit' w/o text in editor
    [Test Location]  C:\Program Files\Microsoft Visual
Studio\MyProjects\Notepad\File\Exit.mst (30)
    [Start Time]     05/31/1998 18:38:01
    [Result]         PASS
    [Elapsed Time]   1.332
    [End Scenario]

    [Start Scenario]
    [Name]              Test #2: 'Exit' with text.  Select
'Cancel'.
    [Test Location]  C:\Program Files\Microsoft Visual
Studio\MyProjects\Notepad\File\Exit.mst (49)
    [Start Time]     05/31/1998 18:38:02
    [Result]         PASS
    [Elapsed Time]   0.300
    [End Scenario]

    [Start Scenario]
    [Name]              Test #3: Verify text in editor didn't
change.
    [Test Location]  C:\Program Files\Microsoft Visual
Studio\MyProjects\Notepad\File\Exit.mst (63)
    [Start Time]     05/31/1998 18:38:03
    [Result]         PASS
```

```
        [Elapsed Time]    0.010
        [End Scenario]

        [Start Scenario]
        [Name]            Test #4: 'Exit' with text.  Select 'No'.
        [Test Location]  C:\Program Files\Microsoft Visual
Studio\MyProjects\Notepad\File\Exit.mst (70)
        [Start Time]      05/31/1998 18:38:03
        [Result]          PASS
        [Elapsed Time]    0.591
        [End Scenario]

        [Start Scenario]
        [Name]            Test #5: 'Exit' w/ text. Select 'Yes' then
'Cancel'.
        [Test Location]  C:\Program Files\Microsoft Visual
Studio\MyProjects\Notepad\File\Exit.mst (95)
        [Start Time]      05/31/1998 18:38:03
        [Result]          PASS
        [Elapsed Time]    0.761
        [End Scenario]

        [Start Scenario]
        [Name]            Test #6: 'Exit' with text.  Select 'Yes'
then 'OK'.
        [Test Location]  C:\Program Files\Microsoft Visual
Studio\MyProjects\Notepad\File\Exit.mst (120)
        [Start Time]      05/31/1998 18:38:04
        [Result]          PASS
        [Elapsed Time]    0.902
        [End Scenario]

      [Case Result]       PASS
      [Elapsed Time]      10.124
      [End Case]

      [Start Case Header]
      [Case Name]         C:\Program Files\Microsoft Visual
Studio\MyProjects\Notepad\File\Open.mst
      [Product Version]   Windows NT 4.0
      [Language]          English
      [Machine]           CHIANTI
      [Start Time]        05/31/1998 18:38:05
      [End Case Header]

        [Start Scenario]
        [Name]            Test #1: File\Open... file when no text in
editor exists.
        [Test Location]  C:\Program Files\Microsoft Visual
Studio\MyProjects\Notepad\File\Open.mst (44)
        [Start Time]      05/31/1998 18:38:12
```

```
     [Result]          PASS
     [Elapsed Time]    0.361
     [End Scenario]

     [Start Scenario]
     [Name]            Test #2: File\Open... file and select
Cancel to Save Changes prompt.
     [Test Location]   C:\Program Files\Microsoft Visual
Studio\MyProjects\Notepad\File\Open.mst (64)
     [Start Time]      05/31/1998 18:38:12
     [Result]          PASS
     [Elapsed Time]    0.330
     [End Scenario]

     [Start Scenario]
     [Name]            Test #3: Verify text didn't change from
previous scenario
     [Test Location]   C:\Program Files\Microsoft Visual
Studio\MyProjects\Notepad\File\Open.mst (78)
     [Start Time]      05/31/1998 18:38:12
     [Result]          PASS
     [Elapsed Time]    0.000
     [End Scenario]

     [Start Scenario]
     [Name]            Test #4: 'Open' file and 'No' to Save
Changes msgbox.
     [Test Location]   C:\Program Files\Microsoft Visual
Studio\MyProjects\Notepad\File\Open.mst (89)
     [Start Time]      05/31/1998 18:38:12
     [Result]          PASS
     [Elapsed Time]    0.461
     [End Scenario]

     [Start Scenario]
     [Name]            Test #5: File\Open... w/ text. Yes to Save
Changes, then Cancel to Open dialog box.
     [Test Location]   C:\Program Files\Microsoft Visual
Studio\MyProjects\Notepad\File\Open.mst (114)
     [Start Time]      05/31/1998 18:38:13
     [Result]          PASS
     [Elapsed Time]    0.681
     [End Scenario]

     [Start Scenario]
     [Name]            Test #6: File\Open... w/o text. Press Yes
then Ok
     [Test Location]   C:\Program Files\Microsoft Visual
Studio\MyProjects\Notepad\File\Open.mst (141)
     [Start Time]      05/31/1998 18:38:14
     [Result]          PASS
```

```
    [Elapsed Time]    0.791
    [End Scenario]

  [Case Result]       PASS
  [Elapsed Time]      9.504
  [End Case]

  [Start Case Header]
  [Case Name]               C:\Program Files\Microsoft Visual
Studio\MyProjects\Notepad\File\Saveas.mst
  [Product Version]   Windows NT 4.0
  [Language]          English
  [Machine]           CHIANTI
  [Start Time]        05/31/1998 18:38:15
  [End Case Header]

    [Start Scenario]
    [Name]            Test #1: File\Save As... w/ text.
Untitled
    [Test Location]   C:\Program Files\Microsoft Visual
Studio\MyProjects\Notepad\File\Saveas.mst (32)
    [Start Time]      05/31/1998 18:38:21
    [Result]          PASS
    [Elapsed Time]    0.771
    [End Scenario]

    [Start Scenario]
    [Name]            Test #2: File\Save As... w/ text.  Saved
instance
    [Test Location]   C:\Program Files\Microsoft Visual
Studio\MyProjects\Notepad\File\Saveas.mst (58)
    [Start Time]      05/31/1998 18:38:21
    [Result]          PASS
    [Elapsed Time]    0.601
    [End Scenario]

    [Start Scenario]
    [Name]            Test #3: Verify text was saved.
    [Test Location]   C:\Program Files\Microsoft Visual
Studio\MyProjects\Notepad\File\Saveas.mst (86)
    [Start Time]      05/31/1998 18:38:22
    [Result]          PASS
    [Elapsed Time]    0.531
    [End Scenario]

  [Case Result]       PASS
  [Elapsed Time]      8.001
  [End Case]

  [Start Case Header]
  [Case Name]               C:\Program Files\Microsoft Visual
```

```
Studio\MyProjects\Notepad\Edit\Slct_all.mst
   [Product Version]   Windows NT 4.0
   [Language]          English
   [Machine]           CHIANTI
   [Start Time]        05/31/1998 18:38:23
   [End Case Header]

    [Start Scenario]
    [Name]             Test #1: Edit\Select All enabled with no
text.
    [Test Location]  C:\Program Files\Microsoft Visual
Studio\MyProjects\Notepad\Edit\Slct_all.mst (31)
    [Start Time]        05/31/1998 18:38:29
    [Result]            PASS
    [Elapsed Time]      0.150
    [End Scenario]

    [Start Scenario]
    [Name]             Test #2: Edit\Select All is a no-op with
no text.
    [Test Location]  C:\Program Files\Microsoft Visual
Studio\MyProjects\Notepad\Edit\Slct_all.mst (40)
    [Start Time]        05/31/1998 18:38:29
    [Result]            PASS
    [Elapsed Time]      0.160
    [End Scenario]

    [Start Scenario]
    [Name]             Test #3: Edit\Select All enabled with
text.
    [Test Location]  C:\Program Files\Microsoft Visual
Studio\MyProjects\Notepad\Edit\Slct_all.mst (52)
    [Start Time]        05/31/1998 18:38:29
    [Result]            PASS
    [Elapsed Time]      0.231
    [End Scenario]

    [Start Scenario]
    [Name]             Test #4: Edit\Select All selects 1 line of
text.
    [Test Location]  C:\Program Files\Microsoft Visual
Studio\MyProjects\Notepad\Edit\Slct_all.mst (62)
    [Start Time]        05/31/1998 18:38:29
    [Result]            PASS
    [Elapsed Time]      0.310
    [End Scenario]

    [Start Scenario]
    [Name]             Test #5: Edit\Select All selects 3 lines
of text.
    [Test Location]  C:\Program Files\Microsoft Visual
```

```
Studio\MyProjects\Notepad\Edit\Slct_all.mst (73)
    [Start Time]      05/31/1998 18:38:30
    [Result]          PASS
    [Elapsed Time]    0.651
    [End Scenario]

  [Case Result]       PASS
  [Elapsed Time]      7.631
  [End Case]

  [Start Case Header]
  [Case Name]         C:\Program Files\Microsoft Visual
Studio\MyProjects\Notepad\Edit\Copy.mst
  [Product Version]   Windows NT 4.0
  [Language]          English
  [Machine]           CHIANTI
  [Start Time]        05/31/1998 18:38:30
  [End Case Header]

    [Start Scenario]
    [Name]            Test #1: Edit\Copy is disabled after
File\New
    [Test Location]  C:\Program Files\Microsoft Visual
Studio\MyProjects\Notepad\Edit\Copy.mst (32)
    [Start Time]      05/31/1998 18:38:36
    [Result]          PASS
    [Elapsed Time]    0.280
    [End Scenario]

    [Start Scenario]
    [Name]            Test #2: Edit\Copy still disabled after
typing.
    [Test Location]  C:\Program Files\Microsoft Visual
Studio\MyProjects\Notepad\Edit\Copy.mst (43)
    [Start Time]      05/31/1998 18:38:37
    [Result]          PASS
    [Elapsed Time]    0.220
    [End Scenario]

    [Start Scenario]
    [Name]            Test #3: Edit\Copy available after
selecting text.
    [Test Location]  C:\Program Files\Microsoft Visual
Studio\MyProjects\Notepad\Edit\Copy.mst (55)
    [Start Time]      05/31/1998 18:38:37
    [Result]          PASS
    [Elapsed Time]    0.291
    [End Scenario]

    [Start Scenario]
    [Name]            Test #4: Edit\Copy the selected text.
```

```
      [Test Location]  C:\Program Files\Microsoft Visual
Studio\MyProjects\Notepad\Edit\Copy.mst (66)
      [Start Time]       05/31/1998 18:38:37
      [Result]           PASS
      [Elapsed Time]     0.671
      [End Scenario]

   [Case Result]         PASS
   [Elapsed Time]        7.752
   [End Case]

   [Start Case Header]
   [Case Name]              C:\Program Files\Microsoft Visual
Studio\MyProjects\Notepad\Edit\Wordwrap.mst
   [Product Version]     Windows NT 4.0
   [Language]            English
   [Machine]             CHIANTI
   [Start Time]          05/31/1998 18:38:38
   [End Case Header]

      [Start Scenario]
      [Name]             Test #1: Type text with WordWrap off.
      [Test Location]  C:\Program Files\Microsoft Visual
Studio\MyProjects\Notepad\Edit\Wordwrap.mst (30)
      [Start Time]       05/31/1998 18:38:44
      [Result]           PASS
      [Reason]           Fail #1: Text wrapped when it shouldn't.
      [Elapsed Time]     0.450
      [End Scenario]

      [Start Scenario]
      [Name]             Test #2: Turn 'WordWrap' on with existing
text.
      [Test Location]  C:\Program Files\Microsoft Visual
Studio\MyProjects\Notepad\Edit\Wordwrap.mst (43)
      [Start Time]       05/31/1998 18:38:44

      [Detail 10]        Selected menu: Edit\Word Wrap
      [Result]           PASS
      [Elapsed Time]     0.211
      [End Scenario]

      [Start Scenario]
      [Name]             Test #3: Type text with WordWrap on.
      [Test Location]  C:\Program Files\Microsoft Visual
Studio\MyProjects\Notepad\Edit\Wordwrap.mst (53)
      [Start Time]       05/31/1998 18:38:45

      [Detail 10]        Selected menu: File\New
      [Result]           PASS
      [Elapsed Time]     0.631
```

```
     [End Scenario]

   [Case Result]        PASS
   [Elapsed Time]       7.500
   [End Case]


   [Start Case Header]
   [Case Name]          C:\Program Files\Microsoft Visual
Studio\MyProjects\Notepad\Edit\Paste.mst
   [Product Version]    Windows NT 4.0
   [Language]           English
   [Machine]            CHIANTI
   [Start Time]         05/31/1998 18:38:46
   [End Case Header]

     [Start Scenario]
     [Name]             Test #1: Edit\Paste disabled when
clipboard is empty.
     [Test Location]  C:\Program Files\Microsoft Visual
Studio\MyProjects\Notepad\Edit\Paste.mst (32)
     [Start Time]     05/31/1998 18:38:52
     [Result]         PASS
     [Elapsed Time]   0.150
     [End Scenario]

     [Start Scenario]
     [Name]             Test #2: Typing should not affect
Edit\Paste
     [Test Location]  C:\Program Files\Microsoft Visual
Studio\MyProjects\Notepad\Edit\Paste.mst (42)
     [Start Time]     05/31/1998 18:38:52
     [Result]         PASS
     [Elapsed Time]   0.240
     [End Scenario]

     [Start Scenario]
     [Name]             Test #3: Edit\Cut enables Edit\Paste
     [Test Location]  C:\Program Files\Microsoft Visual
Studio\MyProjects\Notepad\Edit\Paste.mst (53)
     [Start Time]     05/31/1998 18:38:52
     [Result]         PASS
     [Elapsed Time]   0.481
     [End Scenario]

     [Start Scenario]
     [Name]             Test #4: Edit\Paste text into empty
editor.
     [Test Location]  C:\Program Files\Microsoft Visual
Studio\MyProjects\Notepad\Edit\Paste.mst (68)
     [Start Time]     05/31/1998 18:38:52
     [Result]         PASS
```

```
     [Elapsed Time]    0.160
     [End Scenario]

     [Start Scenario]
     [Name]            Test #5: Edit\Paste text after text.
     [Test Location]  C:\Program Files\Microsoft Visual
Studio\MyProjects\Notepad\Edit\Paste.mst (78)
     [Start Time]     05/31/1998 18:38:53
     [Result]         PASS
     [Elapsed Time]    0.160
     [End Scenario]

     [Start Scenario]
     [Name]            Test #6: Edit\Paste before text.
     [Test Location]  C:\Program Files\Microsoft Visual
Studio\MyProjects\Notepad\Edit\Paste.mst (90)
     [Start Time]     05/31/1998 18:38:53
     [Result]         PASS
     [Elapsed Time]    0.782
     [End Scenario]

     [Start Scenario]
     [Name]            Test #7: File\New then try Edit\Paste
     [Test Location]  C:\Program Files\Microsoft Visual
Studio\MyProjects\Notepad\Edit\Paste.mst (102)
     [Start Time]     05/31/1998 18:38:54
     [Result]         PASS
     [Elapsed Time]    0.370
     [End Scenario]

   [Case Result]        PASS
   [Elapsed Time]      8.533
   [End Case]

   [Start Case Header]
   [Case Name]          C:\Program Files\Microsoft Visual
Studio\MyProjects\Notepad\Edit\Cut.mst
   [Product Version]   Windows NT 4.0
   [Language]          English
   [Machine]           CHIANTI
   [Start Time]        05/31/1998 18:38:54
   [End Case Header]

     [Start Scenario]
     [Name]            Test #1: Edit\Cut is disabled after
File\New
     [Test Location]  C:\Program Files\Microsoft Visual
Studio\MyProjects\Notepad\Edit\Cut.mst (32)
     [Start Time]     05/31/1998 18:39:00
     [Result]         PASS
     [Elapsed Time]    0.150
```

```
     [End Scenario]

     [Start Scenario]
     [Name]            Test #2: 'Cut' still disabled after
typing.
     [Test Location]  C:\Program Files\Microsoft Visual
Studio\MyProjects\Notepad\Edit\Cut.mst (41)
     [Start Time]     05/31/1998 18:39:00
     [Result]         PASS
     [Elapsed Time]   0.221
     [End Scenario]

     [Start Scenario]
     [Name]            Test #3: Edit\Cut available after
selecting text.
     [Test Location]  C:\Program Files\Microsoft Visual
Studio\MyProjects\Notepad\Edit\Cut.mst (52)
     [Start Time]     05/31/1998 18:39:01
     [Result]         PASS
     [Elapsed Time]   0.290
     [End Scenario]

     [Start Scenario]
     [Name]            Test #4: Edit\Cut should remove the text.
     [Test Location]  C:\Program Files\Microsoft Visual
Studio\MyProjects\Notepad\Edit\Cut.mst (62)
     [Start Time]     05/31/1998 18:39:01
     [Result]         PASS
     [Elapsed Time]   0.481
     [End Scenario]

     [Start Scenario]
     [Name]            Test #5: Edit\Cut should put text onto
clipboard.
     [Test Location]  C:\Program Files\Microsoft Visual
Studio\MyProjects\Notepad\Edit\Cut.mst (75)
     [Start Time]     05/31/1998 18:39:01
     [Result]         PASS
     [Elapsed Time]   0.000
     [End Scenario]

   [Case Result]      PASS
   [Elapsed Time]     7.470
   [End Case]

   [Start Case Header]
   [Case Name]        C:\Program Files\Microsoft Visual
Studio\MyProjects\Notepad\Edit\Delete.mst
   [Product Version]  Windows NT 4.0
   [Language]         English
   [Machine]          CHIANTI
```

```
    [Start Time]          05/31/1998 18:39:02
    [End Case Header]

    [Start Scenario]
    [Name]                Test #1: Edit\Delete is disabled in empty
editor.
    [Test Location]  C:\Program Files\Microsoft Visual
Studio\MyProjects\Notepad\Edit\Delete.mst (32)
    [Start Time]     05/31/1998 18:39:08
    [Result]         PASS
    [Elapsed Time]   0.150
    [End Scenario]

    [Start Scenario]
    [Name]                Test #2: Edit\Delete is disabled with no
text selected.
    [Test Location]  C:\Program Files\Microsoft Visual
Studio\MyProjects\Notepad\Edit\Delete.mst (42)
    [Start Time]     05/31/1998 18:39:08
    [Result]         PASS
    [Elapsed Time]   0.230
    [End Scenario]

    [Start Scenario]
    [Name]                Test #3: Edit\Delete is enabled with text
selected.
    [Test Location]  C:\Program Files\Microsoft Visual
Studio\MyProjects\Notepad\Edit\Delete.mst (53)
    [Start Time]     05/31/1998 18:39:08
    [Result]         PASS
    [Elapsed Time]   0.301
    [End Scenario]

    [Start Scenario]
    [Name]                Test #4: Edit\Delete should clear the
selected text.
    [Test Location]  C:\Program Files\Microsoft Visual
Studio\MyProjects\Notepad\Edit\Delete.mst (63)
    [Start Time]     05/31/1998 18:39:08
    [Result]         PASS
    [Elapsed Time]   0.150
    [End Scenario]

    [Start Scenario]
    [Name]                Test #5: Edit\Delete first word of text.
    [Test Location]  C:\Program Files\Microsoft Visual
Studio\MyProjects\Notepad\Edit\Delete.mst (73)
    [Start Time]     05/31/1998 18:39:08
    [Result]         PASS
    [Elapsed Time]   0.250
    [End Scenario]
```

```
   [Case Result]        PASS
   [Elapsed Time]       7.321
   [End Case]


   [Start Case Header]
   [Case Name]          C:\Program Files\Microsoft Visual
Studio\MyProjects\Notepad\Edit\Timedate.mst
   [Product Version]    Windows NT 4.0
   [Language]           English
   [Machine]            CHIANTI
   [Start Time]         05/31/1998 18:39:09
   [End Case Header]


      [Start Scenario]
      [Name]            Test #1: Edit\Time/Date menu is enabled.
      [Test Location]   C:\Program Files\Microsoft Visual
Studio\MyProjects\Notepad\Edit\Timedate.mst (32)
      [Start Time]      05/31/1998 18:39:15
      [Result]          PASS
      [Elapsed Time]    0.150
      [End Scenario]


      [Start Scenario]
      [Name]            Test #2: Put Edit\Time/Date into an empty
editor.
      [Test Location]   C:\Program Files\Microsoft Visual
Studio\MyProjects\Notepad\Edit\Timedate.mst (41)
      [Start Time]      05/31/1998 18:39:15
      [Result]          PASS
      [Elapsed Time]    0.641
      [End Scenario]


   [Case Result]        PASS
   [Elapsed Time]       6.990
   [End Case]


   [Start Case Header]
   [Case Name]          C:\Program Files\Microsoft Visual
Studio\MyProjects\Notepad\Edit\Undo.mst
   [Product Version]    Windows NT 4.0
   [Language]           English
   [Machine]            CHIANTI
   [Start Time]         05/31/1998 18:39:16
   [End Case Header]


      [Start Scenario]
      [Name]            Test #1: Edit\Undo is disabled after
'File/New'.
      [Test Location]   C:\Program Files\Microsoft Visual
Studio\MyProjects\Notepad\Edit\Undo.mst (32)
```

```
     [Start Time]      05/31/1998 18:39:22
     [Result]          PASS
     [Elapsed Time]    0.151
     [End Scenario]

     [Start Scenario]
     [Name]            Test #2: Edit\Undo enabled after typing.
     [Test Location]  C:\Program Files\Microsoft Visual
Studio\MyProjects\Notepad\Edit\Undo.mst (42)
     [Start Time]      05/31/1998 18:39:22
     [Result]          PASS
     [Elapsed Time]    0.260
     [End Scenario]

     [Start Scenario]
     [Name]            Test #3: Edit\Undo typing in a string.
     [Test Location]  C:\Program Files\Microsoft Visual
Studio\MyProjects\Notepad\Edit\Undo.mst (53)
     [Start Time]      05/31/1998 18:39:22
     [Result]          PASS
     [Elapsed Time]    0.150
     [End Scenario]

     [Start Scenario]
     [Name]            Test #4: Edit\Undo again should 'REDO' the
typing.
     [Test Location]  C:\Program Files\Microsoft Visual
Studio\MyProjects\Notepad\Edit\Undo.mst (64)
     [Start Time]      05/31/1998 18:39:23
     [Result]          PASS
     [Elapsed Time]    0.151
     [End Scenario]

     [Start Scenario]
     [Name]            Test #5: Test Edit\Cut is undoable.
     [Test Location]  C:\Program Files\Microsoft Visual
Studio\MyProjects\Notepad\Edit\Undo.mst (74)
     [Start Time]      05/31/1998 18:39:23
     [Result]          PASS
     [Elapsed Time]    0.290
     [End Scenario]

     [Start Scenario]
     [Name]            Test #6: Undoing an Edit\Copy action should
redo the Edit\Cut action.
     [Test Location]  C:\Program Files\Microsoft Visual
Studio\MyProjects\Notepad\Edit\Undo.mst (91)
     [Start Time]      05/31/1998 18:39:23
     [Result]          PASS
     [Elapsed Time]    0.300
     [End Scenario]
```

```
     [Start Scenario]
     [Name]              Test #7: Test that Edit\Paste is undoable.
     [Test Location]  C:\Program Files\Microsoft Visual
Studio\MyProjects\Notepad\Edit\Undo.mst (107)
     [Start Time]      05/31/1998 18:39:23
     [Result]          PASS
     [Elapsed Time]    0.451
     [End Scenario]

     [Start Scenario]
     [Name]              Test #8: Test that Edit\Delete is
undoable.
     [Test Location]  C:\Program Files\Microsoft Visual
Studio\MyProjects\Notepad\Edit\Undo.mst (119)
     [Start Time]      05/31/1998 18:39:24
     [Result]          PASS
     [Elapsed Time]    0.291
     [End Scenario]

     [Start Scenario]
     [Name]              Test #9: Edit\Undo again should 'Redo' the
delete
     [Test Location]  C:\Program Files\Microsoft Visual
Studio\MyProjects\Notepad\Edit\Undo.mst (134)
     [Start Time]      05/31/1998 18:39:24
     [Result]          PASS
     [Elapsed Time]    0.140
     [End Scenario]

     [Start Scenario]
     [Name]              Test #10: Test Time/Date action disables
'Undo'.
     [Test Location]  C:\Program Files\Microsoft Visual
Studio\MyProjects\Notepad\Edit\Undo.mst (144)
     [Start Time]      05/31/1998 18:39:24
     [Result]          PASS
     [Elapsed Time]    0.310
     [End Scenario]

   [Case Result]      PASS
   [Elapsed Time]     8.853
   [End Case]

   [Start Case Header]
   [Case Name]        C:\Program Files\Microsoft Visual
Studio\MyProjects\Notepad\Search\Find.mst
   [Product Version]  Windows NT 4.0
   [Language]         English
   [Machine]          CHIANTI
   [Start Time]       05/31/1998 18:39:25
```

```
[End Case Header]

    [Start Scenario]
    [Name]              Test #1: Search\Find... menu enabled with
no text.
    [Test Location]  C:\Program Files\Microsoft Visual
Studio\MyProjects\Notepad\Search\Find.mst (32)
    [Start Time]        05/31/1998 18:39:31
    [Result]            PASS
    [Elapsed Time]   0.120
    [End Scenario]

    [Start Scenario]
    [Name]              Test #2: Search\Find... brings up 'Find'
DB with no text.
    [Test Location]  C:\Program Files\Microsoft Visual
Studio\MyProjects\Notepad\Search\Find.mst (41)
    [Start Time]        05/31/1998 18:39:31
    [Result]            PASS
    [Elapsed Time]   0.191
    [End Scenario]

    [Start Scenario]
    [Name]              Test #3: Search\Find... the first char of
a string.
    [Test Location]  C:\Program Files\Microsoft Visual
Studio\MyProjects\Notepad\Search\Find.mst (53)
    [Start Time]        05/31/1998 18:39:31
    [Result]            PASS
    [Elapsed Time]   0.631
    [End Scenario]

    [Start Scenario]
    [Name]              Test #4: Search\Find... next occurrence of
SearchText.
    [Test Location]  C:\Program Files\Microsoft Visual
Studio\MyProjects\Notepad\Search\Find.mst (70)
    [Start Time]        05/31/1998 18:39:32
    [Result]            PASS
    [Elapsed Time]   0.020
    [End Scenario]

    [Start Scenario]
    [Name]              Test #5: Search\Find... again will not
find anything.
    [Test Location]  C:\Program Files\Microsoft Visual
Studio\MyProjects\Notepad\Search\Find.mst (81)
    [Start Time]        05/31/1998 18:39:32
    [Result]            PASS
    [Elapsed Time]   0.100
    [End Scenario]
```

```
    [Start Scenario]
    [Name]              Test #6: Check that text found matches
search text.
    [Test Location]  C:\Program Files\Microsoft Visual
Studio\MyProjects\Notepad\Search\Find.mst (94)
    [Start Time]        05/31/1998 18:39:32
    [Result]            PASS
    [Elapsed Time]   0.000
    [End Scenario]

    [Start Scenario]
    [Name]              Test #7: Search\Find... first word of a
string.
    [Test Location]  C:\Program Files\Microsoft Visual
Studio\MyProjects\Notepad\Search\Find.mst (103)
    [Start Time]        05/31/1998 18:39:32
    [Result]            PASS
    [Elapsed Time]   0.320
    [End Scenario]

    [Start Scenario]
    [Name]              Test #8: Search\Find... again should
display message box.
    [Test Location]  C:\Program Files\Microsoft Visual
Studio\MyProjects\Notepad\Search\Find.mst (118)
    [Start Time]        05/31/1998 18:39:32
    [Result]            PASS
    [Elapsed Time]   0.100
    [End Scenario]

    [Start Scenario]
    [Name]              Test #9: Check that text found matches
search text.
    [Test Location]  C:\Program Files\Microsoft Visual
Studio\MyProjects\Notepad\Search\Find.mst (131)
    [Start Time]        05/31/1998 18:39:32
    [Result]            PASS
    [Elapsed Time]   0.000
    [End Scenario]

    [Start Scenario]
    [Name]              Test #10: Search\Find... last word of a
string.
    [Test Location]  C:\Program Files\Microsoft Visual
Studio\MyProjects\Notepad\Search\Find.mst (140)
    [Start Time]        05/31/1998 18:39:32
    [Result]            PASS
    [Elapsed Time]   0.251
    [End Scenario]
```

```
    [Start Scenario]
    [Name]              Test #11: Search\Find... again will not
find another occurrence.
    [Test Location]  C:\Program Files\Microsoft Visual
Studio\MyProjects\Notepad\Search\Find.mst (155)
    [Start Time]        05/31/1998 18:39:33
    [Result]            PASS
    [Elapsed Time]      0.090
    [End Scenario]

    [Start Scenario]
    [Name]              Test #12: Check that text found matches
search text.
    [Test Location]  C:\Program Files\Microsoft Visual
Studio\MyProjects\Notepad\Search\Find.mst (168)
    [Start Time]        05/31/1998 18:39:33
    [Result]            PASS
    [Elapsed Time]      0.000
    [End Scenario]

  [Case Result]         PASS
  [Elapsed Time]        8.192
  [End Case]

  [Start Case Header]
  [Case Name]           C:\Program Files\Microsoft Visual
Studio\MyProjects\Notepad\Search\Findnext.mst
  [Product Version]  Windows NT 4.0
  [Language]            English
  [Machine]             CHIANTI
  [Start Time]          05/31/1998 18:39:33
  [End Case Header]

    [Start Scenario]
    [Name]              Test #1: Search\Find Next with 'Find'
Buffer empty.
    [Test Location]  C:\Program Files\Microsoft Visual
Studio\MyProjects\Notepad\Search\Findnext.mst (32)
    [Start Time]        05/31/1998 18:39:39
    [Result]            PASS
    [Elapsed Time]      0.200
    [End Scenario]

    [Start Scenario]
    [Name]              Test #2: Search\Find Next with next but
Find buffer empty.
    [Test Location]  C:\Program Files\Microsoft Visual
Studio\MyProjects\Notepad\Search\Findnext.mst (44)
    [Start Time]        05/31/1998 18:39:39
    [Result]            PASS
    [Elapsed Time]      0.641
```

```
[End Scenario]

[Start Scenario]
[Name]              Test #3: Check that text found matches
search text.
[Test Location]  C:\Program Files\Microsoft Visual
Studio\MyProjects\Notepad\Search\Findnext.mst (65)
[Start Time]       05/31/1998 18:39:40
[Result]           PASS
[Elapsed Time]     0.010
[End Scenario]

[Start Scenario]
[Name]              Test #4: Search\Find Next with 'Find'
buffer filled.
[Test Location]  C:\Program Files\Microsoft Visual
Studio\MyProjects\Notepad\Search\Findnext.mst (75)
[Start Time]       05/31/1998 18:39:40
[Result]           PASS
[Elapsed Time]     0.141
[End Scenario]

[Start Scenario]
[Name]              Test #5: Check that text found matches
search text.
[Test Location]  C:\Program Files\Microsoft Visual
Studio\MyProjects\Notepad\Search\Findnext.mst (85)
[Start Time]       05/31/1998 18:39:40
[Result]           PASS
[Elapsed Time]     0.010
[End Scenario]

[Start Scenario]
[Name]              Test #6: Search\Find Next should display
'Not Found' message box.
[Test Location]  C:\Program Files\Microsoft Visual
Studio\MyProjects\Notepad\Search\Findnext.mst (94)
[Start Time]       05/31/1998 18:39:40
[Result]           PASS
[Elapsed Time]     0.190
[End Scenario]

[Start Scenario]
[Name]              Test #7: Check that text found matches
search text.
[Test Location]  C:\Program Files\Microsoft Visual
Studio\MyProjects\Notepad\Search\Findnext.mst (106)
[Start Time]       05/31/1998 18:39:40
[Result]           PASS
[Elapsed Time]     0.000
[End Scenario]
```

```
   [Case Result]        PASS
   [Elapsed Time]       7.500
   [End Case]

   [Start Case Header]
   [Case Name]          C:\Program Files\Microsoft Visual
Studio\MyProjects\Notepad\Help\About.mst
   [Product Version]    Windows NT 4.0
   [Language]           English
   [Machine]            CHIANTI
   [Start Time]         05/31/1998 18:39:41
   [End Case Header]

      [Start Scenario]
      [Name]            Test #1: Select the Help\About Notepad...
menu item.
      [Test Location]   C:\Program Files\Microsoft Visual
Studio\MyProjects\Notepad\Help\About.mst (27)
      [Start Time]      05/31/1998 18:39:47
      [Result]          PASS
      [Elapsed Time]    0.290
      [End Scenario]

   [Case Result]        PASS
   [Elapsed Time]       6.570
   [End Case]

   [Start Case Header]
   [Case Name]          C:\Program Files\Microsoft Visual
Studio\MyProjects\Notepad\Help\Topics.mst
   [Product Version]    Windows NT 4.0
   [Language]           English
   [Machine]            CHIANTI
   [Start Time]         05/31/1998 18:39:47
   [End Case Header]

      [Start Scenario]
      [Name]            Test #1: Select the Help\Help Topics menu
item
      [Test Location]   C:\Program Files\Microsoft Visual
Studio\MyProjects\Notepad\Help\Topics.mst (30)
      [Start Time]      05/31/1998 18:39:53
      [Result]          PASS
      [Elapsed Time]    0.922
      [End Scenario]

   [Case Result]        PASS
   [Elapsed Time]       7.000
   [End Case]
```

```
[Suite Result]      PASS
[Elapsed Time]      148.964
[End Suite]
```

✦   ✦   ✦

What's on the CD-ROM

The following ten directories are provided on the CD-ROM that comes with this book:

- ◆ \Apps
- ◆ \Chapters
- ◆ \Interviews
- ◆ \Links
- ◆ \Mainsoft
- ◆ \RWartner
- ◆ \Samples
- ◆ \ST Labs
- ◆ \Other

You can look through these directories as you would normally peruse a CD-ROM's contents, but I urge you to use the INDEX.HTM document found at the root of the CD. If you have a Web browser installed, double-click on INDEX.HTM so that you can view these directories along with more detailed information directly from your browser.

Third-Party Applications

The Apps directory contains some very helpful third-party applications. These include an add-on tool for Visual Test, as well as evaluation copies of software quality assurance-related products. These are found in the \Apps folder on the CD-ROM.

You can install the third-party applications on this CD-ROM manually, or with the INDEX.HTM document at the root directory.

✦ **Adobe Acrobat Reader 3.01:** You will need this to view any documents that have been compiled into the .PDF (portable document format) file format. These include the electronic version of this book and the white paper provided by Mainsoft Corporation.

To install and run Adobe's Acrobat Reader and view the electronic version of this book, start Windows Explorer (if you're using Windows 95) or Windows NT Explorer (if you're using Windows NT), and then open the Acrobat folder. Double click AR32E301.EXE and follow the instructions presented onscreen for installing the application. After you've installed Adobe's Acrobat Reader, start Windows Explorer or Windows NT Explorer and open the chapter folder on the CD-ROM. Double-click the chapter or appendix file you would like to view. All documents in this folder end with a .PDF extension.

✦ **Seapine's TestTrack:** Seapine's TestTrack product is a cross-platform bug tracking system that works on both Macintosh and Microsoft Windows systems. The \Seapine directory contains two files that allow you to evaluate the cross-platform tool along with Seapine's Web-based version of their bug tracking system. Seapine Software's evaluation software can be found in \Apps\Seapine. To install Seapine Software's evaluation software, run TESTTRACK EVAL.EXE. To install the Web version of their software, run TESTTRACK WEB EVAL.EXE. You can also visit them on the Web at `www.seapine.com`. The key or serial to TestTrack Web was not available for us to include by press time for this CD-ROM. So, in order to get the key/serial please call Seapine Software, Inc. at 513-683-6456 or email sales@seapine.com.

✦ **Soffront's TRACK and TRACKWeb:** Soffront is another software company that provides a defect tracking system. The \Soffront directory contains a number of sub-directories that allow you to explore their products further. The first sub-directory is \Documents, which contains the documentation for using their products. The \Track32 directory has the 32-bit version of their bug tracking system. \TrackKB is their knowledge base tool that allows your company to build a knowledge base so that your support staff can have answers to frequently asked questions at their fingertips. \TrackRules allows you to set up rules on notifying people via e-mail of database changes. And finally, \TrackWeb is an HTML/Web page front-end to their database products so that you can enter or access data via any browser.

Soffront's evaluation software can be found in \Apps\Soffront. To install the evalutation of their 32-bit version of their bug-tracking system, go into the Track32 folder and run the SETUP.EXE program. To install the evaluation of their knowledge-base program, go into the TrackKB folder and run SETUP.EXE. To install their notification tool, go into the TrackRules folder and run SETUP.EXE. To install the Web front end for their database products, go into the

TrackWeb folder and run SETUP.EXE. You can also visit them on the Web at
www.soffront.com.

✦ **ST Labs' Test Now 2.0:** Test Now 2.0 is a product created by ST Labs, Inc. It is
an add-on tool that works with Visual Test. The product has been
discontinued, but it contains a number of helpful features that you might want
to put to use in your automation projects. This folder contains both a full
version of Test Now 2.0 and also the source code that was previously not
released. (This is a discontinued product that ST Labs, Inc. is providing for
free as a helpful service, so it is not supported by the company. To install ST
Labs' Test Now 2.0 product, go into the \Apps\Test Now 2.0\Setup directory
and run SETUP.EXE. To use the source code, go into the \Apps\Test Now
2.0\Source directory and copy the files to whichever directory your
development software will be using. *Do not call ST Labs for technical support
on this product.*)

✦ **TeamShare's TeamTrack:** TeamShare's product focuses on bug tracking and
problem tracking, and helps manage product changes made in the life of a
product. TeamTrack is touted as the "only completely Web-based system
available." TeamShare's focus in TeamTrack was to build this product from
the ground up as an intranet (internal company network) solution allowing a
browser to be used for accessing the bug database. If you're interested in a
test drive, run the installer found in the \Apps\TeamShare directory and run
the INSTALL.EXE program. You can also visit them on the Web at
www.teamshare.com.

✦ **Translation Craft's HelpQA and HtmlQA:** Translation Craft has provided an
evaluation copy of their utilities for testing Help files and HTML documents.
These can be found in the \Tcraft subdirectory. If you're interested in testing
HTML documents or Help documents in your Windows-based applications,
check out these tools in the \Apps\TCraft directory. To install their HelpQA
application, go into the HelpQA directory and run the SETPHELP.EXE
program. To install the HtmlQA software, go into the HtmlQA directory and
run the SETPHTML.EXE program. Or visit the company on the Web at
www.tcraft.com.

Note None of these programs are endorsed by me or by IDG Books. These are companies I was able to contact and who were able to respond quickly enough to get
onto the CD. No warranty is provided on installing any of these products. Proceed
at your own risk. If you encounter any problems with installation or use of these
products please contact the individual companies directly.

Electronic Version of this Book

I suggested to IDG Books Worldwide that we should provide this book in electronic
form so that people who are traveling and who don't want to lug the printed book

with them could still have a reference available. They jumped all over the idea, and the result is that all of the chapters of the book are contained in the \Chapters directory of this book's CD-ROM.

These files must be viewed using Adobe Acrobat Reader 3.01 (or newer). The Microsoft Windows 32-bit version of this program is on the CD-ROM in the \Apps directory. If you are running on any other operating system and want to read these electronic files, you will need to visit Adobe Systems' Web site (www.adobe.com) to get the appropriate version of this reader. (They also have a version for UNIX.)

Interviews

ST Labs, Inc. has allowed me to use some of the video footage that I shot while at the company. These interviews are with James Bach and Dr. Cem Kaner. James is well known on the SQA speaking circuit and is often invited to quality assurance conferences to speak about software quality issues. Cem is the author of *Testing Computer Software,* a book that is well known in the testing community. James and Cem are currently collaborating on a new book on quality assurance. Hear what they have to say about software test automation tools and testing in general. These interviews can be found in the \Interviews directory of this book's CD-ROM.

Note   These video clips have been saved in RealNetworks, Inc. RealVideo format, and the RealPlayer application is required to view these files. This player is available on this book's CD-ROM in the \Apps folder.

James Bach

James Bach is one of the leading consultants in the software quality assurance industry. He worked in the QA department at Apple Computer, managed a QA department at Borland International, and helped form ST Labs' QA approaches and methodologies as their chief scientist. Watch these interviews with James (found in the \Bach sub-directory) for great insight on software test automation.

Dr. Cem Kaner

Dr. Cem Kaner is the author of *Testing Computer Software* and is a leading consultant in the software quality assurance industry. In this interview (found in the \Kaner sub-directory) he speaks about using software test automation tools as part of a quality assurance effort.

Links

This directory contains an HTML file called LINKS.HTM. This document will point you to some of the resources available to you as a user of Visual Test. These include hands-on classes, video tapes, freebies, and general information.

References

Following are some references to Visual Test that you may find helpful.

Mainsoft

Mainsoft is a company that specializes in cross-platform development of Windows NT and UNIX applications. A few years ago they signed an agreement with Microsoft, which remains intact today with Rational Software, allowing them to port Visual Test over to run on their MainWin product on UNIX's X-Windows environment. This directory contains a white paper provided by Mainsoft to tell you more about the use of Visual Test when automating testing on cross-platform development projects.

Richard Wartner's online Visual Test book

Richard Wartner is the author of an online Visual Test book (*A Modular Approach to Visual Test 4.0 Programming*) that is provided for free to anyone who wants it. This directory contains a self-extracting file that will install the 1.05 version of his book. To install Richard Wartner's online Visual Test book, go to the \RWartner directory on the CD and run the MAVBK05.EXE program. There is also a README.TXT file that tells you more about how to install his many sample source code files. With both the *Visual Test 6 Bible* and Richard's online book, you've got a huge amount of information available to you on putting Visual Test to use quickly and effectively. Visit www.vtindepth.com for information on any updates he makes to his book.

ST Labs Articles and White Papers

This directory contains a number of articles and white papers written by ST Labs employees and general QA consultants. These are just a sample of what ST Labs has to offer on their Web site, so if you like what you see make sure you visit them on the Internet. You must use a Web browser for easy viewing of these articles. You can do this by double-clicking on the INDEX.HTM document found in this subdirectory, or by using the INDEX.HTM file found at the root of this CD-ROM, which will allow you to navigate to the ST Labs folder. Their Web site can be found at www.stlabs.com.

Source Code from the Book

This directory contains four subdirectories that hold Visual Test source code used as examples in this book. The \Samples directory contains files you can copy to your local hard disk drive and use as you see fit (other than by reselling them as part of another product). The \Samples\Listings folder contains the source code listings shown in the individual chapters. The naming convention followed identifies the text file as a listing, the chapter number, and the position of the listing in that chapter. For example, LST01-02.MST would be the second source code listing in Chapter 1.

Listings

This first sub-directory, \Samples\Listings\, holds the source code listings shown in the book. Although these listings have a .MST file extension so that they can be more easily viewed with Visual Test, they are merely text files and can be viewed with Microsoft Notepad if you don't have Visual Test installed currently.

Microsoft Examples from Chapter 13

Bill Hodghead, a test engineer who focuses a great deal on automation at Microsoft, wrote some great tips for Chapter 13. The source code examples he uses are found in the \Samples\Microsoft folder.

Monkey Examples from Chapter 14

Noel Nyman discusses black box monkey testing in Chapter 14 and includes a sample script on this book's CD-ROM. The entire sample script for that chapter, along with instructions on how to install these scripts so that they will run on your computer, is included in the \Samples\Monkey directory.

The Book's Final Test Suite

The \Samples\Suite directory contains the final version of the Test Suite that is developed throughout this book. If you have Visual Test installed correctly, you will be able to double-click on the NOTEPAD.DSP file to open the project.

The sample driver (DRIVER.MST) uses an initialization file to keep track of the test case files it has been configured to run. This initialization file (TEST.INI) assumes a particular directory structure. The TEST.INI file can either be edited to match the directory structure where you place these sample files, or the files and directories found in the SUITE directory can be copied to your Visual Test SAMPLES directory. You'll only need to do this if you plan to use the DRIVER.MST example program.

Other

The Other directory contains the following items:

✦ SETUPINFO.TXT lists every file and registry setting change made during a full installation of Visual Test 6.0. Use this log file when you need to understand what files are placed where on your computer and what changes are made to your system registry.

✦ The \Digests directory holds an archive of the digest mailings sent by the MT_Info discussion group. These are automatically generated and sent out on almost a daily basis. For more information on joining MT_Info visit `www.vtindepth.com/mt_info.htm`. To get an idea of the types of discussions that go on, view this archive using Microsoft Exchange or Microsoft Outlook. Installation instructions are in the Digests directory along with the archive itself.

✦ The \InDepth directory contains information on a set of video tapes on Visual Test 6.0 from InDepth Productions, Inc. InDepth also maintains the 800-person discussion group that focuses on Visual Test. Information about their training tapes along with information on MT_Info is provided in this directory.

✦　✦　✦

Glossary

ActiveX Another name for OLE custom control. See OLE.

API (Application Programmers Interface) A common set of utilities stored in a DLL to be used by those creating applications to run under a Microsoft Windows operating system.

Application Under Test (AUT) An application that is the focus of testing efforts. It is the application being tested. Many software quality assurance engineers refer to the "test subject" as the Application Under Test.

BASIC Beginners All-Purpose Symbolic Instruction Code. The programming language upon which Visual Test is based.

black box testing A type of testing where the person testing the product is not familiar with any of the source code that makes up the product she is testing.

Boolean A value that evaluates to a TRUE or FALSE result. In most languages FALSE is represented by 0 and TRUE is a 1. In Visual Test, however, TRUE is set to −1. As in other languages, when working with conditional branching in Visual Test, any non-zero number is also treated as a TRUE result.

bug A flaw in the product. Bugs vary in degree of severity. Some bugs may be classified as unlikely to be found by the user and are therefore a low priority and may not be fixed before the product is released. Higher priority bugs that will cause data loss and other issues in using the product are considered show-stoppers and must be fixed before the product can hit a major milestone.

build Refers to the process of compiling the program's executables and libraries into a running version of the product. These are typically referred to as debug or retail builds. A debug build uses debug libraries so that when errors are found it is easier for the developers to track them down. Debug builds also contain intrinsic debug information for use by the debugger. A retail build is a smaller set of libraries that don't contain the debugger information and is the build that will eventually be released for distribution.

callback   A type of function that can be called asynchronously from the rest of the script (typically from outside the script). In the event that a callback function is established and then executed, no matter where the current line of execution is in the Visual Test script, that execution will be interrupted so that the callback function can execute its code. When the callback function completes, normal execution of the script continues. (See Chapter 13 for more information on callback functions.)

case-sensitive   Meaning that a variable, function, or subroutine named aTest is considered completely different than one named atEsT. A case-sensitive compiler looks at those as two separate names. Rational Visual Test's compiler is not case-sensitive.

comment   Information found in a source code file that exists solely for the benefit of the programmer. It is information that is ignored by the Visual Test compiler and run-time engine. Comments help to provide documentation and information in the code base itself.

compiler   The tool that takes the source code (in this case any Test language code (and converts it into a form usable by the interpreter or run-time engine.

conditional compilation   Instructions to the pre-compiler called metacommands allow for sections of code to be included or excluded depending on symbols defined prior to compiling the script, or based on symbols declared in the script itself.

constant   Constants are basically variables that have values that never change and will cause an error to be generated if an attempt is made during the running of the script (run-time) to change a constant's value.

context-sensitive help   When online documentation is accessed through context-sensitive help (the F1 key in Visual Test), the help engine does its best to find information related to the situation the tester is in. For example, pressing F1 on a dialog box will cause the engine to attempt to find help on that specific dialog box. Pressing F1 when a keyword is selected in the editor will cause the help engine to attempt to find information about that keyword.

DAO (Data Access Objects)   A set of pre-defined objects that encapsulate the details of reading and writing database records. For example, in a database this includes indexes, fields, table definitions, query definitions, and so on.

DAM key (Direct Access Method key) These are the underscore marks you see on the letters found in the menu and menu items in a Windows application. Using the Alt key in conjunction with the underlined letter allows you to access a menu, menu item, or control solely through the keyboard.

data hiding The method of data being stored for indirect use by other programmers. Through data hiding, programmers are not allowed to directly affect the value of a variable. This is so that should the way a variable is stored or referenced be changed, the programmer using that data won't need to update the code. An example in secure operating systems would be when a program needs to work with protected information but the programmer should not have direct access to the password for accessing that data. Data hiding also helps keep programmers new to a code base from accidentally manipulating data they shouldn't be touching.

Direct Access Method See DAM key.

dirty bit The variable in a program (such as a graphics editing program or a word processor) tracking whether changes have taken place since the last Save (that will require the program to prompt the user to save their changes) is commonly referred to as the dirty bit.

DLL (Dynamic Link Library) A binary file, created using a computer language compiler, that holds compiled source code or resources sharable with other programs running under the Microsoft Windows operating system. Typically used to store commonly used source code and resources that can be linked to dynamically (during the running of the program as opposed to when the program is compiled, which is static linking) by many different applications. (Windows APIs are in dynamic link libraries.)

driver A program that controls the execution of test case files. A robust driver will report back information such as available memory, duration of execution of scripts, test failures, and so on. Really cool drivers will detect uncompilable scripts and skip them, and will also recover from a crash of the program. Visual Test's Suite Manager utility is a driver.

Easter egg A hidden way to display credits for those who were a part of creating a software product. In Visual Test this is done through a call to the undocumented function VisualTestCredits().

equivalence class Any values, files, and so on that are considered part of an equivalence class are considered equal in the results they provide when testing any one of those members.

explicit declaration A declaration made using the DIM statement. (See also implicit declaration.)

Fast Test   Introduced in Microsoft Test version 1.0 and undocumented in 2.0 so that it could later be removed, Fast Test was an abbreviated form of the Test Basic language.

file number   A unique number associated with a file that has been opened for reading or writing in Visual Test. (See Chapter 13 for more information on using file I/O in Visual Test.)

fixed-length string   A string that is declared to have a specific size and will always take that amount of space in memory even if the value it holds requires less space. (See also variable-length string.)

functional specification   Defines what the end product is going to look like. Describes, many times in technical detail, how each feature of the product is to be implemented, what it will look like, and so on. The functional spec is what QA relies on for its test plan, documentation relies on for online help and printed docs, and management relies on for estimating time-to-market. A functional specification is crucial on a development project but, surprisingly, often missing.

global variable   A variable that is available, or in scope, every place in the test script.

gold release   Once a software product has reached a status where development is finished with features and debugging, and quality assurance has tested everything it can think of testing, and the product is stable and ready for release, this is known as a gold status. This is also referred to as an RTM (Release to Manufacturing) version.

guerilla testing   Ad hoc testing that is done to find the most problems (cause the most damage) in the shortest period of time.

GUI (Graphical User Interface)   The part of a program in which the user interacts is the graphical user interface. Examples include the program's window, menus, dialog boxes, buttons, check boxes, and so on. These are referred to collectively as the GUI.

handle   A value provided by the Windows operating system that can be used to identify a block of memory, window, or control. Handles are used in lieu of pointers and are kept in an internal table in the OS. This way blocks of memory can be moved around by the OS without invalidating the reference to that item (the handle doesn't change while the pointer it refers to can and most likely will). (See "Not Using a Caption or Label" in Chapter 5 for more information on referring to objects by their handles.)

header file   In most languages, such as C or C++, a header file is designated by .H or .HPP and holds common declarations used by the main program files (.C or .CPP in the example of C or C++). This is the same in Visual Test but with a twist. Visual Test uses header files (designated by a .INC file extension) that not only contain declarations, but many times include executable code such as functions and subroutines. (See also Pre-compiled Header File.)

host A term used by the Visual Test Network Distribution Libraries (see Chapter 16). The host computer controls the assignment of testing tasks to the individual stations.

Hungarian notation A naming convention for variables, constants, and functions that allows the programmer, at a glance, to determine what type of value a variable or constant holds, or what kind of value a function will return. (Refer to Chapter 8's Naming Conventions section for examples of this notation.)

ID number The ID number refers to the ID of a control in a dialog box. When a dialog box is created, each control is assigned a unique number that can in turn be used by Visual Test to identify a control. (See "Not Using a Caption or Label" in Chapter 5 for more information.)

IDE (Integrated Development Environment) This is where all of the tools for a development product are hooked into a single application. While the components may be separate standalone executables, they appear more a part of the main product since they are accessible from the main development program. Hence, they're "integrated."

implicit declaration A declaration made on-the-fly instead of declared using the DIM declaration statement. (See the sidebar titled Force Explicit Declarations in Chapter 5 for more on this topic.)

.INC or Include file See header file.

.INI file An initialization file used by a program to store information, such as settings, so that they can be referenced when the program is run again in the future. .INI files were more popular before programs started storing such setting information in the Windows 95, 98, and NT Registry. While most programs use the Registry now, many still use .INI files. (See also Registry.)

Interpreter See run-time engine.

intrinsic Part of the established Test language as opposed to a function provided by a link via the Test language to an external DLL.

Jordanism The effect of attempting to sound intelligent, but completely not succeeding; and wasting peoples' time in the interim.

literal   The actual value (such as a string or number) placed in a script, as opposed to a variable or constant representation of that value.

local variable   A variable accessible only by the function, subroutine, or main block of source code in which it is declared.

metacommand   A directive that issues instructions to the compiler just before compilation. An example would be the '$INCLUDE metacommand, which will place the contents of a file specified by the metacommand at the place in the file where it is referenced.

monkey   An automated program that (given a general set of rules to follow) will work its way through a program, typically providing a random form of test coverage. This term is used because the program is imitating the concept of a monkey at a keyboard randomly pressing keys and clicking on menus, dialog boxes, and so on.

MSDN (Microsoft Developers Network)   A program that developers can join that gets them pre-releases of operating systems, development tools, and online help. In addition to a lot of online help information, it sometimes provides articles, especially for new technology currently under development. See Microsoft's web site at www.microsoft.com for more information.

.MST or script file   Called a .MST file for its original name of "Microsoft Test," this file contains a script written in the Test language. A .MST file may include an .INC file that has common declarations or it may be completely self-contained. This is the file type you will use for writing your automated test scripts.

MTRUN.EXE   See run-time engine.

Network Distribution Libraries   See Test Talk.

Network Distribution Procedures   See Test Talk.

null   Having an empty value. In the case of a number or pointer, this is 0, and in the case of a string it is an empty string (such as ""). In the C programming language, it is represented as '\0'.

null-terminated string   Many of the Windows APIs expect strings that are passed to them to have a CHR$(0) value as the last character in the string. This allows those functions to determine when the end of the string has been reached. Visual Test will null-terminate variable-length strings but not fixed-length strings. If you're using fixed-length strings when calling into Windows APIs and can't figure out why you're getting crashes, or your strings being passed are getting extra garbage appended to them, not having a null-terminator could be the reason. Remember to append CHR$(0) to those strings being passed to Windows APIs.

OCX See OLE.

OLE (Object Linking and Embedding) Also known as an OCX or ActiveX control. An OLE control, or OCX, is simply a *canned* program that performs some kind of function which developers plug into their own applications (see Chapter 13's section on "Testing OLE Controls").

oracle A database, spreadsheet, text file, or any other kind of data store that contains the expected results of a test or tests. An oracle could also be an algorithm that double-checks its results against the expected results it was passed. It is queried by automated tests since it is, by nature, *all knowing*. Discrepancies are usually flagged and reported as errors or bugs by the script that is consulting the oracle.

ordinal A way Visual Test refers to a type of control in a window. A control with an ordinal position of "@3" means that it is the third control of that type (that is of type "button" or "check box") in that window. The order is usually synonymous with the tab order.

ordinal position See ordinal.

.PC6 or pseudo-code file Compiled Visual Test scripts were originally saved in a file with a .PCD extension. This was designated as a compiled script that could be run with the Visual Test interpreter (also known as the run-time engine). In Visual Test 6.0, in order to avoid confusion with older versions of .PCD files and confusion with graphics programs using the same extension, the file extension was changed to .PC6.

.PCD file See .PC6 or pseudo-code file.

P-Code See .PC6 or pseudo-code file.

pointer A variable that holds a memory address.

pre-compiled header file Visual Test allows large header files to be compiled into a .HDR file known as a pre-compiled header file. This cuts down on how long it takes to compile a test script that references an include file since the compilation step for that include file can be skipped.

pre-compiler The step just before compilation of a Test language script. This step goes through the source code looking for any directives that will cause the contents of another file to be included, or sections of code to be skipped based on predefined symbols.

proc   A proc (pronounced "prock") or WndProc is a procedure that handles all the behind-the-scenes messages for a window in the Windows 95 or Windows NT operating system. When a mouse is moved across a window, the WndProc is called with a message (a value representing which event has just occurred) letting it know something is happening. When a control is clicked on, the proc is called with the message, the ID number of the control, and other information.

product manager   This definition varies from company to company. On projects I've worked on at Microsoft and Asymetrix, the product manager has organized the marketing aspects of taking the product to the end user. This includes packaging (art directors, duplication houses), advertising, and distribution. It also includes working with the sales group to get a sales force in place to handle/process orders. Because the product manager is the one doing the marketing and going to the conferences to meet end-users, she communicates with the program manager in regards to what features the end-user wants, and about what the projected release date will be based on the development/QA efforts so that packaging, duplication, and shipping schedules are in place once the product has reached a gold/RTM release status.

program manager   The definition varies from company to company. On projects I've worked on at Microsoft and Asymetrix, the program manager has organized the development, quality assurance, and documentation leads. This person communicates the current development schedule and expected time of release to the product manager. The product manager typically tells the program manager what the users are asking for in regards to features or enhancements.

properties   Values associated with a given object (such as a resource in a resource file). Changing the properties of a given object typically modifies the behavior and even appearance of the object.

pseudo code   A tokenized or compiled form of the Visual Test script that is machine-independent and executed using the MTRUN.EXE program.

redeclaration error   An error generated by the compiler when a variable, subroutine, or function that has already been declared is declared again.

release candidate   Also known as "RC," this is a build of the product that development feels confident will make it out the door. It is handed to quality assurance for a final test pass to verify that no problems have worked their way into the product. It's not uncommon to have four or more release candidates on a large project. Typically they're referred to as RC1, RC2, and so on.

Registry   A central database used by Windows 95 and 98, and Windows NT 3.51, 4.0, and 5.0, for storing program and system settings. Prior to the creation of the Registry, such settings were kept in individual .INI (initialization) files. (See also .INI file.)

regression testing   The process of stepping through all known bugs to verify that they have either been fixed or remain fixed from the last time they were regression tested.

REM or remark   This is how comments are designated in the Test language. (See comments.)

resource   A pre-created object (typically a bitmap, icon, menu definition, list of accelerators, table of strings, or dialog box layout) that can be saved in an external file or, in the case of compiled executable programs, appended to the .EXE file or .DLL, so that it can be referenced and used later without having to create this information on the fly.

RTM   Release to manufacturing. (See gold release.)

run-time   When a script is executing, this is considered its run-time.

run-time engine   A run-time engine is another name for an interpreter. Programs that can't compile down to a computer's native language and must therefore be executed by another program are called interpreted languages. BASIC (Beginner's All Purpose Symbolic Instruction Code) is by nature an interpreted language (although newer versions of Microsoft Visual Basic will run through a translator to create native machine language) and Visual Test's language is very much a form of BASIC. Visual Test's run-time engine is called MTRUN.EXE (similar to Visual Basic's run-time engine which is/was called VBRUN.EXE).

run-time error   An error that is generated through some action of the Test language that is illegal and occurs while the script is executing. The error isn't a syntax error or an error that could have been caught by the compiler, it's an error that could not have been determined to have existed until the script actually executed.

Script Recorder   A tool available in Visual Test and in most automation tools. This feature records the user's actions and generates test scripts based on those actions. Typically a hyped feature since it is the most easy to explain and, to those unfamiliar with automation and the efforts involved, the most impressive. The recorder is very helpful for simple scripts and in learning the Test language.

shorthand notation   Variables in Rational Visual Test can be declared using a shorthand form of the declaration. A $ is used to reference a STRING data type, a % for an INTEGER, a & for a LONG, and so on. (See Chapter 5 for more information.)

smart monkey   An *intelligent* form of a monkey that has more rules and guidelines to follow. (See monkey.)

smoke test   A test scenario that tests the broad areas of the product. It's a test that doesn't go too deeply into the AUT (application under test) but verifies key areas of concern that, if found to have problems, would cause the build to be rejected. It's especially used on a product that is in its early, unstable stages. It's a common term employed throughout the halls of Microsoft.

spaghetti code   Source code that is so jumbled (usually because of the use of GOTOs) that it seems like a jumbled, twisted mass of spaghetti. In short: it is difficult to read, understand, and trace through.

static variable   Typically used only in functions and subroutines, it causes those routines to save the value of a static variable, so that it is still available the next time the function or subroutine is called.

station   A term used by the Visual Test Network Distribution Libraries (see Chapter 16). The station computer communicates with the host computer that it is willing to take on tasks. It then receives those tasks from the host, executes those tasks, and reports the results.

sub-classed control   A control that is based on a standard Windows control but whose behavior has been modified. In these cases the class name of the control is changed and the control is known as a sub-classed control. (For more information on working with sub-classed controls refer to Chapter 5, "Non-standard Class Names.")

symbol   An alpha-numeric string that is created using the '$DEFINE metacommand. Once defined, it can be checked for its existence. It does not take a value, it is only considered to either exist or not exist.

Test Basic   The original name for the language of Microsoft Test 1.0. (Behind the scenes it was known as "Randy Basic," named for the creator of the compiler and interpreter.) The language has since been renamed the "Test language."

test case   A group of related test scenarios. (See test scenario.)

test case file   Designated with a .MST file extension, this file contains a group of related scenarios.

test driver   The program that drives or oversees the running of other test scripts. These can range from a simple script that fires off a list of scripts one at a time to a more complicated driver (such as the Suite Manager that comes with Visual Test) that monitors memory usage, logs results from running the scripts, allows for pausing, and so on.

Test language   The programming language of Rational Visual Test. This form of BASIC was known in previous versions of Visual Test as Test Basic.

test lead   The person in charge of the quality assurance efforts for the application under test. The test lead has years of experience and is the person the test engineers look to for guidance in getting a quality product to market.

test plan   A documented approach describing how the testing/quality assurance work is to be done on a project to ensure that a high-quality product goes to market. To be able to write an effective test plan, a functional specification must be provided by those defining the feature set and reviewed/added to by the developers.

test scenario   A specific set of steps that verify a specific piece of functionality in the application under test. For example, testing that saving a file onto an existing file gives a warning message box is a test scenario.

test suite   A group of test cases. A test suite can have many flavors. It can be a stress-testing suite, a general coverage suite, a benchmark suite, and so on. (See also test case.)

Test Talk   A set of functions in Microsoft Test and Rational Visual Test that allow for testing across a local area network.

UI (User Interface)   Shorthand notation for GUI. (See GUI).

unconditional branch   A change of the current flow of the program through a command that doesn't check for specific conditions before jumping to another line of code (either forward or backward). An example of a conditional branch is the IF/THEN/ELSE statement. An unconditional branch would be the GOTO statement. (See spaghetti code.)

user-defined type   A type not common enough to have already been defined in the programming language. Requires the user to define their own type created from existing types known to the Test language. This is done using the TYPE statement. (See Chapter 5's User-Defined Types section).

Variable-length string   A string type in Visual Test that can shrink and grow in size based on the amount of data it is holding. (See also Fixed-length String.)

Windows API   See API.

WinProc   See Proc.

WIN 16 API   Yet another name for APIs, but of the 16-bit (Windows 3.0, 3.1x) variety.

WIN 32 API   Yet another name for APIs, but of the 32-bit (Windows 95, 98, NT) variety. (See also API.)

wrapper A function or subroutine that typically adds to the capabilities of an existing function. The wrapper function may add extra steps and functionality and then call the existing function. In essence, it is a function or subroutine that envelopes an existing function or subroutine.

zero-terminated string See null-terminated string.

z-order If each control on a dialog box is considered to be on a layer of its own, the layer number a given control is on is its z-order. The ordinal position or value of a control is the same as its z-order. (See the section "Ordinals" in Chapter 5 for more information.) (As my friend Joe Benner likes to point out, "If X is across the screen, and Y is down the screen, the Z is out the screen.")

◆　　◆　　◆

Index

G

IDG BOOKS WORLDWIDE,INC.
END-USER LICENSE AGREEMENT

4. **Restrictions on Use of Individual Programs.** You must follow the individual requirements and restrictions detailed for each individual program in the "What's on the CD-ROM?" section of this Book. These limitations are also contained in the individual license agreements recorded on the Software Media. These limitations may include a requirement that after using the program for a specified period of time, the user must pay a registration fee or discontinue use. By opening the Software packet(s), you will be agreeing to abide by the licenses and restrictions for these individual programs that are detailed in the "What's on the CD-ROM?" section and on the Software Media. None of the material on this Software Media or listed in this Book may ever be redistributed, in original or modified form, for commercial purposes.

5. **Limited Warranty.**

   (a) IDGB warrants that the Software and Software Media are free from defects in materials and workmanship under normal use for a period of sixty (60) days from the date of purchase of this Book. If IDGB receives notification within the warranty period of defects in materials or workmanship, IDGB will replace the defective Software Media.

   (b) **IDGB AND THE AUTHOR OF THE BOOK DISCLAIM ALL OTHER WARRANTIES, EXPRESS OR IMPLIED, INCLUDING WITHOUT LIMITATION IMPLIED WARRANTIES OF MERCHANTABILITY AND FITNESS FOR A PARTICULAR PURPOSE, WITH RESPECT TO THE SOFTWARE, THE PROGRAMS, THE SOURCE CODE CONTAINED THEREIN, AND/OR THE TECHNIQUES DESCRIBED IN THIS BOOK. IDGB DOES NOT WARRANT THAT THE FUNCTIONS CONTAINED IN THE SOFTWARE WILL MEET YOUR REQUIREMENTS OR THAT THE OPERATION OF THE SOFTWARE WILL BE ERROR FREE.**

   (c) This limited warranty gives you specific legal rights, and you may have other rights that vary from jurisdiction to jurisdiction.

6. **Remedies.**

   (a) IDGB's entire liability and your exclusive remedy for defects in materials and workmanship shall be limited to replacement of the Software Media, which may be returned to IDGB with a copy of your receipt at the following address: Software Media Fulfillment Department, Attn.: Visual Test 6 Bible, IDG Books Worldwide, Inc., 7260 Shadeland Station, Ste. 100, Indianapolis, IN 46256, or call 1-800-762-2974. Please allow three to four weeks for delivery. This Limited Warranty is void if failure of the Software Media has resulted from accident, abuse, or misapplication. Any replacement Software Media will be warranted for the remainder of the original warranty period or thirty (30) days, whichever is longer.

(b) In no event shall IDGB or the author be liable for any damages whatsoever (including without limitation damages for loss of business profits, business interruption, loss of business information, or any other pecuniary loss) arising from the use of or inability to use the Book or the Software, even if IDGB has been advised of the possibility of such damages.

(c) Because some jurisdictions do not allow the exclusion or limitation of liability for consequential or incidental damages, the above limitation or exclusion may not apply to you.

7. **<u>U.S. Government Restricted Rights</u>.** Use, duplication, or disclosure of the Software by the U.S. Government is subject to restrictions stated in paragraph (c)(1)(ii) of the Rights in Technical Data and Computer Software clause of DFARS 252.227-7013, and in subparagraphs (a) through (d) of the Commercial Computer — Restricted Rights clause at FAR 52.227-19, and in similar clauses in the NASA FAR supplement, when applicable.

8. **<u>General</u>.** This Agreement constitutes the entire understanding of the parties and revokes and supersedes all prior agreements, oral or written, between them and may not be modified or amended except in a writing signed by both parties hereto that specifically refers to this Agreement. This Agreement shall take precedence over any other documents that may be in conflict herewith. If any one or more provisions contained in this Agreement are held by any court or tribunal to be invalid, illegal, or otherwise unenforceable, each and every other provision shall remain in full force and effect.

Name_____ Company _____

Address _____

City _____ State/Prov. _____ Postal Code _____ Country _____

Phone Day: (_____) _____ Evening: (_____) _____

Order Date: ____/____/_____ E-mail _____

	Qty	Amount
"Visual Test 6 Bible" book (includes CD-ROM) $49	_____	$ _____
Vol. I: The Tool, The Legend (2 tapes) $199	_____	$ _____
Vol. II: Learning the Environment, Utilities and Language (2 tapes) $199	_____	$ _____
Vol. III:Building a Powerful Test Suite (2 tapes) $199	_____	$ _____
Vol. IV:Blowing Past the Basics (2 tapes) $199	_____	$ _____
Vol. V: Breaking Out VT 6's New Features (2 tapes) $199	_____	$ _____

Order the complete set (save $145!) . . . .$899 _____ $ _____
All 10 tapes (5 volumes) plus "Visual Test 6 Bible" book w/CD-ROM

Washington State residents please add 8.6% sales tax . . . . $ _____
Shipping and Handling Charges* (see below for details) . . . . $ _____
Order Total: . . . . $ _____

Payment methods
(Personal checks can delay shipment up to 10 business days until check clears.)
    Mail: ☐ Check   ☐ Money Order   ☐ Cashier's Check
    Payable to: InDepth Productions, Inc.

    Credit Card Information:
    ☐ MasterCard   ☐ Visa   ☐ Amex   ☐ Discover

Expiration MM/YY: ____/_____

Credit Card Number: _____

Signature: _____

Telephone Orders: (425) 644-9827

Fax to 425-747-9164
or mail to:
InDepth Productions Inc.
15600 NE 8th Street
Suite B1-115
Bellevue, WA 98008 USA

*U.S. Shipping and Handling options:
UPS Ground (approx. 5 business days) ....$6/volume............$15 for complete set
FedEx 2nd day..$14/volume..........$32 for complete set
FedEx Overnight ....$20/volume..........$36 for complete set

(Orders outside of the United States, please call for a quote on shipping)

"Our return policy: If you are not satisfied with our video(s) please return the product
in new condition, along with a copy of your receipt, within 90-days from the date of
purchase for a prompt refund. (Note: Refunds do not include shipping and handling
charges. Damaged merchandise subject to less than full refund amount.)"

my2cents.idgbooks.com

Register This Book — And Win!

Visit **http://my2cents.idgbooks.com** to register this book and we'll automatically enter you in our fantastic monthly prize giveaway. It's also your opportunity to give us feedback: let us know what you thought of this book and how you would like to see other topics covered.

Discover IDG Books Online!

The IDG Books Online Web site is your online resource for tackling technology — at home and at the office. Frequently updated, the IDG Books Online Web site features exclusive software, insider information, online books, and live events!

10 Productive & Career-Enhancing Things You Can Do at www.idgbooks.com

- Nab source code for your own programming projects.

- Download software.

- Read Web exclusives: special articles and book excerpts by IDG Books Worldwide authors.

- Take advantage of resources to help you advance your career as a Novell or Microsoft professional.

- Buy IDG Books Worldwide titles or find a convenient bookstore that carries them.

- Register your book and win a prize.

- Chat live online with authors.

- Sign up for regular e-mail updates about our latest books.

- Suggest a book you'd like to read or write.

- Give us your 2¢ about our books and about our Web site.

You say you're not on the Web yet? It's easy to get started with IDG Books' *Discover the Internet*, available at local retailers everywhere.

CD-ROM Installation Instructions

The CD-ROM is provided to you in an uncompressed form, so you need not run an overall program to install its contents. I suggest opening the INDEX.HTM document in the root directory of the CD. It acts as an index to the entire contents of the CD. If you open the INDEX.HTM document on the root of this CD and click a link to install Acrobat Reader or any of the evaluation programs, you will see a dialog box asking whether it should save the program to your local hard drive or open the file from the source. I suggest you select the option to run the program from its current location. This will install the program right from the CD to your local hard drive.

Individual installation instructions for each application are identified in Appendix J.